BEHAVIORAL ASSESSMENT

BEHAVIORAL ASSESSMENT
A PRACTICAL HANDBOOK

Fourth Edition

Edited by

ALAN S. BELLACK
University of Maryland School of Medicine

MICHEL HERSEN
Pacific University

Allyn and Bacon
Boston   London   Toronto   Sydney   Tokyo   Singapore

Series editor: Carla F. Daves
Series editorial assistant: Susan Hutchinson
Manufacturing buyer: Megan Cochran

Copyright © 1998, 1988, 1981, 1976 by Allyn & Bacon
A Viacom Company
Needham Heights, MA 02194

Internet: www.abacon.com
America Online: keyword: College Online

Library of Congress Cataloging-in-Publication Data

Behavioral assessment : a practical handbook / Alan S. Bellack and
    Michel Hersen, editors. -- 4th ed.
        p.   cm.
    Includes bibliographical references and index.
    ISBN 0-205-17194-X
    1. Behavioral assessment.   2. Mental illness--Diagnosis.
I. Bellack, Alan S.   II. Hersen, Michel.
RC473.B43B44   1997   97-27513
616.89'075--dc21   CIP

Printed in the United States of America
10   9   8   7   6   5   4   3   2   02   01   00   99

To Jerry Frank,
who was there at the beginning

CONTENTS

PART III   EVALUATION FOR TREATMENT PLANNING

PART IV   SPECIAL TOPICS

PREFACE

We began our Preface to the Third Edition of this book by indicating how pleased we were at the continuing positive reception the book had received by the field, in general, and by instructors and students in behavioral assessment courses, in particular. We were very fortunate to have had first-rate contributors and an excellent editorial team at Pergamon Press. Continued interest in the book is a reflection of their efforts and scholarship. We are also gratified by the continuing importance of behavioral assessment in the field. It has been more than 20 years since the publication of the first edition of *Behavioral Assessment: A Practical Handbook.* Certainly we were convinced of the importance of the topic at the time, but we would have been loathe to bet that our opinion would be so widely shared a generation later.

Once again, this new fourth edition reflects substantive changes in the field, rather than a simple updating of references and procedures. The number of chapters has been increased from 17 to 20; hence, there is a substantial increase in the breadth of material presented. This modification reflects the expanding focus of behavioral assessment and its continuing integration with a generic, scientifically based biopsychosocial model of human behavior and behavioral disturbance. Only four of the chapters retain the same authors and substantially equivalent focus: Chapter 2, Psychometric Considerations (by John D. Cone); Chapter 7, Psychophysiological Assessment (by Ellie T. Sturgis and Sandra E. Gramling); Chapter 12, Assessment of Health-Related Disorders (by

Donald A. Williamson and two new coauthors); and Chapter 13, Assessment of Appetitive Disorders (by Robert G. Rychtarik and a new coauthor).

Chapters 1, 2, and 4 through 15 retain the primary focus of the previous edition. These encompass the core themes (e.g., behavioral observation, interviewing, assessment of anxiety disorders and depression) in which the content and some of the techniques have evolved, yet remain central to the activities of behavioral therapists and the behavioral assessment process. The material on assessment of child behavior problems has been subdivided into two chapters, reflecting current thinking on the nature and classification of childhood problems: Chapter 16 covers Internalizing Disorders and Chapter 17 deals with Externalizing Disorders. Reflecting changes in both the population and the scope of practice of behavior therapists, we have also added Chapter 18, Assessment of Older Adults. Finally, in response to the increased importance of neurobiology to understanding human behavior, we include Chapter 19, Behavioral Neuropsychology, and Chapter 20, Biological Assessment.

As always, we would like to express our gratitude to those individuals who have played a key role in producing this edition. Our "veteran" contributors have been very responsive about revising and updating their chapters, and the new contributors have uniformly done an excellent job. We are very appreciative of the help and cooperation we have received from Carla Daves, Mylan Jaixen, and their colleagues at Allyn and Bacon, our new publisher, who have picked up admirably from Pergamon Press. Our gratitude is extended also to reviewers Marilyn Bonem, Eastern Michigan University, and C. Richard Spates, Western Michigan University, for their comments on the manuscript. Of course, nothing would get done without the energy of our respective office staffs, including Sonia McQuarters, Christine Apple, Stacy Sanders, and Burt Bolton.

Finally, we wish to remember Jerome B. Frank, our long-time editor and close friend, who passed away prematurely since the publication of the third edition. He was with us in spirit and always will be. Thanks, Jerry!

Alan S. Bellack, Ph.D., ABPP
Michel Hersen, Ph.D., ABPP

ABOUT THE EDITORS

Alan S. Bellack, Ph.D., ABPP, received his Ph.D. from the Pennsylvania State University in 1970. He currently is professor of psychiatry and director of the Division of Psychology at the University of Maryland School of Medicine. He was formerly professor of psychiatry and director of psychology at the Medical College of Pennsylvania, and professor of psychology and director of clinical training at the University of Pittsburgh. He is a former president of the Association for Advancement of Behavior Therapy, and a Diplomate of the American Board of Behavior Therapy and the American Board of Professional Psychology. He is a Fellow of the American Psychological Association, the American Psychological Society, the Association for Clinical Psychosocial Research, and the American Psychopathological Association. Bellack was the first recipient of the American Psychological Foundation Gralnick Foundation Award for his lifetime research on psychosocial aspects of schizophrenia. He is coauthor or coeditor of 27 books and has published over 125 journal articles. He received a NIMH Merit Award and has had continuous funding from NIMH for over 20 years for his work on schizophrenia, depression, and social skills training. He currently serves on a NIDA IRG and is an ad hoc reviewer for several NIMH IRGs. He is editor and founder of the journals *Behavior Modification* and *Clinical Psychology Review,* and serves on the editorial boards of 9 other journals.

Michel Hersen, Ph.D., received his Ph.D. from the State University of New York at Buffalo in 1966. He is professor and dean of the School of Professional Psychology, Pacific University, Forest Grove, Oregon. He is a former president of the Association for Advancement of Behavior Therapy. Hersen has coauthored and coedited 111 books, including the *Handbook of Prescriptive Treatments for Adults* and *Single Case Experimental Designs,* has published more than 220 scientific journal articles, and is coeditor of several psychological journals, including *Behavior Modification, Clinical Psychology Review, Journal of Anxiety Disorders, Journal of Family Violence, Journal of Developmental and Physical Disabilities, Journal of Clinical Geropsychology* and *Aggression and Violent Behavior: A Review Journal.* With Alan S. Bellack, he is coeditor of the forthcoming 11-volume work titled *Comprehensive Clinical Psychology.* Hersen has been the recipient of numerous grants from the National Institute of Mental Health, the Department of Education, the National Institute of Disabilities and Rehabilitation Research, and the March of Dimes Birth Defects Foundation. He is a Diplomate of the American Board of Professional Psychology, Distinguished Practitioner and Member of the National Academy of Practice in Psychology, and recipient of the Distinguished Career Achievement Award in 1996 from the American Board of Medical Psychotherapists and Psychodiagnosticians.

ABOUT THE CONTRIBUTORS

Ron Acierno, Ph.D., received his doctorate in clinical psychology from Nova-Southeastern University. He is currently co-director of the Older Adult Crime Victims Center, located within the National Crime Victims Research and Treatment Center at the Medical University of South Carolina. Acierno has authored over 25 articles and book chapters. His primary area of interest is the assessment and treatment of anxiety-based disorders, particularly PTSD, in older adults. Specifically, he is interested in determining both the response differences to trauma between older and younger adults, and needed modifications to treatments that arise as a function of these differences. Secondary interests include behavioral treatments for adolescent and adult substance use.

John D. Cone, Ph.D., professor of clinical psychology at United States International University, San Diego, earned his B.A. in psychology from Stanford University and his M.S. and Ph.D. degrees from the University of Washington. He has taught at University of Puget Sound, West Virginia University, and University of Hawaii. He is past editor of *Behavioral Assessment* and a contributor to previous editions of this book.

Elizabeth L. Dick, B.S., received her undergraduate degree from the University of Pittsburgh in psychology in 1994. Since then, she has worked as a research associate at Western Psychiatric Institute and Clinic, beginning by collaborating in studies of neuroimaging and cognitive disturbances in chil-

dren with obsessive compulsive disorder. She currently works in the Psychosis Risk Evaluation Program conducting MRI studies of neuroanatomic and neurochemical abnormalities indicative of neurodevelopmental disorders in children who are the offspring of schizophrenic mothers. She will soon begin doctoral studies in physical anthropology.

Raymond DiGiuseppe, Ph.D., a native of Philadelphia, received his B.A. from Villanova University and his Ph.D. from Hofstra University. He then completed a Post Doctoral Fellowship at the Institute for Rational Emotive Therapy with Dr. Albert Ellis. DiGiuseppe has published over 60 journal articles and book chapters and coauthored five books. His present work involves the assessment and treatment of anger, the therapeutic alliance with children and adolescents, and the integration of cognitive and systemic therapies. He is professor of psychology at St. John's University in New York City and director of professional education at the Institute for Rational Emotive Therapy.

Lisa Whipple Drozdick, M.A., is a doctoral student in clinical psychology at West Virginia University. Her research interests include the psychological consequences of falling in older adults, decisional control, and neuropsychological sequelae of adult-residual attention deficit disorder. Other research interests include anxiety, depression, and coping in later life.

Barry A. Edelstein, Ph.D., is professor of psychology at West Virginia University. His current research is focused on decision-making competence among older adults and the psychological consequences of falls among older adults. He is coeditor (with Laura Carstensen and Laurie Dornbrand) of *The Practical Handbook of Clinical Gerontology.*

S. Bunny Falk, Psy.D., is a clinical supervisor for the Nova Community Clinic for Older Adults, as well as an adjunct faculty member at the Center for Psychological Studies, Nova Southeastern University, Fort Lauderdale, Florida. Her research interests include the assessment of PTSD and other clinical disorders in older adults.

Diane Franz is a postdoctoral fellow at the University of Massachusetts Medical Center. Her research interests include child behavior therapy and the treatment of children with chronic illness.

Michael D. Franzen, Ph.D., received his doctorate in clinical psychology from Southern Illinois University at Carbondale. Currently, he is chief of the Section of Psychology and Neuropsychology at Allegheny General Hospital in Pittsburgh and associate professor at Allegheny University of the Health Sciences. His research interests involve the evaluation of neuropsychological assessment instruments.

David M. Fresco, Ph.D., received his doctorate from University of North Carolina at Chapel Hill. He is presently a postdoctoral fellow at Temple University. His research interests include cognitive-behavioral approaches to the etiology and treatment of mood and anxiety disorders, learned helplessness theory, optimism, and content-analysis assessment strategies.

Alan M. Gross is professor of psychology at the University of Mississippi. His research interests include child behavior therapy, self-management, and sexual assault.

Stephen N. Haynes, Ph.D., is professor in the clinical studies program at the University of Hawaii.

He received his Ph.D. from University of Colorado in 1971 and was clinical training director at University of Hawaii and Illinois Institute of Technology. He is editor of *Psychological Assessment* and has published numerous articles and books on assessment.

Debra A. Hope, Ph.D., is associate professor of psychology at University of Nebraska–Lincoln and director of the Psychological Consultation Center. She has published widely on the assessment and treatment of social phobia, social skills, information processing approaches to psychopathology, and the process and efficacy of cognitive-behavior therapy.

Karla Kiper, M.A., is a doctoral student in clinical psychology at Louisiana State University. Her research has emphasized health problems in African Americans. She has conducted studies concerning the relationship between psychological variables and health in ethnic populations.

Jane Null Kogan, M.A., received her B.S. from the University of Pittsburgh and her M.A. in clinical psychology from West Virginia University. She is currently working toward a doctoral degree in clinical psychology at WVU. Her major areas of interest are assessment and treatment of anxiety in older adults and measuring development.

Jean Linscott, Ph.D., is currently working as a staff psychologist at Schneider Children's Hospital, New York, in the Child and Adolescent Day Hospital. She is assistant professor of psychiatry at the Albert Einstein College of Medicine and an associate fellow at the Institute for Rational Emotive Therapy in New York.

Nathaniel McConaghy, M.D., obtained his M.D. by thesis from University of Melbourne in 1966 and a D.Sc. from University of New South Wales in 1990. He is currently visiting professor of psychiatry at University of New South Wales, Sydney, Australia. His research interests center on the assessment and therapy of sexual and impulsive disorders, the relationship of sex-linked behaviors and sexual coercion to sexual orientation, and cognitive styles in normals and schizophrenics. In addition to extensive publications in these areas, McConaghy has published *Sexual Behavior: Problems and Management.*

Neil B. McGillicuddy, Ph.D., received his doctorate in social psychology from the State University of New York at Buffalo in 1989. He is a research scientist at the New York State Research Institute on Addictions, Buffalo, NY. His research interests center on interventions for families of substance abusers.

F. Dudley McGlynn, Ph.D., received his doctorate in clinical psychology from University of Missouri–Columbia in 1968. He has been affiliated with Mississippi State University, University of Florida, and University of Missouri–Kansas City, and is now professor of psychology at Auburn University. He has contributed numerous articles and chapters about behavior therapy and anxiety.

Valerie J. Meier, M.A., received her B.A. from University of Minnesota in 1991 and her M.A. from Mankota State University in 1993. She is currently working toward her doctorate in clinical psychology at University of Nebraska–Lincoln. Her major areas of interest include mood and anxiety disorders.

Jacqueline B. Persons, Ph.D., is director of the Center for Cognitive Therapy in Oakland, California, and associate clinical professor, Department of Psychiatry, University of California, San Francisco. She is author of *Cognitive Therapy in Practice: A Case Formulation Approach,* published by Norton in 1989 and translated into Japanese in 1993, as well as numerous research and clinical articles and chapters. Persons is associate editor of *Cognitive Therapy and Research.*

Michael P. Rose, Ph.D., was graduated by Franklin University in 1976. He entered clinical psychology after a career in business and was graduated with a Ph.D. by Auburn University in 1996. He has coauthored several articles about arousal during *in vivo* exposure. He is assistant professor of psychology at Georgia College, Milledgeville, Georgia.

Robert G. Rychtarik, Ph.D., received his doctorate in clinical psychology from the University of Montana in 1979. He is a senior research scientist at the New York State Research Institute on Addictions, Buffalo, NY. His interests include substance abuse treatment outcome research and research on interventions for families of substance abusers.

David B. Sarwer, Ph.D., received his Ph.D. in clinical psychology from Loyola University, Chicago in 1995. He currently is an instructor of psychology in psychiatry and surgery at Allegheny University of the Health Sciences. His research interests include the psychology of appearance, body image, weight and eating disorders, and sexual dysfunction.

Steven L. Sayers, Ph.D., received his doctorate from University of North Carolina, Chapel Hill and is assistant professor in the Department of Psychiatry, Eastern Pennsylvania Psychiatric Institute (EPPI), Allegheny University of the Health Sciences. He is the director of the Pre-doctoral Psychology Internship at EPPI, and has published numerous articles in the observational assessment of couples.

Daniel L. Segal, Ph.D., is assistant professor in the Department of Psychology at University of Colorado at Colorado Springs, where he teaches courses in diagnostic interviewing, abnormal psychology, and the psychology of aging. Segal also conducts a program of clinical research focusing on diagnosis, assessment, and treatment of older adults. He has published numerous journal articles on interviewing, diagnosis, behavioral assessment, and intervention with the elderly.

Lourdes T. Serafini, M.S., is a doctoral student at Florida International University, Miami. Her research interests are in the area of childhood behavior problems, particularly the internalizing problems.

Wendy K. Silverman, Ph.D., is professor of psychology and director of the Child and Family Psychosocial Research Center at Florida International University, Miami. Silverman has published widely in the area of childhood internalizing disorders, including *Anxiety and Phobic Disorders: A Pragmatic Approach* (coauthored with William M. Kurtines) and *Developmental Issues in the Clinical Treatment of Children* (coedited with Thomas H. Ollendick). She is the recipient of several grants from the National Institute of Mental Health to develop and evaluate psychosocial interventions for children with phobic and anxiety disorders. Silverman also serves on numerous editorial boards and is currently associate editor for *Journal of Clinical Child Psychology*.

Laura Smith-Seemiller, Ph.D., earned her doctoral degree in clinical psychology from Ohio State University. She is currently employed as an instructor of psychology/psychiatry at Allegheny University of the Health Sciences, at Allegheny General Hospital in Pittsburgh, Pennsylvania. Research interests include closed head injury and various aspects of neuropsychological assessment.

Nalini M. Srinivasagam, B.A., received her undergraduate degree from Catholic University of America in 1992, during which time she worked as a research intern at the National Institutes of Health. She then worked as a research associate at Western Psychiatric Institute and Clinic collaborating on studies of eating disorders and schizophrenia. She is now pursuing graduate studies in industrial/organizational psychology at Illinois State University.

John A. Sweeney, Ph.D., received his doctorate in clinical psychology from Syracuse University. He was on the faculty of Cornell University Medical College until 1990 and is now associate professor of psychiatry at the University of Pittsburgh School of Medicine. He is director of the Neurobehavioral Studies Program, which conducts studies of cognitive and eye movement abnormalities in psychiatric and neurologic disorders using behavioral techniques and functional neuroimaging. He also directs the Psychological and Neuropsychological Assessment Program at Western Psychiatric Institute and Clinic.

Warren W. Tryon, Ph.D., received his Ph.D. from Kent State University in 1970, is licensed in New York state, and holds a diploma in Clinical Psychology from the American Board of Professional Psychology (ABPP). He is professor of psychology at Fordham University where he recently became Director of Clinical Training.

Staci Veron-Guidry, Ph.D., is instructor of psychology at Pennington Biomedical Research Center. Her research interests are in the fields of behavior therapy, eating disorders, and obesity. She has recently conducted studies pertaining to psychosocial risk factors for the development of eating disorders in children and preadolescents.

Donald A. Williamson, Ph.D., is professor of psychology at Louisiana State University and at Pennington Biomedical Research Center. He is also director of the Psychological Services Center at LSU. His research interests are in the fields of behavioral medicine and health psychology. Over the past 10 years, his research has focused on eating disorders, obesity, and health. He has published one book and over 100 papers on these topics.

BEHAVIORAL ASSESSMENT

CHAPTER 1

THE CHANGING NATURE OF BEHAVIORAL ASSESSMENT

Stephen N. Haynes
University of Hawaii at Manoa

A *psychological assessment paradigm* is an integrated set of principles, beliefs, values, hypotheses, and methods advocated by the adherents of an assessment discipline. It includes hypotheses about the best level of measurement precision, the causal variables that are most likely to affect behavior, the mechanisms that underlie causal and noncausal functional relationships, the role of assessment in the design and evaluation of treatment, and the best methods for obtaining assessment data. A psychological assessment paradigm also includes guidelines for clinical judgment based on assessment data.

Most psychological assessment paradigms are dynamic in that the elements of the paradigm change over time. Behavioral assessment is perhaps the most dynamic of all psychological assessment paradigms.[1] In the last 10 years, many changes have occurred in the focus and methods of behavioral assessment, in the strategies for integrating assessment data, and in the causal models and treatment of behavior disorders that affect assessment strategies.

The multidimensional changes in behavioral assessment preclude comprehensive coverage. Consequently, the goal of this chapter is to present a sample of the changes that have occurred in the behavioral assessment paradigm. To provide a basis for this presentation, elements of the paradigm will be delineated. Recent changes in several of those elements will then be discussed.

This chapter will examine several dynamic elements: (1) the application and utility of behavioral assessment methods, (2) computerization and other new measurement technologies, (3) clinical case conceptualization and the functional analysis, (4) the application of psychometric principles, and (5) the integration of behavioral and personality assessment. The chapter will emphasize changes that have implications for clinical judgment, particularly for the design and evaluation of treatment programs.

Many developments will not be addressed. For example, nonlinear dynamical modeling and elements of chaos theory have important implications for measurement strategies in behavioral assessment. These have been discussed in recent books by Gilgen and Abraham (1995), Haynes (1992), Vallacher and Nowak (1994), and in articles by Haynes, Blaine, and Meyer (1995), Heiby (1995), and Burton, 1994. Nonlinear multivariate and time-series analyses and multivariate time-series regression analyses strengthen the inferences from time-series data and allow researchers to detect important functional relationships (Gifi, 1990; Serber & Wild, 1989). Developments in cognitive psychology, learning, developmental psychology, psychobiology, and behavior analysis suggest potentially important functional relationships that may account for the onset, maintenance, magnitude, or recovery from behavior problems. Assessment strategies are also affected by developments in intervention strategies and the causal models of behavior disorders. Many of these are outlined in books by Hersen and Bellack (1996), O'Donohue and Krasner (1995), and Sutker and Adams (1993). This chapter will also not address the role of psychiatric diagnosis in behavioral assessment. Readers may consult *Behavioral Assessment* (1988, Vol. 10; 1992, Vol. 14) and *Journal of Abnormal Psychology* (1991, Vol. 100). Behavioral assessment methods increasingly focus on contextual and situational variables and the importance of extended social environments, reflected in many chapters in Hersen and Bellack (1996) (e.g., Franz & Gross, 1996).

INTRODUCTION TO THE BEHAVIORAL ASSESSMENT PARADIGM

Behavioral assessment is a psychological assessment paradigm with methodological and conceptual components. Behavioral assessment emphasizes empirically based, multimethod, multimodal, and multiinformant measurement of lower-level, precisely specified, observable behavior and contemporaneous causal variables.[2] The paradigm emphasizes the application of well-validated, minimally inferential assessment instruments,[3] applied in a time-series format. The variables targeted and the methods used in behavioral assessment are guided by the assumption that antecedent and consequent social/environmental factors are often important sources of variance in behavior and behavior problems. Furthermore, it is assumed that behavior, behavior problems, and extant causal relationships can differ significantly across persons, time, and situations. Characteristics of the behavioral assessment paradigm are outlined in Figure 1.1.

There are differences among behavioral subparadigms in the degree to which they embrace the elements outlined in Figure 1.1. Behavioral assessment sometimes (1) includes nomothetically grounded instruments, (2) focuses on highly inferential variables, (3) applies unvalidated and trait-

Figure 1.1 Characteristics and distinguishing features of behavioral assessment

---

Goals of Assessment

+* To identify and measure precisely specified problem behaviors (as opposed to "diagnosis")

+   To identify and measure specific client goals, strengths and reinforcers (as part of a "constructional" approach to assessment)

+* To provide data for the design intervention programs for individual clients

+   To identify causal variables for behavior problems and goals (e.g., functional relationships involving social/environmental variables)

+   To evaluate the multivariate effects and mediators of intervention programs

+   To facilitate basic research in behavior analysis, learning, psychopathology, cognitive psychology, developmental psychology, and social psychology

Focus of Assessment

*   Observable behavior (as opposed to hypothesized intrapsychic events)

*   Contemporaneous (as opposed to historical) behavior, situations, and environmental factors

Figure 1.1 *(Continued)*

+ Behavior in the natural environment
* Response contingencies, as important factors in the selection of behavior
   Environmental events, settings, and conditions as important sources of variance for behavior (as opposed to historical, trait, or intrapsychic factors)
+ Multiple targets in assessment of treatment outcome (e.g., main treatment effects, side effects, setting and response generalization)
+ Multiple informants (e.g., obtaining data from client, staff, parents, teachers, family, spouse)
   Multiple modes (motoric, verbal, physiological, cognitive)
   Multiple parameters of behavior disorders and functional variables (onset, duration, magnitude, rate)
+ Functional assessment (goals of assessment determine methods and focus)

Inferences from Assessment
+* Lower-level (molecular, precisely defined) behavioral and causal variables
+* Direct (less inferential) measurement of behaviors of interest
* Criterion-referenced, idiographic, and client-referenced (and sometimes norm-referenced) inferences

Empiricism/Scholarly Emphasis
+* Use of time-series assessment (as opposed to single-point or pre-post measurement strategies)
+ An hypothesis testing, disconfirmation, approach to assessment/treatment
+ Multimethod, multiinformant, multisituational measurement of variables to reduce the impact of individual sources of measurement error
+ Empirically accurate and valid measures

Methods of Assessment
* Direct observation (naturalistic and analog settings)
+* Multimethod/informant assessment
+ Frequent, ongoing assessment (time-series assessment)
+* Critical event/situation sampling
   Measurement facilitated by computerization and instrumentation
   A match between assessment methods and the goals of assessment

Assumptions about the Causes of Behavior Problems
+* Social/environmental response contingencies and stimuli are important causal factors
+* There can be significant variance in behavior and its causes across situations and time—behavior and causal variables are dynamic (the conditional nature of causal inferences)
* An emphasis on contemporaneous causes
+ Reciprocal determinism—person-environment interactions are important (bidirectional causality)
   Multiple causality—behavior is affected by multiple, interacting causal factors (mandating a systems focus to assessment)
+* Important differences in the operation of causal factors between persons with the same behavior problems
   Different causal factors may operate for different parameters of behavior problems

+ Characteristics endorsed by almost all subparadigms in behavioral assessment.
* Distinguishing characteristics—those characteristics that most often distinguish between behavioral and nonbehavioral assessment paradigms.

Source: Haynes, 1996. The contents of the table have been influenced by Bandura (1969); Barrios (1988); Bellack and Hersen (1988); Bornstein, Bornstein, and Dawson (1984); Ciminero (1986); Cone (1988); Hartmann, Roper, and Bradford (1979); Haynes (1978, 1989, 1990, 1992); Kratochwill and Shapiro (1988); Mash and Terdal (1988); O'Brien and Haynes (1993); Ollendick and Hersen (1984, 1993); Strosahl and Linehan (1986); and Tryon (1985).

focused assessment instruments, (4) includes retrospective self-report measures, and (5) targets biological and cognitive causal variables. Linscott and DiGiuseppe (1996) have noted significant differences among cognitive subparadigms in type of variables presumed to function as causal factors for behavior problems.

A chapter on "changes" reflects the emphasis of the behavioral assessment paradigm on an empirical, hypothesis-testing, cybernetic approach to psychological assessment. A psychological assessment paradigm with an empirical, hypothesis-testing emphasis must be dynamic: Assessment strategies and foci are amended by new data on causal relationships, causal variables and mechanisms, technological advances, and new methods of clinical intervention.

THE APPLICATION OF BEHAVIORAL ASSESSMENT METHODS

This section will examine the time-course of behavioral assessment applications in (1) treatment outcome research, (2) graduate training programs, and (3) clinical pratice. Issues of power, cost effective-

ness, and incremental utility of behavioral assessment will be noted and addressed further in subsequent sections.

Behavioral Assessment in Treatment Outcome Research

One measure of the impact of a psychological assessment paradigm is the frequency with which assessment methods associated with the paradigm are used in treatment outcome research. Figure 1.2 presents time-course plots of the proportion of articles published in *Journal of Consulting and Clinical Psychology* (*JCCP*) in selected years, that used two classes of assessment methods to evaluate treatment outcome (Bogan, Ignacio, & Haynes, 1996). Figure 1.2 suggests a moderate quadratic function in the use of these two behavioral assessment methods. In contrast, projective techniques and broad-spectrum personality inventories were rarely used (e.g., no treatment outcome study used projective assessment and personality inventories in seven and six of the years surveyed, respectively). Single-trait, aggregated self-report measures were used in more than 75% of the articles.

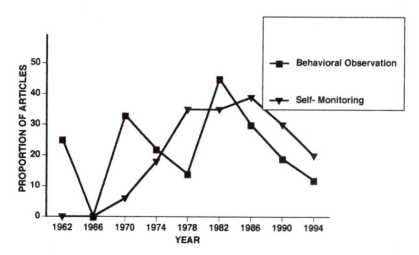

Figure 1.2   The proportion of treatment outcome articles, published in *Journal of Consulting and Clinical Psychology*, in selected years, that used behavioral observation and self-monitoring methods of assessment.

There are many sources of variance in the data presented in Figure 1.2 (e.g., changing editors and editorial policies, the status and publication policies of alternative journals, changes in treatment strategies, alterations in the behavior problems targeted for treatment). However, two inferences may be drawn. First, the two behavioral assessment methods tracked were used in treatment outcome research significantly more than were projective methods and personality inventories. Second, the use of the monitored behavioral assessment methods peaked in the mid 1980s.

A survey of four general-purpose and nonspecialized journals published in 1993 (Haynes, 1996) provides more data about the broad impact of the behavioral paradigm. In that year, 37% of the articles published in *Journal of Consulting and Clinical Psychology*, 25% of the articles published in *Clinical Psychology Review*, 22% of the articles published in *Psychological Assessment*, and 16% of the articles published in *Abnormal Psychology* focused on behavior therapy procedures, specifically addressed conceptual issues in behavior therapy, or primarily addressed issues in behavioral assessment.

Behavioral Assessment in Doctoral Training Programs

The status of behavioral assessment in doctoral training programs provides another index of the impact of the paradigm. Piotrowski and Zalewski (1993) surveyed 13 Psy.D and 67 Ph.D. APA-approved clinical psychology training programs (51% of APA-approved programs) about their required courses in psychological assessment and about their expected changes in required assessment courses. The authors reported that behavioral assessment is taught in about one-half of the doctoral training programs in clinical psychology (compared to 94% for intellectual assessment, 89% for objective personality assessment, and 85% for projective assessment). More important for the future time-course of training in behavioral assessment, over one-third of the program directors expected an increase in the emphasis on behavioral assessment in the future (8% and 45% of the program directors expected an increase and decrease,

respectively, in the emphasis on projective assessment in the near future; 7% expected a decrease in behavioral assessment). The proportion of programs that teach behavioral assessment has likely increased since the early 1980s but behavioral assessment was not included as a response option in a 1984 survey conducted by these authors.

Behavioral Assessment in Clinical Practice

The results of several surveys of practicing clinicians (Piotrowski & Lubin, 1990, survey of 270 members of the Health Psychology Division of APA; Watkins, Campbell, & McGregor, 1989, survey of 41 behaviorally oriented counseling psychologists; Guevremont & Spiegler, 1990, survey of 988 members of the Association for the Advancement of Behavior Therapy) have been consistent: (1) the interview is the most frequently used assessment method (e.g., used by 91% in the Guevremont and Spiegler sample; see also discussion by Sarwer & Sayers, 1996) regardless of the theoretical orientation of the assessor; (2) objective "personality" questionnaires and self-report inventories are used by 50 to 80% of clinicians, regardless of orientation; (3) self-monitoring is used by about half of the behaviorally oriented clinicians; and (4) observations in structured or natural settings are used by a minority (e.g., 15 to 25%) of clinicians.

The application of behavioral assessment can also be estimated by examining its role in research-oriented clinical treatment programs. An edited book by Turner, Calhoun, and Adams (1992), *Clinical Behavior Therapy*, contains overviews of assessment and treatment strategies with 22 classes of behavior disorders. Each chapter is written by scholar-clinicians and most emphasize the integration of behavioral assessment and treatment across sessions. Chapters in an edited book by Bellack and Hersen (1993), *Handbook of Behavior Therapy in the Psychiatric Setting,* provide overviews of "prototypical" and "actual" behavioral assessment for 18 classes of behavior problems. Behavioral observation, particularly in analog settings, was recommended by the authors of 12 chapters; self-monitoring was recommended by authors of 6 of the chapters. Similar recommendations are included in edited books on behavior therapy by Hersen and Ammerman (1994) and Mash and Barkley (1989).

In all of the books cited, behavioral observation was less likely, and trait-focused self-report questionnaires were more likely, to be recommended for the assessment of "internalized" disorders, such as headache, anxiety, or mood disorders. Self-monitoring was less likely to be recommended as an assessment method for child and adolescent behavior disorders. Issues of the practicality, cost effectiveness, and incremental utility of assessment methods were raised in many chapters.

Implications

The data just cited suggest several hypotheses:

1. Viewed across a 30-year time span, the behavioral assessment paradigm is well integrated into, but does not dominate, clinical assessment practices.

2. Behavioral observation is commonly viewed as a valuable but costly method of assessment. The comparatively low rate of use of behavioral observation to aid clinical judgment (see reviews in Tryon, 1996b, and in Suen & Ary, 1989) may vary with the belief by clinicians that the time required for conducting behavioral observations is not warranted by the incremental benefit to clinical judgment. Reid, Baldwin, Patterson, and Dishion (1987) have challenged this belief, noting that the cost for their extensive observational assessment is less than the cost for a typical "personalty assessment."

3. Although self-monitoring is used infrequently with children, many studies support the applicability of self-monitoring for childhood behavior problems. Although self-monitoring requires the ability to track and judge behavior (see reviews in Mash & Terdal, 1988, and in Ollendick & Hersen, 1993), some children can monitor important behaviors, such as their asthma episodes (Creer & Bender, 1993), anxiety episodes and setting events (Beidel, Neal, & Lederer, 1991), study skills, and disruptive classroom behavior (Houghton, 1991).

4. The cost effectiveness of assessment instruments is an important consideration in clinical assessment (e.g., Sobell, Toneatto, & Sobell, 1994). In clinical research settings where cost is less important, more powerful but expensive assessment methods, such as behavioral observation, are used more frequently. More cost-effective and clinically useful methods of behavioral assessment are being developed and some of these are discussed in the next section.

ADVANCES IN THE METHODS OF BEHAVIORAL ASSESSMENT

Behavioral assessment includes diverse methods: observation in the natural and analog environments, participant observation, self-monitoring, behavioral self-report and informant questionnaires and interviews, electrophysiological and other biological measures, and electromechanical recordings. These methods are reviewed in detail in Hersen and Bellack (1996), Cacioppo and Tassinary, (1990), Mash and Terdal (1988), Ollendick and Hersen (1993), Shapiro and Kratochwill (1988), Suen and Ary (1989), and Tryon (1991).

Several recent developments in behavioral assessment methods enhance their accuracy, validity, and clinical applicability. Many of these advances enhance clinical practicality and cost effectiveness by allowing data to be obtained and interpreted more easily. Other advances enhance the sensitivity, accuracy, and power of the assessment instruments. The following subsections discuss (1) computer-aided assessment, (2) other technological aids for the measurement of behavior in the natural environment, and (3) analog assessment instruments.

Computer-Assisted Data Acquisition

Computer-aided interviews and questionnaires facilitate the acquisition of client self-report data. Computers have been used in psychological and psychophysiological assessment (e.g., Angle, 1981; Cacioppo & Tassinary, 1990) for decades. Several reviews (e.g., Butcher, 1987; Eyde, 1987; Farrell, 1991; Honaker & Fowler, 1990) have presented the assets, liabilities, psychometric properties, and utility of computer-assisted interview and questionnaire assessment.

There are two main formats for computer-assisted interviews and questionnaires:

1. Interactive computer-assisted interviews for interviewers in which items are presented on screen to the interviewer. The interviewer verbally presents items to the client and keys in the client responses.

2. Interactive computer-assisted interviews and questionnaires for clients in which items are presented on screen to respondents. The respondents key in their answers, usually in true-false or multiple-choice formats. Other response parameters, such as latency of response, can be measured (Tryon, 1996b). Written responses can also be entered with optical scanning technology

In both formats, computer output can include total scores, scale scores, factor scores, individual item analyses, and diagnoses.

There are many problems associated with computer-assisted questionnaires and interviews. These include discomfort by some clients with computers, error variance associated with the ergonomic aspects of assessment (e.g., font size and type, screen size and coloring), the difficulty of using them in some circumstances or with some clients (e.g., with severely depressed or delusional clients, during crisis situations), insufficient psychometric valuation of some computer-assisted assessment instruments, and the use of unmediated computer-generated reports. In addition, it is difficult to develop interactive software programs that are affordable, cost effective, and sufficiently flexible to address the myriad of behavior problems and controlling variables presented by clients.

Given these caveats, many studies have shown that computer-assisted questionnaire and interview assessment is well accepted by most clients. They also can provide valid and sensitive measures of client problems and functional variables and can increase the cost effectiveness of the assessment process. When properly constructed and carefully developed and evaluated, computer-assisted acquisition of client self-report data can reduce many sources of measurement error (e.g., Sarwer & Say-

ers, 1996). Many computer programs also follow logical branching operations more accurately than interviewers and can interact flexibly with users. Visual analog scales are particularly amenable to presentation and scoring via computer.

More important for the goals and focus of behavioral assessment, computers can greatly simplify the collection and analysis of *behavioral observation and self-monitoring data* (Farrell, 1991) by increasing their cost effectiveness. An important component of the behavioral assessment paradigm is the collection of data on multiple dependent and independent variables using a time-series assessment strategy. For example, measures of back pain, headaches, mood, anxiety, physical activity, social interactions, blood pressure, and self-injury are often measured one or more times per day for weeks or months.

Multivariate time-series data are powerful aids to clinical judgments. Time-series measurement strategies can detect and help predict the time-course of variables (Haynes et al., 1995) and the functional relationships among multiple variables across time for a client. Although used sparingly in the behavioral sciences, *multivariate time-series regression designs* strengthen causal inferences because both temporal precedence and covariance of variables can be examined. This measurement strategy is also congruent with the supposition that there can be important between-person differences in causal relationships—it is amenable to the analysis of functional relationships across time for an individual and also for a group of persons. A time-series measurement strategy is also a necessary element of all *interrupted time-series designs* (i.e., single-subject, within-subject, single-case designs).

Difficulties in collecting, reducing, and analyzing time-series data have limited its application in clinical settings. However, computer technology and statistical analysis software facilitate the clinical applicability of time-series assessment. Time-series assessment is aided by computers in three ways: (1) through the use of lap-top or hand-held computers for the collection of data by external observers, (2) through the use of hand-held computers to facilitate the collection of real-time self-monitored data by clients, and (3) through software packages for the statistical analysis of multivariate time-series regression and interrupted time-series data (Farrell, 1991).

A number of *computerized observation systems* are available, ranging from inexpensive and simple to expensive and elegantly flexible. Examples include the Portable Computer Systems for Observational Use (Bush & Ciocco, 1992), a system using bar-code scanning (Eiler, Nelson, Jensen, & Johnson, 1989), the INTERACT system (Dumas, 1987), the Empiricist (McGrath, 1991), the Observer (Hile, 1991), and a system developed by Repp, Harman, Felce, VanAcker, and Karsh, (1989).

Hand-held computers can enhance the power and clinical applicability of self-monitoring (and participant observation). Self-monitoring has several sources of measurement error but it is congruent with three important elements of the behavioral assessment paradigm: (1) it can be used to collect data in the natural environment, (2) it can reduce measurement error associated with retrospective self-report methods, and (3) it can provide data in a real-time format (see reviews by Gardner, & Cole, 1988; Bornstein, Hamilton, & Bornstein, 1986). It is particularly useful for the measurement of low-rate behaviors (e.g., panic episodes, migraine headaches, eating binges and purges) and for multiple time samples within each day. Hand-held computers can prompt respondents at prescribed times during the day with a diverse array of queries. They can also record client responses in real-time and apply decision-trees for subsequent probes. The reduction and analysis of self-monitoring data can also be facilitated because hand-held computers can summarize obtained data in graphic or table form, and download and synchronize obtained data to desk-top computer files.

Computer-assisted self-monitoring has been used in several studies. In a study by Taylor, Fried, and Kenardy (1990), clients who experienced panic episodes used hand-held computers to record panic and anxiety symptoms, cognitive factors, and settings. In a study by Tombari, Fitzpatrick, and Childress (1985) a fifth-grade boy used a computer (desk-top) to monitor his out-of-seat behavior. Obese clients used hand-held computers to monitor their weight, caloric intake, exercise, daily goals, and goal attainment in a study by Agras and colleagues (1990).

The initial cost of hand-held computers is moderate (the full retail price for a MacIntosh Newton 120 is $699 and the "educational" price is $529 at the time of this writing) but software for clinical assessment is not widely available. Hand-held computers are likely to revolutionize methods of self- and participant monitoring and lead to an increase in the clinical utility of these behavioral assessment methods.

Computer-Aided Clinical Judgment

The synthesis of assessment data to aid clinical judgments is one of the most complex tasks facing the clinician (see Functional Analysis section of this chapter). It has been the topic of many studies and several reviews (see Nezu & Nezu, 1989; Turk & Salovey, 1988; and discussion by Persons, 1989). It is also a challenging but promising application of computer technology. The synthesis of assessment data for clinical judgment involves the integration of multiple measures on multiple variables, and multiple hypotheses about functional relationships—an ideal application of computer technology.

Two systems have been developed for computer-assisted clinical judgments that are congruent with a behavioral assessment paradigm. Both systems attempt to increase the efficiency, objectivity, and precision of clinical decision making. Landsheer (1990) developed the ABC computerized functional analysis system. The ABC system helps the clinician identify functional relationships (covariances among antecedent, behavior and consequent events) through client descriptions of important incidents.

Haynes, Richard, and O'Brien (1996) developed the Clinical Case Modeling (CCM) computerized system for functional analysis and clinical case description. Through a series of interactive queries to the clinician, CCM constructs a vector-graphic model of the clinician's treatment-related hypotheses about a client. The system constructs a *functional analytic causal model* (Haynes, 1994; Haynes & O'Brien, 1990) to illustrate the clinician's estimates of the importance of the client's multiple behavior problems, the sequelae of the behavior problems, the sequences of causal and mediating variables, the strength of causal relationships, and the modifiability of causal variables.

From these estimates, the program calculates the expected magnitude of the effect of focusing treatment efforts on various causal variables.

Instrument-Assisted Assessment in the Natural Environment

The behavioral assessment paradigm emphasizes the use of minimally inferential assessment methods. Consequently, direct measurement of a client's behavior is preferred to retrospective reports. However, observation in the natural environment can be costly. Tryon (1991, 1996b) described instrument-assisted data collection that can facilitate the measurement of behavior in the natural environment. For example, several systems (e.g., LogoPort) provide real-time recordings of speech. A speech-sensing unit is typically worn on a chest harness with a sensor placed close to the larynx. Data can be down-loaded for analysis of multiple response parameters, such as frequency, latency, and duration.

Tape recordings of critical events or during critical periods in the natural environment may also provide cost-effective data (Tryon, 1996b). Examples of critical-event recording include dinner-time conversations among family members, bed-time interactions between parents and children, marital arguments, and social interactions on dates. This is a promising technology but psychometric characteristics, coding and sampling schemes, and utility have not been sufficiently investigated.

Other instruments measure motor activity, blood glucose, blood pressure, medication compliance, penile erections, and multiple psychophysiological responses during sleep and waking. For example, wrist *actigraphs* can record movement in real time and, when worn in bed, can provide an estimate of sleep and awake time (Hauri & Wisbey, 1992). *Actometers* and pedometers (Tryon, 1991) provide an aggregated measure of motor activity and can be useful in the clinical assessment of persons for whom motor activity is an important dependent variable (e.g., patients in pain, and hyperactive, medicated, and depressed patients). Instruments that measure motor activity can be easy to use and clinically useful. However, they are often only indirect measures of the behaviors of interest. For example, actigraph measures are correlated with, but are not direct measures of, sleep and wake states.

Psychophysiological assessment of clients in their natural environment has been aided by advances in the technology for *ambulatory monitoring* (Pickering, 1989). For example, Musso and colleagues (1991) used ambulatory monitoring of blood pressure to help evaluate the effects of a thermal biofeedback program for hypertension. Multimodal ambulatory measurement has facilitated the identification of the time course and triggering and maintaining factors for episodes of psychophysiological disorders such as asthma, elevated blood pressure, panic, pain, and blood-glucose changes (see discussions in Gatchel & Blanchard, 1993). Ambulatory monitoring has also been used to examine the relationship between environmental stressors and physical illnesses (Taylor, 1990), the degree to which social interactions mediate behavioral and biological responses to environmental trauma (Heitzmann & Kaplan, 1988), and the triggering and mediating role of various behavioral and social variables for substance use (Henningfield & Obarzanek, 1992).

Analog Assessment Strategies

Analog assessment strategies involve the measurement of behavior in simulated situations—the assessment setting differs from the environment in which the target behavior typically occurs. Analog assessment can involve simulated social interactions (e.g., role-playing social interaction with a surrogate in a clinic setting), the presentation of feared stimuli, and audiotape or videotape presentations of scenarios (e.g., a videotape presentation of difficult social situations to a socially anxious client). They may involve live or recorded surrogates and are amenable to multimodal and multimethod assessment.

Analog assessment increases the probability that clinically significant behaviors can be measured directly and cost effectively. Analog assessment avoids some errors associated with retrospective recall and can be less costly than observation in the natural environment. Although there are many sources of measurement and inferential errors associated with analog assessment (Franz & Gross, 1996)—such as reactive effects, the lack of normative data, and questionable setting generalizability of some inferences—it can be a powerful assessment strategy and is underused in clinical settings.

The clinical utility of analog assessment has been enhanced by the development of several instruments. For example, Davison, Navarre, and Vogel (1995) and Linscott and DiGiuseppe (1996) described analog assessment instruments in which clients view videotapes or audiotapes of simulated stressful social situations. Clients indicate their thoughts at predetermined parts of the presentations. Many other analog assessment instruments have been developed for the evaluation of social skills and performance problems (Glass & Arnkoff, 1989). Sanderson and Wetzler (1990) described a CO_2 challenge test for use in the assessment with panic disorder patients. Marital assessment strategies often include audiotaped or videotaped discussions between spouses in the clinic. These discussions provide an opportunity for the clinician to observe verbal, paralinguistic, and emotional responses during disagreements or problem solving (O'Leary, 1987). Clients can also review these recordings and provide additional information about their emotional reactions and thoughts. Iwata and associates (1994) have developed methods of systematic evaluation of the degree to which various antecedent and consequent factors trigger or maintain self-injurious behavior. Fagot (1992) described a system for the analog assessment of parental discipline. Parents viewed videotapes of children engaging in high-risk behaviors (e.g., riding a tricycle out between parked cars) and then indicated how they would respond to such a situation.

Summary

Advances in measurement technology and in methods of analyzing obtained data enhance the power and clinical utility of the behavioral assessment paradigm. One's understanding of the factors that affect the onset, magnitude, duration, cyclicity, recovery from, and patterns of covariation among behavior problems is aided by enhanced ability to accurately measure behaviors, environmental events, and functional relationships. Measurement technology also affects one's ability to evaluate the effects and mediators of intervention programs. Technological advances in assessment (1) increase the standardization of assessment instruments, (2) increase the efficiency of assessment, (3) reduce many sources of measurement error, (4) facilitate the acquisition of data in the natural environment, (5) facilitate multimodal and multimethod assessment strategies, and (6) facilitate clinical judgments.

ADVANCES IN CLINICAL CASE CONCEPTUALIZATION: THE FUNCTIONAL ANALYSIS

A complex and infrequently researched component of psychological assessment is the integration of assessment information into a clinical case conceptualization—a hypothesized model of a client. Clinical case conceptualizations guide intervention programs in many paradigms but are particularly important in behavior therapy, in which interventions are often tailored for individual clients. Behavioral interventions are often designed to modify variables that trigger, maintain, or mediate problem behaviors and goals (Haynes, Spain, & Oliviera, 1993). Consequently, the identification of a client's behavior problem and the patterns of covariance among multiple behavior problems (e.g., DSM classification) are usually insufficient to guide behavioral interventions. Such typologies do not identify the functional relationships that are extant for a particular client (see Behavioral Assessment special series on DSM and behavioral assessment, 1988 and 1992). Several recent articles and books have discussed ways to facilitate effective clinical case conceptualizations.

Diverse and conflicting terminology characterizes this area. The hypothesized model of a client formulated from pretreatment assessment information has been called a functional analysis (Haynes, 1990; Haynes et al., 1993; O'Brien & Haynes, 1995), case formulation (Persons, 1989, 1992), behavioral case formulation (Wolpe & Turkat, 1985), functional assessment (Sisson & Taylor, 1993), behavioral analysis (Schulte, 1992), structural analysis (Axelrod, 1987), and functional behavioral analysis (Wincze, 1982).[4]

In this chapter, I use the term functional analysis rather than a more generic term, such as case *formulation*, to refer to the pretreatment clinical case conceptualization in behavior therapy. The term *functional analysis* reflects the emphasis in the behavioral assessment paradigm on identifying functional relationships associated with a client's behavior problems and goals. A functional analysis is defined as the identification of important, controllable, causal relationships applicable to specified behaviors for an individual.

The functional analysis is a higher-level (meta) judgment that involves multiple lower-level judgments about a client that are fundamental to the design of behavioral intervention programs. The functional analysis affects decisions regarding the intervention methods used with a client (e.g., whether social skills training and/or exposure training will be used with a socially anxious patient), the components of those intervention methods (e.g., the specific reinforcers used to strengthen prosocial behavior with an aggressive child), and the problem behaviors and alternatives that are the dependent variables in treatment.

The functional analysis consists of two sets of judgments: (1) judgments regarding the specification of, the relative importance of, the relationships among, and the sequelae of a client's *behavior problems and goals* and (2) judgments about the specification, relative modifiability, form of relationship (e.g., causal, noncausal), magnitude of effect, and relationships among the *causal variables* that affect a client's behavior problems and goals. Data from behavioral assessment instruments, along with data from previously published studies (e.g., Persons & Fresco, 1996), provide the information upon which the functional analysis is based. The validity of the functional analysis depends on the degree to which it is based on valid and appropriately selected assessment instruments.

The characteristics of functional analysis are as follows (Haynes et al., 1993):

1. It is a hypothesized model of the client.
2. It is *dynamic* in that the target behaviors, goals, and functional relationships are expected to change over time.
3. It is *probabilistic*, rather than strictly deterministic.
4. It emphasizes *important and controllable* functional relationships.

5. It reflects *unidirectional and bidirectional* causal relationships.
6. It reflects the *relative importance* of multiple client behavior problems.
7. It reflects *stimulus and response classes*.
8. It can be presented at *different levels of specificity*.
9. It reflects the different *strengths of causal relationships* and different *degrees of modifiability* of causal variables.
10. It is *conditional* in that it may be valid in some conditions (e.g., environmental settings, recent reinforcement history, physiological states) and not others.

Reviews and Overviews Relevant to the Functional Analysis and Clinical Judgment

The growing importance of the functional analysis and other clinical judgments is reflected in the publication of several relevant journal series and books. A series of articles, "Clinical Applications of Psychological Assessment," was published in *Psychological Assessment* in 1993 (vol. 5, p. 521). *Behavioral Assessment* published a series, "Behavioral Assessment in the DSM Era," in 1992 (vol. 14, p. 293) and a series, "Selection of Target Behaviors," in 1988 (vol. 7, p. 3). A special issue on "Case Formulation" from different perspectives was published in *In Session, Psychotherapy in Practice*, (1995, volume 1/2). The *Journal of Applied Behavior Analysis* published a series of articles on functional analysis of self-injurious behaviors in 1994 (vol. 27, p. 131). Four books (e.g., Brehmer & Joyce, 1988; Kanfer & Schefft, 1988; Nezu & Nezu, 1989; Turk & Salovey, 1988) focus on clinical decision making and human judgment.

Limitations of the Functional Analysis

Despite the logical basis and frequent advocacy for the functional analysis, or its elements, as important determinant of treatment strategies (e.g., Franzen & Smith-Seemiller, 1996; Williamson, Veron-Guidry, & Kiper, 1996), the functional analysis is limited in three ways:

1. *The methods for selecting the best assessment instruments* to develop a functional analysis for a particular client have not been delineated. General parameters for clinical assessment are well established. These include an emphasis on multiple methods, multiple response modes, multiple informants, content validity of an assessment strategy, and incremental utility and psychometric characteristics of assessment instruments. Additionally, research on the parameters and causes of behavior disorders (e.g., Persons & Fresco, 1996; Williamson, Veron-Guidry, & Kiper, 1996) provide the clinician with arrays of possible assessment instruments and targets. However, there are no validated methods for selecting assessment methods and instruments to develop a functional analysis for a particular client.

Sisson and Taylor (1993), Persons and Fresco (1996), and many others have suggested a "multiple gating" or "funnel" approach in which more precisely focused assessment instruments are selected on the basis of data derived from less costly, broadly focused (usually aggregated self-report) instruments. Others have suggested that expensive assessment instruments may be warranted only when standardized treatment protocols are ineffective.

2. *The methods for integrating data* from behavioral assessment into a functional analysis have not been developed.

3. *The incremental utility and cost-effectiveness* of the functional analysis have yet to be proved for many behavior problems and have been questioned by some (e.g., Schulte, 1992).

Advances in Methods of Estimating Functional Relationships

Although functional analyses are often intuitively derived, there have been several advances in the methods of estimating the strength of functional relationships and in organizing assessment data. A series of articles published in the *Journal of Applied Behavior Analysis* in 1994 described the systematic manipulation of situational and response contingency variables, such as positive and negative social responses and task demands, on the self-injurious behaviors of people with developmental disabilities. The data from these manipulations can help detect the degree to which variance in the self-injurious behaviors is associated with social and other environmental contingencies and antecedent conditions. Importantly, the authors noted between-person differences and the conditional nature of causal relationships. For example, the degree to which the rate of an individual's self-injurious behavior can be affected by positive social attention can be influenced by concomitant task demands and the degree of impoverishment of the client's social environment (Iwata et al., 1994).

Systematic manipulation of hypothesized causal variables is a powerful but underutilized assessment strategy. It has been used to identify the role of social contingencies in the maintenance of aggressive behaviors; the relationship between emotional responses and dyadic communication behaviors; fear-, sexual arousal-, and panic-eliciting stimuli; and many other clinically useful functional relationships. It can be used in natural settings, psychophysiological laboratories, and during assessment/therapy sessions.

Self-report questionnaires and interviews usually focus on the parameters (probability, rate, magnitude, duration) of behavior problems (Franz & Gross, 1996; Sarwer & Sayers, 1996; Segal & Falk, 1996). They are infrequently designed to identify functional relationships. However, several self-report instruments provide information about functional relationships. For example, some questionnaires measure the expected effects of drug and alcohol ingestion (e.g., Sobell et al., 1994), social and cognitive factors associated with chronic pain (Keefe, Dunsmore, & Burnett, 1992), asthma knowledge and management (Creer & Bender, 1993), and fear stimuli (Glass & Arnkoff, 1989). Interviews have been developed to identify contextual factors in self-injurious (Durand & Crimmins, 1988) and other maladaptive behavior, socially distressing situations, and behavioral and environmental causes of sleep disturbances (see review in Haynes et al., 1993).

As noted earlier in this section, it is difficult to select the best assessment strategies and foci for a client and to integrate assessment results. O'Brien (O'Brien & Haynes, 1995) noted that there are at least 126 ways that a causal variable and behavior problem can interact, if one considers the multiple parameters of the behavior problem and causal variable, setting factors, intraindividual factors, and different levels of specificity of the variables. For clients with multiple behavior problems with multiple interacting causal factors, the task of gathering and integrating data for a functional analysis exceeds the bounds of deductive abilities of most professionals (Nezu & Nezu, 1989) and mandates the use causal presuppositions.

Tryon (in press), in a refinement and expansion of Woods's (1974) taxonomy of instrumental conditioning, outlined a system for classifying response contingencies that can guide the selection of some assessment targets. He classified contingencies on dimensions of response emission-omission, signaled-unsignaled events, accelerative-decelerative functions, and contingent-noncontingent events. He also noted the conditional nature of contingency effects (e.g., the effects of a specific contingency can vary with learning history). The contingency classes have differential treatment implications and Tryon emphasized the importance of multiple and response omission contingencies.

The differential magnitude of functional relationships is a cardinal component of the functional analysis. Schlundt and colleagues (1993), Whitehurst and colleagues (1986), and others have suggested that the magnitude of some functional relationships can be estimated with *contingency and transitional matrices,* particularly with nominal data collected in a time-series format (e.g., the relative probabilities of a binge/purge episode, a critical comment, or a high blood pressure episode, given particular environmental contexts or social stimulus). Several authors (Collins & Horn, 1991; Gottman & Roy, 1990) have described important advances in sequential analysis, multiple linear and nonlinear regression, and time-series regression analysis methods of estimating the conditional probabilities and magnitude of shared variance between variables.

One element of a *latent-variable measurement strategy* (Loehlin, 1992) is consistent with the behavioral assessment paradigm and may enhance the validity of the resultant clinical judgments. If we presume that the variables in a functional analysis are "constructs" (see discussions of the nuances and complexities of this assumption in Foster & Cone, 1995; Haynes et al., 1995; Messick, 1993) that are imperfectly measured by any assessment instrument, the validity of our inferences regarding those constructs will be enhanced to the degree that one employs multiple (i.e., composite) measures rather than single measures of each construct.

The incremental validity of a composite variable measurement strategy depends on the validity of the data derived from each component instrument and the degree to which the measurement errors are uncorrelated. For example, Patterson (1993) discussed inferential errors that can be associated with only a single source of data of adolescent aggression and recommended using multiple informants to enhance the validity of inferences about the parameters of and changes in adolescent aggressive behavior. A composite measurement strategy incurs other inferential problems associated with aggregated measures. As Cone (1996) has noted, the interest in behavioral assessment is often on the determinants of a particular measure (e.g., the determinants of a teacher's report of the rate of a child's aggressive behavior, rather than on the determinants of the construct "aggressive behavior"). In such cases, composite measures may mask important functional relationships relevant to the component measure of interest.

It can be difficult to organize and describe multiple-complexed interacting variables in a functional analysis. *Functional analytic causal models (FACMs)* help organize assessment-based judgments and promote less intuitive intervention decisions. FACMs are graphic-vector models of a functional analysis (see examples in Haynes, 1994; Haynes et al., 1996; O'Brien & Haynes, 1995). They illustrate hypotheses about a client's behavior problems and goals and their relative importance, interrelationships, sequela, and the strength, modifiability, and direction of action of causal variables. A FACM allows the clinician to estimate the relative magnitude of effect of a particular treatment focus, given the clinician's hypothesized functional analysis.

In summary, recently published articles have addressed the components of the functional analysis. However, methods of determining the best assessment strategies for a functional analysis, the methods of integrating assessment data into a functional analysis, and the incremental utility of the functional analysis warrant additional research. Assessment instruments focused on functional relationships, time-series regression analysis, contingency matrices, composite variable measurement strategies, and functional analytic causal models may enhance the validity and utility of the functional analysis.

BEHAVIORAL ASSESSMENT, PSYCHOMETRIC PRINCIPLES, AND PERSONALITY ASSESSMENT

As noted earlier, some elements of the behavioral assessment paradigm are compatible with other psychological assessment paradigms and measurement principles. Furthermore, behavioral and non-behavioral assessment methods are often used concurrently in clinical practice and research. This section will briefly review recent developments in two areas of multidisciplinary interaction: (1) the applicability of psychometric principles to behavioral assessment and (2) the use of personality assessment instruments in behavioral assessment.

Psychometric Principles

Several authors (Cone, 1988, 1996; Foster & Cone, 1995; Haynes & Waialae, 1994; Silva, 1993) have discussed the application of psychometric principles to behavioral assessment. Psychometric principles were originally developed in reference to the measurement of intelligence, abilities, and academic achievement, and later extended to the measurement of personality traits. However, *psychometry* is an evaluative process applicable to any method of psychological assessment, including behavioral assessment.

The *construct validity* of assessment instruments (more precisely, the construct validity of the data and inferences derived from assessment instruments[5]) is the primary focus of psychometric evaluation. Although often applied to higher-level constructs, construct validity is a supraordinate evaluative dimension that refers to the degree to which data and inferences derived from an assessment instrument are representative of the targeted construct (Messick, 1993).

The validity of data derived from an assessment instrument establishes the upper limit to the validity of contingent clinical judgments. The validity of inferences about the relative importance of and maintaining factors for a client's multiple behavior problems, the best treatment strategy for a client, risk factors for relapse, and the degree of treatment effectiveness depends on the validity of assessment data.

The application of psychometric principles to the behavioral assessment paradigm is affected by several factors associated with methods, targets, and tenets of the paradigm:

1. The constructs targeted in behavioral assessment differ in *level of molarity*. Obtained data differ in the degree to which they are presumed to mark a higher-level (e.g., aggregated, synthetic) construct or a lower-level less inferential variable of independent interest to the assessor. Behavioral assessment, compared to personalty assessment, more often targets lower-level variables. The relevance of some psychometric indices—such as internal consistency, factor structure, convergent and discriminant validity, and accuracy—varies with the level of inferences ascribed to obtained data.

2. The validity of data from an assessment instrument can vary with the purpose of assessment, and obtained data in behavioral assessment can be *accurate but invalid*. For example, accurate data may be obtained from analog observation of clients social interactions, but the data may display low levels of covariance with the same behaviors measured in natural settings. Particularly in idiographic assessment, accuracy of data is more important than some dimensions of validity (see Cone, 1996).

3. The *situational and temporal instability* of some phenomena measured in behavioral assessment (e.g., appetitive disorders, Rychtarik & McGillicuddy, 1996) complicate the interpretation of stability coefficients and place additional demands on time-sampling methods. Indices of instability can reflect variability due to true change

in the variable as well as measurement error and are weak indices of invalidity.

4. Behavioral assessment often involves *multimethod assessment* to access different modes and parameters of a phenomena. However, causal mechanisms and sources of measurement error vary across assessment methods and response modes. Estimates of covariance, often used as indices of validity, can be attenuated in comparison to monomethod or monomode assessment strategies (see discussion of psychometric indices of multiple methods in Rychtarik & McGillicuddy, 1996)

5. *Time-series assessment*, strategies often used in behavioral assessment, are associated with unique sources of inferential error, particularly those associated with autocorrelation, cyclicity, and chaotic patterns in data sets. Time-series assessment also accentuates the importance of matching sampling parameters to the dynamic characteristics (e.g., rate of change) of the measured phenomena.

6. The *individualized (idiographic) nature* of some behavioral assessment strategies enhances the importance of some construct validity elements such as accuracy, content validity, and interobserver agreement. It reduces the importance of other construct validity elements such as nomothetically based discriminant and convergent validity.

In summary, some psychometric evaluative dimensions are applicable to the behavioral assessment paradigm. However, other dimensions of psychometric evaluation may be less applicable to some behavioral assessment applications, in some situations, or for some purposes of assessment. Many behavior assessment instruments—particularly idiographic self-monitoring, participant observation, and observation-based instruments—are developed and applied on the basis of "face validity" without sufficient evaluation of their construct validity and sources of error variance.

Behavioral and Personality Assessment Paradigms

Many chapters in Hersen and Bellack (1996) and other recently published behavioral assessment books promote assessment methods that have not traditionally been considered "behavioral." For example, some chapters in Hersen and Bellack (1996) reference many retrospective, self-report, aggregated measures of personality traits. Other chapters focus on complimentary assessment methods and foci, cognitive assessment (Linscott & DiGiuseppe, 1996), and medical and physiological assessment (McConaghy, 1996; Rychtarik & McGillicuddy, 1996; Williamson, Veron-Guidry, & Kiper, 1996). Franzen and Smith-Seemiller (1996) noted that neuropsychological and behavioral assessment have many common tenets but that the data from neuropsychological assessment are more often representational.

The multimodal nature of behavior problems and causal variables supports the inclusion in behavioral assessment of validated instruments that target physiological and cognitive phenomena. These phenomena can be viewed as "behavior" and subjected to the same covariance analyses as motoric behavior.

As noted by many authors, the incremental utility and cost effectiveness of assessment instruments, particularly personality assessment instruments, will vary across clients and settings and have been insufficiently investigated.[6] The use of personality assessment instruments may be warranted on some assessment occasions. However, they are likely to be of most value if they are applied judiciously, if they are selected on the basis of their congruence with current empirically based models of the targeted behavior problems and causal variables, and when their results are interpreted in the context of their many sources of measurement and inferential errors.

The complexity of self-report personality trait-focused assessment and the impact of different personality assessment instruments on inferences are well recognized. For example, many respected personality researchers have noted that inferences about the stability and sources of variance of personality traits are affected by (1) the level of precision of variables that are considered as "personality," (2) the instruments used to measure the personality variables, (3) the time-sampling parameters of the measurement strategy, and (4) the type of statistical analysis to which the data are subjected (Heatherton & Weinberger, 1994).

Many behavioral scholar-clinicians support the use of personality measures as part of an "assessment funnel" approach and view personality and behavioral assessment as compatible (see special series on personality and behavioral assessment in *Behavior Modification*, 1993, vol. 17). However, there are several problems associated with the use of personality assessment instruments (Haynes & Uchigakiuchi, 1993):

1. Many constructs measured with personality assessment instruments are poorly defined and faddish.
2. Personality instruments focusing on the same construct vary in their content validity—the degree to which their elements are representative of and relevant to the targeted construct.
3. They often provide dysfunctionally aggregated, highly inferential, measures that are often insufficiently specific for treatment design or outcome evaluation.
4. Personality constructs are often imbued with causal properties and reified.
5. They often provide data that are insensitive to important dynamic and conditional characteristics of behavior.
6. There are insufficient data on the persons, situations, purposes, and methods, for which personality assessment may be useful.

SUMMARY

This chapter briefly reviewed basic characteristics of the behavioral assessment paradigm and noted the status and recent changes in several methodological and conceptual elements of the paradigm. Because of its empirical emphasis, behavioral assessment is a dynamic paradigm, and some differences between subparadigms were noted. Behavioral assessment plays an important but not dominant role in clinical assessment, in treatment outcome valuation, and in graduate psychology training programs.

There have been several advances in the methods of behavioral assessment: (1) computer-aided assessment, (2) technological aids for measurement in the natural environment, and (3) clinically useful analog assessment instruments. Advances have also occurred in the concepts and methods of the functional analysis in behavior therapy. Several limitations and advances were noted in the methods of gathering data for the functional analysis, integrating obtained data, estimating functional relationships, and drawing clinical judgments from the functional analysis.

Finally, the applications of psychometric principles and the integration of personality and behavioral assessment were addressed. The applicability of various psychometric evaluative dimensions vary across assessment methods, foci, and goals. Personality assessment is frequently used in conjunction with behavioral assessment, but there are many constraints associated with the interpretation of obtained personality assessment data.

ENDNOTES

1. Significant advances have also occurred in psychophysiological assessment (Andreassi, 1995), neuropsychological assessment (Franzen & Smith-Seemiller, 1996; Slomka & Tarter, 1993), and biomedical assessment (although Sweeney, Dick, & Srinivasagam, 1996, noted that the utility of some advances in biomedical assessment is yet to be shown).
2. Two variables have a causal relationship when (a) they demonstrate covariance (i.e., when they have a mathematically describable functional relationship), (b) the causal variable reliably precedes its effect, (c) there is a logical mechanism for the causal relationship, and (d) alternative explanations for the observed covariance can reasonably be excluded (Asher, 1976; Haynes, 1992).
3. A behavioral assessment "instrument" refers to any specific method of acquiring data. Thus, a particular questionnaire, a particular method of acquiring ambulatory blood pressure measures, and a particular strategy for the systematic manipulation of response contingencies in a clinic setting are all assessment "instruments."
4. Most of these terms have multiple definitions. For example, *functional assessment* has also been used to refer to the assessment of abilities in neuropsychology and rehabilitation. The term *functional analysis* has also been used to refer to the systematic manipulation of hypothesized controlling variables in applied and experimental behavior analysis.
5. Indices of validity are conditional, not necessarily generalizable, and do not unconditionally reside

with the assessment instrument. Data derived from an assessment instrument may be valid for some but not other ethnic or age groups, settings and client states, and purposes (e.g., data from an assessment instrument may not be equally valid for large scale community screening, treatment outcome evaluation, and the development of a functional analysis) (see also Silverman & Kurtines, 1996, for a discussion of contextual issues in assessment).

6. The incremental utility of cognitive variables is a contentious issue among behavioral scholars. Discussions of this issue can be found in Linscott and DiGiuseppe (1996) and Tryon, (1995b). Erudite exchanges have occurred on the Internet (sscp-net@bailey.psych.nwu.edu).

REFERENCES

Agras, W. S., Taylor, C. B., Feldman, D. E., Losch, M., & Burnett, K. F. (1990). Developing computer-assisted therapy for the treatment of obesity. *Behavior Therapy, 21*, 99–109.

Andreassi, J. L. (1995). *Psychophysiology: Human behavior and physiological response* (3rd ed.). Hillsdale, NJ: Lawrence Erlbaum.

Angle, H. V. (1981). The interviewing computer: A technology for gathering comprehensive treatment information. *Behavior Research Methods & Instrumentation, 13*, 607–612.

Asher, H. B. (1976). *Causal modeling*. Beverly Hills: Sage.

Axelrod, S. (1987). Functional and structural analyses of behavior: Approaches leading to the reduced use of punishment procedures? *Research in Developmental Disabilities, 8*, 165–178.

Bandura, A. (1969). *Principles of behavior modification*. New York: Holt, Rinehart and Winston.

Barrios, B. (1988). On the changing nature of behavioral assessment. In A. S. Bellack & M. Hersen (Eds.), *Behavioral assessment: A practical handbook* (pp. 3–41). New York: Pergamon.

Beidel, D. C., Neal, A. M., & Lederer, A. S. (1991). The feasibility and validity of a daily diary for the assessment of anxiety in children. *Behavior Therapy, 22*, 505–517.

Bellack, A. S., & Hersen M. (1988). Future directions of behavioral assessment. In A. S. Bellack & M. Hersen (Eds.), *Behavioral assessment: A practical handbook* (3rd ed.) (pp. 610–615). New York: Pergamon.

Bellack, A. S., & Hersen, M. (Eds.). (1993). *Handbook of behavior therapy in the psychiatric setting*. New York: Plenum.

Bogan, K., Ignacio, L., & Haynes, S. N. (1996). Time-source of assessment strategies in treatment outcome research. Manuscript submitted for publication.

Bornstein, P. H., Bornstein, M. T., & Dawson, D. (1984). Integrated assessment and treatment. In T. H. Ollendick & M. Hersen (Eds.), *Child behavioral assessment: Principles and procedures* (pp. 223–243). New York: Pegamon.

Bornstein, P. H., Hamilton, S. B., & Bornstein, M. T. (1986). Self-monitoring procedures. In A. R. Ciminero, C. S. Calhoun, & H. E. Adams (Eds.), *Handbook of behavioral assessment* (pp. 176–222). New York: John Wiley & Sons.

Brehmer, B., & Joyce, C. R. B. (Eds.). (1988). *Human judgement: The SJT View*. New York: North-Holland.

Burton, S. (1994). Chaos, self-organization, and psychology. *American Psychologist, 49*, 4–14.

Bush, J. P., & Ciocco, J. E. (1992). Behavioral coding and sequential analysis: The portable computer systems for observational use. *Behavioral Assessment, 14*, 191–197.

Butcher, J. N. (Ed.). (1987). *Computerized psychological assessment: A practitioner's guide*. New York: Basic Books.

Cacioppo, J. T., & Tassinary, L. G. (1990). *Principles and psychophysiology, Physical, social, and inferential elements*. New York: Cambridge University Press.

Ciminero, A. R. (1986). Behavioral assessment: An overview. In A. R. Ciminero, K. S. Calhoun, & H. E. Adams (Eds.), *Handbook of behavior assessment* (2nd ed.) (pp. 446–495). New York: John Wiley & Sons.

Collins, L. M., & Horn, J. L. (Eds.). (1991). *Best methods for the analysis of change*. Washington, DC: American Psychological Association.

Cone, J. D. (1988). Psychometric considerations and the multiple models of behavioral assessment. In A. S. Bellack & M. Hersen (Eds.), *Behavioral assessment: A practical handbook* (pp. 42–66). New York: Pergamon.

Cone, J. D. (1996). Psychometric considerations: Concepts, contents and methods. In M. Hersen & A. S. Bellack (Eds.), *Behavioral assessment: A practical handbook* (4th ed.). Boston: Allyn and Bacon.

Creer, T. L., & Bender, B. G. (1993). Asthma. In R. J. Gatchel & E. B. Blanchard (Eds.), *Psychophysiological disorders: Research and clinical applications* (pp. 151–204). Washington, DC: American Psychological Association.

Davison, G. C., Navarre, S., & Vogel, R. (1995). The

articulated thoughts in simulated situations paradigm: A think-aloud approach to cognitive assessment. *Current Directions in Psychological Science, 4,* 29–33.

Dumas, J. E. (1987). INTERACT—A computer-based coding and data management system to assess family interactions. In R. J. Prinz (Ed.), *Advances in behavioral assessment of children and families.* (Vol. 3, pp. 177–202). New York: Jai Press.

Durand, V. M., & Crimmins, D. M. (1988). Identifying the variables maintaining self-injurious behaviors. *Journal of Autism and Developmental Disorders, 18,* 99–117.

Eiler, J. M., Nelson, W. W., Jensen, C. C., & Johnson, S. P. (1989). Automated data collection using bar code. *Behavior Research Methods, Instruments & Computers, 21,* 53–58.

Eyde, L. D. (Ed.). (1987). Computerized psychological testing (special issue). *Applied Psychology Int. Rev., 36,* 3–4.

Fagot, B. I. (1992). Assessment of coercive parent discipline. *Behavioral Assessment, 14,* 387–406.

Farrell, A. D. (1991). Computers and behavioral assessment: Current applications, future possibilities, and obstacles to routine use. *Behavioral Assessment, 13,* 159–179.

Foster, S. L., & Cone, J. D. (1995). Validity issues in clinical assessment. *Psychological Assessment, 7,* 248–260.

Franz, D., & Gross, A. M. (1996). Assessment of child behavior problems: Externalizing disorders. In M. Hersen & A. S. Bellack (Eds.), *Behavioral assessment: A practical handbook* (4th ed.). Boston: Allyn and Bacon.

Franzen, M. D., & Smith-Seemiller, L. (1996). Behavioral neuropsychology. In M. Hersen & A. S. Bellack (Eds.), *Behavioral assessment: A practical handbook* (4th ed.). Boston: Allyn and Bacon.

Gardner, W. I., & Cole, C. L. (1988). Self-monitoring procedures. In E. S. Shapiro & T. R. Kratochwill (Eds.), *Behavioral assessment in schools: Conceptual foundations and practical applications* (pp. 206–246). New York: Guilford.

Gatchel, R. J., & Blanchard, E. B. (Eds.). (1993). *Psychophysiological disorders, research and clinical applications.* Washington, DC: American Psychological Association.

Gifi, A. (1990). *Nonlinear multivariate analysis.* Somerset, NJ: John Wiley & Sons.

Gilgen, A., & Abraham, F. (Eds.). (1995). *Chaos theory in psychology.* Westport, CT: Praeger.

Glass, C. R., & Arnkoff, D. B. (1989). Behavioral assessment of phobia. *Clinical Psychology Review, 9,* 75–90.

Gottman, J. M., & Roy, A. K. (1990). *Sequential analysis: A guide for behavioral researchers.* New York: Cambridge University Press.

Guevremont, D. C., & Spiegler, M. D. (1990, November). *What do behavior therapists really do? A survey of the clinical practice of AABT members.* Paper presented at the 24th Annual Convention of the Association for Advancement of Behavior Therapy, San Francisco, CA.

Hartmann, D. P., Roper, B. L., & Bradford, D. C. (1979). Some relationships between behavioral and traditional assessment. *Behavioral Assessment, 1,* 3–21.

Hauri, P. J., & Wisbey, J. (1992). Wrist actigraphy in insomnia. *Sleep, 15,* 293–301.

Haynes, S. N. (1978). *Principles of behavior assessment.* New York: Gardner.

Haynes, S. N. (1991). Behavioral assessment. In M. Hersen, A. Kazdin, & A. Bellack (Eds.), *The clinical psychology handbook* (pp. 430–464). New York: Pergamon.

Haynes, S. N. (1990). Behavioral assessment of adults. In G. Goldstein & M. Hersen (Eds.), *Handbook of psychological assessment* (2nd ed.) (pp. 423–463). New York: Pergamon.

Haynes, S. N. (1992). *Models of causality in psychopathology: Toward synthetic, dynamic and nonlinear models of causality in psychopathology.* New York: Macmillan.

Haynes, S. N. (1994). Clinical judgment and the design of behavioral intervention programs: Estimating the magnitudes of intervention effects. *Psychologia Conductual. 2,* 165–184.

Haynes, S. N. (1996). *Principles of behavioral assessment.* Book submitted for publication.

Haynes, S. N., Blaine, D., & Meyer, K. (1995). Dynamical models for psychological assessment: Phasespace functions. *Psychological Assessment, 7,* 17–24.

Haynes, S. N., Richard, D., & O'Brien, W. O. (1996). *Clinical case modeling: A vector graphic interactive computer software system.* Honolulu: Hawaii Office of Technology Transfer.

Haynes, S. N., Spain, H., & Oliviera, J. (1993). Identifying causal relationships in clinical assessment. *Psychological Assessment, 5,* 281–291.

Haynes, S. N., & Uchigakiuchi, P. (1993). Incorporating personality trait measures in behavioral assessment: Nuts in a fruitcake or raisins in a mai tai? *Behavior Modification, 17,* 72–92.

Haynes, S., N., & Waialae, K. (1994). Psychometric foundations of behavioral assessment. In R. Fernandez-Ballestros (Ed.), *Evaluacion conductual hoy: (Behavioral assessment today).* Madrid: Ediciones Piramide.

Heatherton, T. F., & Weinberger, J. L. (Eds.). (1994). *Can personality change*. Washington, DC: American Psychological Association.

Heiby, E. M. (1995). Chaos theory, nonlinear dynamic models, and psychological assessment. *Psychological Assessment, 7*, 5–9.

Heitzmann, C. A., & Kaplan, R. M. (1988). Assessment of methods for measuring social support. *Health Psychology, 7*, 75–109.

Henningfield, J. E., & Obarzanek, E. (1992). Task force 2: Methods of assessment, strategies for research. *Health Psychology, 11 (Suppl.)*, 10–16.

Hersen, M., & Ammerman, R. T. (Eds.). (1994). *Handbook of prescriptive treatments for adults*. Plenum: New York.

Hersen, M., & Bellack, A. S. (Eds.). (1996). *Behavioral assessment: A practical handbook* (4th ed.). Boston: Allyn and Bacon.

Hile, M. G. (1991). Hand-held behavioral observations: The Observer. *Behavioral Assessment, 13,* 187–196.

Honaker, L. M., & Fowler, R. D. (1990). Computer-assisted psychological assessment. In G. Goldstein & M. Hersen (Eds.), *Handbook of psychological assessment* (pp. 521–546.) New York: Pergamon.

Houghton, S. J. (1991). Promoting generalization of appropriate behaviour across special and mainstream settings: A case study. *Educational Psychology in Practice, 7*, 49–54.

Iwata, B. A. et al. (1994). The functions of self-injurious behavior: An experimental-epidemiological analysis. *Journal of Applied Behavior Analysis, 27*, 215–240.

Kanfer, F. H., & Schefft, B. K. (1988). *Guiding the process of therapeutic change*. Champaign, IL: Research Press.

Keefe, F. J., Dunsmore, J., & Burnett, R. (1992). Behavioral and cognitive-behavioral approaches to chronic pain: Recent advances and future directions. *Journal of Consulting and Clinical Psychology, 60*, 528–536.

Kratochwill, T. R., & Shapiro, E. S. (1988). Introduction: Conceptual foundations of behavioral assessment. In E. S. Shapiro & T. R. Kratochwill (Eds.), *Behavioral assessment in schools: Conceptual foundations and practical applications* (pp. 1–13). New York: Guilford.

Landsheer, J. A. (1990). ABC 0.9. *Behavioral Assessment, 12*, II.

Linscott, J., & DiGiuseppe, R. (1996). Cognitive assessment. In M. Hersen & A. S. Bellack (Eds.), *Behavioral assessment: A practical handbook* (4th ed.). Boston: Allyn and Bacon.

Loehlin, J. C. (1992). *Latent variable models: An introduction to factor, path, and structural analysis*. Hillsdale, NJ: Lawrence Erlbaum.

Mash, E. J., & Barkley, R. A. (1989). *Treatment of childhood disorders*. New York: Guilford.

Mash, E. J., & Terdal, L. G. (1988). Behavioral assessment of child and family disturbance. In E. J. Mash & L. G. Terdal (Eds.), *Behavioral assessment of childhood disorders* (pp. 3–65). New York: Guilford.

McConaghy, N. (1996). Assessment of sexual dysfunction and deviation. In M. Hersen & A. S. Bellack (Eds.), *Behavioral assessment: A practical handbook* (4th ed.). Boston: Allyn and Bacon.

McGrath, M. L. (1991). The empiricist. *Behavioral Assessment, 13*, I.

Messick, S. (1993). Validity. In R. L. Linn (Ed.), *Educational measurement* (2nd ed.). Phoenix: American Council on Education and the Oryx Press.

Musso, A., Blanchard, E. B., & McCoy, G. C. (1991). Evaluation of thermal biofeedback treatment of hypertension using 24-hr. ambulatory blood pressure monitoring. *Behaviour Research and Therapy, 29*, 469–478.

Nezu, A. M., & Nezu, C. M. (1989). *Clinical decision making in behavior therapy: A problem solving perspective*. Champaign, IL: Research Press.

O'Brien, S. N., & Haynes, S. N. (1995). Functional analysis. In Gualberto Buela-Casal (Ed.), *Handbook of psychological assessment*. Madrid: Sigma.

O'Donohue, W., & Krasner, L. (1995). *Theories of behavior therapy*. Washington, DC: American Psychological Association.

O'Leary, K. D. (1987). *Assessment of marital discord*. Hillsdale, NJ: Lawrence Erlbaum.

Ollendick, T. H., & Hersen, M. (1984). An overview of child behavioral assessment. In T. H. Ollendick & M. Hersen (Eds.), *Child behavioral assessment: Principles and procedures* (pp. 3–19). Elmsford, NY: Pergamon.

Ollendick, T. H., & Hersen, M. (1993). Child and adolescent behavioral assessment. In T. H. Ollendick & M. Hersen (Eds.), *Handbook of child and adolescent assessment* (pp. 3–14). Boston: Allyn and Bacon.

Patterson, G. R. (1993). Orderly change in a stable world: The antisocial trait as a chimera. *Journal of Consulting and Clinical psychology, 61*, 911–919.

Persons, J. B. (1989). *Cognitive therapy in practice: A case formulation approach*. New York: Norton.

Persons, J. B. (1992). A case formulation approach to cognitive-behavior therapy: Application to panic disorder. *Psychiatric Annals, 22,* 470–473.

Persons, J. B., & Fresco, D. M. (1996). Assessment of depression. In M. Hersen & A. S. Bellack (Eds.),

Behavioral assessment: A practical handbook (4th ed.). Boston: Allyn and Bacon.

Pickering, T. G. (1989). Ambulatory monitoring: Applications and limitations. In N. Schneiderman, S. M. Weiss, & P. G. Kaufmann (Eds.), *Handbook of research methods in cardiovascular behavioral medicine* (pp. 261–272). New York: Plenum.

Piotrowski, C., & Lubin, B. (1990). Assessment practices of health psychologists: Survey of APA division 38 clinicians. *Professional Psychology: Research and Practice, 21,* 99–106.

Piotrowski, C., & Zalewski, C. (1993). Training in psychodiagnostic testing in APA-approved PsyD. and PhD. clinical psychology programs. *Journal of Personality Assessment, 61,* 394–405.

Reid, J. B., Baldwin, D. V., Patterson, G. R., & Dishion, T. J. (1987). Some problems relating to the assessment of childhood disorders: A role for observational data. In M. Rutter, A. H. Tuma, & I. Lann (Eds.), *Assessment and diagnosis in child psychopathology.* New York: Guilford.

Repp, A. C., Harman, M. L., Felce, D., VanAcker, R., & Karsh, K. G. (1989). Conducting behavioral assessments on computer-collected data. *Behavioral Assessment, 11,* 249–268.

Rychtarik, R. G., & McGillicuddy, N. B. (1996). Assessment of appetitive disorders: Status of empirical methods in alcohol, tobacco, and other drug use. In M. Hersen & A. S. Bellack (Eds.), *Behavioral assessment: A practical handbook* (4th ed.). Boston: Allyn and Bacon.

Sanderson, W. C., & Wetzler, S. (1990). Five percent carbon dioxide challenge: Valid analogue and marker of panic disorder? *Biological Psychiatry, 27,* 689–701.

Sarwer, D., & Sayers, S. L. (1996). Behavioral interviewing. In M. Hersen & A. S. Bellack (Eds.), *Behavioral assessment: A practical handbook* (4th ed.). Boston: Allyn and Bacon.

Schlundt, D. G., Virts, K. L., Sbrocco, T., Pope-Cordie, J., & Hill, J. O. (1993). A sequential behavioral analysis of craving sweets in obese women. *Addictive Behaviors, 18,* 67–80.

Schulte, D. (1992). Criteria of treatment selection in behaviour therapy. *European Journal of Psychological Assessment, 8,* 157–162.

Segal, D. L., & Falk, S. B. (1996). Structured diagnostic interviews and rating scales. In M. Hersen & A. S. Bellack (Eds.), *Behavioral assessment: A practical handbook* (4th ed.). Boston: Allyn and Bacon.

Serber, G. A. F., & Wild, C. J. (1989). *Nonlinear regression.* Somerset, NJ: John Wiley & Sons.

Shapiro, E. S., & Kratochwill, T. R. (1988). Analog assessment: Methods for assessing emotional and behavioral problems. In E. S. Shapiro & T. R. Kratochwill (Eds.), *Behavioral assessment in schools: Conceptual foundations and practical applications* (pp. 290–321). New York: Guilford.

Silva, F. (1993). *Psychometric foundations and behavioral assessment.* Newbury Park, CA: Sage.

Silverman, W. K., & Kurtines, W. M. (1996). Anxiety and phobic disorders: A pragmatic perspective. In M. Hersen & A. S. Bellack (Eds.), *Behavioral assessment: A practical handbook* (4th ed.). Boston: Allyn and Bacon.

Sisson, L. A., & Taylor, J. C. (1993). Parent training. In A. S. Bellack & M. Hersen (Eds.), *Handbook of behavior therapy in the psychiatric setting* (pp. 555–574). New York: Plenum.

Slomka, G. T., & Tarter, R. E. (1993). Neuropsychological assessment. In T. H. Ollendick & M. Hersen (Eds.), *Handbook of child and adolescent assessment* (pp. 208–223). Boston: Allyn and Bacon.

Sobell, L. C., Toneatto, T., Sobell, M. B. (1994). Behavioral assessment and treatment planning for alcohol, tobacco, and other drug problems: Current status with an emphasis on clinical applications. *Behavior Therapy, 25,* 523–532.

Strosahl, K. D., & Linehan, M. M. (1986). Basic issues in behavioral assessment. In A. Ciminero, K. S. Calhoun, & H. E. Adams (Eds.), *Handbook of behavioral assessment* (2nd ed.) (pp. 12–46). New York: Wiley.

Suen, H. K., & Ary, D. (1989). *Analyzing quantitative behaviotal observation data.* Hillsdale, NJ: Lawrence Erlbaum.

Sutker, P., & Adams, H. E. (Eds.). (1993). *Comprehensive handbook of psychopathology* (2nd ed.). New York: Plenum.

Sweeney, J. A., Dick, E. L., & Srinivasagam, N. S. (1996). Biological assessment. In M. Hersen & A. S. Bellack (Eds.), *Behavioral assessment: A practical handbook* (4th ed.). Boston: Allyn and Bacon.

Taylor, C. B., Fried, L., & Kenardy, J. (1990). The use of a real-time computer diary for data acquisition and processing. *Behaviour Research and Therapy, 28,* 93–97.

Taylor, S. E. (1990). Health psychology: The science and the field. *American Psychologist, 45,* 40–50.

Tombari, M. L., Fitzpatrick, S. J., & Childress, W. (1985). Using computers as contingency managers in self-monitoring interventions: A case study. *Computers in Human Behavior, 1,* 75–82.

Tryon, W. W. (1985). *Behavioral assessment in behavioral medicine.* New York: Springer.

Tryon, W. W. (1991). *Activity measurement in psychology and medicine*. New York: Plenum.

Tryon, W. W. (1995). Resolving and cognitive behavioral controversy. *The Behavior Therapist, 18*, 83–86.

Tryon, W. W. (in press). Observing contingencies: Taxonomy and methods. *Clinical Psychology Review*.

Tryon, W. W. (1996b). Behavioral observation. In M. Hersen & A. S. Bellack (Eds.), *Behavioral assessment: A practical handbook* (4th ed.). Boston: Allyn and Bacon.

Turk, D. C., & Salovey, P. (1988). (Eds.). *Reasoning, inference, and judgment in clinical psychology*. New York: The Free Press.

Turner, S., Calhoun, K. S., & Adams, H. E. (1992). *Clinical behavior therapy* (2nd ed.). New York: Wiley.

Vallacher, R., & Nowak A. (Eds.) (1994). *Dynamical systems in social psychology*. San Diego: Academic Press.

Watkins, C. E., Jr., & Campbell, V. L., & McGregor, P. (1989). Personality assessment and counseling psychology. *Journal of Personality Assessment, 53*, 296–307.

Whitehurst, G. H., Fischel, J. E., DeBaryshe, B., Caulfield, M. R., & Falco, F. L. (1986). Analyzing sequential relations in observational data: A practical guide. *Journal of Psychopathology and Behavioral Assessment, 8*, 129–148.

Williamson, D. A., Veron-Guidry, S., & Kiper, K. (1996). Assessment of health-related disorders. In M. Hersen, & A. S. Bellack, *Behavioral assessment: A practical handbook* (4th ed.). Boston: Allyn and Bacon.

Wincze, J. P. (1982). Assessment of sexual disorders. *Behavioral Assessment, 4*, 257–271.

Wolpe, J., & Turkat, I. D. (1985). Behavioral formulation of clinical cases. In I. Turkat (Ed.), *Behavioral case formulation* (pp. 213–144). New York: Plenum.

Woods, P. J. (1974). A taxonomy of instrumental conditioning. *American Psychologist, 29*, 584–597.

CHAPTER 2

PSYCHOMETRIC CONSIDERATIONS
CONCEPTS, CONTENTS, AND METHODS

John D. Cone
United States International University

Careful operationalization of major constructs and collection of high-quality data are the sine qua non of any substantive research enterprise. No methodologies, no matter how powerful allow researchers to study phenomena they have not measured well. One cannot make a silk purse out of a sow's ear, no matter how powerful the sewing machine. . . . Does the use of several measures of a construct improve the measurement of that construct if each measure is poor—if the aim is to produce a silk purse, are 10 sows' ears better than one? (Martin, 1987, p. 36)

The request to revise this chapter is a stimulus to reflect on developments in the psychometrics of behavioral assessment since the last appearance of this book in 1988. Consistent with earlier versions (Cone, 1981, 1988), the opening quote underscores the importance of psychometric considerations. Indeed, one purpose for writing the chapter is to help the reader develop silk purses and to recognize sow's ears so they can be avoided or transformed.

Psychometric considerations are essentially about the quality of assessment information.

Whether this information is any good requires answering "good for what?" For this reason, the chapter begins with a discussion of five common reasons for doing assessment. Once we know *why* we are assessing, it is easier to determine *what* we should assess. For example, if our task is to describe the characteristics of persons applying for public safety jobs in a major U.S. city, we are likely to select personality variables (e.g., responsibility, self-control, conflict avoidance) and compare the applicants with norms in the population or with applicants for other types of positions. Knowing our purpose led to the identification of the personality characteristics as our subject matter. Had our purpose been to teach someone the social skills necessary for successful public safety work, we would have identified specific social behavior as the subject matter of our assessment activities.

Knowing why we are assessing and, therefore, what we need to assess, allows us to select appropriate assessment methods. We are then in a position to evaluate the adequacy of different methods and select ones of the highest quality. The criteria we apply in distinguishing among the available methods will depend on the assessment purpose and subject matter. For example, if our purpose is to describe the personality characteristics of public safety job applicants, we will select methods designed to assess personality traits or latent variables. Furthermore, we will select those methods that meet acceptable standards with respect to the classical psychometric criteria of reliability and validity. If our purpose is to teach specific social skills, we will select methods aimed at identifying specific behavior. In this case, we will select methods meeting acceptable standards with respect to accuracy and other criteria appropriate to measures of behavior.

At this point in the process, it is possible to classify our activities as assessors. That is, it is now apparent that we are acting as latent variable assessors or as behavior assessors, given these examples. We might classify ourselves in different ways, of course, if we are pursuing activities other than those characterized in the preceding examples.

It might be expected that a chapter on the psychometrics of behavioral assessment would start with a definition of the field. Understanding assessment logic is enhanced by delaying definitional considerations, however, until the reasons for assessment and the appropriate subject matters have first been clarified. Thus, definitions of behavioral assessment make up the third section of the chapter. A distinction is made between the *logic* of behavioral assessment and its instrumentation. It is noted that instrumentation is often overemphasized to the detriment of behavioral assessment logic. The instruments (methods) of behavioral assessment are then described briefly, followed by the meat of the chapter, a section devoted to the measurement concepts needed to evaluate the quality of these methods. Accuracy, reliability, generalizability theory, and validity concepts are discussed in this section. Finally, a few thoughts on evaluating the *process* of behavioral assessment, as distinct from its methods, are considered.

PURPOSES OF ASSESSMENT

Various reasons for conducting assessments have been suggested (Cone & Hawkins, 1977; Evans,

1993; Mash & Terdal, 1976, 1980, 1981). It is useful to consider five of them here.

Description/Classification

Fundamentally, assessment is undertaken for descriptive purposes. Here, the goal is to represent or characterize an entity or some portion of an entity's behavioral repertoire. The most useful descriptions are objective ones (i.e., representations that can be repeated). Description provides the basis for all forms of assessment. Indeed, it is difficult to think of assessment that does not include this aspect. For example, a goal to change something about a client requires describing exactly what is to be changed. This is because description is needed for comparison purposes. Some of the obvious comparisons include differences over time (e.g., from the beginning to later points in an intervention, from morning to afternoon), differences between the client and others (e.g., normative comparisons), differences across situations, and differences between various aspects of the person being assessed (e.g., between social and intellectual repertoires). Description may lead to classification or to the assignment of the behavior (or the person) to some category or group. Classification is arbitrarily considered with description here, as is common (e.g., Shaughnessy & Zechmeister, 1990). A case can also be made for viewing classification as a separate purpose of assessment. In any event, description occurs first.

Understanding

A second reason for assessing is to further our understanding of a particular phenomenon. Enhanced knowledge can come from making the comparisons mentioned earlier. For example, we learn more about adolescents' social skills by describing them and then comparing groups independently said to be skillful and unskillful, respectively. Kumar and Beyerlein (1991) developed and evaluated a measure of ingratiatory behavior to learn more about the upward influence techniques of subordinates in organizations. Assessing a number of persons with their newly developed scale and then looking at the structure of the scale via factor-analytic techniques led to greater understanding of the construct of ingratiation.

Prediction

Another reason for assessing is to predict performance at some other time or place. For example, clinicians predict the likelihood of improvements in clients assigned to various forms of intervention (or to no intervention at all). Academicians predict the success of applicants for admission to graduate school (e.g., Dollinger, 1989). Industrial/organizational psychologists predict the productivity of workers or the quality of their work (e.g., Hoffman, Nathan, & Holden, 1991). Note that predicting behavior can be one of the more atheoretical purposes of assessment. Prediction is often a purely practical or economic pursuit, with no concern for advancing scientific understanding of either the construct being assessed or the performance being predicted.

Control

A fourth reason for assessing is to achieve control over some aspect of a person or the person's repertoire. Generally, an interest in control serves the larger purposes of furthering scientific understanding or effecting clinical improvement. When behavioral assessors undertake functional analyses, for example, it is to discover the variables controlling behavior so it can be changed.

Monitoring Change

Finally, assessment can be undertaken to evaluate differences in behavior over time. This is particularly common in time-series analyses in which repeated assessment of a behavior provides data to evaluate the impact of systematic changes in potential controlling variables (Barlow, Hayes, & Nelson, 1984; Kazdin, 1992). A more limited form involves measurements taken before and after intervention.

These five purposes are identified because the assessment methods one uses will depend on the reason for undertaking assessment in the first place. Measures useful for simple descriptive purposes may not suffice for monitoring change over time, for example (Messick, 1983). Likewise, those designed for predicting future behavior may not be

sensitive enough to be useful in functional analyses. These purposes cover most of the reasons psychologists do assessments, but they are admittedly arbitrary, and there may be others that are not represented.

It is also likely that assessment will be undertaken for multiple purposes. For example, assessment might move from a general mapping phase through successively more and more specific phases to the ultimate identification of intervention targets (Hawkins, 1979). At each phase, a different type of method might be appropriate, with broad-band, low-fidelity instruments (Cronbach, 1970) used for general mapping where many different behaviors are being considered, and narrower-band, higher-fidelity ones reserved for the handful of specific behaviors ultimately selected for change. The psychometric issues of greatest interest with interviews used for mapping will differ from those of direct observations used for pinpointing and monitoring change in intervention targets. The point is that evaluating the quality of behavioral assessment devices is accomplished best in a context that includes the reasons for using them.

THE CONTENT OF BEHAVIORAL ASSESSMENT

Psychometric issues will vary with the purpose of assessment. They will also vary with the content (i.e., the subject matter) being assessed which, in turn, depends on assessment purpose. In its infancy, behavioral assessment was contrasted with more "traditional" forms of assessment in terms of content (e.g., Barrios, 1988; Goldfried & Kent, 1972; Hartmann, Roper, & Bradford, 1979; Mischel, 1968). In those comparisons, the subject matter of the former was said to be "behavior," whereas that of the latter was said to be "traits." That is, behavioral assessors were seen to view assessment responses as samples of a repertoire not completely available at the time. Traditional assessors were seen to view those responses as signs (Goodenough, 1949) of a hypothetical construct or trait underlying assessment performance. To some extent, this distinction holds today (e.g., Galassi & Perot, 1992). It is important to be clear whether behavior or latent traits are the ultimate assessment interest, because the design of one's measures and their evaluation depend on the nature of the subject matter (Cone, 1978, 1981; Johnston & Penny-packer, 1980).

It is not enough to espouse *interest* in or the *intention* to assess behavior. For example, one might state an interest in assessing behavior characterized as "assertive." If high scores on a measure of it are subsequently referred to as reflecting high levels of "assertion," it sounds as though the speaker has switched subject matters. Consistency is important. Is behavior per se or something underlying behavior the focus of assessment?

Understanding what is being assessed has been clarified in recent years with the application of structural equation modeling to the development and evaluation of assessment instruments (Bollen, 1989; Bollen & Lennox, 1991). Though directed at more traditional, latent variable forms of assessment, work in this area has definite implications for behavioral assessment as well. Bollen and Lennox's (1991) distinction between effect indicator and causal indicator models of assessment is one example. In the first, responses to stimuli (indicators) on assessment devices are seen to be the result (effect) of underlying latent constructs. Thus, responses to true-false items in a self-report measure of social anxiety are more or less likely to be in the trait-keyed direction depending on the "amount" of the trait the respondent possesses. The responses can be said to be controlled by the trait or construct underlying the instrument.

In the second, or causal indicator, model, responses to stimuli (indicators) on assessment devices are seen to be causes of the construct being assessed rather than the other way around. Bollen and Lennox (1991) give the example of socioeconomic status (SES), the items of which might include level of education, type of job, location of residence, and so on. It is not reasonable to assume one's job type was determined by one's socioeconomic status. Rather, the construct of SES can be seen to be determined by job type, education, and other items in the index. DeVellis (1991) has suggested calling such measures *indices* rather than *scales*.

The instruments of behavioral assessors fall principally in the index category. This is because we are concerned with defining constructs from the client's perspective (Kelly, 1955; Mischel, 1968). When a client complains of being depressed, we look for the sources of control over the complaint and we generally confine our search to events in the client's current environment. We do not assume an underlying construct or trait within the client is causing the complaints. Instead, we do a more or less formal functional analysis to identify causes, typically external ones. For example, we might find the client ingests substances leading to reduced states of physiological arousal. We might also discover the client rarely interacts socially and has low frequencies of vigorous exercise. When we alter the environment to arrange changes in these behaviors, we also see the client's reports of "depression" vary in predictable ways. Our conclusion might be that participating in these activities "causes" variations in depression.

The distinction between effect indicator and causal indicator models is helpful in understanding the applicability of traditional psychometric concepts in behavioral assessment. As Bollen and Lennox (1991) make evident, some of our customary assumptions do not apply so clearly when we move from one model to the other. For example, the effect indicator model assumes responses to test stimuli are the result of a latent trait. Moreover, all indicators are considered equal in that each is comparably determined by the trait. Thus, the expectation that responses will be consistent across test stimuli is a logical outgrowth and the basis for expecting internally consistent measures. When the construct underlying test performance is seen as *determined by* rather than *determining* responses to test stimuli, there is no logical requirement for internal consistency. In the preceding example, whether the client ingests depressogenic substances has no necessary relationship to whether he or she is socially interactive or involved in regular exercise.

If behavior is the subject matter, we are dealing with something that has properties that are more or less objectively definable. If behavior is viewed as matter in motion (Johnston & Penny-packer, 1993), measures of it can be evaluated in terms of the same principles of measurement as are applied to matter in the physical sciences. Thus, whether behavior occurred, how frequently, how fast, how intensely, and so on are all aspects to be determined by assessment instruments, and the adequacy of the instruments for making these determinations can be evaluated. As pointed out previously, the principal characteristic of measuring devices in the physical sciences, and thus, of those applied to behavior, is their accuracy (Cone, 1988).

If latent traits are the subject matter, we are dealing with something having no physically definable properties. We make assumptions about the nature of the trait, develop measures based on these assumptions, and evaluate the adequacy of the measures in terms of how closely their performance matches the assumptions. Johnston and Pennypacker (1980, 1993) make clear that variability in scores on our measures becomes the principal characteristic used both to define the trait *and* to establish the adequacy of the measures. In a latent variable measurement context, reliability and associated concepts related to "true" scores become the most important concepts for evaluating measurement quality.

From the latent trait perspective, classical measurement assumptions stem from the notion of parallel tests (DeVellis, 1991). The assumption is that responses to each item in an assessment device are equally determined by the underlying trait, as mentioned earlier. Thus, they are essentially "parallel tests" of the trait. Additional assumptions include that other influences on item responses are essentially random error and that this error is not correlated across items nor associated with the "true" score. Furthermore, the error associated with each item is assumed to be equal to that associated with any other item (Novick, 1966). The orthodox parallel tests model in classical psychometric theory has been supplemented by models that involve relaxing its assumptions. Relaxing the requirement that items have equal error variances results in "tau-equivalent" measures, for example (DeVellis, 1991; Novick & Lewis, 1967). Loosening classical requirements even further results in the congeneric model (Joreskog, 1971) in which

the only restriction is that items assumed to be measuring the same thing be perfectly correlated.

Structural equation modeling and confirmatory factor analysis provide ways of testing the adequacy of any of these views of the relationship between item responses and the trait assumed to underlie them (Nunnally & Bernstein, 1994). Regardless of the model, however, it is crucial to realize they apply to latent variables and the notion that responses on assessment devices are determined by the traits themselves. Thus, tau-equivalent, essentially tau-equivalent, congeneric, and various factor models may be viewed as subcategories of Bollen and Lennox's (1991) effect indicator model. It is not clear that causal modeling has strong implications for, or applicability to, causal indicator models that are the more relevant to behavioral assessment (Ozer & Reise, 1994).

To summarize, assessment purpose determines assessment subject matter. It also determines the relationship between assessment responses and the subject matter (construct) they are supposed to represent. If latent variables are the subject matter, responses may be the effect or the cause of the variable, and causal modeling and confirmatory factor analysis may be relevant psychometric tools. If behavior is the subject matter, these tools are not so clearly relevant, and accuracy is the central consideration.

Now that we know *why* we are assessing and, therefore, *what* we need to assess, we can classify our assessment activities. In other words, we know what to call ourselves! To assist in this labeling process, let us look at some issues involved in defining the field.

DEFINING BEHAVIORAL ASSESSMENT

A chapter on the psychometric considerations of behavioral assessment presupposes a delimited field of scientific and applied activity on which there is general agreement. Unfortunately, as pointed out elsewhere (Cone, 1986, 1988; Silva, 1993a), *behavioral assessment* is a misunderstood term that has been defined in various ways (Cone, 1987; Nelson & Hayes 1981; O'Leary & Wilson,

1975). According to Silva (1993a), the majority view is similar to that of O'Leary and Wilson (1975), who long ago defined behavioral assessment as "an attempt to identify the environmental and self-imposed variables which are *currently* (emphasis in the original) maintaining an individual's maladaptive thoughts, feelings, and behaviors. . . . The emphasis in behavioral assessment is on analyzing specific environmental events which are controlling behavior" (pp. 18–19). A similar definition is provided in Nelson and Hayes (1981) who noted that behavioral assessment is "the identification and measurement of meaningful response units and their controlling variables (both environmental and organismic) for the purposes of understanding and altering human behavior" (p. 3). A contrasting point of view, described by Silva (1993a) as "diametrically opposed to the views of many authors" (p. 8) defines behavioral assessment as at least "the objective description of specific human responses that are considered to be controlled by contemporaneous environmental events and whose consistency and/or variability are directly related to the consistency and/or variability of their environment. . . . Behavioral assessment can be seen to be an important part of, but not synonymous with behavior analysis" (Cone, 1987, pp. 2–3).

The last definition of behavioral assessment seems very close to *topographic analysis* as described by Ferster (1965), a term he distinguished from functional analysis. It is also very close to defining behavioral assessment in terms of its contents (i.e., the subject matter being assessed). This can be a problem when that subject matter (i.e., behavior) is narrowly restricted to overt motor actions. The difficulty stems from a tendency among lay and professional communities to see behavior as "only a subset of the dependent variables addressed by psychology" (Hayes & Follette, 1993, p. 183), the larger set including such things as attitudes, emotions, thoughts, and feelings. From a content-focused perspective, it is easy to view behavioral assessment as merely one of several types of assessment, complemented by personality assessment, cognitive assessment, and so on.

The restriction of behavioral assessment to assessment of overt motor responses is an even

narrower definition than that proposed by Cone (1987), however. Elsewhere, and consistently, cognitive and physiological events are also treated as behavior (Cone, 1977, 1978, 1979, 1988, 1995). As such, all of the dependent variables of psychology come under the purview of behavioral assessment (Hayes & Follette, 1993). Indeed, the reductionist characterization given Cone's (1987) definition by Silva (1993a) might be challenged in that the definition admits assessment activity involved in functional analyses and is not limited to it. In other words, functional analyses include the topographic descriptions emphasized in Cone's definition. Topographic descriptions are undertaken for lots of reasons that do not include functional analyses, however. Thus, the topographic characterization of behavioral assessment leads to the inclusion of any objective description of the dependent variables of psychology, whether for functional analytic purposes or not. The activities of psychopharmacologists carefully documenting the behavioral effects of nicotine withdrawal in rats (e.g., Helton, Modlin, Tizzano, & Rasmussen, 1993) would be included, for example—so would those of comparative psychologists studying the behavior of genetically different mice (e.g., Paylor, Johnson, Papaioannou, & Spiegelman, 1994).

Unfortunately, it is still true that equating behavioral assessment with its contents can be limiting. This is because even though many more assessment activities are covered, the character of those activities does not always include what many consider to be the central emphasis in behavioral assessment (i.e., to discover the purposes served by behavior so that it can be controlled and better understood).

Thus, part of the reason for the very pluralistic nature of behavioral assessment is the lack of consensus on its subject matter. The present writer and others (e.g., Hayes & Follette, 1993) take the radical behavioral perspective that admits all activities of the organism. Others do not share this inclusiveness, however, limiting the subject matter of behavioral assessment to observable motor responses (e.g., Johnston & Pennypacker, 1993). Indeed, as Hayes and Follette (1993) have noted, the syndromal approach underlying the *DSM* relegates behavioral assessment to an approach focusing on motor activities.

BEHAVIORAL ASSESSMENT METHODS

As we have just seen, what one is willing to allow to be the subject matter of behavioral assessment has profound implications for the definition and inclusiveness of the field. Moreover, the instrumentation seen as relevant to behavioral assessors will vary with the subject matter. Thus, if one holds to the "motor behavior only" view, the use of indirect assessment methods (interviews, self-reports, ratings by others) will seem foreign and inappropriate. Holding the more ecumenical view, such methods will often be seen as the best one can do when assessing less accessible aspects (e.g., thoughts, feelings, physiological responses) of the complete behavior repertoire. Here again, however, behavioral assessors differ in their interpretation of the behavior actually observed in assessment activities. On the one hand, observed responses may be viewed as the effects of something unseen (e.g., social anxiety, fear). On the other hand, they may be seen as samples of behavior that is important in its own right, and the understanding of which involves manipulating contemporary environmental events. The issue in each case is the source of influence on the assessed behavior.

To undertake functional analyses of clients' complaints, it is necessary to make observations of other client behavior in various environmental contexts. Objectifying these observations requires instrumentation. In behavioral assessment, as in other forms of assessment, it has become customary to rely on interviews, self-reports, ratings by others, self-observation, and direct observations by others. As pointed out some years ago (Cone, 1978), each of these methods is more or less suitable to assessing the three forms of behavior (e.g., cognitive, motor, and physiological) mentioned earlier. Because cognitive behavior is equated with private events (i.e., as language that occurs subvocally), ratings by others and direct observation cannot be used with it. Otherwise, the crossing of method and content produces a complete taxonomy (the Behavioral Assessment Grid [Cone, 1978]) for organizing

our thinking about behavioral assessment. For example, physiological responses might be assessed via simple questions directed to a person in the context of an interview. "What do you notice about your breathing when you find yourself speaking with a stranger of the opposite sex?" might be asked. Of course, more direct assessment might occur in the form of the person's observing and rating their breathing when in such encounters in the course of their daily activities. Or, one might "observe" even more directly by attaching sensors to the person's chest and noting the behavior of the sensors when the person is in these situations.

EVALUATING THE METHODS OF BEHAVIORAL ASSESSMENT

Regardless of the methods one uses to objectify observations of behavior, and whether for functional or topographic analyses, the quality of the resulting observations must be established. This is a potentially complex undertaking when conducting functional analyses, as there are invariably multiple behaviors involved and multiple persons producing them. The problem is simpler in the case of topographic analyses because the focus can be limited to the quality of the observations of the response whose topography is being described. Thus, reports of depression can be examined for their adequacy alone. It is not necessary to look at behavior thought to be related to complaints of depression.

There are essentially three questions to ask when evaluating the quality of behavior observations: (1) To what extent was the observation controlled by the behavior itself? (2) Can the observation be repeated? and (3) Does the observation have any relevance? These three questions are dealt with in behavioral assessment via the concepts of accuracy, reliability, and validity, each of which will be discussed in turn.

Accuracy

Johnston and Pennypacker (1993) define accuracy as "the extent to which observed values approximate the 'true' state of nature" (p. 138). They note further that "perfect accuracy [is] a limiting condition, unattainable in any specific instance but approachable with ever-diminishing error" (p. 138). If an observation of a behavior is the result of the behavior's occurrence, the observation can be said to be accurate. The most accurate observations are those influenced by the behavior alone.

Behavior occurs or it does not. It occurs repeatedly, at different times, and at different places or it does not. These facts about behavior are more or less observable. A professor makes a positive comment to a student or he or she does not. The occurrence of the comment can be observed with varying degrees of fidelity. The higher the fidelity, the more accurate the observation. Thus, accuracy can be defined as the extent to which observations are sensitive to objective topographic features and dimensional quantities (i.e., frequency, latency, duration, magnitude) of behavior.

Accuracy is the most important characteristic of measures in the physical sciences. When a biologist examines the structure of a particular cell, he or she does so with a microscope capable (i.e., accurate enough) of revealing the composition of the cell as it exists in nature. The biologist has confidence in the accuracy of the microscope because it has met certain standards, and the limits of its accuracy are known. Similarly, when we purchase sound-reproducing equipment, we are provided information on the accuracy (fidelity) with which the device reproduces the sound. For example, we are given signal to noise ratios (s/n) or percent total harmonic distortion (%THD) data to use in judging instrument quality.

When behavior is viewed from a physical science perspective (e.g., as matter in motion), it is reasonable to apply physical science measurement concepts to it as well. Thus, the most important characteristic of observations of behavior is their accuracy. As noted elsewhere, the accuracy of measures in the behavioral sciences should be established in advance of their use to determine facts about behavior (Cone, 1981, 1987; Foster & Cone, 1986). This will help avoid Type II errors resulting from measurement problems. The prior determination of accuracy is referred to as *derivation* accuracy. It establishes the limits of the fidelity of the measure under optimally controlled laboratory conditions. When the measure is then used for sci-

entific or practical purposes, the adequacy of the data it produces under these less than optimally controlled conditions must be determined as well. Referred to as *application* accuracy, this will usually lead to data of lower fidelity than those of the derivation conditions because there is less control of relevant variables.

To establish accuracy, two things are needed: (1) an incontrovertible index of behavior and (2) rules/procedures for using the measure. When a measure is used in accord with rules and procedures written by its developers, it will be shown to reflect the incontrovertible index with more or less fidelity. If fidelity is high, the measure is said to be accurate. If fidelity is low, it is said to be inaccurate, though it is really a matter of degree. The important point is that, like the microscope of the biologist, the accuracy limits of the assessment instrument of the behavioral scientist can be known ahead of time. When they are, the scientist can make an informed decision as to whether the instrument is likely to produce data of sufficient quality for the task at hand. Measures will vary in accuracy. It is also generally true that accuracy will vary inversely with cost. The degree of accuracy needed will depend on the assessment purpose. For example, a direct observation measure might result in scores on a category called "total deviant" or "total aversive behavior" that are sufficiently accurate to describe the problem behavior of children in a special classroom relative to that of children in regular classes. It may not yield data sufficiently accurate to permit a functional analysis of the specific behavior of an individual child, however. Another instrument may serve this purpose. That instrument is likely to be more expensive in terms of observer training time, prior observer experience, number of observations needed, data-entry equipment needed, and the required frequency and intensity of ongoing quality assurance.

The biggest challenge to routine use of accuracy to evaluate the adequacy of behavioral measures is the need for incontrovertible indices (i.e., the need to know what is "really true" about behavior). Kazdin (1977) suggested consensus could be used as an approximation, and, indeed, observers have often been trained and recalibrated by comparing their data against those of standard protocols generated by averaging the data of multiple observations (e.g., Borman & Hallam, 1991; Cunningham & Tharp, 1981; Mash & McElwee, 1974). Perhaps consensus criteria make the most sense in a postmodernist, constructivist era. The advent of high technology, stop action, multimedia, and computer-controlled video should make these criteria even more important in the future.

More representative of "true" states of nature, however, are electromechanically generated indices such as those involving preprogrammed performances from puppets or animated characters. These criteria require taking on "faith"—only the adequacy of the programming operations and the equipment used to time the performance. The use of scripts in which behavior is predetermined is perhaps an improvement over consensus criteria, but does not escape social construction altogether because of the need to determine whether the script was faithfully enacted. Finally, comparing observers' data with those produced by mechanical counters (e.g., Bechtel, 1967) provides another means of establishing accuracy.

The requirement to show a measure's accuracy has not been fully appreciated in the behavioral assessment literature. In addition to giving increased confidence that observations are the result of the activity being observed, accuracy serves another important purpose in advancing science. It provides a basis for enhanced replicability. When a particular assessment instrument such as the Marital Interaction Coding System (Weiss & Summers, 1983) is developed and used to produce substantive findings in research on couples, other researchers are likely to use it. When they do, their use must be comparable to the original use so their findings can be interpreted appropriately. For maximum replicability, written instructions accompanying assessment instruments must be explicit. That is, they must control user behavior consistently. One way of assessing whether instructions are explicit is to examine the accuracy of data produced from users of an instrument whose training consists solely of reading the instructions. High levels of accuracy are evidence of the adequacy of the instructions. Thus, purveyors of new measures would do well to provide information as to the accuracy of the measure and the adequacy of written instructions for its use.

Derivation accuracy is more easily established than application accuracy. This is because in the derivation condition, an accuracy criterion can usually be produced. Accuracy criteria do not usually present themselves in application conditions, however. Indeed, if an incontrovertible index of behavior existed in application contexts, there would be no need for the assessment instrument itself. The best one can hope for is that high levels of accuracy are shown in derivation conditions, that instructions for using the measure are explicit, and that subsequent applications of the measure do not deviate greatly from the derivation conditions. Periodic calibration checks (Reid, 1982) in the use of direct observation assessment are one way of examining application accuracy. The reactivity of such checks is likely to be a problem, as it is with agreement checks, however (e.g., Romanczyk, Kent, Diament, & O'Leary, 1973; Taplin & Reid, 1973). This is especially likely when live observations are being made. When observers are coding from taped records, accuracy recalibration can be undertaken with greater confidence. For example, unknown to observers, tapes for which a consensus accuracy criterion has been produced previously can be included randomly among those being scored. Accuracy slippage can then be determined.

Accuracy is the preeminent characteristic of any assessment method for which the subject matter is behavior. It has been given most attention when direct observation methods are at issue, but is just as important when other types of method are being used (Cone, 1981). Of course, special difficulties occur when observations cannot be verified independently. This is especially evident when cognitive behavior (or so-called private events) is being assessed. When the observer is reporting something only he or she can see, there is no way to determine the accuracy of the report. This problem is not averted by changing the nature of the assessment process. For example, we do not escape by saying our real interest is in the observer's report rather than what is referred to in that report. When a person makes a statement referring to other behavior of his or hers, we are interested in the sources of control over that statement. If it is completely controlled by the behavior referred to, it is accurate and can be said to represent the behavior with a high degree of fidelity.

In uses of self-report to assess private events or cognitive behavior, we have a legitimate interest in the quality of our assessment. Unfortunately, the accuracy of such observations cannot be known. That is, we cannot assess the extent of control private behavior exerts over public behavior. If we shift focus to the self-report itself, however, we have changed the nature of the assessment activity. The subject matter is now the speech of the reporter, and the observations are made by the assessor who is not the reporter and whose observations can be verified independently. In effect, we have introduced direct observation of motor behavior, and the previous discussion of the accuracy of direct observation assessment methods applies.

We *can* know the extent of control over public behavior exerted by other public behavior, however. That is, we can determine the accuracy of self-reports when they refer to behavior that others can see. When someone says they tremble while giving a speech before an audience of unfamiliar persons, their statement can be verified objectively. Thus, the accuracy of self-reports of motor behavior can be relatively easily established. The same can be said of self-reports of physiological behavior. Whether a person's heart rate really does increase while giving a speech before an audience of unfamiliar persons can be determined. The requirement to use special sensors and amplifiers to detect some physiological activity does not change the fact that it is behavior and that measures of it can be subjected to tests of their accuracy.

To summarize, the preeminent characteristic of assessment methods used with behavior as their subject matter is accuracy. Accuracy reflects the extent to which observations of behavior tact that behavior. Accuracy is best established under derivation conditions that are carefully controlled and that involve an incontrovertible index and explicit rules/procedures for using the measure. Subsequent applications of the instrument implicitly assume generalization of the accuracy previously established. These assumptions are more or less tenable depending on the comparability of derivation and application conditions. They should be tested when possible, however, via the use of recalibration to guard against accuracy drift. The accuracy of all instruments used to assess behavior can be determined, whether self-report, ratings by others, or direct observation. Accuracy is limited to the assessment of publicly observable behavior. There is a great deal of conceptual similarity between accuracy and the classical notion of reliability, a subject to which we now turn our attention.

Reliability

In classical psychometric theory dating to Spearman (1904), the reliability of a measure is the proportion of variance in scores on the measure that is attributable to true variance on the latent trait (DeVellis, 1991). Reliability can be conceptualized, therefore, as a ratio of true to observed score variances:

$$r_{xx} = \frac{\sigma_t^2}{\sigma_x^2}$$

where σ_t^2 is true score variance and σ_x^2 is observed score variance.

The denominator can be decomposed into true score and error variance, making it clear that a measure approximates perfect reliability when its scores are maximally determined by the latent variable underlying them. This appears perfectly analogous to the earlier definition given to *accuracy*, but more on that later.

The difficulty with the mathematical representation of reliability is that the equation cannot be solved. That is, it cannot be used by itself to estimate reliability because it contains a major unknown (i.e., the variance in true scores). One solution to this difficulty requires using the correlation between alternate measures of the same latent trait to estimate their individual reliabilities (Pedhazur & Schmelkin, 1991). To do this involves assuming the measures are alike (i.e., parallel). If they are parallel, they will have the same true scores and equivalent error variances, assumptions that were discussed when describing the parallel tests model previously. It will be recalled that the rather restrictive assumptions of the strictly parallel tests approach have been relaxed, with the result that alternative models (e.g., tau equivalent, congeneric) have been proposed and tested successfully.

Classical test theory concepts of reliability resolve to estimates of true scores that cannot be known with certainty because of the very hypothetical nature of the traits they represent. Indeed, the reliability index has been referred to as the *theoretical validity* of a measure because it deals with the relationship between observed scores and scores on a latent trait (Pedhazur & Schmelkin, 1991). The higher the reliability, the more the measure may be said to be reflecting the underlying trait. Thus, reliability in classical test theory can be seen to have epistemological implications (Northrop [1947] as cited in Pedhazur & Schmelkin, 1991, p. 85).

Responses to items in traditional trait measures are thought to be caused by latent traits. Given this assumption, it is not unreasonable to expect them to be equally determined thereby. Furthermore, if they are equally determined, they will be correlated with one another. This logic is the basis for the importance placed on internal consistency in classical assessment models. Items in a scale should be highly correlated with one another from this perspective. Various ways of representing inter-item relationships and the internal consistency or homogeneity of measuring instruments are well known to psychologists. Among these are split-half techniques in which the resulting correlation is stepped up using the Spearman-Brown prophecy formula (Nunnally & Bernstein, 1994). Methods based on the mean of all possible item splits (i.e., Kuder-Richardson formulae 20 and 21) are also familiar to psychologists, and it is generally known that the K-R 20 is a special case of Cronbach's coefficient alpha, applicable when a measure calls for dichotomous responses (DeVellis, 1991). Alternate form reliability is conceptually comparable to internal consistency and can be useful when repeated assessment is needed to document change while minimizing carryover effects.

Another estimate of reliability results from correlations between sets of scores obtained from a group of persons at two or more points separated in time. Referred to as *test-retest reliability* or *temporal stability* (Cronbach, 1947), the assumption is that items reflecting a latent trait should do so comparably from one occasion to the next (DeVellis, 1991). Thus, correlations between sets of scores obtained at different times should provide estimates of the extent to which those scores are the effect of the latent trait. Lately, problems with the logic of using stability of scores over time to estimate reli-

ability have become apparent. The difficulty is with the assumption that consistent scores reflect anything about the precision with which the latent trait is measured. There may be other reasons than trait-determined ones for scores being stable, such as biases due to carryover effects (Pedhazur & Schmelkin, 1991). In addition, variance in scores caused by trait-irrelevant constructs (e.g., social desirability) might lead to stability over time when the trait itself (e.g., anxiety) has actually changed (Nunnally, 1978). Kelly and McGrath (1988) have identified four possibilities when comparing scores from one time to the next: (1) real change in the latent trait, (2) systematic variations in the construct (as in chemically dependent mood changes throughout the day), (3) differences related to changes in the people taking the test (fatigue-related carelessness) or instrument calibration issues that are unrelated to the latent trait, and (4) instability due to measurement error and problems with the unreliability of the instrument itself. Obviously, only differences over time that are the result of the last of these reflect reliability (or lack of it) per se. Difficulties such as these have led some to recommend the test-retest approach not be used to estimate reliability (e.g., Pedhazur & Schmelkin, 1991).

Problems in applying classical reliability concepts in behavioral assessment have been discussed repeatedly (e.g., Cone, 1981; Johnston & Pennypacker, 1980; Nelson, Hay, & Hay, 1977; Silva, 1993a). In the physical sciences, reliability relates more specifically to the repeatability of scores. Thus, if repeated observations of the same phenomenon agree, they are said to be reliable. Put another way, a reliable measure is one "that yields the same value when brought into repeated contact with the same state of nature" (Johnston & Pennypacker, 1993, p. 138).

This is a much more limited view of reliability than classically espoused. It can be entertained because reliability in behavioral assessment is not based on theories of error and true scores, and is not needed to define the subject matter being assessed. In behavioral assessment, just as in the physical sciences, we are first interested in the fidelity with which our measures represent some aspect of reality. Measures that do this are said to be accurate.

Accuracy may vary over time. More specifically, it may deteriorate—an occurrence referred to earlier as *accuracy drift*. If an instrument remains accurate, it is said to be reliable. In other words, the measure's accuracy is consistent or the measure is consistently accurate.

A second way reliability is used in behavioral assessment is to describe the quality of measurement when there is no incontrovertible index or independent way of knowing what is really true concerning a particular behavior occurrence. Johnston and Pennypacker (1993) give the example of repeatedly scoring permanent records of a behavior such as would be available from audiotapes or videotapes. If comparable scores result from multiple observations, scoring can be characterized as reliable. Note that no information about what "really" occurred is necessary. Scores that under- or overestimate actual occurrences could still be reliable, so long as their estimates are consistent over time. Such scores would not be accurate, but their errors would be systematic, thus leading the scores to be termed reliable.

It should be clear that accuracy and reliability are quite different concepts. The former has epistemic implications in behavioral assessment, the latter in latent trait assessment. Reliability is *not* used in behavioral assessment to define its subject matter. Rather, it is used to characterize the consistency of observations of behavior, and these observations may vary in accuracy. Reliability *is* used to define latent traits, however, though its importance in the repeated observations or temporal sense is questionable, as noted earlier.

In the "psychometrics" of behavioral assessment, accuracy and reliability are doubtless the two most important characteristics. There will be times, however, when neither can be determined. As Johnston and Pennypacker (1993) note, this does not mean the data and the measurement system producing them are worthless. It simply means we cannot be sure what they represent. We are then left with the task of convincing others of the usefulness of data the accuracy and reliability of which we cannot attest. Johnston and Pennypacker (1993) introduce the concept of *believability* for such circumstances. They point to interobserver agreement as one way of enhancing the believability of

data for which accuracy and reliability cannot be established. Joining others (e.g., Gewirtz & Gewirtz, 1969; Kazdin, 1977), they emphasize the difference between interobserver agreement and accuracy. They go further than others, however, in pointing out the importance of accuracy and warning against an easy reliance on interobserver agreement as an inappropriate substitute.

Johnston and Pennypacker (1993) make clear that believability has nothing to do with the adequacy of the data themselves. Rather, it "focuses on influencing the user's disposition to believe that the data represent what they are intended to represent and thus warrant interpretation" (p. 142). There are numerous approaches to using observer agreement to influence believability. These include graphical (e.g., Birkimer & Brown, 1979) and mathematical (e.g., Berk, 1979) representations. The latter are more common and include simple percentage agreement measures (Kelly, 1977) as well as more complex statistics such as kappa (Cohen, 1960), weighted kappa (Cohen, 1968), Pearson product moment correlation (McNemar, 1962), and the intraclass correlation coefficient (Bakeman & Gottman, 1986). Space does not permit detailed treatment of the many alternatives available. It is important to remember the purpose of representing observer agreement when choosing the best way to do it. Because you want to convince consumers of the research that your data warrant their serious consideration, you are well advised to consider who these consumers are and what will impact them the most. For example, end-point users might be more impressed with straightforward graphical representations showing that data are essentially the same from one phase of a study to the next whether primary or calibrator observers data are used. This is obvious to such users when information from both observers is presented jointly in graphs showing changes in participants' data over time.

If the consumers of your research are academically oriented, they are likely to be more impressed with mathematical representations of agreement. Kelly (1977) reports the most popular of these is simple percentage agreement, where agreements between observers are divided by agreements plus disagreements and multiplied by 100. The major decision here is defining agreement. It is well known that defining it liberally (i.e., both observers agreeing that a behavior occurred or both agreeing that it did not occur) results in capitalizing on chance. Thus, it is relatively easy to obtain high levels of agreement because chance alone produces it (Hartmann, 1977; Johnson & Bolstad, 1973). More conservative definitions of agreement protect against chance inflation. For example, when behavior occurs infrequently, restricting agreement to occurrences only (i.e., not considering agreement that the behavior did *not* occur) effectively minimizes chance influences. Similarly, when behavior occurs frequently, restricting agreement to nonoccurrences only (i.e., not considering agreement that the behavior *did* occur) effectively minimizes chance (Suen & Ary, 1989).

Statistical procedures are available that eliminate chance altogether. Among the most versatile of these is Cohen's (1960, 1968) kappa. Simply put, kappa is equal to the ratio of actual nonchance agreements to total possible nonchance agreements. It requires the calculation of chance agreement, which is then subtracted from both observed and total possible agreement. The resulting value can range from -1.00 (meaning complete disagreement between observers, even less than would be expected by chance) through 0 (meaning no more agreement than would be expected by chance) to 1.00 (meaning perfect agreement). There is disagreement as to just how high a resulting value constitutes adequate agreement, with values from .60 to .80 variously seen as acceptable. Even with this ambiguity, however, Suen and Ary (1989) describe kappa as the "single least controversial index" (p. 113) and recommend it as the index of choice. Formulae for computing kappa and more extensive discussions of it can be found in Hartmann (1977), Foster and Cone (1986), and Suen and Ary (1989).

The procedures for influencing data believability discussed thus far assume an interest in showing agreement between observers for specific events being recorded. This is accomplished most easily when the observation interval is small and few events are possible within it. What procedures are available when specific events cannot be isolated? For example, when the total number of self-stimulatory behaviors by a child with autism during some time interval is of interest, how do we establish consistency between observers? Other examples include observations of events/commodities not easily distinguishable (e.g., amounts of litter in different public areas [Burgess, Clark, & Hendee, 1971] or kilowatts of electricity used per hour [Hayes & Cone, 1977]). Observer consistency under these circumstances can be shown most simply by comparing totals. Again, percentage agreement can be computed by dividing the smaller total by the larger and multiplying by 100. If multiple frequencies are of interest, as when frequency counts of behavior occur over different sessions, days, or weeks, correlational procedures can be used. The Pearson product moment correlation is best known, but others (e.g., intraclass correlation [Lindquist, 1953]) have also been suggested. The more recent elaboration of generalizability theory (Cronbach, Gleser, Nanda, & Rajaratnam, 1972) has expanded our appreciation of the applicability of analysis of variance procedures beyond intraclass correlation to interobserver reliability more generally. Readers interested in a lucid treatment of these alternatives are referred to Suen and Ary (1989).

The existence of so many different ways to show interobserver consistency reflects the need to consider the measurement context carefully before choosing. Again, the most important variables may be your audience and the uses to be made of the data. With respect to the latter, it is useful to address the *functional* reliability of a set of scores. That is, if the data from two observers lead to identical conclusions, they may be said to be functionally equivalent. To illustrate, independent observers watching a particular applicant for an elementary teaching job might produce total teaching sequences correct per minute of .40 and .55, respectively. These may appear to be substantially different rates, calling into question the adequacy of the observation system. If the criterion rate for a positive hiring decision is .40, however, the same outcome results regardless of which observer's data are used. In this very practical context, esoteric mathmatical agreement measures might be superfluous.

This returns us to Johnston and Pennypacker's (1993) observation that believability has nothing to do with the adequacy of the data themselves. Given the criterion-referenced assessment context of the preceding example, consumers of the two observers' data will be equally influenced by either. Thus, simply showing the consumers the functional reliability (e.g., the percentage of identical hiring recommendations) of the data might be sufficient. The trick is to show who it is one is trying to influence and what will be most impressive to them. This is logically the case when the task is to convince others of the utility of your interpretation of the data.

Agreement between independent observers results in greater believability because there is a noble tradition in psychology to define phenomena in terms of agreement. Watson (1919), for example, viewed events for which consensus could not be established as outside the realm of psychology. As long as observations were objective (i.e., consistent between at least two independent observers), their subject was admissable. Further evidence that interobserver agreement influences believability is to be found in the vast number of published articles in which it is reported. Apparently, journal editors are more likely to believe data that have been shown not to depend on the observer producing them.

To summarize, reliability has different meanings and is used for different reasons when the subject matter of one's assessment can be known independently of the measures of it, and when the subject matter has no such independence. In the latter situation (i.e., when latent traits are the subject matter), reliability is of fundamental importance in *defining* the trait. Consistent with parallel tests assumptions, the emphasis is on homogeneous instruments, and internal consistency measures are of most importance. In contrast, the use of temporal consistency (test-retest reliability) indices to evaluate latent trait measures has been associated with significant conceptual difficulties in recent years. When behavior is the subject matter, reliability relates to the repeatability of observations of the same state of nature. As nature is unlikely to remain constant, reliability is most applicable when records of behavior are available for repeated observation. It is clear that accuracy is the most important characteristic of behavioral assessment devices, and that reliability can be shown for observations that are not accurate. It is also noted that reliability and

agreement between observers are not the same conceptually or operationally, and that agreement has more to do with influencing the believability of data than with establishing how adequately they represent behavioral phenomena.

Relevance of Classical Reliability for Behavioral Assessment

All of the foregoing might leave the impression that *classical* reliability concepts have no place in behavioral assessment. That is essentially correct (Nelson, 1983). Nonetheless, there are times when the *logic* of classical concepts can be useful. For example, one might have an interest in describing the extent to which preschool children behave independently. Such children can be observed to see whether their behavior reflects dependence/independence on adults. "Being near adults," "asking for assistance," "touching/holding onto adults," and "asking for praise," might be viewed as members of a general class of *dependency* behaviors. The comparability of these behaviors might be examined. Defining comparability in terms of covariation, interbehavior correlations might be computed, much as when exploring the internal consistency of latent trait measures. Spearman-Brown corrected split-half reliabilities or coefficient alphas might even be computed. The purpose for using these statistics would be different, of course, than the purpose for which they were originally developed. This should not matter, however, because statistical procedures are merely tools of investigation and do not really "care" how they are used. The coherence of response classes has obvious scientific as well as practical implications for behavioral assessors, and there are occasions in which this coherence can be documented using statistics developed for other disciplines and subject matters.

Another example involves consistency of behavior over time. Suppose the developmental course of the dependent/independent behavior just described were of interest. There are various ways its temporal course might be charted, including the use of classical temporal stability estimating techniques. That is, correlations could be computed for a group of children assessed on at least two separate occasions. High values would indicate children retain their relative positions with respect to this particular type of behavior over the time interval chosen.

Note that the use of classical reliability procedures in these examples has nothing to do with evaluating the quality of assessment devices per se. The interest is in learning more about the behavior itself. For example, are behaviors organized on a rational basis organized similarly when examined empirically? Are the relative positions of children manifesting these behaviors stable over time? In other words, classical procedures can be useful in behavioral assessment, but not for their original purpose. Behavioral assessment devices are not more or less valuable based on their levels of internal consistency or temporal stability.

Generalizability Theory

The existence of different types of reliability reflects the fact that different questions can be asked about the consistency of scores. Are they consistent across observers/scorers? Are they consistent within all parts of a measure? Can different forms of the measure be developed that will yield consistent scores between them? Are scores consistent over time? The classical notion of reliability represented by Spearman's (1904) formula partitions observed scores into true and error components. Factors that influence scores (other than the latent variable) are assumed to do so randomly. The very acknowledgment of different reliabilities suggests the possibility that these multiple influences might be systematic, however. Unfortunately, there is no mechanism within classical theory to permit identifying what these influences might be.

Cronbach and colleagues (Cronbach, Gleser, Nanda, & Rajaratnam, 1972) proposed a general framework for exploring these influences and determining how much they affect observed scores. For example, items comprising stimuli for a test might be selected at random from a domain of content. If all items in a measure represent the content domain consistently, they will correlate with one another and their combination will result in an instrument with high internal reliability. In Cronbach and colleagues' (1972) parlance, we say the score obtained on the measure does not *depend* on

which particular items were responded to in the keyed direction. Similarly, there are numerous persons who might score a test. If multiple persons independently examine a set of responses and come up with the same number, we say the score does not depend on the scorer. Each influence on scores can be thought of as a *facet* whose impact can be studied separately and in combination with other facets. The *person* facet represents the influence contributed by actual differences among people in the construct being assessed, and is analogous to the classical concept of true score (Shavelson, Webb, & Rowley, 1989). Cronbach and colleagues propose the use of analysis of variance procedures as a comprehensive way of conducting generalizability or G-studies of multiple influences on scores. In such studies, the impact of different variables on scores can be studied individually and in combination.

Generalizability theory is especially compatible with behavioral conceptions of assessment that have never recognized the importance of classical notions of reliability in which observed scores are composed of variance due to the latent variable and random error. The behavioral concept of accuracy acknowledges multiple influences on scores, the largest being the behavior itself. Influences on scores other than the behavior are not thought of as random, however. The following formula represents the logic of the behavioral view of accuracy:

$$X = B + V_1 + V_2 + V_3 + \ldots + V_n$$

where X is an observed score, B is behavior, and $V_{1 \ldots n}$ are other variables systematically influencing the observed score. The perfectly accurate score would be one in which $X = B$, and there were no contributions from other variables. Using the logic of G-studies, if not their analytic procedures, the behavioral assessor can determine the factors to suppress or control if perfect accuracy is to be achieved. This would occur at the instrument development or derivation stage. Identified influences, the extent to which they affect accuracy, and ways of controlling and minimizing their effect would be incorporated into the rules/procedures for using the device. In other words, the quality of the data obtained in application conditions would be appropriately qualified in terms of the "facets" found influential in the derivation conditions. For more extensive treatments, interested readers are referred to excellent discussions of generalizability theory and its application by Crocker and Algina (1986) and Shavelson and associates (1989).

Accurate, reliable, or generalizable scores will have varying degrees of usefulness, ranging from none to considerable. The usefulnesss of scores from assessment measures is represented by their validity, a subject to which we now turn.

Validity[1]

It is customary to define validity as whether a test measures what it is supposed to measure (Anastasi, 1988). However, there is merit in taking Cronbach and Meehl's (1955) broader view of validity as the *meaning* of the data resulting when an instrument or assessment procedure is used. This meaning is to be found in the relations into which scores from a measure enter with those from other measures.

Cronbach (1971) called attention to the fact that it is interpretations of the data produced by a measure, rather than the measure itself, that are validated. This view has been elaborated by Messick (1989, 1994) and others (e.g., Kane, 1992; Pedhazur & Schmelkin, 1991). Messick (1994) has recently argued for a unified concept of validity, placing it under the general rubric of construct validity. From a behavioral perspective, validity may be seen as a value judgment. It is verbal behavior reflecting the believability of empirical and theoretical evidence supporting the characterization of assessment instruments as discriminative for certain behaviors of persons having contact with them. These behaviors might include judgments of whether the measure looks like it can be put to particular uses (face validity) or whether it is composed of stimuli calling for construct relevant responses (content-related validation). Other behavior for which instruments might be discriminative include predictions from responses to the test stimuli to other types of responses, either concurrently available or to be available sometime in the future (criterion-related validation), or judgments of whether relationships entered into by scores on the test are consistent with theory (construct-related valida-

tion). Finally, assessment instruments and responses to them can be discriminative for certain behaviors of other persons toward the respondents. Messick (1994) refers to this as the consequential aspect of measure validation, and it deals with the impact (consequences) of using the assessment procedure. *Consequential validation* treats the larger questions of test use and goes beyond whether it meets its original objectives. Consequential validation asks whether use of the instrument is consistent with other social values. A behavioral assessment subcategory of consequential validation could be intervention or treatment validity (Evans & Nelson, 1977; Hayes, Nelson, & Jarrett, 1987; Silva, 1993b). If use of the information from a measure leads to beneficial intervention outcomes for persons providing it, it is said to have treatment validity. There can be benefits of other types, of course, which is why consequential validation is the more general concept.

When dealing with validation, we are generally asking two major questions about assessment data: (1) Do they represent the subject matter adequately? and (2) Do they mean anything? Answers to these questions can be summarized under representational and elaborative forms of validation (Cone, 1995). *Representational validation* has a logical priority in that it deals with the extent to which responses on a measure are controlled by the variable being assessed. In behavioral assessment, this type of validation is synonymous with accuracy. In latent trait assessment, representational validation deals with how completely assessment responses are determined by the underlying trait. *Elaborative validation* establishes whether a measure, once shown to represent its construct adequately, has any usefulness.

It is possible for an instrument to represent something well, and yet for its scores not to enter into relationships with scores on measures of other constructs. The operationists referred to this as having *meaning without significance* (Bechtoldt, 1959). For them, a concept's meaning is to be found in the operations that define it. Its significance is to be found in the network of relationships involving it and other variables. Thus, defined concepts will have meaning, by definition, though they may not have significance. L. J. Cronbach (personal communication, May 1, 1995) has recently noted similarities between the representational-elaborative validation distinction and Campbell and Fiske's (1959) distinction between trait validity and nomological validity.

The traditional concepts of content, convergent, and discriminant validation are relevant to representational validation. Content-related validation has generally not been seen as very informative when evaluating measures of latent traits (Anastasi, 1988). In part, this is because of the hypothetical nature of such variables. Systematic observation of the content of a trait measure really provides little more than hypotheses about the author's definition of the trait. Content-related validation has generally been of greater importance in evaluating tests of achievement, where defined bodies of content exist, and inspection of items in an assessment instrument can reveal how adequately content domains have been sampled. Similarly, content-related validation is useful in evaluating behavioral assessment measures that are seen as providing samples of behavior from larger domains or repertoires. Haynes and colleagues provide an extensive treatment of content-related validation, and interested readers are encouraged to consult their very thorough paper (Haynes, Richard, & Kubany, 1995).

Representational validation is likely to start with content-related validation, as this provides the easiest initial evidence concerning whether the subject matter one hopes to assess is adequately reflected by the measure. According to Messick (1994), the content aspect of unified validity "includes evidence of content relevance, representativeness, and technical quality" (p. 3). In addition to content, attention should also be directed to structural aspects of the measure (Messick, 1994). Referring to Loevinger's (1957) earlier work, Messick argues that the scoring structure of an instrument should reflect the "structure of the construct domain at issue" (p. 3). A related issue is that the assessment method selected should be appropriate to the subject matter of interest. To illustrate, the title "Construction and Validation of an Instrument for Measuring Ingratiatory Behaviors in Organizational Settings" (Kumar & Beyerlein, 1991) implies a direct observation measure of motor behavior.

Interestingly, a self-report method is described instead.

The format of the method is also relevant to representational validation. Format should be consistent with the nature of the construct being assessed, whether actual behavior or latent trait. For example, the amount of time husbands engage in conversation with their wives is likely to be assessed best with a direct observational measure that records conversational responses and their duration. Such a measure represents the behavior and dimensional quantity of interest with greater fidelity than a self-report of wives' perceptions of the behavior. It is also a better representative than a direct observation system of the momentary time sampling variety. Similarly, when self-report methods are used, response alternatives can be chosen to represent the construct most appropriately. Binary options would seem more reasonable when "ever engaged in" is the information wanted. Likert-type continua seem more reasonable when "how frequently" or "how long" is being assessed. Comrey (1988) argues the superiority of multiple response alternatives, generally. His argument is not addressing representational validation issues, however, but is concerned with facilitating factor analyses of item intercorrelations.

When latent traits are the subject matter, representational validation is advanced with evidence showing convergent and discriminant validation. It has been clear for some time that traits should be shown to be more than the measures of them (Campbell & Fiske, 1959). This is best demonstrated by showing correlations between alternative methods of assessing the traits. When these methods are maximally different, convergent validation arguments are most convincing. Unfortunately, there have never been clear guidelines for judging when methods are different (Pedhazur & Schmelkin, 1991). It is generally agreed, however, that a minimum of two traits assessed by two or more different methods is needed for convergent validation.

Sharpening the differences between one trait (especially a newly proposed one) and others, especially well established ones, is accomplished via discriminant validation arguments. In pursuing discriminant validation, differences are sought between traits said to be theoretically distinct (e.g., conscientiousness and dependability) and between traits and pervasive characteristics known to relate to many individual difference variables (Campbell, 1960). One of the most pervasive characteristics with which latent variable measures are likely to correlate is social desirability (SD; Edwards, 1957). Extensive research documents the pervasive involvement of social desirability in self-report measures of personality (Edwards, 1970, 1990). For example, it is well established that factor analyzing large numbers of scales produces a first principle component with a high loading by social desirability (Edwards, Diers, & Walker, 1962). Because self-report responding is saturated with the social desirability response set, special provisions are often taken to minimize the relationship at the very beginnings of item generation and subsequent refinement of the measure (Jackson, 1984).

The social desirability scale value (SDSV) is an important characteristic of any personality scale item. In fact, the earliest applications of item response theory in personality assessment relied on the SDSV to explain item performance. For example, it is known that the likelihood that persons will endorse items as true of themselves is highly linearly related to the SDSVs of the items. It is also known that the internal consistency of a scale is related to the proportion of items in the scale that have midrange values on the SDSV continuum (Edwards, Walsh, & Diers, 1963). Indeed, one of the tricky aspects of refining scales by eliminating items with too high item-SD Scale correlations is that these items are likely to be at the extremes in terms of their SDSVs. Eliminating them produces a scale with items having medium SDSVs. It also produces a scale with lower internal consistency. SDSVs are a property of all items and can easily be determined. They have been published for some of the more common personality inventories, such as the MMPI (Messick & Jackson, 1961), the California Personality Inventory (Mees, Gocka, & Holloway, 1964), and the Edwards Personal Preference Schedule (Edwards, 1959).

In the representational phase of scale development there are other variables that are sometimes controlled, including inconsistent responding (Butcher, Dahlstrom, Graham, Tellegen, & Kaemmer,

1989; Tellegen, 1988), "yea" and "nay" saying (Couch & Keniston, 1960), and lying (Hathaway & McKinley, 1943). A great deal of research centered on response styles in the 1950s and early 60s. After Rorer (1965) called attention to some major problems with the research, however, it declined significantly. Basically, Rorer concluded there was very little evidence that response styles affect responding on the typical self-report instrument. He distinguished response styles from response sets, though, confining his dismissal to research on styles. The evidence supporting the importance of response sets (i.e., deliberate attempts to portray oneself in particular ways) is much more compelling.

One of these sets, lying, has been shown to account for much less variability in scale responding than social desirability does (Edwards, 1970). In this regard, it is noteworthy that authors of new scales often confuse social desirability and lying (e.g., Kumar & Beyerlein, 1991). Others writing in the area of personality assessment fail to distinguish between them (e.g., Hogan & Nicholson, 1988). It has been shown that a popular measure of social desirability, the Marlowe-Crowne Scale (Crowne & Marlowe, 1960), is uncorrelated with the more general form of SD defined by Edwards (1957). Instead, it correlates with lying as defined in the MMPI (e.g., Edwards & Walsh, 1964). Thus, to show the independence of one's measure from SD as Campbell (1960) recommends, the "right" form of social desirability must be included. Moreover, care must be taken to distinguish between responding in a socially favorable way on the one hand and lying on the other. One is reminded of the hazards of the jingle fallacy (Kelley, 1924) when observing the frequency with the Marlowe-Crowne scale is used to assess social desirability. Just because the names given tests make them sound like they measure the same thing does not mean they do.

Multitrait-multimethod matrices (Campbell & Fiske, 1959; Fiske & Campbell, 1992) have long been the most popular means of jointly considering convergent and discriminant validation arguments. Extensive treatments of these arrangements are available and do not need replication here (Bagozzi, 1993a; Ozer & Reise, 1994; Pedhazur & Schmelkin, 1991). Their application in behavioral assessment has also been described previously (Cone,

1979). In that treatment, it was noted that many attempts to show the relationships between different types of behavior (e.g., cognitive and motor) suffer from confounding behavior and method. Thus, findings of greater within-system (e.g., cognitive-cognitive) than between-system (e.g., cognitive-motor) correspondence might simply reflect the use of the same and different assessment methods, respectively.

It is tempting to elaborate this argument, but space is limited. Suffice it to say that, whether latent variables or observable behaviors are being related in order to further scientific aims, it is useful to show that relationships are more than the fortuitous use of common measurement methods. Various analytic techniques applied to multitrait-multimethod matrices attempt to show the contributions to such relationships made by method variance alone (Bagozzi, 1993b; Goffin & Jackson, 1988; Kenny & Kashy, 1992).

To summarize, content, convergent, and discriminant validation all have to do with establishing the adequacy with which a measure represents the construct it is supposed to measure, be it behavior or latent trait. Additional structural issues (Messick, 1994), method-construct match, and item format considerations also bear on the strength of representational validation arguments. Representational validation precedes elaborative validation (Cone, 1995), with evidence concerning the latter being easier to interpret in the context of evidence concerning the former. When observable behavior is the subject matter, accuracy is shown via representational validation.

An assessment instrument may do an excellent job of *representing* a construct. Whether the construct has any *significance*, however, is argued via the gathering of elaborative validation evidence. Well-measured constructs may have no significance, and constructs can have no significance unless measured well.

Elaborative validation involves arguing the usefulness of constructs by showing relationships entered into by measures of them. Thus, when performance on an assessment instrument is shown to relate systematically to some other type of performance, the usefulness of the instrument and its underlying construct are enhanced. Elaborative validation subsumes evidence gathering activities customarily referred to as construct and criterion-related validation. *Construct validation* typically focuses on expanding nomological networks composed of theoretically meaningful relationships. *Criterion-related validation* is typically more practical, and the criteria are of greater interest than the constructs being used to predict them (AERA, APA, & NCME, 1985).

Consistent with this is a focus on the quality of the criterion measure itself. Often referred to as *the prediction problem* (Nunnally & Bernstein, 1994), the point is that prediction will only be as good as the separate qualities of predictor and criterion. It is generally known that coefficients of determination have upper limits set by the square root of the product of the reliabilities of the two measures being correlated (Kaplan & Saccuzzo, 1993). Therefore, elaborative validation requires the use of criteria and predictors for each of which representational validation evidence has been obtained. In other words, we need some advance confidence in how well the measure of the criterion actually represents that criterion. Incidentally, the requirement for symmetry of measurement quality is not unique to criterion-related validation. Science advances by showing relationships among variables. Its progress is hampered when measures of these variables lack representational validation, whether theoretical or applied questions are being raised.

It has been said that when studying behavior, accuracy is the preeminent characteristic of one's measures and validity is unimportant (Johnston & Pennypacker, 1993). The strength of this argument appears to stem from equating validity with accuracy. In other words, validity is being defined as the extent to which an instrument assesses what it is supposed to assess. In terms of the logic presented in this chapter, this is tantamount to equating accuracy with representational validation and stopping there. Elaborating the validation evidence for accurate measures is important in showing the measure's usefulness, however. It provides evidence as to whether there is any reason to assess the behavior in the first place. Further, it is of substantial value when the purpose of assessment is enhanced understanding of the behavior being assessed.

In behavioral assessment, elaborative validation takes many forms. A measure of social skills might gain value by showing differences between independently defined groups of skillful and unskillful adolescents, for example. Showing differences between contrasted groups on a particular measure is referred to as *discriminative validation,* and is distinguished from *discriminant validity,* a form of representational validation discussed earlier (Foster & Cone, 1995). The same measure of social skills might be useful in predicting the impression made by applicants on college admissions interviewers or on personnel interviewers. Or, it might be useful in predicting rate of promotion of management trainees. Similarly, it might lead to the identification of specific behaviors to change in a client complaining of an unsatisfactory social life. There are countless other ways the data from a particular behavioral assessment device might be shown to have value. The point is that all of these extend or elaborate the validation evidence of the measure. Furthermore, the elaborative validation is best undertaken after we are confident the measure represents the behavior accurately.

EVALUATING THE *PROCESS* OF BEHAVIORAL ASSESSMENT

Most of the foregoing discussion treats the quality of the observations made by behavioral assessors. What they do with these observations is another matter. One of the purposes of behavioral assessment discussed earlier was to control behavior. It was noted that when control is a major purpose, observations of behavior are used in conducting functional analyses. In a sense, functional analyses can be seen as a form of elaborative validation in which the usefulness of observations is related to the success of the functional analysis. That is, if a particular direct observation code is used to assess behavior, the functions of which are subsequently identified, that code has been shown to be useful, and its validation has been elaborated.

The success of functional analyses is related to the representational adequacy of the observations on which they are based. Accurately observed behavior will not necessarily yield to functional analysis, however. The skill of the analyst in choosing contextual variables, the quality of *their* representation, and the adequacy with which they are manipulated are all important features of functional analysis. These can be evaluated independently, of course, but it is more common to consider the success of the aggregate. That is, the functional analysis itself is evaluated in terms of whether the target behavior has been successfully analyzed (i.e., manipulated and controlled). Assuming the functional analysis has been part of a successful behavior change attempt, we say treatment validity has been shown. When treatment validity is not established because appropriate behavior change has not occurred, we might profitably decompose the behavioral assessment process, examining each component individually. Deficient aspects of the process can be identified and corrected. If the earlier arguments have made any impact, the behavior observation component of the functional analysis will be spared scrutiny, as it will already have been shown to be accurate.

The point has been made that behavioral assessment be evaluated functionally rather than structurally (Nelson, 1983; Silva, 1993a). Perhaps this is the basis for arguing the benefits of treatment validity, as Silva (1993a) has noted. In any event, a functional evaluation of behavioral assessment is not the same as conducting functional analyses in the context of behavioral assessment. That is, strictly topographic behavioral assessments could be subjected to functional evaluation. If assessment produced data describing topography that was then used successfully for some purpose, the assessment would be seen as functionally useful.

SUMMARY AND CONCLUSIONS

The pluralistic nature of behavioral assessment makes it extremely difficult to treat psychometric considerations concisely. Confining the field to assessment of behavior would help, but it would be unrepresentative of the myriad activities of those calling themselves behavioral assessors. Therefore, the foregoing has included suggestions for evaluating the quality of both latent variables and specific behavior. Moreover, it has dealt with behavior more broadly than simple motor responses. The argument has been that the process of assessment starts with identifying a purpose. The purpose makes clear the subject matter, which in turn, leads to the selection of appropriate assessment methods. The psychometric considerations of relevance in evaluating which methods are of highest quality depend on what is being assessed: latent variables or behavior. Classical measurement concepts are necessary in the first case, and their relevance has been clarified recently depending on whether instrument content is seen as the effect or the cause of the underlying variable. Accuracy is the important issue when behavior is assessed, with reliability having a different, less substantial role. The usefulness of measures is argued via validation evidence, and it was suggested that distinguishing representational from elaborative forms of validity evidence can be helpful.

It seems important to be clear that behavioral assessment is not synonymous with the interest in assessing behavior. That is, the discipline is more than its subject matter. Neither is it sufficient to equate behavioral assessment with the use of particular methods (e.g., direct observation). A variety of methods will be useful, depending on the form of the behavior being assessed. Moreover, behavioral assessment is more than the conduct of functional analyses. One uses behavioral assessment to *do* functional analyses, but one also uses behavioral assessment to do other types of analysis (e.g., topographic ones). It is also conceivable that functional analyses can be accomplished from other than strictly behavioral perspectives, as when the manifestation of a particular trait (e.g., hostility), functions to mask certain other traits (e.g., insecurity or shyness).

It may be that the bottom line in evaluating behavioral assessment is whether it makes any difference. That is, our ultimate criteria might be functional ones. Whether behavioral assessment proves functional (i.e., effective), however, depends ultimately on the quality of the observations generated

in its use. It is this quality that this chapter has attempted to address.

ENDNOTE

1. Much of the material in this section can be found in a recent paper devoted specifically to validity (Foster & Cone, 1995). The reader is invited to examine that treatment for a more detailed discussion of the subject.

REFERENCES

American Educational Research Association, American Psychological Association, & National Council on Measurement in Education. (1985). *Standards for educational and psychological testing.* Washington, DC: APA.

Anastasi, A. (1988). *Psychological testing* (6th ed.). New York: Macmillan.

Bagozzi, R. P. (1993a). Assessing construct validity in personality research: Applications to measures of self-esteem. *Journal of Research in Personality, 27,* 49–87.

Bagozzi, R. P. (1993b). An examination of the psychometric properties of measures of negative affect in the PANAS-X scales. *Journal of Personality and Social Psychology, 65,* 836–851.

Bakeman, R., & Gottman, J. M. (1986). *Observing interaction: An introduction to sequential analysis.* London: Cambridge University Press.

Barlow, D. H., Hayes, S. C., & Nelson, R. O. (1984). *The scientist practitioner: Research and accountability in clinical and educational settings.* New York: Pergamon.

Barrios, B. A. (1988). On the changing nature of behavioral assessment. In A. S. Bellack & M. Hersen (Eds.), *Behavioral assessment: A practical handbook* (3rd ed.) (pp. 3–41). New York: Pergamon.

Bechtel, R. B. (1967). The study of man: Human movement and architecture. *Transaction, 4,* 53–56.

Bechtoldt, H. (1959). Construct validity: A critique. *American Psychologist, 14,* 619–629.

Berk, R. (1979). Generalizability of behavior observations: A clarification of interobserver agreement and interobserver reliability. *American Journal of Mental Deficiency, 83,* 460–472.

Birkimer, J. C., & Brown, J. H. (1979). A graphical judgmental aid which summarizes obtained and chance reliabilty data and helps assess the believability of experimental effects. *Journal of Applied Behavior Analysis, 12,* 523–533.

Bollen, K. (1989). *Structural equations with latent variables*. New York: Wiley.

Bollen, K., & Lennox, R. (1991). Conventional wisdom on measurement: A structural equation perspective. *Psychological Bulletin, 110*, 305–314.

Borman, W. C., & Hallam, G. L. (1991). Observation accuracy for assessors of work-sample performance: Consistency across task and individual-differences correlations. *Journal of Applied Psychology, 76*, 11–18.

Burgess, R. L., Clark, R. N., & Hendee, J. C. (1971). An experimental analysis of antilitter procedures. *Journal of Applied Behavior Analysis, 4*, 71–75.

Butcher, J. N., Dahlstrom, W., Graham, J., Tellegen, A., & Kaemmer, B. (1989). *Manual for administering and scoring the MMPI-2*. Minneapolis: University of Minnesota Press.

Campbell, D. T. (1960). Recommendations for APA test standards regarding construct, trait and discriminant validity. *American Psychologist, 15*, 546–553.

Campbell, D. T., & Fiske, D. (1959). Convergent and discriminant validation by the multitrait-multimethod matrix. *Psychological Bulletin, 56*, 81–105.

Cohen, J. (1960). A coefficient of agreement for nominal scales. *Educational and Psychological Measurement, 20*, 37–46.

Cohen, J. (1968). Weighted Kappa: Nominal scale agreement with provision for scaled disagreement or partial credit. *Psychological Bulletin, 70*, 213–220.

Comrey, A. L. (1988). Factor analytic methods of scale development in personality and clinical psychology. *Journal of Consulting and Clinical Psychology, 56*, 754–761.

Cone, J. D. (1977). The relevance of reliability and validity for behavioral assessment. *Behavior Therapy, 8*, 411–426.

Cone, J. D. (1978). The Behavioral Assessment Grid (BAG): A conceptual framework and a taxonomy. *Behavior Therapy, 9*, 882–888.

Cone, J. D. (1979). Confounded comparisons in triple response mode assessment research. *Behavioral Assessment, 1*, 85–95.

Cone, J. D. (1981). Psychometric considerations. In M. Hersen & A. S. Bellack (Eds.), *Behavioral assessment: A practical handbook* (2nd ed.) (pp. 38–68). New York: Pergamon.

Cone, J. D. (1986). Idiographic, nomothetic, and related perspectives in behavioral assessment. In R. O. Nelson & S. C. Hayes (Eds.), *Conceptual foundations of behavioral assessment*. New York: Guilford.

Cone, J. D. (1987). Consideraciones "psicometricas" en la evaluacion conductual. In R. Fernandez-Balles-teros & J. A. I. Corrobles (Eds.), *Evaluacion conductual. Metodologia y aplicaciones*. Madrid: Piramide.

Cone, J. D. (1988). Psychometric considerations and the multiple models of behavioral assessment. In A. S. Bellack & M. Hersen (Eds.), *Behavioral assessment: A practical handbook* (3rd ed.) (pp. 42–66). New York: Pergamon.

Cone, J. D. (1995). Assessment practice standards. In S. C. Hayes, V. M. Follette, R. M. Dawes, & K. E. Grady (Eds.), *Scientific standards of psychological practice: Issues and recommendations* (pp. 201–224). Reno, NV: Context Press.

Cone, J. D., & Hawkins, R. P. (Eds.). (1977). *Behavioral assessment: New directions in clinical psychology*. New York: Brunner/Mazel.

Couch, A., & Keniston, K. (1960). Yeasayers and naysayers: Agreeing response set as a personality variable. *Journal of Abnormal and Social Psychology, 60*, 150–174.

Crocker, L., & Algina, J. (1986). *Introduction to classical and modern test theory*. New York: Holt, Rinehart and Winston.

Cronbach, L. J. (1947). Test "reliability": Its meaning and determination. *Psychometrika, 12*, 1–16.

Cronbach, L. J. (1970). *Essentials of psychological testing* (3rd ed.). New York: Harper and Row.

Cronbach, L. J. (1971). Test validation. In R. L. Thorndike (Ed.), *Educational measurement* (2nd ed.) (pp. 443–507). Washington, DC: American Council on Education.

Cronbach, L. J., Gleser, G. C., Nanda, H., & Rajaratnam, N. (1972). *The dependability of behavioral measurements: Theory of generalizability for scores and profiles*. New York: Wiley.

Cronbach, L. J., & Meehl, P. E. (1955). Construct validity in psychological tests. *Psychological Bulletin, 52*, 281–302.

Crowne, D. P., & Marlowe, D. (1960). A new scale of social desirability independent of psychopathology. *Journal of Consulting Psychology, 24*, 349–354.

Cunningham, T. R., & Tharp, R. G. (1981). The influence of settings on accuracy and reliability of behavioral observation. *Behavioral Assessment, 3*, 67–78.

DeVellis, R. F. (1991). *Scale development: Theory and applications*. Newbury Park, CA: Sage.

Dollinger, S. J. (1989). Predictive validity of the Graduate Record Examination in a clinical psychology program. *Professional Psychology: Research and Practice, 20*, 56–58.

Edwards, A. L. (1957). *The social desirability variable in personality assessment and research.* New York: Dryden.

Edwards, A. L. (1959). *Manual for the Edwards Personal Preference Schedule* (rev. ed.). New York: Psychological Corporation.

Edwards, A. L. (1970). *The measurement of personality traits by scales and inventories.* New York: Holt, Rinehart and Winston.

Edwards, A. L. (1990). Construct validity and social desirability. *American Psychologist, 45,* 287–289.

Edwards, A. L., Diers, C. J., & Walker, J. N. (1962). Response sets and factor loadings on sixty-one personality scales. *Journal of Applied Psychology, 46,* 220–225.

Edwards, A. L., & Walsh, J. A. (1964). Response sets in standard and experimental personality scales. *American Educational Research Journal, 1,* 52–61.

Edwards, A. L., Walsh, J. A., & Diers, C. J. (1963). The relationship between social desirability and internal consistency of personality scales. *Journal of Applied Psychology, 47,* 255–259.

Evans, I. (1993). Constructional perspectives in clinical assessment. *Psychological Assessment, 5,* 264–272.

Evans, I. M., & Nelson, R. O. (1977). Assessment of child behavior problems. In A. R. Ciminero, K. S. Calhoun, & H. Adams (Eds.), *Handbook of behavioral assessment.* New York: Wiley.

Ferster, C. B. (1965). Classification of behavioral pathology. In L. Krasner & L. P. Ullmann (Eds.), *Research in behavior modification* (pp. 6–26). New York: Holt, Rinehart and Winston.

Fiske, D. W., & Campbell, D. T. (1992). Citations do not solve problems. *Psychological Bulletin, 112,* 393–395.

Foster, S. L., & Cone, J. D. (1986). Design and use of direct observation systems. In A. Ciminero, K. S. Calhoun, & H. E. Adams (Eds.), *Handbook of behavioral assessment* (2nd ed.) (pp. 253–324). New York: John Wiley.

Foster, S. L., & Cone, J. D. (1995). Validity issues in clinical assessment. *Psychological Assessment, 7,* 248–260.

Galassi, J. P., & Perot, A. R. (1992). What you should know about behavioral assessment. *Journal of Counseling and Development, 70,* 624–631.

Gewirtz, H. N., & Gewirtz, J. L. (1969). Caretaking settings, background events and childrearing environments: Some preliminary trends. In B. M. Foss (Ed.), *Determinants of infant behaviour* (Vol. IV). London: Methuen & Co.

Goffin, R. D., & Jackson, D. N. (1988). The structural validity of the Index of Organizational Reactions. *Multivariate Behavioral Research, 23,* 327–347.

Goldfried, M. R., & Kent, R. (1972). Traditional versus behavioral personality assessment: A comparison of methodological and theoretical assumptions. *Psychological Bulletin, 77,* 409–420.

Goodenough, F. L. (1949). *Mental testing: Its history, principles, and applications.* New York: Rinehart.

Hartmann, D. P. (1977). Considerations in the use of interobserver reliability estimates. *Journal of Applied Behavior Analysis, 10,* 103–116.

Hartmann, D. P., Roper, B. L., & Bradford, D. C. (1979). Some relationships between behavioral and traditional assessment. *Journal of Behavioral Assessment, 1,* 3–21.

Hathaway, S. R., & McKinley, J. C. (1943). *The Minnesota Multiphasic Personality Inventory* (rev. ed.). Minneapolis: University of Minnesota Press.

Hawkins, R. P. (1979). The functions of assessment: Implications for selection and development of devices for assessing repertoires in clinical, educational, and other settings. *Journal of Applied Behavior Analysis, 12,* 501–516.

Hayes, S. C., & Cone, J. D. (1977). Reducing residential electrical energy use: Payments, information, and feedback. *Journal of Applied Behavior Analysis, 10,* 425–435.

Hayes, S. C., & Follette, W. C. (1993). The challenge faced by behavioral assessment. *European Journal of Psychological Assessment, 9,* 182–188.

Hayes, S. C., Nelson, R. O., & Jarrett, R. B. (1987). Treatment utility of assessment: A functional approach to evaluating the assessment quality. *American Psychologist, 42,* 963–974.

Haynes, S. N., Richard, D. C. S., & Kubany, E. S. (1995). Content validity in psychological assessment: A functional approach to concepts and methods. *Psychological Assessment, 7,* 238–247.

Helton, D. R., Modlin, D. L., Tizzano, J. P., & Rasmussen, K. (1993). Nicotine withdrawal: A behavioral assessment using schedule controlled responding, locomotor activity, and sensorimotor reactivity. *Psychopharmacology, 113,* 205–210.

Hoffman, C. C., Nathan, B. R., & Holden, L. M. (1991). A comparison of validation criteria: Objective versus subjective performance measures and self-versus supervisor ratings. *Personnel Psychology, 44,* 601–619.

Hogan, R., & Nicholson, R. (1988). The meaning of personality test scores. *American Psychologist, 43,* 621–626.

Jackson, D. N. (1984). *Personality Research Form manual.* Port Huron, MI: Research Psychologists Press.

Johnson, S. M., & Bolstad, O. D. (1973). Methodological issues in naturalistic observation: Some problems and solutions for field research. In L. A. Hamerlynck, L. C. Handy, & E. J. Mash (Eds.), *Behavior change: Methodology, concepts, and practice.* Champaign, IL: Research Press.

Johnston, J. M., & Pennypacker, H. S. (1980). *Strategies and tactics of human behavioral research.* Hillsdale, NJ: Erlbaum.

Johnston, J. M., & Pennypacker, H. S. (1993). *Strategies and tactics of behavioral research* (2nd ed.). Hillsdale, NJ: Erlbaum.

Joreskog, K. G. (1971). Statistical analysis of sets of congeneric tests. *Psychometrica, 36,* 109–133.

Kane, M. T. (1992). An argument-based approach to validity. *Psychological Bulletin, 112,* 527–535.

Kaplan, R. M., & Saccuzzo, D. P. (1993). *Psychological testing: Principles, applications, and issues* (3rd ed.). Pacific Grove, CA: Brooks/Cole.

Kazdin, A. E. (1977). Artifact, bias, and complexity of assessment: The ABC's of reliability. *Journal of Applied Behavior Analysis, 10,* 141–150.

Kazdin, A. E. (1992). *Research design in clinical psychology* (2nd ed.). Boston: Allyn and Bacon.

Kelley, T. (1924). *Statistical method.* New York: Macmillan.

Kelly, G. A. (1955). *The psychology of personal constructs* (vols. 1 & 2). New York: Norton.

Kelly, J. R., & McGrath, J. E. (1988). *On time and method.* Beverly Hills: Sage.

Kelly, M. B. (1977). A review of the observational data-collection and reliability procedures in *The Journal of Applied Behavior Analysis. Journal of Applied Behavior Analysis, 10,* 97–101.

Kenny, D. A., & Kashy, D. A. (1992). Analysis of the multitrait-multimethod matrix by confirmatory factor analysis. *Psychological Bulletin, 112,* 165–172.

Kumar, K., & Beyerlein, M. (1991). Construction and validation of an instrument for measuring ingratiatory behaviors in organizational settings. *Journal of Applied Psychology, 76,* 619–627.

Linquist, E. F. (1953). *Design and analysis of experiments.* New York: Houghton Mifflin.

Loevinger, J. (1957). Objective tests as instruments of psychological theory. [Monogr. No. 9]. *Psychological Reports, 3,* 635–694.

Martin, J. E. (1987). Structural equation modeling: A guide for the perplexed. *Child Development, 58,* 33–37.

Mash, E. J., & McElwee, J. D. (1974). Situational effects on observer accuracy: Behavioral predictability, prior experience, complexity of coding categories. *Child Development, 45,* 367–377.

Mash, E. J., & Terdal, L. G. (1976). *Behavior therapy assessment: Diagnosis, design, and evaluation.* New York: Springer.

Mash, E. J., & Terdal, L. G. (1980). Follow-up assessments in behavior therapy. In P. Karoly & J. J. Steffen (Eds.), *The long-range effects of psychotherapy: Models of durable outcome.* New York: Gardner Press.

Mash, E. J., & Terdal, L. G. (1981). *Behavioral assessment of childhood disorders.* New York: Guilford.

McNemar, Q. (1962). *Psychological statistics* (3rd ed.). New York: John Wiley.

Mees, H. L., Gocka, E. F., & Holloway, H. (1964). Social desirability scale values for California Personality Inventory items. *Psychological Reports, Monograph Supplement, 15,* 147–158.

Messick, S. (1983). Assessment of children. In P. H. Mussen (Ed.), *Handbook of child psychology* (4th ed.) (pp. 477–526). New York: Wiley.

Messick, S. (1989). Validity. In R. L. Linn (Ed.), *Educational measurement* (3rd ed.) (pp. 13–103). New York: Macmillan.

Messick, S. (1994). Foundations of validity: Meaning and consequences in psychological assessment. *European Journal of Psychological Assessment, 10,* 1–9.

Messick, S., & Jackson, D. N. (1961). Desirability scale values and dispersions for MMPI items. *Psychological Reports, 8,* 409–414.

Messick, S., & Jackson, D. N. (1967). *Problems in human assessment.* New York: McGraw-Hill.

Mischel, W. (1968). *Personality and assessment.* New York: Wiley.

Nelson, R. O. (1983). Behavioral assessment: Past, present, and future. *Behavioral Assessment, 5,* 195–206.

Nelson, R. O., Hay, L. R., & Hay, W. M. (1977). Comments on Cone's "The relevance of reliability and validity for behavioral assessment." *Behavior Therapy, 8,* 427–430.

Nelson, R. O., & Hayes, S. C. (1981). Nature of behavioral assessment. In M. Hersen & A. S. Bellack (Eds.), *Behavioral assessment: A practical handbook* (2nd ed.) (pp. 3–37). New York: Pergamon.

Northrop, F. S. C. (1947). *The logic of the sciences and the humanities.* New York: Macmillan.

Novick, M. R. (1966). The axioms and principal results of classical test theory. *Journal of Mathematical Psychology, 3,* 1–18.

Novick, M. R., & Lewis, C. (1967). Coefficient alpha and the reliability of composite measurements. *Psychometrika, 32,* 1–13.

Nunnally, J. C. (1978). *Psychometric theory* (2nd ed.). New York: McGraw-Hill.

Nunnally, J. C., & Bernstein, I. H. (1994). *Psychometric theory* (3rd ed.). New York: McGraw-Hill.

O'Leary, K. D., & Wilson, G. T. (1975). *Behavior therapy: Application and outcome.* Englewood Cliffs, NJ: Prentice-Hall.

Ozer, D. J., & Reise, S. P. (1994). Personality assessment. *Annual Review of Psychology, 45,* 357–388.

Paylor, R., Johnson, R. S., Papaioannou, V., & Spiegelman, B. M. (1994). Behavioral assessment of c-fos mutant mice. *Brain Research, 651,* 275–282.

Pedhazur, E. J., & Schmelkin, L. P. (1991). *Measurement, design, and analysis: An integrated approach.* Hillsdale, NJ: Erlbaum.

Reid, J. B. (1982). Observer training in naturalistic research. In D. P. Hartmann (Ed.), *Using observers to study behavior* (pp. 37–50). San Francisco: Jossey-Bass.

Romanczyk, R. G., Kent, R. N., Diament, C., & O'Leary, K. D. (1973). Measuring the reliability of observational data: A reactive process. *Journal of Applied Behavior Analysis, 6,* 175–184.

Rorer, L. G. (1965). The great response style myth. *Psychological Bulletin, 63,* 129–156.

Shaughnessy, J. J., & Zechmeister, E. B. (1990). *Research methods in psychology* (2nd ed.). New York: McGraw-Hill.

Shavelson, R. J., Webb, N. M., & Rowley, G. L. (1989). Generalizability theory. *American Psychologist, 44,* 922–932.

Silva, F. (1993a). *Psychometric foundations and behavioral assessment.* Newbury Park, CA: Sage.

Silva, F. (1993b). Treatment utility: A reappraisal. *European Journal of Psychological Assessment, 9,* 222–226.

Spearman, C. (1904). General intelligence: Objectively determined and measured. *American Journal of Psychology, 15,* 201–293.

Suen, H. K., & Ary, D. (1989). *Analyzing quantitative behavioral observation data.* Hillsdale, NJ: Lawrence Erlbaum.

Taplin, P. S., & Reid, J. B. (1973). Effects of instructional set and experimental influences on observer reliability. *Child Development, 44,* 547–554.

Tellegen, A. (1988). The analysis of consistency in personality assessment. *Journal of Personality, 56,* 621–663.

Watson, J. B. (1919). *Psychology from the standpoint of a behaviorist.* Philadelphia: Lippincott.

Weiss, R. L., & Summers, K. J. (1983). Marital Interaction Coding System-III. In E. Filsinger (Ed.), *Marriage and family assessment.* Beverly Hills: Sage.

CHAPTER 3

PRESCRIPTIVE ASSESSMENT AND TREATMENT

Ron Acierno
Michel Hersen
Vincent B. Van Hasselt
Nova-Southeastern University

Contemporary classification systems such as the *Diagnostic and Statistical Manual of Mental Disorders (DSM)* (American Psychiatric Association, 1994) and *Research Diagnostic Criteria (RDC)* (Spitzer et al., 1978) assign diagnoses on the basis of data that are almost exclusively symptom oriented. Although the reliability of these diagnostic schemes has been strongly supported, their construct and predictive validity (corresponding to the abstract theoretical definition of a psychopathology and its relation to differential outcome, respectively [Nunneley & Bernstein, 1994]) are less well established. That is, usefulness of current diagnostic systems in selecting and implementing highly focused, prescriptive interventions, characterized by intentionally circumscribed effects, is limited. Illustrative are the large number of treatment-outcome and meta-analytic studies employing *DSM* diagnoses that have failed to demonstrate the superiority of one treatment over another in the amelioration of general psychopathology (e.g., Luborsky et al., 1975; Smith & Glass, 1977). This has led to the widely held, albeit ill-informed, conclusion that all

treatments are, for the most part, "equal." However, equivalence of treatments across disorders is counterintuitive and in conflict with clinical observation. An equally tenable explanation for the noted lack of differential treatment effects is inappropriate heterogeneity of patients within diagnostic classes that are presumed to be homogeneous. This, naturally, has the effect of inhibiting clear measurement of varied treatment response. Indeed, a failure to obtain data supporting differential efficacy among interventions is very likely attributable to "an uncritical and simplistic reliance on diagnostic labels and subject selection criteria . . . based on the erroneous assumption that once persons have been assigned a diagnostic label, they are sufficiently similar to be randomly assigned to different-treatment conditions" (Eifert, Evans, & McKendrick, 1990, p. 164).

Essentially, classification systems currently in use by psychologists conducting assessment and treatment-outcome research fail to adequately attend to subtypes within diagnostic classes of psychopathology. This obscurement of effects due to "noise" or imprecision in the psychodiagnostic measurement strategy results in a loss of experimental control (Annis, 1988; Beutler, 1991; Bielski & Friedel, 1976; Eifert, Evans, McKendrick, 1990; Finney & Moos, 1986; Hayes, Nelson, & Jarrett, 1987; Wolpe, 1977, 1986a, 1990). Admittedly, the *DSM* and *RDC* do supply criteria for identification of patient subtypes for a few disorders (e.g., melancholic subtype of depression). However, these subtypes are also unidimensional in that they are based primarily on overt symptomatology (Davidson & Pelton, 1988; Ley, 1992; Young et al., 1987; Zimmerman, Stangl, & Coryell, 1985). Ultimately, the "treatment utility" (Hayes, Nelson, & Jarrett, 1987) of formal classification schemes such as the *DSM* and *RDC* is severely constrained by inherent heterogeneity of patients diagnosed with identical disorders. Consequently, conclusions derived from treatment outcome studies using these diagnostic criteria are also "rendered nugatory by the imprecision of the data" (see Hersen, 1981; Wolpe, 1977).

Departures from *DSM*- and *RDC*-defined diagnoses (in an attempt to identify homogeneous subtypes of patients within general diagnostic categories) have frequently resulted in assessment schemes with enhanced predictive validity. Initial efforts to evaluate differential treatment response among heterogenous diagnostic groups included classification systems that extended beyond simple overt symptomatology, yet were still largely univariate in nature (e.g., subtyping alcoholics on measures of internal/external locus of control). The progression to multivariate subtyping (Donovan, Kivlahan, & Walker, 1986) has occurred only recently and is still in its nascent stage. Importantly, precise specification of the conditions under which a given treatment will be most effective requires a much more thorough measurement of patient and pathology than is possible through simple univariate symptom assessment. Along these lines, clinicians for decades have been advocating various forms of "multimodal" assessment (Lazarus, 1973, Maier, Philipp, & Hueser, 1986) as a means to increase treatment efficacy and efficiency.

Examination of medical and psychological models of treatment reveals four basic areas that must be addressed in any attempt to develop or refine prescriptive assessment and intervention. These include precise specification and concurrent measurement of (1) symptoms, (2) maintaining factors, (3) etiological factors, and (4) subject characteristics and treatment history. Assessment, however thorough, along only one parameter ignores the possibility that reliable and valid patient subtypes exist along other parameters, and increases the likelihood that interventions of less than optimal effectiveness will be used to treat an individual's pathology.

PRESCRIPTIVE ASSESSMENT: SYMPTOMS

The largely overt and relatively apparent aspects of psychopathology have historically combined to give symptom assessment a position of primacy over other potential areas of measurement. Comprehensive symptomatic assessment involves appraisal of motoric behavior, cognitions, and physiology (Lang, 1968), and is routinely conducted through behavioral observation, subject self-report, and psychophysiological monitoring. Accurate assessment and analysis of symptomatology potentially increase the precision with which prescriptive treatments are applied.

For example, research with alcoholics has revealed the utility of subclassifying patients as either externalizers or internalizers on the basis of cognitive and behavioral symptoms. Specifically, individuals characterized by impulsivity, sociopathy, aggressiveness, interpersonal dysfunction, episodic binge drinking, increased negativity, and an external locus of control are considered externalizers. In contrast, alcoholics evincing relatively less dependence, aggressiveness, and impulsivity, but increased self-reflection and anxiety, and an internal locus of control are classified as internalizers Using these distinctions, Cooney and colleagues (1991) found that externalizers responded better to structured cognitive behavior therapy while internalizers (characterized by relatively less impaired interpersonal functioning) improved most with an interpersonally based treatment. Notably, this treatment by subtype interaction effect was evident at the two-year follow-up point.

Employing a similar system of symptom subclassification, Kadden and colleagues (1989) evaluated the relative efficacy of group coping skills training (including problem solving, relaxation, urge/mood control training, and relapse prevention) and interactional group therapy (with a focus on interpersonal interactions as they occurred in session and a concomitant avoidance of skills training). These investigators predicted that individuals with higher global psychopathology (i.e., externalizers) would fail to benefit from a treatment relying heavily on interpersonal interaction and would instead respond positively to "coping style" instruction given in a more directive format. In contrast, patients low in global pathology (i.e., internalizers) were expected to benefit most from an interpersonally based treatment. As was the case with Cooney and associates (1991), a significant intervention by symptom-subtype interaction effect was noted, with coping skills training producing more positive results in alcoholics high in sociopathy, and interactional treatment producing more positive results in similarly diagnosed alcoholics low in sociopathy.

Additional support for the utility of conducting comprehensive symptom assessment comes from Annis and Davis (1989), who employed subject self-report of behavior to classify patients as having "generalized" or "differentiated" drinking patterns, based on their ability to delineate specific situations in which drinking occurred. Subjects received either focused relapse prevention or traditional substance-abuse counseling. Results again supported presence of an interaction effect that would not have been identified through the use of standard *DSM* diagnostic classification. Specifically, subjects with "differentiated" drinking patterns responded to a relatively greater extent following relapse prevention, while "generalized" drinkers responded to both treatments equally well. Relatedly, Vaglum and Fossheim (1980) found that adolescent drug use behavior patterns also predicted differential treatment response. For youth who abused psychedelic drugs, increased quantities of family and individual therapy were associated with improved outcome, whereas increased amounts of confrontational milieu therapy were associated with negative outcome. Treatment response was somewhat different for adolescents who used opiates and/or stimulants, with increased

levels of confrontational milieu therapy predicting the strongest improvement.

Similar symptom subtypes, validated by their differential treatment response, have been identified within *DSM*-defined categories of anxiety disorders. For example, Öst, Johansson, and Jerrermalm (1982) classified claustrophobic subjects according to their primary mode of activation during exposure to phobic stimuli. Individuals who responded to exposure with increased heart rate, but few escape behaviors were considered "physiological" responders. However, subjects for whom exposure produced escape behaviors with little concomitant increases in heart rate were designated "behavioral" responders. Half of the patients in each subgroup received an intervention that was largely behavioral in nature, whereas remaining patients were given treatment that was primarily "physiological. Once again, a treatment by symptom-subtype interaction was revealed by this more intensive mode of assessment: Phobic subjects classified as physiological responders improved to a relatively greater extent when treated with a physiologically oriented treatment. Phobic individuals classified as behavioral responders improved most following a behavior-based intervention. Treatment by symptom-subtype interactions within *DSM*-defined anxiety disorder categories have also been demonstrated with mildly anxious college outpatients (Abramowitz et al., 1974) and other social phobics (Elder, Edelstein, & Fremouw, 1981; Öst, Jerrernalm, & Johansson, 1981).

In addition, thorough assessment of symptoms has also revealed differential treatment effectiveness in psychosomatic medicine. In this area, Martelli and associates (1987) classified coping styles of individuals preparing to undergo dental surgery as either problem focused, in which a preference for information about medical procedures was evident, or emotion focused, in which such a preference was not demonstrated. Prior to surgery, patients in both groups received either a "problem-focused" or an "emotion-focused" treatment. In the former, information about probable sensory/stimulus events and surgical procedures was provided, and patients were taught to engage in logical analyses of problem situations, complemented by action-planning and solution-implementation strategies. In the latter intervention, emphasis was on direct palliative measures for dysphoric states elicited by aversive situations, with no effort made to train patients to engage in problem analysis and solution. Impressively, pain and treatment satisfaction ratings by the patient, and adjustment to surgery ratings by a physician, were higher for problem-focused patients when they received problem-focused treatment and for emotion-focused patients when they received an emotion-focused program. Importantly, "responses were relatively poor when [patient/treatment] mismatches occurred" (Martelli et al., 1987, p. 201).

Comparable symptom subtypes of affective disorders also appear to exist, although these largely correspond to etiological subtypes (discussed later). Anxiety level is among the clearest and most clinically relevant symptom with which to sub-classify depressive illness. Although overlooked as an important factor in depression by the DSM-IV, anxiety level has been found to reliably differentiate and predict treatment response for a large subgroup of depressives (e.g., McKnight, Nelson, Hayes, & Jarrett, 1984; Paykel et al., 1973; Wolpe 1977, 1979, 1986a). Moreover, anxiety level appears to provide a means by which to discriminate some endogenous from nonendogenous depressions, with endogenous depressives evincing significantly less anxiety than their nonendogenous counterparts (Heerlein, Lauer, & Richter, 1989; Wolpe 1986a) and responding to a significantly greater extent following somatically oriented therapy (Brown & Shuey, 1980; Nelson et al., 1989; Prusoff et al., 1980; Woggon, 1993).

Convergent validation of the endogenous/anxious-nonendogenous classification scheme is provided by disparate sedation thresholds of the two groups. Specifically, individuals with anxious-depression evince above-average sedation thresholds (as do anxiety-disordered patients), whereas nonanxious-depressed patients evince below average sedation thresholds. Consequently, these depressive subtypes appear to represent qualitatively rather than simply quantitatively (i.e., in terms of severity) different pathologies. Indeed, Conti and colleagues (1987) noted that while nonanxious-depressives required only antidepressant medica-

tion to significantly diminish negative affect, anxious depressives responded no better to antidepressant treatment than to placebo. Logically, appropriate prescriptive interventions for anxious depression will combine strategies to reduce anxiety with techniques to enhance mood (Hersen, 1981; Wolpe 1986a).

Although the *DSM* and *RDC* do not employ anxiety level as a primary means by which to discriminate endogenous from nonendogenous depression, and are widely considered ineffective in this endeavor (de Jonghe et al., 1988; Robbins et al., 1989; Young et al., 1987; Zimmerman, Stangl, & Coryell, 1985), several other core symptoms have been identified as markers for endogenous depression. These include guilt, disinterest in people, early morning insomnia, lack of appetite, weight loss, and psychomotor retardation (de Jonghe et al., 1988; Gunther et al., 1988; Musa, 1986; Robbins et al., 1989; Zimmerman, Stangl, & Coryell, 1985). Importantly, level of depressive severity, despite widespread practice of using this variable, does not reliably differentiate endogenous from nonendogenous depression (Robbins et al., 1989; Gallagher-Thompsen et al., 1992; Willner et al., 1990).

In addition to physiological (e.g., sedation threshold tests) and behavioral (e.g., psychomotor retardation) symptom markers of endogenous depression, cognitive markers may also exist. For example, Simons, Lustman, Wetzel, and Murphy (1985) evaluated depressed subjects' "learned resourcefulness," or their skill in monitoring, controlling, and changing unpleasant internal events, and found that those high in learned resourcefulness (presumably cognitively-oriented) evinced greater improvement following cognitive treatment than subjects with "low resourcefulness." By contrast, low-resourceful subjects responded better to pharmacotherapy than those high in resourcefulness, thereby illustrating an interaction between treatment type and cognitive style.

Clearly, adequate symptom assessment potentiates selection of optimal psychological interventions by permitting clinicians to "fine tune" their general treatments to meet specific requirements of the psychopathology at hand. That is, precise symptomatic assessment facilitates intra- as well as inter-categorical differential diagnosis and treatment. Note that many of the aforementioned examples demonstrate benefits of "first-order" subtyping on the basis of symptomatology. Yet, greater accuracy of classification is achieved when tripartite symptom assessment (including behavior, cognition, and physiology) is conducted. Importantly, the impact on treatment of such "second-order" symptom assessment has yet to be thoroughly evaluated. However, prescriptive assessment must not conclude at the level of symptomatology. Instead, contextual assessment of factors that serve to maintain psychopathology enhances the "treatment utility" of diagnosis processes even further.

PRESCRIPTIVE ASSESSMENT: MAINTAINING FACTORS

Assessment of maintaining factors, sometimes referred to as *functional analysis*, entails delineation of discriminant stimuli and/or contingencies of reinforcement that exist in a patient's natural environment and serve to consistently elicit or perpetuate problematic behavior. Specification of the actual target behavior is achieved through measurement of symptoms, but functional assessment reveals the "purpose" a particular behavior fulfills, or illustrates possible reasons for its continued existence. With these data, prescriptive treatments can be chosen that both reduce overt psychopathology and prevent its future recurrences, by providing individuals with alternative means by which to achieve a given end (e.g., in the case of a child misbehaving in order to receive parental attention, elimination of negative behavior would be accompanied by training the child to obtain attention in a more socially appropriate manner).

A patient's symptomatic presentation will determine, in large part, the manner in which functional assessment of maintaining factors is conducted. Characteristic of all comprehensive assessments of maintaining factors, however, is (1) specification of antecedents and consequents of problem behaviors (Wolpe, 1986b); (2) specification of effects problem behaviors have on significant others, and their responses to these effects; and (3) delineation of environmental stimuli that vary

as a function of the problem behavior. The complexity of a functional assessment of maintaining factors may vary widely across disorders, yet its usefulness in both achieving and prolonging treatment gains is exceptional.

Meichenbaum, Gilmore, and Fedoravicius (1971) indirectly demonstrated the potential usefulness of complementing symptom assessment with even a cursory measurement of maintaining variables in their study of patients with public speaking fears. Subjects were treated by either a cognitively oriented regimen in which they were trained to attend to and alter self-verbalizations in an anxiety-producing situation, or standard desensitization. Interestingly, those suffering from more pervasive social fears benefitted to a relatively greater extent after receiving a cognitive-insight therapy. In contrast, desensitization treatment was more effective with individuals for whom anxiety was confined to specific public speaking situations. Arguably, patients with more generalized fears experienced anxiety that was maintained by a larger number of conditioned stimuli in the social environment. For such pathology, the intentionally focused effects of desensitization were, predictably, limited to only a few "triggers" of fear. However, the cognitive-insight intervention appeared to impart useful coping skills, which were then applied to overcome a variety of anxiety-producing situations and stimuli.

Additional support for the utility of assessing maintaining factors is provided by controlled single-case studies, in which pathology, maintaining factors, and subject characteristics are routinely described in great detail. Along these lines, Kallman, Hersen, and O'Toole (1975) presented the case of a 42-year-old male with hysterical paralysis. Over the five years preceding treatment, the patient reported multiple episodes of paralysis lasting for periods of one to two weeks, during which he was unable to walk or even move his legs. Symptom onset appeared to have corresponded with the subject's early retirement and assumption of his wife's former household responsibilities. Moreover, assessment revealed that several episodes of past paralysis closely followed increases in familial conflict. Additionally, it was apparent that, once paralyzed, the patient received significantly increased levels of social reinforcement and relief from household duties.

Following hospitalization, the patient entered a treatment regimen characterized by differential contingent reinforcement of standing and walking behaviors by attractive research assistants. Predictably, both standing and walking behaviors returned, the frequency and duration of which were directly related to the reinforcement level provided by the research assistants. The patient was discharged and remained problem free for only four weeks, at which point he was readmitted to the hospital, again unable to move his legs. Because initial functional assessment of maintaining factors revealed discriminative stimuli for paralytic responses (i.e., family discord) as well as responses on the part of significant others that served to maintain and increase the likelihood that future paralytic episodes would occur (i.e., positive reinforcement through familial attention and negative reinforcement through relief from household duties), a relatively more comprehensive prescriptive treatment was implemented. Specifically, family members were trained to differentially reinforce appropriate motor behaviors and extinguish paralytic behavior. Familial application of these new contingencies of reinforcement resulted in lasting therapeutic gains. Obviously, assessment at only the symptom level would have been insufficient to generate an intervention with such effects.

Benefits of addressing clinically relevant discriminative stimuli and contingencies of operant reinforcement are also evident in Azrin and associates' (1994) controlled outcome study of two substance-abuse treatments. In this experiment, standard supportive counseling was compared to a behaviorally oriented, individually customized treatment package in which extensive effort was devoted to identifying stimuli that elicited drug use, followed by training to decrease the frequency and magnitude of time spent in the presence of those stimuli. Additionally, existing patterns of contingent reinforcement of drug use (other than reinforcement through ingestion of the drug, of course) were identified for each patient and altered specifically so that drug use resulted in high response cost of previously obtained social reinforcement (i.e.,

provided by parent or spouse) and abstinence resulted in increased social reinforcement.

Note again that both associative and instrumental aspects of learned pathological behavior were addressed for each patient by this intervention. Not surprisingly, subjects receiving the behavioral treatment that addressed maintaining factors of drug use evinced significantly greater reductions in substance use than counterparts receiving the less individualized, supportive counseling treatment. Most importantly, these differential gains were maintained at the nine-month follow-up (Azrin et al., in press).

As mentioned, in order to thoroughly assess the variables that maintain psychopathology, clinicians must attend to both the contingencies that sustain a behavior, as well as the learned discriminative stimuli that reliability elicit the problem response (Wolpe, 1986b). That is, awareness of both instrumental and associative relationships within which psychopathology persists permits application of comprehensive, multidimensional prescriptive treatments. Importantly, this awareness is achieved through functional assessment of both pathological behavior and the context in which it exists. However, assessment must not end with maintaining factors, for as Wolpe (1986a) noted, "The most effective treatments of diseases are usually based on knowledge of their etiology" (p. 499).

PRESCRIPTIVE ASSESSMENT: ETIOLOGY

The highly focused, intentionally circumscribed effects produced by many prescriptive treatments necessitate precise and conceptually consistent diagnosis. Such precision and consistency are attained by complementing assessment of symptoms and maintaining factors with assessment of etiology (Agras, 1987; Eifert, Evans, & McKendrick, 1990; Hersen, 1981; Wolpe 1986a). Rationally,

it would seem that in cases where faulty habits have been conditioned, a therapeutic strategy directed toward their deconditioning would be most appropriate. On the other hand, where cognitive misperceptions predominate, a therapeutic strategy directed toward correcting such misperceptions would seem warranted. (Hersen, 1981, p. 21)

Delineation of etiologic pathways is routinely, albeit informally, conducted in applied practice. Indeed, most clinicians attempt to concurrently identify the "how" as well as the "what" of their patients' psychopathology. Ironically, such informative data are neither obtained or utilized in the great majority of empirical outcome studies (Hersen, 1981; Wolpe, 1977, 1979, 1990). Consequently, treatment conditions in most controlled clinical trials are comprised of etiologically heterogeneous groups of patients, and intervention effects (or lack thereof) are confounded by etiological differences among subjects.

For example, in their meta-analysis of treatment-outcome studies involving "standard" antidepressants, "newer" antidepressants, and placebo, Greenberg, Bornstein, Greenberg, and Fisher (1992) found that effects of medication did not exceed those of placebo. However, these results are misleading in that study subjects were not consistently differentiated along etiological lines. Further, of the 41% of studies that did attempt to control for etiology, a majority employed methods of subclassification that were based primarily on overt symptom correlates rather than existing objective biological indicators. As a result, treatment effects were confounded by potential etiological differences within conditions.

Avoidance of etiological assessment in the empirical realm is partially a function of the *DSM*'s rejection of theory-based etiological speculation as a means to avoid theoretical bias when subclassifying patients within diagnostic categories. It is also a function of many behavior therapists' overreliance on mere symptomatic presentation when conducting clinical assessment. Unfortunately, the move to an overwhelmingly symptom-defined diagnostic system appears to have been both premature and in conflict with existing data that support the existence, and more importantly, differential treatment response, of patients with similar overt symptom presentations but differing psychopathological origins. Moreover, assessment of etiology is essential to the appropriate application of any prescriptive treatment in that it directs

clinicians to those aspects of an intervention that are most relevant to a particular presenting problem.

Usefulness of etiological assessment is best illustrated by the extensive existing literature on affective disorder subtypes. Although a large number of researchers have obtained data that strongly indicate existence of a biologically based, endogenous subtype of depression that is reliably differentiated from nonendogenous depression (Conti et al., 1987; Feinberg & Carroll, 1982; Kupfer & Thase, 1983; Thase et al., 1983; Wolpe, 1986a), many have failed to detect a treatment-specific response between these two groups. However, the apparent absence of an interaction between etiology and treatment may be a function of faulty or insufficient etiological assessment strategies employed by systems such as the *DSM, RDC,* Newcastle 1 (Carny et al., 1965) and 2 (Gurney, 1971) Indices, Michigan Discriminant Index (Feinberg & Carroll, 1982), and so on. Indeed, in their study of inter-test diagnostic agreement with *DSM-III, DSM-III-R, RDC,* and the Newcastle Index, Gallagher-Thompson and associates (1992) concluded that "these criteria are not all measuring the same construct" (p. 300).

Other investigators have also questioned the validity of *RDC* classifications of endogenous depression, including de Jonghe and colleagues (1988), Young and colleagues (1987), Zimmerman, Coryell, and Black (1990), and Zimmerman, Stangl, and Coryell (1985). Along these lines, Davidson and Pelton (1988) compared the Newcastle Index 1, the Newcastle Index 2, and the Michigan Index and found diagnostic agreement in only 30% of subjects. Using the Newcastle Index 1, 57% of the sample of depressed patients was classified as endogenous, compared to 23% for the Newcastle Index 2, and *78%* for the Michigan Index.

Clearly, categorization on the basis of these scales is problematic in that they obviously describe very different populations. As a result, identification of etiologically based differential treatment response is precluded by "looseness" of the measures. This concern was validated by Davidson and Pelton (1988), who found that use of some definitions of endogenous depression revealed an MAOI-by-diagnosis interaction, while use of others did not. In their study, subjects classified as having endogenous depression by the Newcastle I scale responded to a relatively greater extent following low-dose MAOI, while subjects diagnosed by this scale as nonendogenous responded more favorably to high-dose MAOI. No such interaction was recorded when patients were classified by the Michigan Index. Notably, between-groups main effects were not significant for any scale, and use of the Newcastle Index 2 or the Michigan Index would have led to the erroneous conclusion that both treatments were equally effective, irrespective of diagnosis.

As mentioned, a major weakness of the preceding scales is their overreliance on overt symptom and severity ratings to define subtypes. Fortunately, additional methods of etiological assessment of endogenous depression can be used to supplement these symptombased scales and offer convergent validity for diagnostic subgrouping. Foremost among these is the dexamethasone suppression test (DST). Nonsuppression on the DST appears to be a characteristic of endogenous depression (Chadhury, Valdiya, & Agustine, 1989; Robbins, Alessi, & Colfer, 1989; Zimmerman, Stangl, Coryell, 1985; Zimmerman, Coryell, & Black, 1990). Indeed, when the DST is used as an external grouping criterion (in contrast to using *DSM* or *RDC* as reference criteria), a reliable and seemingly homogeneous subset of depressives are identified, characterized by middle or early morning insomnia, worsened mood in the morning, poor appetite, psychomotor retardation, low anxiety, and positive response to tricyclic medication (Zimmerman, Stangl, & Coryell, 1985; Robbins, Alessi, & Colfer, 1989).

Some investigators have questioned the usefulness of the DST in distinguishing endogenous from nonendogenous depression (e.g., Klein & Berger, 1987). Yet, an obvious factor responsible for its intermittent failure in achieving high inter-test reliability with other measures is the "nonuniform" application of comparison criteria across settings and investigators. In fact, Zimmerman, Coryell, and Black (1990) noted that experimenters employing "narrow" versions of *RDC* definitions consistently find a strong association between endo-

genous depression and nonsuppression on the DST, whereas researchers using "broad" interpretations have failed to find such an association. Obviously, if the measure serving and the criterion reference is unreliable, then any test's sensitivity and specificity relative to that criterion cannot be accurately evaluated.

In addition to the DST (and the aforementioned sedation threshold test), other biological markers for endogenous depression have been identified, further validating this etiological subtype. For example, Maes, de Ruyter, and Suy (1987) used a combination of objective biological tests—including the DST, 1-tryptophan competing amino acid ratio, and the 3-methoxy-4-hydroxyphenylglycol flow in 24-hour urine, as well as age—to classify, with 82% accuracy, subjects into depressive subgroups. Convergent biologically based validation of the endogenous/nonendogenous distinction in depression was also supplied by Bertschy and colleagues (1989) who found that cardiac beta-adrenergic sensitivity was significantly lower in patients diagnosed with endogenous depression. Importantly, this relationship was independent of depression severity. Overall, it would appear that a combination of objective methods will result in enhanced reliability of the diagnosis of endogenous depression.

Although the argument has been made that endogenous depression is, in itself, a homogeneous subtype of depression, Wolpe (1990) postulates the existence of at least four subtypes of nonendogenous depression resulting from: (1) severe conditioned anxiety (recall that endogenous depression was characterized by a lack of anxiety) (Heerlein, Lauer, & Richter, 1989; Wolpe, 1986a), (2) devaluative cognitions, (3) interpersonal inadequacy or social skills deficits, and (4) severe bereavement. Craighead (1980) offers a fifth etiological depressive subtype presumed to result from marital discord. Relatively less empirical attention has been directed toward identification of nonendogenous subtypes of depression and evaluation of differential treatment response. Indeed, these subgroups are wholly ignored in *RDC* and *DSM* diagnostic schemes.

Prescriptive assessment of depressive etiology is useful insofar as it facilitates effective application of prescriptive interventions. Several investigators have provided support for the position that nonendogenous and endogenous depressive subtypes require different prescriptive treatments. For example, Robbins, Alessi, and Colfer (1989) treated 38 adolescent depressives with a psychosocial intervention to which 47% responded. The remaining nonresponders were treated with a combined package of tricyclics and psychosocial therapy, to which 92% responded. Notably, DST nonsuppression (indicating endogenous depression) was predictive of failure to respond to psychosocial treatment alone. Relatedly, Raskin and Crook (1976) noted that endogenous depressives improved when treated with antidepressant medication but not when treated by placebo, whereas nonendogenous depressives improved in response to both treatments.

Moreover, Kiloh, Ball, and Garside (1977) found that endogenous depressives maintained gains following treatment by antidepressant medication to a significantly greater extent than nonendogenous depressives undergoing an identical treatment. Along similar lines, Paykel and associates (1973) divided subjects as anxious depressives, psychotic depressives, hostile depressives, and young depressives with personality disorders. Following treatment with amitriptyline, those patients with the most severe depression at pretreatment evinced the greatest improvement with medication, *unless* they were diagnosed as anxious (i.e., nonendogenous) depressives, who responded to pharmacotherapy with the least improvement of all groups. Further, Davidson and Pelton (1988) found that endogenous depressives improved to a relatively greater extent with low-dose MAOIs, whereas nonendogenous depressives responded more favorably to high-dose MAOI treatment. Similar interactions between depressive subtype and treatment were demonstrated by Bech and colleagues (1980), Brown and Shuey (1980), McKnight and colleagues (1984), Woggon (1993), and Prusoff and colleagues (1980).

The predictive utility of the endogenous/nonendogenous distinction is also evident from a study by Buchholtz-Hansen and associates (1993). In their 10-year follow-up of pharmacologically treated patients, these investigators found the sui-

cide rate of nonendogenous depressives to be 100 times that of a normal reference group, compared to endogenous depressives, who committed suicide at 20 times the rate of the normal group. Clearly, prescriptive treatment for the former group will require continued therapeutic maintenance in addition to psychotropic medication or, at the least, continued assessment of affective state following pharmacotherapy.

In the area of nonendogenous depression, Heiby (1986) employed a controlled single-case crossover design to evaluate the relative efficacy of social-skills training and self-control training with depressed subjects low in either social or self-control skills. Predictably, "treatment matched to the deficit appeared to be more effective than treatment that was not specifically matched to the depressed individuals' deficits" (p. 165). Similarly, McKnight, Nelson, Hayes, and Jarrett (1984) demonstrated that depressed subjects characterized by depressogenic cognitions, but not social-skills deficits, displayed greater improvement on both measures of depression and irrational cognitions following a cognitively oriented treatment than did similarly diagnosed subjects receiving social-skills training. In contrast, subjects with social-skills deficits, but not depressogenic cognitions, improved to a relatively greater extent on measures of social-skill and depression after receiving social-skills training than did similarly categorized subjects receiving cognitive therapy. Overall, it is clear that assessment of etiological factors in depression facilitates appropriate application of prescriptive treatments. Therefore, empirical investigations of interventions for depression must attend to the confounding effects of subject heterogeneity resulting from absent or insufficient etiological analysis and control in order to yield meaningful results.

Comparable findings of diagnostic heterogeneity have been noted within *DSM*-defined anxiety disorders. For example, individuals with identical specific phobic symptom presentations may vary with respect to psychopathological etiology (Öst, 1991). Indeed, Wolpe (1981), Öst and Hugdahl (1983), Rachman (1977), and Kleinknecht (1994) noted that circumscribed phobic responses may be acquired through either conditioning or misinformation and/or faulty logic. Öst and Hugdahl (1983) differentiated conditioned from cognitively based fears with their Phobic Origins Questionnaire, which attempted to verify the existence of traumatic conditioning experiences or negative information and instruction.

On the other hand, Wolpe and colleagues (1985) categorized phobic etiology as having cognitive origins when a patient truly believed that a feared stimulus was dangerous. In contrast, they considered conditioned fears to be those in which the patient felt as if exposure would cause danger, but did not actually believe the stimulus itself was harmful, or the object of fear was panic associated with a feared stimulus, rather than the stimulus itself. As was the case with depressive subtypes, an interaction appears to exist between mode of phobic acquisition and method of treatment applied. For example, Öst (1985) classified subjects as having either conditioned or cognitive fears with his Phobic Origins Questionnaire and found that those with conditioned fears improved to a relatively greater extent following counterconditioning/extinction interventions than did similarly classified phobics receiving cognitive restructuring. Along these lines, Trower and associates (1978) demonstrated that socially phobic subjects with skills deficits responded more favorably to social-skills training than unskilled social phobics receiving systematic desensitization. In contrast, both treatments were equally efficacious for socially anxious patients with no significant skills deficits.

Analogous subtypes of patients diagnosed with *DSM-IV* panic disorder also appear to exist and are differentiated through prescriptive assessment. Russel and colleagues (1991) described an interesting subgroup of patients who met *DSM* criteria for panic disorder, but for whom attacks were unaccompanied by fear. These patients differed from most panic-disordered individuals along other diagnostic and treatment parameters as well. Indeed, all of the nonfearful panickers in the sample responded to lactate-infusion challenges with attacks, while none demonstrated such a response to a placebo-infusion challenge. Most importantly, *all* patients experienced a 75% or greater reduction in symptoms over a 6-month period following treatment with imipramine or clonazepam, a reduction in excess of that typically seen in fearful panickers receiving this course of pharmacotherapy (Mavis-

sakalian, Michelson, & Dealy, 1983). These findings are indicative of a panic subgroup with a strongly biological etiology. Indeed, the unusual uniform responses of these patients to both placebo and lactate challenges, and to antipanic medication, offer convergent evidence for the validity of this symptom-defined (i.e., lack of overt fear during attacks) class of panic.

Along slightly different lines, Ley (1992) has hypothesized that at least three additional subtypes of panic disorder exist and likely evince differential treatment response. In Type I, "classical" panickers, hyperventilation is presumed to be responsible for each panic attack (e.g., Maddock & Carter, 1991). In Type II panic, hyperventilation or another discrete event causes initial panic, and contiguous interoceptive stimuli become conditioned stimuli for future panic attacks. In Type III panic, interoceptive stimuli characteristic of arousal are erroneously considered to be evidence of impending mental and physical disaster. Such missattribution leads to increased arousal and anxiety, which reaffirms the distressing nature of the initial missattribution, until the cycle results in a panic attack.

Although "second-order" empirical studies have not yet been conducted, it would seem logical that the appropriate prescriptive treatment for Type I, or hyperventilatory panic, will involve strategies aimed at reducing the incidence of inappropriate breathing in the patient (e.g., Ley, 1993). Similarly, appropriate treatment for Type II panic will necessarily involve some form of interoceptive exposure, thereby permitting extinction or counterconditioning of learned anxiety response (e.g., Griez & Van den Hout, 1986). Finally, prescriptive treatment for Type III panics will likely involve cognitive interventions aimed at altering the nature of catastrophic missattributions of somatic symptoms (e.g., Beck et al., 1992).

Again, the relevance of etiological assessment in defining subgroups of disorders with similar symptomatic presentations is great, and permits focused application of specific treatments to specific problems. Moreover, the variance accounted for in treatment outcome by etiology appears to be very significant, particularly with affective and anxiety disorders. Therefore, attention to this area increases the likelihood that appropriate treatment will be employed. A final important area of prescriptive assessment remains to be described, however, and includes specification of subject characteristics and treatment history.

Prescriptive Assessment: Subject Characteristics and Treatment History

Assessment of subject characteristics and treatment history, long a *sine qua non* of diagnostic processes in the medical field, is only given cursory attention by psychologists. Indeed, physicians will regularly consider patient response history to antibiotics when forming treatment recommendations for an individual with a bladder infection; however, clinical psychologists (including those conducting outcome research) frequently fail to investigate a depressed patient's previous response to a particular treatment before initiating a course of preferred therapy for depression. Clearly, such a line of inquiry would be extremely useful, in that interventions with demonstrated past efficacy for an individual should be selected in favor of those lacking such positive response histories.

Additionally, our general failure to consider more than grossly defined subject characteristics is somewhat ironic in fight of the specific epidemiological data often supplied in Subject sections of most published research. This apparent contradiction lies in the fact that most of these data—including socioconomic status, ethnicity, age, level of social support, previous psychiatric history, length of current illness, and familial status (exception: gender and race)—are not utilized in a manner that would isolate their interactive effects with treatment. However, this information is potentially relevant to treatment outcome. For example, initial erectile failure in a 70-year-old male demands a very thorough physiological assessment and is likely to predict an organic etiology, whereas identical symptoms in a newly married 20-year-old are more likely to indicate problems of a psychological nature.

Subject characteristics are also potentially useful in highlighting prevalence of particular psychopathologies for specific subgroups of individuals. This, in turn, may guide the assessor to examine those potential problem areas more closely. For instance, incidence of many disorders varies as a function of social-cultural background, with higher rates of alcoholism in the Russian, Irish, and French than in those of Italian or Jewish descent (Swinson & Eaves, 1978). Similarly, young Native Americans are at greatly increased risk for suicide relative to other ethnic groups (May, 1987). Organic disorders and complications due to bereavement are more likely to occur in older than younger adults experiencing similar life events. Finally, patients from lower SES levels appear to be at greater risk for almost all psychopathology compared to individuals from higher socioeconomic status levels (Dohrenwend & Dohrenwend, 1974; Noyes et al., 1993).

As was the case with etiological and maintaining factors (albeit to a relatively lesser extent), heterogeneous patient samples naturally arise when variables with potentially powerful effects, such as marital status and SES, remain uncontrolled. In illustration of this point, Azrin and associates (1982) demonstrated that marital status interacted strongly with treatment for alcoholism. Specifically, these investigators found that a "disulfiram assurance" program was as effective as a more comprehensive (and expensive) disulfiram assurance + community reinforcement intervention for married men. However, only the combined treatment was effective in producing near-total sobriety in unmarried men. Obviously, failure to consider marital status when employing these interventions has potentially strong consequences.

Unfortunately, Azrin and colleagues' (1982) demonstration is among the few that address this area in substance-abuse treatment. Subject characteristics also play a role in treatment responses of depressives. Bielski and Friedel (1976) showed that higher social class (as well as symptoms of endogenous depression) predicted improved response to tricyclics. George, Blazer, Hughes, and Fowler (1989) reported that older adult depressed males with weak social support networks were at increased risk of relapse 6 to 32 months after treatment relative to those with strong social support. Similarly, Dumas and Wahler (1983) noted that parent training to reduce oppositional behavior in children was significantly less effective for low SES mothers with restricted or insular social networks compared to low SES mothers with more positive interpersonal support systems.

It is clear from our review that the focused nature of many contemporary, manualized prescriptive treatments necessitates comprehensive, multidimensional assessment. In sharp contrast to general therapy (e.g., psychodynamic therapy or cognitive-behavioral therapy), prescriptive interventions involve specific procedures that vary according to the disorder and patient. That is, prescriptive treatments are those with effects that change as a function of symptoms, maintaining factors, etiology, and subject characteristics. Because of their intentionally circumscribed effects, however, the therapeutic outcomes of these techniques are largely limited to targeted areas. Therefore, problems that are targeted must be well defined. Importantly, though, patients rarely present with only a singly, circumscribed complaint. Indeed, their problems are routinely complex and require complex solutions (Hersen, 1981), such that application of multiple prescriptive treatments is often necessary to alleviate suffering in an individual.

The level of complexity of an intervention package should be determined through repeated evaluation of the patient and pathology variables specified earlier. At no time during treatment should prescriptive assessment cease. (To illustrate this point, consider the case we recently supervised in which an anxious septagenarian admitted, in the twentieth treatment session, that 50 years prior he had engaged in an incestual relationship with his adolescent sister, and that her recent death was related to his level of distress.) Rather, measurement is continuous and flexible, changing according to the communications and requirements of the patient, producing prescriptive interventions that are refined and modified in step with the needs of the patient.

CONCLUSION

Several investigators have noted that current symptom-defined assessment systems such as the *DSM* necessarily limit the extent to which prescriptive treatments can be evaluated. A sampling of selected quotations illustrates the current status of the field: "A second explanation for the apparent limited efficacy of [alcoholism] treatment suggests that what is needed is not so much better methods of treatment, but more judicious matching of patients to available treatment options" (Annis, 1988, p. 153). "A good classification system is essential to any matching experiment" (Gibbs & Hollister, 1993, p. 43). "From this clinical standpoint, greater appreciation of the distinctiveness of certain subgroups of alcoholics could be used to tailor more appropriate and effective interventions" (Donovan, Kivlahan, & Walker, 1986, p. 208). "There are undoubtably many functionally distinct subgroups of patients currently mixed together in popular diagnostic systems" (Bielski & Friedel, 1976, p. 971). "The failure of literature reviews to find differential treatment effects may be a result of their failure to evaluate homogenous patient samples" (Beutler, 1979, p. 882).

Effects of contemporary psychological treatments are increasingly focused and intentionally circumscribed. Importantly, such prescriptive interventions require precise prescriptive assessment along multiple parameters in order to achieve maximum efficacy. Logically, such assessment will address those factors accounting for the greatest variance in treatment response. Consequently, variables included in prescriptive assessment are symptom presentation, maintaining factors, etiology, and subject characteristics and history. Assessment and control along these parameters permits identification of homogeneous patient subgroups within heterogenous *DSM* disorder classes.

The argument has been made, however (e.g., Nelson et al., 1989), that employing componential treatments that ultimately address different needs of patient subtypes effectively eliminates the necessity of thorough assessment and specific matching of patient and treatment. Yet, as Eifert, Evans, and McKendrick (1990) state, "Casting an ever widening therapeutic net is not the answer" (p. 166) in terms of both temporal or economic efficiency, particularly in light of contemporary third-party reimbursement practices. Indeed, it is neither in the best interest of the patient or the field to pursue the study of componential *over* that of prescriptive treatments.

Clinical psychology has largely completed the initial phase, or "first-order" investigation of treatment efficacy with general, univariately defined patient groups. Indeed, the American Psychological Association's Task Force on Promotion and Dissemination of Psychological Procedures (1995) provides a list of interventions with demonstrated efficacy in the treatment of several generally defined disorders. However, research to answer Paul's (1967) ultimate question—"What treatment, by whom, is most effective for this individual with that specific problem under which set of circumstances" (p. 118)—is still very much in its nascent stage. Such second-order, multivariate investigations necessary to answer this query have been undertaken only rarely and are forestalled by diagnostic systems that both preclude necessary subclassification of psychopathology and obliterate pathological subtype by treatment interactions.

Importantly, some progress has been made, as is evident from the many examples provided in this chapter, and from the large, federally funded, multisite study Project Match (Project Match Group, 1993), developed and implemented for the express purpose of identifying differential response indicators in alcoholism treatment. Additional outcome studies are needed with affective and anxiety disorders, in which classification is conducted in a more refined and systematic manner, along one or more (preferably more) of the parameters outlined here, with control over treatment interaction effects of symptoms, maintaining factors, etiology, and subject characteristics. These need to be achieved *a priori* through modifications in experimental design, rather than post hoc as secondary analyses. It is at that point that we will be able to claim true prescriptive assessment and treatment.

REFERENCES

Abramowitz, C. V., Abramowitz, S. I., Roback, H. B., & Jackson, C. (1974). Differential effectiveness of directive and non-directive group therapies as a function of client internal-external control. *Journal of Consulting and Clinical Psychology 42*, 849–853.

Agras, W. S. (1987). So where do we go from here? Behavior *Therapy, 18*, 203–217.

American Psychiatric Association. (1994). *Diagnostic and statistical manual of mental disorders* (4th ed). Washington, DC: American Psychiatric Association.

Annis, H. (1988). Patient-treatment matching in the management of alcoholism. 50th annual scientific meeting of the committee on problems of drug dependence. *National Institute on Drug Abuse Research Monograph, 90*, 152–161.

Annis, H., & Davis, L. (1989). Relapse prevention. In R. Hester & W. Miller (Eds.), *Handbook of alcoholism treatment approaches*. New York: Pergamon.

Azrin, N. H., Acierno, R., Kogan, E. S., Donohue, B., Besalel, V., & McMahon, P. (in press). Follow-up results of supportive versus behavioral therapy for illicit drug use. *Behaviour Research and Therapy*.

Azrin, N. H., McMahon, P., Donohue, B., Besalel, V., Lapinski, K., Kogan, E., Acierno, R., & Galloway, E. (1994). Behavior therapy for drug abuse: A controlled treatment-outcome study. *Behaviour Research and Therapy, 32*, 857–866.

Azrin, N. H., Sisson, R., Meyers, R., & Godley, M. (1982). Alcoholism treatment by disulfuram and community reinforcement therapy. *Journal of Behavior Therapy and Experimental Psychiatry, 13*, 105–112.

Bech, P., Gram, L. F., Reisby, N., & Rafaelsen, O. J. (1980). The WHO depression scale: Relationship to the Newcastle scales. *Acta Psychiatrica Scandinavica, 62*, 140.

Beck, A. T., Sokal, L., Clark, D., Berchick, R., & Wright, F. (1992). A crossover study of focused cognitive therapy for panic disorder. *American Journal of Psychiatry, 149*, 778–783.

Bertschy, G., Vandel, S., Puech, A. Vandel, B, Sandoz, M., & Allers, G. (1989). Cardiac beta-adrenergic sensitivity in depression: Relation with endogenous subtype and desipramine response. *Neuropsychobiology, 21*, 177–181.

Beutler, L. E. (1979). Toward specific psychological therapies for specific conditions. *Journal of Consulting and Clinical Psychology, 47*, 882–897.

Beutler, L. E. (1991). Have all won and must all have prizes? Revisiting Luborsky et al.'s verdict. *Journal of Consulting and Clinical Psychology, 59*, 226–232.

Bielski, R., & Friedel, R. O. (1976). Predictions of tricyclic response. *Archives of General Psychiatry, 33*, 1479-1489.

Brown, W. A., & Shuey, I. (1980). Response to dexamethasone and subtype of depression. *Archives of General Psychistry, 37*, 747–751.

Buchholtz-Hansen, P. E., Wang, A. G., & Sorensen, P. (1993). Mortality in major affective disorder: Relationship to subtype of depression. *Acta-Psychiatrica-Scandinavica, 87*, 329–335.

Carney, M., Roth, M., & Garside, R. (1965). The diagnosis of depressive syndromes and the prediction of ECT response. *British Journal of Psychiatry, III*, 659.

Chadhury, S., Valdiya, P. S., & Augustine, M. (1989). The dexamethasone suppression test in endogenous depression. Indian *Journal of Psychiatry, 31*, 296–300.

Conti, L., Placidi, G. R., Dell'Osso, L., Lenzi, A., & Cassano, G. B. (1987). Therapeutic response in subtypes of major depression. *New Trends in Experimental and Clinical Psychiatry, 3*, 101–107.

Cooney, N. L., Kadden, R. M., Litt, M. D., & Getter, H. (1991). Matching alcoholics to coping skills, or interactional therapies: Two year follow up results. *Journal of Consulting and Clinical Psychology, 59*, 598–601.

Craighead, W. C. (1980). Away from a unitary model of depression. *Behavior Therapy, II*, 122–128.

Davidson, J. R., & Pelton, S. (1988). A comparative evaluation of three discriminant scales for endogenous depression. *Psychiatry Research, 23*, 193–200.

de Jonghe, F., Ameling, E., & Assies, J. (1988). An elaborate description of the symptomatology of patients with research diagnostic criteria endogenous depression. *Journal of Nervous and Mental Disease, 176*, 475–479.

Dohrenwend, B. P., & Dohrenwend, B. S. (1974). Social and cultural influences upon psychopathology. *Annual Review of Psychology, 25*, 417–452.

Donovan, D. M., Kivlahan, D. R., & Walker, R. D. (1986). Alcoholic subtypes based on multiple assessment domains: Validation against treatment outcome. *Recent Developments in Alcoholism, 4*, 207–222.

Dumas, J. E., & Wahler, R. G. (1983). Predictors of treatment outcome in parent training: Mother insularity and socioeconomic status. *Behavioral Assessment, 5*, 301–313.

Eifert, G. H., Evans, I. M., & McKendrick, V. G. (1990). Matching treatments to client problems not diagnostic labels: A case for paradigmatic behavior therapy. *Journal of Behavior Therapy and Experimental Psychiatry, 21*, 163–172.

Elder, J. P., Edelstein, B. A., & Fremouw, W. J. (1981). Client by treatment interactions in response acquisitions and cognitive restructuring approaches. *Cognitive Therapy and Research, 5*, 203–210.

Feinberg, M., & Carroll, B. J. (1982). Separation of subtypes of depression using discriminant analysis: I. Separation of unipolar endogenous depression from non-endogenous depression. *British Journal of Psychiatry, 140*, 384–391.

Finney, J. W., & Moos, R. H. (1986). Matching patients with treatments: Conceptual and methodological issues. *Journal of Studies on Alcohol, 47*, 122–134.

Gallagher-Thompson, D., Futterman, A., Hanley-Peterson, P., Zeiss, A., Fronson, G., & Thompson, L. (1992). Endogenous depression in the elderly: Prevalence and agreement among measures. *Journal of Consulting and Clinical Psychology, 60*, 300–303.

George, L. K., Blazer, D. G., Hughes, D. C., & Fowler, N. (1989). Social support and the outcome of major depression. *British Journal of Psychiatry, 154*, 478–485.

Gibbs, L. E., & Hollister, C. D. (1993). Matching alcoholics with treatment: Reliability, replication, and validity of a treatment typology. *Journal of Social Service Research, 17*, 41–72.

Greenberg, R. P., Bornstein, R. F., Greenberg, M. D., & Fisher, S. (1992). A meta-analysis of antidepressant outcome under "blinder" conditions. *Journal of Consulting and Clinical Psychology, 60*, 664–669.

Griez, E., & van den Hout, M. (1986). CO_2 inhalation in the treatment of panic attacks. *Behaviour Research and Therapy. 24*, 145–150.

Gunther, W., Gunther, Streck, P., Romig, H., & Rodel, A. (1988). Psychomotor disturbances in psychiatric patients as a possible basis for new attempts at differential diagnosis and therapy: III Cross validation study on depressed patients: The psychotic motor syndrome as a possible state marker for endogenous depression. *European Archives of Psychiatry and Neurological Sciences, 237*, 65–73.

Gurney, C. (1971). Diagnostic scales for affective disorders. *Proceedings of 4th World Congress of Psychiatry*, Mexico City, p. 130.

Hayes, S. C., Nelson, R. O., & Jarrett, R. B. (1987). The treatment utility of assessment: A functional approach to evaluating assessment quality. *American Psychologist, 42*, 963–974.

Heerlein, A., Lauer, G., & Richter, P. (1989). Alexithymia and affective expression in endogenous and non-endogenous depression. *Nervenarzt, 60*, 220–225.

Heiby, E. M. (1986). Social versus self-control skills deficits in four cases of depression. *Behavior Therapy, 17*, 158–169.

Hersen, M. (1981). Complex problems require complex solutions. *Behavior Therapy, 12*, 15–29.

Kadden, R. M., Cooney, N. L., Getter, H., & Litt, M. D. (1989). Matching alcoholics to coping skills or interactional therpies: Posttreatment results. *Journal of Consulting and Clinical Psychology, 57*, 698–704.

Kallman, W. M., Hersen, M., & O'Toole, D. H. (1975). The use of social reinforcement in a case of conversion reaction. *Behavior Therapy, 6*, 411–413.

Kiloh, L. G., Ball, J. R., & Garside, R. F. (1977). Depression: A multivariate study of Sir Aubrey Lews's data on melancholia. *Australian and New Zealand Journal of Psychiatry, 11*, 149–156.

Klein, H. E., & Berger, M. (1987). The pitfalls of the dexamethasone suppression test: A biological marker of endogenous depression? *Human Psychopharmacology Clinical and Experimental, 2*, 85–103.

Kleinknecht, R. A. (1994). Aquisition of blood, injury, and needle fears and phobias. *Behaviour Research and Therapy, 32*, 817–823.

Kupfer, D. L., & Thase, M. F. (1983). The use of the sleep laboratory in the diagnosis of affective disorders. *Psychiatric Clinics of North America, 6*, 3–25.

Lang, P. J. (1968) Fear reduction and fear behavior: Problems in treating a construct. In J. M. Shlien (Ed.), *Research in psychotherapy* (vol. 3). Washington, DC: American Psychological Association.

Lazarus, A, (1973). Multimodal. behavior therapy and treating the basic id. *Journal of Nervous and Mental Disease, 156*, 404–411.

Ley, R. (1992). The many faces of Pan: Psychological and physiological differences among three types of panic attacks. *Behaviour Research and Therapy, 30*, 347–357.

Ley, R. (1993). Breathing retraining in the treatment of hyperventilatory complaints and panic disorder: A reply to Garssen, De Ruiter, and van Dyck. *Clinical Psychology Review, 13*, 393–408.

Luborsky, L., Singer, B., & Luborsky, L. (1975). Comparative studies of psychotherapy: Is it true that "Everyone has won and all must have prizes"? *Archives of General Psychiatry, 32*, 995.

Maddock, R. J., & Carter, C. S. (1991). Hyperventilation-induced panic attacks in panic disorder with agoraphobia. *Biological Psychiatry, 29*, 843–854.

Maes, M. H., de Ruyter, M., & Suy, E. (1987). Prediction of subtype and severity of depression by means of dexamethasone suppression test, 1-tryptophan: Competing amino acid ration, and MHPG flow. *Biological Psychiatry, 22*, 177–188.

Maier, W., Philipp, M., & Heuser, 1. (1986). Dimensional assessment of endogenous depression based on a polydiagnostic approach. *Psychopathology, 19*, 267–275.

Martelli, M. F., Auerbach, S. M., Alexander, J., & Mercuri, L. G. (1987). Stress management in the health care setting: Matching interventions with patient coping styles. *Journal of Consulting and Clinical Psychology, 55*, 201–207.

Mavissakalian, M., Michelson, L., & Dealy, R. S. (1983). Pharmacological treatment of agoraphobia: Imipramine versus imipramine with programmed prac-

tice. *British Journal of Psychiatry, 143*, 348–355.

May, P. (1987). Suicide and self destruction among American Indian youths. *American Indian and Alaska Native Mental Health Research, 1*, 52–69.

McKnight, D., Nelson, R., Hayes, S., & Jarrett, R. (1984). Importance ot treating individually assessed response classess of depression. *Behavior Therapy, 15*, 315–335.

Meichenbaum, D., Gilmore, J., & Fedoravicius, A. (1971). Group insight versus group desensitization in treating speech anxiety. *Journal of Consulting and Clinical Psychology, 36*, 410–421.

Musa, M. N. (1986). Higher steady-state plasma concentration of imipramine in endogenous compared to nonendogenous depression. *Research Communications in Psychology, Psychiatry, and Behavior, 11*, 11–22.

Nelson, R. O., Herbert, J. D., Herbert, D. L., Sigmon, S. T., & Brannon, S. (1989). Effectiveness of matched, mismatched, and package treatments of depression. *Journal of Behavior Therapy and Experimental Psychiatry, 20*, 281–294.

Noyes, R., Clancy, J., Woodman, C., Holt, C., Suelzer, M., Christiansen, J., & Andersen, D. (1993). Environmental factors related to the outcome of panic disorder: A seven year follow-up study. *Journal of Nervous and Mental Disease, 181*, 529–538.

Nunnally, J. C., & Bernstein, I. H. (1994). *Psychometric theory* (3rd ed.). New York: McGraw-Hill.

Öst, L. G. (1985). Ways of acquiring phobias and outcome of behavioral treatment. *Behaviour Research and Therapy, 23*, 683–689.

Öst, L. G. (1991). Acquisition of blood and injection phobia and anxiety response patterns in clinical patients. *Behaviour Research and Therapy, 29*, 323–332.

Öst, L. G., & Hugdahl, K. (1983). Acquisition of agoraphobia, mode of onset and anxiety response patterns. *Behaviour Research and Therapy, 21*, 623–631.

Öst, L. G., Jerremalm, A., & Johansson, J. (1981). Individual response patterns and the effects of different behavioral methods in the treatment of social phobia. *Behaviour Research and Therapy, 19*, 1–16.

Öst, L. G., Johansson, J., & Jerremalm, A. (1982). Individual response patterns and the effects of different behavioral methods in the treatment of claustrophobia. *Behaviour Research and Therapy, 20*, 445–560.

Paul, G. L. (1967). Outcome research in psychotherapy. *Journal of Consulting Psychology, 31*, 109–118.

Paykel, E. S., Prusoff, B. A., Klerman, G. L., Haskell, D., & Dimascio, A. (1973). Clinical response to amitriptyline among depressed women. *Journal of Nervous and Mental Disease, 156*, 149–165.

Project MATCH Research Group. (1993). Project match: Rationale and methods for a multisite clinical trial matching patients to alcoholism treatment. *Alcoholism Clinical and Experimental Research, 17*, 1130–1145.

Prusoff, B. A., Weissman, M. M., Klerman, G. L., & Rounsaville, B. J. (1980). Research diagnostic criteria subtypes of depression. *Archives of General Psychiatry, 37*, 796–801.

Rachman, S. (1977). The conditioning theory of fear-acquisition: A critical examination. *Behaviour Research and Therapy, 15*, 375.

Raskin, A., & Crook, T. H. (1976). The endogenous-neurotic distinction as a predictor of response to antidepressant drugs. *Psychological Medicine, 6*, 59–70.

Robbins, C. J., Block, P., & Peselow, E. D. (1989). Specificity of symptoms in RDC endogenous depression. *Journal of Affective Disorders, 16*, 243–248.

Robbins, D. R., Alessi, N. E., & Colfer, M. V. (1989). Treatment of adolescents with major depression: Implications of the DST and the melancholic subtype. *Journal of Affective Disorders, 17*, 99–104.

Russell, J. L., Kushner, M. G., Beitman, B. D., & Bartels, K. M. (1991). Nonfearful panic disorder in neurology patients validated by lactate challenge. *American Journal of Psychiatry, 148*, 361–364.

Simons, A. D., Lustman, P. J., Wetzel, R. D., & Murphy, G. E. (1985). Predicting response to cognitive therapy of depression: The role of learned resourcefulness. *Cognitive Therapy and Research, 9*, 79–89.

Smith, M., & Glass, G. V. (1977). Meta-analysis of outcome studies. *American Psychologist, 32*, 752–760.

Spitzer, R. L., Endicott, J., & Robbins, E. (1978). Research diagnostic criteria: Rationale and reliability. *Archives of General Psychiatry, 35*, 773–782.

Swinson, R. P., & Eaves, D. (1978). *Psychiatric topics for community Workers: Alcoholism and addiction*. England: Woburn Press.

Task Force on Promotion and Dissemination of Psychological Procedures. (1995). *The Clinical Psychologist, 48*, 3–23.

Thase, M. E., Hersen, M., Bellack, A. S., Hirmmelhoch, J. M., & Kupfer, D. J. (1983). Validation of a Hamilton subscale for endogenomorphic depression. *Journal of Affective Disorders, 5*, 267–278.

Trower, P., Yardley, K., Bryant, B., & Shaw. (1978). The treatment of social failure: A comparison of anxiety reduction and skills aquisition procedures for two social problems. *Behavior Modification, 2*, 41–60.

Vaglum, P., & Fossheim, I. (1980). Differential treatment of young abusers: A quasi-experimental study of a "therapeutic community" in a psychiatric hospital. *Journal of Drug Issues, 10*, 505–516.

Willner, P., Wilkes, M., & Orwin, A. (1990). Attributional style and perceived stress in endogenous and reactive depression. *Journal of Affective Disorders, 18*, 281–287.

Woggon, B. (1993). The role of moclobermide in endogenous depression: A survey of recent data. Third International symposium: RIMAs in subtypes of depression: Focus on moclobemide. *International Clinical Psychopharmacolgy, 7*, 137–139.

Wolpe, J. (1977). Inadequate behavior analysis: The achilles heel of outcome research in behavior therapy. *Journal of Behavior Therapy and Experimental Psychiatry, 8*, 1–3.

Wolpe, J. (1979). The experimental model and treatment of neurotic depression. *Behaviour Research and Therapy, 17*, 555–565.

Wolpe, J. (1981). The dichotomy between classically conditioned and cognitively learned anxiety. *Journal of Behavior Therapy and Experimental Psychiatry, 12*, 35–42.

Wolpe, J. (1986a). The positive diagnosis of neurotic depression as an etiological category. *Comprehensive Psychiatry, 27*, 449–460.

Wolpe, J. (1986b). Individualization: The categorical imperative of behavior therapy practice. *Journal of Behavior Therapy and Experimental Psychiatry, 17*, 145–153.

Wolpe, J. (1990). *The practice of behavior therapy* (4th ed.). New York: Pergamon.

Wolpe, J., Lande, S. D., McNally, R. J., Schotte, D. (1985). Differentiation between classically conditioned and cognitively based neurotic fears: Two pilot studies. *Journal of Behavior Therapy and Experimental Psychiatry, 16*, 287–293.

Young, M. A., Keller, M. B., Lavori, P. W., Scheftner, W. A., Fawcett, J., Endicott, J., & Hirschfeld, R. (1987). Lack of stability of the RDC endogenous subtype in consecutive episodes of major depression. *Journal of Affective Disorders, 12*, 139–143.

Zimmerman, M., Coryell, W. H., & Black, D. W. (1990). Variability in the application of contemporary diagnostic criteria: Endogenous depression as an example. *American Journal of Psychiatry, 147*, 1173–1179.

Zimmerman, M., Stangl, D., & Coryell, W. (1985). The research diagnostic criteria for endogenous suppression and the dexamethasone suppression test: A discriminant function analysis. *Psychiatry Research, 14*, 197–208.

CHAPTER 4

BEHAVIORAL INTERVIEWING

David B. Sarwer
Steven L. Sayers
Allegheny University of the Health Sciences

The behavioral interview is the foundation of the behavioral assessment process. Despite the technological advances in behavioral assessment such as observational coding and analysis (e.g., Bakeman & Casey, 1995), the interview is still the most essential step in examining the reasons for and planning the treatment of patients' difficulties. It is still guided by the need for a clinician to start from the patient's complaints and discover the relations between the person's environment and his or her individual responses to it. The interviewer still applies basic behavioral principles and assumptions to these data and formulates a treatment plan. However, there are no "standards" for conducting a behavioral interview, only a general consensus among behaviorally oriented clinicians and theorists about what the interview involves. Furthermore, the issues that arise in each interview can be quite diverse. Thus, learning how to conduct a behavioral interview can be a daunting task. Fortunately, some progress has been made in specifying the elements of a behavioral interview and examining what training components are needed to help

beginning clinicians learn these skills. The goal of this chapter is to clarify what concepts should guide a behavioral interview, how this may affect the way the interview is conducted, and specifically how a behavioral interview can be implemented.

Because the behavioral interview is usually the first step in behavioral assessment, it provides the first opportunity for the behavior therapist to set the tone and direction of the therapy. The behavioral interviewer should consider carefully what is subtly communicated to the patient about what therapy will be like and how the patient will be regarded in this therapy. On the other hand, the behavioral interview also needs to yield specific information crucial to understanding why the patient was presented for treatment and how to help him or her. We will hopefully make it clear that the skilled behavioral interviewer accomplishes these goals simultaneously.

This chapter is divided into three major sections. First, we present a definition and description of behavioral interviewing. This will cover what assumptions and theoretical principles of behavioral treatments guide these methods as well as the content and range of behavioral interviewing. We will also briefly discuss the empirical literature on the training and evaluation of behavioral interviewing. Then, we discuss the specifics of how to conduct a behavioral interview, including illustrative case examples. Finally, we will review aspects of interviewing affected by the "participants"—the stable and interactional characteristics that each interviewer and each patient bring into the interview that determine the outcome of the assessment.

GENERAL ISSUES IN BEHAVIORAL INTERVIEWING

What Is a "Behavioral" Interview?

A behavioral interview reflects the viewpoint that a patient's difficulties can be understood through the learning principles that govern the individual's behavior. Essential to this idea is that the patient has learned inappropriate responses, or not learned appropriate responses, to specific situations or problems. This does not blame the patient for these problems—it merely provides the therapist and patient a way to understand and respond to these difficulties in search of a more satisfactory outcome. The interviewer applies concepts from operant conditioning, classical conditioning, and social learning perspectives to the information provided by the patient. Using these frameworks, the interviewer attempts to elicit the information necessary to perform a functional analysis of the problem— that is, understand what environmental conditions or events are functionally related to the patient's behavior so as to result in unhappiness with his or her life.

The difficulties that bring the patient to therapy are not always seen by the patient as potentially influenced by his or her own behavior, but instead as something visited on an unsuspecting victim. In fact, this may be literally true in cases such as post-traumatic stress disorder (PTSD) that develops subsequent to an automobile accident or a sexual assault. However, the clinician still must use careful interviewing to understand the factors that may determine the maintenance of the PTSD symptoms in order to develop a plan for treating the patient. Thus, when a patient voices a com-

plaint (e.g., "I'm always anxious since I had the accident"), the behavioral interviewer attempts to understand the "ABCs" of the problem (O'Leary & Wilson, 1975): antecedents (A) to the problem behavior or situation, the behavioral responses (B) of the patient, and the consequences (C). For example, the patient who complains of PTSD symptoms is asked to describe antecedents, or the circumstances in which he or she feels anxious and any event that may precipitate this subjective state.

Further, the patient is asked to describe his or her responses, which includes subjective emotional states, overt behavioral responses (e.g., avoidance of the situation), and other covert phenomena such as thoughts and interpretations of the situation. Consequences that are examined might be immediate (e.g., reduced anxiety after avoidance of a situation), self-generated (e.g., intrusive disturbing memories and images), or delayed (e.g., reduced social contact and reduced social support). The clinician attempts to rely on as little inference as possible in the process of this analysis. The patient is asked to report specifically on internal states and to describe situations in detail so that the clinician does not make an erroneous assumption about what actually happens with the patient outside the office.

To a great extent, the goal of the interview is to develop specific and detailed descriptions of observable events that are potentially connected to the problems the patient brings to the initial interview. Patients can often be vague in their complaints and are generally not skilled at observing the events in a highly specific way. Thus, the interviewer often needs to describe to patients why such behavioral specificity is important and help them provide the data that are needed. In the end, this detailed information is used to tie in the patient's complaints to specific and measurable goals of the treatment, as well as to evaluate the success of the treatment in achieving these goals.

Clinicians who use a behavioral interview acknowledge that problematic behavior has multiple determinants and that the most important determinants are often the most proximal in time. For instance, an individual with social conflicts has learned inappropriate social skills over a period of time, likely starting in his or her early years. Whereas this might suggest to some an analysis of these early conditions, it is actually more important (and practical) to examine the current conditions that maintain these behaviors. Importantly, it is the current social context that the therapist and patient will examine in order to determine what behavior change is possible and likely to be effective in improving the patient's social difficulties. Furthermore, the behavioral interviewer assumes that the patient's stated problems, problem behavior, and the environmental context that influences them is not a static model, but a dynamic and interactive system (O'Brien & Haynes, 1993). In other words, the patient's environment (particularly his or her *social* environment) provides antecedents and consequences to his or her behavior. In turn, the patient behaves in ways that may influence the behavior of others in his or her environment. Since there are potentially many influential factors for each person in this scenario that naturally change over time, the result can be a complex, multileveled model of the patient's behavior that can shift with these changing circumstances.

The interviewer can acknowledge the potential influence of biological and neurodevelopmental conditions on a patient's symptoms yet still determine the environmental conditions functioning as stimuli or consequences of the patient's behavior. Patients whose social skills result from the negative symptoms of schizophrenia can still potentially be helped through teaching family members to provide structure and appropriate reinforcements for improvements in the patient's social behavior within the home (Mueser & Glynn, 1995). Low reinforcement of the patient's behavior on the part of family members may be understood as the result of having a relative with schizophrenia; however, determining that family members can provide more reinforcement to the patient's social behavior may be crucial in improving family relations and ultimately improving the course of the illness.

What Does a Behavioral Interview Cover?

Like any skilled clinical interview, the behavioral interview must provide enough information for an understanding of the problems presented by the patient and must guide the clinician in the development of a treatment plan. Unlike some other theoretical approaches, the behavioral interview is only the first step in the assessment process. (The other chapters in this book describe many other techniques that are used in behavioral assessment.) Therefore, the interview can be thought of as comprehensive but not exhaustive, covering the ABCs of the problem, the history of the problem, and any other relevant information about the patient that has a bearing on treatment. Admittedly, this could be fairly broad. Some guidelines concerning the areas one might cover are presented here.

The behavioral interview must reflect a multifaceted view of the patient's complaints. As implied earlier, the interviewer should assess cognitions, behaviors, affects, and the patient's social relationships as they relate to the problem. Lazarus (1973) provided a highly useful framework (and acronym) for areas needing assessment in preparation for therapy: behavior (B), affect (A), sensation (S), imagery (I), cognitions (C), interpersonal relationships (I), and the possible need for drugs (D) or BASIC ID. A thorough examination of each of these domains will help the clinician identify the factors that are influencing the problem. In other words, what does the patient do, feel, think, and imagine, when X happens? What do others do? Who are the people he or she interacts with and what do these contacts lead the patient to do, feel, or think? What influences do other people have on the problem? In addition, what does the patient believe is causing the problem, and what can be done about it?

The history of the problem is also quite important: How long has it occurred? Has it varied in intensity? What has the patient done about it thus far? The history of the problem is relevant from a number of perspectives. It may be useful to know the circumstances that led to the patient learning inappropriate responses, so that the therapist can estimate what reinforcers may be needed to help the patient learn new responses. For example, a patient who has learned to be abrupt, demanding, and controlling in interactions with co-workers may have been positively reinforced by relative success in convincing others to acquiesce to him or her by using this interpersonal approach. The interviewer should attempt to understand the value of this acquiescence as a reinforcer, relative to the value of reinforcers associated with a more cooperative style.

Likewise, the chronicity of any problem behavior may inform the therapist and patient how difficult it may be for the patient to learn a different approach.

One important reason that such a broad sweep of the patient's complaints is conducted is that the problem ultimately addressed in therapy may not be the initial problem cited by the patient. For example, a patient treated by one of the present authors initially complained of social anxiety. She reported a history of chronic acne that had resulted in severe facial scarring. She was predictably anxious about others' perceptions of her at dances and parties, and had requested the therapist to teach her relaxation techniques. Upon further detailed questioning, it was apparent that her responses to others' initiations in social settings were often defensive and sarcastic. It also seemed that her pessimistic beliefs about the outcome of social encounters and her own angry affect going into these situations led to ineffective behavior on her part. The problem was then reformulated as a difficulty in responding to the casual social encounters that held potential for relationship development, and led to further assessment of her skills in that area. In the end, it was found that the patient's beliefs and behavior in social encounters were highly complex and self-defeating, and the initial statement of the problem had little bearing on the goals of treatment.

The role of the patient's history in a behavioral interview needs to be considered carefully. The vast majority of behavioral treatments focus primarily on current situations and events as determinants in the problematic behaviors of the patient. In contrast, the hallmark of psychodynamic approaches is the great emphasis on early childhood events as causes of the patient's current problems. The reason for the emphasis on recent events in behavioral treatment is straightforward—after all, only the most current situations are potentially modifiable, and it is only relevant for the patient to learn new behaviors to respond to current, rather than past, situations. As cognitive therapy has become more well developed, more attention has been placed on the development of cognitions. For example, what early childhood experiences led the patient to believe that he or she was basically inadequate? Can the therapist help the patient change his or her cognitions by directly dealing with the patient's memories that led to the belief? Beck (1995) describes the use of patients' early history in ways that have been considered antithetical to the behavioral approach. Specifically, the patient is asked to recall the events in childhood associated with a particular target feeling or thought (e.g., feelings of depression or inadequacy when yelled at by mom). Working with the patient to draw more realistic conclusions about the event(s) is aimed at changing the core belief interfering with the patient's current functioning. It is sufficient here to say that the assessment of memories for this purpose may be useful. Interested readers should consult Beck (1995) for the methods associated with this type of assessment.

Nevertheless, traditional behavioral interviewing focuses primarily on the here and now of the problematic behavior. To that end, the behavioral interview should also cover other information relevant to the success of behavioral treatment. What is the overall life context of the problem? Do the mother/adolescent conflicts presented to the therapist, for example, pale in comparison to the fact that the family might soon have the power and the telephone services terminated? Patients may have life circumstances that prevent them from completing behavioral assignments, such as overwhelming parenting or job demands. Furthermore, the interviewer should be fully aware of the patient's education and socioeconomic status (SES); less highly educated and lower SES patients may expect less active involvement in treatment, and not assume the importance of assignments and other "homework." This characteristic should lead the interviewer to examine the patient's beliefs and expectations of treatment so that the treatment rationale can address the patient's role adequately. In contrast, patients with very high SES may feel that they are above doing "homework" for therapy—an inquiry about these attitudes might also prevent problems with the implementation of behavior therapy. Further discussion about complications in the behavioral assessment and treatment of a variety of disorders can be found in the interesting volume, *Failures in Behavior Therapy* (Foa & Emmelkamp, 1983).

As with any comprehensive interview, the behavioral interview should address the current medical status of the patient. There are many medical conditions that have psychiatric consequences, and many medical conditions may mimic psychiatric conditions. This suggests that a complete medical evaluation may be necessary to eliminate either of these possibilities. Furthermore, psychiatric patients may be less adequately evaluated by primary-care physicians for a variety of reasons (O'Boyle & Cincirpini, 1993). Thus, the behavioral interviewer should be aware of the role of medical complications in evaluation, treatment, and work in conjunction with primary-care physicians to clarify the patient's medical status. The volume titled *Medical Factors and Psychological Disorders* (Morrison & Bellack, 1987) is an excellent resource for this purpose.

Research on Behavioral Interviews

Given the relevance of the behavioral interview for actual treatment of the patient, it is difficult to understand why more research has not been devoted to such issues as the content of interviews, training, and establishing reliability and validity for behavioral interviews. The few existing studies do point to the usefulness and feasibility of studying this important assessment method.

Only a few interview guidelines have been developed for the content of behavioral interviews that approach the specificity of current structured diagnostic interviews (e.g., the Structured Clinical Interview for the *DSM*; Spitzer, Williams, Gibbon, & First, 1990). Structured interviews, of course, can lead to generally enhanced reliability in conducting the interview, as well as more rigorous tests of the reliability and validity of the interview itself. One early interview guide, the Behavioral Interview, was developed for the assessment of hyperactivity in children through an interview with the child's mother (Golinko, 1978). A pilot study reported good inter-rater reliabilities for the instrument; unfortunately, no further studies adopted the measure to investigate its usefulness more fully.

Two other studies have produced specific lists of the types of questions that should be part of a behavioral interview. Miltenberger and Veltum (1988) examined methods for training relatively inexperienced psychology students in behavioral interviewing using a list of 30 target therapist responses (e.g., "[Interviewer] uses an open-ended question to ask client what happens just following the occurrence of the problem behavior"). Keane, Black, Collins, and Vinson (1982) examined the training of pharmacy externs in behavioral interviewing using a list of open-ended questions regarding antecedents, behaviors, and consequences that was similar to that of Miltenberger and Veltum. The simulated interviews were conducted with assistants in the role of seizure patients and focused on both the seizures and medication compliance. (Additional behavioral interview guides for children's problem behaviors can be found in Murphy, Hudson, King, & Remenyi [1985] and O'Neill, Horner, Albin, & Sprague [1990].) Although the guidelines in these studies do not represent structured interviews, they have the advantage of providing behavioral targets against which the interviewer's behavior can be judged.

These studies cited by Miltenberger and Veltum (1988) and Keane and colleagues (1982) demonstrate that with training, interviewers can learn to conduct behavioral interviews with a high degree of proficiency. However, modeling and behavioral rehearsal seem to be crucial training elements. Miltenberger and Veltum showed that psychology students with a basic understanding of behavioral analysis and no training used only 21% of the behavioral interviewing responses on the target list developed by the authors. After receiving written instruction, audiotaped modeling, and feedback regarding the responses necessary in a behavioral interview, the students used an average of 94% of these responses. Only trainees that received modeling of the skills improved to a high level—written instruction was not sufficient. Keane and associates (1982) demonstrated the importance of behavioral rehearsal in addition to modeling for training interviewers. The pharmacy externs who received training exclusively with a modeling videotape improved relative to a control group in the number of target content areas addressed. However, the trainees who also received behavioral rehearsal training addressed significantly greater number of target areas. In addition, interviewers trained with behavioral rehearsal improved in the general use of open-ended questions, and this effect also generalized to interviews of actual patients.

Despite the research on the training of behavioral interviewing, there has been a limited number of studies demonstrating the validity of behavioral interviews. This is not surprising, given the studies that suggest that the reliability of the selection of target behaviors by different interviewers can be somewhat limited (Hay, Hay, Angle, & Nelson, 1979; Wilson & Evans, 1983). Nevertheless, another study has indicated some consistency between information gained from a behavioral interview, a direct observational assessment, and an experimental analysis of problem behaviors of five children (Arndorfer, Miltenberger, Woster, Rortvedt, & Gaffaney, 1994). Using the Functional Analysis Interview Form (O'Neill, Horner, Albin, & Sprague, 1990), a descriptive analysis was developed using an interview with the each child's parents and an observational assessment in the child's home. This descriptive analysis was then confirmed using an experimental analysis in the home by involving the parents in the manipulation of the variables that had been hypothesized to control the problem behavior. The authors noted that the data from each assessment source led to the same conclusion about the function of each child's problem behavior. Future studies should take these findings as a starting point in trying to establish the reliability and validity for behavioral interviews so that clinicians can have relatively greater faith in interview assessment when direct observational assessment is not possible.

STARTING THE INTERVIEW

Starting a behavioral interview is often the first step in the behavioral assessment process for a new patient. The interviewer may have a broad range of information available to him or her prior to the initial meeting with the patient, such as an existing chart in the case of inpatient work or a treatment summary provided by another mental health professional. In other instances, the interviewer may have little, if any, information beyond demographic information from a referral form. It is often better for the interviewer to have as much information available prior to the initial meeting as possible, so that he or she can begin to develop hypotheses about the patient as well as tailoring the structure of the interview to the presenting problem. For example,

if the interviewer is aware that the patient reports experiencing anxiety in social situations, he or she can be prepared to devote more time in the interview to the nature of the social situations that the patient encounters.

If the interview is the patient's initial contact with a mental health provider, the patient may approach the interview with numerous preconceived notions or questions about what may occur, which may influence the patient's responses to the interviewer's queries: What will the interviewer look like? Will I be asked to lay on a couch and talk about my dreams or my mother? Will the therapist say anything to me or just listen and scratch his chin? Will she cure me in one session? Even patients with previous exposure to mental health professionals may be somewhat surprised by the goal-directed interaction style used by a behavioral interviewer. Often these beliefs of what will occur in a session are shaped by television and movie portrayals of therapists, which are often stereotyped or comical and are not an accurate representation of what occurs in an interview or therapy session. It is useful for the interviewer to consider the preconceived notions that a patient may bring into an initial session and the influence that such beliefs may have on the patient's responses.

In order to facilitate rapport, the interviewer should also consider some of the logistical and situational elements of the setting in which the interview will be conducted. Although behavioral interviews can take place in settings ranging from inpatient rooms to outpatient offices, the interviewer should strive to ensure that certain structural elements will be maintained. The interview should be conducted in a private environment in which the potential for disturbance is minimized. Both the patient and the interviewer should be seated, ideally in chairs of equal height, and directly facing each other. To convey an open environment, the patient and interviewer should not be separated from one another by a desk or table. If the interviewer takes notes, it should be done so in a manner that involves minimal distraction to the patient and maximizes the degree of eye contact maintained with the patient.

At the onset, the interviewer should introduce himself or herself using the manner in which he or she prefers to be addressed. It may be useful to summarize briefly for the patient the information the interviewer already has about the patient. In addition, the patient should be told that the purpose of the interview is to gather information about the problem, so that the patient will be prepared for the direction of the interview. Then, the interviewer will want to give the patient an opportunity to speak about his or her presenting concern and may ask the patient, "I know a little about you, but why don't you tell me in your own words what has brought you here today." Although the specifics of such a statement may vary from setting to setting, such a transitional statement conveys some understanding of the patient's concerns and gives the patient the opportunity to state the concern in his or her own words. Additionally, it is often useful to provide the patient more structure by briefly outlining of the format of interview. For example, the interviewer might say, "After hearing what you'd like help with, I will ask you about your history; that might help us understand the problem. Then we'll go over the problem in a more detailed manner. So, what is it that you would like help with?" Although interviewers who will later serve as therapists to the patient may wish to discuss the general behavioral approach to therapy at this time, it may be more useful to save such a discussion until the end of the interview, thus allowing the patient to discuss his or her concerns as early as possible in the session.

Patients may respond to an invitation to discuss why they sought an evaluation or therapy in many ways. Some may embark on a long, detailed story involving several years of history, whereas others may answer the question by simply saying, "I'm anxious." Regardless of how the patient responds to the query, the interviewer should summarize the patient's disclosure and provide empathy to the patient. Not only does this indicate to the patient that the interviewer is listening but it also begins to establish rapport. Often this initial response by the patient generates an endless supply of subsequent issues to examine. Although some of the details of the situation described may remain unclear, it may be better to continue probing with open-ended questions, allowing the patient to direct the early stages of the interview. It may be best for the interviewer to save more specific closed-ended questions, which might yield more precise information, for later in the discussion. The

interviewer should inquire about other difficulties that the patient may have. These are noted, in turn, and the interviewer should continue asking about further problems until the patient indicates that there are none.

As the patient continues to describe the reason he or she is in the interviewer's office, the interviewer should continue to summarize what is being said and provide empathy to him or her. After the patient concludes a general description of his or her problems, the interviewer should summarize the list of problems just presented. In addition, the interviewer may wish to make a comment about the process of the interview to this point. For example, the interviewer might comment on the patient's plight, showing some appreciation for the difficulty he or she might have had in sharing such information or in deciding to address the problem by entering into therapy.

THE BODY OF THE INTERVIEW

As a first step to conducting a functional analysis of the problematic behavior, the interviewer works with the patient to identify the first difficulty to develop a problem list. What does the patient think is the most distressing problem or area of his or her life? As noted earlier in discussing the patient with chronic acne, the eventual problem identified differed somewhat from the patient's original description. This may not be of any great concern at this point, in that the interviewer's inquiry will serve to highlight for the patient and the therapist the most important factors in the problem. In the earlier example, the patient's original problem statement of social anxiety was quickly recognized by the patient to be only a small feature of the difficulty in her casual social contacts after all of the other features of the situation were examined. In any event, the interviewer should consider other problems related to the patient's original complaints. The interviewer should maintain additional working hypotheses about the patient as the interview precedes and can adjust further questioning to test these hypotheses.

Many patients with previous therapeutic experience are familiar with the "language of therapy" but are probably not aware of the specific concepts and terms utilized in behavioral theory and intervention. In addition, patients may use terms such as *anxious* or *depressed* in ways that are very different from those of the interviewer. The interviewer may wish to operationalize these terms, perhaps through asking about physiological changes the patient notices or by asking the patient to rate their subjective experience on a 1 to 10 scale. Following is an example of how a clinician can quantify a patient's difficulties and incorporate behavioral terms in an interview of a patient who reports having trouble getting along with others.

Interviewer: It sounds like you have been having difficulty in a number of areas, but your conflicts with your roommate are the most trouble right now.

Patient: Like I said, he's inconsiderate and I can't stand being around him.

Interviewer: I'd like to ask some more questions about what happens when you are the most bothered about it. Can you pick a particular disagreement and tell me how you felt at the time?

Patient: He really pissed me off when I came in last night and wanted to go to sleep. He wouldn't turn the TV off, and I can't sleep with the light and the noise.

Interviewer: How angry were you? Can you rate it, from 1 to 10, with 10 being the most angry you've ever been?

Patient: I guess about a 6. What does that matter?

Interviewer: Well, I'm wondering if you also felt anything else, like tension, nervousness, anxiety, apprehension? If so, how much?

Patient: I was tense, too. About a 6, I guess. We don't really talk much except about the TV and superficial things about school.

Interviewer: When do you feel the most angry, and also the most tense? For example, when you were walking into the room, before? After he didn't turn down the TV?

Patient: I was getting tense coming into the room, thinking what a drag this roommate situation was, and then when he kept watching TV, I was so pissed off I couldn't sleep.

It is useful early in the interview process to introduce the language of behavior theory through the style of questioning and through asking for specific types of responses from the patient. The patient's verbal behavior and thinking will begin to be shaped by doing this, and it will facilitate information gathering crucial to the functional analysis. Although some will argue that such an influence on the patient's discussion of the problem may conflict with the patient's world view, the patient's explanation is redefined in terms of measurable constructs that will then be incorporated into a behavioral model of treatment.

Many times it is important to ask patients to be very specific about their thoughts and their activities related to a problem. Following is an example of this inquiry with a patient who has identified severe social anxiety about going out with friends as a major problem. The patient is encouraged to provide enough detail to identify factors influencing her behavior in the situation.

Interviewer: I'd like to ask you a few more details about this situation in which you became anxious. You told me that last Friday you went out with your friends and at first were very anxious, but later felt a little more comfortable. I'd like to hear more detail about how that occurred so we can understand what may influence how you feel. First, when did you start to feel anxious about going out?

Patient: It always starts about three hours before I go out. I just get more and more tense about it.

Interviewer: Is that when it started this time? Three hours before?

Patient: Approximately. Probably less because these are friends I was going out with. Why should I be anxious about them? I don't get it, and I just can't control it.

Interviewer: When did you start to notice you were particularly anxious?

Patient: Some time in the afternoon, when I started getting ready, I think by about two hours before leaving.

Interviewer: Can you describe for me what you were doing and what kind of thoughts were going through your head?

Patient: I was trying to pick something to wear, and hating everything I own. Also, I wasn't sure who was going out with us and where we were going.

Interviewer: Let's try to get down to the exact thoughts as you were looking over your clothes. Something like, "I really hate my clothes" and "I wonder who else will be there" and "I have no idea where we're going tonight"? These may not be exactly right—maybe you can tell *me* what the thoughts were more accurately.

Patient: Yeah, something like that, and "They're always bringing people along I don't know—it's less fun that way. It's someone else I have to get used to, and they will see the stupid clothes that I have."

Interviewer: What else were you thinking? Anything about being anxious or something unpleasant happening once you went out?

Patient: Yeah, I thought about them always teasing me about turning red, which happens to me in groups.

At this time the interviewer may wish to inquire about time-sequence issues, asking the patient what occurred directly before a given event and what occurred directly after the event. Special attention should be given to variations in the intensity of negative affect because, in the current example, reductions in the level of anxiety may reinforce avoidance behavior. Furthermore, the inquiry should cover interactions with others (i.e., "My boyfriend made fun of me because I changed clothes several times"). The interviewer should also be aware that most problems identified by patients involve several stimulus-behavior sequences, or complex chains of behaviors (Mullinix & Galassi, 1981; Voeltz & Evans, 1982).

Interviewer: When did your anxiety peak? What was happening at the time?

Patient: Right when we all started to leave from my girlfriend's house. We were splitting up to ride in two cars. I don't really know Susan and Cathy that well so I didn't want to ride with them. I managed to ride with my friend Beth.

Interviewer: When did the anxiety start to lessen? Where were you and what was happening then?

Patient: Once we sat down in the restaurant I was OK. Nothing was really happening—we were just talking about the summer.

Interviewer: Who were you sitting next to? Did it matter to you?

Patient: Beth. I always try to sit next to her. She knows me a lot better than the others do—she is the only one who I've told about my anxiety.

Through careful questioning, the interviewer learns that the patient's anxiety is stimulated by thoughts and images about the night out, her attempts to control or lessen her anxiety through avoidance of being in threatening situations (e.g., sitting next to relatively unfamiliar people), and the resulting diminution of her negative affect. Further inquiry would reveal other important thoughts and beliefs about the situation that may determine the patient's level of anxiety (e.g., "They will think there's something wrong with me if my face flushes or if I sweat"). In addition to behavior that may be maladaptive (e.g., avoidance), the patient may exhibit behavioral excesses or deficits in the problem situation (Kanfer & Grimm, 1977). Further questions of the patient in the preceding scenario might focus on the frequency and type of social behavior the patient displays. For example, does she ask questions with appropriate frequency? Does she exhibit appropriate eye contact? Does she drink water or alcohol with greater frequency when anxious? Does she exhibit repetitive motions, such as shaking her leg or tapping with her silverware?

The interviewer should then inquire about the situational specificity of the patient's behavior relevant to the problem (Kazdin, 1979). What social situations do not lead to anxious thoughts and mood, avoidance behavior, or nervous twitching? This may include the type of people involved in the problem, the time of day, the place or type of place, or the type of activity that may be required. Using the previous example, the patient may not be particularly anxious if the social event is a party that requires her to help with serving food, because of the reduced demands for unstructured social behavior.

The onset and history of the problem is the next aspect for the interviewer to address. Straightforward questions such as "When did you first have problems like the one we just discussed?" are often sufficient to elicit the context giving rise to the problem. Some patients, however, may respond to this inquiry with vagueness or with the statement that "things have always been this way." Such responses should prompt specific questions of various time-points in the patient's history to stimulate the patient's memory. The interviewer should keep in mind that many patients are not accustomed to thinking systematically about their problems, and that maintaining rapport is more important than obtaining detailed historical information in the first contact. It may also be convenient to inquire about family and social history at this point.

The role of the patient's beliefs about his or her problems, and more generally, his or her world-view, has been recognized from early on in the history of behavior therapy (Lazarus, 1971). At this point, it may be helpful to inquire about the patient's beliefs about the cause of his or her problems. In the most direct way, a patient's belief about his or her problem may lead to noncompliance to the clinician's request during therapy. For example, if a patient believes his or her depression is primarily determined by biological factors, the relevance of behavioral methods of intervention may not be immediately clear to the patient. Many patients will have already hinted about their beliefs about the cause of the problem during the type of detailed discussion that was illustrated previously. The interviewer can use this information to prompt the patient to expand on these ideas. For example, the clinician may say, "You mentioned that you wondered whether there was something physically wrong with your body. Do you have an idea of what that might be? Was there anything other doctors have told you, or something you read, which may lead you to consider that possibility?" On another level, the clinician needs to understand the patient's world-view in order to guide the assessment and treatment appropriately. What are the patient's values connected to the problem? Did the reported problem arise from the patient's failure to achieve his or her own behavioral expectations in life? This type of information will help the clinician appreciate how the patient prioritizes problems and how willing he or she might be to achieve therapeutic goals. For example, the reduction of social conflict for one patient who expects to have a high level of social competence may take a differ-

ent course than for a patient whose career achievement is tantamount.

After the presenting problem has been identified and redefined in behavioral terms, the interview should begin to widen the spectrum of questioning to other areas of the patient's life. Asking how the problematic behavior affects other areas of the patient's life, such as employment and other social relationships not already discussed, will allow the interviewer to understand further the extent of difficulty the presenting problem is causing. As noted earlier, the patient's medical status should be addressed first by inquiring about when the patient last went to a medical doctor, had a medical examination, or whether the patient had recently been sick. The connection between the patient's presenting complaints and any possible medical illness should be explored fully. The interviewer can consult Morrison and Bellack (1987) or other similar volumes for information on the association between psychological syndromes and medical difficulties.

Although the patient's report of difficulties is essential, it may also be necessary to collect information about the patient's behavior from outside sources. The interviewer may arrange to interview other individuals, such as relatives, who interact with the patient concerning the problem behavior. Patients with obsessive-compulsive disorder, for example, may be sufficiently embarrassed or distressed about their symptoms to underestimate the frequency of their compulsive behaviors or the degree of impact of this maladaptive behavior on family relationships.

CLOSING THE INTERVIEW

As the interview comes to a close, the interviewer should provide a summary to the patient of the information collected. The summary provides another opportunity for the interviewer to explain to the client the presenting problem in behavioral terms. Some interviewers may wish to describe explicitly the antecedent/behavior/consequence relationship to the patient as an element of treatment. The patient will leave the office with a behaviorally based conceptualization of his or her presenting problem and a basic idea of how the problem may be addressed in treatment.

Not only will the summary demonstrate understanding to the patient but it can be a useful bridge into a discussion of the need for further assessment. Additional assessment may include asking the patient to monitor his or her behavior prior to the next session and may include observations of the patient in situations in which the problematic behavior is occurring. The reasons for these techniques need to be addressed fully using the initial behavioral conceptualization of the problem. Patients unfamiliar with behavioral assessment and therapy may be surprised that treatment will involve tasks such as behavioral monitoring and other "homework" assignments. Some patients may be uncomfortable with such an approach to assessment and treatment, whereas others may not be willing to engage in this type of treatment due to the time commitment sometimes involved. Still other patients may be critical of behavioral interventions due to issues of freedom and control. The interviewer should be prepared to address these concerns. However, if the patient remains resistant after this discussion, the interviewer should be prepared to make a referral to a therapist whose approach to the presenting problem is more in line with the patient's expectations.

Finally, the interviewer may wish to provide encouragement to the patient by commenting on the previous distress of the patient and applaud his or her courage for seeking help. In addition, the interviewer may want to leave the patient with a sense of optimism by discussing the existing empirical support for the behaviorally based treatment of the presenting problem.

THE PARTICIPANTS IN THE BEHAVIORAL INTERVIEW

The behavioral interview is an interactive process whose product—the information relevant to the patient's complaint—is a function of the interaction of many elements. This interaction is influenced to a large extent by the characteristics of the patient and the interviewer. In addition, other elements of the process affect the end product, including the environmental setting of the interview or the manner in which additional information about the patient is collected. This section focuses on the effect that the actual participants in the interview—the interviewer and the patient—have on the interview.

Interviewers' Characteristics and Behaviors

There are several aspects of interviewing style about which the behavioral interviewer should take note. As described in a previous section, behavioral interviews can be more efficient when the patient is provided some structure to present his or her difficulties. The interviewer is the "leader" in the interview; consistent with this metaphor, the patient cannot be forced to follow. Again, the interviewer must be prepared to follow the patient's lead at times, exercising the flexibility in the goals he or she has for the interview. We have placed great emphasis on the information one needs to gather in a behavioral interview, how to help the patient provide detailed information, and how to help the patient understand his or her difficulties through a behavioral "lens." Many patients will already have definite ideas about their difficulties and the solutions, however, despite having consulted a clinician for an evaluation. Some patients will have a firm agenda for the initial session that may differ from the agenda of the interviewer. It is important to remember that there need not be a struggle for the control of the session because patients who present in this way are doing so for reasons that are paramount to them, and important for the interviewer to understand. This type of behavior may be, in itself, a relevant sample of the patient's behavior.

The interviewer can inquire about the range and frequency of assertive/directive type of behavior by saying the following: "It sounds like you have a good idea about the things you feel I should know, and how you want to present them. I'm wondering if this would be your approach, in general, or if this is an uncommon circumstance? For example, are you fairly systematic like this at work, when talking to a co-worker or to your boss?" Furthermore, the patient's cognitions and affect related to his or her way of presenting can be assessed in the following way: "I was wondering what you thought might happen if you did not arrive as organized as you have been. Some people are afraid they won't be able to get everything across; others fear that they will not be organized enough. What was your motivation?" Although this example illustrates the use of a decidedly broad, nonbehavioral term (i.e., "motivation"), the patient will likely respond with clues about his or her thoughts and feelings that can be followed up with questions by the interviewer.

Second, the effective interviewer must have well-developed listening skills (Wilson, Spence, & Kavanagh, 1989). This includes good eye contact, a relaxed but appropriate body posture, appropriate turn taking in speaking, and summarizing and asking for clarification for the information conveyed by the patient. As mentioned briefly in an earlier section, the interviewer can facilitate the development of rapport through structural aspects of the interview—the placement of chairs, appropriate posture, and appropriate eye contact even if the therapist takes notes during the interview. In addition, the interviewer must be careful to exhibit appropriate turn taking in speaking, particularly during the first statements on the part of the patient. Although interruptions may be necessary at a later point in order to guide the direction of the conversation, interruptions early in the interview can convey an exaggerated sense of hierarchy (i.e., "What I am saying is more important that what you are saying") and lack of respect for the problems as seen by the patient. Some patients may be initially reticent in describing their problems, and the interviewer can "help" patients along by allowing for pauses before speaking. Furthermore, the interviewer can facilitate the telling of the "story" by briefly summarizing what was related and asking for clarifications about particular elements. For example, an interviewer might say, "So the most recent instance of fighting with your brother was the most upsetting, and led most directly to feeling separated from your family. What was different this time from the other times?"

The communication of warmth, positive regard, and genuineness through the expression of accurate empathy is of paramount importance. This is a subtle and difficult-to-specify aspect of the patient/therapist relationship that was emphasized several decades ago by Rogers (1961). Indeed, current texts on interviewing continue to emphasize this basic process (e.g., Craig, 1989; Turner & Hersen, 1994), so there are a few points the behavioral interviewer should keep in mind. Exhibiting accurate empathy and acceptance can be facilitated by the interviewer focusing on the emotions and moods expressed by the patient, in addition to the facts of the problem situation. When summarizing the patient's statements through paraphrasing, empathy and acceptance is conveyed when the emotions are highlighted rather than facts. This is a fundamentally different process than summarizing and clarifying where gathering information is the goal. The effective interviewer uses one or the other of these types of reflections, depending on what is needed at that particular moment. If the interviewer judges that the patient is conveying something particularly intense or unpleasant, then exhibiting empathy about these feelings may facilitate rapport more readily than focusing on the facts of the situation.

Another aspect of interviewer behavior that can determine the direction of the interview is the relative use of open- versus closed-ended questions (Craig, 1989; Turner & Hersen, 1994). The most important feature of open- versus closed-ended questions is the degree of structure that is placed on the response. Thus, the more closed-ended the question, the more restrictive and directive it is regarding the patient's response. An open-ended question that provides a good deal of freedom in the patient's response might be: "Can you tell me about what it has been like for you when on dates in the past?" A question that provides more restrictions to the patient's response is the following: "When you were at the movie with Liz last Friday night, what thoughts and feelings were you having about the date?" The most closed-ended type of question calls for a yes/no or numerical response, and is illustrated by the following: "How many drinks did you have on Monday? How about on Tuesday? (etc.)" or "Did you go to any parties this week?"

The closed-ended questions tend to get specific responses, but they are "conversation stoppers." Open-ended questions may get specific *or* general answers, and may or may not address the desired content area. However, they tended to draw out information that is particularly important to the patient. The behavioral interviewer should keep in mind the general response style of the patient and the nature of the information desired at that point in the interview when deciding to use closed- versus open-ended questions. Typically, there will be more open-ended questions in the beginning of the interview than at the end as the interviewer narrows down the most important content areas to address.

Both novice and expert interviewers often forget that they have developed a highly specialized vocabulary for describing psychological difficulties and often may use these technical words with the patient. Jargon should be avoided because it is distracting and often confusing to the patient because of the existence of alternate meanings in everyday language. Examples of problematic terminology include *affect*, *obsession*, and *reinforcement*. Using common wording instead of jargon is not "dumbing down" the presentation of ideas in a way that insults the patient's intelligence. The interviewer might recognize that if an idea or concept cannot be described in nontechnical language to an interested nonprofessional person, then it is unlikely to be a useful idea.

The use of humor in clinical interviewing has a controversial history. The psychoanalytic position on the use of humor suggests that it is inappropriately injecting one's own personality and psychological conflicts into the assessment session; indeed (the patient's) humor should be the subject of psychotherapeutic interpretation. Similarly, self-disclosure has often been seen as taboo, in that it may disturb the "blank slate" that allows the transference relationship to form. However, the concepts of the interpretation of humor and of transference have limited utility in behavior therapy. In behavioral interviewing, it is important to establish a rationale for the use of humor and self-disclosure. In general, humor and self-disclosure should be used judiciously, particularly because the interviewer may not be able to know how the statement may be viewed by the patient. If humor or self-disclosure is used, the clinician should always understand the goal. Reasonable goals for both humor and self-disclosure include the following: (1) to put the patient at ease, (2) to provide a release in the tension of the session, (3) to build rapport by demonstrating a commonality or empathy (specifically, self-disclosure), and (4) to build rapport by showing genuineness.

Patients' Characteristics and Behaviors

Numerous factors or variables of the patient can influence the behavioral interview process. At the most elementary level, a patient's demographic characteristics can influence the information conveyed to the interviewer. Gender, age, race, religion, marital status, employment history, and socioeconomic conditions are just some of the variables that may affect the information given to a behavioral interviewer. These characteristics in part influence a patient's world-view, in that each patient's concerns are formed by his or her experiences. For example, the interviewer must recognize that the concerns voiced by a devout Catholic patient about the possibility of a marital separation may take on a radically different meaning than for the relationship separation voiced by a nonreligious individual who has never been married.

In addition, the manner in which these variables compare and contrast with those of the interviewer may influence the information collected. For example, a depressed, unemployed patient who attends sessions casually dressed in jeans may be embarrassed or resentful in discussing his or her financial problems with an interviewer wearing a suit. Another example might be a Jewish patient that may be reluctant to discuss the role personal religious beliefs have in his or her anxiety to a non-Jewish interviewer. The interviewer should keep in mind the role of diversity in the interview process. Is the patient tailoring or limiting the presentation of his or her concerns to the interviewer based on the patient's concept of the interviewer's demographics? Although this may not be accurately anticipated, the interviewer should be sure to maintain an open and accepting stance so that the patient will be encouraged to reveal as much as needed to address the presenting problem. This stance can be communicated by the interviewer limiting a skeptical tone or implication in his or her questions; alternatively, a persistent, interested, and inquisitive manner might be more productive.

Along these lines, the interviewer must be careful not to make assumptions about the patient based on superficial demographic characteristics, especially when the patient appears to be from a culture that differs from his or her own. The family of a schizophrenia patient treated by one of the authors had emigrated from Pakistan and the family constellation was unusually close-knit by U.S. standards. However, in this case, it was important to avoid assuming the conventional wisdom was true (and the family members' report) that it is normative that Pakistani families are more closely knit. A detailed inquiry about the functioning of the family, the expectations of each family member, and the needs of the patient was necessary to help the patient function as well as possible.

The manner in which patients convey information to the interviewer also can influence the interview process. Patients often have their own understandings or hypotheses about their presenting problems and their importance or relevance in their lives. Although these self-generated hypotheses have their own truth for the patient, patients also may have little understanding of how their presenting problem is affected by ongoing behavioral contingencies. As discussed earlier, some patients may describe vaguely the effects of the presenting problem on their behavior, whereas others may be able to spontaneously pinpoint antecedents and consequences to their problems. Given the possible range of styles patients may use, it is clear that at times it is beneficial for the interviewer to begin to reframe the patient's problem in behavioral terms. The interviewer must remain flexible regarding the direction of the interview and flexible regarding the level of information gained in any single interview. Without this flexibility, the interviewer will become frustrated, which will begin to erode the rapport that is necessary for an effective interview.

All clinicians will, at some time during their career, interview difficult or challenging patients. Of course, the type of patient that is difficult to interview differs from interviewer to interviewer, but some reliably difficult patient characteristics

include hostility, social inappropriateness, guardedness, or defensiveness. Most of these ways of presenting result from two sources: the patient dislikes the situation he or she is in and/or the patient is presenting a behavioral style that is somewhat representative of his or her behavior outside the session. Thus, the behavioral interviewer's task is still to understand the contingencies that govern the patient's behavior.

One key to gathering as much information as possible about a difficult patient's behavior is for the interviewer to limit his or her own overt emotional responses, thus not reciprocating strong negative affect. The interviewer should develop a sense of which in-session problematic behaviors are truly consequential. At one extreme of this continuum, patients can be physically threatening or actually violent. At the other extreme, a patient could be mildly insulting or rude. Where the interviewer draws the line between these extremes will determine to what extent the patient's behavior and associated affect can be eplored in the session, as opposed to limited. Does the interviewer need to respond to a patient's feet on the coffee table in the office? Does it really matter if the patient takes books off the interviewer's shelf when entering the office? A limit may be a polite request to cease a behavior ("I would appreciate it if you would put your feet on the floor rather than on my desk") or an indication that the session would be stopped if the behavior does not change ("You will have to stop yelling and take a seat or we will have to stop for now").

Patients who are hostile or upset at an interviewer generally prompt the least effective behavior from the clinician. We do not intend to upset our patients, so when this happens we often respond defensively (e.g., "The behavioral approach *happens* to be the most effective way of conceptualizing and treating patient's with anxiety problems"), argumentatively (e.g., "But that's really not what I meant"), or with an interpretation (e.g., "Maybe you are generalizing to me the things your husband has said to you"). There is no harm, and usually great long-term benefit, to simply acknowledging the error and demonstrating acceptance of the patient's feelings through accurate empathy. This requires practice because the interviewer's first response is usually highly emotional and very difficult to retrain.

Another way for the interviewer to limit his or her own destructive responses is to concentrate on being curious about what is precipitating and maintaining the patient's negative responses to the situation. As suggested earlier, it is important first to acknowledge and empathize with the patient's negative response. Questions such as the following can then solicit useful information, without indicting the patient's reasoning or feelings: "I'm glad that you told me about being so angry about the question that was insulting to you. Now I'd like to understand what you didn't like about it so I can avoid doing that in the future. Can you tell me what about it made the question hit you so hard? Were there other things that I did or even someone else did that really made it all worse?"

SUMMARY

Behavioral interviewing is a crucial aspect of behavioral assessment and treatment. It is a complex process that requires the interviewer to assess the patient's difficulties, abilities, and resources, while at the same time developing a supportive working relationship. The behavioral interviewer uses the framework of learning principles in order to understand what precipitates and maintains problematic behavior. Although existing research provides some support for the usefulness of the behavioral interview, only a general consensus has been developed about the specific elements necessary in the this type of assessment. A great deal of additional research is needed to support the reliability and validity of the selection of target behaviors as well as the functional analysis that behavioral interviews yield.

A skillful behavioral interview has a beginning, a middle, and an end. In most instances, the interviewer finds that the interview will flow better with some structure, which can be provided by suggesting to the patient the general sequence of the interview. During the discussion of the patient's complaints, the interviewer helps the patient provide detailed information about the frequency of difficulties, the antecedents and consequents of the patient's behavior occurring in problem situations, and the interpersonal context in which the problem occurs. Several difficulties may be examined in this way until the primary difficulties of the patient are understood. The patient's history is also examined to the extent that it may be relevant to the patient's difficulties. The interviewer closes the session with a summary of the information covered, some comment on the next step, and general support and encouragement for his or her desire for treatment.

It should be recognized that both patient and therapist characteristics influence the course of the interview. The interviewer should keep in mind the general goals of the discussion, but remain flexible to account for the needs of the patient. Successful interviewers develop good listening skills such as eye contact and appropriate posture. Rapport between the patient and the interviewer is built through using accurate empathy, especially when empathic reflections are focused on the patient's emotions. In addition, interviewers will tend to use open-ended questions in the beginning of the interview but use more close-ended questions in order to get more specific information as the interview progresses. Although the use of humor and self-disclosure has been seen as taboo in the past, judicious use by the interviewer can actually help build rapport.

Patients' goals and expectations of the evaluation and treatment process are the result of their respective cultures and life experiences. However, interviewers should be careful not to make assumptions about patients based on superficial demographic information—detailed inquiry is usually needed to understand fully how patients perceive their problems and the treatment setting. Patients sometimes present difficulties for the interviewer by being hostile, defensive, or inappropriate. Interviewers should clearly understand within themselves what specific behaviors are unacceptable in the office, versus actions that are unpleasant but may be valuable samples of the patients' behavior outside the session. When confronted by hostile patients, many clinicians fail to be appropriately empathic and do not sufficiently examine the reasons for the patient's criticism. Despite the discomfort associated with the negative affect directed toward the interviewer, it is still important that the interviewer try to understand the precipitants of the conflict situation, as well as the factors maintaining it.

REFERENCES

Arndorfer, R. E., Miltenberger, R. G., Woster, S. H., Rortvedt, A. K., & Gaffaney, T. (1994). Home-based descriptive and experimental analysis of problem behaviors in children. *Topics in Early Childhood Special Education, 14,* 64–87.

Bakeman, R., & Casey, R. L. (1995). Analyzing family interaction: Taking time into account. *Journal of Family Psychology, 9,* 131–143.

Beck, J. (1995). *Cognitive therapy: Basics and beyond.* New York: Guilford.

Craig, R. J. (1989). The clinical process of interviewing. In R. J. Craig (Ed.), *Clinical and diagnostic interviewing* (pp. 3–34). Northvale, NJ: Jason Aronson.

Foa, E. B., & Emmelkamp, P. M. G. (1983). *Failures in behavior therapy.* New York: John Wiley & Sons.

Golinko, B. E. (1978). Hyperactivitiy: Operationalization of traits using a structured behavioral interview: A pilot study. *Journal of Pediatric Psychology, 3,* 35–43.

Hay, W. M., Hay, L. R., Angle, H. V., & Nelson, R. O. (1979). The reliability of problem identification in the behavioral interview. *Behavioral Assessment, 1,* 107–118.

Kanfer, F. H., & Grimm, L. G. (1977). Behavioral analysis: Selecting target behaviors in the interview. *Behavior Modification, 4,* 419–444.

Kazdin, A. E. (1979). Situational specificity: The two edged sword of behavioral assessment. *Behavioral Assessment, 1,* 57–75.

Keane, T., Black, J. L., Collins, F. L., & Vinson, M. C. (1982). A skills training program for teaching the behavioral interview. *Behavioral Assessment, 4,* 53–62.

Lazarus, A. A. (1971). Notes on behavior therapy, the problem of relapse and some tentative solutions. *Psychotherapy, 8,* 192–196.

Lazarus, A. A. (1973). Multimodal behavior therapy: Treating the "BASIC ID." *The Journal of Nervous and Mental Disease, 156,* 404–111.

Miltenberger, R. G., & Veltum, L. G. (1988). Evaluation of an instructions and modeling procedure for training behavioral assessment interviewing. *Journal of Behavioral and Experimental Psychiatry, 19,* 31–41.

Morganstern, K. P. (1976). Behavioral interviewing: The initial stages of development. In M. Hersen &

A. S. Bellack (Eds.), *Behavioral assessment: A practical handbook.* New York: Pergamon.

Morrison, R. L., & Bellack, A. S. (1987). *Medical factors and psychological disorders: A handbook for psychologists.* New York: Plenum.

Mueser, K. T., & Glynn, S. M. (1995). *Behavioral family therapy for psychiatric disorders.* Boston: Allyn and Bacon.

Mullinix, S. D., & Galassi, J. P. (1981). Deriving the content of social skills training with a verbal response components approach. *Behavioral Assessment, 3,* 55–66.

Murphy, G. C., Hudson, A. M., King, N. J., & Remenyi, A. (1985). An interview schedule for use in the behavioural assessment of children's problems. *Behaviour Change, 2,* 6–12.

O'Boyle, M., & Cincirpini, P. (1993). Medical complications with adults. In A. S. Bellack & M. Hersen (Eds.), *Handbook of behavior therapy in the psychiatric setting* (pp. 165–175). New York: Plenum.

O'Brien, W. H., & Haynes, S. N. (1993). Behavioral assessment in the psychiatric setting. In A. S. Bellack & M. Hersen (Eds.), *Handbook of behavior therapy in the psychiatric setting* (pp. 39–71). New York: Plenum.

O'Leary, K. D., & Wilson, G. T. (1975). *Behavior therapy: Application and outcome.* Englewood Cliffs, NJ: Prentice Hall.

O'Neill, R. E., Horner, R. H., Albin, R. W., Storey, K., & Sprague, J. R. (1990). *Functional analysis of problem behavior: A practical guide.* Sycamore, IL: Sycamore.

Rogers, C. R. (1961) *On becoming a person.* Boston: Houghton Mifflin.

Spitzer, R. L., Williams, J. B. W., Gibbon, M., & First, M. B. (1990). *User's guide for the structured clinical interview for DSM-III-R: SCID.* Washington, DC: American Psychiatric Press.

Turner, S., & Hersen, M. (1994). The interviewing process. In M. Hersen & S. Turner (Eds.), *Diagnostic interviewing* (pp. 3–24). New York: Plenum.

Voeltz, L. M., & Evans, I. M. (1982). The assessment of behavioral interrelationships in child behavior therapy. *Behavioral Assessment, 4,* 131–165.

Wilson, F. E., & Evans, I. M. (1983). The reliability of target-behavior selection in behavioral assessment. *Behavioral Assessment, 5,* 15–32.

Wilson, P. H., Spence, S. H., & Kavanagh, D. J. (1989). *Cognitive-behavioral interviewing for adult disorders: A practical handbook.* Baltimore, MD: Johns Hopkins University Press.

CHAPTER 5

BEHAVIORAL OBSERVATION

Warren W. Tryon
Fordham University

Direct observation of behavior has been the mainstay of behavioral assessment from its inception. Although behavioral observation has a long history in developmental psychology, formerly called child psychology, clinical psychologists mainly relied on objective and projective personality assessment to evaluate clients prior to treatment, to make treatment recommendations, and to evaluate the results of intervention. Anastasi (1988) correctly observed that "a psychological test is essentially an objective and standardized measure of a sample of behavior" (p. 23). Intelligence, achievement, and personality tests present the subject with standard stimuli and provide for recording the subject's responses. The test manual indicates how the subject's behavior is to be scored and provides norms for interpreting test results. Data on test reliability and validity are also presented in the manual to aid in test result interpretation.

A major criticism of standardized testing concerns the inferences drawn from the behavioral sample. Consider Binet's intelligence test. The goal was to predict performance of children enrolled in the middle-class Paris school system. Binet identified tasks teachers routinely asked students to do, obtained behavioral samples from children, and correlated performance with academic grades. Those subtests most highly correlated with grades were retained in the final test. Not surprisingly, subsequent validation studies confirmed that scores on Binet's test correlate substantially with academic grades because this is what the test was constructed to do. To this point, behavioral assessment, observation, and traditional psychometric test construction are congruent. Both infer typical behavior from a representative sample.

The two assessment approaches differ on the issue of how test results should be used. Psychometricians use test results to infer underlying traits, such as intelligence, as was the case for Binet's test. The explanation for why Binet's behavioral test successfully predicted academic achievement was that it measured intelligence. Persons with especially low scores were said to be retarded, when it might alternatively been concluded that they lacked the necessary behaviors and skills to do well in middle-class Paris schools. Such children were excluded from mainstream education rather than taught the necessary skills, thereby setting the occasion for protest.

Behavioral assessment argues against using behavioral samples as signs of underlying traits, reminding investigators that test results provide information only about a subject's current behavioral repertoire under specific environmental conditions (Barrios, 1988). This admonition is consistent with the behavioral perspective that behavior is presumed to be a function of the environment. The important implication here is that standard psychometric tests can be interpreted from a behavioral perspective and avoid much of the criticism that has been leveled against testing.

In condemning the "sign" interpretation of test results, a conceptual problem has been created regarding the interface of behavioral assessment and medicine. I wish to resolve that problem now. Medicine has long distinguished between signs and symptoms (Teicher, 1995). *Symptoms* are subjective reports about feelings, such as pain, soreness, stiffness, fatigue, nausea, and blurred vision. *Signs* are physical manifestations of disease that can be *directly observed* and examined by the physician. Although the physician can use his or her hands to feel for swollen glands, lumps, and so on, they often use instruments to aid their physical examination. Thermometers are used to confirm fever that might have first been suspected through touch. The stethoscope augments sounds originating within the body. X-rays and advanced scanning procedures such as MRI and PET are used to look inside the body. Given this distinction, behavioral observation is concerned with signs rather than symptoms. This distinction will be most important for psychologists who work with physicians.

Personality tests exclusively rely on self-reported symptoms. Although some of these symptoms pertain to potentially observable behaviors such as psychomotor retardation or agitation or slowed speech, the test per se is limited to the subject's self-report about these symptoms. Efforts by physicians to directly observe relevant aspects of disorder and to use technology to further quantify these facets of illness are congruent with the goals and objectives of behavioral assessment. Conse-

quently, behavioral observation can legitimately be used to provide independent information about *behavioral signs* of physical illness and/or psychological disorder. Technology has enabled behavioral measurement of activity (Tryon, 1991a; in press a, in press b) and speech (Darby, 1981; Greden & Carroll, 1981; Siegman & Feldstein, 1987; Tryon, 1991b), thereby enhancing behavioral assessment of directly observable clinically relevant events.

Testing has traditionally entailed examining all subjects under the same standardized conditions so that inter-individual variation can be almost entirely attributed to subjects and almost none to the test circumstances, the nature of the stimuli, the order of presentation, or the manner of stimulus presentation. This decision is consistent with a trait-theoretic position. It also maximizes discriminability among subjects because all other sources of variation have been methodologically minimized. Collecting behavioral data under highly controlled situations is also a useful strategy when attempting to classify persons into groups on the basis of observed behavior or to determine if subjects previously classified into groups using clinical criteria differ behaviorally. This approach was used by Halperin, Matier, Bedi, Sharma, and Newcorn (1992), Halperin and associates (1993), and Matier, Halperin, Sharma, Newcorn, and Sathaye (1992) to show that children with attention-deficit hyperactivity disorder (ADHD) are characterized by motor excess and that this behavior decreases in response to medication, especially for nonaggressive ADHD children. Their strategy was to measure activity only during psychological testing lasting approximately one hour.

Behavioral assessment seeks to describe behavior occurring under natural as well as artificial laboratory testing circumstances. Patterson and colleagues routinely send observers into the home and school to obtain behavioral samples under natural conditions for the purpose of identifying antecedents and consequents that occasion and reward particular behaviors for the purpose of evaluating functional relationships and deriving therapeutic interventions (Patterson, 1979, 1982, 1986; Patterson, & Cobb, 1973; Patterson & Reid, 1970). Sometimes it is sufficient to track a specific behavior over time, such as when one wishes to determine pre-post change. Technological advancements have made it possible to obtain objective activity measurements for two weeks (Futterman & Tryon, 1994; Pinto & Tryon, 1993), every minute of the day and night if desired (Porrino, Rapoport, Behar, Sceery, Ismond, & Bunney, 1983; Porrino, Rapoport, Behar, Ismond, & Bunney, 1983; Teicher, 1995; Tryon, 1991a). The latest technology can record activity every minute of the day and night for 22 days (Tryon & Williams, 1996).

Taking extended behavioral samples under natural conditions over a wide range of environmental settings allows one to evaluate behavioral consistency. For example, Porrino, Rapoport, Behar, Sceery, Ismond, and Bunney (1983) reported that ADHD children are consistently more active than normal children at nearly all times, including night times when they are asleep! Pinto and Tryon (1993) reported consistent day-time motor excess in children rated as hyperactive by their teachers. These data contradict the main effect situational-specificity hypothesis and implicate person characteristics.

Instruments are useful to quantify some things, such as the physical correlates of behavior, but are unable to classify behaviors into qualitative categories. Consequently, direct observation by a human observer still plays an important role in behavioral assessment. The primary purpose of this chapter is to describe the practical details associated with conducting behavioral observation and evaluating the obtained results. Direct observation of operant contingencies leading to assessment conclusions and treatment recommendations will also be discussed. The secondary purpose of this chapter is to recognize the practical limitations associated with direct observation and to indicate how technology is solving this problem. Applications of instrumented behavioral assessment of activity and speech will be discussed.

OBSERVATIONAL SYSTEM

A behavioral observation system is a method for classifying the contents of a behavioral sample into a predefined set of behavioral categories. This process can be done on-line in real time or the behav-ior can be videotaped and classification conducted off-line.

Determining What to Observe

It is virtually impossible to repeat exactly the same behavior twice. Even simple behaviors such as standing up or reaching for an object cannot be duplicated exactly, nor does the investigator usually care about minute and trivial physical differences among acts of the same general kind. Skinner (1953, p. 66) used the term *operant* to describe a set of functionally similar behaviors. Constructing a behavioral coding system entails defining a set of operants. Exactly which operants are to be defined and how they are to be defined is largely a function of the purposes for conducting the behavioral assessment.

One starts by defining one or more target behaviors of interest. Clinically, this usually involves some behavioral excess or deficit—something the person does too frequently or not frequently enough. Behavioral observation in residential programs often reduces to defining operants that earn points and perhaps other operants that earn demerits, cause points to be deducted, or cause other actions to be taken by staff. Staff usually implement the code on a daily basis, points are recorded, and the person's progress is evaluated over time.

Instruments can be used to define operants. The lever or key in an operant chamber requires that the animal press with more than the required threshold force to close the associated switch. The construction characteristics of human activity monitors selects what they will respond to (Tryon, 1985a, 1991a). Schulman, Stevens, and Kupst (1977) constructed a "biomotometer" capable of producing a beeping signal through a crystal earphone every time that the number of activity counts exceeded a predetermined level per unit time. Schulman, Stevens, Suran, Kupst, and Naughton (1978) and Schulman, Suran, Stevens, and Kupst, (1979) reported activity reductions in hyperactive children wearing this device. It is noteworthy that this device both provides treatment and records the necessary data to evaluate treatment effectiveness.

If the objective of behavioral assessment is to identify interactions that increase or decrease the frequency of target behaviors, then one must conceptualize the range of possible events capable of these functional effects and carefully define each of them. In addition to observing the target person's behavior, it is often useful to examine the behavior of other relevant people in the target person's environment. For example, if one is interested in what controls the rate with which a child hits or strikes another child, it will often be useful to observe whether other adults and/or children hit the child.

The next step is to survey other operants on the part of other people with whom the subject interacts in various settings in order to capture important causal information. One can either use behavioral definitions created by other investigators researching or treating the same or similar behavior problems or turn to one's own clinical experience to derive appropriate behavioral categories.

Defining Behaviors

Once behavioral categories have been conceptually identified, the next step is to operationally define each category so that it can be written into a manual and observers can be trained to recognize each category with an acceptable degree of reliability. Every effort should be made to reduce inference on the part of the observer. Refer to what the senses can detect, to what is able to be videotaped. Hence, one can record yelling, pushing, or hitting but not anger; similarly, smiling but not happiness can be recorded. The extent to which untrained observers can agree after reading the manual defining the behavioral codes is a good test of the adequacy of the behavioral definitions (Hawkins & Dobes, 1977). Development of workable behavioral codes usually requires several cycles of pilot data collection followed by revision before acceptable interobserver reliability is achieved.

Response Dimensions

Most frequently, observers are asked to tally the *frequency* with which each of the designated behavioral categories occurs. It is also possible, but more difficult, to record the *duration* of each behavior.

Techniques for *time stamping* the occurrence of behavior (discussed later) can be used to infer duration if one stamps both the onset and offset of each behavior.

Subject Consent

Informed consent must be obtained from the subject prior to behavioral observation unless the person is in a public situation (because observation violates his or her right to privacy). The consent form should include why observation has been recommended; type, extent, and scope of behavioral categories being observed; who will be observing; times observation will occur; how confidential results will be; and who will see the data or any report based on the data.

In clinical settings, the subject to be observed is identified initially. In research contexts, it is less clear who should be observed to draw appropriate conclusions. All of the issues associated with subject inclusion and exclusion criteria are relevant. In what ways do the experimental and control subjects differ and is the coding system adequate to detect these differences? Suen and Ary (1989, pp. 33–58) consider subject sampling and assignment at length.

Situation Sampling

The assumption of situational specificity places the burden of generalizability from the assessment situation to the patient's life circumstance on the clinician or investigator. It cannot be assumed that behaviors observed in the office are representative of behaviors exhibited in school and at home. It is often easiest for clinicians or investigators to observe in their offices or laboratories. They may have special facilities and/or equipment in their offices or nearby observation facilities. Sometimes this practice is defended on the basis that all subjects are observed under standard conditions. Danforth, Barkley, and Stokes (1991) challenge the content validity of convenient assessment: "At issue still is whether the results accurately represent long term behavior in the home" (p. 716).

Generalizability of office and laboratory observations to natural settings remains assumed rather than demonstrated. Generalization is expected only to the extent that the test and natural settings are equivalent in behaviorally important ways. It behooves the clinician and/or investigator to identify specific behaviorally relevant dimensions and to demonstrate adequate equivalence between the test and natural situation to which the test results are to be generalized (Tryon, 1993a) or to qualify office and laboratory observations accordingly. Obtaining significant relationships between behavioral observations and interventions, such as drug treatments, does *not* establish the generality of the treatment effect. It only establishes that treatment changes behavior in the test situation. Generalization to school or home must either be directly assessed or argued for on the basis of environmental similarity between the test and natural situations. Trait theorists assume generalizability across assessment contexts. Behavioral clinicians have too often assumed rather than demonstrated generalizability.

Psychometricians encountered the sampling problem with respect to items. They concluded that test construction should ensure adequate sampling of items across the domain of interest and they labeled this issue *content validity*. Behavioral assessment has increasingly recognized the general relevance of psychometric considerations (Cone, 1988; Tryon, 1993a) and the particular importance of content validity. Just as psychometric tests must sample items across a content domain, so should behavioral assessment sample relevant settings in order to be content valid (Linehan, 1980; Nelson & Hayes, 1979, 1981; Strosahl & Linehan, 1981).

The main point of this section is that one should obtain behavioral samples from one or more naturalistic settings in addition to any test settings in order to determine the extent to which findings obtained under test conditions generalize to natural conditions.

Behavioral Sample Size

How long should observation continue? How large should the behavioral sample be? This is equivalent to asking how many items should be on a test. It is well known that test reliability is directly proportional to its length. I am unaware of a research literature upon which to base an answer to the question of observation duration. Behavioral sample size appears to be determined entirely on pragmatic grounds. If the person will be interviewed for 20 minutes, then behavioral observations are made for this amount of time. If testing takes one hour, then behavioral observation is for one hour.

If the goal is clinical repeatability (Tryon, 1991a, pp. 11–14), then duration should be directly proportional to variability. More variable behaviors require larger, longer, behavioral samples to achieve the same degree of temporal stability/ reliability as less variable behaviors.

A small behavioral sample can detect extreme behavioral differences and therefore may legitimately be used to support a hypothesis provided the generalizability issue has adequately been addressed. However, concluding that two groups do not differ regarding some behavior on the basis of a small, short, behavioral sample is very questionable because a longer behavioral sample may well reveal a difference and contradict the equivalence conclusion. The problem of proving no difference is the same for behavioral assessment as it is for psychometric assessment. Investigators must show that their measurements, observations, and procedures are sufficiently powerful to detect a minimally important finding most of the time, at least 80%, and still no difference is discovered. A real difference could still have been missed, but replication by other investigators will reduce uncertainty regarding this possibility.

Behavioral Sampling

Event Sampling
The observer tallies the occurrence of each event. Recording the time of day each instance occurred is preferable because it enables one to calculate interbehavior intervals. This will reveal whether the events were evenly distributed in time or if they occurred in bursts and, if so, how long a typical burst lasts, which allows one to calculate interburst intervals.

Duration and Latency Recording

Event sampling responds to onset of a behavior. However, behaviors also have a point of offset, which can be recorded, enabling one to calculate the duration of each behavior and the latency between one event and another.

Time Sampling

All time-sampling methods attempt to infer the entirety of what occurred on the basis of sampled observations. Different methods detect different parts of the whole. Each sampling method interacts with the ongoing behavioral stream, and therefore no absolute conclusions can be made about one method or another, since they are all dependent on the behavior being observed. All sampling methods fail under some circumstances.

The more rapid the sampling interval, the less is missed. However, the more complex and comprehensive the coding scheme, the slower sampling will occur, given relatively fixed human information processing capacities.

It is important to control when observation periods occur. This is especially true when reliability is being evaluated. One method is to have observers listen to a tape on which something like the following is recorded: "Interval 1, observe. . . . interval 1, record" (Hartmann & Wood, 1990, p. 115). This procedure has the added benefit of explicitly identifying the exact entry number to be completed, which guards against being off by one interval when recording observations. If behavior has been videotaped and observers are rating from the tape, then displaying the time index during replay will be helpful.

Technological Aids

Horner and Storey (1989) and Farrell (1991) discuss the use of computers to aid behavioral observation. Bush and Ciocco (1992) review a Portable Computer Systems for Observational Use (PCS). Eiler, Nelson, Jensen, and Johnson (1989) discuss a bar-code system for basic observation. Bloom, Hursh, Wienke, and Wolf (1992) present research showing that computers facilitate the use of systematic behavioral observation by teachers.

General-purpose computers can be programmed to detect when a particular key is pressed and to record the time of day when each key is pressed. This enables one to use a laptop or hand-held computer as an elaborate event recording device. This approach avoids the expense of purchasing costly dedicated timing hardware and has the advantage of creating a computer-readable file during the observation period, thereby saving the time that would otherwise be required to enter the data and precluding possible data-entry errors.

Microsoft's QuickBASIC can do real-time event trapping. The relevant code is as follows:

```
TIMER ON
SB$ = CHR$(32)
DO
A$ = INKEY$
LOOP UNTIL A$ = SB$
```

An alternate test loop is:

```
DO
A$ = INPUT$(1)
LOOP  UNTIL  A$ = SB$  or  A$ = "Q"  or
    A$ = "q"
IF A$ = SB$ THEN
    T! = TIMER
    [Take desired action]
END IF
IF A$ = "Q" or A$ = "q" THEN END
TIMER OFF
```

The TIMER ON command initiates event trapping. The space bar is identified as the string variable SB$. CHR$ is the QuickBASIC command to return a one-character string whose ASCII code is given in parentheses. The number 32 is the ASCII decimal equivalent of the space bar. The INKEY$ command can be used to detect a key press. The first DO LOOP UNTIL command executes until the space bar is pressed. Pressing any other key will not terminate this loop. Alternatively, the INPUT$(1) command reads 1 byte from the keyboard. The DO LOOP UNTIL command tests to see if the keyboard buffer contains a space bar press (SB$) or whether an uppercase Q or lowercase q has been pressed. T! is a single precision variable equal to the cumulative number of seconds past midnight. The "Take desired action" code might entail writing T! to an array or to a disk file or a subroutine could be called to take more extensive action. If a Q or q is pressed, then the program will branch to the END statement, which terminates execution. Additional keys can be identified and tested for. Additional IF THEN statements can be used to record the time stamps associated with the occurrence of these other behaviors.

Initiating the observation session by a single reference key press allows all subsequently recorded cumulative second measurements to be converted into the number of seconds since the observation period began or into the number of seconds between consecutive instances of each behavior. Because the system clock is updated 18.2 times each second, all times are accurate to $1/18.2 = .05449$ seconds $= 54.49$ milliseconds.

Multiple behaviors can be tracked by enabling a different key for each behavior. The 12 function keys are excellent candidates for 12 specific behaviors. All of the keys plus their shift, control, and alt combinations can be enabled for real-time event trapping using Quick BASIC.

Behavior is often complex and can occur remarkably fast, thereby taxing even well-trained observers. Videotaping behavioral samples for subsequent analysis allows one to slow down or stop time and to discuss what is occurring prior to making each data entry, if necessary. Audiotapes provide less information but are still useful. Soskin and John (1963) attached radio transmitters to subjects to monitor spontaneous talk. Bernal, Gibson, Williams, and Pesses (1971), Johnson and Bolstad (1975), and Purcell and Brady (1965) also discuss the use of audiotape recording to obtain behavioral samples. Johnson, Christensen, and Bellamy (1976) recorded 15-minute behavioral samples of five children at random and parent-specified times using a radio transmitter attached to the child's belt. Audio information was telemetered to tape recorders contained in a trunk stored in a closet in the child's home. Recorded data were subsequently scored in 10-second blocks using 16 discrete codes. Clicks were recorded on a second channel of each tape to ensure that observers responded to the same content. The authors conclude that random reliability checks enables "completely generalizable reliability assessments" (p. 217).

Observer Training

The first step in training observers is to present them with written definitions of the behavioral codes, discuss the limits of each code, and provide video samples of clear and borderline positive and negative examples of each behavioral code.

The second step is to have observers code videotaped behavioral samples and compare their data with a criterion code for the same sample. All differences should be discussed until the observer clearly understands how they differed from the criterion. This step is repeated until acceptable agreement with the criterion is reached.

The third step is to observe the actual behavior in real time. It is best if the behavioral sample can be video- or audiotaped so that a criterion data set can be generated for the purpose of evaluating observer accuracy. If this cannot be accomplished, then a veteran observer should simultaneously observe along with the novice observer. All differences should be discussed and the process repeated until acceptable agreement is obtained.

Observer drift refers to the fact that trained observers rate the same events differently over time (Foster & Cone, 1986; Johnston & Bolstad, 1973; Reid, 1970; Taplin & Reid, 1973). Pairs of observers can also drift, thereby preserving high interobserver agreement but inaccurate results. Johnston and Bolstad (1973) refer to this as *consensual observer drift*. The solution is periodically to retrain all observers back to criterion and to check continuously for observer drift.

Observer Reactivity

Presence of observers can influence the behavior being observed. Hartmann and Wood (1990) discuss factors that contribute to reactivity. Subjects increase socially desirable behaviors and decrease undesirable behaviors. Conspicuous observation practices can be especially reactive. The observer's characteristics may make them stand out (e.g., a large man in a kindergarten class).

Observer Bias

Observer bias occurs when behavioral observation is systematically distorted by the observer's expectations and prejudices and/or as a result of the observer's cognitive characteristics (Hartmann & Wood, 1990; Haynes & Horn, 1982). Observers tend to see what they expect in accordance with their implicit or explicit hypotheses about what they are observing. Observers also have a central tendency due to a reluctance to use the extreme categories or ratings. Naturally, observers can fatigue if they are asked to observe rapidly and continuously without a break.

DATA ANALYSIS

Behavioral observations were initially assumed to be reliable and valid (Cone, 1977). It is now believed that both reliability and validity must be demonstrated for all measurement systems (Suen & Ary, 1989, pp. 99–192). *Reliability* refers to the consistency with which data are recorded. We first consider agreement between two independent observers and then agreement for a single observer with themselves.

Observer Reliability

Interobserver reliability is the product of at least two factors. The first factor pertains to the sampling method and how consistently it makes contact with the actual behavior. The second factor concerns how consistently each observer records the behaviors he or she observes. Suen and Ary (1989, pp. 101–102) review four different ways the term *reliability* has been used regarding behavioral observation. This diversity of opinion is reflected in the following indices of agreement.

Smaller/Larger Index

With two observers, one can divide the smaller frequency by the larger frequency for every recorded behavior and get a value ranging from 0 to 1.0 (Suen & Ary, 1989, pp. 104–105). A criticism of this approach is that it evaluates the extent to which two observers saw the same number of events in each behavioral category but does not ensure that the exact same events were observed. Two observers could report 20 instances of a behavior resulting in S/L = 1 but only concurred on 15 of the events (each observer reporting 5 events at the time the other reported nothing).

Percent Agreement

Two observers can agree or disagree on the presence and absence of a target response. Percent agreement is calculated by dividing the number of occurrence agreements plus the number of nonoccurrence agreements by the number of total number of agreements and disagreements, multiplying the resulting proportion by 100 to obtain a percentage. This index can be calculated from a 2 • 2 table of the frequency of occurrence and nonoccurrence for both observers. It is possible that observers agree highly about occurrences, but disagree regarding nonoccurrences of a target behavior or vice versa. Therefore, one can calculate percent agreement for occurrences separately from nonoccurrences. Percent occurrence equals the number of occurrence agreements divided by the number of occurrence agreements plus disagreements, multiplying the resulting proportion by 100 to obtain a percentage. Percent nonoccurrence equals the number of nonoccurrence agreements divided by the number of nonoccurrence agreements plus disagreements, multiplying by 100 to obtain a percentage (Suen & Ary, 1989, pp. 110–111).

Kappa

Two observers who complete observation forms at random will agree to some extent, especially if they both record many instances of the target behavior. When the rate of a particular behavior is high, two observers will frequently tally its occurrence, making the number of occurrences a large fraction of the number of occurrences and nonoccurrences and therefore resulting in a high percent agreement. Kappa corrects for chance agreement. It equals the proportion of observed agreement minus the proportion of chance agreement, divided by the quantity 1, minus the proportion of chance expectation. Suen and Ary (1989, pp. 111–114) provide worked examples and discuss the relationship between proportion of agreement and kappa.

Other Indices of Agreement

Suen and Ary (1989, pp. 116–117) present 12 additional agreement formulas testifying the diversity of opinion in this area.

ANOVA (Generalizability Theory). Cronbach, Gleser, Nanda, and Rajaratnam (1972) reframed the question of reliability in terms of generalizability. When two or more people observe two or more subjects at one or more times or one subjects at two or more times, Analysis of Variance (ANOVA) can be used to calculate variance components due to observers, subjects, and an error term (Suen & Ary, 1989, pp. 131–139). Observer variance reflects systematic differences between observers. The error term reflects random measurement error.

Validity

Validity concerns how accurately the recorded data reflect what they purport to measure. Despite many different formulas for calculating reliability, evaluating validity is more difficult because it entails an epistemological problem. One cannot directly know reality but must depend on one's measurements, the validity of which is in question. Hence, validation is necessarily a bootstrap process that depends on indirect evidence. The literature on validation assessment is much smaller than for reliability assessment.

Observer validity is the product of at least the following two factors. The first factor pertains to the sampling method and how consistently it makes contact with the actual behavior. The second factor concerns how accurately observers record behavior they observe.

Content
A behavioral observation system is content valid if the definitions of the behavioral categories is consistent with the general understanding of what is being measured. Peculiar operational definitions of a behavior compromise content validity.

Criterion
A behavioral observation system has criterion validity to the extent that it covaries meaningfully with a "gold standard" index such as a master scoring derived from multiple observers viewing a video or audiotaped behavioral sample. Agreement with the criterion is termed *observer accuracy*.

Time-Series Analysis

Behavioral observation is almost always conducted over time, thereby giving rise to multiple measurements over time, commonly referred to as a *time series*. These data can be analyzed both graphically and quantitatively.

Graphic Methods
It is highly recommended to graph the data prior to conducting any other analyses. There are often many ways to graph data. The simplest approach is to graph the cumulative frequency for each behavior observed. More frequently occurring behaviors will have steeper slopes than less frequently occurring ones. Aggregate cumulative plots can be produced by summing the tallies for a single behavior over subjects.

When the same subjects are observed on two or more occasions, two graphic options exist. One approach is to create a within-session graph of each observation period. The other option is to plot the average across sessions. This assumes that the same number of observations have been made each time observation was conducted.

Crosbie (1993) reviews the visual inference literature and reports that inter-rater reliability regarding degree of experimental control evidenced by a graph can be as low as .61 even by experienced raters. Concluding in favor of a significant effect when none exists can range from 16% to 84%. Concluding that no significant effect exists when one does can occur 22% of the time, though most often about 10% of the time.

Digital Filters (Smoothers)
The greatest impediment to interpreting graphs accurately is correctly estimating and adjusting conclusions for the effects of variability, or uncertainty. Velleman (1980) and Velleman and Hoaglin (1981) discuss simple numerical methods for stabilizing data sets by computing running averages, running medians, and Hanning. These techniques often substantially clarify the presence or absence of any trends.

ARIMA Methods
AR stands for *autoregressive,* which means self-predicting; one part of the time series is predicted from, regressed on, another part of itself. The lagged correlation coefficient is used to index nature and degree that a given data point is predictable from a prior data point. The Lag 1 autocorre-

lation coefficient is calculated as follows. Label the original series X. Label its duplicate Y. Place them side by side and slide the Y series up one position so that the observation taken at time t is being correlated with the observation taken at time $t + 1$. The resulting Lag 1 correlation coefficient will be based on $N - 1$ observations. The Lag 2 correlation coefficient is obtained similarly by sliding the Y series up one more position so that the observation taken at time t is being correlated with the observation taken at time $t + 2$. This correlation will be based on $N - 2$ observations. Suen and Ary (1989, pp. 197–199) describe how to test autocorrelation coefficients for significance. Data are said to be autocorrelated when one or more lagged correlation coefficients are significant.

Crosbie (1987) indicates that autocorrelation creates two problems for traditional statistical analyses such as the t test, the ANOVA, or the binomial tests (which assume that all data points are independent of one another, not autocorrelated at all). First, autocorrelation reduces the degrees of freedom from their normally computed values. Second, positive autocorrelation means that consecutive data points are more similar to each other than they are to the mean. This spuriously reduces error variance from computed values. Negative autocorrelation indicates that consecutive data points are more dissimilar to each other than they are to the mean (Crosbie & Sharpley, 1989). This spuriously increases error variance. Huitema (1985) found that although autocorrelation is nearly zero on average, it can be substantially positive or negative. The combined effect of these problems is that the null hypothesis is rejected at times when it should be accepted.

The letter I represents differencing, which entails finding consecutive differences among data points. The observed data points are replaced by differences between them. This is done to remove trend and establish stationarity, which is assumed when estimating the autoregressive and moving average parameters.

The letters MA stand for *moving average*. This refers to the number of previous points used to predict a given point in the series. For example, MA(1) indicates that point 2 is predictable from point 1 and point 3 from 2, and so on, whereas

MA(2) indicates that point 3 is predictable from points 2 and 1, and point 4 is predictable from points 3 and 2.

ARIMA methods are used to evaluate and extract autocorrelation from time series and then evaluate the data for a change in slope and/or intercept associated with treatment. Model identification and specification are the first phase of ARIMA analysis. It attempts to specify the correct $AR, I,$ and MA parameters for the series at hand. This information can be used to calculate a residual series containing only random error and treatment effects. Ostrom (1978), McDowall, McCleary, Meidinger, and Hay (1980), and Suen and Ary (1989, pp. 215–262) provide additional details. Unfortunately, 50 to 100 data points per phase are recommended (Crosbie, 1993). Suen and Ary (1989) discuss evaluating intervention after collecting 100 baseline data points, implying that at least another 100 data points were obtained during intervention. Behavior therapists rarely collect this many data points across the entire experiment, let alone during baseline.

Small Samples
Crosbie (1993) discusses a method of conducting time-series analysis with as few as 5 scores per phase, but preferably 10 to 20 points per phase, called ITSACORR. A DOS format computer program is available from John Crosbie, Department of Psychology, West Virginia University, Morgantown, West Virginia 26506-6040 for $99 (check made payable to John Crosbie) that will conduct this analysis. An omnibus F test for intercept and slope is first conducted followed by separate tests for the intercept and slope for each of two phases.

LIMITATIONS

Behavioral observation is not easy to carry out and has significant limitations even when adequate resources are available. Human observers tend to be reactive, in that they are often easily noticed and serve as a discriminative stimulus to the persons being observed, thereby changing the behavior of interest. Observers can be biased by their expectations and prejudices. Observers drift and need to be retrained periodically. Because one never knows when observer drift is going to be a significant problem, one must continually evaluate its presence.

The ability to slow time through slow motion or frame-by-frame videotape replay, described as an advantage earlier, is now appreciated as a significant expense. The practical question becomes: How many hours of videotape analysis can clinicians expect to bill clients for in addition to therapy contact hours?

Human observers have a finite information processing capacity that can rapidly be exceeded if too many behaviors are tracked too often or if too many persons are to be observed in the same setting. Human observers are often effective at detecting the presence or absence of a behavior but are often poor at judging magnitude. For example, observers can reliably tell if a child gets out of his or her seat but not be able to accurately quantify the degree of activity shown. Human observers may be able to reliably identify when one person interrupts another while talking, but almost certainly will not be able to reliably or accurately report how many milliseconds the second person continued talking before yielding the floor to the first speaker. Observations such as these are better left to instruments specially designed for these purposes.

Human observers violate the client's right to privacy to some degree. Clients consent to being observed because it is in their therapeutic interest to do so. The extent of this problem is directly proportional to the size of the proposed behavioral sample. Being observed while in the therapist's office is arguably the least invasive case. Being observed in school might set the occasion for being treated differently by other children and or teachers. Being observed at home during meal time is not as invasive as being followed all day long and into the latter evening.

Instrumented recordings are less invasive precisely because they are not human. For example, it is less intrusive to have activity level recorded by a small monitor worn at the waist than to have several different observers constantly watching the subject's every move.

Personnel costs associated with trained observers are high and increases over time, especially when medical and retirement benefits are included. Few clinical facilities can afford to hire,

train, and continuously retrain observers. The cost of audio and video recorders, computers, and computer-based instruments is modest by comparison and decreases with time. The future of behavioral observation may well depend on our ability to constructively use new technology.

BEHAVIORAL MEASUREMENT

Some aspects of behavior are especially well suited for measurement rather than observation. The two most easily instrumented clinically interesting behaviors are activity and speech.

Activity

Teicher (1995) and Teicher, Ito, Glod, and Barber (in press) used an infrared motion analysis stem to track the movements of the head, shoulders, and right arm of ADHD and normal control children while taking a computerized continuous performance test. They found that ADHD children were 2.3 to 3.8 times more active than normal control children. Small portable sophisticated actigraphs are available for ambulatory monitoring of activity levels under natural conditions (Tryon, 1991a, Tyron & Williams, 1996). Although activity can be observed, measurement has at least the following advantages:

1. *Objectivity.* instruments are not influenced by the person's age, sex, race, prior history, or diagnosis. Instruments do not have expectations nor do they respond to demand characteristics.

2. *Unidimensionality.* Response characteristics are engineered into devices and consequently can be made unidimensional, which makes data more readily interpretable.

3. *Validity.* Tryon (1991a, pp. 23–51) used the term *construction validity* to indicate that instruments validly measure what they were engineered to measure. How the device is constructed determines what it will validly measure.

4. *Portability.* Small devices can be attached to the person's waist, wrist, or ankle that can measure activity every minute of the day and night for up to 22 days before data need to be down-loaded and the device reset for another 22 days of data col-

lection. This provides clinicians and investigators with the ability to obtain very large behavioral samples while the subject behaves in his or her natural environment.

5. *Reliability.* Instrument reliability can best be determined under laboratory conditions. Attempting to estimate instrument reliability by placing activity monitors on people confounds *instrument reliability* with *clinical repeatability* (Tryon, 1991a, pp. 9–14).

6. *Stability.* Although instruments require periodic recalibration, they maintain their measurement characteristics far longer than human observers, who are known to drift soon after training (Foster & Cone, 1986; Johnston & Bolstad, 1973; Reid, 1970; Taplin & Reid, 1973).

7. *Privacy.* Obtaining large behavioral samples while the subject behaves in his or her natural environment is intrusive. Small portable instruments are ethically preferable.

8. *Cost effectiveness.* Obtaining large behavioral samples from the subject's natural environment is exceptionally expensive and usually impracticable for practicing clinicians. Cost, as well as the difficulty in recruiting and training and retraining observers, are perhaps the largest impediments to the widespread use of behavioral observation outside the office or clinic. Simple step-counters can be purchased from Radio Shack for approximately $25. Over time, their cost reduces to pennies per hour, per day, and per week. Sophisticated actigraphs cost more but they also provide time-stamped minute-by-minute readings (1,440 readings per 24 hours over multiple days). Tryon (1991a) discusses applications of activity measurement to mood disorders, schizophrenia, attention-deficit hyperactivity disorder, eating disorders, sleep disorders, drugs, and chronic disease. Newer applications include assessment of patients with chronic fatigue syndrome and evaluating recovery after surgery (Redeker, Mason, Wykpisz, Glica, & Miner, in press). Activity-measuring devices are rapidly becoming more sophisticated, able to store more data, and more cost effective.

Speech/Sound Pressure Levels

Psychologists have long recognized the social and psychological importance of speech. Several literature reviews are available (Siegman, 1987a; Feldstein & Welkowitz, 1987; Siegman & Feldstein, 1979). Kupfer, Maser, Blehar, and Miller (1987), Rehm (1987), Scherer (1987), and Siegman (1987b) have discussed the relationships between speech and affective disorder. Speech can be analyzed for content or for other properties such as presence versus absence and speech pause times, which are much easier to quantify than content. Investigators have either studied the properties of monologues or conversations between two speakers.

Monologues

Godfrey and Knight (1984), Greden, Albala, Smokler, Gardner, and Carroll (1981), Hinchliffe, Lancashire, and Roberts (1970), Kanfer (1960), Pope, Blass, Siegman, and Raher (1970), Szabadi, Bradshaw, and Besson (1976), Teasdale, Fogarty, and Williams (1980), and Weintraub and Aronson (1967) have all reported reductions in speech rate associated with depression. Greden and Carroll (1980), Greden, Albala, Smokler, Gardner, and Carroll (1981), Hardy, Jouvent, and Widlocher (1984), and Hoffmann, Gonze, and Mendlewicz (1985) also reported that pause times decreased during hospitalization from pretreatment through discharge.

Stitzer, Griffiths, and Liebson (1978) used a voice-operated relay with a response time of 160 millisecond and a hold duration of 1.5 seconds to increment a counter and cumulative recorder. They measured speech rate before and after oral administration of 5, 10, 15, or 20 milligrams d-amphetamine and reported reliable drug-induced speech rate changes in three of four subjects.

More complex analyses of voice require signal processing analyses called *power spectrograms,* which provide an intensity-by-frequency plot for each, usually small, time period. Williams and Stevens (1972) reported fundamental frequency changes associated with anger, fear, and sorrow. Hargreaves, Starkweather, and Blacker (1965) evaluated voice quality in depressed subjects using sound spectrography.

Sound spectrography has been applied to infants. Ostwald and Peltzman (1974) analyzed 356 distress cries from 13 infants and discovered clear-cut differences between the crying sounds made by abnormal versus normal infants. Zeskind and Marshall (1988) reported that the mean fundamental frequency of 16 newborn infant cries best predicted maternal ratings of how urgent, arousing, and distressing these cries were; higher pitch was associated with greater disturbance. Gustafson and Green (1989) reported correlations from .64 to .83 between sound spectrographic parameters of 12 spontaneous cries from 12 different 1-month-old infants on the perceptions of urgency, distress, arousal, sickness of the infants, and how grating, discomforting, piercing, and aversive their crying was by 20 parents (10 married couples) and 22 nonparent adults (11 men, 11 women). Lester (1987) reported significant correlations between the sound spectograms of 20 normal healthy full-term and 20 preterm infants and the Bayley Scales of Infant Development and McCarthy General Cognitive Index.

Andreasen, Alpert, and Martz (1981) measured the fundamental frequency of 31 schizophrenic patients rated as having flat affect and 30 schizophrenics rated as not having flat affect, and reported that flat affect is associated with reduced variance in both speech amplitude (intensity) and fundamental frequency. Alpert (1981, 1989) has reported similar variance attenuation associated with flat affect ratings.

Alpert, Merewether, Homel, Martz, and Lomask (1986) describe a Voxcom system for analyzing natural speech in real time. Several speech-analysis products, capable of sophisticated speech analysis, are commercially available for personal computers. Ariel Corporation (Highland Park, NJ, 201-249-2900) sells a fully integrated software and hardware mouse-driven package called SpeechStation.[TM] Kay Elemetrics Corporation's (Pine Brook, NY, 800-289-5297) CSL[TM] / Computerized Speech Lab system is capable of many sophisticated analyses. Their DSP Sona-Graph[TM] workstation is extremely powerful and can conduct complex analyses in real time. Kay Elemetrics also sells a biofeedback voice system called Visi-Pitch.[TM] GW Instruments's (Somerville, MA, 617-625-4096) SoundScope[TM] offers Macintosh users with point and click access to sophisticated speech processing.

Conversations

Cappella (1981), Jaffe and Feldstein (1970), and Siegman and Feldstein (1979, 1987) extensively document that adult conversations entail coordinated interpersonal timing (CIT; Crown, 1991) or vocal congruence (Beebe, Alson, Jaffe, Feldstein, & Crown, 1988) using an Automatic Vocal Transaction Analyzer (AVTA) (Feldstein & Welkowitz, 1987). For example, the length of uninterrupted speech by one person directly influences the uninterrupted speech of his or her partner. When one person pauses longer, so does the other. CIT characterizes mother/infant interactions as early as four months after birth (Beebe et al., 1988; Feldstein et al., 1993). Jasnow, Crown, Feldstein, Taylor, Beebe, and Jaffe (1988) demonstrated that CIT is delayed in Down syndrome infants at 4 months of age but approach normality by 9 months of age.

Breznitz and Sherman (1987) used the AVTA to measure the speech of depressed and healthy mothers as they spoke to their young children. They reported significantly less vocalization and significantly longer switching times in the speech of depressed mothers.

Feldstein and Crown (1990) analyzed speech samples from 44 undergraduate men, half Canadian (whose first language was English) and half Oriental (whose first language was Cantonese). Oriental speakers took significantly more speaking turns, used nearly twice as many switching pauses, and made shorter vocalizations than did Canadian speakers. Both groups were similar as to duration of pauses and simultaneous speech. Orientals paused significantly more often when speaking English than Chinese.

Group conversations have been studied using the AVTA by Dabbs, Ruback, and Evans (1978)—an extension of social psychological group process analysis. Possibilities for speakers to take turns with each other, to interrupt each other, and to give way to each other increase rapidly with group size. One method has been to assign a problem to mixed-sex groups of five persons and record their conversation while solving the problem. The potential of this technology for analyzing the behavior of distressed couples and families appears great.

Ambulatory Monitoring

These studies were conducted in a laboratory. It is now possible to collect ambulatory speech data using a device called the LogoPort[TM] (Kruger, 1987, 1989) now commercially available from

Ambulatory Monitoring, Inc. (800-341-0066). It measures 164 • 108 • 30 millimeters, weighs 800 grams, and is worn with a shoulder strap. A small condenser microphone is taped to the subjects throat and connected to one channel of the Logo-Port.^{TM} If desired, EKG can be recorded on a second channel. A 40-megahertz quartz clock samples the microphone every millisecond. If speech is present in 8 consecutive samples, then speech is scored present for the entire interval. This results in 125 samples per second written to memory. Speech can be recorded for 6.5 hours. Two or more Logo-Ports^{TM} can be synchronized by setting their internal clocks to the same time.

The LogoPort^{TM} could be used to advance research published by Hayes and Cobb (1979) on "ultradian biorhythms in social interaction." Circadian rhythms have regularly been studied by continuously monitoring activity as just described. Hayes and Cobb have taken the same approach to speech. They had eight pairs of subjects live in a special apartment for a week and telemetered their speech to a nearby recording studio using equipment attached to a golf hat. Speech duration per 10-minute epochs was calculated from 10 to 20 waking hours per day for seven days. Spectral analyses were made of each day's speech activity. A prominent 183-minute cycle was discovered along with a 91- and 46-minute speech cycle. Such studies could be conducted in a subject's natural environment using the LogoPort.^{TM}

Response Latency

Computer administration of personality and other self-report inventories enables one to measure the time taken to read and respond to each item, thereby measuring an important aspect of the subject's behavior during testing. Administering personality tests by computer does not compromise their reliability. Holden, Fekken, and Cotton (1990) reported that reliability (alpha) coefficients ranged from .79 to .92 for the basic and factor scales of the microcomputerized version of the Basic Personality Inventory (Jackson, 1976). Retesting 26 subjects nine weeks latter yielded alpha coefficients ranging from .78 to .92. Good psychopathological test items have fast response times (Holden &

Fekken, 1990). Affective content also appears to influence response time. Temple and Geisinger (1990) reported shorter response times to arousing than neutral stimuli. Tryon and Mulloy (1993) replicated this finding.

Items that are clearly true or false of oneself should be answered more rapidly than other items. Popham and Holden (1990) computer administered the MMPI to 40 students and found a significant correlation ($r(38) = -.27$, $p < .01$) between scale score and response latency. Persons with higher scale scores endorsed item content faster than did subjects with lower scale scores. Holden, Fekken, and Cotton (1991) report on an unpublished paper by Erdle and LaLonde (1986), who found that persons with relatively high scores on personality dimensions responded faster to test items they endorsed and slower to test items they rejected than did persons with relatively low scores on the same personality dimensions. They also found that persons with relatively low scores on personality dimensions responded faster to test items they rejected than did persons with relatively high scores on the same personality dimensions. Holden, Fekken, and Cotton (1991) further confirmed this finding.

Hsu, Santelli, and Hsu (1989) measured response times of 100 undergraduates to MMPI items under one of five instructional sets: (1) standard reporting, (2) fake good with no incentive, (3) fake bad with no incentive, (4) fake good with incentive, and (5) fake bad with incentive. Faking good and bad were always associated with shorter latencies than standard (honest) reporting. Following orders was viewed as less cognitively complex than examining self-relevance.

Holden, Kroner, Fekken, and Popham (1992) divided 84 college students to respond to three MMPI instructional sets: (1) standard self-report, (2) fake good, and (3) fake bad. The authors hypothesized that instructions established a response schema that would facilitate responding. Results supported this conjecture in that subjects instructed to fake good responded significantly faster to nonpathological than to pathological items. The standard self-report subjects responded similarly. Subjects instructed to fake bad responded significantly faster to pathological than nonpathological items. A discriminant analysis correctly classified 58.33% of the subjects into the three instructional groups versus a chance expectation of 33.33%. The authors replicated these findings on 72 additional students taking the Basic Personality Inventory (BPI; Jackson, 1976). Administering the BPI to 87 prison inmates under the same three instructional sets replicated the fake good and standard self-report but not the fake-bad condition, which yielded similar response times for psychopathological and nonpsychopathological content.

Holden and Kroner (1992) administered the BPI to 87 male prison inmates under the same three instructional sets. Differential latencies to endorse or reject psychopathology with true and false responses were found to correctly discriminate 59.77% of the subjects. Congruence between the instructional set and response time was again found.

Eye Movements

Normal reading entails brief fixations followed by small quick jumps to the right until reaching the end of the line, where upon scanning quickly returns to the left margin. Pavlidis (1981, 1985a, 1985b) reported that children with reading problems have abnormal eye movement patterns. In particular, they show an abnormal number of regressive movements. Filippi and Tryon (1997) have recently replicated this finding. Modern equipment can monitor eye movements without attaching any sensors to the subject. One only need sit within a few feet of the equipment.

DSM-IV

Behavioral assessment is consistent with the *DSM-IV* (APA, 1994) emphasis on observable behaviors as inclusion and exclusion criteria (First, Frances, Widiger, Pincus, & Davis, 1992). The *DSM-IV* list of specific psychosocial stressors (Axis IV, pp. 29–30) is consistent with the emphasis behavioral assessment places on environmental factors.

DSM-IV is based on *syndromes*, defined as "a group of symptoms that collectively characterize a disease or disorder" (*American Heritage Dictionary,* 1983, p. 691) (Krasner, 1992). The term *dis-*

ease generally connotes an internal cause. However, *DSM-IV* is atheoretical as to etiological causation and therefore does not actively exclude any explanation of behavior disorder, including those based on conditioning principles or cognitive theory. *DSM-IV* remains open to the possibility that syndromes arise because of external, environmental, experiential factors. For example, coercive family processes—negative reinforcement—can result in aggressive children who meet *DSM-IV* (APA, 1994, p. 85) inclusion criteria for conduct disorder (312.8).

Behavioral assessment has historically sought to go beyond documenting the frequency, intensity, and duration of target behaviors and symptoms to a better understanding of behavior disorder through functional analysis. Hayes and Follette (1992) have considered the possibility of supplementing *DSM* categorization with a functional analysis. They discussed problems with functional analysis and recommended possible solutions.

Perhaps the primary impediment limiting the widespread clinical use of behavioral observation is logistic. Behavioral observation methodology requires an observer to record behavior, and this increases the cost of treatment by the amount necessary to recruit, train, and support observers. Additional costs are associated with data entry and the calculation of conditional probabilities (Patterson, 1982; Patterson & Cobb, 1973; Tryon, 1989), transition matrices (Whitehurst, Fischel, DeBaryshe, Caulfield, & Falco, 1986), and/or regression analyses (Martin, Maccoby, Baran, & Jacklin, 1981) to identify reinforcement contingencies. The time and expense associated with this methodology has precluded its incorporation into everyday clinical practice. The next section describes a more feasible method of identifying and recording contingent events.

OBSERVING CONTINGENCIES

Behavioral observation can form the empirical basis for a *functional analysis*, which Haynes and O'Brien (1990) define as "the identification of important, controllable, causal functional relationships applicable to a specified set of target behaviors for an individual client" (p. 654). Said otherwise, O'Brien and Haynes (1995) indicate that "the first goal is to obtain valid and useful measures of target behaviors and controlling factors" (p. 111). Haynes and O'Brien (1990) cite the "lack of efficient and clinically useful methods" (p. 659) as one reason why only 20% of the case studies published between 1985 and 1988 based treatment on a functional analysis. The percentage of daily clinical services based on functional analysis is probably much lower (perhaps a fraction of 1%). One reason for such neglect is that trained observers are expensive and often unavailable to clinicians. The use of home tape recording as an inexpensive and practical means of obtaining naturalistic behavioral samples is considered in this section. Another reason why functional analysis is not performed more often is that evidence of elevated conditional probabilities is desired (Patterson, 1982; Patterson, & Cobb, 1973; Schlundt, 1985; Tryon 1989) but requires data-entry and analysis skills and resources not generally available in clinical settings. We will consider more feasible alternative methods for identifying contingent relationships.

Tryon (1996) describes a method for directly observing contingent events. Space limitations preclude a complete reiteration of all details, so a general overview will be given. An expanded version of Woods's (1974) taxonomy of instrumental conditioning constitutes the core of the recommended procedure. Tryon (1976a) described eight models of behavior disorder using Woods's original system; Tryon (1976b) first recommended that the taxonomy be used as a diagnostic system.

Principles of operant conditioning constitute sufficient conditions for behavior change. Contingent consequences can predictably increase or decrease the frequency, duration, and/or intensity of a target behavior. Martin and Pear (1992) discuss how conditioning principles can produce behavior problems by well-meaning parents, teachers, clinicians, and others who are unaware of conditioning principles. They discuss "pitfalls" of positive reinforcement, extinction, shaping, intermittent reinforcement, schedules for decreasing behavior, stimulus discrimination training, fading, conditioned reinforcement, chaining, generalization, punishment, and escape and avoidance conditioning. In sum, both theoretical and practical

reasons exist for identifying contingent events supporting the emission of undesirable behavior and the omission of desirable behavior.

Reporting observed contingencies using a formal taxonomy serves several useful purposes. The first purpose is *descriptive*. A descriptive profile can be created for each client by identifying and categorizing the presence of contingencies supporting behavior disorder and the absence of contingencies supporting desirable behavior. For example, Patterson (1982, 1986) finds that the coercive family process entails high levels of negative reinforcement and low levels of positive reinforcement. First, Frances, Widiger, Pincus, and Davis (1992) and Hersen (1988) indicate that description is one of the main benefits of the *DSM* series. The common reference point provided by the *DSM* series is deemed valuable, even though it lacks both etiological significance and prescriptive implications.

The second purpose a taxonomy of contingencies serves is *explanatory*. Given that contingencies causally modify behavior, they can be used to explain why a particular behavior disorder persists. For example, positive reinforcement for school avoidance can partly explain school phobia.

The third purpose a taxonomy of contingencies serves is *prescriptive*. This contribution is corollary to the explanatory contribution. Tryon (1996) identifies eight behavioral prescriptions. The first four behavioral diagnoses pertain to single contingencies. They involve (1) absence of contingencies that increase positive behaviors, (2) presence of contingencies that decrease the presence of positive behaviors, (3) presence of contingencies that increase negative behaviors, and (4) absence of contingencies that decrease negative behaviors. A behavioral prescription follows from each diagnosis. For example, given the first diagnosis (1), one would prescribe the presence of contingencies that increase positive behaviors. Given the third diagnosis (3), one would prescribe removing contingencies that increase negative behaviors.

The second four behavioral diagnoses pertain to binary contingencies (the joint occurrence of two contingencies). They involve (5) a contingency that decelerates the emission of a response plus a contingency that accelerates the same response (learned helplessness), (6) a contingency that accelerates the emission of a response occurring jointly with a contingency that decelerates the emission of the same response (approach-avoidance conflict), (7) a contingency that accelerates omission of a response occurring jointly with a contingency that decelerates the omission of the same response resulting in a second type of approach-avoidance conflict (neurotic paradox— that self-defeating behavior is self-perpetuating, [Mowrer, 1948]), and (8) a contingency that accelerates the emission of a response occurring jointly with a contingency that accelerates the omission of a response (superstitious behavior). The four associated behavioral prescriptions all have the same logical form; remove one or the other of the two contingencies or substitute a compatible second contingency. For example, given diagnosis (6), one could choose either to accelerate the emission or decelerate the emission of a response. If acceleration of response emission was chosen, then a second compatible contingency such as omission penalty or punishment could be added to more strongly accelerate response emission.

The previous paragraphs are based on an expanded version of Woods's (1974) taxonomy of instrumental conditioning to categorize and explain behavior disorder and to prescribe behavioral interventions. This analytic system retains its theoretical merit despite practical difficulties associated with behavioral observation. It provides a conceptual basis for describing and communicating about behavior disorder that has both etiological and prescriptive implications. The remaining paragraphs in this section concern more efficient methods for observing contingencies.

One must first obtain a behavioral sample for analysis. Real-time observation using trained observers is beyond the means of most clinicians. Technological advances in both audio and video recording allow clients to obtain their own behavioral samples and mail or bring them to the clinician for review and analysis. Bernal, Gibson, Williams, and Pesses (1971), Johnson and Bolstad (1975), Johnson, Christensen, and Bellamy (1976), Purcell and Brady (1965), and Soskin and John (1963) discuss using audiotapes to collect behavioral samples. Small high-fidelity audio and video

systems are becoming increasingly more capable and less expensive. Invasion of privacy is less when recording is done using an instrument than with a human observer and can be minimized by allowing the clients to record what they choose.

The simplest clinical use to which these tapes can be put is to review them with the client during the session to better understand who does what to whom and under what conditions. Contingent events can be verbalized by both the client(s) and therapist(s) and written up as part of the case notes. Tapes can be mailed to the therapist who can review them prior to the next session in preparation for that session. Tapes may be archived if clients so consent, serving at least two purposes. The tape contains much more detail than the notes ever could and can serve as ongoing documentation of therapeutic progress or the lack of it. Earlier tapes can be replayed at a latter time to demonstrate to the client or other professionals the changes associated with treatment.

Formal analysis can be conducted in the following way. Clinical interview and judgment based on the previously mentioned informal review of the tapes and self-report can be used to identify one or more target behaviors and probable discriminative stimuli plus positive and negative reinforcers. Procedures described by Timberlake and Farmer-Dougan (1991) can also be used to identify reinforcers. Using an incident-recording approach, the observer waits until one of the target behaviors occurs. Important antecedents, discriminative stimuli, and consequents/reinforcers are noted or an entry is made on a recording form published by Tryon (1996). If the target behavior is requested by another person, then the observer distinguishes between its emission and omission (Did the person comply or not?). A more complete analysis of omission conditioning requires that the observer make entries at fixed or random sampled times to evaluate what happens during specified time windows when the target behavior does not occur. Tryon (1996) provides additional details and an example of a completed observation form.

In conclusion, identification of contingent events supporting behavior disorder and documenting the absence of supporting contingencies for desirable behavior are important to all forms of behavior therapy because reinforcement contingencies causally modify behavior. The well-documented large effect sizes associated with reinforcement contingencies indicates that they must be evaluated as part of any comprehensive behavioral assessment and that they must be considered as part of any comprehensive behavioral intervention. Clinicians who neglect contingencies do so at their own peril, as exemplified by Martin and Pear's (1992) "pitfalls" mentioned earlier. Cognitive treatments undoubtedly work better when their goals and objectives are not compromised by competing reinforcement contingencies.

SUMMARY

Behavioral assessment seeks to obtain observable evidence regarding the frequency, intensity, and duration of specific behaviors in standardized and natural environments. Traditional procedures are sufficiently time consuming and expensive that they are not commonly used in clinical practice. Current trends in health service delivery suggest even less chance of their inclusion in the foreseeable future. The vitality of behavioral observation may well be linked to the extent to which technological advances can be used to obtain behavioral samples and/or used to make behavioral measurements. Behavioral measurement entails the use of instruments to quantify behavior. Sophisticated devices are currently capable of quantifying the intensity of behavior 10 times a second and integrating these measurements over each of the 1,440 minutes per 24-hour day for three consecutive weeks, thereby providing comprehensive behavioral measurements of diurnal and nocturnal activity (Tryon, 1991). Speech samples can be recorded under many clinically interesting circumstances and objectively analyzed with computer software. Response latency to computer-administered tests can be obtained and eye movements can be accurately and unobtrusively monitored.

DSM-IV is consistent with behavioral assessment through its emphasis on observable symptomatology. Behavioral observation can therefore contribute to making *DSM* diagnoses. However, behavioral assessment has always sought to do more than tabulate the frequency, intensity, and duration of target behaviors (symptoms). I refer to the analysis of reinforcement contingencies. They entail important causal conditions that can theoretically explain the origin, modification, and treatment of behavior disorders. Although cognitive treatments remain far more popular than reinforcement treatments, clinicians ignore these well-documented large sources of behavioral variance at their own peril. Cognitive interventions undoubtedly work better when their goals and objectives are not sabotaged by competing reinforcement contingencies.

The *DSM* series has been enormously popular despite the fact that it is mainly a descriptive nosology. It does not reveal etiology and carries few clear treatment implications. An expanded version of Woods's (1974) taxonomy of instrumental conditioning (Tryon, 1996) can also serve this descriptive function. The taxonomy carries explanatory and prescriptive implications because it concerns causal sources of behavior variance. Theoretical analysis of behavior disorder based on the taxonomy is important despite logistic and technical difficulties associated with behavioral observation. Efficient methods of obtaining information about contingencies that can be used clinically to educate clients about behavior change further enhance the clinical utility of this approach. Home audio- and videotaping increasingly provide cost-effective methods of obtaining behavioral specimens capable of serving both clinical and research objectives.

There is a growing trend toward limiting behavior therapy to procedures validated by two or more well-controlled clinical trials (Barlow, 1993). This is useful because organized health-care officials increasingly demand empirical support for reimbursable services. Behavior therapy has always emphasized the importance of empirical support for clinical intervention. It is notable that the American Psychological Association has published test-user guidelines that prohibit the use of unvalidated tests but remains silent regarding the use of unvalidated clinical procedures.

There are at least four problems with the controlled clinical trial standard for certifying therapeutic efficacy and limiting practice. First, it is a "one size fits all" approach designed for a modal client that few clinicians will ever meet. It assumes that individual variations are small and/or unimportant relative to the standardized procedures. Treatment packages are expected to be applied to all persons in the same group in the same way. This approach has been justified by comparing it to surgical procedures. Surgery entails a set of procedures that need to be carried out in a particular way. Surgery involves more than just skilled cutting. This defense is problematic because it assumes that variability of behavioral problems is comparable to the variability of human physiology; that people suffering from *DSM* disorders are no more variable in quality or quantity than are people in need of a specific operation (e.g., a hernia repair). Human physiology is much more similar from person to person than are behavior patterns and reinforcement histories. Therefore, surgeons can more readily write surgical manuals than psychologists can write behavioral treatment manuals baring gross oversimplification or excessive departures from the formulary. The problem of client variability can be diminished by constructing subgroups and modifying treatment to fit special needs up to a point. How many subgroups are needed is an empirical issue but the number is likely to be large if more than a few person variables are jointly considered.

Second, behavioral assessment is reduced to determining which package should be administered and whether the treatment has any effect. This is a much diminished role for behavioral assessment. Determining if reinforcement contingencies support problematic behaviors and/or if they fail to support desired behaviors (functional analysis) is not central to standardized treatment packages because this information can lead in many directions not anticipated by prepared intervention manuals. Nor is it easy to write specific manuals for addressing highly individualistic functional-analytic results. The proposed taxonomy serves to reduce the spectrum of possible outcomes to a set of categories or contingencies that can be present singly or in pairs. Perhaps future manuals can be written on this basis.

Third, the immense well-controlled literature on the powerful and meaningful effects of condi-

tioning procedures on a vast array of target behaviors is ignored. That reward conditioning predictably increases the frequency, rate, or probability of a target behavior is among the most, if not the most, empirically supported clinically relevant intervention known to behavioral science. Conditioning procedures consistently modify the behavior of individuals to a substantial degree. Regardless of a person's view about the validity of conditioning explanations, he or she identifies sufficient conditions for altering the frequency, rate, or probability of behavior. These conditions can be directly observed, and when they support behavior disorder or fail to support adaptive behaviors, clinicians are warranted to intervene and correct them. Such customized clinical care is scientifically validated by numerous single-subject research designs. Taken one by one, single-subject studies may have limited generalizability, but taken as a whole, their collective impact is much greater than one or two controlled clinical trials.

Connectionistic neural networks provide a new theoretical context for properly interpreting conditioning explanations. Tryon (1993b, 1993c, 1994, 1995a, 1995b, 1995c) introduces psychologists to neural networks and details how they foster theoretical unification between the cognitive and behavioral perspectives and how both are integrated with neuroscience. These theoretical developments may revitalize clinical interest behavioral contingencies and therefore in behavioral observation and assessment.

Fourth, demonstrating that selected clinicians participating in controlled trials can produce significant treatment effects does not mean that every person receiving a doctorate from a clinical psychology program can produce equivalent results. It is necessary, but not sufficient, to prove that therapeutic procedures are effective. One must also certify that practitioners are skilled in the application of these procedures. Perhaps more attention should be paid to certifying clinicians in behavioral assessment, including the recommended methods for observing contingencies, since this assessment procedure leads to empirically validated conditioning treatments.

REFERENCES

Alpert, M. (1981). Speech and disturbances of affect. In. J. K. Darby (Ed.), *Speech evaluation in psychiatry* (pp. 359–367). New York: Grune & Stratton.

Alpert, M. (1989). Vocal acoustic correlates o flat affect in schizophrenia: Similarity to Parkinson's disease and right hemisphere disease and contrast with depression. *British Journal of Psychiatry, 155,* 51–56.

Alpert, M., Merewether, F., Homel, P., Martz, J., & Lomask, M. (1986). Voxcom: A system for analyzing natural speech in real time. *Behaviour Research Methods Instruments & Computers, 18,* 267–272.

American Psychiatric Association (1994). *Diagnostic and statistical manual of mental disorders* (4th ed.). Washington DC: Author.

Andreasen, N. C., Alpert, M., & Martz, M. J. (1981). Acoustic analysis: An objective measure of affective flattening. *Archives of General Psychiatry, 38,* 281–285

Anastasi, A. (1988). *Psychological testing* (6th ed.). New York: Macmillan.

Barrios, B. A. (1988). On the changing nature of behavioral assessment. In A. S. Bellack & M. Hersen (Eds.), *Behavioral assessment: A practical handbook* (3rd ed.) (pp. 3–41). Elmsford, NY: Pergamon.

Barlow, D. H. (1993). *Clinical handbook of psychological disorders: A step-by-step treatment manual* (2nd ed.). New York: Guilford.

Beebe, B., Alson, D., Jaffe, J., Feldstein, S., & Crown, C. (1988). Vocal congruence in mother-infant play. *Journal of Psycholinguistic Research, 17,* 245–259.

Bernal, M. E., Gibson, D. M., Williams, D. E., & Pesses, D. I. (1971). A device for recording automatic audio tape recording. *Journal of Applied Behavior Analysis, 4,* 151–156.

Bloom, L. A., Hursh, D., Wienke, W. D., & Wolf, R. K. (1992). The effects of computer assisted data collection on students' behavior. *Behavioral Assessment, 14,* 173–190.

Breznitz, Z., & Sherman, T. (1987). Speech patterning of natural discourse of well and depressed mothers and their young children. *Child Development, 58,* 395–400.

Bush, J. P., & Ciocco, J. E. (1992). Behavioral coding and sequential analysis: The portable computer systems for observational use. *Behavioral Assessment, 14,* 191–197.

Cappella, J. N. (1981). Mutual influence in expressive behaviour: Adult and infant-adult interaction. *Psychological Bulletin, 89,* 101–132.

Cone, J. D. (1977). The relevance of reliability and validity for behavior assessment. *Behavior Therapy, 8,* 411–426.

Cone, J. D. (1988). Psychometric considerations and the multiple models of behavioral assessment. In A. S. Bellack & M. Hersen (Eds.). *Behavioral assessment: A practical handbook* (3rd ed.) (pp. 42–66). New York: Pergamon.

Cronbach, L. J., Gleser, G. C., Nanda, H., & Rajaratnam, N. (1972). *The dependability of behavioral measurements: Theory of generalizability for scores and profiles.* New York: Wiley.

Crosbie, J. (1987). The inability of the binomial test to control type I error with single-subject data. *Behavioral Assessment, 9,* 141–150.

Crosbie, J. (1993). Interrupted time-series analysis with brief single-subject data. *Journal of Consulting and Clinical Psychology, 61,* 966–974.

Crosbie, J., & Sharpley, C. F. (1989). DMITSA: A simplified interrupted time-series analysis program. *Behavior Research Methods, Instruments & Computers, 21,* 639–642.

Crown, C. L. (1991). Coordinated interpersonal timing of vision and voice as a function of interpersonal attraction. *Journal of Language and Social Psychology, 10,* 29–46.

Dabbs, Jr., J. M., Ruback, R. B., & Evans, M. S. (1978). "Grouptalk": Sound and silence in group conversation. In A. W. Siegman & S. Feldstein (Eds.), *Nonverbal behavior and communication* (2nd ed.) (pp. 501–520). Hillsdale, NJ: Lawrence Erlbaum.

Danforth, J. S., Barkley, R. A., & Stokes, T. F. (1991). Observations of parent-child interactions with hyperactive children: Research and clinical implications. *Clinical Psychology Review, 11,* 703–727.

Darby Jr., J. K. (Ed.). (1981). *Speech evaluation in psychiatry.* New York: Grune & Stratton.

Donahoe, J. W. (1991). The selectionist approach to verbal behavior: Potential contributions of neuropsychology and connectionism. In L. J. Hayes & P. N. Chase (Eds.), *Dialogues on verbal behavior: The first international institute on verbal relations* (pp. 119–150). Reno, NV: Context Press.

Eiler, J. M., Nelson, W. W., Jensen, C. C., & Johnson, S. P. (1989). Automated data collection using bar code. *Behavior Research Methods, Instruments, & Computers, 21,* 53–58.

Erdle, S., & LaLonde, R. N. (1986, June). *Processing information about the self: Evidence for personality traits as cognitive prototypes.* Paper presented at the Canadian Psychological Association Annual Convention. Toronto, Ontario, Canada.

Feldstein, S., & Crown, C. L. (1990). Oriental and Canadian conversational interactions: Chronographic structure and interpersonal perception. *Journal of Asian Pacific Communication, 1,* 247–265.

Feldstein, S., Jaffe, J., Beebe, B., Crown, C. L., Jasnow, M., Fox, H., & Gordon, S. (1993). Coordinated interpersonal timing in adult-infant vocal interactions: A cross-site replication. *Infant Behavior and Development, 16,* 455–470.

Feldstein, S., & Welkowitz, T. (1987). A chronography of conversation: In defense of an objective approach. In A. W. Siegman & S. Feldstein (Eds.), *Nonverbal behavior and communication* (pp. 435–499). Hillsdale, NJ: Erlbaum.

Filippi, A. D., & Tryon, W. W. (1997). *Regressive eye movements found in reading disabled boys.* Manuscript submitted for publication.

First, M. B., Frances, A., Widiger, T. A., Pincus, H. A., & Davis, W. W. (1992). DSM-IV and behavioral assessment. *Behavioral Assessment, 14,* 297–306.

Foster, S. L., Bell-Dolan, D. J., & Burge, D. A. (1988). Behavioral observation. In A. S. Bellack & M. Hersen (Eds.), *Behavioral assessment: A practical handbook* (3rd ed.) (pp. 119–160). New York: Pergamon.

Foster, S. L., & Cone, J. D. (1986). Design and use of direct observation. In A. R. Ciminero, K. S. Calhoun, & H. E. Adams (Eds.), *Handbook of behavioral assessment* (2nd ed.) (pp. 253–324). New York: Wiley.

Futterman, C. S., & Tryon, W. W. (1994). Psychomotor retardation found in depressed outpatient women. *Journal of Behavior Therapy and Experimental Psychiatry, 25,* 41–48.

Godfrey, H. P. D., & Knight, R. G. (1984). The validity of actometer and speech activity measures in the assessment of depressed patients. *British Journal of Psychiatry, 145,* 159–163.

Greden, J. F., Albala, A. A., Smokler, I. A., Gardner, R., & Carrol, B. J. (1981). Speech pause time: A marker of psychomotor retardation among endogenous depressives. *Biological Psychiatry, 16,* 851–859.

Greden, J. F., & Carroll, B. J. (1980). Decrease in speech pause times with treatment of endogenous depression. *Biological Psychiatry, 15,* 575–587.

Greden, J. F., & Carroll, B. J. (1981). Psychomotor function in affective disorders: An overview of new monitoring techniques. *American Journal of Psychiatry, 138,* 1441–1448.

Gustafson, G. E., & Green, J. A. (1989). On the importance of fundamental frequency and other acoustic features in cry perception and infant development. *Child Development, 60,* 772–780.

Halperin, J. M., Matier, K., Bedi, G., Sharma, V., & Newcorn, J. H. (1992). Specificity of inattention, impulsivity, and hyperactivity to the diagnosis of attention-deficit hyperactivity disorder. *Journal of the American Academy of Child and Adolescent Psychiatry, 31,* 190–196.

Halperin, J. M., Newcorn, J. H., Matier, K., Sharma, V., McKay, K. E., & Schwartz, S. (1993). Discriminant validity of attention-deficit hyperactivity disorder. *Journal of the American Academy of Child and Adolescent Psychiatry, 32,* 1038–1043.

Hardy, P., Jouvent, R., & Widlocher, D. (1984). Speech pause time and the Retardation Rating Scale for Depression (ERD): Towards a reciprocal validation. *Journal of Affective Disorders, 6,* 123–127.

Hargreaves, W. A., Starkweather, J. A., & Blacker, K. H. (1965). Voice quality in depression. *Journal of Abnormal Psychology, 70,* 218–220.

Harlow, H. F., & Suomi, S. J. (1974). Induced depression in monkeys. *Behavioral Biology, 12,* 273–296.

Hartmann, D. P., & Wood, D. D. (1990). Observational methods. In A. S. Bellack, M. Hersen, & A. E. Kazdin (Eds.), *International handbook of behavior modification and therapy* (2nd ed.) (pp. 107–138). New York: Plenum.

Hawkins, R. P., & Dobes, R. W. (1977). Behavioral definitions in applied behavior analysis: Explicit or implicit. In B. C. Etzel, J. M. LeBlanc, & D. M. Baer (Eds.), *New developments in behavioral research: Theory, method, and applications. In honor of Sidney W. Bijou* (pp. 167–188). Hillsdale, NJ: Lawrence Erlbaum.

Hayes, D. P., & Cobb, L. (1979). Ultradian biorhythms in social interaction. In A. W. Siegman & S. Feldstein (Eds.), *Of speech and time: Temporal speech patterns in interpersonal contexts* (pp. 57–70). New York: Wiley.

Hayes, S. C., & Follette, W. C. (1992). Can functional analysis provide a substitute for syndromal classification? *Behavioral Assessment, 14,* 345–365.

Haynes, S. N., & Horn, W. F. (1982). Reactivity in behavioral observation: A review. *Behavioral Assessment, 4,* 369–385.

Haynes, S. N., & O'Brien, W. H. (1990). Functional analysis in behavior therapy. *Clinical Psychology Review, 10,* 649–668.

Hersen, M. (1988). Behavioral assessment and psychiatric diagnosis. *Behavioral Assessment, 10,* 107–121.

Hinchliffe, M. K., Lancashire, M., & Roberts, F. J. (1970). Depression: Defense mechanisms in speech. *British Journal of Psychiatry, 118,* 471–472.

Hoffmann, G. M., Gonze, J. C., & Mendlewicz, J. (1985). Speech pause time as a method for the evaluation of psychomotor retardation in depressive illness. *British Journal of Psychiatry, 146,* 535.

Holden, R. R., & Fekken, G. C. (1990). Structured psychopathological test item characteristics and validity. *Psychological Assessment, 2,* 35–40.

Holden, R. R., Fekken, G. C., & Cotton, D. H. G. (1990). Clinical reliabilities and validities of the microcomputerized basic personality inventory. *Journal of Clinical Psychology, 46,* 845–849.

Holden, R. R., Fekken, G. C., & Cotton, D. H. G. (1991). Assessing psychopathology using structured test-item response latencies. *Psychological Assessment: A Journal of Consulting and Clinical Psychology, 3,* 111–118.

Holden, R. R., & Kroner, D. G. (1992). Relative efficacy of differential response latencies for detecting faking on a self-report measure of psychopathology. *Psychological Assessment, 4,* 170–173.

Holden, R. R., Kroner, D. G., Fekken, G. C., & Popham, S. M. (1992). A model of personality test item response dissimulation. *Journal of Personality and Social Psychology, 63,* 272–279.

Horner, R. H., & Storey, K. (1989). Putting behavioral units back unto the stream of behavior: A consumer report. *The Behavior Therapist, 12,* 249–251.

Hsu, L. M., Santelli, J., & Hsu, J. R. (1989). Faking detection validity and incremental validity of response latencies to MMPI subtle and obvious items. *Journal of Personality Assessment, 53,* 278–295.

Huitema, B. E. (1985). Autocorrelation in applied behavior analysis: A myth. *Behavioral Assessment, 7,* 107–118.

Jackson, D. N. (1976). *The Basic Personality Inventory.* Port Huron, MI: Sigma Assessment Systems.

Jaffe, J., & Feldstein, S. (1970). *Rhythms of dialogue.* New York: Academic Press.

Jasnow, M., Crown, C. L., Feldstein, S., Taylor, L., Beebe, B., & Jaffe, J. (1988). Coordinated interpersonal timing of Down-Syndrome and nondelayed infants with their mothers: Evidence for a buffered mechanism of social interaction. *The Biological Bulletin, 175,* 355–360.

Johnson, S. M., & Bolstad, O. D. (1973). Methodological issues in naturalistic observation: Some problems and solutions for field research. In L. A. Hamerlynck, L. C. Handy, & E. J. Mash (Eds.), *Behavioral change: Methodology, concepts, and practice* (pp. 7–67). Champaign, IL: Research Press.

Johnson, S. M., & Bolstad, O. D. (1975). Reactivity to home observation: A comparison of audio recorded behavior with observers present or absent. *Journal of Applied Behavior Analysis, 8,* 181–185.

Johnson, S. M., Christensen, A., & Bellamy, G. T. (1976). Evaluation of family intervention through unobtrusive audio recordings: Experiences in "bugging" children. *Journal of Applied Behavior Analysis, 9,* 213–219.

Kanfer, F. H. (1960). Verbal rate, eye blinks, and content in structured psychiatric interviews. *Journal of Abnormal and Social Psychology, 61,* 341–347.

Krasner, L. (1992). The concepts of syndrome and functional analysis: Compatible or incompatible? *Behavioral Assessment, 14,* 307–321.

Kruger, H. P. (1987). *A new measurement device for the study of verbal behavior in the open field.* Paper presented at the meeting of the Eastern Psychological Association, Washington, DC.

Kruger, H. P. (1989). Speech chronemics—A hidden dimension of speech: Theoretical Background, measurement and clinical validity. *Pharmacopsychiatry, 22,* 5–12.

Kupfer, D. J., Maser, J. D., Blehar, M. C., & Miller, R. (1987). Behavioral assessment in depression. In J. D. Maser (Ed.), *Depression and expressive behavior* (pp. 1–15). Hillsdale, NJ: Lawrence Erlbaum.

Lester, B. M. (1987). Developmental outcome prediction from acoustic cry analysis in term and preterm infants. *Pediatrics, 80,* 529–534.

Linehan, M. M. (1980). Content validity: Its relevance to behavioral assessment. *Behavioral Assessment, 2,* 147–159.

Martin, G., & Pear, J. (1992). *Behavior modification: What it is and how to do it* (4th ed.). Englewood Cliffs, NJ: Prentice Hall.

Martin, J. A., Maccoby, E. E., Baran, K. W., & Jacklin, C. N. (1981). Sequential analysis of mother-child interaction at 18 months: A comparison of microanalytic methods. *Developmental Psychology, 17,* 146–157.

Matier, K., Halperin, J. M., Sharma, V., Newcorn, H. H., & Sathaye, N. (1992). Methylphenidate response in aggressive and nonaggressive ADHD children: Distinctions on laboratory measures of symptoms. *Journal of the American Academy of Child and Adolescent Psychiatry, 31,* 219–225.

McDowall, D., McCleary, R., Meidinger, E. E., & Hay, Jr., R. A. (1980). *Interrupted time series analysis.* Beverly Hills: Sage.

Mowrer, O. H. (1948). Learning theory and the neurotic paradox. *American Journal of Orthopsychiatry, 18,* 571–610.

Nelson, R. O., & Hayes, S. C. (1979). Some current

dimensions of behavioral assessment. *Behavioral Assessment, 1,* 1–16.

Nelson, R. O., & Hayes, S. C. (1981). Nature of behavioral assessment. In M. Hersen & A. S. Bellack (Eds.), *Behavioral assessment: A practical handbook* (2nd ed.) (pp. 3–37). New York: Pergamon.

O'Brien, W. H., & Haynes, S. N. (1995). Behavioral assessment. In L. A. Heiden & M. Hersen (Eds.), *Introduction to clinical psychology* (pp. 103–139). New York: Plenum.

Ostrom, Jr., C. W. (1978). *Time series analysis: Regression techniques.* Beverly Hills: Sage.

Ostwald, P. F., & Peltzman, P. (1974). The cry of the human infant. *Scientific American, 230,* 84–90.

Patterson, G. R. (1979). A performance theory for coercive family interaction. In R. Cairns (Ed.), *Social interaction: Methods, analysis, and illustrations.* Hillsdale, NJ: Lawrence Erlbaum.

Patterson, G. R. (1982). *Coercive family process: A social learning approach* (vol. 3). Eugene OR: Castalia.

Patterson, G. R. (1986). Performance models for antisocial boys. *American Psychologist, 41,* 432–444.

Patterson, G. R., & Cobb, J. A. (1973). Stimulus control for classes of noxious behaviors. In J. F. Knutson (Ed.), *The control of aggression: Implications from basic research.* Chicago: Aldine.

Patterson, G. R., & Reid, J. B. (1970). Reciprocity and coercion: Two facets of social systems. In C. Neuringer & J. L. Michael (Eds.), *Behavior modification in clinical psychology* (pp. 133–177). New York: Appleton-Century-Crofts.

Pavlidis, G. T. (1981). Do eye movements hold the key to dyslexia? *Neuropsychologia, 19,* 57–64.

Pavlidis, G. T. (1985a). Eye movement dyslexia: Their diagnostic significance. *Journal of Learning Disabilities, 18,* 42–50.

Pavlidis, G. T. (1985b). Sequencing, eye movements, and diagnosis of dyslexia. In G. T. Pavlidis & T. R. Miles (Eds.), *Dyslexia research and its application to education* (pp. 99–163). New York: Wiley.

Pinto, L. P., & Tryon, W. W. (1993). Children rated as hyperactive manifest motor excess. *Behavior Modification, 17,* 371–406.

Pope, B., Blass, T., Siegman, A. W., & Raher, J. (1970). Anxiety and depression in speech. *Journal of Consulting and Clinical Psychology, 35,* 128–133.

Popham, S. M., & Holden, R. R. (1990). Assessing MMPI constructs through the measurement of response latencies. *Journal of Personality Assessment, 54,* 469–478.

Porrino, L. J., Rapoport, J. L., Behar, D., Ismond, D. R., and Bunney, Jr., W. E. (1983). A naturalistic assessment of the motor activity of hyperactive boys II. Stimulant drug effects. *Archives of General Psychiatry, 40,* 688–693.

Porrino, L. J., Rapoport, J. L., Behar, D., Sceery, W., Ismond, D. R., & Bunney, Jr., W. E. (1983). A naturalistic assessment of the motor activity of hyperactive boys I. Comparison with normal controls. *Archives of General Psychiatry, 40,* 681–687.

Purcell, K., & Brady, K. (1965). Adaptation to the invasion of privacy: Monitoring behavior with a miniature radio transmitter. *Merrill-Palmer Quarterly, 12,* 242–254.

Redeker, N. S., Mason, D. J., Wykpisz, E. M., Glica, B., & Miner. C. (in press). Activity patterns, mood, and recovery in women after coronary artery bypass surgery: The first post-operative week. *Nursing Research.*

Reid, J. B. (1970). Reliability assessment of observation data: A possible methodological problem. *Child Development, 41,* 1143–1150.

Rehm, L. P. (1987). The measurement of behavioral aspects of depression. In A. J. Marsella, R. M. A. Hirschfeld, & M. M. Katz (Eds.), *The measurement of depression* (pp. 199–239). New York: Guilford.

Scherer, K. R. (1987). Vocal assessment of affective disorders. In J. D. Maser (Ed.), *Depression and expressive behavior* (pp. 57–82). Hillsdale, NJ: Lawrence Erlbaum.

Schlundt, D. G. (1985). An observational methodology for functional analysis. *Bulletin of the Society of Psychologists in Addictive Behaviors, 4,* 234–249.

Schulman, J. L., Stevens, T. M., & Kupst, M. J. (1977). The biomotometer: A new device for the measurement and remediation of hyperactivity. *Child Development, 48,* 1152–1154.

Schulman, J. L., Stevens, T. M., Suran, B. G., Kupst, M., & Naughton, M. J. (1978). Modification of activity level through biofeedback and operant conditioning. *Journal of Applied Behavior Analysis, 11,* 145–152.

Schulman, J. L., Suran, B. G., Stevens, T. M., & Kupst, M. J. (1979). Instructions, feedback and reinforcement in reducing activity levels in the classroom. *Journal of Applied Behavior Analysis, 12,* 441–447.

Siegman, A. W. (1987a). The telltale voice: Nonverbal messages of verbal communication. In A. W. Siegman & S. Feldstein (Eds.), *Nonverbal behavior and communication* (2nd ed.) (pp. 351–434). Hillsdale, NJ: Lawrence Erlbaum.

Siegman, A. W. (1987b). The pacing of speech in depression. In J. D. Maser (Ed.), *Depression and expressive behavior* (pp. 83–102). Hillsdale, NJ: Lawrence Erlbaum.

Siegman, A. W., & Feldstein, S. (Eds.). (1979). *Of speech and time: Temporal speech patterns in interpersonal contexts.* Hillsdale, NJ: Lawrence Erlbaum.

Siegman, A. W., & Feldstein, S. (Eds.). (1987). *Nonverbal behavior and communication* (2nd ed.). Hillsdale, NJ: Lawrence Erlbaum.

Skinner, B. F. (1948). "Superstition" in the pigeon. *Journal of Experimental Psychology, 38,* 168–172.

Skinner, B. F. (1953). *Science and human behavior.* New York: Macmillan.

Soskin, W. F., & John, V. P. (1963). The study of spontaneous talk. In R. G. Barker (Ed.), *The stream of behavior* (pp. 228–281). New York: Appleton-Century-Crofts.

Stitzer, M. L., Griffiths, R. R., & Liebson, I. (1978). Effects of d-amphetamine on speaking in isolated humans. *Pharmacology Biochemistry & Behavior, 9,* 57–63.

Strosahl, K. D., & Linehan, M. M. (1981). Basic issues in behavioral assessment. In A. R. Ciminero, K. S. Calhoun, and H. E. Adams (Eds.), *Handbook of behavioral assessment* (2nd ed.) (pp. 12–46).

Suen, H. K., & Ary, D. (1989). *Analyzing quantitative behavioral observation data.* Hillsdale, NJ: Lawrence Erlbaum.

Szabadi, E., Bradshaw, C. M., & Besson, J. A. O. (1976). Elongation of pause-time in speech: A simple, objective measure of motor retardation in depression. *British Journal of Psychiatry, 129,* 592–597.

Taplin, P. S., & Reid, J. B. (1973). Effects of instructional set and experimental influences on observer reliability. *Child Development, 44,* 547–554.

Teasdale, J. D., Fogarty, S. J., & Williams, J. M. G. (1980). Speech rate as a measure of short-term variation in depression. *British Journal of Social and Clinical Psychology, 19,* 271–278.

Teicher, M. H. (1995). Actigraphy and motion analysis new tools for psychiatry. *Harvard Review of Psychiatry, 3,* 18–35.

Teicher, M. H., Ito, Y., Glod, C. A., & Barber, N. I. (in press). Objective measurement of hyperactivity and attentional problems in ADHD. *Journal of the American Academy of Child and Adolescent Psychiatry.*

Temple, D. E., & Geisinger, K. F. (1990). Response latency to computer administered inventory items as an indicator of emotional arousal. *Journal of Personality Assessment, 54,* 289–297.

Timberlake, W., & Farmer-Dougan, V. A. (1991). Reinforcement in applied settings: Figuring out ahead of time what will work. *Psychological Bulletin, 110,* 379–391.

Tryon, W. W. (1976a). Models of behavior disorder: A formal analysis based on Woods's taxonomy of instrumental conditioning. *American Psychologist, 31,* 509–518.

Tryon, W. W. (1976b). A system of behavioral diagnosis. *Professional Psychology, 7,* 495–506.

Tryon, W. W. (1978). An operant explanation of Mowrer's neurotic paradox. *Behaviorism, 6,* 203–211.

Tryon, W. W. (1982). A simplified time series analysis for evaluating treatment interventions. *Journal of Applied Behavior Analysis, 15,* 423–429.

Tryon, W. W. (1985a). The measurement of human activity. In W. W. Tryon (Ed.). *Behavioral assessment in behavioral medicine* (pp. 200–256). New York: Springer.

Tryon, W. W. (1985b). "A simplified time-series analysis for evaluating treatment interventions": A rejoinder to Blumberg. *Applied Behavior Analysis, 17,* 543–544.

Tryon, W. W. (1989). Behavioral assessment and psychiatric diagnosis. In M. Hersen (Ed.), *Innovations in child behavior therapy* (pp. 35–56). New York: Springer.

Tryon, W. W. (1991a). *Behavioral measurement in psychology and medicine.* New York: Plenum.

Tryon, W. W. (1991b). Motor activity and DSM-III-R. In M. Hersen & S. M. Turner (Eds.). *Adult psychopathology and diagnosis* (2nd ed.) (pp. 412–440). New York: Wiley.

Tryon, W. W. (1993a). The role of motor excess and instrumented activity measurement in Attention-deficit Hyperactivity Disorder. *Behavior Modification, 17,* 371–406.

Tryon, W. W. (1993b). Neural networks: I. Theoretical unification through connectionism. *Clinical Psychology Review, 13,* 341–352.

Tryon, W. W. (1993c). Neural networks: II. Unified learning theory and behavioral psychotherapy. *Clinical Psychology Review, 13,* 353–371.

Tryon, W. W. (1994). Synthesis not complementarity. *American Psychologist, 49,* 892–893.

Tryon, W. W. (1995a). Synthesizing psychological schisms through connectionism. In A. Gilgen & F. Abraham (Eds.), *Chaos theory in psychology* (pp. 247–263). Westport, CT: Praeger.

Tryon, W. W. (1995b). Resolving the cognitive behavioral controversy. *The Behavior Therapist, 18,* 83–86.

Tryon, W. W. (1995c). Neural networks for behavior therapists: What they are and why they are important. *Behavior Therapy, 26,* 295–318.

Tryon, W. W. (in press a). Motor activity and DSM-IV. In S. M. Turner & M. Hersen (Eds.), *Adult psycho-*

pathology and diagnosis (3rd. ed.). New York: Wiley

Tryon, W. W. (in press b). Physical activity. In M. Hersen & V. B. Van Hasselt (Eds.), *Handbook of clinical geropsychology.* New York: Plenum.

Tryon, W. W. (1996). Observing contingencies: Taxonomy and methods. *Psychology Review, 16, 215–230.*

Tryon, W. W., & Mulloy, J. M. (1993). Further validation of computer-assisted response time to emotionally evocative stimuli. *Journal of Personality Assessment, 61,* 231–236.

Tryon, W. W., & Williams, R. (1996). Fully proportional actigraphy: A new instrument. *Behavior Research Methods Instruments & Computers, 28,* 392–403.

Velleman, P. F. (1980). Definition and comparison of robust nonlinear data smoothing algorithms. *Journal of the American Statistical Association, 75,* 609–615.

Velleman, P. F., & Hoaglin, D. C. (1981). *Applications, basics, and computing of exploratory data analysis.* Boston: Duxbury Press.

Weintraub, W., & Aronson, H. (1967). The application of verbal behavior analysis to the study of psychological defense mechanisms IV: Speech pattern associated with depressive behavior. *The Journal of Nervous and Mental Disease, 144,* 22–28.

Whitehurst, G. J., Fischel, J. E., DeBaryshe, B., Caulfield, M. R., & Falco, F. L. (1986). Analyzing sequential relations in observational data: A practical guide. *Journal of Psychopathology and Behavioral Assessment, 8,* 129–148.

Williams, C. E., & Stevens, K. N. (1972). Emotions and speech: Some acoustical correlates. *The Journal of the Acoustical Society of America, 52,* 1238–1250.

Wolpe, J. W. (1958). *Psychotherapy by reciprocal inhibition.* Stanford, CA: Stanford University Press.

Woods, P. J. (1974). A taxonomy of instrumental conditioning. *American Psychologist, 29,* 584–597.

Zeskind, P. S., & Marshall, T. R. (1988). The relation between variations in pitch and maternal perceptions of infant crying. *Child Development, 59,* 193–196.

CHAPTER 6

COGNITIVE ASSESSMENT

Jean Linscott
Long Island Jewish Medical Center and St. John's University
Raymond DiGiuseppe
St. John's University

The revelation of thought takes men out of servitude into freedom. (Ralph Waldo Emerson, *The Conduct of Life,* "Fate," 1860)

The utility of cognitive constructs in behavior therapy has been (Skinner, 1945) and continues to be hotly debated (Follette, 1995; Hayes, 1995). The main issue in this debate concerns whether the inclusion of cognitive constructs improves our ability to explain, predict, and change behavior and emotions. If cognitive behavior therapies are to maintain their widespread acceptance in the field, more evidence will need to be accumulated to support the utility of cognitive constructs. Since cognitive constructs are more abstract and more difficult to define operationally than traditional behavior therapy constructs, the assessment of cognitive constructs is more difficult. Therapists cannot plan which cognitive deficits or dysfunctional thoughts to target for intervention unless they can validly assess which cognitions are related to the target behavioral and emotional symptoms. The measurement and assessment of cognitive constructs is crucial for practitioners to plan and implement cognitive interventions effectively.

The goals of this chapter are to provide scientist-practitioners with strategies to guide the practice of cognitive assessment, to suggest areas of future research, and to link research and clinical practice. Multiple methods for assessing cognition are reviewed and recommendations for selection of assessment methods are provided within the context of recommendations for research and clinical strategies.

At this stage of the development of cognitive behavior therapy (CBT), we perceive two major issues that confront the field of cognitive assessment. The first issue concerns which assessment methods provide the most reliable and valid information. The second concerns which cognitions to assess for treatment planning. Little research exists that directly bears on these issues confronting practitioners.

Most research in cognitive assessment has focused on the development of questionnaires to measure specific cognitive constructs. Therefore, most cognitive assessment tools and strategies available to practitioners are based on a nomothetic-trait approach. Widely used cognitive assessment scales such as the Automatic Thought Questionnaire (Hollon & Kendall, 1980), Dysfunctional Attitudes Scale (Weissman & Beck, 1978), the Irrational Belief Test (Jones, 1968), the Attitude and Beliefs Scale (Burgess, 1990; DiGiuseppe, Robin, Leaf, & Gorman, 1989), and dysfunctional core schema (Schmidt, Joiner, Young, & Teich, 1995) have proven useful in their abilities to empirically test theoretical formulations and to distinguish between the cognition endorsed by groups of individuals. However, these existing cognitive assessment measures have limited clinical utility. We propose that most such scales have scientific merit but fail to address the problems confronted by practitioners.

Cognitive behavior therapy is not dominated by one paradigm. Numerous theories exist proclaiming that a particular type of cognition is the mediator of behavioral and emotional dysfunction. Researchers usually measure only the one cognition to which they have some theoretical commitment. As a result, we do not have a body of research that compares the role of different types of cognitions in mediating clinical problems. Practitioners must decide which cognition to assess. This chapter will provide some guidelines for making the decision of which cognition to assess.

A CALL FOR IDEOGRAPHIC COGNITIVE ASSESSMENT

One of the hallmarks of behavioral assessment has been the insistence on empirically based, ideographic methods. Behavior therapists have always emphasized the idiopathic nature of behavior. This philosophy has resulted in individualized assessments and treatment plans. The field of cognitive-behavioral assessment, however, has not always been true to this behavioral philosophy and has focused more on trait assessment.

Cone (1988) cautions that nomothetic measures are (1) too general and (2) insensitive to individual differences critical to clinical practice and single-case research designs. The concerns of the behavioral practitioner are to assess, produce, and evaluate changes in an individual's behavior. The concerns of cognitive-behavioral practitioners are similar. Treatment gains measured by use of nomothetic measures may provide some access to the comparative level of disturbance, but may miss critical changes reported by the individual client. By using assessment measures targeted at the individual client level (vs. the group differences level), the scientist-practitioner, whether behaviorist or cognitive-behaviorist, may begin to answer the questions of which treatment for which client with what specific problems under what circumstances prove effective (Barlow, Hayes, & Nelson, 1984; Kiesler, 1971; Paul, 1961).

Cone (1988) recommends ideographic measures that are sensitive to individual change for use in behavioral assessment. Others have similarly recommended ideographic measures for use in cognitive-behavioral assessment (Muran, 1991; Safran, Vallis, Segal, & Shaw, 1986). The majority of the currently existing cognitive assessment scales do not allow for adequate empirical measurement of individual differences in clients' specific beliefs or for changes in these specific beliefs through treatment. Few ideographic cognitive assessment strategies with adequate empirical backing have been created for use by practitioners. Therefore, practitioners frequently rely on nomothetic assessment instruments to guide their ideographic treatments. We recommend the extensive development of diverse ideographic measures for the continued advancement of both research and clinical applications of cognitive assessment and intervention.

MULTITRAIT/MULTIMETHOD MODEL OF ASSESSMENT

After reviewing the psychometric considerations in cognitive assessment, Glass (1993) recommended that researchers allow for variations in an individual's thoughts across context and time (Lazarus, 1995; Martzke, Anderson, & Cacioppo, 1987) and include the representative cognitions that differ according to the disorder studied. Different methods of assessing the same cognitive constructs, such as endorsement of questionnaire items versus production of thoughts, do not correlate highly with each other (Glass & Furlong, 1990; Myska, Galassi, & Ware, 1986) and therefore cannot be considered equivalent measures of the same construct. Clark (1988) reached a similar conclusion. These findings emphasize the need for a multitrait/multimethod approach to validate cognitive assessment measures and constructs (Campbell & Fiske, 1959; Cook & Campbell, 1978; Webb, Campbell, Schwartz, & Sechrest, 1966). Using this method will assist the researcher in the process of sorting out the degree to which differences in results are explained by the specific cognitive construct as opposed to the methodology for measuring those constructs.

The lack of cross-method convergence on measures of the same construct suggests that clinicians need to be cautious in utilizing research measures in clinical practice. These results also leave open the question of which type of assessment instrument best measures clinical change. The failure to find agreement among various type of measures also questions the validity of information extracted from self-report questionnaires.

WHAT TO MEASURE

Cognitive behavior therapy is not a unified theory. Numerous cognitive constructs are proposed to mediate psychopathology. The constructs targeted in therapy include automatic thoughts (Beck, 1976), irrational beliefs (Ellis, 1962, 1994), personal constructs (Guidano & Liotti, 1983; Mahoney, 1991), coping self-statements (Meichenbaum & Cameron, 1981), perceptions of self-efficacy (Bandura, 1982), attributions for causation (Seligman, 1975), and social problem-solving skills (Spivack, Platt, & Shure, 1975). The problem facing the practitioner is what construct to measure.

Many cognitive-behavioral treatment programs include interventions aimed at changing several cognitive constructs. For example, a recent program developed by Seligman and Reivich (1995; Gillham, Reivich, Jaycox, & Seligman, 1995) to prevent adolescent depression targeted Ellis's irrational beliefs, Beck's automatic thoughts, Seligman's attributional styles, and social problem-solving skills. Seligman and Reivich's research included excellent methodology and provided important contributions to the field. The program also provided an example of the problems in cognitive assessment that confront clinicians who wish to guide their practice by science. Although Seligman and Reivich's research showed differences between untreated and treated groups, it did not demonstrate that each subject made gains in each of the cognitive constructs targeted. Thus, we do not know which cognitive constructs accounted for what proportion of the change in all subjects. Perhaps different subjects benefited because of changes in different cognitive constructs.

Consider the problems facing practitioners. Suppose a clinician treats a depressed adolescent using Seligman and Reivich's treatment manual. The therapist assesses depression weekly on an objective measure and also includes some ideographic measures of behavior relevant to the client, such as positive socializing experiences, or mastery activities. Suppose the client fails to improve and the clinician had measured one cognitive construct which demonstrated change. The clinician does not know which parts of the treatment package to continue, modify, or stress. Good behavioral practice would dictate assessment on all the cognitive variables to accurately determine if the treatment was having the desired impact. The therapist would have to regularly assess irrational beliefs, automatic thoughts, attributional styles, and problem-solving skills. Using different measures that focus on each of these constructs would challenge the compliance of any client. The clinician might be restricted to rely on more informal interview strategies to assess these constructs.

An additional clinical problem would be the adaptation of the Seligman and Reivich treatment manual to individual clients. Some adolescents may have deficits in only problem-solving skills, others may have only faulty attributions, and still others may hold only negative automatic thoughts or irrational beliefs. Best practice standards would dictate that the clinician design a treatment plan based on an assessment of the problem and the resulting data concerning which particular cognitive constructs are mediating the particular clients' problem. This rarely occurs. Most clinicians and researchers start with an *a priori* theoretical notion of which cognitive constructs mediate the symptoms and assess only that construct. CBT research has failed to demonstrate that focused interventions based on an assessment that indicated which cognitive constructs mediate a particular client's problems can affect outcome. That is, we have failed to demonstrate that individualized treatment, perhaps deduced from manualized principles, leads to effective change. This problem may have risen from the failure of researchers to assess more than one cognitive construct.

No research exists comparing the roles of the various cognitive constructs in mediating behavior or emotions. Most research focuses on simple correlations of the researcher's favored cognitive construct and a measure of some psychopathology, or a comparison of disturbed and normal groups on a measure of the cognitive construct. More research is needed comparing the contribution of the various cognitive constructs. Perhaps attributional style, irrational beliefs, and automatic thoughts share a common path to emotional disturbance and each has little or no unique variance independent of the other. Perhaps they all contribute some unique variance. Perhaps each shows unique variance only with certain populations or certain types of psychopathology. Until researchers answer such questions, clinicians are faced with the question of which cognitive construct to measure.

ASSESSING MORE THAN ONE CONSTRUCT

One strategy to resolve this problem is the development of instruments that can measure different cognitive constructs. One such device is Davison's "articulated thoughts in simulated situations" paradigm (ATSS) (Davison, Navarre, & Vogel, 1995; Davison, Robin, & Johnson, 1983). Subjects are asked to review seven 30-second audiotapes of situations that simulate the eliciting stimuli for their problem. After each situation, they are asked to speak into a microphone all of the thoughts that run through their minds. Subjects' responses to the ATSS can be coded for various cognitive constructs. Thus, one could learn from the assessment that the client thinks global, stable, internal attributions for failure, self-deprecatory self-evaluations, and fails to produce problem-solving strategies or coping statements. The ATSS has been shown to be a valid measure in studying depression, hypertension, speech and social anxiety, smoking relapse,

family conflict, and aggression. It has proved to be superior to standard paper-and-pencil questionnaires in detecting change in cognition from therapeutic interventions (Davison, Navarre, & Vogel, 1995).

ASSESSING SCHEMA-BASED MODEL OF COGNITION

Muran (1991) proposed a revised theory of cognitive mediation of emotional disturbance in which schema are the core cognitions that moderate other cognitive constructs. This model provides an excellent conceptual framework that subsumes most of the existing CBT models. A major strength of this model is its integration of information processing models of cognitive processing with cognitive-behavioral models of emotional disturbance.

The model proposes that individual cognitive processes center around schemata for emotional events. These schemata are defined as "cognitive structures that consist of procedural knowledge about particular events, which the mind extracts in the course of exposure to particular instances of events . . . and exerts an organizing influence on that information" (Muran, p. 405). Types of knowledge represented within schemata identified in the clinical literature include self-schemata (Markus, 1977) and interpersonal schemata (Safran & Greenberg, 1991), each of which includes cognitive, affective, and motoric components. Perceptions, inferences (automatic thoughts), and evaluations of the stimulus situation are viewed as fluid, continuous, intrinsically integrated, and never experienced in isolation of themselves or of their relevant schemata. In addition, the cognitive, affective, and motoric processes are never experienced in isolation, in accordance with other previous integrational models (Ellis, 1962, 1985; Gibson, 1979; Mahoney, 1991; Neisser, 1976; Schwartz, 1982). The schema is proposed to be the cognitive structure that integrates all of the cognitive, affective, and behavioral processes. These schemata are higher-order constructs from which other cognitive constructs are deduced. Most of the cognitive constructs in cognitive-behavioral theoretical models can be integrated and explained according to this schema-based model.

Ellis's (1962, 1994) Rational Emotive Behavior Therapy breaks down emotional and behavioral disturbances along the ABC continuum and divides cognition into at least two separate categories: inferences and irrational beliefs. The A, or Activating Event, can be categorized as either perceptions, inferences, emotions, or behaviors in Muran's model, and the C is easily described by the affective and motoric components. Irrational beliefs (the B) may fit into at least two categories: evaluative cognition (e.g., "It is terrible and awful if I do not have a relationship partner") and schematic beliefs (e.g., "I must have others' love and be involved in a romantic relationship to be a worthwhile human being"). Muran's schemata model therefore includes all of Ellis's constructs.

Beck's (1976) conceptualization of automatic thoughts can be classified as inferences, including the irrational processes of arbitrary inference, selective abstraction, and overgeneralization. The process of magnification/minimization appears to be best described as an evaluative cognitive process. Similarly, Beck's concepts of underlying core beliefs can be classified at both the evaluation and schema level in Muran's model. For example, an individual may have an autonomous schema-level belief connecting one's sense of self-worth to one's achievements. One might also magnify the conditions in the world at an irrational evaluative level (i.e., "The world is a terrible, awful place that is not at all enjoyable"). Thus, Muran's model also includes all of Beck's constructs.

The cognitive conceptualizations of locus of control (Rotter, 1954, 1966), efficacy expectation (Bandura, 1982, 1986), and coping (Lazarus & Folkman, 1984; Lazarus, 1991, 1995) are all best classified as schema-level processes. The distinction between core versus periperheral beliefs (Arnkoff, 1980; Guidano & Liotti, 1983; Kelly, 1955; Mahoney, 1982) is also easily understood according to Muran's model. Kendall's (1985) conceptualization of deficient versus distorted information processing also appears to be related to core schemata. Since core schemata may influence attention to and perception of information that is consistent with the schemata (DiGiuseppe, 1991), Muran's model appears capable of explaining all of the cognitive constructs from information processing models in CBT.

Some cognitive constructs are not easily accounted for according to Muran's model. Values and goal hierarchies (Lazarus, 1995) and social problem-solving skills (Spivack, Platt, & Shure, 1975) have not been related to schemata. These constructs may have to be assessed independently.

Cognitive assessment strategies need to extract information from as many cognitive constructs as possible, so that practitioners and researchers understand which type or types of cognition are mediating the presenting disorder. For example, in treating an anxiety-disordered adult, the assessment and (therefore) treatment would be incomplete if the therapist relied solely on increasing the client's problem-solving skills (Spivack, Platt, & Shure, 1975) or challenging their automatic thoughts (Beck, 1976), without attending to the underlying irrational beliefs for anxiety at the schema level (Beck, Freeman, & Associates, 1990; Ellis, 1994). Multiple cognitive constructs would appear relevant to all cases, regardless of disorder.

Our present cognitive-behavioral theories are inexact, disconnected, and disjointed. There is no unifying construct that adds meaning to the plethora of variables that exist under the present rubric of CBT. Because Muran's model provides a conceptualization to link these disparate constructs, it is an excellent model to guide research and practice in the development of ideographic measures for cognitive assessment. Future research could focus on the assessment of Muran's self and interpersonal schemata and the relationship of such measures with measures of other cognitive constructs. Such research would help confirm whether the cognitive variables are linked. If they are related, practitioners can complete a comprehensive cognitive assessment by measuring only one or a few constructs. If they are not related, we will have a better understanding of which cognitive variables contribute unique variance to psychopathology and can plan assessment accordingly.

CATEGORIZATION OF COGNITIVE ASSESSMENT METHODS

Numerous classification schemes for methods of cognitive assessment have been proposed. Differing classifications attempt to order the content, process, focus, valence, balance, and parameters of the individual's schemata, evaluations, inferences, and perceptions. A review of the existing cognitive assessment methods is instructive because it provides the scientist practitioner with diverse assessment methods from which to choose (Glass, 1993; Heimberg, 1994; Merluzzi, 1991; Parks & Hollon, 1988). Existing methods should be used in combination to strengthen a multitrait/multimethod approach to assessment. The unique strengths of existing measures can be integrated in the development of new, more advanced measures.

Strategies of cognitive assessment are summarized next, including recognition methods, recall methods, prompted recall methods, expressive methods, projective methods, and inferential methods (Merluzzi, 1993; Parks & Hollon, 1988). In addition, methods for measuring schema, clinical interview assessment strategies, and the self-scenario model of assessment (Muran, 1991; Muran & Segal, 1992) are discussed.

Recognition Methods

Recognition methods typically require the subject to endorse thought items according to frequency or degree of belief. Most nomothetic measures of cognitive assessment used in current clinical research and practice fall within this category.

Examples of recognition measures attempting to evaluate cognition at the evaluative and schema levels are the Attitude and Belief Scale (Burgess, 1990, DiGiuseppe, Robin, Leaf, & Gorman, 1989), the Dysfunctional Attitudes Scale (Weissman & Beck, 1978), the Irrational Belief Test (Jones, 1968), and the Personal Beliefs Test (Kassinove 1986). The Automatic Thought Questionnaire (Hollon & Kendall, 1980) and the Checklist of Positive and Negative Thoughts (Galassi, Frierson, & Sharer, 1981) assess cognition at the inference level. The Cognition Checklist (Beck, Brown, Steer, Eidelsen, & Riskind, 1987) and the Social Interaction Self Statement Test (Glass, Merluzzi, Biever, & Larsen, 1982) are inference level, disorde-specific assessment measures. The Cognitive Bias Questionnaire (Hammen & Krantz, 1976; Krantz & Hammen, 1979) attempts to measure both the content and process of distorted cognition at the inference level.

Limitations of Self-Report Questionnaires

Once clinicians decide what to measure, they are faced with choosing a method of assessment. The most common assessment strategy in cognitive assessment is the self-report questionnaire. Such questionnaires exist to measure negative automatic thoughts (Hollon & Kendall, 1980), dysfunctional attitudes (Weissman & Beck, 1978), irrational beliefs (Burgess, 1990; DiGiuseppe, Robin, Leaf, & Gorman, 1989), and dysfunctional core schemata (Schmidt, Joiner, Young, & Teich, 1995).

Such scales are usually developed to test scientific theories. Theoreticians propose that certain cognitive constructs mediate psychopathology. Items for such scales are designed to represent examples of the dysfunctional cognition. Higher scores indicate that an individual endorses more items reflecting the type of cognition the scale measures. Scores indicating higher levels of endorsement of the selected cognition correlate with measures of psychopathology. The development of a psychometrically reliable and valid scale demonstrates the construct validity of the cognitive construct in question. Such scales are used to provide scientific evidence for the proposed construct. Thus, the clinician can assume that persons scoring high on the scale experience the type of cognition the scale assesses. The literature is filled with construct-specific scales and their relationship to certain types of psychopathology. A review of the psychometric and scientific merit of this body of research is beyond the scope of this chapter and inconsistent with its goals.

The problem with all such cognitive-assessment scales is that they were not designed for clinical practice but to validate constructs. Self-report scales rely on retrospective memory. What the client reports *post hoc* may not be what goes through his or her mind at the time of the target problem. Self-report scales are always structured in some way, and clients are constrained by the items presented. Each scale measures only one cognitive construct. Clinicians have to make *a priori* decisions concerning what cognition mediates the target problem when they design the assessment battery. Thus, the measures may fail to disconfirm the clinician's bias that a particular cognitive construct is the one that mediates the clinical problem.

Questionnaires also allow for false negative findings. Most cognitive theories propose that a given process of thinking is related to psychopathology. Given a specific activating event, and given the patient's disposition to use the cognitive process, one can expect psychopathology. If the client fails to endorse the examples of the cognitive construct included on the scale, the assessor cannot necessarily conclude that the client does not hold such thoughts. The client may endorse thoughts similar to those cognitive constructs assessed on the test, but his or her thoughts are not directly represented in the sample of items included on the test (Wessler & Wessler, 1980). A high score on such a test may mean that the person frequently performs the type of process measured by the test (e.g., overgeneralization, selective abstraction, irrational thinking). A low score may mean that the person does not employ the cognitive process measured by the test, or that the person does hold such beliefs but holds a rare or idiosyncratic version of that belief not sampled by the test.

Another issue is whether cognitive therapies target change in the cognitive processes or change in the specific cognition that mediates the client's particular target problem. Beck's cognitive therapy (CT) or Ellis's REBT (1994) may identify a type of cognitive process as leading to psychopathology, such as selective abstraction and demandingness, respectively. Is the goal of therapy to eliminate that cognitive process altogether, or to eliminate the particular example of that cognitive process that precedes or mediates the target behavior? It appears that targeting the cognitions that immediately precede the presenting problem is the primary goal of most forms of cognitive therapy, especially those that focus on changing various dysfunctional or irrational beliefs. Helping the client eliminate the thought process completely may be an ultimate goal to prevent the client from having further problems.

Several cognitive-behavior therapists have pointed out that people can hold or endorse dysfunctional thoughts without these thoughts leading to emotional or behavioral disturbance, or without the dysfunctional thoughts being related to the particular disturbance the person presents with (Freeman, Pretzer, Fleming, & Simon, 1990; Walen, DiGiuseppe, & Dryden, 1992). Cognitive theories specify that psychopathology is caused by the interaction of the presence of an eliciting stimulus and a dysfunctional cognition. Ellis's (1994) ABC model provides that people must have both the activating event and the irrational belief to experience emotional disturbance. Beck (Beck, Freeman, & Associates, 1990) has proposed a similar model. He believes that dysfunctional thoughts or schema are activated by the presence of certain events or stimuli. The beliefs can remain dormant and may not lead to disturbance unless activated by critical events. The identification of dysfunctional or irrational beliefs by a self-report questionnaire may lead clinicians to target beliefs that clients hold but that are unrelated to the presenting problem.

This does not mean that self-report questionnaires have no treatment utility. Rather, it means that they have limited treatment utility. Self-report measures can provide the clinician with good hypotheses about what cognitions are mediating the target problems. However, these are only hypotheses. The relationship between the hypothesized target cognition and the clients' identified emotional and behavioral problems needs to be tested.

Recall Methods

Recall or production methods require the subject to list, orally or in writing, his or her thoughts that occurred before, during, or after a selected event. Examples of this method include the RET Self-Help Form (Sichel & Ellis, 1984) and the Daily Record of Dysfunctional Thoughts (Beck, Rush, Shaw, & Emery, 1979). Thought-listing methods are an integral part of most cognitive-behavioral treatments.

Disadvantages to recall methods include greater susceptibility to social reactivity and developmental-cognitive limitations. Subjects may edit the content of responses so as to present in a more socially desirable manner, record relatively few cognitions, and exclude lower-frequency cognitions that may have high relevancy (Cacioppo & Petty, 1981). The subject's written expressive skills, especially in the case of children and those with limited education or intellectual ability, may in turn limit the usefulness of this approach. An advantage of this method is its flexibility across varying events, contexts, and times.

Prompted Recall Methods

An alternative recall strategy is the prompted recall method. Here, the subjects' thoughts are elicited by means of situational stimulus cues rather than retrospective reports. Two examples of the prompted recall methods are thought dubbing (Smye & Wine, 1980) and articulated thoughts (Davison, Robins, & Johnson, 1983). Each involves the video- or audiotaped presentation of a person in a conflict scenario. The subject is asked either to dub in the thoughts as if he or she was the person in the video, or to provide the thoughts and feelings of the person during intermittent pauses inserted every 30 seconds on the tape. Subject reactivity may be decreased in this method, but construct validity remains problematic. It is unclear whether the subjects' reports of the stimulus characters thoughts are reflective of their own thoughts in that situation, as self and other schema may differ substantially.

Expressive Methods

Expressive or concurrent cognitive assessment methods require the subject to think aloud as he or she is performing a task. Variations of the method include having the subject think aloud during imagined social interactions (Craighead, Kimball, & Rehak, 1979; Goldfried & Sobocinski, 1975) and a time-sampling method (Hurlburt & Melancon, 1987; Pope & Singer, 1978). Another variation is to have the subject review an audiotape of himself or herself in an actual conversation and to stop the tape whenever a thought that occurred during the conversation is recalled (Johnson & Glass, 1989). The assessment of private speech (Kendall & Hollon, 1981b; Roberts & Tharp, 1980) used by children during task performance can also be classified as a concurrent expressive method.

Although this method is recommended by some as the best overall method of cognitive assessment (Merluzzi, 1993; Merluzzi & Boltwood, 1989), its limitations remain. The actual performance of the think-aloud task may distort the content of cognition as compared to when the subjects' thoughts remain private (Kendall & Hollon, 1981a). Certain tasks do not lend well to reporting thoughts aloud concurrent with performing the actual task, such as in social interactions (Kendall & Hollon, 1981a; Kendall & Ellsas Chansky, 1991), public speaking, or performing arts. Davison, Navarre, and Vogel (1995) point out that traditional think-aloud strategies are limited because subjects may report only a portion of their thoughts, and highly relevant but low frequency thoughts may be omitted.

Davison and colleagues have altered the think-aloud method and developed the Articulated Thoughts in Simulated Situations (ATSS) paradigm (see Davison, Navarre, & Vogel [1995] for a review). The subjects are asked to listen to simulated two- to three-minute audiotapes of scenarios relevant to the presenting problem and to imagine that they are in the situation. The audiotapes pause at crucial spots and subjects are asked to verbalize their thoughts into a microphone. The ATSS paradigm has been used with numerous clinical problems, and reliable coding schemes have been developed to rate different cognitive constructs. Results of the ATSS have been shown to change in response to therapy.

The ATSS appears to be one of most promising methods of cognitive assessment for both research and practice. Clinicians can devise simulated situations from the client's report of actual problem scenarios. Clients can then articulate what they are thinking when they replay the scenario on tape. This strategy allows clinicians to assess several different cognitive constructs in situations relevant to the clients' presenting problems.

Measuring Schema

The assessment methods noted thus far are primarily used to assess cognitions in the stream of consciousness. Recent discussions in CBT have focused on the schemata as a coreunifying construct (Beck, Freeman, & Associates, 1991; Freeman, Pretzer, Fleming, & Simon, 1991; Muran, 1991; Persons, 1989; Young, 1995). Schemata are not usually stream-of-consciousness beliefs, but are best described as underlying cognitive structures that are accessible to language. They usually are inferred from automatic thoughts or other cognition uncovered in recall or expressive assessment (Beck, Freeman, & Associates, 1990; DiGiuseppe, 1991; Persons, 1989; Young, 1995). The assessment of cognition in recall and expressive strategies would still require some inference to identify such constructs.

The assessment of schematic cognition creates unique problems in cognitive assessment for behavior therapists since one is measuring a construct that cannot be directly observed or reported. Rather, it must be inferred from other stream-of-consciousness thoughts, behaviors, and emotions. Given the increasing popularity of schematic-based approaches to CBT, the reliable and valid assessment of schemata is crucial if the field is to maintain its credibility. Research and clinical strategies in this area of assessment cannot be separated from the inference process of the assessor. Thus, procedures should focus on the data gatherer who does the inferring, and the cognitive processes involved in his or her inference development.

Projective Methods

One popular method of inferential assessment in clinical psychology has been projective tests. In the application of projective methods to cognitive assessment, subjects are asked to state what a person in a picture or vignette might be thinking. Examples of such methods are Sobel's (1981) Cancer Problem Solving Projective Test and the Cognitive Response Test (Watkins & Rush, 1983), an open-ended sentence completion task. These projective methods rely on inferences made by the subject and require little interpretation by the clinician or researcher. The issue of construct validity is highly problematic with projective measures. However, the problem of social desirability responding may be decreased when one is asked to describe someone else's reactions in a more ambiguous yet conflict-related scenario. The potential for projective assessment appears yet untested.

Inferential Methods

Inferential methods (see discussion by Parks & Hollon, 1988) are perhaps better than projective

methods in addressing the problems of response bias and demand characteristics. They are typically indirect, since the cognitive constructs being tested are not readily apparent to the subject. Two common methods include social categories and category-judgment tasks. In the first, subjects are presented with a general social category and asked to provide its features. In the second, subjects are presented with specific features and asked to name the category to which the features belong. Examples of inferential assessment measure of self-schemata are the Self Referent Encoding Task (Derry & Kuiper, 1981; Kuiper, Olinger, MacDonald, & Shaw, 1985), and an adaptation of the Stroop color naming task (Segal, 1988; Segal & Vella, 1990). These methods rely on a combination of number and type of self-descriptive adjectives and response-latency measures to infer underlying self-schemata.

Other inferential methods outlined in Parks and Hollon (1988) include organization in free recall tasks (in which information recalled is interpreted as being clustered along schematic lines), autobiographical memory, and the mapping of psychological space. The subjects' personal metaphors (DiGiuseppe & Muran, 1992; Muran & DiGiuseppe, 1990) are an additional inferential cognitive assessment approach. Imagery can also be employed in the assessment of daydreams and fantasies (Beck, 1970; Tower & Singer, 1981) in order to infer underlying cognitive constructs. Although many of the inferential techniques are more in line with a psychoanalytic, enduring trait approach to assessment, they can serve to complement other traditional behaviorally based cognitive assessment methods within a multimethod assessment approach (Merluzzi, 1993).

Clinical Interview Format of Cognitive Assessment

A final category of cognitive assessment is the clinical interview. This method may take the form of a structured, semistructured, or unstructured interview. The clinician may simply ask the subject to recall an upsetting situation and what he or she was thinking and feeling at the time and then infer the client's more tacit cognitions (Ellis 1994; Arnkoff & Glass 1989; Walen, DiGiuseppe, &

Dryden, 1992). Other methods, such as inference chaining (Moore, 1983), attempt to access the subject's core irrational beliefs and dysfunctional schemata. In the inference-chaining technique, the therapist explores the client's automatic thoughts and purposefully avoids challenging them. Rather, the therapist asks the client to imagine what would happen if the inference were true until the schema level beliefs are accessed. Variations on the inference-chaining production methods include systematic evocative unfolding (Rice, 1984), vertical exploration (Safran, Vallis, Segal, & Shaw, 1986), chaining (DiGiuseppe, 1991; Dryden, 1989; Moore, 1983), and guided imagery through the restructuring of early memories (Edwards, 1990).

After reviewing the literature on schema models of CBT, it appears that most authors utilize or recommend an inductive interpretation approach to assessing these constructs (DiGiuseppe, 1991). This strategy involves collecting clients' automatic thoughts either during the interview or through automatic thought logs. The therapist then inductively infers the common theme that runs through the collection of automatic thoughts. In this method, the client collects the automatic thoughts, and the inference is made by the therapist through induction. Despite the widespread popularity of these approaches, surprisingly little research has occurred in schema-focused CBT to understand the process by which clinicians infer their clients' cognitions. Also, research has not addressed how the reliability of clinicians' inferences, or the accuracy of schema identification, affects therapy outcome.

Combining Interview and Recognition Methods

Muran and Segal (1992) developed the self-scenario model of assessment (Muran, 1991; Muran & Segal, 1992; Muran, Segal, & Wallner Samstag, 1994), which combines the inferential and recognition methods that is an ideographic measure of schema. The self-scenarios are designed according to the specific cognition of each individual client from clinical interviews with each client. The measure includes situation-specific cognitive, affective, and motoric components. The items constructed for each client are rated on multiple dimensions, including frequency of scenario occur-

rence, preoccupation, accessibility of alternatives, self-efficacy, self-view, interpersonal view, and chronicity. Also, each item contains components of situation-specific cognitive perceptions, inferences, evaluations, and schemata. The self-scenario method may lead to increased construct validity, which has been most often cited as problematic for previously existing self-report/recognition measures (Abelson, 1981; Glass, 1993; Muran & Siegal, 1992).

Instead of relying solely on the subject's recognition of a belief, information generated directly from clinical interviews is formulated into individual self-scenarios. Each scenario contains components of the individual client's problematic stimulus situation, cognitive responses, affective responses, and motoric responses.

During the initial sessions, the therapist or researcher generates a number of possible scenarios that represent the core schema the interviewer believes the client holds. Next, the therapist, client, and a third-party observer rate the client's scenarios, and the scenarios of clients with similar problems, for relevancy and reliability. The most clinically relevant self-scenarios for the individual client are selected and readministered in a repeated measures fashion across sessions. For each successive assessment, the client is presented with the same self-scenario(s) and asked to rate it (them) on the following parameters on five-point Likert scales (Muran & Segal, 1992, p. 528):

1. *Frequency:* "How often has such a scenario occurred recently?"
2. *Preoccupation:* "How concerned have you been about this happening recently?"
3. *Accessibility:* "How easily can you imagine such a scenario?"
4. *Alternatives:* "How easily can you imagine alternatives for you in this scenario?"
5. *Self-efficacy:* "How confident are you about your ability to act on these alternatives?"
6. *Self-view:* "How well does this scenario describe you?"
7. *Interpersonal view:* "How well does this scenario describe your relationship with others?"
8. *Chronicity* (one-time rating only): "How far back in your life can you recall this scenario occurring?"

Clients' ratings of the different aspects of their beliefs in the schemata is a recognition task. However, it differs from other questionnaires since the items were directly constructed from each client's experience. Clients' repeated answers to the self-scenario questionnaire provides the therapist with information on the progress in changing the schema and what aspects need further attention. Other treatment outcome measures can be obtained to assess the degree to which change in schemata co-vary or precede changes in treatment outcome measures.

Evaluating Inferences

The problem with clinician-inference methods of assessment is the potential error in clinician judgments and the failure to collect additional evidence to falsify or corroborate the clinician's hypotheses. DiGiuseppe (1991) points out that although all clinical inference may rely on psychological induction, there is an inherent error in relying on logical induction to confirm inferences. Inference concerning clients' core schemata are the clinicians' hypotheses. Data are required to confirm or falsify such hypotheses. Clinicians easily and quickly formulate hypotheses concerning their client's core schemata in CBT. Reliance on inductive data collection processes fails to provide a process to disconfirm clinicians' hypotheses because of the common human foible of confirmatory bias in memory and data collection.

DiGiuseppe (1991) suggested that clinicians could guard against adopting invalid schemata by adapting Popper's (1968) philosophy of science to clinical practice. Clinicians need to acknowledge that their inferences about clients' schemata are only hypotheses that need to be evaluated. According to Popper's model, one can only adequately test a hypothesis by allowing for its falsification. Once a clinician draws a hypothesis concerning a client's core schema, he or she needs to devise interview questions or data collection strategies to allow this hypothesis to be falsified. If the hypothesis is falsified, more data are collected until a new hypothesis is formed and attempts at falsification are tried again. If the hypothesized schema is not falsified, and corroborating evidence is obtained, the therapist targets interventions to change the schema. It

should be noted that these hypotheses can never be proved. Continued assessment of a measure of the schema and the specific behaviors and emotions that the schema supposedly mediates simply provides further evidence that the clinician chose the correct construct.

Muran and Segal's (1992) scenario model follows these procedures. The inferences drawn by the therapist, as well as other closely related items, are rated by three people for relevance. This provides an opportunity for the therapist's inferences to be falsified. The resulting scale constructed from the scenario allows ongoing assessment for the construct to evaluate its reaction to therapy and its relationship to other outcome measures. DiGiuseppe, Hutchinson, and Naiditch (1995) utilized a similar strategy to assess client core irrational beliefs in a study to evaluate Ellis's rational emotive behavior therapy. They developed several ideographic items reflecting Ellis's core irrational beliefs for each client. Alternative forms of these beliefs were developed. These ideographic measures were given to 10 clients at the beginning of each session to test Ellis's hypothesis that challenging demanding irrational beliefs would result in change in other types of irrational beliefs.

Selection of Cognitive Assessment Measures

The selection of cognitive assessment measures needs to be theory driven, disorder specific, and developmentally appropriate (DiGiuseppe, 1989; Kendall, 1991; Kendall & Hollon, 1981a; Segal & Shaw, 1988). For example, a researcher or clinician who subscribes to a multidimensional conceptualization of disturbed emotion would look for a measure(s) that included cognitive, affective, and behavioral components of perceptions, inferences, evaluations, and schema. He or she would choose a measure in which the situation, cognition, emotions, and behaviors were relevant to a specific individual with a specific problem. In addition, the methodology would be easily understood and adequately performed in accordance with the subject's cognitive abilities and developmental level. Thus, the researcher would steer away from assessment techniques with complex written expressive demands when assessing children or adults with bor-derline-level cognitive abilities.

Multiple methods of measuring convergent and divergent constructs should be selected. Reliability concerns would focus less on test-retest reliability, due to the expected variation in cognition across settings and time (Glass, 1993). If a recognition method was employed, internal consistency versus inter-rater reliability would be a prominent criteria for evaluating reliability (Glass, 1993). In attempts to establish the predictive validity of the measure, one could select from among combinations of both concurrent and future measures of cognition, affect, and behavior.

It appears to be important to compare measures of different cognitive constructs. Although research and practice are theory driven, assessing only the cognitive constructs consistent with one's theory fails to allow for falsification. Providing measures for multiple constructs allows for evidence that other cognitions may account for the change in the target variables better than the hypothesized variable.

Research Recommendations

Based on the considerations mentioned here, we recommend the following guidelines for future research in cognitive assessment:

1. The selection of assessment instruments should be theory driven, disorder specific, and developmentally guided.

2. Develop diverse ideographic measures of cognitive assessment to add to the relatively few existing models. These measures should attempt to account for hierarchical levels of schemata (Muran, 1991), idiosyncratic attitudes and higher-level constructs (Safran et al., 1986), and the distinction between vulnerability versus episodic schemata (Hammen, Marks, DeMayo, & Mayol, 1985; Beck, 1976; Kovacs & Beck, 1978).

3. Use multiple methods of cognitive assessment within the same study (Blackwell, Galassi, Galassi, & Watson, 1985) and use alternatives to the commonly employed assessment methods. Innovative, alternative methods include an adaptation of the Stroop Color Naming Task (Segal, 1988; Segal

& Vella, 1990; Warren 1972), the ATSS (Davison, Navarre, & Nagel, 1995), and the self-scenarios method (Muran, 1991; Muran & Siegel, 1992; Muran, Segal & Wallner-Samstag, 1994).

4. Combine Muran and colleagues' self-scenario method of assessment with DiGiuseppe's hypothesis-driven model of assessment (DiGiuseppe, 1991). Muran's model provides cognitive constructs and parameters to be included in the evaluation of the schema. DiGiuseppe's model provides an interviewing strategy by which clients' schema-level cognitions can be accessed and the clinician's inferential processes involved in developing the self-scenario can be evaluated.

5. Assess cognition on the core level (schema-based irrational beliefs, or core dysfunctional beliefs), and at the periphery (automatic thoughts, inferences, perceptions) to determine the degree of common versus specific variance such thoughts contribute to emotional disturbance. Evaluate treatment efficacy when treatment is focused at the core level of cognition, the periphery level of cognition, or both in combination.

6. Assess the impact of context and demand characteristics on cognitive assessment (Merluzzi & Boltwood, 1989).

7. Develop ecologically valid cognitive assessment measures (Merluzzi & Boltwood, 1989).

Recommendations for Clinical Practice

Cognitive-behavioral clinicians should incorporate the integrational models of cognitive constructs and research-based methods of cognitive assessment into their practice. Muran's (1991) model for emotional episodes can serve as an integrational model to guide the cognitive assessment process. In selecting their assessment tools, practitioners need to choose ideographic measures that will be sensitive to individual change across treatments.

Adaptations of empirically based methods of cognitive assessment such as the self-scenario method (Muran, 1991; Muran & Segal, 1992; Muran, Segal, & Wallner Samstag, 1994) and the ATSS (Davison, Navarre, & Nagel, 1995) can be used in clinical practice. The individual practitioner may not have the time or resources available to have independent interviewers and raters assist in constructing and validating the self-scenarios. However, the practitioner can devise effective self-scenarios based on the client's report by assuring that the key factors and parameters of the self-scenario model are included. Once the scenarios have been constructed, the practitioner could use these scenarios as ideographic measures across sessions. Multiple methods of assessment in addition to the self-scenario method should be employed to enhance the validity of the assessment procedure and thereby the efficacy of treatment interventions.

Clinicians can effectively and efficiently develop ideographic measures to assess clients' situation-specific perceptions, inferences, evaluations, and schema in their attempts to develop a self-scenario measure. Such measures could serve to guide interventions and assess treatment progress across sessions. We recommend an active-directive hypothesis-driven model of assessment as outlined by DiGiuseppe (1991). This model of clinical interviewing allows for cognitive assessment at the individual client level and can easily be included in each therapy session. In the hypothesis-driven model, the therapist actively guides the client in accessing his or her inferences, evaluations, and tacit schema-level cognition. The therapist's hypothesis-driven, guided inquiries allow for the client's preconscious-level schema to be accessed in an individualized manner, while making allowances for situation specificity of cognition, falsifiability of hypotheses, and modification of hypotheses based on client feedback on a session-by-session basis. The major components of this model include:

1. Assessment is an ongoing process across the duration of treatment. Intervention is begun as soon as relevant cognition and disturbed emotions and behaviors are presented by the client.

2. Traditional logical-positivist, medical models of assessment are rejected. Instead, the therapist employs a combination of psychological induction to formulate hypotheses regarding the clients' difficulties, and hypothesis-driven deduction, in which the therapist actively attempts to falsify his or her inductively derived hypotheses.

3. The therapist's influence on the data gathering process—including preferential memory for, interest in, and reinforcement of hypothesis-supporting information—is acknowledged. Recommendations for avoiding such errors include (a) deducing facts that would be expected to be true if the hypothesis is true, and false if the hypothesis is false; (b) active collaboration with the client to confirm or disconfirm the hypotheses; (c) the therapist's willingness to accept that his or her hypotheses and interpretations, no matter how profound, may in fact be false (and not simply the client's resistance); and (d) the therapist's active generation of new, diverse hypotheses, which in turn can be falsified or confirmed by the client.

Inference chaining is recommended as the most efficient means for assessing irrational disturbed cognition or core schema (DiGiuseppe, 1991; Walen, DiGiuseppe, & Dryden, 1992). For a clear review on the distinctions between inferences and evaluative beliefs and schema, see Muran (1991). Inferences are automatic thoughts. Inference chaining can quickly help the client become aware of his or her core, underlying dysfunctional schemata. Inference chaining involves the therapist requesting that the client assume that the inference is true. The therapist then follows with Socratic inquiries as to what would happen next, what it would mean to the client, or what it would mean about the client if the inference were true (Ellis, Young, & Lockwood, 1987).

The critical difference between the inference-chaining approach and other cognitive assessment methods such as inductive awareness and inductive interpretation (Beck & Emery, 1985) is that the inference-level cognitions are *not* challenged directly. Also, the therapist does not gather numerous related inferences in hopes of inductively interpreting the client's underlying core beliefs.

In addition, we propose these assessment methods can be employed to access dysfunctional schemata through assessing not only dysfunctional cognition but also emotions and behaviors. The therapist need not rely on following a distinct cognitive chain that is free from verbal references to behavior and affect. In keeping with Muran's integrational model (1991), the therapist would do better to direct the client through cognitive, emotive, and behavioral chaining in order to achieve a more complete understanding of their underlying schemata. The client may have difficulty verbalizing cognition, but might access more easily the related emotions or behaviors associated with core-level schemata. Client process indicators that occur as the therapist's deductive inquiries proceed are critical factors in the assessment process. A client's nonverbal cues and changes in voice intonation may be as important as the client's verbal confirmations of the therapist's hypotheses.

For example, clinical experience suggests that when the therapist has touched on a core-disturbed belief system, the client will frequently exhibit emotional and behavioral reactions. The client who was previously actively engaged in the conversation with the therapist may abruptly begin to avoid the therapist's questions, make little eye contact, evidence disturbed facial expressions, and work to change the subject. Or the client may become enlivened, as if a light bulb has been illuminated by the therapist's inquiries. The client may speak more, provide more rich and detailed information, have an animated facial expression, and work persistently with the therapist along this line of reasoning. In addition, the client's sudden anger and confrontational arguments with the therapist may also signal that a core belief has been elicited. It is these in-session "hot" emotions, cognition, and behaviors that may provide the most direct access to the client's schematic beliefs (Beck, Rush, Shaw, & Emery, 1979; Bower, 1981; Safran et al., 1986; Walen, DiGiuseppe, & Dryden, 1992).

The following is a dialogue of a therapist and client engaged in the hypothetico-deductive cognitive assessment process detailed here. This example involves the first session with a 40-year-old, socially phobic male client. He becomes highly anxious when asked to do monthly team presentations at his job, and he believes his difficulty may lead to the loss of his job. The inference-chaining dialogue begins after the point in the session where the therapist and client have established an agreement on treatment goals and tasks.

This model can also be applied to both internalizing and externalizing difficulties, and can be modified to accommodate clients of varying ages and cognitive ability levels. For specific modifications suggested for assessment with children, see DiGiuseppe (1989), Bernard and DiGiuseppe (1990), Bernard and Joyce (1984), and Linscott and DiGiuseppe (1994).

Case Example

Therapist: Can you give me an example of the last time the problem occurred?

Client: Yesterday we had a team conference at work, just like we do every month. It was terrible! My heart was pounding and I was sweating, and I knew everyone was noticing. I just can't handle any sort of meeting like this; it happens every time. And when the boss asks for my input, all I can say is "I'm not sure." I kept thinking, they'll fire me soon if I don't shape up!

Therapist: I'd like to help you learn ways to handle that intense anxiety you put yourself through whenever you're in a group setting.

Client: I don't think I'll ever learn how to handle it. Speaking in front of people just makes me nuts, and it always has.

Therapist: When you say "nuts," what does that mean?

Client: Like unbearable, like all tense and frozen.

Therapist: Would you say you mean anxious when you say nuts?

Client: Definitely.

Therapist: OK, so let's see if we can help you with that. We're going to try to figure out what you do to get yourself so anxious, instead of just appropriately concerned, when you speak in front of groups. Does that make sense?

Client: Yes, I think so.

(NOTE: At this point, the therapist begins the inference-chaining process.)

Therapist: OK, so now in these meetings, you feel anxious *because . . . ?*

Client: I see everyone there.

(The client reports a perception.)

Therapist: And when you see everyone there, you feel anxious *because . . . ?*

(The therapist repeats the client's perception and works to elicit a related cognition by use of conjunctive phrasing).

Client: Because they're all watching me and listening to me!

(The client reports an inference.)

Therapist: The worst thing about everyone watching and listening to you is . . . ?

(The therapist repeats the client's inference and adds conjunctive phrase in a different form).

Client: I might screw up in front of them! I'd start stuttering and messing up facts, and sounding totally stupid.

(The client reports more inferences.)

Therapist: And if you did screw up, *it would mean* . . . ?

(The therapist continues to repeat the inference and add a conjunctive phrase in an attempt to elicit core-level disturbed cognition.)

(NOTE: At this point, the client has reported several inferences. The therapist has not challenged these automatic thoughts, but rather works to connect the chain of inferences to the underlying disturbed schema.)

Client: They'd see that I screwed up and think how incompetent I was.

(Inference)

Therapist: So let's assume that's true. You screw up and they think you are incompetent. In fact, someone says, "Could someone else speak in his place? We don't have time to waste here!" Then how would you feel?

(NOTE: The therapist has changed the inference-chaining strategy from cuing the client for related thoughts, to cuing for related emotions. The therapist adds information to the scenario in an attempt to elicit a strong emotional response from the client in session.)

Client: I'd feel humiliated!

Therapist: And if you felt humiliated, what would you *do* then?

(The therapist's chaining strategy is now directed toward dysfunctional behaviors associated with the client's reported emotions and cognitions. By cuing the client for relevant affective, behavioral, and cognitive responses, the therapist has a greater likelihood of accessing

the client's underlying, situation-specific schema.)

Client: I'd probably choke up and turn red so I'd have to leave the room.

Therapist: You'd have to leave the room *because* . . . ?

(NOTE: At this point, the therapist has strong hypotheses that the client's self-schema revolve around the need for achievement and the need for others' approval in achievement-related areas. The client's self-acceptance is highly contingent on accomplishments (and lack of failures) and others' acknowledgment of accomplishments. The therapist will now attempt to confirm or disconfirm these hypotheses.)

Client: They would have seen how stupid I was, and they'd all be thinking that I was an idiot!

(Inference)

Therapist: If they did all think you were stupid, how would you *feel*?

(The inference is repeated and the therapist cues for an emotional reaction associated with this inference if it were true.)

Client: Terrible! I couldn't take it!

(The client reports an evaluative cognition.)

Therapist: And you couldn't take it if people thought you were stupid *because* . . . ?

(The therapist repeats the evaluative cognition and chains for further related, schema-level cognition.)

Client: What, are you kidding!! Would you like it? How awful! The whole room of people at work thinking you're a stupid idiot. They'd probably go tell other people all about it, and then other people at work not even on my team soon would know!!

(NOTE: At this point, the client continues to report evaluations and inferences. The therapist observes that the client's voice has raised and he is speaking more quickly and forcefully. The therapist has some evidence to support the hypothesized dysfunctional schema. The next step is to define the schema-level hypotheses for the client and to allow the client to provide confirming or disconfirming reactions to the hypotheses.)

Therapist: OK, let's assume they did go tell

other people, and the others began to think you were stupid. What would that mean to you?

Client: I couldn't take it. I mean, you have to get other people to think well of you at work!

(The client reports the first schema-level cognition regarding conditions of one's self-worth as related to others' acceptance and approval.)

Therapist: But wait, let's just pretend for a minute that you did your absolute best. You spoke clearly in the group and made some important points. Most of the people in the room told you afterwards you did a nice job today. But some whispered behind your back and looked at you as you were leaving the room with a disapproving face. Then how would you feel?

(NOTE: At this point, the therapist assumes that a relevant schema-level belief system has been activated. The therapist then attempts to further specify the schema at an individual level. This information will help in the intervention process wherein the therapist will challenge the client's schematic beliefs.)

Client: Terrible! I'd want to run away and hide!

Therapist: But there were still more people who told you that you did a good job? What does that mean?

Client: Nothing. They were just probably trying to be polite.

Therapist: OK, so if you don't get everyone at work to approve and compliment what you've said, what does that mean about you?

(NOTE: At this point, the therapist has clearly stated the client's disturbed schema and has begun to challenge schema-related beliefs. Intervention occurs as the assessment process continues.)

Client: That I'm totally incompetent.

Therapist: Would it make you incompetent in every way? At all of your job? At home? With friends? Or would it mean you had yet to develop adequate group presentation skills at this point in time in this particular job?

Client: OK, not in every way. But in the ways that really matter.

Therapist: What do you mean 'the ways that really matter'?

Client: Your performance at work is probably the most important thing about a person. If others think you're incompetent, there's a good chance that you are. And if I'm incompetent at my job, it's pointless. What good am I?

(NOTE: With the therapist's guiding questioning, inference chaining, and hypothesis testing, the client has accessed core schematic disturbed beliefs and is able to clearly state the schema in the first session.)

Therapist: So, people who are only average at speaking in groups are totally incompetent workers and are less worthwhile people than others who do well at that?

Client: Without a doubt.

(NOTE: The therapist will continue to clarify the parameters of the client's schema while disputing the client's core beliefs. New, alternative beliefs will be collaboratively developed and practiced in session.)

Once the therapist has obtained the client's situation-specific perceptions, inferences, evaluations, and schema, a brief self-scenario can be devised, as is discussed in Muran's (1991) research-based method of cognitive assessment. Questions assessing the frequency, preoccupation, accessibility, alternatives, self-efficacy, self-view, interpersonal view, and chronicity of the self-scenarios can then be added. The practitioner would develop multiple, problem-specific self-scenarios as new problems were revealed and assess the client's ratings of these self-scenarios at the end of each session. Each problem could be assessed and tracked in a similar manner. Clinicians might also wish to break down the cognitive responses contained within the scenarios into specific cognitive construct categories, such as automatic thoughts or irrational beliefs. They could then have the client rate the separate cognitive constructs, in addition to the entire scenario, in an attempt to determine which constructs may require further intervention.

Figure 6.1 contains a summary of the self-scenario components obtained from the clinical interview with the socially phobic client. The clinician would combine each of the components in the figure into paragraph form, and then ask the client to

Figure 6.1 Social phobic client's self-scenario as developed from
hypothesis-driven, inference-chaining interview format

Stimulus Situations

1. I have great difficulty when I have to present in front of my team at work.
2. I have great difficulty when my team watches and listens to me.

Cognitive Responses

1. I worry that I might stutter, mess up facts, and sound stupid.
   They'll know how incompetent I am at speaking in public!
   It's terrible if others do not rate my performance at work in a totally positive way.
2. If my co-workers have negative evaluations of me, it proves I'm totally incompetent at all tasks.

Affective Responses

1. I become anxious and worried.
2. I feel stupid and humiliated.

Motoric Responses

1. My heart pounds, my hands sweat, and I feel tense.
2. I have trouble speaking and concentrating.

Final Scenarios for Questionnaire

I have great difficulty when I have to present in front of my team at work. I worry that I might stutter, mess up facts, and sound stupid. They'll know how incompetent I am at speaking in public! It's terrible if others do not rate my performance at work in a totally positive way. I become anxious and worried. My heart pounds, my hands sweat, and I feel tense. I have great difficulty when my team watches and listens to me. If my co-workers have negative evaluations of me, it proves I'm totally incompetent at all tasks. I feel stupid and humiliated. I have trouble speaking and concentrating.

---

assess the scenario on a Likert scale according to the frequency, preoccupation, accessibility, alternatives, self-efficacy, self-view, and interpersonal view of the scenario (Figure 6.2). For an example of a question format to assess these parameters, see the discussion of Muran and Segal's (1992) method earlier. The chronicity parameter would also be assessed, but only during the first administration of each new scenario, as recommended in Muran's method.

SUMMARY

A multitrait/multimethod model of cognitive assessment, in which innovative idiographic assessment practices are employed, is recom-

mended for the future research and practice of cognitive-behavioral therapy. Further integration of existing theories and development of unified theories of cognitive-behavioral constructs will be critical to this process. Muran and colleagues' schema-based theoretical model and self-scenario assessment method, and DiGiuseppe's hypothesis-driven model of assessment provide models for future developments in the field of cognitive assessment. We encourage researchers and clincians to integrate and clarify the components of existing cognitive-behavioral theoretical models and assessment techniques reviewed in this chapter. In this fashion, we will continue to develop more comprehensive techniques that address the limitations of currently existing cognitive assessment strategies.

Figure 6.2   Likert scales for scenario in Figure 6.1

1. How often has such a scenario occurred recently?

1	2	3	4	5	6	7

   not at all   extremely

2. How concerned have you been about this happening?

1	2	3	4	5	6	7

   not at all   extremely

3. How easily can you imagine such a scenario?

1	2	3	4	5	6	7

   not at all   extremely

4. How well does the scenario describe you and your relationship with others?

1	2	3	4	5	6	7

   not at all   extremely

5. How far back in your life can you recall this scenario occurring?

1	2	3	4	5	6	7

   not at all   extremely

6. How easily can you imagine alternatives for you in this scenario?

1	2	3	4	5	6	7

   not at all   extremely

7. How confident are you about your ability to act on these alternatives?

1	2	3	4	5	6	7

   not at all   extremely

8. How often have you acted out these alternative scenarios recently?

1	2	3	4	5	6	7

   not at all   extremely

REFERENCES

Abelson, R. P. (1981). Psychological status of a script concept. *American Psychologist, 36*, 715–729.

Arnkoff, D. B. (1980). Psychotherapy from the perspective of cognitive theory. In M. Mahoney (Ed.), *Psychotherapy process: Current issues and future directions* (pp. 339–361). New York: Plenum.

Arnkoff, D. B., & Glass, C. R. (1989). Cognitive assessment in social anxiety and social phobia. *Clinical Psychology Review, 9,* 61–74.

Bandura, A. (1982). Self-efficacy mechanisms in human agency. *American Psychologists, 37* (2), 122–147.

Bandura, A. (1986). *Social foundations of thought and action: A social cognitive theory.* Englewood Cliff, NJ: Prentice Hall.

Barlow, D., Hayes, S. C., & Nelson, R. (1984). *The scientist practioner: Research and accountability in clinical and educational settings.* New York: Pergamon.

Beck, A. T. (1970). Role of fantasies in psychotherapy and psychopathology. *Archives of General Psychiatry, 9*, 324–333.

Beck, A. T. (1976). *Cognitive therapy and the emotional disorders*. New York: International Universities.

Beck, A. T., Brown, G., Steer, R. A., Eidelson, J. I., & Reskind, A. (1987). Differentiating anxiety and depression: A test of the cognitive content specificity hypothesis. *Journal of Abnormal Psychology, 96*, 179–183.

Beck A. T., & Emery, G. (1985). *Anxiety disorders and phobias: A cognitive perspective*. New York: Guilford.

Beck, A. T., Freeman, A., & Associates (1990). *Cognitive therapy and personality disorders*. New York: Guilford.

Beck, A. T., Rush, A. J., Shaw, B., & Emery, G. (1979). *Cognitive therapy of depression*. New York: Guilford.

Bernard, M. E., & DiGiuseppe, R. (1990). Rational emotive therapy and school psychology. *School Psychology Review, 19*, 267.

Bernard, M. E., & Joyce, M. (1984). *Rational emotive therapy with children and adolescents*. New York: Wiley.

Blackwell, R., Galassi, J., Galassi, M., & Watson, J. (1985). Are cognitive assessment methods equal? A comparison of think aloud and thought listing. *Cognitive Therapy and Research, 9*, 399–413.

Bower, G. H. (1981). Mood and memory. *American Psychologists, 36*, 129–148.

Burgess, P. M. (1990). Towards resolution of conceptual issues in the assesment of beliefs systems in rational emotive therapy. *Journal of Cognitive Psychotherapy: An International Quarterly, 4*, 171–184.

Cacioppo, J., & Petty, R. (1981). Effects of thought on the pleasantness ratings of p-o-x triads: Evidence for the three judgmental tendancies in evaluating social situations. *Journal of Personality and Social Psychology, 40*, 1000–1009.

Campbell, D. T., & Fisk, D. W. (1959). Convergent and discriminant validation by the multitrait-multimethod matrix. *Psychological Bulletin, 56*, 81–105.

Clark, D. A. (1988). The validity of measures of cognition: A review of the literature. *Cognitive Therapy and Research, 12*, 1–20.

Cone, J. P. (1988). Psychometric considerations and the multiple models of behavioral assessment. In A. S. Bellack & S. M. Hersen (Eds.), *Behavioral assessment: A practical handbook* (3rd ed., pp. 42–66). New York: Pergamon.

Cook, T., & Campbell, D. (1978). *Quasi-experimentation: Design and analysis issues for field settings*. Chicago: Boston: Houghton Mifflin.

Craighead, W. E., Kimball, W. H., & Rehak, P. J. (1979). Mood changes, physiological responses, and self-statements during social rejection imagery. *Journal of Consulting and Clinical Psychology, 47*, 385–396.

Davison, G. C., Navarre, S., & Vogel, R. (1995). The articulated thoughts in simulated situations paradigm: A think-aloud approach to cognitive assessment. *Current Directions in Psychological Science, 4*, 29–33.

Davison, G. C., Robins, C., & Johnson, M. K. (1983). Articulated thoughts during simulated situations: A paradigm for studying cognition in emotion and behavior. *Cognitive Therapy and Research, 7*, 17–40.

Derry, P., & Kuiper, N. (1981). Schematic processing and self-reference in clinical depression. *Journal of Abnormal Psychology, 90*, 286–297.

DiGiuseppe, R. (1989). Cognitive therapy with children. In A. Freeman, K. M. Simon, L. E. Butler, & H. Arkowitz (Eds.), *Comprehensive handbook of cognitive therapy* (pp. 249–266). New York: Plenum Press.

DiGiuseppe, R. (1990). A rational emotive model of assessment of school aged children. *School Psychology Review, 19*, 287–293.

DiGiuseppe, R. (1991). A rational-emotive model of assessment. In M. E. Bernard (Ed.), *Using rational-emotive therapy effectively* (pp. 151–172). New York: Plenum.

DiGiuseppe, R., Hutchinson, K., & Naiditch, J. (1995). *The effect of congruent or incongruent disputing strategies on irrational beliefs*. Unpublished manuscript, Albert Ellis Institute for Rational Emotive Behavior Therapy, New York.

DiGiuseppe, R., & Muran, C. (1992). The use of metaphor in rational-emotive therapy. *Psychotherapy in Private Practice, 10*, 151–161.

DiGiuseppe, R. Robin, M., Leaf, R., & Gorman, B. (1989 June). *A discriminative validation and factor analysis of a measure of irrational/rational beliefs*. Presented at the World Congress of Cognitive Therapy. Oxford, England.

Dryden, W. (1989). The use of chaining in rational-emotive therapy. *Journal of Rational-Emotive and Cognitive-Behavior Therapy, 7*, 59–66.

Edwards, D. J. A. (1990). Cognitive therapy and the restructuring of early memories through guided imagery. *Journal of Cognitive Psychotherapy: An International* Quarterly, *4*, 33–50.

Ellis, A. (1962). *Reason and emotion in psychotherapy*. Seacacus, NJ: Lyle Stuart.

Ellis, A. (1994). *Reason and emotion in psychotherapy: A comprehensive method of treating human disturbance revised and updated*. New York: Birch Lane Press.

Ellis, A., Young, J., & Lockwood, G. (1987), Cognitive therapy and rational emotive therapy: A dialogue. *Journal of Cognitive Psychotherapy: An International Quarterly, 1*, 205–255.

Follette, W. (1995) The last visitation of private events. *The Behavior Therapist, 18*, 57–58.

Freeman, A. F., Pretzer, J., Fleming, B., & Simon, K. M. (1990). *Clinical applications of cognitive therapy*. New York: Plenum.

Galassi, J., Frierson, H. & Sharer, R. (1981). Concurrent vs. retrospective assessment in test anxiety research. *Journal of Consulting and Clinical Psychology, 49*, 614–615.

Gibson, J. J. (1979). *The ecological approach to visual perception*. Boston: Houghton Mifflin.

Gillham, J., Reivich, K., Jaycox, L., & Seligman, M. (1995). Prevention of depressive symptoms in school children. *Psychological Science, 6*, 343–351.

Glass, C. (1993). A little more about cognitive assessment. *Journal of Counseling and Development, 71*, 546–548.

Glass, C. R., & Furlong, M. (1990). Cognitive assessment of social anxiety: Affective and behavioral correlates. *Cognitive Therapy and Research, 14*, 365–384.

Glass, C. R., Merluzzi, T.V., Biever, J. L., & Larsen, K. H. (1982). Cognitive assessment of social anxiety: Development and validation of a self-statement questionnaire. *Cognitive Therapy and Research, 6*, 35–55.

Goldfried, M. R., & Sobocinski, D. (1975). Effects of irrational beliefs on emotional arousal. *Journal of Consulting and Clinical Psychology, 43*, 504–510.

Guidano, V., & Liotti, G. (1983). *Cognitive processes and emotional disorder*. New York: Guilford.

Hammen, C., & Krantz, S. (1976). Effect of success and failure on depressive cognitions. *Journal of Abnormal Psychology, 85*, 577–586.

Hammen, C., Marks, T., DeMayo, R., & Mayol, A. (1985). Self-schema and risk for depression: A prospective study. *Journal of Personality and Social Psychology, 49*, 1147–1159.

Hayes, S. C. (1995). Why cognition are not causes. *The Behavior Therapist, 18*, 59–60.

Heimberg, R. G. (1994). Cognitive assessment strategies and the measurement of outcome of treatment for social phobia. *Behavior Research and Therapy, 32*, 269–280.

Hollon, S. D., & Kendall, P. C. (1980). Cognitive self-statements in depression: Development of an automatic thoughts questionnaire. *Cognitive Therapy and Research, 4*, 383–395.

Hurlburt, R. T., & Melancon, S. M. (1987). How are questionnaire data similar, and different from, thought sampling data? Five studies manipulating retrospectiveness, single movement focus, and indeterminacy. *Cognitive Therapy and Research, 11*, 681–704.

Johnson, R. L., & Glass, C. R. (1989). Heterosocial anxiety and direction of attention in high school boys. *Cognitive Therapy and Research, 13*, 509–526.

Jones, R. G. (1968). *A factored measure of Ellis' irrational belief system with personality and adjustment correlates*. Unpublished doctoral dissertation, Texas Technical College.

Kassinove, H. (1986). Self-reported affect and core irrational tinikin: A preliminary study. *Journal of Rational Emotive Therapy, 4*, 119–130.

Kelly, G. A. (1955). *The psychology of personal constructs*. New York: Norton.

Kendall, P. C. (1985). Toward a cognitive-behavioral model of child psychopathology and a critique of related interventions. *Journal of Abnormal Child Psychology, 13*, 357–372.

Kendall, P. C. (1991). Cognitive behavior therapy with children and adolescents. New York: Guilford.

Kendall, P. C., Ellsas, S., & Chansky, T. (1991). Considering cognition in anxiety-disordered children. *Journal of Anxiety Disorders, 5*, 167–185.

Kendall, P. C., & Hollon, S. D. (1981a). *Assessment strategies for cognitive behavioral interventions*. New York: Academic.

Kendall, P. C., & Hollon, S. D. (1981b). Assessing self-referent speech: Methods in the measurement of self-statements. In P. C. Kendall & S. D. Hollon (Eds.), *Assessment strategies for cognitive-behavioral interventions* (pp. 85–118). New York: Academic.

Kendall, P. C., & Korgeski, G. P. (1979). Assessment and cognitive-behavioral interventions. *Cognitive Therapy and Research, 3*, 1–22.

Kovacs, M., & Beck, A. T. (1978). Maladaptive cognitive strutures in depression. *American Journal of Psychiatry, 135*, 525–533.

Krantz, S., & Hammen, C. (1979). Assessment of cognitive bias in depression. *Journal of Abnormal Psychology, 88*, 611–619.

Kuiper, N., Olinger, L., MacDonald, M., & Shaw, B. (1985). Self-schema processing of depressed and non-depressed content: The effect of vulnerability to depression. *Social Cognition, 3*, 77–93.

Lazarus, R. S. (1991). *Emotion and adaption.* New York: Oxford University Press.

Lazarus, R. S. (1995). Cognition and emotion from the RET viewpoint. *Journal of Rational-Emotive and Cognitive-Behavior Therapy, 13*, 29–54.

Lazarus, R. S., & Folkman, S. (1984). *Stress, appraisal and coping.* New York: Springer.

Linscott, J., & DiGiuseppe, R. (1994). RET with children. In C. W. LeCroy (Ed.), *Handbook of Child and Adolescent Treatment Manuals* (pp. 5–40). New York: Lexington.

Mahoney, M. J. (1982). Psychotherapy and human change processes. In *Psychotherapy research and behavior change* (Vol. 1). Washington, DC: APA.

Mahoney, M. J. (1991). *Human change processes.* New York: Basic Books.

Markus, H. (1977). Self-schemata and processing information about the self. *Journal of Personality and Social Psychology, 35*, 63–67.

Martzke, J. S., Anderson, B. L., & Cacioppo, J. T. (1987). Cognitive assessment of anxiety disorders. In L. Michelson & L. M. Ascher (Eds.), *Anxiety and stress disorders: Cognitive-behavioral assessment and treatment* (pp. 62–88). New York: Guilford.

Meichenbaum, D. H., & Cameron, R. (1981). Issues in cognitive assessment. In T. V. Merluzzi, C. R. Glass, & M. Genes (Eds.), *Cognitive assessment* (pp. 42–80). New York: Guilford.

Merluzzi, T. V. (1993). Cognitive assessment: Clinical applications of self-statement assessment. *Journal of Counseling and Development, 71*, 539–545.

Merluzzi, T. V., & Boltwood, M. D. (1989). Cognitive assessment. In A. Freeman, K. M. Simon, L. M. Beutler, & H. Arkowitz (Eds.), *Comprehensive handbook of cognitive therapy* (pp. 249–266). New York: Plenum.

Merluzzi, T. V., & Boltwood, M. D. (1990). Cognitive assessment. In C. E. Watkins & V. L. Campbell (Eds.), *Testing in counseling practice* (pp. 135–176). Hillsdale, NJ: Erlbaum.

Merluzzi, T. V., Glass, C. R., & Genes, M. (1981). *Cognitive assessment.* New York: Guilford.

Moore, R. H. (1983). Inference as "A" in RET. *British Journal of Cognitive Psychotherapy, 1*, 17–23.

Muran, J. C. (1991). A reformulation of the ABC model in cognitive psychotherapies: Implications for assessment and treatment. *Clinical Psychology Review, 11*, 399–418.

Muran, J. C., & DiGiuseppe, R. (1990). Towards a cognitive formulation of metaphor use in psychotherapy. *Clinical Psychology Review, 10*, (1), 69–85.

Muran, J. C., & Segal, Z. V. (1992). The development of an idiographic measure of self-schema: An illustration of the construction and use of self-scenarios. *Psychotherapy, 29*, 525–535.

Muran, J. C., Segal, Z. V., & Wallner Samstag, L. (1994). Self-scenarios as a repeated measures outcome measurement of self-schema in short-term cognitive therapy. *Behavior Therapy, 25*, 255–274.

Myska, M. T., Galassi, J. P., & Ware, W. B. (1986). Comparison of cognitve assessment methods with heterosexually anxious college women. *Journal of Counseling Psychology, 33*, 401–407.

Neisser, U. (1976). *Cognition and reality.* San Francisco: Freeman.

Nelson-Gray, R.O. (1994). The scientist-practitioner model revisited: Strategies for implementation. *Behaviour-Change, 11*, 61–75.

Parks, C. W., Jr., & Hollon, S. D. (1988). Cognitive assessment. In A. S. Bellack & M. Hersen (Eds.), *Behavioral assessment: A practical handbook* (3rd ed., pp. 161–212). New York: Pergamon.

Paul, G. L. (1969). Behavior modification research: Design and tactics. In C. M. Franks (Ed.), *Behavior therapy: Appraisal and status* (pp. 29–62). New York: McGraw-Hill.

Persons, J. D. (1989). *Cognitive therapy in practice: A case formulation approach.* New York: Norton.

Pope, K. H., & Singer, J. L. (Eds.). (1978). *The stream of consciousness: Scientific investigations onto the flow of human experience.* New York: Plenum.

Popper, K. (1968). *Conjecture and refutation.* New York: Oxford.

Rice, L. N. (1984). Client tasks in client-centered therapy. In R. F. Levant & J. M. Shlier (Eds.), *Client-centered therapy and the person-centered approach: New directions in therapy, research, and practice.* New York: Praeger.

Roberts, R. N., & Tharp, R. G. (1980). A naturalistic study of school children's private speech in academic problem-solving task. *Cognitive Therapy and Research, 4*, 341–352.

Rotter, J. B. (1954). *Social learning and clinical psychology.* Englewood Cliffs, NJ: Prentice-Hall.

Rotter, J. B. (1966). Generalized expectancies for internal versus external locus of control of reinforcement. *Psychological Monographs, 80* (1 Whole No. 609).

Safran, J. D., & Greenberg, L. (1991). *Emotion, psychotherapy and change.* New York: Guilford.

Safran, J. D., Vallis, T. M., Segal, Z. V., & Shaw, B. F. (1986). Assessment of core cognitive processes in cognitive therapy. *Cognitive Therapy and Research, 10,* 509–526.

Schmidt, N. B., Joiner, T. E., Young, J., & Teich, M. J. (1995). The schema questionnaire: Investigation of psychometric properties and the hierarchical structure of a measure of maladaptive schema. *Cognitive Therapy and Research, 19,* 295–321.

Schwartz, R. M. (1982). Cognitive behavior modification: A conceptual review. *Clinical Psychology Review, 2,* 267–293.

Segal, Z. V., & Shaw, B. F. (1988). Cognitive assessment: Issues and methods. In K. Dobson (Ed.), *Handbook of cognitive-behavioral therapies* (pp. 39–81). New York: Guilford.

Segal, Z. V., & Vella, D. D. (1990). Self-schema in major depression: Replication and extension of a priming methodology. *Cognitive Therapy and Research, 14,* 161–176.

Seligman, M. (1975). *Helplessness.* San Francisco: Freeman.

Seligman, M., & Reivich, K. (1995). *Optimistic child: Preventing depression and promoting resilience.* Paper presented at the 103rd annual convention of the American Psychological Association, New York.

Sichel, J., & Ellis, A. (1984). *RET Self-Help Form.* New York: Institute for Rational Emotive Therapy.

Skinner, B. F. (1945). The operational analysis of psychological terms. *Psychological Review, 52,* 270–276.

Smye, M. D., & Wine, J. D. (1980). A comparison of female and male adolescents' social behavior and cognition. *Sex Roles, 6,* 213–230.

Sobel, H. J. (1981). Projective methods of cognitive analysis. In T. V. Merluzzi, C. R. Glass, & M. Genes (Eds.), *Cognitive assessment* (pp. 127–148). New York: Guilford.

Spivack, G., Platt, J., & Shure, M. (1975). *The social problems solving approach to adjustment.* San Francisco: Jossey-Bass.

Stein, D., & Young, J. (1992). Schema approach to personality disorders. In D. Stein & J. Young (Eds.), *Cognitive science and clinical disorders.* New York: Academic.

Tower, R. B., & Singer, J. L. (1981). The measurement of imagery: How can it be clinically useful? In P. C. Kendall & S. D. Hollon (Eds.), *Assessment strategies for cognition-behavioral interventions* (pp. 119–159). New York: Academic.

Walen, S., DiGiuseppe, R., & Dryden, W. (1992). *The practitioner's guide to rational emotive behavior therapy* (2nd ed.). New York: Oxford.

Warren, R. E. (1972). Stimulus, encoding and memory. *Journal of Experimental Psychology, 94,* 90–100.

Watkins, J., & Rush, A. J. (1983). Cognitive response test. *Cognitive Therapy and Research, 7,* 425–435.

Webb, E. J., Campbell, D. T., Schwartz, R. D., & Sechrest, L. (1966). *Unobtrusive measures: Nonreactive research in the social sciences.* Chicago: Rand McNally.

Weissman, A., & Beck, A. T. (1978 November). *Development and validation of the dysfunction attitudes scale.* Paper presented at the annual meeting of the Association for Advancement of Behavior Therapy, Chicago.

Wessler, R. A., & Wessler, R. L. (1980). *The principles and practice of rational emotive therapy.* San Francisco: Jossey-Bass.

CHAPTER 7

PSYCHOPHYSIOLOGICAL ASSESSMENT

Ellie T. Sturgis
Virginia Polytechnic Institute and State University
Sandra E. Gramling
Virginia Commonwealth University

A graduate student from another psychology program on campus was taking a course in behavioral assessment and questioned the relevance of a chapter on psychophysiological assessment. She asked, "Why is all of this biology important in understanding why people do the things they do? It seems to me you are just complicating the picture and trying to make psychology sound scientific." We were surprised and then puzzled by the question, particularly given the history of psychology and the current domains in which psychological assessment is currently used. Coverage of psychophysiology appears fundamental to the psychological assessment enterprise, as psychology has always been in the "mind-body" business. Indeed, the field of psychology descended from the school of philosophy, with its emphasis on introspection, and the school of physiology, with its emphasis on observation. As the pursuit of knowledge evolved, these parent disciplines continued to search for answers to basic questions such as whether behavior results from physical or mental sources, whether nature or nur-

ture better explain development, and what limits biology sets on the individuals' capacities. Although the questions asked by both disciplines have often been similar, the methodologies used to answer such questions have differed significantly (cf. Hunt, 1993; Sternberg, 1995).

The conceptualization of the "mind-body question" has evolved through a number of phases. There may have been earlier instances of work on mind-body issues, but written records credit Hippocrates for making the first systematic observations as to this complex relationship. Hippocrates posited that the mind, which he located in the brain, controlled all aspects of behavior. His younger contemporary, Aristotle, founded the school of monism. This school of thought asserted that the mind and body were parts of the same whole and that behaviors could ultimately explained by a single processes. According to this reductionistic approach, in order to explain a behavior, one must trace it back to the most molecular (i.e., basic) mechanism possible. Therefore, biological processes were viewed as the underlying mechanisms from which psychological processes emerged (Sternberg, 1995).

Eighteenth-century philosopher Descartes rejected the concept of monism and emphasized the duality of the mind and body. He viewed the external reality experienced by the individual as being different from the internal perception of that reality. He associated biological forces with the external reality and linked the mind with internal, perceptual processes. According to Descartes, the mind and body were separate from one another but could interact. This dualistic view supported establishment of a hierarchical model of behavior in which basic physiological relationships were viewed as fundamental to the manifestation of psychological phenomena. In addition, the mind and body interacted to produce unique manifestations of any particular behavior. Current views of psychophysiology generally incorporate dualism and interactionism (Turpin, 1989).

APPROACHES TO PSYCHOPHYSIOLOGY

In a critique of psychophysiology, Turpin (1989) suggested that progress in the field of psychopathology has been complicated by the fact that psychophysiology has alternatively been viewed as a method, a mechanism, and a process, with some groups or researchers emphasizing one aspect more than the others. Such differential emphasis, although encouraging various lines of research, has possibly limited the scope and impact of psychophysiology.

The study of psychophysiology as a *method* involves development of reliable and valid assessment tools and procedures. The methods of psychophysiology have advanced substantially throughout this century. For example, early physiologists employed tracings of bioelectric potentials marked on rotating smoked glass cylinders to record physiological activity, whereas current researchers can transmit a host of different physiological measures to a computer located in a laboratory at the same time the individual functions in his or her daily environment. Also, laboratory-based measures of

psychophysiological activities continue to be a major source of information on psychophysiological responses, but types of experimental tasks used to elicit such activity have become more relevant to the specific questions being asked. As well as the more traditional measures of cardiovascular, musculoskeletal, electrodermal, and cortical responses, psychophysiologists can now map patterns of electrocortical activity that are associated with various task performance, measure patterns of regional cerebral blood flow using radioisotopes, assess the structural characteristics of the body using nuclear magnetic resonance imaging techniques, evaluate the metabolic activity of the brain during different stimulus conditions using positron emission tomography, and use assays of biochemical activity in the blood and spinal column to provide information about neurotransmitters, neurohormones, and neuromodulators (Raczynski, Ray, & McCarthy, 1991).

In addition to these technical advances in the measurement of psychophysiological responses, several researchers have concentrated on methodological issues, specifying the most appropriate statistical procedures to be used with physiological data to test varied hypotheses and to identify the complex patterns and relationships existing across time among specified physiological, behavioral, cognitive, and environmental forces (Cacioppo, Berntson, & Andersen, 1991; Coles, Gratten, Kramer, & Miller, 1986; Gottman, 1990; Porges & Bohrer, 1990).

In summary, the methodological approach to psychophysiology has markedly increased the number and types of psychophysiological variables that can be measured as well as the complexity of the questions addressed. In addition, assessment of the reliabilities and validities of these assessment procedures has increased (Arena, Bruno, Brucks, Sherman, & Meador, 1994; Arena & Hobbs, 1995; Arena, Sherman, Bruno, & Young, 1990; Stemmler & Fahrenberg, 1989).

Expanding on the role of psychophysiology as a method, researchers have also examined the field of psychophysiology as an important *mechanism* underlying psychological processes (Turpin, 1989). This approach posits a hierarchical model of behavior in which biological substrates underlie psychological and behavioral activity (Wakefield, 1989). The mechanism approach has dominated much psychophysiological research throughout the past century. Indeed, Stern (1964) defined psychophysiology as the application of physiological measurements to the measurement of psychological processes underlying behavior. Coles, Donchin, and Porges (1986) extended this concept of mechanism and suggested that the goals of psychophysiology were (1) to understand psychological phenomena by studying the activity of varied organ systems of the human body and (2) to evaluate the functional significance of physiological variables by exploring in them in a psychological context.

In particular, psychophysiological assessment has been used to identify parallels between inferred psychological processes (e.g., sleep, attention, conditioning, emotions) and observed physiological events, as well as to identify physiological correlates and markers of a variety of pathophysiological conditions (e.g., migraine headaches, hypertension, schizophrenia, anxiety) (Haynes, Gannon, Orimoto, O'Brien, 1991; Haynes, Falkin, & Sexton-Redek; 1989; Iacono, 1991; Turpin, 1989, 1991).

Most recently, however, investigators have found the dichotomous treatment of psychophysiology as either a method or a mechanism to be limiting and have viewed the distinction between mechanism and process as being a blurry one. Pribram (1971) sought to understand mind-body relationships underlying changes in the relationships among biological and psychological variables and concluded that biology (the amygdala) was involved in a number of "fight or flight" (cognitive or behavioral) reactions. He set up the goal of understanding the psychological processes characterizing those reactions. He indicated that if a *process* view of behavior were to be useful, it must explain a number of particulars in biological systems, such as (1) variability existing in the system, (2) ability to respond to novel stimuli, (3) ability to process information made available only in real time (i.e., in conditions in which there was no pre-existing instructional set), and (4) ability to respond adaptively in an unpredictable environment.

Pribram posited that the development of a model of behavior that could accomplish these goals would lead to marked advances in the understanding of behavior. To a considerable extent, the dynamic systems approached developed by several developmental theorists has approached this goal (Gottlieb, 1991; Lickliter & Berry, 1990; Oyama, 1985; Thelen, 1992). A dynamic selective systems view provides a useful framework for understanding the integration of mind and body issues. A simple way to view the nature of this integration can be seen using the example of a rectangle. Just as the area of a rectangle cannot be described by measures of length or width alone, the dynamic systems perspective states that biology cannot be separated from psychology. Knowledge of either alone precludes the effective description of the effects of each. However, since behavior is viewed over time using this approach, a mobile composed of separate, but connected, rectangles might best describe the process of progressive integration. In the case involving a human or animal organism, one must have ongoing knowledge about both biology and experience to understand or describe behavior at any point in time.

According to the dynamic systems view, individual development and behavior represent a hierarchical organization of multiple levels (e.g., genes, cells, organ, organism, behavior, environment, and experience), *all* of which *mutually* influence one other in a bi-directional manner. Different levels of the system can respond to any given stimulus at any point in time, thus leading to a different behavioral trajectory and response pattern, thus behavior has plasticity or the ability to respond adaptively in an unpredictable environment (Gottlieb, 1991). Variability in the system results from operation of the adaptive selection process in any organism-environment interaction. In the field of psychophysiology, the primary levels of interest for explication include the cognitive, behavioral, social, and physiological systems (Bandura, 1978, 1986; Haynes, 1991). The dynamic systems perspective views physiological and psychological operations as being dynamic, always in flux, and truly integrated with one another. The varied aspects of behavior continuously affect and are affected by the other domains.

Thus, the cause of any particular response is determined by a multitude of variables combining in a probabilistic manner, and any given response can be caused by several different combinations or permutations of activity at the different levels of the system. Again, one must remember the importance of bi-directional influences that actually *change* the system in which they are operating. This change is not totally random, as there are some constraints on biological systems. It is through this process that the operation of homeostasis and self-regulating feedback loops operate.

A dynamic selective system accounts for the control of behavior in at least three important ways. First, the behaviors observed (at any level of the system) depend on the specifics of an interaction, the context of that interaction, and the history of the system. Second, the systems operate in hierarchical levels (e.g., processes at one level interact and give rise to processes at the next level, while upper-level processes can in turn be reflected in lower-level ones). Third, the control of behavior changes through time, sometimes being transferred from one process to another one. The system is not represented in some preexisting code (e.g., a genetic code; a trait), but evolves as a complex of interacting influences, internal and external to the organism, tied to the activities of individual and to the stable features of the general environment. In addition, a dynamic systems view predicts that behavior is in constant change and the configuration of biology, context, cognitions, and behavior at one point will be changed by some perturbation or demand in the system.

In relation to psychophysiology, Turpin (1989) suggested that a dynamic process approach should alter the questions to be asked in research and practice and will necessitate the use of different statistical techniques to interpret the data. When a dynamic systems approach is used, one must abandon old conceptions of variables as dependent and independent, for this classification will switch from one sampling episode to another. The traditional linear models upon which much of the science of psychology is based must be abandoned in favor of time series and nonlinear dynamical models, which will be needed to describe and explain the changing behaviors of the system over time. In addition, mul-

tiple measurement episodes or snapshots of the behavior are required to inform cause and effect relationships (Heiby, 1995); thus, longitudinal and case study designs are useful (Fogel, 1992).

Until recently, perhaps as a consequence of the different conceptualizations of psychophysiology employed by different researchers, no over-arching theory of psychophysiology has organized the questions asked, the methods used, the observations made, or the interpretation of obtained results. Indeed, the field of psychophysiology, while fundamental to the subject matter of psychology, has not yet permeated the mainstream of psychological research or clinical practice. In responding to the need for clinical psychophysiology to embrace the issues of method, mechanism, *and* process, Turpin (1989) proposed an integrative definition of psychophysiology that may significantly advance research during the next 30 years of work in the area. He defined *clinical psychophysiology* as "the application of psychophysiological techniques, concepts, and theories to the explanation of psychological factors which influence health behaviors and risks. Health, in this context, is taken to mean a state of both physical and psychological well-being" (p. 7).

This integrative view of psychophysiology has already influenced the field, as can be seen in a series of seminal articles published in *Psychological Assessment* in 1991 (Anderson & McNeilly, 1991; Cacioppo et al., 1991; Fredrikson, 1991; Haynes et al., 1991; Iacono, 1991; Steptoe & Johnson, 1991; Turpin, 1991). These articles have articulated a number of important issues in the field of psychophysiology and illustrate new, potentially more exciting research directions. These increasingly sophisticated methodologies, theories, and paradigms set the stage for renewed interest in the usefulness of psychophysiological theories and methodologies in the explanation of a variety of psychological processes. In the remainder of this chapter, the authors will review key issues related to the measurement and interpretation of several common methods of psychophysiological assessment, review some of the literature highlighting the importance of psychophysiology in the conceptualization of normal and dysfunctional behavior, and provide an example of a case study in which a multimodal assessment paradigm employing psycho-physiological assessment was used to clarify the nature of the pain problem and to assess the effectiveness of an intervention strategy.

MEASUREMENT ISSUES

Research Questions

The choice of appropriate psychophysiological measure(s) to assess the phenomenon of interest ranks among the most important responsibilities of any investigator involved in psychophysiological research. Turpin (1989) summarized several issues that should inform the decision to employ psychophysiological methodologies in assessment. The research clinician should be able to (1) explain the rationale underlying the decision to employ a psychophysiological approach to an assessment problem, (2) evaluate the appropriateness of the measures selected to assess the targeted construct, (3) specify the scale and time course characteristic of physiological index of interest, (4) describe and understand the physiological context in which the measurement, and (5) temper the ideal assessment by consideration of the practical or clinical aspects of the assessment process. An elaboration and example of each of these features problems.

The choice of selecting a psychophysiological rationale for assessment suggests that the assessor recognizes the complex causal models of any behavior. Such models typically involve complex interactions among behavioral, cognitive, emotional, physiological, and social components of behavior, interacting in a dynamic relationship with one another. According to this approach, the process of assessment should clarify the patterns, identify the relevant moderating factors, and establish the boundary conditions surrounding the observed results. These boundary conditions may present threats to the external validity of the finding.

The choice of particular variables for assessment depends on several factors, including the relationship between the psychological construct of interest and the proposed physiological response(s), the activation of pattern of the particular response, and an understanding of how the response(s) relate to the construct. The investigator

utilizing psychophysiological assessment procedures should be able to specify whether targeted responses are considered primary defining characteristics of the construct or dysfunction being evaluated or are only a part of the nomological net associated with the construct. For example, if the evaluator is directly observing a clinically relevant physiological behavior, the target variables are those that define that behavior (e.g., blood pressure in hypertension, digital vasoconstriction in Raynaud's phenomenon). Alternatively, psychophysiological variables could be considered to be indirect components of a construct if they constitute only a portion of the nomological net defining the psychological construct (e.g., increased heart rate and anxiety). In either case, selection of targets should be guided by theoretical understanding of the psychophysiological dysfunction or construct of interest as well as past research assessing the concurrent and construct validity of such measures (Turpin, 1989).

Once the particular physiological response set for assessment is selected, the evaluator must still select the most appropriate dimension of the responses (i.e., amplitude or frequency, lability, latency, or recovery time) to be used (Haynes et al., 1991). Previous research should guide selection of the parameters; however, pilot testing of the options is also desirable. Nonetheless, one must remain mindful that comparisons of response amplitude or frequency alone often are not the best representation of the action of the variable (Haynes et al., 1991).

In addition, physiological responses are affected by the context in which they are made. Because of these context-dependent relationships and the fact that activity is multidetermined, other sources of response variability must be clarified. For example, cardiovascular activity, a commonly measured correlate of anxiety, reflects both autonomic and somatic activity. Indeed, Obrist (1981) hypothesized that cardiovascular measures are largely determined by metabolic demands resulting from both anticipated and actual physical movements. Thus, in assessment paradigms in which motor activity is expected to vary (e.g., in vivo exposure for agoraphobics), additional measures of skeletal or metabolic activity would be needed to elucidate the meaning of cardiovascular findings (Turpin, 1989). Unfortunately, until recently, most of the context-dependent relationships in psychophysiological research have been controlled but not explored (Cacioppo et al., 1991).

The scale and time course of the measure of interest must also be considered when selecting a variable for measurement. Measures can either be obtained as short-term, event-locked phasic changes or as long-term, time-locked tonic changes (Turpin, 1989). For example, in the human body, physiological stress responses occur through two interdependent pathways: (1) the autonomic nervous system (ANS), particularly the sympathetic division; and (2) the hypothalamus-pituitary-adrenal (HPA) cortex system. Sympathetically mediated arousal is organized by the hypothalamus and is characterized by a rapid onset, a short equilibrium rate, and a relatively quick recovery rate. Measurement of such activity is most appropriate in situations involving short duration stressors, and the response is characterized by increased norepinephrine levels, decreased cortisol levels, and enhanced immune functioning. The ANS responds to almost any stimulus creating a startle effect or requiring cognitive or physical effort. Exposure to a transient mild electric shock also elicits ANS activation.

On the other hand, activity resulting from chronic stressors is mediated by the HPA cortex system and results in decreased levels of norepinephrine and increased cortisol, which result in decreased immune functioning. This chronic stress response is activated when stressors are psychologically salient, subjectively distressing, and uncontrollable (Fredrikson, 1991; Haynes, 1991). As a consequence of such differences in the response to stress, selection of the responses for measurement should be guided by the types of stressors involved as well as the questions to be asked.

Finally, practical and clinical concerns should inform the process of measurement selection. For example, the investigator must consider the instrumentation and transducers required for measurement as well as the nature of the paradigm to be tested. For instance, heart rate can be measured using an electrocardiogram or a polygraph or it may be measured using a transducer that is attached to the finger or ear and is electrically coupled with a brief display device. In the first case, the measurement may be slightly more sensitive and precise. However, the measurement process itself is more invasive, for it involves placing a number of electrodes on the chest or the limbs and hooking these electrodes to a recording instrument. In the latter case, the measurement process is much less intrusive and may be more acceptable to the subject. As another example, cortisol levels can be assessed using blood or saliva assays. Again, one procedure is more invasive and uncomfortable than the other. Such differences in convenience and acceptability, given appropriate reliability estimates, may change the methodology.

In summary, intrusiveness of a measure, ease and accuracy of measurement, and susceptibility of the measure to movement and other artifacts should all be considered when choosing the responses to be evaluated. Advantages of one technique may need to be sacrificed for benefits of another.

Measurement

The goal of most psychologists in collecting physiological data is to make inferences about theoretical constructs such as anxiety, stress, or pain based on the patterns of responses measured. Thus, establishment of the construct validity of the measures is needed in the field of psychophysiology; however, such a goal has not yet been achieved for most of the measures of interest.

Coles and associates (1986) and Stemmler and Fahrenberg (1989) discussed a number of statistical issues of importance when multicomponent explanatory model is used to assess constructs. First, one must determine how to measure change. This measurement is particularly problematic when there are only pre- and poststimulus conditions. Lacey (1959) criticized use of the simple change score because it contains variances attributable to both prestimulus and poststimulus levels of activity and is also affected by the law of initial values. This law, first proposed by Wilder in 1950, stated that magnitude of a particular physiological response to a given stimulus depends on the prestimulus level of the system being measured (i.e., the higher the prestimulus level of the response, the smaller the increase in the response following stimulation). Lacey suggested use of regression (or residualized change scores) to control for the initial values effect. However, use of residualized change scores does not eliminate the possible error present in the prestimulus and poststimulus conditions.

Second, Berntson, Cacioppo, and Quigley (cited in Cacioppo et al., 1991) found there are a number of sources of autonomic restraint on both the direction and the magnitude of autonomic responses that were not adequately handled by the use of residualized change scores. Several other statistical procedures have been proposed to deal with these problems:

1. Use noninvasive measures to provide information about the functional neural input underlying a physiological response and adjust the obtained scores accordingly (Porges & Bohrer, 1990).

2. Compare prestimulus values across conditions. If these values are statistically equivalent, then comparisons can be made among the poststimulus measurements to assess treatment effects.

3. Use the different conditions (prestimulus, stimulus, poststimulus) as within-subject factors in a repeated measures design. Significant interaction effects will then signal treatment effects.

4. Use multivariate solutions (MANOVAS and MANCOVAS) with repeated measures to analyze treatment effects if more than two physiological measures are recorded.

5. Express physiological activity in standard units of measurement (e.g. z scores) and analyze differential activity across treatment conditions as well as within-subject variation (Cacioppo et al., 1991).

An extensive discussion of these issues is not possible given the space constraints of the chapter, thus readers are referred to the methodological resources identified earlier. More recently, as researchers have moved toward a process approach to psychophysiology, several methodologists have strongly encouraged a need to use nonlinear statistical models to test results (Haynes, Blaine, & Meyer, 1995; Heiby, 1995)

Conditions of Assessment

If one accepts a process model of psychophysiology, it quickly becomes apparent that there is an in-

terdependence among measurement conditions (the cognitive, behavioral, and physiological responses of the individual) and the task demands of the situation. Cacioppo and colleagues (1991) examined a number of issues to be considered as one conducts a psychophysiological assessment. One issue these authors addressed was the reconsideration of the dimensions of psychophysiological activity.

Lacey (1959) originally specified three dimensions of autonomic activity to be considered in the assessment process: (1) autonomic tension (i.e., the current level of the physiological response); (2) autonomic lability or the transient change in the level of a physiological function in response to some external stimulus; and (3) spontaneous autonomic activity (i.e., fluctuations in the momentary level of a response as a function of some internal, not externally imposed, stimulus.) Lacey maintained that these dimensions of a response were independent and provided different types of information to the examiner. However, further research indicated these dimensions were neither orthogonal nor exhaustive of the array of potentially relevant physiological responses (Cacioppo et al., 1991).

Based on Lacey's classification system, however, much research has been conducted that has examined the temporal relationship between environmental stimuli and subsequent responses (i.e., event-related responses). Responses that cannot be easily associated with an external stimulus have been termed *spontaneous responses* and are frequently viewed as a source of error. However, such a classification does not consider the finding that stimuli can be external or internal, and it also ignores the fact that the context of the assessment itself may moderate the impact of a potential stimulus.

For example, an agoraphobic client accompanied by her therapist on an exposure trial may show muted levels of cardiovascular reactivity during the task relative to her levels of reactivity when she travels alone. Indeed, the measurement process is often reactive. Two former clients indicated that they did not have panic attacks when driving over a bridge when wearing a Holter monitor because they believed the therapist would come help them if they got in trouble. Unfortunately, cognitions are not always rational, for in this case, evaluation of cardiovascular function was performed after the individuals returned the tape, a time in which intervention on the bridge would have occurred too late! Cacioppo and colleagues (1991) have criticized the event-related interpretation of psychophysiology with its strong emphasis on tonic and phasic activity and suggested that efficacy of identifying psychological and biological mechanisms underlying behavior is reduced when the social and contextual characteristics of the assessment are ignored.

According to Cacioppo and associates (1991), psychologists have recognized the issue of social influences and context on psychophysiology, but have typically chosen to hold social factors and contextual conditions constant across subjects and conditions. However useful such a technique is in controlling sources of variance, it does not eliminate the effects of social and contextual variables and potentially obfuscates important context-variable information. From a process model, it is the reciprocal interdependence of context, stimuli, physiological responsivity, and behavior transacting over time that is of importance in explaining biological-experiential relationships. As a result of these criticisms, Cacioppo and associates (1991) proposed a model of psychophysiological response space to inform the research process. Using this three-dimensional model, one can represent different characteristics of the research question. One dimension on the model represents the antecedent(s) of the physiological event (both event-related and spontaneous), the second represents the nature of the stimulus (both discrete and contextual), and the final dimension represents the time course of the physiological event. The authors hypothesized that the resulting physiological response patterns occurred as an integration of the response with its context. Specific response patterns will likely vary from those in another portion of the space as a result of the different context. However, by using the dimensional approach, one could group more homogeneous conditions (both physically and psychologically) and potentially demonstrate increased consistancy in the findings, potentially clarifying some of the frequently observed inconsistancies in psychophysiology.

Another proposal made by Cacioppo and colleagues is that the dimensional information about psychophysiological responses should help identify the psychological and biological mechanisms associated with a particular response pattern and clarify the nature of response differences both across and within individuals. Finally, the authors proposed that a dimensional approach to the definition of a psychophysiological response characteristics would help to identify the features of physiological response *patterns* associated with specific psychological contexts, thus furthering our understanding of the psychophysiological process.

Steptoe and Johnson (1991) also addressed important aspects of the assessment conditions. First, one must carefully consider the procedures used for collecting resting or control values, since the responses to tasks are typically compared with control values. Stable resting measures are typically difficult to achieve in psychophysiological research because people often take a considerable amount of time to adapt to the laboratory setting. Several issues relate to this difficulty. First, there is typically a dramatic reduction of physical activity when one arrives at the lab, since subjects are typically required to remain immobile during the assessment period. Second, the physiology of the subject may change as a function of the measurement process itself. The more artificial the setting and the more complicated the accouterments of the assessment (e.g., number of transducers, placement of transducers, video cameras, immobilizing devices, experimental chambers with heavy doors that close to attenuate sound, etc.), the more physiological activation is likely to be induced by the setting itself.

Although setting effects can typically be assessed by the use of additional separate adaptation periods, such separation introduces time artifacts into the assessment process, since a process model proposes that people are constantly changing as a function of the interdependence of their biology and experience. At different points in time, they are literally different biological entities reacting to their experiences. To further complicate the picture, most subjects show habituation of a physiological response over time and different physiological responses often show different habituation patterns. It is sometimes tricky to provide sufficiently adequate baseline periods to accomplish adaptation without exhausting the subject and/or initiating the habituation process.

One must also be concerned about the duration of exposure to stimuli and the timing of responses to be measured. If one assesses reactivity to a stimulus, one should ensure that the participant has time to interact with and respond to the stimulus. It is also important to know the typical event-related time course for maximal reactivity, especially if one is sampling responses at specific time intervals rather than performing continuous recordings. Failure to sample during the correct time period could lead to inaccurate data with erroneous conclusions.

The type of experimental tasks or conditions used in the assessment is also important. A wide range of protocols has been used across varied studies to assess various reactions to stress. This diversity makes comparisons across studies difficult. In addition, there is typically a lack of normative data for performance on the task of interest (Fredrikson, 1991; Steptoe & Johnson, 1991). Krantz, Manuck, and Wing (1986), in noting this problem, attempted to classify mental stress tasks along a variety of dimensions, including active versus passive behavioral coping, task engagement versus detachment, control versus lack of control, and level of workload. Such distinctions are important, given the different musculoskeletal, hemodynamic, and metabolic demands of varied situations. More work along these lines in areas other than the cardiovascular arena appears warranted. Finally, the choice of task, like the choice of measures, is likely determined by the questions being asked. When standardization is not possible, the inclusion of explicit explanations of the procedures used should inform the analyses of the obtained results.

A consideration of subject characteristics, such as age, gender, and ethnicity, is also important in the assessment process. Given the unique effects of such variables, a discussion of these factors (as well as a discussion of drug effects) will be provided later.

Instrumentation

Precise measurement and quantification of covert psychophysiological events usually requires sensitive equipment. Often, the physiological signal of interest is very small, measured in microvolts (EMG, EEG), and requires equipment that can both detect the signal and filter out extraneous signals that would constitute "noise" in the data. Therefore, adequate instrumentation in psychophysiological assessment permits detection of otherwise covert physiological events, and, through proper filtering and amplification, these events are meaningfully quantified and displayed. The basic issues regarding instrumentation in psychophysiological assessment have changed little in the last decade, although the actual instruments employed have changed a great deal. The three major categories of equipment in psychophysiological assessment include the stand-alone physiograph, the turn-key computerized psychophysiological assessment system, and ambulatory recording equipment. Each of these are discussed in the sections that follow along with issues surrounding their use.

Physiograph. The large stand-alone physiograph (polygraph) with multiple channels—each comprised of preamplifiers, amplifiers, and drivers—has been the cornerstone of psychophysiological instrumentation for decades. These machines are literally called *polygraphs* by their manufacturers and were so named long before lie detection technology gave the term a negative connotation. The term *polygraph* simply means "many graphs," but because patients/clients participating in a psychophysiological assessment often become anxious when they see the label *polygraph* on the equipment, many psychophysiologists (including the authors) tape over the word or otherwise obscure it from view. The equipment of interest when using a physiograph includes (1) the electrodes or transducers that detect the signal; (2) the physiograph proper, which receives the signal from the sensors and includes preamplifiers and amplifiers to filter and amplify the signal; (3) the output devices, which traditionally included penwriters (which produce "many graphs") and oscilloscopes; and (4) integrators, magnetic tape, and computers to quantify the output.

Electrodes and transducers. Electrodes and transducers detect the physiological signal and transmit that information to the physiograph. Many physiological response systems are electrical in nature (e.g., electrocardiogram [EKG], electromyography [EMG], electrodermal activity [EDR], and electrocortical activity [EEG]; thus surface electrodes are able to detect these signals directly.

Surface electrodes are typically constructed of silver/silver chloride metal disks encased in plastic housings, which are attached to the subject/client with adhesive collars. Proper preparation of the electrodes, preparation of the skin, and electrode placement are critical in obtaining valid and reliable measurements and to ensure the safety of the subject. There are a number of good sources to obtain detailed information on these topics (e.g., Andreassi, 1989, Hassett, 1978; Martin & Venables, 1980; Fridlund & Cacioppo, 1986).

Transducers are used when the physiological response system of interest does not manifest itself as an electrical signal. In general, a transducer is a sensor that converts one type of energy into another type of energy. Respiration, blood volume, and hand temperature are all examples of physiological processes of interest to psychophysiologists that are not bioelectric signals and therefore must be transduced into an electrical signal that is compatible with the physiograph. Transducers and electrodes are attached to wires or "leads," which allow the electrical energy to be transmitted to the physiograph. There are also telemetry-based systems that send the information via radio waves, infrared light, and so forth, but space does not permit a full discussion of these systems.

Physiograph. The physiograph typically consists of several components that process, filter, and amplify the signal. This process is often called *signal conditioning* and the amount and type of conditioning needed depend on the type of input signal. For example, EKG is a relatively high-amplitude, low-frequency signal compared to the low-amplitude, high-frequency EEG signal observed in an awake and alert subject. Filtering out extraneous electrical "noise" is more important when measuring EEG than it is when measuring a relatively strong high-amplitude signal like EKG. The components of most physiographs offer a great deal of flexibility in the types of preamplifiers available

and the range of settings to allow the user to faithfully record the signal of interest with minimal distortion and noise. Careful study of the operating manual and diligent practice are needed to record meaningful psychophysiological data with a physiograph.

Output devices. Once processed, the signal is amplified so that it can be meaningfully displayed. For many years, the most common output device was the penwriter, which typically accompanies the physiograph. The penwriter produces a tracing of the physiological signal on paper, providing a permanent record of the recording. Over time, the computer terminal has become an equally common display device as well as a data storage device.

Data quantification. Tracings from a penwriter can be quantified by hand but the process is tedious, time intensive, and subject to substantial error. One of the earliest uses of the computer in psychophysiology has been in the area of data storage and quantification

In the section that follows, the rise of the computer in psychophysiology from a data storage device to a replacement of the traditional physiograph is briefly traced.

Computers. The tremendous growth in computer technology has vastly changed the landscape of psychophysiological assessment in the last decade. Although the physiograph is still a frequently utilized instrument in many psychophysiology labs, computer-based systems are now at least as common. In a review of computers and human psychophysiological research, three phases of computer instrumentation are described (McArthur, Schandler, & Cohen, 1988).

During the early period of computer-aided psychophysiological research (early 60s to early 70s), utilization of computers was scant due to their relatively high cost and rudimentary capabilities. Much of the programming was at the assembly-language level and only the most highly trained computer programmers could understand and utilize computers and understand their role in the psychophysiological assessment setting (McArthur et al., 1988). The prevailing view at this point was that the data storage capabilities of the computer could make it a useful supplement to instruments such as the physiograph, but not a replacement for them. In the early 1970s, a rapid acceleration in the development of computer applications in psychophysiology occurred as a growing interest in biofeedback spurred a multitude of manufacturers to develop equipment suitable for clinical practice (McArthur et al., 1988). The second phase (mid-70s to mid-80s) was characterized by computers that were easier to use, less bulky, and less expensive. Psychophysiologists began to see the value of the computer not only as a means of data storage but also as a useful tool to measure psychophysiological processes (McArthur et al., 1988). Phase three denoted the move toward the computer as the central piece of equipment in a psychophysiology laboratory. Psychophysiological studies involving computers are now the norm, and most of the published articles measuring psychophysiological variables use the computer as the primary or only source of psychophysiological data collection (McArthur et al., 1988).

Since publication of McArthur and colleagues' (1988) review, use of computers in psychophysiological assessment has only continued to expand. Turnkey systems are readily available, which typically include their own control board and microprocessor, sensor modules, and electrodes/transducers capable of handling all aspects of psychophysiological assessment. The move toward user friendly software and hardware that are compact and easily coupled to the computer board has made psychophysiological assessment available to any practitioner or researcher with a relatively modest financial investment.

Ambulatory Psychophysiological Measurement. Expanding computerization allows for increasingly complex laboratory experiments and sophistication in data reduction and analysis of psychophysiological data. Proliferation of computer technology has also helped foster the growth of the ambulatory measurement of psychophysiological processes. Miniaturization of electronic components and the tremendous drop in prices associated with the growth of the computer industry has led to the development of ambulatory monitoring devices that are practical, both in terms of size and expense.

Recently, there has been a call from many sectors for the development of more ecologically valid assessment procedures (Farrell, 1991; Hatch et al., 1992; Arena & Hobbs, 1995; Steptoe & Johnson, 1991). Development and use of ambulatory psychophysiological recording equipment in naturalistic settings would be a significant move in that direction. Numerous studies suggest that psychophysiological measures recorded in vivo provide more relevant information and often reveal more complex relationships than are observed in a laboratory or clinic setting (e.g., Steptoe & Johnson, 1991; Shapiro, Jamner, & Goldstein, 1993). While the call for more ecologically valid measurements cannot be ignored (Steptoe & Johnson, 1991; Anderson, Coyle, & Haythornwaithe, 1992) neither can the traditional issues of reliability and validity in psychophysiological assessment (Arena, Bruno, Brucks, Searles, Sherman, & Meador, 1994; Arena, Sherman, Bruno, & Young, 1990; Steptoe & Johnson, 1991).

Reliability has been a key issue in laboratory-based psychophysiological research where many sources of artifact and "noise" can be controlled (Arena, Blanchard, Andrasik, Cotch, & Meyers, 1983). These issues are more pronounced in naturalistic settings, where it is often impossible to control variables that may lead to spurious effects on the measure of interest. For example, movement artifact and environmental conditions—such as temperature, food, and beverage intake—can all affect various psychophysiological measures and are difficult to control in naturalistic settings. Despite these problems, advances have been made in the area of ambulatory psychophysiological assessment. In the sections that follow, some of the more recent applications of ambulatory monitoring across a variety of physiological response systems are briefly highlighted.

Heart Rate and Blood Pressure. Cardiovascular measures such as heart rate and blood pressure are relevant to many disorders of interest in behavioral health (e.g., hypertension, cardiovascular reactivity, and so-called type-A behavior) and the assessment and treatment of various anxiety disorders. Ambulatory monitoring of these measures has received considerable attention. Steptoe and Johnson

(1991) reviewed ambulatory measurement of cardiovascular function and came to several conclusions. Heart rate (HR) is both the easiest measure to record in ambulatory settings and is also the most reliable. Blood pressure (BP) is more difficult to measure because it cannot be recorded continuously in a noninvasive manner. Therefore, most ambulatory blood pressure systems take measures relatively infrequently (e.g., once every 15 minutes). Since BP measurement is sensitive to movement, the subject is required to be still during the measurement procedure, thereby decreasing, to some extent, the ecological validity of the measures. Steptoe and Johnson (1991) concluded that with proper data-analytic techniques, there are moderately strong relationships between measures taken in the field with those in the laboratory. This type of work is expanding to include measures of endocrine functioning, as reported in a study of the relationship between cardiovascular and catecholamine reactions to laboratory and real-life stress (vanDoornen & vanBlokland, 1992).

Ambulatory measurement of HR and BP in naturalistic settings has provided information that would be completely inaccessible in traditional laboratory settings. An excellent example is a study assessing the relationships between HR and BP reactivity and preferred coping styles among paramedics across three different settings (Shapiro, Jamner, & Goldstein, 1993). The extent of cardiovascular reactivity varied a great deal depending on the setting (i.e., riding in the ambulance, during a rescue, at the hospital) and preferred coping style (i.e., active or passive) of the individual paramedics. Similarly, ambulatory monitoring has revealed interesting results in the assessment of anxiety. For example, panic-prone individuals assessed in real-life settings do not have unusually high HR in high-risk situations (Margraf, Taylor, Ehlers, Roth, & Agras, 1987; Roth, Telch, Sachitano, Gallen, Kopell, McClenahan, Agras, & Pfefferbaum, 1986). Utility of ambulatory cardiovascular response monitoring has also been documented in other published reports as well (Myrtek, 1990).

Respiration. The technical challenges associated with ambulatory measurement of some key parameters of respiration (i.e., tidal volume, minute ventilation) have only recently been surmounted (Anderson & Frank, 1990). A study using a device based on this technology successfully studied inhibitory breathing among healthy adult subjects (Anderson, Coyle, & Haythornwaithe, 1992). This promising technology may prove very useful in the psychophysiological assessment of anxiety disorders and psychophysiological disorders associated with disturbed breathing patterns.

EMG. In rehabilitation settings, portable EMG scanners are frequently used in "work-hardening" programs but there has been little empirical research regarding the reliability of these devices. Advancement of ambulatory EMG recording that meets criteria for adequate reliability has been vigorously advanced by Arena and colleagues (e.g., Arena et al., 1994; Arena et al., 1990). Arena and colleagues (1994) tested an ambulatory EMG device designed to measure two channels of surface EMG while controlling for peak and integral motion. They found that the device demonstrated adequate reliability among healthy subjects and studies with musculoskeletal pain patients are currently being conducted.

SCR. The feasibility of ambulatory measurement of the skin conductance response has been documented since at least the early 1980s (Turpin, Shine, & Lader, 1983). Applications that permit virtually unrestricted daily activities by subjects, and more intensive computer-aided data reduction have been reported in the assessment of menopausal hot flashes (Freedman, 1989 Woodward & Freedman, 1994). The pattern of SCR during spontaneous hot flashes recorded in the laboratory versus ambulatory settings was similar in terms of both the magnitude and time course of the SCR response (Freedman, 1989).

Hand temperature. Ambulatory measurement of hand temperature is one area where inexpensive portable devices have been available for many years. Inexpensive electronic devices are frequently used for home training in hand temperature biofeedback protocols in the treatment of headache (e.g., Musso, Blanchard, & McCoy, 1991). Ambulatory hand temperature monitoring has been used in the assessment of a variety of other psychophysiological disorders, including Raynaud's disease, diabetes, and hypertension (Freedman, 1995).

Conclusions. The published reports continue to demonstrate the power of ambulatory psychophysiological recordings. Assessing psychophysiological responses in naturalistic settings reveals, in many cases, a fairly strong relationship between laboratory and naturalistic observations (e.g., Steptoe & Johnson, 1991). Sometimes, however, unique relationships between psychophysiological and psychological variables have been revealed by the use of ambulatory recordings in the naturalistic environment that would have been very difficult in a laboratory assessment (e.g., Shapiro et al., 1993). We believe that the real benefit of increased use of ambulatory recording procedures will accrue in daily clinical practice. The need for psychophysiological assessment in treating the various anxiety disorders is widely accepted (Turpin, 1991), yet the routine collection of these data, either in the clinic or in more naturalistic settings, has not been commonplace. To use the growth of computers in psychophysiology as an analogy, we seem to be in the "second phase" of ambulatory recordings in psychophysiology. Hopefully, the trend toward affordable, reliable, and more user-friendly ambulatory devices will continue and the use of these instruments will proliferate. These technical advancements may well have even more impact than the proliferation of computers in psychophysiological assessments in that it seems likely that ambulatory devices would be more applicable for the needs of the private practitioner relative to turnkey computerized systems.

COMMON PSYCHOPHYSIOLOGICAL ASSESSMENT PARADIGMS

As noted earlier, techniques useful in clarifying psychophysiological processes have increased substantially, but this chapter will emphasize some of the more easily accessible and commonly employed measures used to explain the psychophysiological process. The important anatomical and

physiological bases for each measure will be briefly described and the authors will then discuss the different response indices applicable for the measure. A synopsis of potential threats to the validity of the measure will be presented. Finally, a selection of studies illustrating the use in the assessment process will be highlighted.

Cardiovascular Psychophysiology

The cardiovascular system is one of the most basic of the physiological systems, for it provides the oxygen and nutrients required by all cells of the body in order to sustain life. Cardiac activity can be evaluated in several ways, including heart rate, blood pressure, stroke volume, cardiac output, and pulse contour analysis (Steptoe & Johnson, 1991). Measures of heart rate and blood pressure have heretofore been of greatest interest to the fields of clinical psychology and behavioral medicine. In particular, the study risk factors and the development of behaviorally based life-change strategies for use in the management of hypertension and coronary heart disease, as well as the assessment and treatment of vascular-related conditions (e.g., Raynaud's syndrome, migraine headaches), have proven to be fruitful areas of endeavor for those interested in behavioral medicine (Steptoe & Johnson, 1991). For psychopathologists, a thorough understanding of cardiovascular functioning is important if one is to understand the multifactorial nature of the varied anxiety states (e.g., anxiety, phobias, panic) as well as the processes involved in emotional functioning (Foa & Kozak, 1986 Hugdahl, 1989; Ost, 1989; Sartory, 1989; Turpin, 1991). Thus, it is prudent to review the major characteristics of cardiovascular activity and to consider issues related to the assessment of these responses.

Anatomy and Physiology

The heart is a four-chambered muscular structure whose primary purpose is to supply blood to all cells in the body. The blood then transfers nutrients and oxygen to the body's tissues, enabling the continuing life and functioning of the individual (Andreassi, 1989). The control of heart rate (HR) involves mechanisms internal and external to the heart. The efficiency of the heart as a pumping system is a function of the sequential pattern of excitation and contraction coordinated by specialized fibers, including (1) the sinoatrial (S-A) node, (2) the atrioventricular (A-V) node, (3) the A-V bundle, and (4) the left and right bundles of conducting fibers (Andreassi, 1989). The SA node is located in the right atrium. The regular discharge of the S-A node produces normal rhythmic contractions of the entire heart and functions as the pacemaker for the system. The normal rate of contractions is 120 beats per minute (bpm). However, the vagus nerve inhibits the activity of the S-A node and slows the average heart rate to about 70 to 80 bpm. Impulses are slightly delayed at the A-V node before passing into the ventricles of the heart. The A-V bundle then conducts the electrical impulse into the ventricles. Here, the Purkinje fibers conduct the impulse for contraction to all parts of the ventricles. The contraction phase of the heart is termed *systole,* whereas the relative relaxation phase is termed *diastole* (Andreassi, 1989).

These internal structures of the heart are also influenced by external factors from both the central (CNS) and autonomic (ANS) nervous systems. The parasympathetic (PNS) system influences both the A-V and S-V nodes through activation of the vagus nerve, which results in a decrease in heart rate. This effect is produced by the release of the neurotransmitter acetylcholine at the vagal nerve endings, which then slows cardiac activity at the S-A node, which in turn slows down the action of the ventricles. Activation of the sympathetic nervous system releasing norepinephrine and epinephrine, however, increases heart rate. Increased sympathetic activity increases the rate of discharge at the S-A node, increases the excitability of heart tissue, and increases the contractile force for both atrial and ventricular musculature. As a result of these changes, sympathetic activation increases cardiac output in certain stressful situations and at extreme levels of exercise, a finding that makes cardiovascular functioning attractive as part of an index of emotional arousal. However, increased rate is also related to decreased activation of the vagal nerve, which is related to decreases in parasympathetic activity (Andreassi, 1989).

Regulation of cardiovascular activity, then, is not a simple process; it requires coordination of local, reflexive, and central nervous system activities. Central nervous system structures involved in the regulation of cardiovascular activity include the hypothalamus, cerebellum, and amygdala. Central nervous system activation is regulated by both neurotransmitter and neurohormonal effects. The SNS also controls the degree vascular tone (e.g., degree of vasodilation vs. constriction) of the blood vessels. Normal sympathetic activity maintains the blood vessels at about half of their maximal diameter. The SNS activation generally leads to vasoconstriction with decreases leading to vasodilation (Andreassi, 1989).

Blood pressure is regulated by five major factors: (1) the cardiac factor describes the volume of blood produced each time the left ventricle contracts; (2) the peripheral resistance is produced by the arterioles, which vary in diameter; (3) a drop in blood volume (the relative constant volume of blood cells and plasma contained in the vascular system) reduces blood pressure; (4) an increase in viscosity, which affects ease with which the blood flows; raises arterial pressure; and (5) when elasticity of the arterial walls decreases, the systolic pressure rises (Jacob & Francone, 1970).

The baroreceptors (stretch receptors of the carotid sinuses and aorta) transmit signals to the vasomotor of the brain stem to regulate blood pressure. The cardiovascular system works to ensure an adequate supply of blood and nutrients to the brain, both through the control of heart rate and through this baroreceptor system. The baroreceptors are located in the neck at about the level of the chin and are innervated by fibers from the glossopharyngeal (IX) cranial nerve. If the blood pressure is low, the pressure on the walls of the carotid sinus is low. The medulla responds to such information by accelerating the heart rate through the activation of sympathetic nerve fibers. Once pressure increases to an acceptable level, the feedback mechanism slows down the acceleration. Thus, the function of the baroreceptors is to guarantee sufficient blood gets to the brain to maintain effective functioning.

Blood volume measures assess the amount of blood present in body tissue at a given time. The blood volume measure changes as a function of local metabolic requirements. Shifts in blood volume are dependent on the arterial blood flow to an area and venous flow from an area. The SNS effects on constriction and dilation affect local blood flow.

Measurement

Heart Rate (HR). Several measures of cardiac functioning are of particular interest to psychophysiologists. The assessment of heart rate is considered to be the most common measure of cardiac functioning. This measure can be determined from any cardiac signal (e.g., blood pressure or blood flow) that fluctuates at regular intervals in the cardiac cycle. The most common measure of heart rate, however, is obtained from the electrocardiogram (EKG). In addition to providing information about heart rate, an EKG can provide information about the integrity of the heart muscle. The electrocardiogram is used to trace the electrical impulse that passes through the heart during contraction. Electrodes are placed on the skin and an electrical waveform is recorded. The electrodes may be made of stainless steel or silver, typically measure 1/2 to 2 inches across, and are attached to the individual in a variety of ways, including the use of rubber straps, suction cups, surgical tape, or plastic adhesive strips. When possible, the electrodes should be attached to hairless sits. The area of application should be cleaned and lightly abraded and the electrode jelly and electrodes applied. Larsen, Schneiderman, and Pasin (1986) provide recommendations for electrode placement. Following electrode placement the waveform resulting from the depolarization of the heart can be measured using a physiograph, turnkey computer system, or ambulatory system. Heart rate data are typically measured by counting the heart rate, measuring the interbeat interval, or examining the contours of the signal.

Blood Pressure. Blood pressure can be assessed using both invasive and noninvasive techniques. The BP is the force built up in the arteries as blood encounters resistance in the peripheral circulatory system. It is usually measured in terms of systolic pressure and diastolic pressure. The systolic pressure is the force that results as muscles contract and blood leaves the heart. Diastolic pressure is the

force with which blood flows back to the heart and represents the residual pressure present in the vascular system when the cardiac muscle relaxes between contractions. Factors affecting blood pressure include heart rate, muscular contractility, stroke volume, elasticity of the arteries, veins and capillaries, viscosity of the blood, and volume of the blood supply (Hassett, 1978). Blood pressure can be measured using a sphygmomanometer and stethoscope; using a physiograph or computer and a microphone designed to pick up the sound of blood flowing through and being occluded by the pressure cuff; using intraarterial cannulas, which are inserted into the vessel and are coupled with a pressure transducer; and using indirect measures that estimate pressure by measuring the rate of propagation of a pulse-wave through the arterial system.

Blood Volume. The two most common measures of vasomotor activity include blood volume and pulse volume. Blood volume reflects the slowly changing absolute amount of blood in a vascular bed at a particular point in time, whereas pulse volume reflects the blood flow through the tissue with each cardiac contraction and represents the combined blood volume and pulse volume (Brown, 1967). The measures are commonly recorded using photosensitive plethysmography, a technique that measures the amount of light transmitted through or reflected back from a section of tissue. The blood volume response is typically measured with a DC electrical amplifier as it represents a slowly changing signal, whereas the pulse volume is measured through an AC amplifier.

Applications

Heart rate appears to be particularly sensitive to the effects of fear and anxiety, perhaps because the client can perceive his or her heart rate and appraise the meaning of such physiological change. Appraisal of the significance of a change in heart rate can trigger anxious thoughts, particularly regarding danger and safety, and these thoughts often lead to increases in anxiety level. The typical cardiac response to fear and anxiety is an increase in heart rate and blood pressure, signs of the traditional "fight or flight reaction." Although sympathetic activation is usually seen as the cause of increases in cardiovascular activity, decreased vagal activation could also lead to similar results.

Increased heart rate and blood pressure responses have been documented in patients with phobias (Turner, Beidel, Dancu, & Keyes, 1986; Lader & Matthews, 1970; Shear, Polan, Harshfield, Pickering, Mann, Frances, & James, 1992); however, this is not always the case (Taylor, Sheikh, Agras, Roth, Margraf, Ehlers, Maddock, & Gossard, 1986). Heart rate increases have also been found to discriminate veterans with post-traumatic stress disorder from a variety of control subjects when the participants are exposed to tapes of combat sounds (Pallmeyer, Blanchard, & Kolb, 1986). Interestingly, however, a pattern of increased heart rate has not been found to characterize patients with panic disorder (McNally, 1994). A pattern of heart rate increases, coupled with decreases in blood pressure has been found to be somewhat unique to individuals who experience problems with blood and injury fears (Ost, Sterner, & Lindahl, 1984). In a recent article, Haynes and colleagues (1991) have challenged the traditional paradigm of looking for increases in rate or changed activity as being the optimal index of a psychophysiological variable and have suggested incorporation of recovery time as being a potential way of looking at physiological activity, including cardiovascular activity, in a more effective way.

Assessment of cardiovascular activity is also important in several areas as behavioral medicine, including hypertension and coronary artery disease. Psychophysiological studies have been used to identify the mechanisms through which psychosocial factors influence the cardiovascular system. In a large review study, Fredrikson and Matthews (1990) reported that hypertensives generally show greater HR and BP activation when exposed to mental stress, particularly in the early phases of hypertension relative to individuals with no cardiac history. An analysis of heart rate variability suggests a sympathetic predominance with vagal dampening in individuals who have hypertension (Alicandri, Fariello, Bon, Zaninelli, Minotti, Guarienti, Orsatti, Cinquegrana, & Muiesan, 1985). Research targeting risk factors for individuals with a high risk of hypertension continues (Steptoe &

Johnson, 1991). Research evaluating effectiveness of treatment studies for hypertension (which have included cardiovascular monitoring) has documented some beneficial effect of regular aerobic exercise in reducing tonic levels of blood pressure, although results have been somewhat inconsistent. Use of relaxation and stress management techniques with this popuation is more questionable, since several well-controlled studies have not been able to demonstrate reliable reductions in blood pressure. There is little information available on the effects of multifactorial treatments for hypertension (Rosen, Brondolo, & Kostis, 1993)

The finger and blood volume response measures have been used primarily in the study Raynaud's disorder, headache activity, and sexual responsiveness (Geer & Castille, 1989; Sturgis, Tollison, & Adams, 1978; Freedman, 1989b). Data supporting the validity of vascular and skin temperature biofeedback in Raynaud's disease has been particularly strong (Freedman & Ianni, 1983; Surwit, Pilon, & Fenton, 1977), with at least one study showing maintenance of voluntary control at one-year follow-up with continued symptom reduction through the third year of follow-up (Freedman, Ianni, & Wenig, 1983).There are some data supporting the fact that one can condition vasomotor and/or skin temperature activity in the biofeedback treatment of migraine headaches (Feuerstein & Adams, 1978; Friar & Beatty, 1976). However, specific mechanisms of treatment effectiveness are not clear. Studies of long-term improvement show inconsistent findings (Blanchard, Andrasik, Guarnieri, Neff, & Rodichok, 1987; Guathier & Carrier, 1991).

Studies of vascular activity have provided significant information about the nature of male and female sexual responsiveness, but several issues complicate research in this area. First, devices currently used to measure responsiveness may be directly or indirectly reactive, thus confounding results (Geer & Castille, 1989). Wolchik, Spencer, and Lisi (1983) have questioned the potential bias introduced by using volunteer subjects. Given the current danger of sexually transmitted diseases, the issue of sterilization of transducers is critical (Geer, 1978). In addition, the emotional concerns of subjects may again distort results. However, given the strong interdependence of emotions, cognitions, and physiological activity, a psychophysiological process emphasizing a time-series methodology could lead to significant advances in our understanding of this very important area.

Although clinicians and researchers have long emphasized the need to assess physiology, behavioral responses, and subjective appraisals in the assessment of fear and anxiety (Lang, 1971), more recent work has shown that these responses are only loosely coupled. However, the unexpected desynchrony among these measures has spawned a significant body of research predicting who should profit most from which treatment based on differential target behaviors (Rachman & Hodgson, 1974). Such studies have shown inconsistent findings (Sartory, Rachman, & Grey, 1977; Craske, Sanderson, & Barlow, 1987). In reviewing these inconsistencies, Foa and Kozak (1986) developed a theory that posits that the extent of the psychophysiological activation within exposure-based treatments is strongly associated with emotional processing. Using this model, Foa and Kozak suggest that exposure-based treatments should be guided by physiological information that reflects the thoroughness with which clients process the emotional material related to the feared situation. Greater physiological activation is associated with more thorough processing and is hypothesized to be related to greater therapeutic gains, provided the individual will stay in therapy long enough for physiological habituation to occur and for more efficacious cognitions to develop. Despite the strong association with cardiovascular functioning and phobic or fearful behavior, the association between cardiovascular activation and panic disorder is much less clear, with the majority of studies finding no real differences in heart rate among panic patients and normals (Margraf et al., 1987; Steptoe & Johnson, 1991).

Research using cardiovscular measures has gained increased sophistication over the past few years. The examples cited here represent only a few of the ares in which a more detailed examination of cardiovascular activity, especially as measured over time and integrated with more cognitive and behavioral data, should increase our understanding of the psychophysiological process.

Factors Influencing Cardiovascular Activity. Epidemiological and laboratory studies have documented general decreases in heart rate while blood pressure tends to increase with age. Blood pressure levels are consistently higher in African-Americans than their White counterparts, and African Americans typically show more reactivity in blood pressure response than do control subjects. The resting heart rate for women is faster relative to that in age-matched populations of men. However, the cardiac reactivity response shows inconsistent patterns across gender. There are also inconsistent racial differences in heart rate, with African American infants demonstrating faster resting heart rates than White newborns. This effect is not typically observed during childhood or adolescence. Young African American males tend to show slower heart rates; however, this difference disappears with age. The research on heart rate responses in African American adults engaged in mentally challenging laboratory tasks has been inconsistent (Anderson & McNeilly, 1991).

Electromyography (EMG)

EMG is used to assess the activity of the musculoskeletal system. An EMG recording reflects the electrical activity (action potentials) of stimulated muscle fibers associated with muscle contraction. EMG is typically measured with surface electrodes placed on the skin over the muscle group of interest. Health psychologists in applied research and clinical settings use EMG recordings most commonly in the assessment and treatment of stress-related muscular disorders such as muscle contraction headaches (Schwartz, 1995), temporomandibular disorders (Flor & Birbaumer, 1993), and low back pain (Fogel, 1995). EMG is also frequently used in various muscular rehabilitation settings (Agras, 1984; Krebs, 1995).

Anatomy and Physiology

The muscles of interest in EMG recordings are the striated muscles. The functional unit of the striated muscle is the motor unit, which is comprised of an alpha motor neuron, its axon, and associated muscle fibers. A single muscle (e.g., masseter muscle) is comprised of many interrelated motor units.

When stimulated, the motor neuron "fires" (initiates and action potential) and a wave of depolarization passes along the associated muscle fibers, causing them to contract. The number of motor units activated and the frequency of firing determines both the total amount of contraction observed and the strength of the signal detected at the EMG recording site. For example, clenching the teeth tightly results in activation of more motor units than biting down gently on the molars, and therefore would result in higher levels of EMG at a masseter muscle placement.

Measurement

Recording meaningful EMG data begins with proper skin preparation and electrode placement. The skin should be rubbed vigorously with an alcohol pad and then gently abraded with an abrasive material (e.g., abrasive skin buff, fine sandpaper). This removes skin oil and the high impedance dead surface layer of skin. Typically, preparation of the electrodes involves coating or filling them with an electrode jelly. Adhesive collars are usually used to attach the electrode to the skin. The skin should be dry before attaching the electrode to ensure that the adhesive collar will stick to the skin, thereby providing the best skin-to-electrode contact.

The purpose for all of these procedures is to reduce electrical impedance as much as possible. Once the electrodes are attached to the skin, electrical impedance between electrodes should ideally be less than 5,000 ohms (Stern, Ray, & Davis, 1980) and definitely no higher than 10,000 ohms (Andreassi, 1989). If impedance exceeds these levels, the electrodes should be removed and the preparation repeated. With some currently available equipment, skin abrasion may not be necessary to yield an electrical impedance between electrodes of less than 10,000 ohms (Fridlund & Cacioppo, 1986). The user must be familiar with the characteristics and of the psychophysiological recording instruments in order to properly prepare subjects/clients for EMG recordings.

The site of electrode placement depends on the purpose of the psychophysiological assessment. In general, as the distance between electrodes increases, the number of motor units included in the recording increases. More specific localized recordings are obtained the closer the active electrodes are placed. Whenever possible, the electrodes should be placed in a line parallel with the muscle fiber. The convention of placing one electrode above each eyebrow in frontalis (forehead) EMG recordings violates this principle and therefore has been questioned by some researchers in the field (e.g., Davis, Brickette, Stern, & Kimball, 1978). Other researchers report that for many applications, such as evaluating changes in EMG levels for individual subjects (as is the case in frontalis EMG biofeedback) placement per se is of little importance (Williamson, Epstein, & Lombardo, 1980; van Boxtel, Goudswaard, & Schomaker, 1984). An EMG electrode placement atlas, as well as a thorough review of other measurement issues in EMG recordings (e.g., signal filtering and amplification) can be found in Fridlund and Cacioppo's (1986) review of this topic.

Applications

EMG recordings have been an integral part of the assessment of various stress-related musculoskeletal disorders (headache, facial pain, back pain), muscle rehabilitation and training (e.g., neuromuscular problems associated with stroke, injury, or disease), and in more basic research such as the study of facial expressions and emotion. There are several books that review various applied and basic research applications of EMG assessment (Andreassi, 1989; Schwartz, 1995). This discussion attempts only to highlight some of the interesting applications of EMG recordings among the stress-related musculoskeletal disorders.

High levels of muscle tension are presumed to play a causal role in the development of stress-related musculoskeletal chronic pain problems (i.e., stress leads to muscle hyperreactivity and subsequent pain). Consequently, EMG biofeedback aimed at teaching clients to reduce the level of tension in the affected muscles has been a frequently employed treatment modality.

Recent studies indicate that EMG biofeedback may be more effective than either cognitive behavior therapy or conservative medical interventions in the treatment of chronic musculoskeletal problems such as back pain and temporomandibular joint pain (Flor & Birbaumer, 1993; Turk, Zaki, &

Rudi, 1993). More general reviews of the treatment literature for tension headache (Blanchard & Andrasik, 1985; Schwartz, 1995), temporomandibular disorders (Gevirtz, Glaros, Hopper, & Schwartz, 1995), and low back pain (Fogel, 1995; Feuerstein, Papciak, & Hoon, 1987) all endorse the utility of EMG biofeedback in the treatment of these various disorders. Ongoing assessment of the psychophysiological response of interest is, of course, inherent in any biofeedback application.

Although there is general consensus as to effectiveness of EMG biofeedback with many musculoskeletal problems, a continuing assessment question in EMG research has been the mechanism of change that accounts for the beneficial effects of biofeedback (e.g., Schwartz, 1995; Martin, Marie, & Nathan, 1992). The data are inconsistent regarding whether these musculoskeletal problems are, in fact, associated with elevated levels of muscle tension (Andreassi, 1989; Schwartz, 1995). A great deal of research has focused on assessing pain patients in pain versus no-pain conditions, during stressful and nonstressful conditions, and pain patients relative to nonpain patients, to ascertain the role of elevated muscle tension in these disorders (e.g., Hatch, Moore, Borcherding, Cyr-Provost, Boutros, & Seleshi, 1992). Increasing sophistication in experimental protocols and instrumentation has provided more convincing evidence that patients with musculoskeletal pain problems do, in fact, have elevated levels of muscle tension. For example, assessing patients in different postures and from multiple EMG cites seems to be important in observing EMG elevations in pain patients versus pain-free controls (Schoenen, Gerard, DePasqua, & Juprelle, 1991). This line of research is a good example of how refinements in our measurement procedures and methods of data quantification have facilitated our understanding of psychophysiological processes.

Psychophysiological assessment strategies are also critical in increasing our understanding of the other etiological factors in these musculoskeletal disorders. For example, maladaptive oral habits (e.g., teeth clenching, jaw jutting) have been implicated in the etiology of certain types of head and facial pain (Laskin, 1992; Moss, Sult, & Garrett,

1984; Moss, Ruff, & Sturgis, 1984). Unfortunately, assessment of these behaviors has relied almost solely on self-report data. A recent study in our laboratory (Gramling, Grayson, & Sullivan, 1996) employed a multimodal assessment of oral habits that included masseter EMG recordings, behavioral observation data, and self-report of oral habits among facial pain subjects and controls during a frustrating task.

Results revealed a general convergence of the three types of data, although the EMG data provided unique information. Namely, self-report of oral habits was higher during task relative to baseline and this effect was stronger among facial pain subjects. Overt oral behavior was generally higher among facial pain subjects across baseline and task phases. EMG data revealed that significantly more of the facial pain subjects engaged in scheduled-induced (adjunctive) masseter muscle contractions, an observation that would have been impossible to detect with self-report or behavioral observation data alone.

We hypothesize that many people who suffer from facial pain, specifically TMD, engage in oral habits (e.g., teeth clenching) under conditions of intermittent insufficient reinforcement—for example, when frustrated with the waiting associated with many of the naturally occurring fixed-interval schedules of daily living (Schwartz & Gramling, 1994). The utility of multimodal assessment, and psychophysiological data in particular, is revealed in a separate study recently completed in our laboratory to test this hypothesis (Gramling, Nicholson, Townsend, Grayson, Sullivan, & Neblett, 1996). Masseter EMG was recorded while TMD patients recruited from the community participated in a four-phase EMG reactivity assessment (adaptation, free-play baseline, scheduled-play baseline, recovery). During the scheduled-play condition, subjects competed with the experimenter in alternating one-minute turns on a slot machine-style electronic poker game. EMG, self-reported oral habits, and negative affectivity were significantly higher during the scheduled-play relative to free-play baseline. Moreover, EMG was significantly higher during the one-minute intervals when the subject waited to play, compared to the one-minute intervals when the subject was actually playing the game. Our hypothesis that oral behaviors may be, in part, schedule-induced is bolstered by both the EMG data and the pattern of results obtained across these various assessment modalities.

These are just a few examples from the diverse literature of EMG applications. EMG biofeedback has been called the workhorse of biofeedback (Schwartz, 1995), and promising new applications such as single-muscle unit biofeedback (Donaldson, 1994) and neuromuscular reeducation and gait training (1995) continue to emerge. The increasing sophistication of these clinical applications can be attributed, in part, to the advances in psychophysiology data acquisition, reduction, and analysis technology developed in more basic research areas (e.g., facial expression and emotion) (Waterink & van Boxtel, 1994). Space limitations, not lack of appreciation, precludes a full discussion of these more basic research applications.

Electrodermal Activity

One of the earliest forms of psychophysiological research involved the measurement of sweat gland, or electrodermal, activity. In 1888, a French neurologist found that he could measure the electrical activity of skin by passing a small electrical current between two electrodes. He then presented the subject with a variety of sensory and emotional stimuli and noted differences in the electrical current. Feré believed the resulting changes in electrical conductivity were instances of nervous system excitement or "arousal" (Andreassi, 1989). The Russian scientist Tarchanoff extended the work in 1890 and found that the stimulated subject would show similar changes in electrical potential between two electrodes without passing an electrical current through the skin. These findings stimulated much early work in psychophysiology as they were seen as providing proof of a mind-body interaction.

Skin resistance (SR), the most commonly used measure of electrodermal activity in early research, represents the measure that results when an external source of voltage is passed through the skin and changes in electrical resistance are recorded. Skin conductance (SC) is the reciprocal of skin resis-

tance and is more easily analyzed in statistical analyses, since it is more likely to conform to the normal distribution required for many analyses. The conductance response also increases with higher levels of arousal and decreases with lower levels of arousal (Andreassi, 1989). Skin potential (SP) measures electrical activity at the surface of the skin with no current passed through it. This measure usually yields a biphasic response curve with an initial negative component followed by a positive phase. Each of the electrodermal measures can be expressed as responses or as levels. Levels represent basal, tonic, or ongoing levels of the response, whereas responses represent phasic or temporary changes in activity that result from exposure to specific stimuli. Investigators are also interested in spontaneous electrodermal activity that occurs in the absence of any known stimulation (Stern, Ray, & Davis, 1980).

Anatomy and Physiology

The electrodermal measures are recorded from the surface of the skin. Skin, the largest organ of the body, has several functions: (1) to form a protective barrier for the organism against environmental agents such as bacteria, chemical pollutants, and so on; (2) to keep fluids inside the body; and (3) to regulate the body's temperature by increasing sweat gland activity and blood vessel dilation when the individual becomes overheated, and decreasing sweat gland activity and constricting the vasculature when the individual is chilled (Andreassi, 1989). The skin is composed of two layers, the epidermis and the dermis, which contain a number of different structures necessary for protection, temperature regulation, and nourishment (e.g., hair follicles, blood vessels, nerves, lymph nodes, smooth muscles).

The eccrine sweat glands, widely distributed across the body, are simple tubular structures with a rounded secretory portion and a duct leading to the epidermis. Innervation of the eccrine glands results from a complex interaction of activity at the prefrontal cortex, the limbic and hypothalamic areas (associated with motivation and emotional behavior), and the reticular system. Eccrine innervation occurs solely within the sympathetic branch of the autonomic nervous system; however, the synaptic transmission involves the neurotransmitter acetylcholine, not noradrenaline, the more typical sympathetic nervous system neurotransmitter (Venables & Christie, 1980).

Generalization of information about the sympathetic nervous system obtained from the eccrine glands may be somewhat limited, given the different pattern of neurochemical innervation. With increased sympathetic nervous system innervation, sweat rises toward the surface of the skin in varying amounts and in varying numbers of sweat glands. The greater the rise of sweat in a given gland, the lower the SR and the higher the SC. However, the measure of electrodermal activity is also affected by the hydration of the tubule, thus it is not an exact measure of sympathetic nervous system activity. Overflow of the sweat to the surface of the skin increases not only skin conductance but also skin potential. In order to interpret electrodermal activity, one must know the resting or tonic response pattern, the pattern following stimulation, the maximal change in the response pattern, and/or the time required for the response to return to its tonic state.

Measurement

Two types of circuits are used to measure the SC and SR response: constant voltage and constant current circuits. The constant voltage measure hold the voltage across the surface constant while the current varies with changes in the resistance or conductance of the skin (Stern, Ray, & Davis, 1980). Electrodes should be constructed of a non-polarizing metal, typically with a salt of that metal adhered to the surface. The most commonly used electrodes in electrodermal recording are silver/silver chloride or zinc/zinc sulfate. Most investigators recommend that the electrode paste contain a potassium chloride or sodium chloride electrolyte. Electrode placement sites vary as a function of the response being measured. In the measurement of the SC or SR response, one should use the palms, fingertips, and soles of the feet when necessary. Another common choice for SC/SR recording is the thenar and hypothenar eminence of the palm (Hassett, 1978). Skin potential recordings reflect a potential difference between the sweat glands and internal body tissues. A monopolar placement is most common. For best recording, one electrode is placed on an "emotionally active" site (such as the thenar eminence) while the other electrode is placed over a small hole drilled into the skin, typically on the forearm (Venables & Christie, 1980).

Signal filtering and amplification are more difficult for the electrodermal responses. One frequent annoyance to the EDA investigator is the fact that, for many subjects, level changes may be of a relatively large magnitude compared to the responses, thus necessitating a change in the baseline scale. One way to avoid this necessity is to filter out the level changes that have a slower frequency through the use of a high-pass filter of 3 Hz. While this procedure assists in locating a detectible range in which to detect the change in level, information about the level and data concerning the topography of the electrodermal response are lost, thus information concerning the amplitude of the true response is not available. Another way to cope with this change in baseline is to use a dual recording procedure, with one channel of the physiograph measuring the levels of the response with the second amplifier set with a high gain so that small changes in the response are recorded. Other procedures for scoring the EDR may be found in Andreassi (1989), Boucsein (1992), Fowles, Christie, Edelberg, Grings, Lykken, and Venables (1981), Venables and Christie (1980), and Hassett (1978).

Applications

Electrodermal activity has been widely investigated in a number of areas. The electrodermal response has been extensively studied in the context of discriminating the orienting and defensive responses (Sokolov, 1963). The frequency and amplitude of skin conductance responses (SCRs) are influenced by changes in stimuli, particularly when the change involves increasing the intensity or the tonal frequency of a stimulus (Bernstein, 1969; Siddle & Heron, 1978). Wingard and Maltzman (1980) expanded the orienting paradigm to include a measure of interest in the stimuli and found that recreational interests influenced the reaction to stimuli. Individuals showed significantly larger SCRs and orienting responses to slides depicting their hobbies. Ohman (1979) has extended work on the use of electrodermal measures in indexing the information processing of the individual.

Dawson, Nuechterlein, and Adams (1989) summarized a host of studies employing electrodermal measures in the study of schizophrenia. In particular, studies have emphasized habituation rates of SCRs as well as orienting responses. A host of studies has found that 40% to 50% of schizophrenic subjects fail to orient to innocuous stimuli, and this failure to respond does not appear related to the medication state of the individual. In schizophrenics who do show an orienting response, the majority habituate quite quickly. Of clinical importance, nonresponders are generally rated by observers in other settings as being more disorganized, emotionally withdrawn, and lower on excitement (negative symptoms of schizophrenia that typically index poor prognosis) (Straub, 1979; Bernstein, Taylor, Starkey, Juni, Lubowsky, & Paley, 1981). Those who show orienting responses with slow habituation rates are generally rated as being more manic, anxious, belligerent, and attention seeking than the nonresponders. Finally, schizophrenics in remission have been noted to develop the blunted SCR response to stimulation prior to a relapse, thus this response pattern might be useful in the ongoing monitoring of schizophrenic patients in the community (Dawson, 1990).

Factors Affecting EDA Measurement

Research has also indicated that the interpretation of electrodermal activity is complicated by several factors. There are age changes in skin conductance activity, with older individuals showing reduced levels (Anderson & McNeilly, 1991). Hormonal fluctuations in progesterone also decrease eccrine gland sweat output (Andreassi, 1989). In addition, there are several studies of ethnic differences in the magnitude of the skin conductance response with African American subjects exhibiting lower levels (Johnson & Corah, 1963). Finally, the experimental context—including the sociocultural, interpersonal, and situational context of the study—may alter electrodermal activity.

Electrocortical Activity

During the past quarter century, recordings of brain activity by psychophysiologists has increased substantially. Several factors have contributed to this increase: (1) development of fast Fourier transformation algorithms, which make it possible to perform spectral analyses of EEG activity simultaneously with data collection; (2) increased sophistication and low cost of computers that can serve as multipurpose laboratory instruments presenting data while simultaneously recording data and performing unique analytic functions; (3) and increased yield of information from cortical measures as investigators have begun to use electroencephalographic activity to index cortical processes in addition to their use as diagnostic tools of brain injury (Johnson, 1980).

Anatomy and Physiology

The brain is composed of over 1 billion neurons, each capable of two types of electrical responses: (1) graded potentials and (2) action potentials. *Graded potentials* are small gradual changes in the neuronal membrane potential resulting from synaptic activity When the sum of those graded potentials exceeds a critical threshold, the neuron "fires" or initiates an action potential. Action potentials are electrical pulses that fire in an all-or-none fashion. The impulse originates at the axon hillock, travels along the axon, and then releases neurotransmitter substances into the synaptic cleft. The EEG actually measures electrical potential differences between any two electrodes placed on the surface of the scalp. The EEG reflects the combined electrical activity of millions of neurons and measures the summation of the ongoing, spontaneous electrical activity (graded and action potentials) across a given area.

Measurement

EEG Response. The EEG is a measure of the electrical potential difference between any two electrodes placed on the scalp. Since EEG reflects the combined electrical activity of millions of neurons, changes in voltage that characterize the EEG are relatively large. Therefore, surface electrodes placed on the scalp are suitable signal detectors, even though the scalp is several millimeters from the surface of the brain, the surface of interest. However, the scalp area where the electrodes are to be placed must be thoroughly cleaned and abraded in order to obtain a clear signal. Electrode placement has been standardized by the International Federation of Societies for Electroencephalography and Clinical Neurophysiology with the "10-20" system of electrode placement (Jasper, 1958). This system of electrode placement allows for individual differences in skull size by specifying that electrodes be placed on the scalp either 10% or 20% of the distance from common cranial landmarks (Hassett, 1978; Johnson, 1980).

Once EEG wave forms are obtained, they can be analyzed several ways. The first efforts of EEG interpretation included frequency and amplitude analysis. The waveforms comprising the EEG record traditionally have been classified according to specified frequency along four to five band-wave dimensions. Each band-wave was assumed to reflect different levels of cortical arousal. Frequencies of less than 4 Hz are classified as delta waves and are often associated sleep. Theta waves (4 to 8 Hz) are associated with drowsiness and are commonly seen in children. Alpha waves (8 to 13 Hz) are associated with the experience of relaxation. Finally, all EEG patterns exceeding 13Hz are Beta waves and are typically associated with the awake, alert state.

Frequency analysis of the EEG, combined visual analyses of wave-forms which can show spontaneous spike waves, paroxysmal bursts, and spike and slow wave discharges have been used diagnostically primarily by medical professionals to diagnose convulsive disorders, sleep difficulties, substance use patterns, and other forms of cerebral dysfunction. More sophisticated analyses using computer reduction and collapsing of EEG patterns across similar time periods has allowed more sophistication in the questions addressed by electrocortical responses. Such spectral procedures can allow the examiner to estimate the density and periodicities of different waveforms.

Applications. Spectral analyses of EEG have allowed examiners to study differences in reaction time, attention, mental activity, emotional functioning, temperament, and hemispheric differences during different types of cortical and emotional activity. These analyses have been quite useful in clarifying the processes of information processing used by normals and schizophrenics (Dawson, Nuechterlein, & Adams, 1989). These approaches have also yielded information regarding the relative specificity of different areas of the brain as well as provided information useful in the rehabilitation of chronic head injury. However, emergence of the MRI and PET-scan methodologies have largely surpassed the diagnostic utility of EEG evaluations of nervous system dysfunction (Parsons & Nixon, 1993).

The Evoked Potential Response. The event related potential response (ERP), rather than representing random activity, is an time-locked electrical response of the cortical system generated by some event in the external environment. The ERP waveform is recorded from the scalp in a manner similar to the EEG and consists of the analysis of transient series of voltage oscillations that are time-locked to a particular stimulus. However, since the magnitude of the ERP is typically small relative to the background noise, the signal event is typically repeated a number of times and the signal averaged across multiple trials to distinguish the ERP from the background EEG. Because of its ability to allow psychophysiologists to make associations between discrete psychological states and events and physiological responses, the ERP is of particular interest to psychophysiologists (Dawson et al., 1989).

Applications. Some of the more interesting brain responses are termed *slow potentials* because they take relatively longer to develop than other ERPs. An examination of ERP responses has shown deficits in selective attentional processes in a number of clinical populations, including individuals with schizophrenia, hyperactivity, a learning disability, senile dementia, and dissociative disorders (Hillyard & Hansen, 1986). There is some promising research indicating that abnormalities in the P-300 response may provide promising markers for schizophrenia and alcoholism in the young children of schizophrenics or alcoholics (Begleiter, Porjesz, & Bihari, 1987; Schuckit, Gold, Finn, & Polich, 1988). However, results are inconclusive at present since it is not known how and in what ways the psychophysiological reactivity of children is similar to adults (Iacono & Ficken, 1991). Were EEG measures, combined with information on other risk factors including current behaviors patterns, found to be reliable markers of a disorder, the use of primary prevention efforts could be significantly advanced (Iacono & Ficken, 1991).

Factors Affecting Electrocortical Activity

Interpretation of electrocortical data can be complicated by a number of factors. Alcohol, heroin, marijuana, the hypnotics, tranquilizers, and nicotine all alter EEG activity in specific ways. Indeed, the EEG analysis is viewed as a major way to objectively determine psychoactive drug activity (Andreassi, 1989). This research approach has also gained prominence in the field of affective psychoses, psychosomatic disorders, and anxiety-related disorders (Gruzelier, 1989). While the data suggest an understanding of electrocortical activity is not sufficient to explain these more complex psychological states, one must consider cortical factors among the systems being examined if a psychophysiological understanding is to be gained (Turpin, 1989).

Unfortunately, space limitations prohibit an examination of the varied types of psychophysiological assessment that can be useful in the understanding of behavior. We have necessarily been brief in what we have presented and have ignored measures such as respiration, eye movement, and pupillary responses, (measures often employed in psychological research) as well as the more sophisticated methodologies currently being used in many medical centers and major research laboratories. Work in these areas will continue to inform our understanding of the psychophysiological process. However, by highlighting work in a few traditional areas, our intent has been to introduce the reader to many of the issues that need to be considered as one employs psychophysiological assessment in research and clinical practice. We close the chapter with a case study that will provide addi-

tional information about the potential utility of this most important area.

CASE STUDY IN PSYCHOPHYSIOLOGICAL ASSESSMENT

The following case study illustrates the use of psychophysiological assessment in a comprehensive assessment and treatment program for individuals suffering from temporomandibular joint disorder (TMD). TMD is a stress-related disorder where stress presumably leads to parafunctional oral habits (e.g., teeth clenching, lip biting), which in turn results in increased tension in the muscles of mastication. The prevailing etiological model of TMD suggests that this stress-related increase in muscle tension causes the facial pain experienced by TMD sufferers (Laskin, 1969; Parker, 1990). Numerous psychophysiological assessment studies have tested the adequacy of this model with mixed results. Some studies show increased EMG reactivity among TMD patients relative to controls, whereas others do not. However, treatments that target muscles of mastication (e.g., masseter EMG biofeedback, relaxation training) have consistently been reported to be effective in treating the TMD client, and these findings have generally been used as evidence to support the stress→→ muscle tension →→ pain hypothesis. In addition to pain ratings and measures of psychological functioning, treatment studies with TMD clients frequently use pre-post reductions in masseter EMG as a key outcome measure.

Case Study

Janice, the subject of the case study, participated in a psychophysiological reactivity evaluation in conjunction with her participation in a structured group treatment program for TMD patients offered by the Behavioral Health Institute at Virginia Commonwealth University. The seven-session treatment emphasized habit reversal and cognitive restructuring. Participants learned both to detect their maladaptive oral habits and substitute incompatible responses and to detect and change their maladaptive stress-inducing cognitions. The psychophysiological assessment procedure used a stressful task to assess baseline EMG, EMG reactivity, and return-to-baseline levels before and after treatment.

At the time of testing, Janice was a 35-year-old married Caucasian female who presented with facial pain of eight years' duration. She was married with two children (a 12-year-old daughter and 8-year-old son). She worked full time and reported major stressors in the areas of parenting, finances, and career satisfaction. During the two-month pretreatment phase, she experienced zero pain-free days and her average daily pain rating was in the moderate range (3 on a 5-point scale). Location of her pain was localized in the left and right masseter area. When her pain was at its maximum, the pain was predominantly on the left side. She reported engaging in several oral habits that have been linked to facial pain, including lip biting, resting the head on hands while sitting, and holding the telephone receiver between the chin and shoulder while talking on the telephone (average frequencies of 6 to 8 on a 10-point scale). Her maladaptive beliefs included catastrophizing and perfectionism.

The primary physiological measure of interest in this case was masseter EMG. With facial pain clients (and other musculoskeletal pain patients such as tension headache and many chronic back pain clients), we are interested in the extent to which EMG is elevated at baseline, the extent to which EMG is reactive during stress, and whether resting levels of EMG return to baseline levels or stay elevated after exposure to a stressor. Other psychophysiological measures are often collected as more general measures of arousal. In Janice's case, we collected hand temperature (HT measured in degrees Fahrenheit) and skin conductance (SCR measured in mmhoms) as well as electromyography (EMG measured in microvolts)

A pretreatment psychophysiological assessment protocol was used to assess masseter EMG reactivity during a laboratory stressor. Janice gave her informed consent to participate, completed several self-report measures of psychological functioning, and was then prepared for the psychophysiological assessment. Since her pain was predominantly on the left side, masseter EMG recordings were taken from the left side. The skin was vigorously cleansed with alcohol, gently abraded

with a skin buff, and silver/silver chloride electrodes prepared with electrolyte were attached to the skin with adhesive collars. One active electrode was placed ¾ inch anterior to and ½ inch above the angle of the jaw, and the second active electrode was placed over the same muscle group 2 inches above the first electrode, as recommended by Stern, Ray, and Davis (1980). The ground electrode was attached to the chin. Hand temperature was recorded by taping a thermistor to the middle finger of the left hand. Skin conductance was assessed with electrodes, prepared with electrolyte, and attached to the palmer surface of the left hand at the hypothenar eminence and thenar eminence with adhesive collars. A Velcro-covered stiff wooden bar was placed across the palm of the Velcro surface of the back of the electrodes and then a Velcro strap attached to the wooden bar was wrapped around the palm and attached at the other end of the bar. The client kept her hand palm up resting on the chair's arm rest throughout the experiment. The data were collected, stored, and reduced with a computer system for psychophysiological recordings (Biocomp 2001).

The stressor used in the reactivity assessment involved a gambling game where the client and experimenter competed against each other to win points by accumulating the most winning jackpots on a small electronic slot machine. The experimenter and client took turns playing the game in two-minute trials, with both parties getting two turns each. This task involved competition but the outcome was determined solely by chance. The task involved taking turns in order to mimic daily life situations where people are required to wait before responding. TMD clients tend to be more reactive to this task relative to control subjects. We hypothesize that the TMD clients find the waiting associated with taking turns in this task particularly frustrating.

Psychophysiological assessment began with a 15-minute adaptation period wherein Janice was asked to sit quietly and relax. The data from the last 3 minutes of the adaptation phase were used as baseline. Following baseline, Janice participated in the 8-minute gambling task, which was followed by a 10-minute recovery period. The results of the pretreatment assessment were as follows:

	Baseline	Gambling	Recovery
EMG	4.14	15.52	5.92
HT	91.80	87.30	85.81
SCR	2.92	7.85	7.91

Although Janice's baseline EMG was somewhat elevated, the elevation observed during the gambling task was fairly dramatic. Decreasing hand temperature and increasing SCR also suggest physiological arousal during the gambling task. After the seven-week treatment program, Janice's reaction to arousing stimuli was strikingly reduced and her baseline measures suggested lower levels of arousal as well.

The results of the posttreatment assessment were as follows.

	Baseline	Gambling	Recovery
EMG	2.85	3.6	3.0
HT	96.4	96.2	96.5
SCR	1.67	4.3	2.5

The treatment seemed to have a powerful effect on Janice's level of stress reactivity, and these changes were paralleled by substantial reductions in ratings of facial pain. During the first five weeks of treatment, Janice reported pain everyday, although of a diminishing intensity. At the sixth week of treatment, she began experiencing pain-free days. At the time of the postpsychophysiological assessment, her average pain intensity was .35 on a 5-point scale, her number of pain-free days in the preceding week was 5 and her maximum pain was a 2. Her ratings of treatment satisfaction were excellent (7 on a 7-point scale) and she improved on measures of psychological functioning as well. At one-year follow-up, Janice continues to report virtually no pain.

We cautiously infer that the treatment led to a reduction in EMG stress reactivity and that this reduction in reactivity, in turn, accounts for the reduction in pain reported by Janice. As with any single-case design there are threats to internal validity (e.g., sensitization to testing procedures and historical effects) that limit our confidence in this conclusion. In Janice's case, we have additional information that increases our confidence in these findings. She was one of 10 clients that par-

ticipated in the treatment study. Relative to a comparison group of untreated TMD clients, those like Janice who received the treatment improved significantly on measures of pain relative to the controls. Moreover, controls who participated in psychophysiological assessments seven weeks apart without intervening treatment did not show a change in psychophysiological reactivity. Taken together, these findings bolster our confidence that treatment affected psychophysiological reactivity per se. At the very least, these results illustrate the utility of multimodal assessment procedures that include psychophysiological measures.

SUMMARY

Although psychologists have been sensitive to mind-body interactions since inception of the discipline, to date, an emphasis on psychophysiology has not had the impact on psychology one might predict. In this chapter, we advocate that users rethink how and why they wish to include psychophysiological measures in the assessment process. We suggest the measures that will be most useful when studied in the total context of the assessment process and in an ongoing fashion rather than being used to clarify substrates of particular behavior patterns. We also suggest the adoption of a process approach to psychophysiology, emphasizing that the dynamic nature of biological, cognitive, emotional, and behavioral factors may prove more useful than have other approaches. To do so, however, we must rethink the experimental designs as well as the statistical analyses used to analyze the data. Until recently, most studies have investigated psychophysiology as a method or a mechanism underlying behavior. As we move into the next millennium, a reconceptualization of the classic questions about mind-body relations may lead to significant advances in our understanding of human behavior.

REFERENCES

Agras, W. S. (1984). The behavioral treatment of psychological disorders. In W. D. Gentry (Ed.), *Handbook of behavioral medicine* (pp. 479–530). New York: Guilford.

Alicandri, C., Fariello, R., Boni, E., Zaninelli, A., Minotti, F., Guarienti, P., Orsatti, D., Cinquegrana,

A., & Muiesan, G. (1985). Autonomic nervous system control of heart rate in essential hypertension. *Journal of Hypertension, 3,* S117–S119.

Anderson, D. E., Coyle, K., & Haythornwaithe, J. A. (1992). Ambulatory monitoring of respiration: Inhibitory breathing in the natural environment. *Psychophysiology, 29,* 551–557.

Anderson, D. E., & Frank, L. B. (1990). A microprocessor system for ambulatory monitoring of respiration. *Journal of Ambulatory Monitoring, 3,* 11–20.

Anderson, N. B., & McNeilly, M. (1991). Age, gender, and ethnicity in psychophysiological assessment: Sociodemographics in context. *Psychological Assessment, 3,* 376–384.

Andreassi, J. L. (1989). *Psychophysiology: Human behavior and physiological response* (2nd ed.). Hillsdale, NJ: Lawrence Erlbaum.

Arena, J. G., Blanchard, E. B., Andrasik, F., Crotch, P. A., & Meyers, P. E. (1983). Reliability of psychophysiological assessment. *Behaviour Research and Therapy, 13,* 407–460.

Arena, J.G., Bruno, G. M., Brucks, A. G., Searle, J.R., Sherman, R. A., & Meador, K. J., et al. (1994). Reliability of an ambulatory electromyographic activity device for musculoskeletal pain disorders. *International Journal of Psychophysiology, 17,* 153–157.

Arena, J.G., & Hobbs, S. H. (1995). Reliability of psychophysiological responding as a function of trait anxiety. *Biofeedback and Self-Regulation, 20,* 19–37.

Arena, J. G., Sherman, R. A., Bruno, G. M., & Young, T. R. (1990). Temporal stability of paraspinal electromyographic recordings in low back pain and non-pain subjects. *International Journal of Psychophysiology, 9,* 31–37.

Bandura, A. (1978). The self system in reciprocal determinism. *American Psychologist, 33,* 344–358.

Bandura, A. (1986). *Social foundations of thought and action: A social cognitive theory.* Englewood Cliffs, NJ: Prentice-Hall.

Begleiter, H., Porjesz, B., & Bihari, B. (1987). Auditory brainstem potentials in sons of alcoholic fathers. *Alcoholism: Clinical and Experimental Research, 11,* 477–480.

Bernstein, A. S. (1969). The orienting response and direction of stimulus change. *Psychonomic Science, 112,*127–128.

Bernstein, A. S., Taylor, K. W., Starkey, P., Juni, S., Lubowsky, J., & Paley, H. (1981). Bilateral skin conductance, finger pulse volume, and EEG orienting response to tones of differing intensities in chronic schizophrenics and controls. *Journal of Nervous and Mental Disease, 169, 513–528.*

Blanchard, E. B., & Andrasik, F. (1985). *Management of chronic headaches: A psychological approach.* New York: Pergamon.

Blanchard, E. G., Andrasik F., Guarnieri, O., Neff, D. F., & Rodichok, L. D. (1987). Two, three, and four-year follow-up on the self-regulatory treatment of chronic headache. *Journal of Consulting and Clinical Psychology, 55,* 257–259.

Brown, C. C. (1967). The techniques of plethysmography. In C. C. Brown (Ed.), *Methods in psychophysiology* (pp. 54–74. Baltimore: Waverly.

Bouscein, W. (1992). *Electrodermal activity.* New York: Plenum.

Cacioppo, J. T., Berntson, G. G., & Andersen, B. L. (1991). Psychophysiological approaches to the evaluation of psychotherapeutic process and outcome, 1991: Contributions from social psychology. *Psychological Assessment: A Journal of Consulting and Clinical Psychology, 3,* 321–336.

Coles, M. G. H., Donchin, E., & Porges, S. W. (1986). Preface. In M. G. H. Coles, E. Donchin, & S. W. Porges (Eds.), *Psychophysiology: Systems, processes, and applications* (pp. ix–x). New York: Guilford.

Coles, M. G. H., Gratton, G., Kramer, A. F., & Miller, G. A. (1986). Principles of signal detection and analysis. In M. G. H. Coles, E. Donchin, & S. W. Porges (Eds.), *Psychophysiology: Systems, processes, and applications* (pp. 183–221). New York: Guilford.

Craske, M. G., Sanderson, W. C., & Barlow, D. H. (1987). How do desynchronous response systems related to the treatment of agoraphobia: A follow-up evaluation. *Behaviour Research and Therapy, 25,* 117–122.

Davis, C. M., Brickette, P., Stern, R. M., & Kimball, W. H. (1978). Tension in two frontales: Electrode placement and artifact in the recording of the forehead EMG. *Psychophysiology, 15,* 591–593.

Dawson, M. E. (1990). Psychophysiology at the interface of clinical science, cognitive science, and neuroscience. *Psychophysiology, 27,* 243–255.

Dawson, M. E., Nuechterlein, K. H., & Adams, R. M. (1989). Schizophrenic disorders. In G. Turpin (Ed.), *Handbook of clinical psychophysiology* (pp. 393–418). Chichester, England: Wiley.

Donaldson, S., Romney, D., Donaldson, M., & Skubick, D. (1994). Randomized study of the application of single motor unit biofeedback training to chronic low back pain. *Journal of Occupational Rehabilitation, 4,* 23–37.

Donchin, E., Karis, D., Bashore, T. R., Coles, M. G. H., & Gratton, G. (1986). Cognitive psychophysiology and human information processing. In M. G. H.

Coles, E. Donchin, & S. W. Porges (Eds.), *Psychophysiology: Systems, processes, and information* (pp. 244–267). New York: Guilford.

Farrell, A. D. (1991). Computers and behavioral assessment: Current applications, future possibilities, and obstacles to routine use. *Behavioral Assessment, 13,* 159–179.

Feurstein, M., & Adams, H. E. (1978). Cephalic vasomotor feedback in the modification of migraine headache. *Biofeedback and Self–Regulation, 2,* 241–253.

Feuerstein, M., Labbe, E. E., & Kuczmierczyk, A. (1988). *Health psychology: A psychobiological perspective.* New York: Plenum.

Feuerstein, M., Papciak, A. S., & Hoon, P. E. (1987). Biobehavioral mechanisms of chronic low back pain. *Clinical Psychology Review, 7,* 243–273.

Flor, H., & Birbaumer, N. (1993). Comparison of the efficacy of electromyographic biofeedback, cognitive behavior therapy and conservative medical interventions in the treatment of chronic musculoskeletal pain. *Journal of Consulting and Clinical Psychology, 61,* 653–658.

Foa, E. B., & Kozak, M. J. (1986). Emotional processing of fear: Exposure to corrective information. *Psychological Bulletin, 99,* 20–35.

Fogel, A. (1992). The process of developmental change in infant communicative action: Using dynamic systems theory to study individual ontogenies. In L. B. Smith & E. Thelen (Eds.), *A dynamic systems approach to development applications* (pp. 341–353). Cambridge, MA: MIT Press.

Fogel, E. R. (1995). Biofeedback-assisted musculoskeletal therapy and neuromuscular re-education. In M. S. Schwartz (Ed.), *Biofeedback: A practitioner's guide* (pp. 560-593). London: Guilford.

Fogel, A. (1992). The process of developmental change in infant communicative action: Using dynamic systems theory to study individual ontogenies. In L. B. Smith & E. Thelen (Eds.), *A dynamic systems approach to development applications* (pp. 341–353). Cambridge, MA: MIT Press.

Fogel, E. R. (1995). Biofeedback-assisted musculoskeletal therapy–and neuromuscular re-education. In M. S. Schwartz (Ed.), *Biofeedback: A practitioner's guide* (pp. 560-593). London: Guilford.

Fowles, D. C., Christie, M. J., Edelberg, R., Grings, W. W., Lykken, D. T., & Venables, P. H. (1981). Committee Report: Publication recommendations for electrodermal measurements. *Psychophysiology, 18,* 232–239.

Fredrickson, M. (1991). Physiological responses to stressors: Implications for clinical assessment. *Psychological Assessment: A Journal of Consulting and Clinical Psychology, 3,* 350–355.

Fredrikson, M., & Matthews, K. A. (1990). Cardiovascular responses to behavioral stress and hypertension: A meta-analytic review. *Annals of Behavioral Medicine, 12,* 30–30

Freedman, R. R. (1989a). Laboratory and ambulatory monitoring of menopausal hot flashes. *Psychophysiology, 26,* 573–579.

Freedman, R. R. (1989b). Raynaud's disease. In G. Turpin (Ed.), *Handbook of clinical psychophysiology* (pp. 469–494). Chichester, England: Wiley.

Freedman, R. R., & Ianni, R. (1983). Self-control of digital temperature: Physiological factors and transfer effects. *Psychophysiology, 20,* 682–688.

Freedman, R. R. (1995). Raynaud's disease and phenomenom. In A. J. Goreczny (Ed.), *Handbook of health and rehabilitation psychology* (pp. 117–131). New York: Plenum.

Freedman, R. R., Ianni, R., & Wenig, P. (1983). Behavioral treatment of Raynaud's disease. *Journal of Consulting and Clinical Psychology, 51,* 539–549.

Friar, L. R., & Beatty, J. (1976). Migraine: Management by trained control of vasoconstriction. *Journal of Consulting and Clinical Psychology, 44,* 46–53

Fridlund, A. J., & Cacioppo, J. T. (1986). Guidelines for human electromyographic research. *Psychophysiology, 23,* 567–589.

Gauthier, J. G., & Carrier, S. (1991). Long-term effects of biofeedback on migraine headaches: A prospective follow-up study. *Headache, 31,* 605–612.

Geer, J. H. (1978). Sterilization of genital devices. *Psychophysiology, 15,* 385.

Geer, J. H., & Castille, C. O. (1989). Sexual disorders. In G. Turpin (Ed.), *Handbook of clinical psychophysiology* (pp. 419–440). Chichester, England: Wiley.

Gevirtz, R. N., Glaros, A. G., Hopper, D., & Schwartz, M. S. (1995). Temporomandibular disorders. In M. S. Schwartz (Ed.), *Biofeedback: A practitioner's guide* (pp. 411–428). London: Guilford.

Gottlieb, G. (1991). Experimental canalization of behavioral development: Theory. *Developmental Psychology, 27,* 4–13.

Gottman, J. (1990). Time-series analysis applied to physiological data. In J. T. Cacioppo & L. G. Tessinary (Eds.)., *Principles of psychophysiology: Physical, social, and inferential elements* (pp. 754–774). Cambridge: Cambridge University Press.

Gramling, S. E., Grayson, R., & Sullivan, T. N. (1996, March). *Tri-modal assessment of oral habits in facial pain.* Poster presented at the 17th Annual Meeting of the society of Behavioral Medicine.

Gramling, S. E., Nicholson, R., Townsend, D., Grayson,

R., Sullivan, T. N., & Neblett, J. (1996, March). *Schedule induced EMG muscle reactivity among facial pain patients.* Poster presented at the 17th Annual Meeting of the Society of Behavioral Medicine.

Gruzelier, J. H. (1989). Lateralization and central mechanisms in clinical psychophysiology. In G. Turpin (Ed.), *Handbook of clinical psychophysiology* (pp. 135–174). Chichester, England: Wiley.

Hassett, J. (1978). *A primer of psychophysiology.* San Francisco: Freeman.

Hatch, J. P., Moore, P. J., Borcherding, S., Cyr-Provost, M., Boutros, N. N., & Seleschi, E. (1992). Electromyographic and affective responses of episodic tension-type headache patients and headache-free controls during stress task performance. *Journal of Behavioral Medicine*, 15, 89–112.

Haynes, S. N. (1991). Clinical application of psychophysiological assessment: An introduction and overview. *Psychological Assessment: A Journal of Consulting and Clinical Psychology, 3,* 307–308.

Haynes, S. N., Blaine, D., & Meyer, K. (1995). Dynamical models for psychological assessment: Phase space functions. *Psychological Assessment, 7,* 17–24.

Haynes, S. N., Falkin, S., & Sexton-Radek, K. (1989). Psychophysiological assessment in behavior therapy. In G. Turpin (Ed.), *Handbook of clinical psychophysiology* (pp. 175–214). Chichester, England: Wiley.

Haynes, S. N., Gannon, L. R., Orimoto, L., & O'Brien, W. H. (1991). Psychophysiological assessment of poststress recovery. *Psychological Assessment: A Journal of Consulting and Clinical Psychology, 3,* 356–363.

Heiby, A. M. (1995). Chaos theory, nonlinear dynamical models, and psychological assessment. *Psychological Assessment, 7,* 5–9.

Hillyard, S. A., & Hansen, J. C. (1986). Attention: Electrophysiological approaches. In M. G. H. Coles, E. Donchin, & S. W. Porges (Eds.), *Psychophysiology: Systems, processes, and information.* (pp. 227–243). New York: Guilford.

Hugdahl, K. (1989). Simple phobias. In G. Turpin (Ed.), *Handbook of clinical psychophysiology* (pp. 283–308). Chichester, England: Wiley.

Hunt, M. (1993). *The story of psychology.* New York: Doubleday.

Iacono, W. G. (1991). Psychophysiological assessment of psychopathology. *Psychological Assessment: A Journal of Consulting and Clinical Psychology, 3,* 309–320.

Iacono, W. G., & Ficken, J. W. (1989). Research strategies employing psychophysiological measures: Identifying and using psychophysiological markers. In G. Turpin (Ed.), *Handbook of clinical psychophysiology* (pp. 45–70). Chichester, England: Wiley.

Jacob, S. W., & Francone, C. A. (1970). *Structure and function in man* (2nd ed.). Philadelphia: Saunders.

Jasper, H. H. (1958). The ten-twenty electrode system of the International Federation. *EEG Clinical Neurophysiology, 10,* 371–375.

Johnson, L. C. (1980). Measurement, quantification, and analysis of cortical activity: Recordings and analysis of brain activity. In I. Martin & P. H. Venables (Eds.), *Techniques in psychophysiology* (pp. 329–357). New York: Wiley.

Johnson, L. C., & Coria, N. L. (1963). Racial differences in skin resistance. *Science, 139,* 766–767.

Krantz, D. S., Manuck, S. B., & Wing, R. R. (1986). Psychological stressors and task variables as elicitors of reactivity. In K. A. Matthews, S. M. Weiss, T. Detre, T. M. Dembroski, B. Faulknew, S. B. Manuck, & R. B. Williams (Eds.), *Handbook of stress reactivity and cardiovascular disease* (pp. 85–107). New York: Wiley-Interscience.

Krebs, D. E. (1995). Biofeedback in neuromuscular re-education and gait training. In M. S. Schwartz (Ed.), *Biofeedback: A practitioner's guide* (pp. 525–559). London: Guilford.

Lacey, J. I. (1959). Psychophysiological approaches to the evaluation of psychotherapeutic process and outcome. In E. A. Rubinstein & M. B. Parloff (Eds.), *Research in psychotherapy.* (pp. 161–208). Washington, DC: American Psychological Association.

Lader, M., & Mathews, A. (1970). Physiological changes during spontaneous panic attacks. *Journal of Psychosomatic Research*, 14, 377–382.

Lang, P. J. (1971). The application of psychophysiological methods in the study of psychotherapy and behavior modification. In A. E. Bergin & S. S. Garfield (Eds.), *Handbook of psychotherapy and behavior change: An experimental analysis* (pp. 75–125). New York: Wiley.

Larsen, P. B., Schneiderman, N., & Pasin, R. D. (1986). Physiological bases of cardiovascular psychophysiology. In M. G. H. Coles, E. Donchin, & S. W. Porges (Eds.), *Psychophysiology: Systems, processes, and applications* (pp. 122–165). New York: Guilford.

Laskin, D. M. (1969). Etiology of pain-dysfunction syndrome. *Journal of the American Dental Association, 79,* 147–153.

Laskin, D. M. (1992). Temporomandibular disorders: Diagnosis and etiology. In B. G. Sarnat & D. M. Laskin (Eds.), *The temporomandibular joint: A biological basis for clinical practice* (4th ed.) (pp. 316–328). Philadelphia: Saunders.

Lickliter, R., & Berry, T. (1990). The phylogeny fallacy: Developmental psychology's misapplication of evolutionary theory. *Developmental Review, 10,* 348–364.

Margraf, J., Taylor, C. B., Ehlers, A., Roth, W. T., & Agras, W. S. (1987). Panic attacks in the natural environment. *The Journal of Nervous and Mental Disease, 175,* 558–565.

Martin, I., & Venables, P. (Eds.). (1980). *Techniques in psychophysiology.* Chichester, England: Wiley.

Martin, P. R., Marie, G. V., & Nathan, P. R. (1992). Psychophysiological mechanisms of chronic headache: Investigation using pain induction and pain reduction procedures. *Journal of Psychosomatic Research, 36,* 137–148.

McArthur, D. L., Schandler, S. L., & Cohen, M. J. (1988). Computers and human psychophysiological research. *Computers in Human Behavior, 4,* 111–124.

McNally, R. J. (1994). *Panic disorder: A critical analysis.* New York: Guilford.

Moss, R. A., Ruff, M. H., & Sturgis, E. T. (1984). Oral behavioral patterns in facial pain, headache, and nonheadache populations. *Behaviour Research and Therapy, 22,* 683–687.

Moss, R. A., Sult, S., & Garrett, J. C. (1984). Questionnaire evaluation of craniomandibular pain factors among college students. *Journal of Crainiomandibular Practice, 2,* 364–368.

Musso, A., Blanchard, E. B., & McCoy, G. C. (1991). Evaluation of thermal biofeedback treatment of hypertension using 24-HR ambulatory blood pressure monitoring. *Behaviour Research and Therapy, 29,* 469–478.

Myrtek, M. (1990). Covariation and reliability of ECG parameters during 24-hour monitoring. *International Journal of Psychophysiology, 10,* 117–123.

Obrist, P. A. (1981). *Cardiovascular psychophysiology: A perspective.* New York: Plenum.

Ohman, A. (1979). The orienting response, attention, and learning: An information processing perspective. In H. D. Kimmel, E. H. Van Olst, & J. F. Orlebecke (Eds,), *The orienting reflex in humans* (pp. 443–471). Hillsdale, NJ: Lawrence Erlbaum.

Ost, L. G. (1989). Panic disorder, agoraphobia, and social phobia. In G. Turpin (Ed.), *Handbook of clinical psychophysiology* (pp. 309–327). Chichester, England: Wiley.

Ost, L. G., Sterner, V., & Lindahl, I. L. (1984). Physiological responses in blood phobics. *Behaviour Research and Therapy, 20,* 109–117.

Oyama, S. (1985). *The ontogeny of information: Developmental systems and evolution.* Cambridge: Cambridge University Press.

Pallmeyer, T. P., Blanchard, E. B., & Kolb, L. C. (1986). The psychophysiology of combat-induced posttraumatic stress disorder in Vietnam veterans. *Behaviour Research and Therapy, 24,* 645–652.

Parker, M. W. (1990). A dynamic model of etiology in temporomandibular disorder. *Journal of the American Dental Association, 120,* 283–290.

Parsons, O. A., & Nixon, S. J. (1993). Behavioral disorders associated with central nervous system dysfunction. In P. B. Sutker & H. E. Adams (Eds.), *Comprehensive handbook of psychopathology* (2nd ed.) (pp. 689–733). New York: Plenum.

Porges, S. W., & Bohrer, R. E. (1990). Analyses of periodic processes in psychophysiological research. In J. T. Cacioppo & L. G. Tessinary (Eds.), *Principles of psychophysiology: Physical, social, and inferential elements* (pp. 754–774). Cambridge: Cambridge University Press.

Pribram, K. H. (1971). *Languages of the brain.* New York: Brandon House.

Rachman, S., & Hodgson, R. (1974). I. Synchrony and desynchony in fear and avoidance. *Behaviour Research and Therapy, 12,* 311–318.

Raczynski, J. M., Ray, W. J., & McCarthy, P. (1991). Psychophysiological assessment. In M. Hersen, A. E. Kazdin and A. S. Bellack (Eds.), *The clinical psychology handbook* (4th ed.) (pp. 465–490) New York: Pergamon.

Rosen, R. C., Brondolo, E., & Kostis, J. B. (1993). Essential hypertension. In R. J. Gatchel & E. B. Blanchard (Eds.), *Phychophysiological disorders: Research and clinical applications* (pp. 63–110). Washington, DC: American Phychological Association.

Roth, W. T., Telch, M. J., Taylor, C. B., Sachitano, J. A., Gallen, C. C., Kopell, M. L., McClenahan, K. L., Agras, W. S., & Pfefferbaum, A. (1986). Autonomic characteristics of agoraphobia with panic attacks. *Biological Psychiatry, 21,* 1133–1154.

Sartory, G. (1989). Obsessional-compulsive disorder. In G. Turpin (Ed.), *Handbook of clinical psychophysiology* (pp. 329–356). Chichester, England: Wiley.

Sartory, G., Rachman, S., & Grey, S. J. (1977). An investigation of the relation between reported fear and heart rate. *Behaviour Research and Therapy, 15,* 435–438.

Schoenen, J., Gerard, P., De Pasqua, V., & Juprelle, M. (1991). EMG activity in pericranial muscles during postural variation and mental activity in healthy volunteers and patients with chronic tension-type headache. *Headache, 31,* 321–324.

Schuckit, M. A., Gold, E. O., Croot, F., Finn, P., & Polich, J. (1988). P-300 latency after ethanol ingestion in sons of alcoholics and in controls. *Biological Psychiatry, 24,* 942–945.

Schwartz, M. S. (1995a). Headache: Selected issues and considerations in evaluation and treatment: Part A: Evaluation. In M. S. Schwartz (Ed.), *Biofeedback: A practitioner's guide* (pp. 313–353). London: Guilford.

Schwartz, M. S. (1995b). Headache: Selected issues and considerations in evaluation and treatment: Part B: Treatment. In M. S. Schwartz (Ed.), *Biofeedback: A practitioner's guide* (pp. 354–407). London: Guilford.

Schwartz, S., & Gramling S. (1994, March). Integration of the adjunctive behavior paradigm with etiological models of myofascial pain disorder. *The Mississippi Psychologist,* pp. 9, 19, 22.

Shapiro, D., Jamner, L. D., & Goldstein, I. B. (1993). Ambulatory stress psychophysiology: The study of "compensatory and defensive counterforces" and conflict in a natural setting. *Psychosomatic Medicine, 55,* 309–323.

Shear, M. K., Pilkonis, J. J., Harshfield, G., Pickering, T., Mann, J. J., Frances, A., & James, G. (1992). Ambulatory monitoring of blood pressure and heart rate in panic patients. *Journal of Anxiety Disorders, 6,* 213–221.

Siddle, D. A., & Heron, P. A. (1978). Effects of length of training and amount of tone frequency change on amplitude of autonomic components of the orienting reflex. *Phychophysiology, 13,* 281–287.

Sokolov, E. N. (1963). *Perception and the conditioned reflex.* New York: Macmillan.

Stemmler, G., & Fahrenberg, J. (1989). Psychophysiological assessment: Conceptual, psychometric, and statistical issues. In G. Turpin (Ed.), *Handbook of clinical psychophysiology* (pp. 71–104). Chichester, England: Wiley.

Steptoe, A. (1989). Psychophysiological interventions in behavioural medicine. In G. Turpin (Ed.), *Handbook of clinical psychophysiology* (pp. 215–214). Chichester, England: Wiley.

Steptoe, A., & Johnston, D. (1991). Clinical applications of cardiovascular assessment. *Psychological Assessment: Journal of Consulting and Clinical Psychology, 3,* 337–349.

Stern, J. A. (1964). Toward a definition of psychophysiology. *Psychophysiology, 1,* 90–91.

Stern, R. M., Ray, W. J., & Davis, C. M. (1980). *Psychophysiological recording.* New York: Oxford.

Sternberg, R. J. (1995). *In search of the human mind.* Fort Worth: Harcourt Brace.

Straub, E. R. (1979). On the meaning of electrodermal nonresponding in schizophrenia. *Journal of Nervous and Mental Diseases, 167,* 601–611.

Sturgis, E. T., Tollison, C. D., & Adams, H. E. (1978). Modification of combined migraine-muscle contraction headaches using BVP and EMG feedback. *Journal of Applied Behavioral Analysis, 11,* 215–233.

Surwit, R. S., Pilon, R. N., & Fenton, C. H. (1977, October). *Behavioral treatment of Raynaud's Disease.* Paper presented at the 17th Annual Meeting of the Society for Psychophysiological Research, Philadelphia, PA.

Taylor, C. B., Shiekh, J., Agras, W. S., Roth, W. T., Margraf, J., Ehlers, A., Maddock, R. J., & Gossard, D. (1986). Ambulatory heart rate changes in patients with panic attacks. *American Journal of Psychiatry, 143,* 478–482.

Turk, D., Zaki, H., & Rudy, T. (1993). Effects of intraoral appliance and biofeedback/stress management alone and in combination in treating pain and depression in patients with temporomandibular disorders. *Journal of Prosthetic Dentistry, 70,* 158–164.

Turner, S. M., Beidel, D. C., Dancu, C. V., & Keys, D. J. (1986). Psychopathology of social phobia and comparison to avoidant personality disorder. *Journal of Abnormal Psychology, 95,* 389–394.

Turpin, G. (1989). An overview of clinical psychophysiological measures: Identifying and using psychophysiological markers. In G. Turpin (Ed.), *Handbook of clinical psychophysiology* (pp. 3–44). Chichester, England: Wiley.

Turpin, G. (1991). The psychophysiological assessment of anxiety disorders: Three-systems measurement and beyond. *Psychological Assessment: Journal of Consulting and Clinical Psychology, 3,* 366–375.

Turpin, G., Shine, P., & Lader, M. (1983). Ambulatory electrodermal monitoring. Effects of ambient temperature, general activity, electrolyte media, and length of recording. *Psychophysiology, 20,* 219–224.

van Boxtel, A., Goudswaard, P., & Schomaker, L. R. B. (1984). Amplitude and bandwidth of the frontalis surface EMG: Effects of electrode parameters. *Psychophysiology, 21,* 699–707.

van Doornen, L. J. P., & van Blokland, R. W. (1992). The relationship between cardiovascular and catecholamine reactions to laboratory and real-life stress. *Psychophysiology, 29*, 173–181.

Venables, P. M., & Christie, M. J. (1980). Electrodermal activity. In I. Martin & P. H. Venables (Eds.), *Techniques in psychophysiology* (pp. 3–67). New York: Wiley.

Wakefield, J. C. (1989). Levels of explanation. In D. M. Buss & N. Cantor (Eds.), *Personality psychology: Recent trends and emerging directions.* New York: Springer-Verlag

Waterink, W., & van Boxtel, A. (1994). Facial and jaw-elevator EMG activity in relation to changes in performance level during a sustained information processing task. *Biological Psychology, 37*, 183–198.

Wilder, J. (1950). The law of initial value. *Psychosomatic Medicine, 12,* 392–400.

Williamson, D. A., Epstein, L. H., & Lombardo, T. W. (1989). EMG measurement as a function of electrode placement and level of EMG. *Psychophysiology, 17,* 279–282.

Wingard, J. A., & Maltzman. (1980). Interest as a predeterminer of the GSR reflex of the orienting reflex. *Acta Psychologia, 40,153–160.*

Wolchick, S. A., Spencer, S. L., & Lisi, I. S. (1983). Volunteer bias in research employing vaginal measures of sexual arousal. *Archives of Sezual Behavior, 12,* 399–408.

Woodward, S., & Freedman, R. (1994). The thermoregulatory effects of menopausal hot flashes on sleep. *Sleep, 17,* 407–501.

CHAPTER 8

STRUCTURED INTERVIEWS AND RATING SCALES

Daniel L. Segal
University of Colorado at Colorado Springs

S. Bunny Falk
Nova Southeastern University

Over the past two decades, the behavioral assessment of psychiatric signs and symptoms has undergone significant change and evolution. During this time, numerous structured diagnostic interviews and rating scales have been developed for clinical and research applications, and these measures have strongly contributed to the advancement in behavioral assessment. Structured interviews have been devised to assist in diagnosis of most major Axis I (clinical syndromes) and Axis II (personality) disorders. Several interviews have been directly tied to *DSM* criteria and updated to match refinements in that classification system. Rating scales, focusing on dimensional aspects of psychopathology, have also proliferated over the past two decades of psychiatric research. Indeed, rating scales have been developed for almost every conceivable disorder, syndrome, and important clinical construct (i.e., assertiveness, social support, expressed emotion). Overall, these scales and structured interviews have improved clinical and research endeavors by providing a more standardized, scientific, and quantitative approach to the evaluation of psy-

chiatric symptomatology. The purpose of this chapter is to review the prominent structured interviews and rating scales that have been designed to assess psychopathology. For each instrument, the purpose, construction, characteristics, psychometric properties, and clinical applications will be discussed.

STRUCTURED DIAGNOSTIC INTERVIEWS

Impetus for Development of Structured Interviews

A major problem in psychiatric research has historically been the lack of agreement between two diagnosticians concerning presence or absence of a psychiatric diagnosis. Early attempts in the 1950s and 1960s to achieve adequate reliability of diagnosis consistently produced results that were below scientifically acceptable limits (Frank, 1975; Hersen & Bellack, 1988). In their thorough review of early reliability studies, Grove, Andreason, Mc-

Donald-Scott, Keller, and Shapiro (1981) rightly characterized this task as a "hopeless undertaking." Indeed, credible results from many early investigations were lacking for the even best-known and most prevalent diagnostic categories, such as major depression and schizophrenia (Grove et al., 1981; Grove, 1987; Hersen & Bellack, 1988).

This pervasive lack of agreement between clinicians and researchers when diagnosing patients is particularly troublesome, given that reliability is a necessary, but insufficient, prerequisite for validity. Indeed, reliability refers to replicability and stability. If a diagnostic instrument (such as a structured interview) does not provide reproducible data when readministered under identical conditions (i.e., poor reliability), what the instrument purports to measure is inconsequential (Magnusson, 1966). Acceptable levels of reliability must be documented before conclusions about validity can be drawn. However, even if adequate reliability is attained, validity is not guaranteed, as two clinicians can have perfect agreement but still be incorrect about all cases.

Two primary reasons have been elucidated to account for this historically poor state of affairs. The first targets the diagnostic criteria themselves, suggesting that inadequate nosology and poorly defined criteria play a substantial role in poor reliability (Ward, Beck, Mendelson, Mock, & Erbaugh, 1962). In the classic report by Ward and associates, 80% of all diagnostic disagreements was attributed to inadequate diagnostic criteria. This source of disagreement has been referred to as "criterion variance" (Spitzer, Endicott, & Robins, 1975). For example, disagreement about a diagnosis could result when two interviewers have different interpretations about the same criteria for a disorder.

Indeed, early classification systems, such as the original *Diagnostic and Statistical Manual of Mental Disorders* (*DSM*; American Psychiatric Association, 1952) and its revision *DSM-II* (American Psychiatric Association, 1968), lacked explicit diagnostic criteria for many disorders, provided a theoretical focus with respect to etiology, and had many inconsistencies. Interviewers faced the formidable task of rating general or vague symptoms that often represented a theoretical construct that was difficult to operationalize. This particular problem was addressed with publication of the *DSM-III* (American Psychiatric Association, 1980), which greatly operationalized criteria and took a more descriptive, objective, and atheoretical approach regarding signs and symptoms of disorders. The current multiaxial diagnostic system was also adopted by the *DSM-III*, which provided five separate axes upon which diagnostic data could be recorded. Most notably here, clinical syndromes, such as bipolar disorder and generalized anxiety disorder, were recorded on Axis I, whereas personality disorders reflecting chronic interpersonal and self-image deficits were denoted separately on Axis II. Inclusion and exclusion criteria for many disorders were also more objectively defined in clear behavioral terms. These innovations have continued to be refined in subsequent versions of *DSM*, including *DSM-III-R* (American Psychiatric Association, 1987) and *DSM-IV* (American Psychiatric Association, 1994). Overall, these improvements in diagnostic criteria have greatly reduced criterion variance.

A second factor accounting for historically poor agreement rates between clinicians concerns the lack of standardization of questions that are asked to patients to assess psychiatric symptomatology and ultimately to arrive at a formal diagnosis. Prior to standardized structured interviews, the unstructured psychosocial interview format prevailed. With unstructured interviews, clinicians were entirely responsible for asking whatever questions they decided were necessary for them to reach a diagnostic conclusion. The amount and kind of information gathered, as well as the way clinicians probed and assessed psychiatric symptoms during an interview, was largely determined by their theoretical model, view of psychopathology, training, and interpersonal style, which varied widely from clinician to clinician.

The source of error involved when different clinicians obtain different information from the same patient has been called "information variance" (Spitzer et al., 1975). The impetus for development of structured interviews was generated by the need to standardize questions asked of patients and provide guidelines for categorizing or coding responses. Adoption of such procedures served to increase coverage of many disorders, better determine if a particular symptom is present or absent, and reduce variability among interviewers (i.e., reduce information variance). Clearly, introduction of operationalized, specified, and standardized criteria for mental disorders in conjunction with construction of standardized structured diagnostic interviews has served to substantially improve diagnostic reliability and validity.

Structured Diagnostic Interviews for Adults, Axis I Disorders

This section will be limited to coverage of the major structured instruments that are tied to a major classification system, cover a wide range of Axis I disorders, yield categorical diagnoses, and are employed with adult respondents. Assessment devices for children are not discussed here, due to their coverage in other chapters of this book. The three primary diagnostic interviews we will review are the Schedule for Affective Disorders and Schizophrenia (SADS), the Diagnostic Interview Schedule (DIS), and the Structured Clinical Interview for *DSM-IV* (SCID).

The Schedule for Affective Disorders and Schizophrenia (SADS)

The SADS (Endicott & Spitzer, 1978) is a semistructured diagnostic interview designed to evaluate symptoms of psychiatric disorders as specified by the Research Diagnostic Criteria (RDC; Spitzer, Endicott, & Robins, 1978). Indeed, the SADS was developed in conjunction with the RDC, which predated publication of the *DSM-III*, and was a significant predecessor of that system. The SADS is intended to be used with adult psychiatric respondents and to be administered by trained mental health professionals. It focuses heavily on the differential diagnosis of affective and psychotic disorders, but also covers anxiety, alcohol use, and drug use disorders.

The full SADS is divided into two parts, each focusing on a different time period. Prior to those sections, a brief overview of the respondents problems is elicited in an open-ended inquiry. Then, Part I provides for a thoroughly detailed evaluation of

all *current* psychiatric conditions and impairment in functioning, as well as functioning during the week preceding the interview. For the current episode, symptoms are rated when they were at their worst levels to increase diagnostic sensitivity and validity. In contrast, Part II evaluates prior episodes of psychopathology and treatment. Overall, the SADS covers over 20 RDC diagnoses in a systematic and comprehensive fashion, and provides for diagnosis of both current and lifetime RDC psychiatric disorders. Some examples include schizophrenia, manic disorder, major depressive disorder, minor depressive disorder, panic disorder, alcoholism, and antisocial personality disorder. In addition to collecting information to diagnose specific RDC disorders, the SADS also yields scores for eight clinically relevant dimensional "Summary Scales" that were identified through factor analysis: depressive mood and ideation, endogenous features, depressive-associated features, suicidal ideation and behavior, anxiety, manic syndrome, delusions—hallucinations, and formal thought disorder (Endicott & Spitzer, 1978).

In the SADS, questions are clustered according to specific diagnoses, to approximate the natural flow in a less structured interview. Indeed, for each disorder, standard probes are specified to evaluate specific symptoms of that disorder. Questions are rated on a Likert scale, which allows for standardized documentation of levels of severity, persistence, and functional impairment associated with each symptom. For example, the mania syndrome criterion of "elevated mood" can be rated from "(1) normal or depressed mood" to "(6) extremely elated mood." Items are rated 0 if no information is available. To supplement patient self-report and obtain the most accurate symptom picture, the SADS allows for consideration of all available sources of information (i.e., chart records, relatives input). Additionally, SADS interviewers are instructed to ask as many general and specific probes and gently challenge as necessary to accurately rate the symptom.

To reduce length of administration and evaluation of symptoms that are not diagnostically significant, most diagnostic sections begin with screening questions, which provide for "skip-outs" to the next disorder if the respondent shows no evidence of having the disorder. Administration of the SADS typically takes between 1.5 and 2.5 hours, but can be extended if the respondent is currently severely mentally impaired or has an extensive psychiatric history. After all symptoms are rated and the interview is completed, interviewers consult the RDC and make diagnostic appraisals according to specified criteria. At present, no reliable computer scoring applications have been designed due to the complex nature of the diagnostic process and the SADS' strong reliance on clinical judgment.

As noted, the SADS was designed for use by trained clinicians. Indeed, considerable clinical judgment, interviewing skills, and familiarity with diagnostic criteria and psychiatric symptoms are requisite for competent administration of the SADS. As such, it is recommended that the interview only be conducted by professionals with graduate degrees and clinical experience, such as clinical psychologists, psychiatrists, and psychiatric social workers (Endicott & Spitzer, 1978). Training in the SADS is intensive and can encompass several weeks. The process includes reading articles about the SADS and the RDC, and the most recent SADS manual. Then, practice is provided in rating written case vignettes and videotaped SADS interviews. Additionally, trainees typically watch and score live interviews as if participating in a reliability study with a simultaneous-rating design. Throughout, discussion and clarification with expert interviewers regarding diagnostic disagreements or difficulties add to the experience. Finally, trainees conduct their own SADS interviews, which are observed and critiqued by the expert trainers.

Numerous additional versions of the SADS have been devised, each with a distinct focus and purpose. Perhaps the most common is the SADS-L (Lifetime version), which can be used to make both current and lifetime diagnoses, but has significantly less details about current psychopathology than the full SADS. The SADS-L generally is used with nonpsychiatric samples, where there is no assumption of a significant current disturbance. Reduced emphasis on current symptoms of the SADS-L results in a quicker administration time. Two offshoots of the SADS-L are the SADS-LA and SADS-LB, for comprehensive and detailed evaluation of anxiety and bipolar disorders, respec-

tively. Also popular is the SADS-C (Change version), which provides for measurement of change in symptom levels over time that can be used in treatment and outcome studies. For family studies, the Family History-RDC (FH-RDC) version collects information from family members about other relatives who are not present. The Family Informant Schedule and Criteria (FISC) is a revision of the FH-RDC with expanded focus on anxiety disorders.

Early psychometric data on the SADS came from its developers who evaluated interrater reliability of SADS summary scales in two samples (Endicott & Spitzer, 1978). In the first study, 150 inpatients were jointly evaluated by two raters who made independent diagnostic appraisals. Reliability was excellent, with intraclass correlation coefficients (ICC) ranging from .82 (formal thought disorder) to .99 (manic syndrome). Similarly, internal consistency was high for all composite scales except formal thought disorder and anxiety. In the second study, which employed a test-retest design with 60 hospitalized subjects, agreement rates were slightly lower than in the joint evaluations, but still substantial for all summary scales except formal thought disorder (ICC = .49).

With the same sample, Spitzer and colleagues (1978) reported test-retest concordance rates for many major diagnostic categories of the RDC. Agreement rates (kappa coefficients) were high for all eight current disorders, ranging from .65 for schizophrenia to 1.00 for alcoholism, while kappas for lifetime diagnoses tended to be lower, ranging from .40 for bipolar I to .95 for alcoholism. In a similar test-retest investigation, reliability generally was good for the SADS-L (Lifetime) version (Andreason et al., 1981). Later, in a small multicenter investigation, Andreason and associates (1982) used a videotape design with eight patients. Their results indicated excellent agreement rates for schizophrenia (ICC = 1.00) and major depression (.84), whereas a moderate value was found for manic disorder (.64). Taken together, these studies suggest that sufficiently high diagnostic reliability can be achieved for summary scales and most major diagnoses of the SADS.

Interestingly, although the SADS is tied to the RDC system, some versions can be modified to make *DSM*-based diagnoses, although this is not easy or possible for some disorders. Due to its ties to the RDC system, the SADS is not currently being revised to match *DSM-IV* criteria, although many such disorders are tapped by SADS items. The SADS has been translated into several languages, has been widely used in clinical research over the past three decades, and subsequently has a large body of empirical data associated with it. As such, it is often the instrument of choice for clinical researchers interested in depression, schizophrenia, and anxiety. However, due to its length and complexity, the SADS is less often chosen for use in pure clinical settings.

For information on SADS materials, training, and related procedures, the interested reader should contact Dr. Jean Endicott, Department of Research Assessment and Training Unit 123, New York State Psychiatric Institute, 722 West 168th Street, New York, NY, 10032; telephone (212)-960-5536.

The Diagnostic Interview Schedule (DIS)

The Diagnostic Interview Schedule (DIS; Robins, Helzer, Croughan, & Ratcliff, 1981) is a *fully structured* diagnostic interview specifically designed for use by lay, nonprofessional interviewers. It was developed by Robins and colleagues at Washington University Department of Psychiatry in St. Louis at the request of the National Institute of Mental Health (NIMH) Division of Biometry and Epidemiology. The DIS was designed for use in a set of large-scale epidemiological investigations of mental illness in the general adult population (age 18 and older), as part of the Epidemiological Catchment Area (ECA) Program. Variables to be assessed included incidence and prevalence of specific mental disorders and utilization profiles of health and mental health services. With this purpose in mind, development of a structured interview that could be administered by nonclinicians was imperative due to the prohibitive cost of using professional clinicians for these expansive community studies. The original DIS provided for determination of diagnoses according to three different, but popular, sets of criteria: the "Feighner criteria," associated with the St. Louis group (see Feighner et al., 1972); the Research Diagnostic Criteria (Spitzer et al., 1978); and the *DSM-III* (American Psychiatric Association, 1980).

To compensate for use of nonclinical lay interviewers, the DIS is a fully structured interview. Indeed, the exact wording of all symptom questions and follow-up probes are delineated in an interview book, items are read verbatim to the respondent in a standardized order, and clarification or rephrasing of questions is generally not permitted, although DIS interviewers can repeat any question as necessary to ensure that it is understood by the respondent. Further, all questions are written to be closed ended, and replies are coded with a forced choice yes/no format, which eliminates the need for clinical judgment to rate responses. Given the yes/no format, clarification of responses is neither needed nor required. Unlike other structured interviews, the DIS gathers all necessary information about the subject from the subject; collateral sources of information are not used, which again obviates the need for advanced clinical skills.

As the DIS was designed for epidemiological research with normative samples, DIS interviewers do not elicit a presenting problem or chief complaint from the subject, but rather begin by asking questions about symptoms in a standardized order. Like other structured interviews, the DIS has sections that cover different disorders. Once a symptom is reported to be present, further close-ended questions are pursued to assess additional diagnostically relevant information such as severity, frequency, time frame, and possibility of organic etiology of the symptom. Indeed, the original DIS had approximately 200 core questions asked to each respondent, and over 800 contingent questions that are administered only if the preceding core question is endorsed. DIS interviewers utilize a Probe Flow Chart that indicates which probes to use in which circumstances. Due to its highly structured format, administration of the DIS interview typically requires between 60 and 75 minutes, with a three-hour maximum for severely ill or loquacious subjects.

For each symptom, the respondent is asked to state whether it has ever been present and how recently. All data about presence/absence of symptoms and time frames of occurrence are coded and then entered into a computer for scoring. Indeed, consistent with its use of lay interviewers who may not be familiar with the *DSM* or psychiatric diagnosis, diagnostic output of the DIS is generated by a computer that analyzes the coded data from the completed interview. Output of the computer program provides estimates of prevalence for two time periods: current and lifetime. The original DIS covered criteria for over 30 *DSM-III* diagnoses, and more have been added as the instrument has been updated.

Although designed for use by lay administrators, training for competent administration of the DIS is intensive and includes several components. Trainees typically attend a week-long training program at Washington University, during which they review the DIS manual; listen to didactic presentations about the format, structure, and conventions of the DIS; and view videotaped vignettes. Additionally, many role-play practice interviews are conducted with extensive feedback and review to ensure that trainees master the material. Finally, a supplemental week of supervised practice is also recommended.

Since its inception, there have been several revisions and adaptations of the original DIS. One highly significant adaptation was to revise the questions and diagnostic algorithms to match new criteria presented in *DSM-III-R* (DIS Version III-R; Robins, Helzer, Cottler, & Goldring, 1989). Complete computerized administration, computer-prompted administration (interviewer uses computer program as a guide), as well as quick computerized versions of the DIS are also now available and have been applied successfully (Blouin, Perez, & Blouin, 1988; Erdman et al., 1992). Similarly, modifications are currently underway to establish compatibility with *DSM-IV* (American Psychiatric Association, 1994), and the updated version (DIS-IV) will surely add to the researchers' arsenal for large-scale community-based psychiatric research. Like all revised instruments, this new adult version will require its own reliability and validity evaluation.

The psychometric properties of the original DIS and its revisions have been evaluated in numerous investigations. Initial reliability results from St. Louis were encouraging (Robins et al., 1981), as

concordance between lay administration and psychiatrist administration was assessed in a test-retest design with 216 patients. Psychiatrist interviews were employed as the criterion measure. For *DSM-III* diagnoses, mean kappa was .69, mean sensitivity was 75%, and mean specificity was 94%. In a more recent study (Blouin et al., 1988), 80 psychiatric patients and 20 normal controls completed a self-administered computerized version of the DIS (C-DIS) on two occasions. Results showed generally acceptable test-retest reliability for the computerized DIS. With a similar test-retest design, Semler and associates (1987) examined 60 psychiatric inpatients on two occasions with a mean interval 1.7 days. Results indicated acceptable agreement values (kappa over .5) for all but two disorders: dysthymic disorder and generalized anxiety disorder. Further, Semler and associates noted that their results were improved over earlier versions of the DIS, especially for anxiety disorders.

More recently, Vandiver and Sher (1991) investigated the temporal stability of the DIS by administering it to 486 college students at baseline and again approximately 9 months later. Findings suggested that the DIS is a moderately reliable instrument for assessing lifetime psychopathology, although reliability estimates tended to be lower for 12-month and 6-month diagnoses than for lifetime diagnoses. Unreliability was attributed to "borderline" cases, which historically have hampered reliability in categorical diagnostic systems.

Validity of the DIS has been evaluated in several studies that typically compare DIS diagnoses to clinician-generated diagnoses. Taken together, results have generally been quite variable, depending on the sample, diagnosis, and criterion measure. An early study by Robins, Helzer, Ratcliff, and Seyfried (1982) compared DIS diagnoses to medical chart diagnoses, with generally poor concordance. With lay administration, mean agreement was 55%, whereas psychiatrist-administered DIS resulted in a 63% success rate. Anthony and associates (1985) compared lay-administered DIS diagnoses to standardized *DSM-III* diagnoses made by psychiatrists in a sample of 810 community residents. Their results also were discouraging, with agreement rates (kappa) ranging between −.02 (panic disorder) to .35 (alcohol-use disorder), with a mean of .15. In another study, psychiatrist-administered DIS diagnoses were examined in relation to clinical diagnoses from a *DSM-III* checklist (Helzer et al., 1985). Subjects were 370 community residents. Results were generally higher in this report, as kappas ranged from .12 to .63, with an average unweighted kappa of .40.

Most recently, when chart diagnosis for 220 psychiatric patients was used as the criterion measure, agreement (kappas) ranged from –.03 (schizophreniform) to .39 (bipolar disorder) and averaged .14 for 13 diagnostic categories (Erdman et al., 1987). In summarizing research examining the performance of the DIS in *clinical* settings (as opposed to epidemiological research), Erdman and colleagues raised questions about the appropriateness for the DIS in the clinical context, noting its "consistently poor agreement with clinical diagnosis is cause for concern" (p. 1479). As such, it is suggested that DIS data be supplemented with other data to make clinical diagnoses in individual cases.

Overall, the DIS and its numerous versions and adaptations have proven to be popular and useful diagnostic assessment tools for large-scale epidemiological research. The DIS has been translated into numerous languages, used in many countries for epidemiological research, and served as the basis for the Composite International Diagnostic Interview (CIDI/DIS) employed by the World Health Organization. Presently, it is the only well-validated case finding strategy that can make *DSM*-based diagnoses in large-scale epidemiological research.

For information on DIS materials, training, and related procedures, the interested reader should contact Dr. Lee Robins, Department of Psychiatry, Washington University School of Medicine, 4940 Children's Place, St. Louis, MO, 63110; telephone (314)-362-2469.

The Structured Clinical Interview for DSM-IV (SCID)

The original Structured Clinical Interview for *DSM-III* (SCID; Spitzer & Williams, 1984) was the first comprehensive *semistructured* diagnostic interview that was specifically designed to match *DSM-III* criteria for Axis I mental disorders. The SADS (Endicott & Spitzer, 1978), in contrast, was

based on Research Diagnostic Criteria (RDC; Spitzer et al., 1978) and was published prior to *DSM-III* and its clear-cut standardized criteria. Although the DIS (Robins et al., 1981) provided for diagnostic evaluations based on *DSM-III* criteria, its fully structured format, administration by nonclinicians, and computer scoring has caused debate over whether obtained diagnoses are valid (Spitzer, 1983). Indeed, an oft-quoted paper by Spitzer (1983) suggested that clinicians were necessary to the diagnostic process, thus questioning the apparent value of the DIS.

Four years after its initial appearance in the literature, the SCID was updated (Spitzer, Williams, Gibbon, & First, 1988) to reflect modifications that appeared in *DSM-III-R*, and most recently, a version tied to *DSM-IV* criteria has been published (First, Spitzer, Gibbon, & Williams, 1995). With each revision, the SCID has been broadened to encompass Axis I disorders that were not evaluated in the original SCID. Interestingly, a computer-administered screening version for the SCID for *DSM-IV*, the Mini-SCID, has also been produced. A complementary version has been designed to assess *DSM-IV* personality disorders (SCID-II; First, Spitzer, Gibbon, Williams, & Benjamin, 1994), located on Axis II. Additionally, specialized editions of the SCID have been developed to provide a two-tiered categorical and dimensional assessment of psychotic disorders (SCID-PANSS; Kay et al., 1991), to specifically evaluate panic disorder and panic subtypes (SCID-Upjohn version; Williams, Spitzer, & Gibbon, 1992), and to assess PTSD and combat experiences of veterans. Since its inception, the SCID has enjoyed widespread popularity as an instrument to obtain reliable and valid psychiatric diagnoses for clinical and research purposes.

Two standard versions of the SCID exist for assessment of Axis I disorders, each targeting a different population: patients and nonpatients (Spitzer, Williams, Gibbon, & First, 1992). The SCID-P (patient version) is used with psychiatric inpatients and outpatients, and includes full coverage of psychotic disorders. For settings where psychotic disorders are unlikely to be seen, an abridged version (SCID-P with psychotic screen) can be employed that screens for hallucinations and delusions but does not provide for a differential diagnosis of psychotic disorders. The SCID-NP (nonpatient version) is designed for application with normal control subjects or community surveys where no assumption of mental illness is made. Logically, this version does not ask for a chief complaint and it employs the shorter psychotic screen format.

Both standard versions of the SCID (patient/nonpatient) contain broad "modules" of major diagnostic categories (e.g., Mood Disorders, Anxiety Disorders) under which specific disorders (e.g., major depression, panic disorder) are subsumed. Disorder coverage of the SCID-P and SCID-NP are similar, except that for the SCID-NP version, the Psychotic Module is replaced by the Psychotic Screening. Most of the major Axis I disorders for adults are covered in the *DSM-IV* version, and these are shown in Figure 8.1.

The format and sequence of the SCID was designed to approximate the flowchart and decision trees followed by experienced diagnostic interviewers. As such, questions are grouped by major diagnostic category (e.g., Mood, Anxiety, Somatoform) under which specific disorders are covered independently. Disorders are evaluated for two time periods: current (meets criteria for past month) and lifetime (ever met criteria). The SCID begins with an "overview" portion, during which the development and history of the present psychological disturbance are elicited and tentative diagnostic hypotheses generated. Then, the SCID systematically presents modules that allow for assessment of specific disorders and symptoms. Consistent with its anchor in *DSM*, formal diagnostic criteria are embedded in the context of the SCID, thus permitting interviewers to make direct queries about specific features that contribute to the overall diagnostic picture. This unique feature also makes the SCID an excellent training device for administrators as it facilitates the learning of diagnostic criteria and appropriate probes.

Unlike the fully structured DIS, the SCID has many open-ended prompts that encourage respondents to elaborate about their symptoms. At times, open-ended prompts are followed up by closed-ended questions to fully clarify a particular symptom. While the SCID provides structure to cover criteria for each disorder in each module, its flexible *semistructured* format provides for considerable latitude for interviewers to restate questions, ask for further clarification, probe, and challenge if the initial prompt was misunderstood by the interviewee or clarification is needed to fully rate a symptom. SCID interviewers are encouraged to use all sources of information about a respondent, and gentle challenging of the respondent is encouraged if discrepant information is suspected.

Each symptom criteria is rated 1, 2, 3, or ?. The 1 indicates that the criterion was clearly absent, 2 refers to subthreshold levels of the symptom, 3 means that the criterion was clearly present and clinically significant, and the ? denotes that inadequate information was obtained to code the criterion. Like the SADS, the SCID flowchart instructs interviewers to "skip-out" of a particular diagnostic section when essential symptoms are judged to be absent or false. These skip-outs result in decreased time of administration, as well as the passing over of items with no diagnostic significance. Administration of the SCID typically requires between 60 and 90 minutes, although the Psychotic Module or a seriously disturbed subject can add considerable length.

Spitzer and associates (1992) suggest that the SCID is optimally administered by trained interviewers who have knowledge about psychopathology, *DSM* criteria, and diagnostic interviewing. Indeed, with its semistructured format, proper administration often requires that interviewers restate or clarify questions in ways that are sometimes not clearly outlined in the manual in order to accurately judge if particular symptom criteria have been met. The task requires that SCID assessors have working knowledge of psychopathology and *DSM-III-R/DSM-IV*, as well as basic interviewing skills. Standard procedures for training to use the SCID include carefully reading the SCID, consulting an instruction manual (Spitzer, Williams, Gibbon, & First, 1989), role-playing practice administrations, and viewing videotape training materials that are available from the SCID authors at Biometrics Research Department. Following this, trainees administer the SCID to representative subjects, who are jointly rated so that a discussion about sources of disagreements can ensue. Finally, a test-retest reliability study is completed, with further discussion and remediation of problem areas.

Figure 8.1   Diagnoses covered by the Structured Clinical Interview
for Axis I *DSM-IV* Disorders- Patient edition (SCID-I/P), by modules

Mood Disorders

Bipolar I Disorder
Bipolar II Disorder
Other Bipolar Disorder
    (includes Cyclothymic Disorder, Intermittent
    Hypomanic Episodes, and Manic or Hypomanic Epi-
    sode Superimposed on Psychotic Disorder)
Major Depressive Disorder
Dysthymic Disorder
Other Depressive Disorder
    (includes Postpsychotic Depressive Disorder of
    Schizophrenia, Premenstrual Dysphoric Disorder,
    Minor Depressive Disorder, Recurrent Brief Depres-
    sive Disorder)
Mood Disorder Due to a GMC
Substance-Induced Mood Disorder

Psychotic Disorders

Schizophrenia
Schizophreniform Disorder
Schizoaffective Disorder
Delusional Disorder
Brief Psychotic Disorder
Psychotic Disorder Due to a GMC
Substance-Induced Psychotic Disorder
Psychotic Disorder NOS

Psychoactive Substance Use Disorders
(Abuse or Dependence)

Alcohol
Sedative-Hypnotic-Anxiolytic
Cannabis

Stimulant
Opioid
Cocaine
Hallucinogen/PCP
Polysubstance (Dependence only)
Other Substances

Anxiety Disorders

Panic Disorder
Agoraphobia without History of Panic Disorder
Social Phobia
Specific Phobia
Obsessive Compulsive Disorder
Posttraumatic Stress Disorder
Generalized Anxiety Disorder
Anxiety Disorder Due to a GMC
Substance-Induced Anxiety Disorder
Anxiety Disorder NOS

Somatoform Disorders

Somatization Disorder
Pain Disorder
Undifferentiated Somatoform Disorder
Hypochondriasis
Body Dysmorphic Disorder

Eating Disorders

Anorexia Nervosa
Bulimia Nervosa
Binge Eating Disorder

Adjustment Disorder

The reliability of the SCID in adult populations with diverse disorders has been evaluated in a number of investigations. Although a review of this literature has recently been completed (see Segal, Hersen & Van Hasselt, 1994), data will be summarized here. An extensive multisite project included test-retest reliability interviews of 592 subjects in four patient and two nonpatient sites in the United States and one patient site in Germany (Williams et al., 1992). Randomly matched pairs of two professionals independently evaluated and rated the same subject within a two-week period. The sample was divided into patient ($N = 390$) and nonpatient

($N = 202$) subjects for whom levels of agreement for current and lifetime disorders were reported. Results for the patient sample indicated that kappas for current and lifetime disorders ranged from a low of .40 (dysthymia) to a high of .86 (bulimia nervosa). Kappas were above .60 for most of the major disorders (e.g., bipolar disorder = .84; alcohol abuse/dependence = .75; schizophrenia = .65; major depression = .64). Combining all disorders yielded a mean kappa of .61 for current and .68 for lifetime disorders. In the nonpatient sample, agreement generally was poorer, with an overall weighted kappa of .37 for current and .51 for lifetime disorders. Overall, obtained kappas were judged to be comparable to data from other structured interviews (Williams et al., 1992)—namely, the SADS and DIS.

Riskind, Beck, Berchick, Brown, and Steer (1987) videotaped 75 psychiatric outpatients to assess interrater reliability of *DSM-III* major depression and generalized anxiety disorder. They found that the SCID can reliably differentiate between the two disorders (major depression, kappa = .72; generalized anxiety disorder, kappa = .79). In another study, Skre, Onstad, Torgerson, and Kringlen (1991) assessed reliability using audiotaped SCID interviews of 54 adults participating in a larger Norwegian twin study of mental illness. Excellent interrater agreement (kappa above .80) was obtained for many disorders (e.g., schizophrenia, major depression, dysthymia, generalized anxiety disorder, panic disorder, and alcohol use disorder), whereas moderate levels were found for most other disorders (e.g., cyclothymia, PTSD, social phobia, simple phobia, bipolar disorder, and adjustment disorder). Poor reliability was indicated for obsessive-compulsive disorder (kappa = .40) and agoraphobia without history of panic disorder (.32), and somatoform disorder (−.03). Interestingly, Skre and associates (1991) also tested reliability for combinations of diagnoses (e.g., mood and anxiety disorders) and concluded that reliability was generally good for combinations of two disorders (range = .53 to 1.00) and poorer for combinations of three disorders (range = .38 to .87).

Reliability has also been established for the Upjohn version of the SCID (panic disorder and subtypes) in a large, multinational, test-retest project (Williams, Spitzer, & Gibbon, 1992). Of the 72 patients who participated in the investigation, 52 (72%) were retested within one week of the initial administration. Agreement on the diagnosis of panic disorder was very good (kappa = .87), although this base rate was very high (86%). Agreement was only fair to good for subtypes of panic disorder: uncomplicated (.73), panic disorder with limited phobic avoidance (.61), and agoraphobia with panic attacks (.66).

In our earlier review (Segal et al., 1994), we called for increased evaluations of the reliability of the SCID in minority populations, including older adults. Our research group has conducted two such reliability studies with elderly individuals. In the first study (Segal, Hersen, Van Hasselt, Kabacoff, & Roth, 1993), subjects consisted of older inpatients and outpatients ($N = 33$; age range = 56 to 84 years; mean = 67.3 years). SCID interviews were administered by graduate-level clinicians and audiotaped for retrospective review by an independent rater. Reliability estimates (kappa) were calculated for current major depressive episode (47% base rate, kappa = .70), and the broad diagnostic categories of anxiety disorders (15% base rate, kappa = .77) and somatoform disorders (12% base rate, kappa = 1.0).

The second investigation (Segal, Kabacoff, Hersen, Van Hasselt, & Ryan, 1995) targeted older psychiatric outpatients exclusively ($N = 40$; age range = 55 to 87 years; mean = 67.0 years) and evaluated a larger number of diagnoses. Diagnostic concordance was determined for the broad diagnostic categories of mood disorder (60% base rate), anxiety disorder (25% base rate), somatoform disorder (9% base rate), and psychoactive substance use disorder (9% base rate). Specific diagnoses evaluated included major depressive disorder (58% base rate), dysthymia (9% base rate), and panic disorder (15% base rate). Results for the broad diagnostic group of somatoform disorder (kappa = .84) suggests almost perfect agreement. Agreement was slightly lower, but still substantial, for mood disorder (.79) and anxiety disorder (.73). Psychoactive substance use disorder (.23) had the lowest agreement, reflecting poor agreement. For specific disorders, almost perfect agreement was obtained for major depressive disorder (.90) and panic disorder (.80), whereas agreement for dysthymia (.53) was moderate. Taken together, these two studies suggest that reliability of the SCID administered by graduate-level clinicians to older adults appears very promising, although additional research with larger samples obviously is warranted.

The latest and most comprehensive version of the SCID (First et al., 1995) mirrors diagnostic refinements made in the recently published *DSM-IV* (American Psychiatric Association, 1994) classification system. Interestingly, the *DSM-IV* version of the SCID has been split into two components, research and clinical. The research version covers more disorders, subtypes, and course specifiers than the *DSM-III-R* version, and as such is considerably longer. However, it provides for a wealth of diagnostic data that is particularly valued in the research setting. The clinical version has been trimmed down to encompass only those *DSM-IV* disorders that are most typically seen in clinical practice. Undoubtedly, the *DSM-IV SCID* can be expected to enjoy widespread application in psychiatric research, service, and training for many years to come, and studies are needed to evaluate and document its psychometric properties. At this time, however, no data on the latest version have been published.

For information on SCID materials, training, and related procedures, the interested reader should contact Miriam Gibbon, M.S.W., Biometrics Research Department, Unit 74, New York State Psychiatric Institute, 722 West 168th Street, New York, NY, 10032; telephone (212)-960-5524.

RATING SCALES

Rating scales have been used with increased regularity during the last decade by mental health professionals to assess for presence or absence of symptoms and/or behaviors associated with most types of psychopathology. Indeed, assessment of severity of disturbance or symptomatology with rating scales often serves as a vital supplement to psychiatric diagnosis, treatment, and discharge planning. Additionally, by providing validated and quantifiable measures of symptom severity, rating scales enhance the meaningfulness of treatment outcome research. As the subject sample is specified with greater clarity, a smoother transition from research to clinical application is facilitated. Therefore, both researchers and clinicians alike find rating scales to be valuable instruments.

Reliability and Validity

According to Kerlinger (1973), "Rating scales are the most ubiquitous of measuring instruments probably because they are seemingly easy to construct and more important, easy and quick to use" (p. 547). The author cautions, however, that lack of

reliability and/or validity is often the "heavy price" paid for such ease. Reliability and validity are important psychometric qualities to consider when determining inferences to be made on the basis of information obtained from rating scales. As Wilson and Prentice-Dunn (1981) point out, "Often the assumption is made that behavioral observations are automatically valid due to the obvious face validity and reduced rate of inference inherent in most behavioral observation procedures" (p.122). They emphatically state, however, that "neither reliability nor validity is permanently established, for each must be assessed for new populations and situations" (p.122). We will briefly focus on the concepts of reliability and validity as they relate to our examination of rating scales.

Reliability

Reliability refers to consistency (Anastasi, 1988) or stability (Naglieri & Flanagan, 1992) of test scores across time and situations. The degree to which measurement of a characteristic or behavior is error free provides the level of confidence one can have in any instrument. In its broadest sense, reliability indicates the extent to which differences in individual rating scores are due to true differences in the characteristics being examined or attributable to chance errors (Anastasi, 1988; Naglieri & Flanagan, 1992). The consistency of measurement in rating scales can be affected by three sources of error: (1) internal consistency reliability, (2) test-retest reliability, and (3) inter-rater reliability (Wilson & Bullock, 1989). Ideally, all three types of reliability estimates should be provided by test authors.

Internal Consistency Reliability. Estimates of the degree of internal consistency provide an indication of the homogeneity of test items, or the extent to which individual test items measure similar symptom characteristics or types of behavior. The more homogeneous a group of items, the lesser the potential for error variance (Corcoran & Fischer, 1987).

Test-Retest Reliability. Test-retest reliability is the consistency of test scores over time (Naglieri & Flanagan, 1992). Reliability coefficients provide an indication of the similarity between sets of ratings by the same rater for the same individual, but made at two different points in time. With respect to rating scales, when individual items on the scale are difficult to interpret, raters may not maintain consistent scoring from one administration to the next (Wilson & Bullock, 1989). For that reason, detailed descriptions or definitions of items to be rated should be provided by the test author. Without such aids, the resulting stability error will seriously impact reliability.

Inter-Rater Reliability. Estimates of inter-rater reliability provide an indication of consistency between sets of ratings on the same individual performed by two or more raters. This type of reliability is especially relevant with scales that involve subjectivity, as is the case with most rating scales. In fact, for rating scales, the most commonly quoted reliabilities are inter-rater reliabilities (Flemenbaum & Zimmerman, 1973).

Inter-rater reliability is influenced by the specifics of the rating situation (Flemenbaum & Zimmerman, 1973; Gabbard et al., 1987) (i.e., whether two [or more] raters jointly interview and then independently evaluate the patient at a single session, or each rater interviews and evaluates the patient separately with a period of time elapsing between the separate interviews). In the latter scenario, reliability is influenced by day-to-day patient variability and the specific dynamics of the rating situations (i.e., time of day, environmental changes, etc.).

Another factor exerting considerable influence on inter-rater reliability is rater-baseline effect. Flemenbaum and Zimmerman (1973) noted that significant differences between the means of pathology ratings of different raters are almost always present across a patient sample. Each rating point on a continuous rating scale has a descriptive adjective that corresponds with a number on that scale. For example, on a continuous scale from 0 to 6, "absent" or "not present" may be associated with 0; "very mild" with 1; "mild" with 2, and so on. However, because each rater is influenced by his or her "own mental continuum of psychopathology and baseline," the actual clinical correlates of the descriptive adjectives may vary between raters (Gabbard et al., 1987). Moreover, Flemenbaum

and Zimmerman (1973) suggest that the "principal factors determining the reproducibility of the ratings are probably associated, not with the rating scale, but with the rater using the scale" (p. 784). Experience/training in the use of subjective rating scales, rater-client rapport, ability to elicit pathology during rating session, and overall clinical experience are important factors noted by these researchers.

Validity

Validity refers to the quality of a scale, or how well it measures the characteristics it purports to measure. With respect to rating scales, inferences are drawn from the rating of individuals on some behavior variable of practical importance called a *criterion*. Indeed, the primary reason for employing a rating scale is to examine a patient for presence of psychopathology. Therefore, the most relevant criterion is a measure of psychopathology obtained by means *other* than the rating scale being validated. The rating scale is referred to as the *predictor*. Variables that could be used as the criterion include adaptive behavior, adequate social skills, or successful interpersonal relationships, all of which would show negative correlations to various types of psychopathology. But the goal of rating scales is to provide a determination of the level of psychopathology; therefore, a criterion should be some indication of the level of asynchronous manifestation of psychopathology.

Predictive validity and concurrent validity are two kinds of predictor-criterion relationships that are especially relevant to rating scales (Crocker & Algina, 1986). *Concurrent validity* refers to the extent to which scores of a given instrument correlate with the scores of an established instrument that was administered simultaneously (Naglieri & Flanagan, 1992). *Predictive validity* refers to the degree to which individual rating scores can predict a specified criterion situation over a time interval. In other words, a temporal estimate is obtained from rating scales administered to patients on whom other criterion data are already available (Anastasi, 1988). Indeed, the purpose of rating scales is to aid clinicians or researchers in making some determination about present and future psychopathological behavior of patients.

Our discussion will focus on three popular rating scales of general psychiatric adjustment in adults: the Brief Psychiatric Rating Scale (BPRS; Overall & Gorham, 1962), the Global Assessment Scale (GAS; Endicott, Spitzer, Fleiss, & Cohen, 1976), and the Nurses Observation Scale for Inpatient Evaluation (NOSIE; Honigfeld, Gillis, & Klett, 1966). Interestingly, each scale derives its score in different ways. The BPRS is scored on the basis of a structured interview, whereas the GAS utilizes information from several sources (patient interview, any reliable informant, or case record). By contrast, the NOSIE derives scores from frequency-of-occurrence ratings that originally were performed by nurses, but can currently be rated by lay administrators with specialized training. Numerous other rating scales restricted to more specific subsets of psychiatric symptoms have been developed and validated (e.g., Child Behavior Checklist; Achenbach, 1978; Hamilton Rating Scale for Depression; Hamilton, 1960; Scale for the Assessment of Negative Symptoms; Andreason, 1982; Yale-Brown Obsessive-Compulsive Scale; Goodman, Price, & Rasmussen, 1989). Due to their coverage in other chapters, these scales will not be reviewed here.

Brief Psychiatric Rating Scale (BPRS)

The BPRS was originally developed to evaluate psychiatric subjects involved in psychopharmacological research (Overall & Gorham, 1962). On the basis of a brief, unstructured interview, trained clinicians rate subjects on 16 diverse symptom constructs. All ratings are made on a scale of increasing severity (range: 0 to 6). Two other items (Psychomotor Agitation and Disorientation/Confusion) were later added to the BPRS, resulting in the final 18-item version that is currently widely used in a variety of research endeavors that examine change in symptomatology over time. The original 16 scales are defined and described by Overall and Gorham (1962) in their introductory publication. Additionally, Bech, Kastrup, and Rafaelsen (1986) also have provided concise and useful descriptions of each of the original and added scales.

The 18 symptom areas/scales of the BPRS are briefly described here:

1. Somatic Concerns (frequency and severity of physical complaints are rated). Here, the degree to which patients perceive physical ailments to play a key role in their overall lack of well-being is evaluated.

2. Anxiety (Psychic) refers to the *subjective* experience of worry, overconcern, insecurity, tenseness, irritability, fear, or apprehension. Interestingly, the report of physiological manifestations of anxiety (i.e., sweating, palpitations, hyperventilation, etc.) are not rated in this scale.

3. Emotional Withdrawal refers to the ability of the patient to relate to the examiner *during the interview* and is the sole basis of this rating. Eye contact, facial expression, voice quality and variability, and expressive movements or gestures are considered in making the judgment.

4. Conceptual Disorganization refers to disruption of normal thought processes as evidenced by confusion, inconsistencies, blocking, confabulation, autistic behavior, and loosening of associations.

5. Guilt Feelings include self-deprecatory behavior associated with lowered selfesteem. Such guilt feelings must relate to specific past behavior that the patient now believes to have been wrong.

6. Anxiety (Somatic)/Tension scale is restricted to rate the *physiological* and motor signs commonly associated with anxiety. Raters are instructed to attend to number and nature of physiological concomitants of anxiety reported by the patient.

7. Specific Motor Disturbances refers to "mannerisms and posturing." Manifestations include unusual and/or bizarre motor behaviors that would set that patient apart from other patients in a room. Odd, indirect, repetitive movements, or movements lacking normal coordination and integration are rated. Strained, distorted, or abnormal postures that are maintained for extended periods of time are also rated.

8. Grandiosity describes to degree of discrepancy between self-appraisal and reality. Verbal report by the patient and not simply patient's demeanor should be used to determine rating.

9. Depressive Mood includes only the affective component of depression. Ratings are based on verbal expressions of discouragement, pessimism, sadness, hopelessness, and helplessness. Facial expression, crying, and other modes of communicating dysphoric moods are also considered.

10. Hostility represents the patient's verbal report of hostile feelings or actions toward others outside of the interview. Note that evidence of hostility toward the examiner during the session is *not* reflected in the Hostility score, but rather is rated on the Uncooperativeness scale (item 14).

11. Suspiciousness; this rating reflects the degree to which the patient tends to project blame and accusations onto others. Manifestations can range from lack of confidence in others to florid persecutory delusions.

12. Hallucinations refer to presence of sensory perceptions without corresponding external stimuli.

13. Psychomotor Retardation relates to a general reduction in motor activity, including verbal activity and ability to perform voluntary acts.

14. Uncooperativeness, as previously mentioned, refers to overt signs of hostility toward the interviewer during the interview session.

15. Unusual Thought Content, this scale focuses on *content* of the patient's verbalizations and *not* organization of language.

16. Blunted Affect represents a reduced ability or motivation to express normal feelings or involvement. Emotional expressions from patients may be absent, and as such, are scored here.

17. Psychomotor Agitation represents a marked increase in motor activity evidenced by such behaviors as pacing, pressured speech, or inability to remain seated during interview.

18. Disorientation and Confusion refers to deficits in one or more spheres of sensorium (person, place, and/or time).

Presence and degree of most individual items are evaluated at the time of the interview; however, 6 items (Anxiety/Psychic, Hostility, Suspiciousness, Hallucinatory Behavior, Unusual Thought Content, and Blunted Affect) are rated on the basis of retrospective judgment of the previous three days. If necessary, the rater can elicit information from family members and/or The treatment team to assist in the accurate evaluation of the patient on each scale. Ratings of 7 symptoms (Tension, Emotional Withdrawal, Mannerisms and Posturing, Motor Retardation, Uncooperativeness, Disorientation and Confusion, and Psychomotor Agitation) are based on the clinician's observation of the patient. The remaining 11 scales (Conceptual Disorganization, Unusual Thought Content, Psychic Anxiety, Guilt Feelings, Grandiosity, Depressive Mood, Hostility, Somatic Concerns, Suspiciousness, Hallucinatory Behavior, and Blunted Affect) are rated primarily on the basis of verbal report of the patient or other source (Overall & Gorham, 1962). In addition to obtaining individual scale/symptom scores, the 18 ratings can be summed to yield a "total pathology" score. Overall and Gorham (1962) recommend using this "total" score when evaluating patient change during treatment.

Additionally, four composite "syndrome factor" scores can be derived: thought disturbance, withdrawal-retardation, hostility-suspiciousness, and anxiety-depression (Overall & Klett, 1972). Subscales assessing depressive, manic, and schizophrenic symptoms have also been developed and used empirically (see Anderson et al., 1993). Despite derivation of many useful and descriptive scales, the BPRS should *not* be used in isolation to assign formal psychiatric diagnoses. Indeed, we concur with Bech and colleagues (1986), who previously noted that "the scale is basically quantitative; it has been constructed for the sole purpose of rating the actual clinical picture, and is not to be considered a diagnostic tool" (p. 32).

In their initial report, Overall and Gorham (1962) indicated that inter-rater reliability coefficients for the 16 original scales ranged from .56 to .87, with a mean of .78. However, these figures have been challenged by other investigators (see Gabbard et al., 1987; Andersen et al., 1992), who suggest that it is unlikely that most later studies will employ raters with the extensive training and experience of the raters in the first investigation. Gabbard and colleagues (1987) examined the inter-rater reliability problem, not only as a function of having raters of varying disciplines and levels of clinical expertise but also as it related to the method of scoring (or rating) and the inherent problem in the descriptive adjectives associated with their numerical designations (e.g., 0= "not present"; 1= "very mild"; 2= "mild"; 3= "moderate"; 4= "moderately severe"; 5= "severe"; 6= "extremely severe"). These investigators hypothesized that by assigning more detailed, behaviorally anchored descriptions to scale points, baseline differences among raters would be attenuated and scale-point choice agreement would be enhanced.

After describing the various symptom gradations behaviorally that encompass the BPRS, Gabbard and colleagues assigned two teams of raters who were "roughly matched" for clinical experience and training with the BPRS. One team had additional training with the BPRS with the added anchor points, whereas the second team received only its original BPRS training. Both teams rated 10 videotaped structured interviews with the BPRS. Results indicated an improved inter-rater reliability on 15 of the 18 symptoms with the added descriptive anchor points. Three symptoms (Guilt Feelings, Motor Retardation, and Blunted Affect), however, showed no improvement in inter-rater reliability. The investigators argued that the latter two symptoms are more difficult to assess via videotape and that problems with the former seem related to the question of degree of pathology associated with slowing of speech or motor activity. Overall, Gabbard and associates concluded that modifying the BPRS with descriptive anchor points and utilizing such a modified version will greatly enhance inter-rater reliability of the instrument.

In a more recent study of BPRS reliability, Andersen and colleagues (1992) attempted to determine amount of practice required to attain uniform agreement in the use of this instrument. Seven psychiatrists evaluated 103 patients once a week in joint rating sessions. Forty-five minute interviews/ sessions were conducted at the same time of day, followed by a discussion of possible disagreements on individual symptoms or items. Results indicated that raters did not achieve a stable level of agreement in the BPRS total score and the Schizophrenia subscale until after 30 rating sessions. By contrast, high and stable correlations of the depressive symptoms (.80) were attained after only 10 practice rat-

ing sessions. For symptoms of Mania, however, three times as many patients had to be rated to reach maximum agreement (.70). The four symptoms of the BPRS rendering the greatest disagreement among raters were Tension, Mannerisms and Posturing, Uncooperativeness, and Blunted Affect. In critiquing their own work, Andersen and associates (1992) noted that their methodology did not clarify whether the disagreement among raters on these symptoms specifically (or in general) was due to scale construction or to difficulty in the observation of related behaviors. The researchers concluded that future investigations should "be required to document the degree of interrater reliability obtained" (p.131).

Foster, Sclan, Welkowitz, Boksay, and Seeland (1988) examined whether inter-rater reliability of the BPRS (and other scales) remains constant across settings and populations. These investigators, noting the paucity of literature concerning rating-scale performance with patients in long-term care facilities (LTCF), sought to compare inter-rater reliability of the BPRS with a LTCF sample assessed during psychiatric consultation where "complexities of combined medical and psychiatric morbidity are continually interacting" (p. 230). Forty patients were selected to represent a wide range of diagnoses that included organic mental disorders, a variety of psychotic and affective disorders, adjustment disorders, personality disorders, and uncomplicated bereavement. Subjects were assessed by eight raters representing various mental health professions in two studies of 20 patients each. Foster and colleagues reported inter-rater reliability coefficients of the BPRS for the two studies as .94 and .98, confirming the inter-rater reliability of the scale in a LTCF. These researchers also argue that the data documents that raters with different training and experience can reliably be used in LTCFs.

As a means of highlighting the importance of adequate inter-rater reliability, clinicians and researchers need only refer to studies wherein the predictive qualities of rating scales are explored. Palmstierna, Lassenius, and Wistedt (1989) examined the relationship of psychopathology and aggression. This was done specifically to determine the ability of separate item of the BPRS to predict number of serious aggressive incidents in patients during acute involuntary hospitalizations. Ratings on three items (Hostility, Grandiosity, and Anxiety) were significantly correlated with aggressive behavior. Grandiosity was negatively correlated (-0.43) and hostility and anxiety were positively correlated (0.58 and 0.37, respectively). Palmstierna and colleagues concluded that the constellation of high scores on hostility and anxiety, together with the low scores on grandiosity, offers an effective model for predicting violent behavior within a brief time frame. Identifying patients who have a sum of scores exceeding 8 on BPRS ratings for hostility and anxiety, and who also have a 0 on ratings of grandiosity, provides useful short-term predictive ability.

The Global Assessment Scale (GAS)

The Global Assessment Scale (GAS) was designed by Endicott, Spitzer, Fleiss, and Cohen (1976) to provide clinicians with a procedure for measuring the global severity of psychiatric disturbance in their patients. In essence, the GAS is a rating scale for evaluating the overall functioning of a patient during a specified time period on a continuum from severe psychological sickness to complete mental health (Endicott et al., 1976). Generally, the time period assessed by the GAS is the week prior to evaluation. Patients are rated on a scale from 1 to 100, with 1 being sickest or lowest functioning and 100 being healthiest or highest functioning. Dividing the 100-point scale into 10 equal parts (1 to 10, 11 to 20, etc.), Endicott and associates provide the rater with defining characteristics for each of 10 intervals. These investigators describe the two highest intervals (81 to 90 and 91 to 100) as being reserved for those "unusually fortunate individuals who ... exhibit many traits referred to as positive mental health" (p. 766). Such attributes include superior functioning, having a wide range of interests, social effectiveness, warmth, and integrity. The interval represented by scores of 71 to 80 is for individuals without psychopathology but who lack the "positive mental health features" just mentioned. The vast majority of individuals receiving psychiatric or psychological services will be rated between 1 and 70 (Endicott et al., 1976). More spe-

cifically, Endicott and colleagues relate that most outpatients will be rated between 31 and 70, and that most inpatients will be rated 1 to 40.

Ratings on the GAS may be made on the basis of information from the patient directly, any other reliable informant, or case records. Although little information may be necessary to assign a low rating, a high-end rating in the 90 to 100 range would require confirming not only absence of psychopathology and impairment but also presence of signs of positive mental health. Inter-rater reliability is enhanced by the provision of a number of specific behavioral descriptions that exemplify each interval range.

Endicott and associates (1976) found inter-rater reliability coefficients ranging from 0.61 to 0.91 in studies that utilized interview ratings of inpatient and aftercare patients, and ratings based on case records. In another study employing a diagnostically more heterogeneous inpatient sample, these researchers report a quite high agreement rate of 0.85. However, it has also been reported that inter-rater reliability coefficients obtained by researchers generally were higher than those obtained by clinicians (Endicott et al., 1976; Plakun, Muller, & Burkhardt, 1987).

Validity of GAS scores is evidenced in Endicott and associates' (1976) report of moderate correlations between GAS scores and overall severity of illness scores from other measures (i.e., Mental Status Examination, Psychiatric Status Schedule), and between GAS scores and symptom dimensions on other measures. GAS scores have their highest correlations with independent measures of symptoms dimensions that measure psychosis and overt behavioral disorganization at the time of admission, whereas measures of subjective distress have little, if any, relationship with GAS scores. At six months, however, all three kinds of symptom measures are related to GAS scores. Additionally, the GAS shows greater sensitivity to change (from admission to six-month evaluation) than measures of single-symptom dimensions (Endicott et al., 1976).

More recently, Dworkin and colleagues (1990) described their experience with the GAS in an outpatient setting with chronically mentally ill clients. The GAS was used by multiple clinician/raters to evaluate 108 chronically mentally ill patients from 1 to 11 times over a period of 18 months. Training in use of the GAS was provided to all clinicians and is reported to have facilitated high inter-rater reliabilities (.80 to .92). The GAS was also found to be sufficiently sensitive to real changes in patient functioning in that patient means were correlated with psychiatric decompensation over the 18-month period. Additionally, a high degree of internal consistency (Cronbach's alpha = .89) was found, which further supports the notion of the sensitivity of the GAS.

Notably, the 1987 revision of the *Diagnostic and Statistical Manual of Mental Disorders (DSM-III-R*; American Psychiatric Association, 1987) added the Global Assessment of Functioning (GAF) Scale to the multiaxial classification system on Axis V. The GAF rating scale was derived from the GAS, and allows clinicians to rate an individual's overall level of symptoms and psychological, social, and occupational functioning as part of his or her diagnostic determinations. The GAF Scale has also been included in the most recent version of the *DSM (DSM-IV*; American Psychiatric Association, 1994) and appears to be a stable and important component of the multiaxial system.

The Nurses Observation Scale for Inpatient Evaluation (NOSIE)

The NOSIE is a 30-item behavior rating scale that was developed by Honigfeld, Gillis, and Klett (1966) almost 30 years ago. Since its introduction, the scale has been widely used in inpatient settings evaluating token-economy procedures (Elliott, Barlow, Hooper, & Kingerlee, 1979; McMordie & Swint, 1979) and in psychopharmacological studies (e.g., Honigfeld, 1974; Kane, Honigfeld, Singer, & Melzer, 1988). More recently, the NOSIE has been demonstrated to be a valuable global indicator of patient change (Hafkenscheid, 1991).

The NOSIE consists of 30 items that are rated on a five-point frequency-of-occurrence scale. The items are grouped into seven subscales: social competence, social interest, neatness, irritability, psychosis, retardation, and depression. Hafkenscheid (1991) reported that, with the exception of the competence and neatness subscales, the other subscales

can be distinguished reasonably well from each other. Internal consistency coefficients of the NOSIE are high (Cronbach's alpha ranging from 0.74 to 0.89), with the somewhat lower, but still moderate reliability (0.70) of the depression scale as an exception (Hafkenscheid, 1991). Inter-rater reliability for subscales taken individually was variable, ranging from 0.41 (depression) to 0.78 (neatness). Global scale level of inter-rater agreement was moderate (0.71). Hafkenscheid (1991) also reports that NOSIE ratings at both the subscale and global scale levels demonstrate good test-retest reliability, therefore providing sound pre- versus posttherapy score differences. Global scale scores are reported to have adequate discriminatory power in that they were able to distinguish psychotic patients from those in the neurotic range, as well as short-term patients from long-term patients. Predictive ability of the NOSIE, however, was found to be limited with respect to treatment outcome (Hafkenscheid, 1991).

SUMMARY

This chapter suggests that although structured interviews have been widely and successfully employed in controlled research for several years, gaps in the research data still exist. For example, there are few studies in which diagnoses from one structured interview are compared to other structured interviews for assessing validity. Further, a complicating factor here is that even if one interview is compared to another, it is unclear which one will serve as the criterion measure. Indeed, lack of a "gold standard" in diagnostic research prevents firm conclusions about validity to be drawn. The *lead* standard proposed by Spitzer (1983) as a means to establish procedural validity of a diagnostic instrument in the absence of clear-cut external validators provides appropriate methodology for validity evaluation, but unfortunately has been infrequently applied.

Another issue in research on reliability of structured interviews is the degree to which many studies address the topic of clinical and practical utility, an issue also quite relevant to rating scales. For example, some investigations have been conducted in a research context rather than in an ongoing clinical setting, and high inter-rater agreement rates of rating scales reported in the literature should be viewed with considerable caution. Too often, clinical application does not allow or provide for the same level of administrative abilities as with research application of the various scales. For structured interviews, raters in many cases are experienced clinical researchers who are well trained and committed to the development and success of the instrument. Such raters have exceptional familiarity and training with regard to psychopathology, *DSM* criteria, and interviewing skills. Unfortunately, this is not the typical situation in standard clinical practice (i.e., typical mental health center), where clinicians who might use these measures are neither as committed nor well trained as clinical researchers participating in reliability studies. At this point in time, the effect of using standard clinical service providers (as compared to clinical researchers) on reliability is largely unknown, although results from two studies conducted by our research group (Segal et al., 1993; Segal et al., 1995) are promising. These findings await further empirical support from research with larger and more diverse patient populations.

Yet another issue deserving attention is that two of the three major structured interviews (SCID and DIS) have recently undergone significant revision in order to correspond with some of the altered diagnostic criteria in *DSM-IV*. Much current research still is evaluating psychometric properties of these interviews based on *DSM-III-R* criteria, so it cannot be assumed that these findings will apply to the updated versions. Thus, reliability and validity data as to future versions of the these instruments inevitably will lag behind establishment of *DSM-IV* criteria.

It has been noted in the literature that reliability of a structured interview is not a static statistic that remains constant from one study or situation to the next. To the contrary, the reliability of interviewer-administered instruments is affected by many factors, such as the characteristics of the interviewers and the subject sample, the type of reliability assessed (e.g., inter-rater or test-retest), and the reliability of the diagnostic criteria (Williams et al., 1992). Thus, it cannot automatically be assumed that any structured interview will be reliable if

administered to untested populations, such as minorities or older adults. In a recent review of the SCID, Segal and colleagues (1994) emphasized the need for future investigations to focus on (1) the lack of studies in which SCID diagnoses are compared to diagnoses from unstructured interviews or other structured interview formats, (2) the need for a more natural evaluation of this instrument, and (3) the importance of establishing norms and obtaining reliability data for underserved clinical populations such as African Americans, older adults, and those adults who are physically and developmentally disabled. Indeed, these comments can well apply to other structured interviews such as the SADS and DIS. Although our two studies that have investigated applicability of the SCID with older adults have found promising results (see Segal et al., 1993; Segal et al., 1995), similar studies are needed with other interview schedules and additional minority groups.

The information in this chapter is intended to provide a broad overview of the many standardized structured interviews and rating scales that are available to the clinician and researcher. Basic descriptions, guidelines for use, and evidence for reliability and validity have been summarized for each instrument. Application of structured interviews has greatly enhanced diagnostic reliability and validity, with substantially improved results over earlier efforts with unstructured interviews. Use of rating scales has similarly enhanced clinical research as symptoms of clinical disorders can be more clearly quantified and measured. This allows for a better measurement of changes over time as specific symptoms are targeted in intervention studies. Together, these instruments have placed psychiatric research on a more empirical foundation. It is hoped that this review will lead to increased application of structured interviews and rating scales and also enable clinicians and researchers to choose an instrument that will most appropriately suit their needs.

REFERENCES

Achenbach, T. M. (1978). The Child Behavior Profile: I. Boys aged 6 through 11. *Journal of Consulting and Clinical Psychology, 46,* 478–488.

Anastasi, A. (1988). *Psychological testing* (6th ed.). New York: Macmillan.

American Psychiatric Association. (1952). *Diagnostic and Statistical Manual of Mental Disorders*. Washington, DC: Author.

American Psychiatric Association. (1968). *Diagnostic and Statistical Manual of Mental Disorders* (2nd ed.). Washington, DC: Author.

American Psychiatric Association. (1980). *Diagnostic and Statistical Manual of Mental Disorders* (3rd ed.). Washington, DC: Author.

American Psychiatric Association. (1987). *Diagnostic and Statistical Manual of Mental Disorders* (3rd ed.- revised). Washington, DC: Author.

American Psychiatric Association. (1994). *Diagnostic and Statistical Manual of Mental Disorders* (4th ed.). Washington, DC: Author.

Andersen, J., Korner, A., Larsen, V., Schultz, B., Neilsen, K., Behnke, E., Munk-Andersen, E., & Bjorum, N. (1993). Agreement in psychiatric assessment. *Acta Psychiatrica Scandinavica, 87,* 128–132.

Andreason, N. C. (1982). Negative symptoms in schizophrenia: Definition and reliability. *Archives of General Psychiatry, 39,* 784–788.

Andreason, N. C., Grove, W. M., Shapiro, R. W., Keller, M. B., Hirschfeld, R. M. A., & McDonald-Scott, P. (1981). Reliability of lifetime diagnosis. *Archives of General Psychiatry, 38,* 400–405.

Andreason, N. C., McDonald-Scott, P., Grove, W. M., Keller, M. B., Shapiro, R. W., & Hirschfeld, R. M. A. (1982). Assessment of reliability in multicenter collaborative research with a videotape approach. *American Journal of Psychiatry, 139,* 876–882.

Anthony, J. C., Folstein, M., Romanoski, A. J., Von Korf, M. R., Nestadt, G. R., Chahal, R., Merchant, A., Brown, C. H., Shapiro, S., Kramer, M., & Gruenberg, E. M. (1985). Comparison of the lay Diagnostic Interview Schedule and a standardized psychiatric diagnosis. *Archives of General Psychiatry, 42,* 667–675.

Bech, P., Kastrup, M., & Rafaelsen, O. (1986). Mini-compendium for states of anxiety, depression, mania, and schizophrenia with corresponding DSM-III syndromes. *Acta Psychiatrica Scandinavica, 73,* 7–37.

Blouin, A. G., Perez, E. L., & Blouin, J. H. (1988). Computerized administration of the Diagnostic Interview Schedule. *Psychiatry Research, 23,* 335–344.

Corcoran, K., & Fischer, J. (1987). *Measures for clinical practice: A sourcebook.* New York: The Free Press.

Crocker, L., & Algina, J. (1986). *Introduction to classi-cal and modern test theory.* New York: Holt, Rinehart and Winston.

Dworkin, R., Friedman, L., Telschow, R., Grant, K., Moffic, H. S., & Sloan, V. (1990). The longitudinal use of the Global Assessment Scale in multiple-rater situations. *Community Mental Health Journal, 26,* 335–344.

Elliott, P., Barlow, F., Hooper, A., & Kingerlee, P. (1979). Maintaining patients improvement in a token economy. *Behavior Research and Therapy, 17,* 355–367.

Endicott, J., & Spitzer, R. L. (1978). A diagnostic interview: The Schedule for Affective Disorders and Schizophrenia. *Archives of General Psychiatry, 35,* 837–844.

Endicott, J., Spitzer, R. L., Fleiss, J., & Cohen, J. (1976). The Global Assessment Scale. *Archives of General Psychiatry, 33,* 766–771.

Erdman, H. P, Klein, M. H., Greist, J. H., Bass, S. M., Bires, J. K., & Machtinger, P. E. (1987). A comparison of the Diagnostic Interview Schedule and clinical diagnosis. *American Journal of Psychiatry, 144,* 1477–1480.

Erdman, H. P, Klein, M. H., Greist, J. H., Skare, S. S., Husted, J. J., Robins, L. N., Helzer, J. E., Goldring, E., Hamburger, M., & Miller, J. P. (1992). A comparison of two computer-administered versions of the NIMH Diagnostic Interview Schedule. *Journal of Psychiatric Research, 26,* 85–95.

Feighner, J. P., Robins, E., Guze, S. B., Woodruf, R. A., Winokur, G., & Munoz, R. (1972). Diagnostic criteria for use in psychiatric research. *Archives of General Psychiatry, 26,* 57–63.

First, M. B., Spitzer, R. L., Gibbon, M., & Williams, J. B. W. (1995). *Structured Clinical Interview for Axis I DSM-IV Disorders–Patient Edition (SCID-I/P, Version 2.0).* New York: Biometrics Research Department, New York State Psychiatric Institute.

First, M. B., Spitzer, R. L., Gibbon, M., Williams, J. B. W., & Benjamin, L. (1994). *Structured Clinical Interview for DSM-IV Axis II Personality Disorders (SCID-II, version 2.0).* New York: Biometrics Research Department, New York State Psychiatric Institute.

Flemenbaum, A., & Zimmerman, R. (1973). Inter and intra-rater reliability of the Brief Psychiatric Rating Scale. *Psychological Reports, 36,* 783–792.

Foster, J., Sclan, S., Welkowitz, J., Boksay, I., & Seeland, I. (1988). Psychiatric assessment in medical long-term care facilities: Reliability of commonly used rating scales. *International Journal of Geriatric Psychiatry, 3,* 229–233.

Frank, G (1975). *Psychiatric diagnosis*. Oxford: Pergamon.

Gabbard, G., Coyne, L., Kennedy, L., Beasley, C., Deering, C., Shroder, P., Larson, J., & Cerney, M. (1987). Interrater reliability in the use of the Brief Psychiatric Rating Scale. *Bulletin of the Menninger Clinic, 51*, 519–531.

Goodman, W. K., Price, L., & Rasmussen, S. (1989). The Yale-Brown Obsessive-Compulsive Scale (Y-BOCS): Past development, use, and reliability. *Archives of General Psychiatry, 46*, 1006–1016.

Grove, W. M. (1987). The reliability of psychiatric diagnosis. In C. G. Last & M. Hersen (Eds.), *Issues in diagnostic research* (pp. 99–119). New York: Plenum.

Grove, W. M., Andreason, N. C., McDonald-Scott, P., Keller, M. B., & Shapiro, R. W. (1981). Reliability studies of psychiatric diagnosis. *Archives of General Psychiatry, 38*, 408–413.

Hafkenscheid, A. (1991). Psychometric evaluation of the Nurses Observation Scale for Inpatient Evaluation in the Netherlands. *Acta Psychiatrica Scandinavica, 83*, 46–52.

Hamilton, M. (1960). A rating scale for depression. *Journal of Neurology, Neurosurgery, and Psychiatry, 23*, 56–62.

Helzer, J. E., Robins, L. N., McEvoy, M. A., Spitznagle, E. L., Stoltzman, R. K., Farmer, A., & Brockington, I. F. (1985). A comparison of clinical and diagnostic interview schedule diagnoses: Physician reexamination of lay-interviewed cases in the general population. *Archives of General Psychiatry, 42*, 657–666.

Hersen, M., & Bellack, A. S. (1988). DSM-III and behavioral assessment. In A. S. Bellack & M. Hersen (Eds.), *Behavioral assessment: A practical handbook* (pp. 67–84). New York: Pergamon.

Honigfeld, G. (1974). NOSIE-30: History and current status of its use in pharmacopsychiatric research. *Modern Problems in Pharmacopsychiatry, 7*, 238–263.

Honigfeld, G., Gillis, R., & Klett, C. (1966). NOSIE-30: A treatment sensitive ward behavior rating scale. *Psychological Reports, 19*, 180–182.

Kane, J., Honigfeld, G., Singer, J., & Melzer, H. (1988). Clozapine in treatment resistant schizophrenias. *Psychopharmacology Bulletin, 24*, 62–67.

Kay, S R., Opler, L. A., Spitzer, R. L., Williams, J. B. W., Fiszbein, A., & Gorelick, A. (1991). SCID-PANSS: Two-tier diagnostic system for psychotic disorders. *Comprehensive Psychiatry, 32*, 355–361.

Kerlinger, F. (1973). *Foundations of behavioral research* (2nd ed.). New York: Holt, Rinehart and Winston.

Magnusson, D. (1966). *Test theory*. Stockholm: Almqvist & Wiksell.

McMordie, W., & Swint, E. (1979). Predictive utility, sex of rater differences, and interrater reliability of the NOSIE-30. *Journal of Clinical Psychology, 35*, 773–775.

Naglieri, J., & Flanagan, D. (1992). A psychometric review of behavior rating scales. *Comprehensive Mental Health Care, 2*, 225–239.

Overall, J., & Gorham, D. (1962). The Brief Psychiatric Rating Scale. *Psychological Reports, 10*, 799–812.

Overall, J., & Klett, C. (1972). *Applied multivariate analysis*. New York: McGraw-Hill.

Palmstierna, R., Lassenius, B., & Wistedt, B. (1989). Evaluation of the Brief Psychopathological Rating Scale in relation to aggressive behavior by acute involuntarily admitted patients. *Acta Psychiatrica Scandinavica, 79*, 313–316.

Plakun, E., Muller, J., & Burkhardt, P. (1987). The significance of borderline and schizotypal overlap. *Hillside Journal of Clinical Psychiatry, 9*, 47–54.

Riskind, J. H., Beck, A. T., Berchick, R. J., Brown, G., & Steer, R. A. (1987). Reliability of DSM-III-R diagnoses for major depression and generalized anxiety disorder using the Structured Clinical Interview for DSM-III-R. *Archives of General Psychiatry, 44*, 817–820.

Robins, L. N., Helzer, J. E., Cottler, L., & Goldring, E. (1989). *The Diagnostic Interview Schedule Version III-R*. St. Louis: Washington University School of Medicine.

Robins, L. N., Helzer, J. E., Croughan, J., & Ratcliff, K. S. (1981). National Institute of Mental Health Diagnostic Interview Schedule: Its history, characteristics, and validity. *Archives of General Psychiatry, 38*, 381–389.

Robins, L. N., Helzer, J. E., Ratcliff, K. S., & Seyfried, W. (1982). Validity of the Diagnostic Interview Schedule, Version II: DSM-III diagnoses. *Psychological Medicine, 12*, 855–870.

Segal, D. L., Hersen, M., & Van Hasselt, V. B. (1994). Reliability of the Structured Clinical Interview for DSM-III-R: An evaluative review. *Comprehensive Psychiatry, 35*, 316–327.

Segal, D. L., Hersen, M., Van Hasselt, V. B., Kabacoff, R. I., & Roth, L. (1993). Reliability of diagnosis in older psychiatric patients using the Structured Clinical Interview for DSM-III-R. *Journal of Psychopathology and Behavioral Assessment, 15*, 347–356.

Segal, D. L., Kabacoff, R. I., Hersen, M., Van Hasselt, V.

B., & Ryan, C. F. (1995). Update on the reliability of diagnosis in older psychiatric outpatients using the Structured Clinical Interview for DSM-III-R. *Journal of Clinical Geropsychology, 1*, 313–321.

Semler, G., Wittchen, H. U., Joschke, K., Zaudig, M., von Gieso, T., Kaiser, S., von Cranach, M., & Pfister, H. (1987). Test-retest reliability of a standardized psychiatric interview (DIS/CIDI). *European Archives of Psychiatry and Neurological Sciences, 236*, 214–222.

Skre, I., Onstad, S., Torgerson, S., & Kringlen, E. (1991). High interrater reliability for the Structured Clinical Interview for DSM-III-R Axis I (SCID-I). *Acta Psychiatrica Scandinavica, 84*, 167–173.

Spitzer, R. L. (1983). Psychiatric diagnosis: Are clinicians still necessary? *Comprehensive Psychiatry, 24*, 399–411.

Spitzer, R. L., Endicott, J., & Robins, E. (1975). Clinical criteria for psychiatric diagnosis and DSM-III. *American Journal of Psychiatry, 132*, 1187–1192.

Spitzer, R. L., Endicott, J., & Robins, E. (1978). Research diagnostic criteria. *Archives of General Psychiatry, 35*, 773–782.

Spitzer, R. L., & Williams, J. B. W. (1984). *Structured Clinical Interview for DSM-III disorders (SCID-P 5/1/84 Revision).* New York: Biometrics Research Department, New York State Psychiatric Institute.

Spitzer, R. L., Williams, J. B. W., Gibbon, M., & First, M. B. (1988). *Structured Clinical Interview for DSM-III-R-Patient Version (SCID-P 6/1/88).* New York: Biometrics Research Department, New York State Psychiatric Institute.

Spitzer, R. L., Williams, J. B. W., Gibbon, M., & First, M. B. (1989). *Instruction manual for the Structured Clinical Interview for DSM-III-R (SCID, 5/1/89 Revision).* New York: Biometrics Research Department, New York State Psychiatric Institute.

Spitzer, R. L., Williams, J. B. W., Gibbon, M., & First, M. B. (1992). The Structured Clinical Interview for DSM-III-R (SCID): History, rationale, and description. *Archives of General Psychiatry, 49*, 624–629.

Vandiver, T., & Sher, K. J. (1991). Temporal stability of the Diagnostic Interview Schedule. *Psychological Assessment, 3*, 277–281.

Ward, C. H., Beck, A. T., Mendelson, M., Mock, J. E., & Erbaugh, J. K. (1962). The psychiatric nomenclature: Reasons for diagnostic disagreement. *Archives of General Psychiatry, 7*, 198–205.

Williams, J. B. W., Gibbon, M., First, M. B., Spitzer, R. L., Davies, M., Borus, J., Howes, M. J., Kane, J., Pope, H. G., Rounsaville, B., & Wittchen, H. (1992). The Structured Clinical Interview for DSM-III-R (SCID): Multisite test-retest reliability. *Archives of General Psychiatry, 49*, 630–636.

Williams, J. B. W., Spitzer, R. L., & Gibbon, M. (1992). International reliability of a diagnostic intake procedure for panic disorder. *American Journal of Psychiatry, 149*, 560–562.

Wilson, M., & Bullock, L. (1989). Psychometric characteristics of behavior rating scales: Definition, problems, and solutions. *Behavior Disorders, 14*, 186–200.

Wilson, D., & Prentice-Dunn, S. (1981). Rating scales in the assessment of child behavior. *Journal of Clinical Child Psychiatry, 10*, 121–126.

CHAPTER 9

ASSESSMENT OF ANXIETY AND FEAR

F. Dudley McGlynn
Michael P. Rose
Auburn University

Psychological assessment involves providing stimuli and recording subsequent responses. The nature of the stimuli provided and the responses recorded differs markedly across psychologists, owing to fundamental differences in the goals of assessment, in method assumptions, and in the postulated mechanisms that connect responses to stimuli.

Within the arena of psychological assessment, a useful distinction can be made between behavioral assessment and behaviorally oriented clinical assessment. *Behavioral assessment* refers to assessment activities that are congruent philosophically with one or more of several varieties of psychological behaviorism. (In brief, the activities of assessment mirror either the premise that behavior is a determined product of specific environmental control or the premise that behavior is a dynamic product of moment-to-moment interactions between environmental and organismic determinants.) *Behaviorally oriented clinical assessment*, on the other hand, refers to the evolved assessment practices of clinicians who identify themselves as behavior therapists. The distinction between behavioral assessment and behaviorally oriented clinical assessment is nontrivial; allegiance to psychological behaviorism *per se* has not been a major influence in the evolution of behavior therapists' assessment practices (see Barrios, 1988a).

The stimuli used during behavioral assessment are subsets and/or analogues of real-life stimuli. Real-life stimuli are of interest because, as noted, behavioral assessors believe that environmental events exert important influences on behavior. The responses recorded during behavioral assessment are subsets and/or analogues of adaptively significant naturalistic performances. Naturalistic performances are of interest because behavioral assessors seek to understand the governance of problematic behaviors directly (see Cone, 1987; Nelson & Hayes, 1979).

Behaviorally oriented clinical assessors have concerned themselves recently with integrating traditional (personality) assessment systematically into behavioral assessment packages (e.g., Collins & Thompson, 1993; Haynes & Uchigakiuchi, 1993). In traditional assessment, the stimuli used are declarative sentences organized into questionnaires. The responses of interest yield checkmarks next to the declarative sentences. The stimuli and responses used by traditional assessors reflect their belief that meaningful similarities can be discovered among persons who endorse subsets of declarative sentences in the same ways.

Making use of traditional assessment instruments poses a complex dilemma. On the one hand, behavior therapists value empiricism, and some of the instruments of traditional assessment afford empirically trustworthy statements about the populations of which individual patients are members. On the other hand, behavior therapists eschew the actuarial methods that provide the substrate of traditional assessment and reject the notion, historically prominent in personality assessment, that control over behavior resides mainly within persons. The value of empiricism seems to be winning out thus far; behavior therapists are grappling with the problem of how to make use of results from traditional assessment instruments in an intellectually honest way (e.g., Collins & Thompson, 1993).

Behavioral assessment of anxiety occurs in the context of behavior therapy for anxiety disorders. The stimuli used in behavioral assessment of anxiety are subsets and/or analogues of real-life anxiety-cue stimuli. The stimuli can be exteroceptive, as when the patient who displays specific phobia for spiders is presented with caged tarantulas, or when the patient with obsessive-compulsive decontaminating rituals is handed a soiled diaper. The stimuli can be interoceptive or proprioceptive, as when the patient who displays panic attacks is constrained to run-in-place so as to produce cardiac acceleration or is spun in a chair so as to produce dizziness. Inferentially, the "stimuli" for behavioral assessment can also be central, as when the patient with social phobia is instructed to visualize giving a speech to a large audience. The domains of anxiety-cue stimuli used are influenced both by provisional diagnoses and by the type of behavior therapy with which assessment is linked.

The responses recorded during behavioral assessment of anxiety occur in three domains: verbal reports, motor acts, and physiological events. Measurement activities across and within the three domains yield different pictures of anxiety phenomena (e.g., Lacey, 1967; Lang, 1968; Rachman & Hodgson, 1974). Ideally, behavioral assessment makes use of those response domains that are relevant to the description of adaptively significant naturalistic conduct in the individual case. Again, choices among measurement domains will reflect both the provisional diagnoses that apply and the type of behavior therapy with which assessment is linked.

As with the field of behavior therapy at large, behaviorally oriented clinical assessment of anxiety makes use of some assessment modes in which the stimuli are declarative sentences organized into questionnaires, and the responses yield checkmarks next to them. Self-reports about fear have been integral to behavior therapy since its inception, and psychometric assessment has been valuable for several reasons. Therefore, psychometric instruments are included in the review of behaviorally oriented clinical assessment here.

The narrative begins with comparative descriptions of several different approaches to behavior therapy. The descriptions are provided because, as noted, the desiderata of assessment are influenced by the sort of behavior therapy with which assessment is associated. The narrative continues with an overview of modern concepts of anxiety and of anxiety disorders. The conceptual overview is necessary for understanding the strategies used in assessment. Reviews of major assessment strategies are then provided; they are organized into the verbal report, motor behavior, and psychophysiological domains. Finally, the major activities of behavioral assessment for several *DSM-IV* (American Psychiatric Association, 1994) anxiety-disorder categories are described. (Trauma-related stress disorders are omitted due to space limitations and because anxiety assessment is only a component of symptom evaluation.) The organization here recognizes that *DSM-IV* categories influence the types of stimulating conditions used during assessment and, to a lesser extent, the domains of responses recorded.

APPROACHES TO BEHAVIOR THERAPY FOR ANXIETY DISORDERS

Several different approaches to behavior therapy have evolved over the 30-year course of the behavior-therapy movement. Major approaches to behavior therapy for anxiety disorders can be placed into five broad categories.

Orthodox behavior therapy (e.g., Wolpe, 1973, 1990) rests on the twofold assumption that anxiety behaviors reflect sympathetic activation and that stimulus control over sympathetic activation reflects a history of either aversive respondent conditioning or exposure to (mis)information. Even though sympathetic activation is viewed as fundamental, untoward thinking is sometimes important. Emphasis is placed on understanding precisely the anxiety controlling features of clinically focal stimuli (i.e., the elements, dimensions, and abstract themes that influence the vigor of anxiety responses). Assessment that is linked to orthodox behavior therapy provides both actual and imaginal stimuli, and records indices of sympathetic activation as well as motor acts and verbal reports of various kinds.

Exposure technology (Marks, 1975, 1978) does not derive from assumptions about either the nature of anxiety or the ontogeny of anxiety disorders. Its sole guiding principle is that anxiety can be overcome by exposing patients to anxiety-cue stimuli beyond the point at which their anxiety inevitably subsides. Typically, the stimuli used during exposure treatment are representative subsets of the stimuli that pose adaptive hazards in the natural environment. Sometimes the fear stimuli are encountered by the patient hierarchically from events that are less fearsome to events that are more fearsome. Sometimes ungraded fear stimuli are used. The responses recorded during exposure are motor acts indicative of anxiety and of its diminution. Verbal reports of anxiety are used also by many clinicians. Behavioral assessment is based largely on the motor acts (and verbal reports) observed during the therapeutic exposure.

Cognitive therapy (Beck, 1970; Beck & Emery, 1985) rests on the assumption that the fundamental problem in maladaptive anxiety is untoward thinking. The themes of untoward thinking can be related to the uncontrollability of the feared situation (Barlow, 1988), to the likelihood and consequences of deficit performances in the feared situation (Beck & Emery, 1985), and the like. Because thinking presumably drives anxious emotion and anxious behavior, cognitive therapy and associated assessment for anxiety disorders emphasize demonstrable cognitive alteration.

Social-learning approaches (e.g., Bandura, 1977, 1986) also place emphasis on the role of maladaptive thinking in anxious behavior. In this case, expectations of deficit performance and/or expectations of adverse performance outcomes produce anxiety in the form of behavioral inhibition. Therapy is directed toward increasing self-efficacy expectations and reducing adverse performance-outcome expectations via personal mastery experiences such as those that occur during participant modeling. Assessment of constructs such as self-efficacy is central because of the postulate that self-efficacy influences therapeutically pivotal factors, such as the strength and persistence of adjustive and self-change efforts (Bandura, 1977).

A *prescriptive treatment approach* is emerging in clinical psychology—that is, "the prescription of a highly specified, thoroughly evaluated treatment regimen in order to ameliorate a highly specified, thoroughly assessed complaint" (Acierno, Hersen, & Ammerman, 1994, p. 3). By and large, the prescribed treatments involve some combination of exposure technology and/or cognitive therapy and/or pharmacotherapy. Assessment within the prescriptive approach attends to the problem behaviors, to discriminanda and contingencies that influence the problem behaviors, to psychological ontogenies reflected in the problem behaviors, and to relevant characteristics of the persons who exhibit the problem behaviors (see Acierno, Hersen, Van Hasselt, & Ammerman, 1994). Behavioral assessment, functional analysis of behavior, interviewing, and psychometric instruments are used in evaluating patients.

Orthodox behavior therapy, cognitive therapy, and social-learning approaches are derived from different assumptions about how thinking, arousal, and motor acts are organized in complex anxiety displays (see Barlow, 1988). No doctrinal position on that set of issues is taken here. Rather, anxious thinking, physiological arousal, and motor behavior are used simply as behavioral domains that might require assessment in any given instance.

CURRENT CONCEPTS OF ANXIETY DISORDERS

In the earliest days of the behavior therapy movement, the concept of anxiety *per se* was not discussed frequently. Eysenck and others argued that anxiety behaviors are conditioned emotional respondents; thus, the details of anxiety behavior would conform in one way or another to the unconditional respondents elicited by the aversive stimuli of interest. Wolpe (1958) maintained that anxiety is fundamentally a matter of sympathetic activation. These and similar assertions were accepted more or less uncritically. Somewhat later, the routine finding of low intercorrelations between self-report, behavioral, and physiological "measures of anxiety" prompted explicit examination of the anxiety concept. That examination eventuated in the popular view of anxiety as a multidimensional or multireferential construct that serves to organize thinking about diverse events at the self-report and/or behavioral and/or psychophysiological levels of measurement (e.g., Lang, 1968; Rachman & Hodgson, 1974). Clearly, the three-channel anxiety construct remains popular among the verbal community of behavior therapists. At the same time, the concept of anxiety is evolving. Major aspects of that evolution are noted here.

There are ongoing efforts to understand anxiety from within the context of the larger field known as the *psychology of emotion* (e.g., Barlow, 1988; Lang, 1995). Emotion theorists divide emotional experience into separate domains called *cognition* and *affect*. If that division is accepted for anxiety, then anxiety becomes a four-domain construct; it summarizes events in cognition and/or affect and/or behavior and/or physiology. Koskal and Power (1990) have reported beginning psychometric work toward a four-factor construction of anxiety.

Hallam (1978), Klein (1981), and others popularized a distinction between exogenous and endogenous cues for anxiety, and used that distinction to delimit two primary anxiety syndromes. The idea that endogenously cued anxiety (panic) constitutes a primary syndrome was then incorporated into the structure of *DSM-III-R* (American Psychiatric Association, 1987). The anxiety (panic) attack is now a central organizing feature of the anxiety-disorder nomenclature; the classification system "can be usefully seen as a taxonomy of the contexts in which the anxiety attacks occur" (Lipschitz, 1988, p. 43).

Concurrent with the taxonomic developments previously noted, the concept of panic has changed. According to the traditional account, panic attacks occur suddenly, without warning, and for no apparent reason. According to the contemporary account, panic attacks mirror a spiraling vicious cycle in which oftentimes normal somatic events (e.g., tachycardia) occasion catastrophic thinking (e.g., "I am losing control") among persons who monitor their somatic status too closely and who are otherwise predisposed to panic phenomena (Barlow, 1988).

Interest in the role of catastrophic thinking in panic attacks is emblematic of another changed aspect of the contemporary zeitgeist. Cognitive therapy has been with us during most of the evolution of behavior therapy (e.g., Beck, 1970). During the past 15 years, however, cognitive approaches and related concepts have become increasingly influential in the arena of anxiety disorders. There are "complete" cognitive theories of the origin and maintenance of anxiety (see Delprato & McGlynn, 1984). There are also cognitive constructs such as anxiety sensitivity, anxious self-talk (Cacciopo, Glass, & Merluzzi, 1979), and information-processing deficits that play pivotal roles in multielement models of anxiety phenomena. There is important work on the cognitive psychophysiology of anxiety (e.g., Lang, 1979, 1985, 1995).

The evolution of the modern anxiety concept has been paralleled by new developments in anxiety assessment, particularly in cognitive assessment. However, the basic methods of anxiety assessment remain unchanged; they are classified as self-report methods, observation of behavior, and measurement of physiological reactions.

MAJOR ASSESSMENT METHODS

Self-Report Methods

For various reasons, psychologists sometimes forego the direct observation of stimuli and responses and, instead, obtain subjects' reports about relations between stimuli and responses. The accuracy of self-reports has always been controversial. Early behavior therapists were influenced by neo-behavioristic learning theory. Because neo-behavioristic learning theory was grounded in methodological behaviorism, there was a systematic bias against self-report methods. Later, behavior therapists voiced empirical objections to self-report measures. Objections related to "deficiencies in reliability and validity, contamination by faking and bias, low correlations with concurrent behavioral and physiological measures, and error associated with acquiescence, social desirability, and other response sets" (Nietzel, Bernstein, & Russell, 1988, p. 297). More recently, however, the contexts of clinical work have placed a premium on efficient assessment practices. Furthermore, the increasingly cognitive model of anxiety means that self-report measures are sometimes needed because the reporting person is the only observer of the state-of-affairs reported. For these reasons, and others, self-report measures are seen increasingly as valuable components of clinical assessment.

Workers in the psychometric tradition have learned a great deal about how to develop self-report queries that maximize accuracy of the information obtained. For example, questions should contain specific and concrete information, and response choices should be scaled quantitatively as to frequency and/or intensity. Some of the storied inaccuracy of self-report assessment in the individual case derives from the practices of aggregating data across subjects and of focusing questions on presumed internal determinants of behavior. In the final analysis, self-reporting is behavior; as such, its accuracy is subject to various influences in addition to the states-of-affairs being reported (see Bellack & Hersen, 1977).

In assessing anxiety *per se,* self-report measures serve two functions; they provide convenient but inexact information about motor acts and physiology, and they provide criterional information about inherently subjective events (e.g., the content of catastrophic thinking, the intensity of anxious experience). In the narrative here, self-report assessment is divided into structured interviews, questionnaires, protocol analyses, situational ratings, and self-monitoring.

The Structured Interviews

Structured interviews for diagnosis were prompted by the need for improved diagnostic reliability in research. The first major structured interview format was the Present State Examination (Wing, Cooper, & Sartorius, 1974). It prompted questions about a variety of adverse conditions and behaviors, but the primary focus was on psychotic disorders. The second major structured interview format was the Schedule of Affective Disorders and Schizophrenia (Endicott & Spitzer, 1978). It was the major format for psychiatric research during the 1970s. Several broad-band and special-purpose interview formats appeared during the early 1980s (see Hersen & Turner, 1985). Two interview guides have been especially prominent: the Diagnostic Interview Schedule (Helzer, Robins, et al., 1985) and the Structured Clinical Interview for *DSM-III-R* (Spitzer, Williams, & Gibbon, 1987).

The interview structure most commonly used in evaluating anxiety disorders was developed and has been refined over several iterations by Barlow and colleagues. The Anxiety Disorders Interview Schedule (ADIS; Di Nardo, O'Brien, Barlow, Waddell, & Blanchard, 1983) incorporated items developed by Barlow and colleagues with material from the Schedule for Affective Disorders and Schizophrenia (Endicott & Spitzer, 1978), the Hamilton Anxiety Rating Scale (Hamilton, 1959), and the Hamilton Rating Scale for Depression (Hamilton, 1960). The ADIS was developed for use with *DSM-III* (American Psychiatric Association, 1980) and was intended "not only to permit differential diagnosis but also to provide data beyond the basic information required for establishing the diagnostic criteria" (Barlow, 1988, p.

326). The additional information included the history of the anxiety problem, the situational and cognitive factors that influence anxiety, and detailed symptom ratings as well as material about depressive, psychotic, addictive, and organic symptoms. The ADIS-R (DiNardo & Barlow, 1988) and the ADIS-IV (Brown, DiNardo, & Barlow, 1994) were developed later so as to keep pace with the changes in the anxiety-disorder classifications of *DSM-III-R* (American Psychiatric Association, 1987) and *DSM-IV* (American Psychiatric Association, 1994).

Throughout the iterations of the ADIS there has been careful work on fundamentals, such as inter-rater reliabilities of *DSM* diagnoses. The work has produced impressive reliabilities, thus legitimizing the *DSM* anxiety-disorder constructs as well as the ADIS. An early, and conservative, evaluation of the inter-judge reliabilities of *DSM-III* diagnoses among raters who worked with the ADIS was undertaken with 125 consecutive admissions to an anxiety-disorders clinic (Barlow, 1987). The reliabilities were quite impressive; the lowest reliabilities were for categories with few behavioral referents (e.g., panic disorder and generalized anxiety disorder). Similar inter-rater reliabilities were achieved using the ADIS-R; again, reliabilities were lowest for disorders with relatively few behavioral markers (DiNardo, Moras, Barlow, Rapee, & Brown, 1993).

The ADIS-IV interview is structured so as to maintain thematic continuity (e.g., the agoraphobia section follows the panic section). It begins with demographic information, followed by basic questions about the presenting complaint and by queries about recent life stresses. The remainder of the interview deals with anxiety disorders, mood and somatoform disorders, mixed anxiety and depression, substance use, obvious psychotic/conversion symptoms, and medical disorders. The anxiety disorder questions go a long way toward differential diagnosis; the additional questions serve a screening function. There are identified "research" questions about panic disorder, generalized anxiety disorder, and social and specific phobia. There is an ADIS-IV-L (lifetime edition) that provides more in-depth information about previous episodes.

The ADIS is used for assessing anxiety disorders in clinics worldwide. It is recommended here as the state-of-the-art means of deciding which direction(s) behavioral assessment of a given patient should take.

Questionnaires

Notwithstanding the would-be behavioristic posture of the early behavior therapy movement, questionnaires about fear/anxiety have been with us since the beginning (e.g., Geer, 1965; Wolpe & Lang, 1964). For the most part, questionnaires have served research purposes; they are convenient and standardized, they provide for comparisons vis-à-vis normative data, they lend themselves to factor-analytic and related work concerned with the organization of fear, and so on. Most questionnaires are not well suited to clinical work. However, questionnaires are used often as components of multifaceted assessment protocols that are organized around convergent validation strategies.

There are questionnaires that list multiple objects and events (e.g., snakes, thunderstorms, dentists) and that prompt Likert-scale ratings of the degree of fear associated with each. And there are questionnaires that list multiple aspects of encounters with single objects or events and that prompt Likert-scale ratings of the degree of fear associated with each aspect. There are also questionnaires organized around multiple dimensions of a *DSM* diagnostic category (e.g., social phobia, obsessive-compulsive disorder, post-traumatic stress disorder). There are questionnaires, too, that quantify anxiety as an enduring, trans-situational disposition of the individual.

There are several questionnaires that elicit ratings about various bodily (i.e., autonomic) reactions during anxious periods. There are other questionnaires about somatic and/or cognitive phenomena that contribute to the development of anxiety. Many of the questionnaires of interest are noted by Nietzel, Bernstein, and Russell (1988). Narratives about questionnaires related to anxious thinking are provided by Martzke, Anderson, and Cacciopo (1987). Questionnaires that are commonly used currently are described in narratives (later in this chapter) about assessing *DSM-IV* anxiety disorders.

Protocol Analyses

A protocol analysis can be thought of as "a content analysis of self-reported cognitions, with variations occurring in when and how the cognitions are obtained, categorized and analyzed" (Martzke, Anderson, & Cacioppo, 1987, p. 62). In general, patients report on their thought content as they are behaving or as they are later viewing videotapes of their behavior. Major versions of the protocol analysis strategy are the thought-listing technique (Cacioppo & Petty, 1981), videotape reconstruction (e.g., Chiauzzi & Heimberg, 1983), and the think-aloud technique (Ericsson & Simon, 1980).

In thought-listing work, respondents are provided with pencils and structured paper and are instructed to write down all of their thoughts without editing and without concern for spelling, grammar, and so on. The lists can be prepared before and/or after an anxiety-producing encounter. The "thoughts" are then scored along one or more relevant dimensions such as frequency, content, and valence (e.g., Arnkoff, 1980; Huber & Altmaier, 1983). Thought-listing adjuncts to behavioral assessment tasks provide clinicians with more information than they would otherwise have about anxious thinking during targeted performances.

Behavioral assessment performances can be videotaped and patients can be asked to watch the videotapes and provide commentary on their thinking at various points. Sometimes the commentary is provided during videotape viewing (e.g., Hollandsworth, Glazeski, Kirkland, Jones, & van Norman, 1979) and sometimes the commentary is provided afterwards (Burgio, Glass, & Merluzzi, 1981). As with thought listing, videotape reconstruction provides inferentially useful data about various aspects of thinking during anxious performances.

Application of the think-aloud technique (Erricson & Simons, 1980) to the arena of anxiety assessment entails instructing patients to verbalize their thoughts and feelings as they participate in anxiety-related performances. In principle, data acquired from the think-aloud method can be subject to the same scoring and interpretation procedures used in thought-listing work. The think-aloud technique suffers from a substantial problem of reactivity—that is, because the reporting is concurrent with task performance, it interferes with task-related attention and behavior (see Fulkerson, Galassi, & Galassi, 1984). There is the additional consideration that thinking occurs more rapidly than speaking, thus raising concerns over the content validity of spoken renditions.

The narrative here about thought listing, videotape reconstruction, and thinking aloud draws from a review by Martzke, Anderson, and Cacioppo (1987). The techniques sometimes are referred to as *cognitive assessment* and they are usually associated with cognitive therapy (e.g., Beck & Emery, 1985). In the language of cognitive therapy, nouns such as *thoughts* and *feelings* are used so as to connote psychological entities. In the metaphor of cognitive therapy, these entities serve as presumptive causes for subsequent actions and emotions. Alterations in the language and metaphor of cognitive assessment might be useful to behaviorally oriented therapists. Replacement metaphors are found in contextualist metatheories (see Hayes, 1987). In brief, the idea that anxious thoughts cause anxious behavior should be replaced by the idea that anxious thinking *is* anxious behavior; anxious thinking occurs along with physiological arousal and anxious motor behavior in response to specific environmental and/or bodily signals.

Situational Ratings

When questionnaires and interviews are used to prompt reports of fear intensity, the functional stimuli are written or oral statements. Of course, one can use actual stimuli to prompt reports of fear intensity. One can also instruct patients to visualize focal stimuli then prompt reports about the fear intensities associated with imaging. Walk's (1956) Fear Thermometer, and Wolpe's (1973) Subjective Units of Discomfort (SUD) scale are commonly used. The Fear Thermometer prompts fear-intensity ratings from 1 ("completely calm") to 10 ("absolute terror"). In using the SUD scale, the patient is told "Think of the worst anxiety you have ever experienced or can imagine experiencing, and assign to this the number 100. Now think of the state of being absolutely calm and call this zero" (Wolpe, 1973, p. 120). These instructions provide anchor points for subsequent fear ratings before and after exposure to fear cues and/or to fear-imagery instructions.

Visual analogue scales can be used also to prompt ratings of fear intensity before and after real and visualized encounters with feared stimuli. Patients are instructed simply to mark somewhere along a line that has anchors, such as "absolute calm" to "terror" (e.g., McGlynn, Moore, Rose, & Lazarte, 1995). Ratings of fear intensity can also be recorded continuously for research purposes. For example, McGlynn, Rose, and Lazarte (1994) used a system composed of a manual-input dial, a skin-conductance module, software for analogue-to-digital conversion, and a computer. Subjects were instructed to monitor their fear levels continuously by adjusting a dial on the manual input box; the numbers 1 through 4 were placed equidistantly around the dial to signify increasing fear intensity.

Self-rating of fear can be extended beyond the domain of intensity by incorporating semantic-differential methods. In this approach, objects, events, and words are rated on the factor analytically derived affective dimensions of pleasure (valence), arousal, and dominance (Mehrabian & Russell, 1974). An early extension of semantic-differential methods to the arena of fear self-assessment was reported by Husek and Alexander (1963). More recently a human-figure pictorial version of the semantic-differential approach to self-assessment of affect has been developed. (The affective dimension of valence is captured by a human figure that ranges from smiling to frowning; the dimension of arousal involves a figure that varies from wide-eyed excitement to relaxed sleepiness, etc.) The original self-assessment manikin (SAM) is an interactive computer program on which respondents adjust emotion-relevant features of a computer-generated figure to describe their own affect; real-time records of the adjustments are made (Lang, 1980; Cook, Atkinson, & Lang, 1987). More recently, a paper-and-pencil version of SAM has been reported (Bradley & Lang, 1994). The SAM method has been useful to researchers using both anxious patients (Cook, Melamed, Cuthbert, McNeil, & Lang, 1988) and fearful research subjects (Hamm, Globisch, Cuthbert, & Vaitl, 1991). It has been used with imagery (Miller, Levin, Kozac, Cook, McClean, & Lang, 1987) and lends itself to applications where a nonverbal approach is needed.

Many therapists and researchers use ratings of self-efficacy in the context of behavior therapy. Self-efficacy was introduced (Bandura, 1977) as a unifying explanation for the success of behavior therapy for anxiety-related disorders. In brief, its explanatory status rests on observed parallels between the behavioral effects of fear reduction procedures and the levels of self-efficacy vis-à-vis fearsome tasks that result from the procedures (Bandura, 1977, 1986). Acceptance of self-efficacy as an explanatory construct is not widespread among advocates of the various types of behavior therapy described earlier. Among many behavior therapists, however, the self-efficacy of patients vis-à-vis clinically targeted performances is assessed because self-efficacy is thought to influence the intensity and persistence of self-change efforts. Furthermore, there are numerous reports of large correlations between efficacy ratings and subsequent performance attainments (e.g., Lee, 1984; Williams, 1987). Typically, self-efficacy ratings are situation specific (Bandura, Adams, Hardy, & Howells, 1986). When faced with a clinically targeted performance of some kind, the patient is asked to rate (e.g., on a 0 to 100 scale) his or her confidence (level of efficacy) that the performance or various subtasks within the performance will be accomplished. Typically, the patient is asked also to rate his or her confidence in each efficacy rating (strength of efficacy).

Self-Monitoring

In self-monitoring, the patient or subject monitors and records some aspect of the behavior of interest (e.g., frequency, intensity, duration). Usually a standard form for record keeping is provided; often there is an instruction to turn in the record forms on some regular basis (e.g., at each visit).

Self-monitoring was not common in the early anxiety assessment literature. Rather, it appeared in literatures about assessing discrete, repetitive, variables such as cigarettes smoked, foods eaten, times studied, and so forth. More recently, however, self-monitoring has become increasingly prominent in the anxiety literature. Probably this reflects the modern construction of panic as a discrete response as well as influence on assessment practices from protocols for self-management of anxiety (i.e., Marks, 1978).

Self-monitoring is behavior and, as such, it is susceptible to many of the same sources of inaccuracy that influence other assessment-related activities. Self-monitoring also presents problems associated with reactivity (i.e., behavior change wrought by the activities of behavior recording). Fortunately, early interest in self-monitoring prompted considerable research on variables that influence both accuracy and reactivity (see Nelson, 1977). Research on the accuracy of self-monitoring has taken three forms: self-monitored data have been compared (1) with other-monitored data, (2) with data produced by mechanical response transducers, and (3) with data in the form of measured by-products from self-monitored activities. The following generalizations have been produced by the research and can be of value to clinicians working with anxious patients who provide self-monitored data.

1. Accuracy is highest when the self-recorder knows that accuracy is being checked.

2. Accuracy can be enhanced by providing accuracy-based incentives.

3. Descriptions of to-be-recorded behavior should be as concrete as possible.

4. Negatively valenced target behaviors might be self-recorded less accurately than positively valenced ones.

5. Accuracy is likely to suffer when the self-recorder must attend simultaneously to tasks other than self-assessment.

6. Accuracy is enhanced by instructions to record each and every instance of the target behavior, and can be enhanced by training in self-monitoring activities.

Research on the reactivity of self-monitoring has produced differences in self-monitored data that are associated with independent-variable domains such as instructions, goal setting, feedback, and timing (see Nelson, 1977). Many of the conditions that influence reactivity are the same as those that influence accuracy. The following generalizations can be added to those about the accu-

racy of self-monitoring, and are potentially applicable in influencing the reactivity of self-monitored assessment among anxious patients.

7. Reactivity is not necessarily an issue; there are conditions under which reactivity does and does not occur.

8. If reactivity is present, then positively evaluated target behaviors will show reactive increases in frequency; negatively valenced target behaviors will show decreases.

9. Instructions that influence the valence of target behaviors can also produce these increases/decreases in frequency.

10. For some behaviors, prebehavior monitoring will produce stronger reactive effects than will postbehavior monitoring.

Along with increasing use of self-monitoring in clinical assessment, there is a modest research literature about the accuracy of self-monitoring in the area of anxiety behavior. For example, Beidel, Neil, and Lederer (1991) studied the use of a daily diary among children who did and who did not have problems with test anxiety. The children complied with the self-recording instructions satisfactorily, and the self-recorded information discriminated between anxious and nonanxious children. There is also a body of research on anxiety phenomena in which self-monitoring served as a primary source of data. For example, Basoglu, Marks, and Sengun (1992) used self-monitoring to track panic and anxiety phenomena among 39 patients diagnosed as having panic disorder with agoraphobia. The work prompted several generalizations about panic and anxiety phenomena (e.g., panic occurs at the end of long anxious periods, panic occurs more frequently in public places, a categorical distinction between panic and anxiety is not justified). Similarly, Rapee, Craske, and Barlow (1990) had 62 panic-disorder patients self-monitor their symptoms during 285 cumulative panic episodes that occurred during a two-week period. The self-monitoring revealed an average of 2.3 panic attacks per week, and an average of 4.6 symptoms from the *DSM-III-R* checklist for anxiety phenomena.

Compliance with self-monitoring instructions is sometimes problematic. For example, there is weak compliance among some panic patients because they anticipate that the act of self-monitoring will cue a panic episode. In general, however, there is no obvious reason to suppose that otherwise influential self-monitoring variables will act uniquely when anxiety behavior is being monitored. As noted by Nietzel, Bernstein, and Russell (1988), the value of self-monitoring is that, in principle, it provides detailed information about the topography, frequency, and consequences of anxiety behavior, as the patient deals with the ever-changing environments of his or her daily life.

Measures of Anxiety-Related Behavior

Motor behavior in the presence of feared stimuli has been a preferred assessment domain in behavior therapy since the 1960s (e.g., Lang & Lazovik, 1963). Early behavior therapists learned the dual-process fear mediation theory of phobic avoidance (Mowrer, 1939). According to the dual-process view, anxiety is an aversive drive state whose contingent removal or reduction negatively reinforces instrumental escape/avoidance of the cues that produce it. Given a direct connection between anxiety and instrumental escape/avoidance, the original purpose of assessing motor behavior was to "measure fear objectively." After three decades or so, behavior therapists recognized the manifest deficiencies in the dual-process theory (e.g., Bandura, 1969) and abandoned it in favor of the three-channel anxiety concept (Lang, 1968). Hence, the contemporary purpose of assessing motor behavior vis-à-vis feared stimuli is to measure the motoric dimension of the three-channel anxiety construct. Two of the more common venues for assessing fear-related motor behavior are the Behavioral Avoidance Test (BAT) and the Interpersonal Performance Test. In both cases, these are assessment strategies, not particular instruments or procedures.

Contrived Behavioral Avoidance Tests

Motoric behavior vis-à-vis feared circumstances can be assessed in contrived or in naturalistic settings. Assessment within contrived settings is reported frequently. In general, a targeted fear stimulus (e.g., snake, spider, mouse) is caged at the end of a 15- to 20-foot walkway along which distances are indicated. Typically, performance aids such as a pointer or heavy gloves are placed near the cage. Frequently, the patient or subject is provided with a behavioral checklist that describes a number of concrete actions that are called for during the assessment. He or she is then escorted to the far end of the walkway and instructed to perform the actions on the list. There is room for many variations in the content and timing of the instructions as well as in the locations and activities of experimenters or therapists during the assessment. There is room for variation also in the details of behavior that are recorded (e.g., distance remaining at maximum approach, latency to touch the feared specimen, observed fear behaviors during the test).

Performance during a behavioral avoidance test (BAT) is influenced by contextual demand characteristics and by other threats to internal validity (i.e., influential factors that are not related to fear of the specimen housed at the end of the walkway) (Bernstein, 1973). Bernstein and Nietzel (1973) showed, for example, that the same BAT format would yield different assessment results when styled as a "fear assessment" than when styled as a "physiological assessment." Behavior during a single BAT probably is not representative of fear behaviors in various conceivable assessments (i.e., the content validity of a single BAT is weak). Behavior during contrived BATs probably is not representative of behaviors in natural settings (i.e., the external validity of contrived assessment is suspect) (see Lick & Unger, 1977). For these reasons, contrived BAT assessment is best used as a precursor to naturalistic behavioral assessment or as a substitute when naturalistic assessment is not feasible.

Naturalistic Behavioral Avoidance Tests

Naturalistic BATs are used frequently also. For one example, Height Avoidance Tests have been used to assess the behaviors of acrophobics vis-à-vis tall buildings that have multilevel balconies (Williams & Watson, 1985), multilevel parking garages (Williams, Turner, & Peer, 1985), and fire escapes (Marshall, 1985). Ordinarily, patients are instructed to do as much as they can tolerate, and assessors do what they can to facilitate functional as well as nominal exposure to height cues (see Williams, 1988). Data from one-month test-retest assessments (Williams, Turner, & Peer, 1985) show that results from procedurally uniform Height Avoidance Tests are very stable.

For another example, social-encounter avoidance tests have been used to assess the anxiety-related behaviors of social phobics. Mattick and Peters (1988) constructed a unique hierarchical list of moderately to strongly avoided social situations for each of 51 social phobic subjects. They then asked each subject to report whether he or she could attempt each item, and prompted the subject to actually attempt the highest item endorsed. Data were provided in the form of the hierarchical placement of the highest item endorsed, SUDs ratings during the attempt, and outcome of the attempt.

Naturalistic BATs are used often in assessing motor behavior among patients diagnosed as agoraphobic. In the simplest case (e.g., Emmelkamp, 1982), the patient is instructed to walk as far as possible along a specified route and to return immediately when no further progress is anticipated. The route can be specified as one that leaves a place of safety (e.g., home, car, neighborhood) or as one that approaches a place of danger (e.g., crowded supermarket). Sometimes patients are instructed to leave a corroborative marker such as a piece of adhesive tape at the point of maximum progress. In a more complex naturalistic assessment of agoraphobia, an individualized hierarchy of adaptively germane and increasingly fearsome locomotor performances is specified, and the patient is instructed to do each in turn (Mathews, Gelder, & Johnston, 1981). In a still more complex application, termed the *standardized walk*, locomotor behavior among agoraphobics is assessed under standardized conditions so that data can be compared across patients (Agras, Leitenberg, & Barlow, 1968). At the SUNY-Albany Center for Stress and Anxiety Disorders, a standard 1.2-mile course punctuated with 20 or so stopping stations has been set up. Patients are instructed to proceed until they are too uncom-

fortable to continue. Behavioral progress is monitored by appearances at the stopping stations.

In general, the technique and measurement variations that are possible in contrived BATs are possible also in naturalistic assessment. In principle, use of a naturalistic assessment strategy is limited only by the availability of environmental resources, cost, and the creativity of clinicians. Naturalistic assessment solves the problem of external validity and addresses that of content validity. However, insofar as the concept of situational specificity in behavior is taken seriously, multiple naturalistic assessments are required. Decisions about standardized versus individualized assessment procedures rest on the exact purposes of assessment and on matters related to cost.

Interpersonal Performance Tests

Behavioral assessment of interpersonal/performance anxieties is not different fundamentally from the approaches just described. In general, measures of behavior are acquired as patients or subjects are engaged in frightening public performances or in role-plays of anxiety-laden social interactions. These approaches have been very popular since the beginning of the behavior therapy movement. They are used not only to assess socially anxious patients and subjects but also to evaluate social-skill deficits among diversely handicapped populations. The measurement of social skill differs from the measurement of socially cued anxiety. The latter is emphasized here.

Behavioral assessment during a public performance was first undertaken in the landmark research of Paul (1966), who instructed socially fearful subjects to speak to a small audience while trained raters recorded anxiety behaviors such as hand tremors and speech dysfluencies. The raters were provided with a checklist of 20 anxiety-related behaviors and were instructed to record them within specified time intervals. Paul's initial work showed that the procedure produced highly reliable ratings. Use of public speaking as a context for behavioral assessment has continued but has tended to focus on social skills rather than socially cued anxiety behaviors. For example, Marshall, Cooper, and Parker (1979) empirically developed a checklist containing 19 items that describe general behaviors, specific speech behaviors, and body movements that are associated with effective public speaking.

Shyness related to heterosocial interaction has become the most common target for anxiety assessment during public performance. In one approach (Borkovek, Stone, O'Brien, & Kaloupek, 1974), an attractive female confederate sits passively while shy male subjects attempt conversationally to create a favorable impression. Research has shown that the procedure affords behavioral, self-report, and heart-rate measures that discriminate shy from nonshy subjects and that are relatively immune to experimental demand effects (Borkovec et al., 1974; McGlynn, Patterson, Marchetti, & Geisen, 1980).

Obvious problems associated with the artificiality of early laboratory-performance protocols prompted attempts to develop more realistic laboratory procedures for behaviorally assessing shyness. One such procedure (Haemmerlie, 1983) entails recording anxiety behaviors (e.g., number of conversation initiations) from audiotapes made while shy subjects interact with a trained, opposite-sex confederate who is "disguised" as another subject. Ratings of three-minute audiotapes using designated anxiety-behavior categories have been reliable across judges, stable through time, and sensitive to improvements wrought by intervention for shyness.

Role-play performances are used sometimes to evaluate social performance deficits related to social phobia. The Behavioral Situations Test (Barrios, 1983) is a role-play format developed specifically for evaluating interpersonal responses of men during first encounters with women. Twelve scenarios drawn from the Survey of Heterosocial Interactions (Twentyman, Boland, & McFall, 1981) are used. In each, the situation is described, 30 seconds are allowed for preparation, and three minutes are allowed for role-playing one's reactions vis-à-vis a polite but unfamiliar woman. Performances are audiotaped and scored using specific behavioral categories (e.g., refusal to do the role-play, introducing oneself, requesting a future get-together). Self-report and physiological measures are taken as well. Careful psychomet-

ric work with socially isolated males showed high internal consistency and excellent inter-rater reliability for behavioral scores based on the role-play format (see Barrios, 1988b).

Measurement of Physiological Reactions

Psychophysiology began in earnest during the 1950s when equipment for transducing and storing biological signals became available. The early machines were "physiographs" of various kinds with which paper records of physiological events were made. For example, electrodermal flow (discussed next) was amplified, measured, and recorded on moving paper with a pen that was calibrated such that a given amount of pen deflection was equal to known bioelectric equivalents. Physiograph devices are still used, but the advent of computers, bioelectric-signal recording modules, and computer software for digitizing analogue signals has brought about significant changes, as has the advent of ambulatory equipment for bioelectric recording (e.g., Medilog and Holter).

Anxiety phenomena have always been of interest to psychophysiologists. There is considerable information about anxiety in relation to cardiovascular factors such as heart activity, vasomotor activity, and arterial blood pressure. There is substantial information about anxiety also in relation to electrodermal and electromyographic phenomena and to respiratory function. The three most common psychophysiological measures of anxiety are heart rate, electrodermal flow, and respiration rate.

Heart Rate

Heart rate is the most widely used psychophysiological measure of anxiety. Heart beats can be recorded with electrodes that register the bioelectric events associated with myocardial contraction or with sensors that detect changes that are linked directly to heart beats (e.g., finger pulse, arterial blood pressure). There are two methods for heart-rate measurement. In one method, a unit of time is chosen, then the beats within that unit of time are counted (e.g., beats per minute). In the other method, each heart period (the interval between successive heart beats) is measured in milliseconds, and the heart rate is prorated, usually in beats-per-minute values. Heart-rate and heart-period measures do not produce the same picture of what the heart is doing (Jennings, Stringfellow, & Graham, 1974; Montgomery, 1977). Therefore, researchers have argued about the best approaches for various exact purposes (e.g., Graham, 1979). For clinical assessment, however, either approach will suffice. Manual recording of heart rate will necessarily be time based; the details of heart-period recording will be determined by equipment (see Siddle, Turpin, Spinks, & Stevenson, 1980).

Typically in the behavior therapy literature, variations in heart rate have been construed as showing corresponding variations in autonomic output (i.e., heart rate acceleration means heightened beta-adrenergic action). Problematically, heart rate is influenced by peripheral hemodynamic mechanisms and central nervous system factors, among other non-autonomic inputs. Hence, interpretations of heart-rate variations as signaling anxiety variations are oversimplified. Nonetheless, a long history of heart-rate measurement in connection with anxiety phenomena (e.g., White & Gilden, 1937) has yielded three empirical generalizations that are trustworthy and potentially useful to clinicians.

First, anxious patients and patients with panic disorder have higher resting heart rates than do normal comparison subjects. In one study (Kelley & Walter, 1968), 41 chronically anxious patients had resting heart rates of 91 bpm, whereas comparison subjects had rates of 74 bpm. Second, panic attacks are accompanied frequently by sudden heart-rate increases. In one study (Taylor, Sheikh, et al., 1986), heart-rate signatures were observed in 58% of 33 panic attacks recorded naturalistically. Third, patients with anxiety disorders show greater heart-rate reactivity (Borkovec, Stone, O'Brien, & Kaloupec, 1974) during fear-cue exposure, and slower habituation of heart rate responsivity to repeated fear-cue exposures (McGuiness, 1973) than do normal subjects.

Electrodermal Activity

Electrodermal flow is the second most widely used psychophysiological measure of anxiety. Again, there are two basic approaches to measurement. In one method, a very small electrical current is passed between two nonpolarizing electrodes (e.g., silver/silver chloride) on the skin; changes in the electrical properties of the skin are then recorded as alterations in conductance or resistance relative to the constant applied voltage. In the other method, differences in the electrical potential of two electrode placements are compared. One electrode is placed over a presumably active site, such as a palm, and the other is placed over a relatively inert site, such as a forearm. Usually, changes relative to a constant applied voltage are studied and are expressed as conductance changes. *Tonic skin-conductance* level refers to an ongoing property of the skin. *Phasic skin-conductance* response refers to a discrete and short-term reaction of the skin to some external stimulus. Spontaneous skin-conductance response refers to a discrete and short-term reaction that is not known to be due to any external stimulus.

Electrodermal phenomena mirror the action of eccrine sweat glands. These glands occur throughout the surface of the body and are concentrated in the palms of the hands and soles of the feet. They are innervated solely by the sympathetic division of the autonomic nervous system and are activated by acetylcholine. Despite the relatively simple mechanism of sweat gland activation, changes in electrodermal measures should be interpreted cautiously. Electrodermal flow is influenced by subject variables, such as age, sex, race, menstrual phase, and other biological rhythms, and influenced by context variables such as room temperature and humidity. If subject and context variables such as these have been taken into account, then some electrodermal phenomena can be construed as anxiety related; these include pronounced skin-conductance responses to fear-related signals, non-habituating or slowly habituating responses to fear-related signals, and relatively frequent spontaneous electrodermal fluctuations.

Respiration

Measures of respiratory function appear not infrequently in psychophysiological studies of anxiety. Usually, respiratory measures are obtained because they have implications for interpreting simultaneous measures of other variables (e.g., heart rate)

(Grossman, 1983). The technology exists to monitor separately respiratory-response components such as respiratory rate, tidal volume, and thoracic and diaphragmatic movement (Papillo, Pijacki, & Tursky, 1984). Usually, however, only respiration rate and depth are measured; stretchable devices are placed around the thoracic and abdominal regions, and stretches are quantified with a strain gauge, an air-pressure transducer, or an impedance pneumograph. Sometimes a thermistor is attached near the nasal passages so as to record respiration by monitoring temperature differences between inhaled and exhaled air. Respiration can also be monitored manually; reactivity can be circumvented by holding the patient's wrist and telling him or her that heart beats are being counted.

There are several reports of positive correlations between respiration rate and subjective anxiety (e.g., Mathews & Gelder, 1969; Lande, 1981). However, recent interest in respiration has been driven by the idea that respiratory disturbances participate in panic disorder.

An Organizing Framework

Notwithstanding the availability of information about anxiety and psychophysiology, a general recommendation about clinical use of physiological measurement is difficult to articulate. On the one hand, psychophysiological data of reasonable quality are not easy to acquire; interpretation of psychophysiological data is oftentimes problematic; the data themselves might not be "reliable"; and clinical work with anxious patients usually can proceed without information about physiological responding. On the other hand, data acquisition is not insurmountably difficult; some data acquired from individual patients are not difficult to interpret; and anxiety is importantly, if not fundamentally, a matter of physiological activation. Clinicians who work within the orthodox behavior therapy tradition use physiological measurement routinely in choosing from among treatment options.

Clinicians who choose to employ psychophysiological assessment should be guided by a few basic concepts related to somatic response patterning among anxious individuals. Early on, the psychophysiological study of anxiety was governed by activation theory (e.g., Lindsley, 1951), according to which various states of emotional arousal are accompanied by global and unidirectional changes in physiological activation. Soon, however, Lacey (1950) and others reported the phenomenon of directional fractionation (e.g., increasing electrodermal activity in parallel with decreasing heart rate). The phenomenon of directional fractionation could not be accommodated by activation theory; it prompted the development of alternative concepts for organizing the events of emotion and physiology. The concept of individual response stereotypy summarizes the idea that different people respond anxiously in different ways; each person has a characteristic anxiety response pattern that is temporally stable, trans-situationally recognizable, and has a dominant response mode such as cardiac reactivity, electrodermal reactivity, and so on. The concept of stimulus-response specificity summarizes the idea that people respond somewhat differently to different cue stimuli. Taken together, these concepts argue in favor of using multiple anxiety-cue (and comparison) stimuli, and multichannel psychophysiological assessment in order to understand an individual's anxious physiology. Meaningful psychophysiological assessment probably should include both heart-rate and electrodermal recording and, sometimes, respiration rate as well as various special-purpose measures (see Papillo, Murphy, & Gorman, 1988).

ASSESSMENT USING
DSM-IV CATEGORIES

In this section, an attempt is made to describe the major features of behaviorally oriented clinical assessment that are applicable to the *DSM-IV* categories of anxiety disorders. As noted earlier, this organization recognizes that the details of assessment differ somewhat according to the anxiety disorder being evaluated. Behavior therapists object legitimately to the neo-Kraepelinian idea that mental disorders exist inside of persons and control their behavior. Behavior therapists object legitimately also to the related idea that the purpose of assessment is only to arrive at a "correct" diagnosis. At the same time, recent advances in understanding anxiety-related phenomena have rendered the anxiety-disorder sections of the *DSM* superior to virtually all others. Furthermore, the organization of clinical practice in many contexts is necessarily oriented to *DSM* terminology. Therefore, *DSM-IV* (American Psychiatric Association, 1994) categories are used here. The narrative is *not* about comprehensive clinical assessment of patients who present with the various *DSM* disorders. Rather, it is about assessment of anxiety as an aspect of the various disorders. The purpose of assessment in the context of behavior therapy remains that of describing the anxiety-related behaviors of persons and how they interface with events in the environments where persons behave.

As was noted earlier, the ADIS-IV (Brown, DiNardo, & Barlow, 1994) serves nicely as a format for arriving at one or more preliminary *DSM-IV* diagnoses within the anxiety-disorder domain. In this section and those that follow, the assumption is made that an interview structured by the ADIS-IV has been done.

Panic and Agoraphobia

Panic attacks are unexpected episodes of extreme cognitive and physiological anxiety that reach their apex in around 10 minutes then gradually subside. Biological (Carr & Sheehan, 1984), cognitive (Beck, 1988; Clark, 1988), and biopsychosocial (Barlow, 1988) etiologic theories are available that link anxious physiology with anxious cognition. As noted earlier the contemporary viewpoint is that bodily sensations cue catastrophic thinking that feeds into further bodily sensations, further catastrophic thinking, and so on (Clark, 1986). The biopsychosocial perspective adds that the vicious physiological-cognitive cycle occurs among persons who are predisposed to it by chronic autonomic lability, by ingrained modes of thinking, and the like (see Barlow, 1988).

Agoraphobia is actual avoidance of activities and settings where panic attacks are believed to be likely. (Agoraphobia does not usually involve fear of particular settings; rather, it involves fear of panicking in those settings.) The relations between panic and avoidance are often quite complex. Therefore, panic and agoraphobia typically are assessed at the same times. Different clinicians organize the activities of assessing panic/agoraphobia in

different ways, but an orthodox practice is beginning to emerge.

Data about panic attacks can be acquired by self-monitoring. Typically, provision is made for recording frequency and duration of each episode along with the specific symptoms and contexts (see Craske & Waikar, 1994). Self-monitoring record forms, such as those used in the SUNY Albany Center for Stress and Anxiety Disorders, prompt the patient to record whether he or she was alone during the attack or with a spouse, friend, or stranger; to record whether the attack occurred in a stressful situation; and to record whether the attack was or was not expected. Lists of various bodily sensations and various themes of catastrophic thinking also are provided; the patient is prompted to rate each listed bodily event and cognitive theme numerically on a scale of severity. Because compliance with self-monitoring instructions sometimes is a problem, experienced therapists prompt patients to perform self-monitoring activities as an integral aspect of treatment and to provide their self-monitoring records for regular review.

An interesting application of self-monitoring in panic-disorder assessment was reported by Taylor, Fried, and Kenardy (1990). Twenty patients with panic-disorder were provided with a hand-held computer to use in record storage. On each hour from 7:00 A.M. through 11:00 P.M., and during each panic attack, the computer prompted subjects to answer a series of questions. The first question was: "Are you having a panic attack?" The next four questions called for visual analogue ratings about how anxious they felt, their sense of control, their sense of threat or danger, and the likelihood of panic during the upcoming hour. These ratings were followed by 13 yes/no questions about specific anxiety symptoms and by multiple-choice questions about who they were with and where they were. On average, the 20 patients tolerated the procedure well and completed 88% of the prompted ratings.

Data about panic attacks can be acquired also by procedures that deliberately produce panic in the clinic or laboratory. Sodium lactate, caffeine, and yohimbine are among the substances used to produce panic phenomena (Shear & Fyer, 1988). Carbon dioxide has received the most attention recently. In a carbon-dioxide challenge test, the patient usually inhales 5% carbon dioxide for 15 to 20 minutes by means of a canopy over the head, a specialized mouthpiece, or a pressurized mask fitted over the mouth and nose (for a review, see Sanderson & Wetzler, 1990). Group data have shown repeatedly that panic patients report more anxiety and more panic phenomena during carbon-dioxide breathing than do normal comparison subjects. However, there is sufficient variability across reports to raise questions about the diagnostic utility of the carbon-dioxide challenge method; induced panic has ranged from 19% to 90% among panic patients and from 0% to 55% among normal comparison subjects (Sanderson & Wetzler, 1990). Furthermore, there is reason to believe that carbon-dioxide–provoked panic is related to the psychological context of challenge testing as well as to the bodily correlates of carbon dioxide inhalation (see Barlow, 1988). Therefore, there is little support for utilizing carbon-dioxide challenge as a routine procedure for diagnosing panic disorder.

By contrast with biological challenge testing, ambulatory monitoring of heart rate (e.g., Taylor, Telch, & Haavick, 1983) is well suited for panic assessment because it solves the problem of ecological validity that inheres in laboratory assessment procedures and it can be continued throughout the course of treatment and beyond. In their application of hand-held computers to the tasks of self-monitoring Taylor, Fried, and Kenardy (1990) also had 12 of the 20 panic-disorder patients wear a cardiac monitor. The device recorded heart rate continuously and supplied 10-second records of actual ECG data when the software "recognized" atypical signals. There is little doubt that ambulatory bioelectric recording devices will become increasingly prominent in efforts to behaviorally assess panic and other anxiety phenomena. Clinicians should be mindful, however, that some panic attacks occur without identifiable heart-rate signatures and that some apparent heart-rate signatures occur without reports of panic (see Taylor, Sheikh, et al., 1986).

Data about agoraphobic avoidance can be acquired with naturalistic behavioral avoidance tests. Individualized behavioral tests should assess behavior in a representative subset of the actual situations that pose adaptive hazards. The tests can be structured hierarchically in terms of difficulty and

can be scored as task refused, task attempted but failed, and task completed. Situational ratings of fear can be prompted also during the attempted behavioral performances. Self-report data about agoraphobic avoidance can be acquired with the Mobility Inventory (Chambless, Caputo, Jasin, Gracely, & Williams, 1985) and via self-monitoring. The Mobility Inventory produces data about 26 common agoraphobic situations both when alone and when accompanied. Self-monitoring can be structured with behavioral checklists and diaries.

Treatment for agoraphobia often entails self-directed exposure trials of considerable difficulty. Self-efficacy vis-à-vis the various exposure tasks is sometimes measured so as to afford prediction about the strength and persistence of self-exposure efforts. Williams (1990) has provided a standardized format called the Self-Efficacy Scales for Agoraphobia on which patients rate their perceived efficacy vis-à-vis several locomotor performances: walk away from home, bus, movie theater, supermarket, or busy city street. Efficacy scores when alone and when accompanied are obtained. Versions of these scales are beginning to appear in comparative behavior-therapy outcome research because standardized measurement is important (e.g., Hoffart, 1995).

The habitual tendency of a person to display catastrophic thinking in the presence of particular bodily sensations has come to be known as *anxiety sensitivity* (Reiss & McNally, 1985). Anxiety sensitivity, sometimes called *fear of fear*, is measured with the Reiss-Epstein-Gursky Anxiety Sensitivity Index, or ASI (Reiss, Peterson, Gursky, & McNally, 1986), a 16-item self-report questionnaire about fearful preoccupation with 16 potentially adverse consequences of anxiety. Each item is rated on a 0- to 4-point scale; anxiety sensitivity is the total score.

The ASI has received considerable psychometric attention and has performed very well, to date. Data have shown, for example, that ASI scores have adequate test-retest stability, account for unique variance in anxiety ratings, discriminate between normal and anxiety-disordered respondents, and that can be used so as to discriminate between panic-disordered and other anxious respondents

(Taylor, 1995). In general, the ASI is a valid instrument, and anxiety sensitivity is coming to be recognized as a valuable, unitary construct for explicating how thinking participates in panic. Information about the bodily sensations that are most frightening in the individual case, and about cognitive accompaniments to them, can be obtained by using the Body Sensations Questionnaire (Chambless, Caputo, Bright, & Gallagher, 1984).

Social Phobia

Social phobia is characterized by fear and avoidance of scrutinized performance that is prompted by concern over negative evaluation by others. There are indications that social phobics are unusually responsive to physiological changes, such as tachycardia and sweating that accompany scrutiny. Social phobia was not recognized as a distinct psychological problem until the 1960s (Marks, 1969; Taylor, 1966). With publication of *DSM-III* (American Psychiatric Association, 1980), the diagnosis of social phobia was established, but the disorder was described as relatively benign. Research since has shown significant and sometimes pervasive adaptive impairment stemming from fearful avoidance of social situations (Cappe & Alden, 1986; Liebowitz, Gorman, Fyer, & Klein, 1985).

Self-report inventories are used frequently to assess social phobia. Two such inventories were developed not long after social phobia became an identified problem. The Social Avoidance and Distress Scale (Watson & Friend, 1969) is a 28-item true/false scale that assesses anxiety and avoidance vis-à-vis a number of interpersonal-performance contexts. The Fear of Negative Evaluation Scale (Watson & Friend, 1969) is a 30-item Likert scale about fear of negative evaluation by others. Several self-report inventories that deal with social phobia are of more recent vintage. The widely used Fear Questionnaire (Marks & Mathews, 1979) has a subscale for social phobia as well as scales for agoraphobia and blood-injury fears. The Social Phobia and Anxiety Inventory (Turner, Beidel, Dancu, & Stanley, 1989) prompts ratings about subjective, behavioral, and physiological responses in settings related to both social phobia (32 items) and agoraphobia (13 items). The Social Interaction Anxiety

Scale and the Social Phobia Scale are 20-item questionnaires developed by Mattick and Clarke (1989) to assess anxiety in social interactions and anxiety while under scrutiny, respectively. The Social Interaction Self-Statement Test (Glass, Merluzzi, Biever, & Larsen, 1982) seeks to standardize the measurement of adaptive and maladaptive thought content among social phobics as they encounter difficult interactions. It has 15 items about adaptive themes and 15 about maladaptive themes; each is rated on a 5-point scale that reflects the frequency of the theme during social encounters.

The contents of thinking during interpersonal performances have been assessed also with protocol analysis methods (Glass & Furlong, 1990). For example, Turner, Beidel, and Larkin (1986) used protocol analysis to show that social phobics, by contrast with comparison subjects, report fewer positive cognitions and more negative cognitions during interpersonal performances. Thought listing (e.g., Arnkoff & Glass, 1989) is used most frequently. Patients or subjects are instructed to write down their anxiety-related thoughts during specific time periods (e.g., for 20 minutes before giving a speech). Thought-listing efforts produce reliable scores across judges, but there are mixed results for various measures related to construct validity (see Donohue, Van Hasselt, & Hersen, 1994).

Interpersonal Performance Tests and role-plays are used frequently in assessing anxiety in social contexts. The Social Situations Interaction Test (Mersch, Emmelkamp, Bogels, & Van Der Sleen, 1989), for example, is a standardized procedure in which the patient role-plays four vignettes with a male confederate and four with a female confederate. In each case, a narrator describes the situation, then the confederate delivers a prompt to begin. Ratings of the patient's behavior are made by the patients themselves, by the confederates, and by independent raters. Even though the Social Situations Interaction Test is a measure of social skill, not socially cued anxiety, it has been used reliably in clinical assessment of treatment effects among social phobics (Mersch et al., 1989). The Behavioral Situations Test (Barrios, 1988b) is a standardized role-play approach to assessment of social anxiety that was discussed earlier.

Standardized performances and role-plays such as those just discussed are used typically in clinical research, but individualized and less elaborate methods are used typically for clinical assessment. Ideally, the individualized vignettes are realistic and drawn from the patient's actual experience (Bellack, 1983) Basically, the patient is instructed to perform and/or role-play in situations or vignettes that approximate those that pose adjustive hazards; therapists or assistants acquire data from behavioral observation, from ambulatory physiological monitoring equipment, and from retrospective patient reports (see Heimberg, Hope, Dodge, & Becker, 1990; Hope & Heimberg, 1993).

Self-monitoring also has been adapted to the problem of assessing social phobia. Typically, the patient is instructed to record targeted behaviors that occur during social encounters that are clinically relevant. As noted earlier, Mattick and Peters (1988) used a Naturalistic Behavioral Avoidance Test to assess social phobia. During the test, patients self-monitored the number of exposures to problem events, the duration of each exposure, and the level of anxiety produced by each exposure.

Heart rate is the most commonly used physiological measure in assessing social phobia. Before the diagnosis of social phobia was popular, heart rate was used to assess separate target domains such as fear of public speaking (Paul, 1966), heterosocial shyness (Borkovec et al., 1974), and test anxiety (Marchetti, McGlynn, & Patterson, 1977). More recently, heart rates have been recorded among diagnosed social phobics, typically in association with an Interpersonal Performance Test format of some kind (for a brief review, see Donohue, Van Hasselt, & Hersen, 1994).

Specific Phobia

A specific phobia is a peripherally cued anxiety response that is not related to panic or to social phobia. *DSM-IV* organizes specific phobias into categories according to the nature of the fear signal: animal or insect (e.g., cats, spiders), natural phenomena or setting (e.g., storms, water), blood/injury/injection, and human-made event or setting (e.g., tunnels, airplanes). For the most part, there are sound reasons for the *DSM* subcategorization.

There are widespread phobias of sufficient severity to merit *DSM* diagnosis but they usually go untreated; phobic persons develop skillful strategies for avoiding phobia-cue stimuli, thus weakening their motivation for treatment.

Specific phobias have garnered a major share of research and scholarly attention among behavior therapists in spite of the fact that they are not frequently treated. Because of frequent research attention, narratives about assessing phobic subjects are readily available in mainstream behavior-therapy journals. In general, specific phobias lend themselves readily to analysis in S-R terms. On the stimulus side of the S-R equation, assessment is concerned with identifying the specific stimuli for anxiety and describing their anxiety-controlling aspects, dimensions, or themes. On the response side of the S-R equation, assessment is concerned with detailing the subjective, behavioral, and physiological events that manifest anxiety.

Self-report measures are used to assess specific phobias because of their low cost and convenience. Omnibus fear questionnaires such as the Fear Survey Schedules (e.g., Geer, 1965; Wolpe & Lang, 1964) prompt respondents to provide Likert-type fear-intensity ratings about commonly feared objects and events. Responses to omnibus surveys pinpoint areas for further assessment and suggest organizing themes among fear clusters. For example, high-fear ratings on items related to giving a speech and meeting someone for the first time point to social phobia as an organizing dimension.

Many specific phobias were of sufficient interest early on to prompt the development of questionnaires for assessing them (see Borkovec, Werts, & Bernstein, 1977). Ordinarily, such questionnaires are used for research because, by and large, they are insufficiently idiographic for clinical purposes. However, many specific-fear questionnaires have demonstrable reliability and discriminant validity and can be used to provide a comparative picture of a patient's self-reported functioning. In addition, the factor structures of multi-item questionnaires about single phobias sometimes provide information about the anxiety-controlling dimensions of fear stimuli. For example, Johnson, Mayberry, and McGlynn (1990) developed a 60-item, Likert-type questionnaire about fear of various activities involved in seeking and receiving dental care. Exploratory factor analysis pointed to fear of pain (algophobia), anticipatory fear, social phobia, and control-related fears as underlying response dimensions. Self-monitoring can be adapted to assessing specific phobias. Marks (1978) provides standardized formats and instructions for self-assessment of anxiety.

Contrived Behavioral Avoidance Tests have been used frequently to assess specific phobias. Notwithstanding the validity problems noted earlier, such behavioral tests are preferred to self-reports because they are less subject to voluntary distortion. Contrived tests are also easy to arrange because many fear stimuli are portable. Traditionally, measures such as Fear Thermometer ratings have been added into behavioral avoidance testing, sometimes at each step of the behavioral gradient, sometimes at the beginning and end of progress. More recently, ambulatory devices for physiological monitoring have been included in contrived behavioral testing. Naturalistic Behavioral Avoidance Tests are being used with increasing frequency. They are preferred over contrived tests, when feasible, because they afford opportunities for measuring physiologic, cognitive, and motoric fear behaviors vis-à-vis subsets of the actual situations that are adaptively problematic in the individual case.

Orthodox behavior therapists evaluate physiological responding before and after instructions to imagine phobia cues (e.g., Wolpe, 1990). Usually heart rate and/or skin-conductance reactivity are recorded. First, the patient is given some training in progressive muscle relaxation. Instructions to visualize phobia-relevant scenes are then provided and followed by pause periods for psychophysiological recording during imaging. Sometimes instructions to visualize control scenes are used. Ideally, the control scenes correspond closely to the phobia-relevant scenes in terms of complexity and visualized activity. McGlynn and Vopat (1994), for example, reported an imaginal assessment of a patient suffering from severe fear of dental treatment. After brief relaxation training, she was instructed to visualize various activities involved in seeking and receiving dental care. At other times, she was instructed to visualize going to a hair salon where the operator's

behaviors corresponded closely to those of the dentist in the other scenes. Instructions to imagine dental scenes, by contrast with instructions to imagine very similar hair-salon scenes, were followed by increased heart rate and skin conductance. Thus, imaginal behavior was identified as a potentially important component of her phobia.

Obsessive-Compulsive Disorder

Obsessive-Compulsive Disorder (OCD) is typified by repetitive contents of thinking that produce anxiety by signifying danger, and by repeated attempts to reduce or control the anxiety by restoring safety (Foa & Tillmans, 1980). Episodes of repetitive thinking are experienced as uncontrollable and distressing, are aggressive and/or sexual in content, and are recognized as irrational. Attempts to deal with obsessional thinking and its associated distress are voluntary, purposeful behaviors, including private/cognitive behaviors, that are preceded by a sense of urgency and are recognized as irrational and as potentially embarrassing. Among OCD patients, 90% show this pattern (Foa & Tillmans, 1980).

As with specific phobias, analysis of OCD phenomena lends itself readily to the S-R metaphor. Assessment is concerned with identifying the cue stimuli for obsessive behavior and with pinpointing the details of that behavior (see Steketee, 1993; Turner & Beidel, 1988). Stimuli for OC behavior can be peripheral as well as central. For example, a cleansing ritual can be cued by discovering a chipped piece of glassware as well as by obsessional thinking about one's spouse ingesting broken glass. Compulsive responses can be central as well as peripheral. For example, the distress occasioned by obsessional thinking about one's spouse ingesting broken glass can be defended against by deliberately attempting to think of something else as well as by inspecting all the glassware in the house.

Individualized target ratings have been useful in clinics worldwide to assess OCD phenomena and monitor the effects of treatment. Ideally, the response dimensions of anxiety, avoidance, and rituals are assessed separately, and are assessed vis-à-vis each of the various cues for OC behavior identified in the individual case. Riggs and Foa (1993), for example, describe an approach in which an 8-point Likert-type rating is assigned to each of three subdomains within anxiety, avoidance, and ritual behavior. Though useful clinically, various individualized rating formats suffer from inadequate psychometric underpinnings.

Some standardized target-rating scales are used by therapists, patients, and independent raters to quantify the severity of OCD symptoms on the basis of interview data. The Yale-Brown Obsessive-Compulsive Scale (Goodman, Price, et al., 1989a, 1989b) is one standardized format. There are 5 items about obsessional thinking and 5 items about compulsive behavior. Each item is rated on a 0- to 4-point scale of severity. Rating dimensions include the time occupied by the obsession or compulsion, the degree of interference with functioning, the level of distress, specific attempts to resist symptoms, and the level of control over the symptoms. Reliability and some validity data were provided in the original reports. The Compulsive Activity Checklist (Marks, Hallam, Connelly, & Philpott, 1977) contains 37 items devoted to assessing the degree of interference with functioning. It is sometimes recommended as a supplement to the Yale-Brown Obsessive-Compulsive Scale.

Questionnaires that are used to assess OCD are similar to the rater checklists just described. A self-report version of the Compulsive Activity Checklist was reported by Freund, Steketee, and Foa (see Riggs & Foa, 1993). It contains 38 items and has been found reliable, valid, and sensitive to change from treatment (Freund, 1986). The Maudsley Obsessional Compulsive Inventory (Hodgson & Rachman, 1977) is a 30-item true/false questionnaire. It yields a total score and subscale scores for checking, washing, slowness, and doubting. There are adequate normative and reliability data, and data that show sensitivity to treatment improvement (e.g., Sternberger & Burns, 1990a, 1990b). It is most useful in quantifying OCD phenomena among patients whose disorder fits the expected patterns. The Padua Inventory (Sanavio, 1988) is a 60-item instrument that assesses control of thinking and of motor behavior, checking, and contamination. Psychometric work is beginning to appear (e.g., van Oppen, 1992).

Because of its factor content, the Padua Inventory might supplement instruments such as the Maudsley Obsessional Compulsive Inventory in self-report assessment of atypical OCD patients. The Leyton Obsessional Inventory (Cooper, 1970) began as a yes/no card-sort procedure in which 46 items evaluated obsessive symptoms such as checking, cleaning, and repetition, whereas 23 items assessed obsessive personality traits such as punctuality and hoarding. It yielded four scores reflecting the number of obsessional symptoms, the number of trait manifestations, the strength of attempts to resist the symptoms and traits, and the degree of interference created by them. Snowdon (1980) produced a questionnaire version of the scale that is gaining in popularity. Psychometric work (e.g., Stanley, Prather, et al., 1993) suggests that the Leyton inventory has adequate psychometric properties but room exists for further psychometric characterization.

Self-monitoring is a prominent feature of the OCD assessment literature. Attempts are made to acquire self-ratings of the frequencies and durations of episodes, of the cues for the episodes, and of the levels of associated anxiety (e.g., Steketee, 1993). Self-monitored data are supplied for each significant ritual separately using record forms. The patient is pretrained in self-monitoring activities such as timing a performance, writing down a terse description of the ritual-cue context, and so on (see Riggs & Foa, 1993). Reactivity is a unique problem in self-monitoring assessment of OCD because the activities of self-monitoring can replace those of the ritual. Some therapists (e.g., Barlow, 1988) recommend, therefore, that urges to perform rituals be monitored as well as rituals themselves.

Contrived Behavioral Avoidance Tests are used in some clinics to assess OCD even though the requisite psychometric information is not available. In principle, these tests do not differ from those used to assess phobias; that is, they can be used to quantify levels of approach and rated fear vis-à-vis contaminated objects, ability to suspend ritual behaviors after contamination, and so on.

There is evidence that obsessional thinking is accompanied by increases in heart rate and in spontaneous skin-conductance responses (Boulougouris, Rabavilas, & Stefanis, 1977). There is evidence also that contact with contaminated stimuli produces heart rate increases (Rachman & Hodgson, 1980). Nonetheless, psychophysiological assessment has not been an important feature of clinical work with OCD patients.

Generalized Anxiety Disorder

Generalized Anxiety Disorder (GAD) first appeared as a diagnostic category in *DSM-III* (American Psychiatric Association, 1980). Its characteristic features are chronic, worry (apprehensive expectation), and chronic anxiety. For worry behavior to qualify as a symptom of GAD, it must be experienced as difficult to control, it must occur for at least 6 months, and it must be unrelated to worries occasioned by other Axis I conditions. In turn, the anxiety behaviors in GAD tend to be those related to motor tension and to vigilance scanning (see Brown, O'Leary, & Barlow, 1993). Unlike other anxiety disorders, GAD often shows a lifelong developmental course without identifiable beginnings.

Worry and tension-related physiological symptoms are the targets of treatment and therefore of assessment. The Penn State Worry Questionnaire, or PSWQ (Meyer, Miller, Metzger, & Borkovec, 1990), is an increasingly popular instrument for quantifying worry behavior among GAD patients. The PSWQ has only 16 items, but it is psychometrically sound; internal consistency, temporal stability, and adequate convergent and discriminant validity were shown in the original report about the scale. Discriminant validity for GAD versus other anxiety-disorder groups was shown independently in a fairly large-scale study by Brown, Antony, and Barlow (1992), who also provided normative data from clinic patients in various anxiety-disorder categories.

The report of Brown, Antony, and Barlow (1992) also highlighted the DASS (Lovibond & Lovibond, 1992) as a potentially worthwhile approach for assessing GAD. The DASS is a 42-item measure that, among other things, yields a subscale score for anxious tension during the preceding week. Brown, Antony, and Barlow (1992) reported that scores on the DASS tension subscale discriminated GAD patients from others and were correlated with scores from the PSWQ. The latter finding ties together the two main dimensions of GAD: tension and worry. The Trait version of the State-Trait Anxiety Inventory (Spielberger, Gorsuch, et al., 1983) should be useful as a measure of GAD, given the "characterological" appearance of the disorder. Scores afford bases for comparing GAD patients before and after treatment with thousands of patients and subjects who have contributed data to the literature in which the State-Trait Anxiety Inventory was used.

An application of self-monitoring to assessment of GAD-related behavior is described by Brown, O'Leary, and Barlow (1993). Their record form provides for daily ratings of average anxiety, maximum anxiety, average depression, average pleasantness, and percent-of-day worried. Patients are trained to use the form and prompted to complete it each evening before retiring. A self-monitoring approach based on a daily diary is overviewed by Borkovec and Roemer (1994). In their protocol, records are made four times daily of average anxiety level during the preceding few hours, of acute anxiety episodes, and of the internal and external events associated with the episodes.

There is only infrequent mention of physiological assessment in connection with GAD. Given that chronic overarousal is a defining feature of the disorder, the deemphasis of psychophysiological assessment is interesting. Psychophysiology is a complex arena, and doubts have been expressed about the "reliability" and clinical relevance of psychophysiological data (e.g., Arena, Blanchard, Andrasik, Cotch, & Myers, 1983). These and other factors have worked against psychophysiology in clinical work with GAD patients and others. However, muscle tension is elevated in GAD patients, and GAD is associated with identifiable curtailments of normal heart rate and skin-conductance responsivity to challenge. Therefore, psychophysiological assessment of GAD should be revisited.

ASSESSMENT IN AN ILLUSTRATIVE CASE

Instructive case studies about fear of dental treatment are available (McGlynn & Vopat, 1994; Nietzel, Bernstein, & Russell, 1988). However, fearful avoidance of dental treatment is a significant cultural problem. In addition, dental fear presents a microcosm of the issues involved in assessing phobias because themes related to social phobia, claustrotophobia, and diminished fate control can be present, as well as fear of pain. Therefore, a case of dental fear is used here.

Case Study

The patient, Bob, was a 48-year-old Caucasian male with a high school education. He was self-referred for treatment to overcome his long-standing avoidance of dental-care settings. His initial history was unremarkable except for two epochs of adversity related to dental treatment. As a preteen, he had feared oral infiltrations so much that he had endured restorative dentistry "every Saturday for two years" without benefit of anesthesia. As a young adult, he had been forced to receive oral infiltrations and had endured dental-office treatment described as "harsh" at the hands of dentists in the U.S. Navy. He presented for treatment, saying that "just the thought of going to a dentist makes me break out in a sweat . . . makes me sick to my stomach . . . makes my heart stick in my throat." He was highly motivated to seek dental care due to deteriorating oral health and worry about the social impact of dentures.

There was no hint of frank psychopathology at any point during an unstructured first interview. Therefore, structured assessment was begun with the ADIS-R. Follow-up queries in connection with the ADIS-R interview indicated that thinking about or attempting dental-office visits always occasioned fear and avoidance. The interview data also pointed to a complete absence of panic-like phenomena other than those related to dental-office settings. Thus, the ADIS-R interview served to identify specific phobia for dental treatment as the main diagnosis. During the GAD section of the ADIS-R interview, Bob described himself as a worrier, and he indicated he had worried more days than not for the preceding six months. Further questioning suggested that much of his worry was occasioned by episodic pains in various teeth. Nonetheless, GAD was identified as a problem to be ruled out. No other anxiety-related problems were noted.

At the second visit, Bob responded to a Fear Survey Schedule (Geer, 1965) and to the Penn State Worry Questionnaire (Meyer et al., 1990). His fear-survey ratings did not identify additional fear-related problems. His raw score of 36 on the PSWQ was very near the mean of 34. 90 obtained by 32 nonanxious subjects described in Brown, Antony, and Barlow (1992). Because Bob's worry had initially seemed focused on his teeth and on related phobic and interpersonal concerns, the normal score on the PSWQ prompted dismissal of GAD as an issue. The remaining time was devoted to beginning to describe Bob's dental fear in detail.

Bob responded to two questionnaires about fear of dentistry and one questionnaire about his perceived somatic response to dental stimuli. The first, the Dental Fear Survey (Kleinknecht, Klepac, & Alexander (1973), is a 20-item Likert-type fear questionnaire about the major events in receiving dental treatment. It is useful for evaluating dental-fear complaints because it has a replicated factor structure (Kleinknecht, Thorndike, McGlynn, & Harkavy, 1984) and it has good psychometric properties and normative data (McGlynn, McNeil, Gallagher, & Vrana, 1987). Bob's fear ratings were highest on factor analytically derived subscales for fear of pain and physiological arousal, and were above the 90th percentile for both subscales.

The second questionnaire, a 60-item Likert-type scale about fear of dentistry (Johnson, Mayberry, & McGlynn,1990), was mentioned earlier. Some psychometric characterization of the questionnaire remains but, as already noted, the factor structure provides subscales for fear of pain, anticipatory fear, fear of negative evaluation (social phobia), and concern over giving up control. Bob's responses yielded very high raw scores on subscales related to fear of pain and anticipatory fear.

Taken together, Bob's answers on the two questionnaires implicated fear of pain, anticipatory fear, and physiological arousal as components of his fearful avoidance of dental treatment. Because Bob had remarked about his heart being in his throat, he was asked to respond to the Autonomic Nervous System Response Inventory (Waters, Cohen, Bernard, Buco, & Dreger, 1984) according to a protocol described by Waters, Bernard, and Buco (1989). Bob's ratings of his bodily reactions during one specifically remembered dental visit impli-cated both cardiac and electrodermal responses as features of his perceived anxiety pattern. After the self-reports were completed, Bob was handed the telephone number of a cooperating dentist and in-vited to call for an appointment. He reported inabil-ity to do so even though the first appointment would have entailed an oral examination only.

During the next visit, Bob's physiological responsivity during dental and control imagery was evaluated. First, Bob received brief relaxation instructions that were presented verbatim from the manual provided by Bernstein and Borkovec (1973). Next, he was instructed to visualize, for three-minute periods, a series of personally relevant dental scenarios constructed from his experiences with Navy dentists. These scenes were alternated with a series of personally detailed barbershop scenes in which the barber's behaviors corre-sponded to those of the navy dentist. A series of idyllic scenes (e.g., pastures, blue skies, a flowing stream) were interspersed as well. Bob's heart rate and skin conductance were recorded throughout the imagery periods. There was no observable physio-logical reactance during the dental scenes by con-trast with the others.

The absence of physiological responding fol-lowing dental-imagery instructions argued against using an orthodox behavior-therapy approach in which imagery was a prominent feature. Because orthodox behavior therapy was rejected, there was no attempt to assess the fine grain of stimulus con-trol of Bob's anxiety behaviors. Rather, the choice was made to use a graduated, in vivo exposure for-mat in overcoming his fear, and to adapt assess-ment to the exposure-technology orientation. A 30-item Naturalistic Behavioral Avoidance Test was constructed. It began with "Calling to make an appointment." It ended with "Sitting while the den-tist drills on my tooth." Among the intervening items were "Turn into the dentist's office, park, and get out," and "Walk up to the receptionist's window and say "I'm Bob _____.""

Multiple copies of a behavioral checklist that contained the 30 items on the avoidance test were made. They included Fear Thermometer ratings of each step when alone and when accompanied. A corresponding set of 30-item self-efficacy scales

based on the model of Williams (1990) also was made. A graduate student was assigned to accom-pany Bob during daily trials with the behavioral checklist, to structure the goals of each trial based on trial-specific self-efficacy ratings, and to keep separate records. From this point on, Bob's treat-ment entailed continued in-office relaxation train-ing and repeated behavioral trials—first when ac-companied, then when alone. Trial-to-trial progress through the 30 steps and/or reductions in Fear Ther-mometer ratings produced lavish praise and en-couragement. The last 11 items on the behavioral checklist took place in the dental-practice setting. The dentist and dental-office staff cooperated with this part of the plan. The dentist also prescribed a diazepam premedication that Bob did not use.

SUMMARY

Psychological assessment involves presenting stimuli and recording subsequent responses. In behavioral assessment of anxiety, the stimuli used are subsets and/or analogues of anxiety-cue stimuli encountered in adaptively significant natural set-tings. The responses recorded during behavioral assessment are subsets and/or analogues of subjec-tive and/or physiological and/or motoric behavior. Increasingly, the methods of traditional (personal-ity) assessment are being used by clinical behavior therapists.

There are five systematically different ap-proaches to the behavioral treatment of anxious pa-tients. Use of the concept of anxiety itself is con-tinuing to evolve. The perspective of cognitive psychology is increasingly influential in conceptu-alizing anxiety and its treatment. Assessment activ-ities can be classified as entailing self-report, be-havioral, or psychophysiological methods.

Self-report methods include structured inter-views, questionnaires, protocol analyses, situa-tional ratings, and self-monitoring. A structured interview known as the ADIS-IV (Brown, DiNardo, & Barlow, 1994) is styled as a foundation for anxiety assessment; other self-report methods are used for many specific purposes. Question-naires and situational ratings are traditional in anx-iety assessment. Recent interest in protocol-analysis methods is emblematic of an increasingly cognitive perspective. Increased use of self-monitoring mirrors change in the way anxiety (panic) is conceptualized, as well as interest in self-managed approaches to intervention.

Assessment of anxiety-related behavior is undertaken with Contrived Behavioral Avoidance Tests, with Naturalistic Behavioral Avoidance Tests, and with Interpersonal Performance Tests, including role-plays. Naturalistic tests call on patients to attempt problematic locomotor performances in adaptively germane settings. Naturalistic tests are increasingly popular because they solve the problem of external validity and address the problem of content validity in measurement. However, insofar as control over behavior is construed as "situation specific," content validity will always be of concern. Contrived behavioral tests are convenient and popular but they suffer from serious validity shortcomings. Contrived tests should be used when naturalistic assessment is not feasible. When interpersonal performances and role-plays are used in anxiety assessment, the focus typically is on social phobia. Interpersonal performances and role-plays afford venues for obtaining self-report and psychophysiological data as well as information about anxiety-related performance deficits.

Psychophysiology has been more useful to researchers than to clinicians, but orthodox behavior therapists evaluate patients' anxiety-related cardiac and electrodermal responses when evaluation is feasible. Respiration and special-purpose measures are obtained not infrequently. Recent interest in the various phenomena of panic, combined with increased availability of ambulatory bio-electric signal recorders, might usher in an era of clinical psychophysiology. Psychophysiological assessment should take into account individually unique and stimulus-specific somatic response patterning.

The major activities of assessing anxiety across several diagnostic categories were reviewed. Also, assessment of a patient who presented with dental fear of many years' duration was described.

REFERENCES

Acierno, R., Hersen, M., & Ammerman, R. T. (1994). Overview of the issues in prescriptive treatments. In M. Hersen & R. T. Ammerman (Eds.), *Handbook of prescriptive treatments for adults* (pp. 3–27). New York: Plenum.

Acierno, R., Hersen, M., Van Hasselt, V. B., & Ammerman, R. T. (1994). Remedying the Achilles heel of behavior research and therapy: Prescriptive matching of intervention and psychopathology. *Journal of Behavior Therapy and Experimental Psychiatry, 25,* 179–188.

Agras, S., Leitenberg, H., & Barlow, D. H. (1968). Social reinforcement in the modification of agoraphobia. *Archives of General Psychiatry, 19,* 423–427.

American Psychiatric Association. (1980). *Diagnostic and statistical manual of mental disorders* (3rd ed.). Washington, DC: Author.

American Psychiatric Association. (1987). *Diagnostic and Statistical Manual of Mental Disorders* (3rd ed. rev.). Washington, DC: Author.

American Psychiatric Association. (1994). *Diagnostic and Statistical Manual of Mental Disorders* (4th ed.). Washington, DC: Author.

Arena, J. G., Blanchard, E. B., Andrasik, F., Cotch, B. A., & Myers, P. E. (1983). Reliability of psychophysiological assessment. *Behaviour Research and Therapy, 21,* 447–460.

Arnkoff, D. B. (1980). Psychotherapy from the perspective of cognitive theory. In M. Mahoney (Ed.), *Psychotherapy process: Current issues and future directions* (pp. 339–361). New York: Plenum.

Arnkoff, D. B., & Glass, C. R. (1989). Cognitive assessment in social anxiety and social phobia. *Clinical Psychology Review, 9,* 61–74.

Bandura, A. (1969). *Principles of behavior modification.* New York: Holt, Rinehart & Winston.

Bandura, A. (1977). Self-efficacy: Toward a unifying theory of behavioral change. *Psychological Review, 84,* 191–215.

Bandura, A. (1986). *Social foundations of thought and action: A social-cognitive perspective.* Englewood Cliffs, NJ: Prentice-Hall.

Bandura, A., Adams, N., Hardy, A., & Howells, G. (1986). Tests of the generality of self-efficacy theory. *Cognitive Therapy and Research, 4,* 39–66.

Barlow, D. H. (1987). The classification of anxiety disorders. In G. L. Tischler (Ed.), *Diagnosis and classification in psychiatry: A critical appraisal of DSM-III* (pp. 223–242). Cambridge: Cambridge University Press.

Barlow, D. H. (1988). *Anxiety and its disorders: The nature and treatment of anxiety and panic.* New York: Guilford.

Barrios, B. A. (1983). The role of cognitive mediators in heterosocial anxiety: A test of self-efficacy theory. *Cognitive Therapy and Research, 7*, 543–554.

Barrios, B. A. (1988a). On the changing nature of behavioral assessment. In A. S. Bellack & M. Hersen (Eds.), *Behavioral assessment: A practical handbook* (3rd ed.) (pp. 3–41). New York: Pergamon.

Barrios, B. A. (1988b). Behavioral Situations Test. In M. Hersen & A. S. Bellack (Eds.), *Dictionary of behavioral assessment techniques* (pp. 69–72). New York: Pergamon.

Basoglu, M., Marks, I. M., & Sengun, S. (1992). A prospective study of panic and anxiety in agoraphobia with panic disorder. *British Journal of Psychiatry, 160*, 57–64.

Beck, A. T. (1970). Cognitive therapy: Nature and relation to behavior therapy. *Behavior Therapy, 1*, 184–200.

Beck, A. T. (1988). Cognitive approaches to panic disorder: Theory and therapy. In S. Rachman & J. D. Maser (Eds.), *Panic: Psychological perspectives* (pp. 91–109). New York: Basic Books.

Beck, A. T., & Emery, G. (1985). *Anxiety disorders and phobias: A cognitive perspective*. New York: Basic Books.

Beidel, D. C., Neal, A. M., & Lederer, A. S. (1991). The feasibility and validity of a daily diary for the assessment of anxiety in children. *Behavior Therapy, 22*, 505–517.

Bellack, A. S. (1983). Recurrent problems in the behavioral assessment of social skill. *Behavioral Assessment, 1*, 157–166.

Bellack, A. S., & Hersen, M. (1977). Self-report inventories in behavioral assessment. In J. D. Cone & R. P. Hawkins (Eds.), *Behavioral assessment: New directions in clinical psychology* (pp. 52–76). New York: Brunner/Mazel.

Bernstein, D. A. (1973). Situational factors in behavioral fear assessment: A progress report. *Behavior Therapy, 4*, 41–48.

Bernstein, D. A., & Borkovec, T. D. (1973). *Progressive relaxation training*. Champaign, IL: Research Press.

Bernstein, D. A., & Nietzel, M. T. (1973). Procedural variation in behavioral avoidance tests. *Journal of Consulting and Clinical Psychology, 41*, 165–174.

Borkovec, T. D., & Roemer, L. (1994). Generalized anxiety disorder. In M. Hersen & R. T. Ammerman (Eds.), *Handbook of prescriptive treatments for adults* (pp. 261–281). New York: Plenum.

Borkovec, T. D., Stone, N. M., O'Brien, G. T., & Kaloupek, D. G. (1974). Evaluation of a clinically relevant target behavior for analogue outcome research. *Behavior Therapy, 5*, 505–514.

Borkovec, T. D., Werts, T. C., & Bernstein, D. A. (1977). Assessment of anxiety. In A. R. Ciminero, K. S. Calhoun, & H. E. Adams (Eds.), *Handbook of behavioral assessment* (pp. 367–428). New York: Wiley.

Boulougouris, J. C., Rabavalis, A. D., & Stefanis, C. (1977). Psycho-physiological responses in obsessive-compulsive patients. *Behaviour Research and Therapy, 15*, 221–230.

Bradley, M. M., & Lang, P. J. (1994). Measuring emotion: The self-assessment manikin and the semantic differential. *Journal of Behavior Therapy and Experimental Psychiatry, 25*, 49–59.

Brown, T. A., Antony, M. M., & Barlow, D. H. (1992). Psychometric properties of the Penn State Worry Questionnaire in a clinical anxiety disorders sample. *Behaviour Research and Therapy, 30*, 33–37.

Brown, T. A., DiNardo, P. A., & Barlow, D. H. (1994). *Anxiety disorders interview schedule for DSM-IV (ADIS-IV)*. Albany, NY: Graywind Publications.

Brown, T. A., O'Leary, T. A., & Barlow, D. H. (1993). Generalized anxiety disorder. In D. H. Barlow (Ed.), *Clinical handbook of psychological disorders* (2nd ed.) (pp. 137–188). New York: Guilford.

Burgio, K. L., Glass, C. R., & Merluzzi, T. V. (1981). The effects of social anxiety and videotape performance feedback on cognitions and self-evaluations. *Behavioral Counseling Quarterly, 1*, 288–301.

Cacioppo, J. T., Glass, C. R., & Merluzzi, T. V. (1979). Self-statements and self-evaluation: A cognitive response analysis of heterosocial anxiety. *Cognitive Therapy and Research, 3*, 249–262.

Cacioppo, J. T., & Petty, R. E. (1981). Social psychological procedures for cognitive response assessment: The thought-listing technique. In T. V. Merluzzi, C. R. Glass, & M. Genest (Eds.), *Cognitive assessment* (pp. 309–342). New York: Guilford.

Cappe, R. F., & Alden, L. E. (1986). A comparison of treatment strategies for clients functionally impaired by extreme shyness and social avoidance. *Journal of Consulting and Clinical Psychology, 54*, 796–801.

Carr, D., & Sheehan. D. (1984). Panic anxiety: A new biological model. *Journal of Clinical Psychiatry, 45*, 323–330.

Chambless, D. L., Caputo, G., Bright, P., & Gallagher, R. (1984). Assessment of fear in agoraphobics: The Body Sensations Questionnaire and the Agoraphobic Cognitions Questionnaire. *Journal of Consulting and Clinical Psychology, 52*, 1090–1097.

Chambless, D. L., Caputo, G., Jasin, S. E., Gracely, E. J., & Williams, C. (1985). The Mobility Inventory for Agoraphobia. *Behaviour Research and Therapy, 23*, 1090–1097.

Chiauzzi, F., & Heimberg, R. G. (1983). The effects of subjects' level of assertiveness, sex, and legitimacy of request on assertion-relevant cognitions: An analysis by post-performance videotape reconstruction. *Cognitive Therapy and Research, 7*, 555–564.

Clark, D. M. (1986). A cognitive approach to panic. *Behaviour Research and Therapy, 24*, 461–470.

Clark, D. M. (1988). A cognitive model of panic attacks. In S. Rachman & J. D. Maser (Eds.), *Panic: Psychological perspectives* (pp. 71–89). Hillsdale, NJ: Erlbaum.

Collins, F. L., & Thompson, K. J. (1993). The integration of empirically derived personality assessment data into a behavioral conceptualization and treatment plan: Rationale, guidelines, and caveats. *Behavior Modification, 17*, 58–71.

Cone, J. D. (1987). Behavioral assessment: Some things old, some things new, some things borrowed? *Behavioral Assessment, 9*, 1–4.

Cook, E. W. III, Atkinson, L., & Lang, P. J. (1987). Stimulus control and data acquisition for IBM PCs and compatibles. *Psychophysiology, 24*, 726–727.

Cook, E. W. III, Melamed, B. G., Cuthbert, B. N., McNeil, D. W., & Lang, P. J. (1988). Emotional imagery and the differential diagnosis of anxiety. *Journal of Consulting and Clinical Psychology, 56*, 734–740.

Cooper, J. (1970). The Leyton Obsessional Inventory. *Psychological Medicine, 1*, 48–64.

Craske, M. G., & Waikar, S. V. (1994). Panic disorder. In M. Hersen & R. T. Ammerman (Eds.), *Handbook of prescriptive treatments for adults* (pp. 135–155). New York: Plenum.

Delprato, D. J., & McGlynn, F. D. (1984). Behavioral theories of anxiety disorders. In S. M. Turner (Ed.), *Behavioral theories and treatment of anxiety* (pp. 1–49). New York: Plenum.

DiNardo, P. A., & Barlow, D. H. (1988). *Anxiety Disorders Interview Schedule-Revised (ADIS-R)*. Albany: Phobia and Anxiety Disorders Clinic, State University of New York at Albany.

DiNardo, P. A., Moras, K., Barlow, D. H., Rapee, R. M., & Brown, T. (1993). Reliability of DSM-III-R anxiety disorder categories using the Anxiety Disorders Interview Schedule-Revised (ADIS-R). *Archives of General Psychiatry, 50*, 251–256.

DiNardo, P. A., O'Brien, G. T., Barlow, D. H., Waddell, M. T., & Blanchard, E. B. (1983). Reliability of DSM-III anxiety disorder categories using a new structured interview. *Archives of General Psychiatry, 40*, 1070–1074.

Donohue, B. C., Van Hasselt, V. B., & Hersen, M. (1994). Behavioral assessment and treatment of social phobia: An evaluative review. *Behavior Modification, 18*, 262–288.

Emmelkamp, P. M. G. (1982). *Phobic and obsessive-compulsive disorders: Theory, research and practice*. New York: Plenum.

Endicott, J., & Spitzer, R. L. (1978). A diagnostic interview: The Schedule for Affective Disorders and Schizophrenia. *Archives of General Psychiatry, 35*, 837–844.

Endicott, J., & Spitzer, R. L. (1979). Use of the Research Diagnostic Criteria and Schedule for Affective Disorders and Schizophrenia. *Archives of General Psychiatry, 35*, 837–844.

Ericcson, K. A., & Simon, H. A. (1980). Verbal reports as data. *Psychological Review, 82*, 215–251.

Foa, E. B., & Tillmanns, A. (1980). The treatment of obsessive-compulsive neurosis. In A. Goldstein & E. B. Foa (Eds.), *Handbook of behavioral interventions: A clinical guide* (pp. 416–500). New York: Wiley.

Freund, B. (1986). *Comparison of measures of obsessive-compulsive symptomatology: Rating scales of symptomatology and standardized assessor- and self-rated*. Unpublished doctoral dissertation, Southern Illinois University, Carbondale.

Fulkerson, K. E., Galassi, J. P., & Galassi, M. D. (1984). Relation between cognitions and performance in math anxious students: A failure of cognitive theory? *Journal of Counseling Psychology, 34*, 376–382.

Geer, J. H. (1965). The development of a scale to measure fear. *Behaviour Research and Therapy, 3*, 45–53.

Glass, C. R., & Furlong, M. (1990). Cognitive assessment of social anxiety: Affective and behavioral correlates. *Cognitive Therapy and Research, 14*, 365–384.

Glass, C. R., Merluzzi, T. V., Biever, J. L., & Larsen, K. H. (1982). Cognitive assessment of social anxiety: Development and validation of a self-statement questionnaire. *Cognitive Therapy and Research, 6*, 37–55.

Goodman, W. K., Price, L. H., Rasmussen, S. A., Mazure, C., Fleischmann, R. L., Hill, C. L., Heninger, G. R., & Charney, D. S. (1989a). The Yale-Brown Obsessive-Compulsive Scale I. Development, use, and reliability. *Archives of General Psychiatry, 46*, 1006–1011.

Goodman, W. K., Price, L. H., Rasmussen, S. A., Mazure, C., Delgado, P., Heninger, G. R., & Charney, S. S. (1989b). The Yale-Brown Obsessive-Compulsive Scale II. Validity. *Archives of General Psychiatry, 46*, 1012–1016.

Graham, F. K. (1979). Distinguishing among orienting, defense, and startle reflexes. In H. D. Kirimal, E. H. van Olst, & J. F. Orlebile (Eds.), *The orienting reflex in humans* (pp. 137–167). Hillsdale, NJ: Lawrence Erlbaum.

Grossman, P. (1983). Respiration, stress, and cardiovascular function. *Psychophysiology, 20*, 284.

Haemmerlie, F. M. (1983). Heterosocial anxiety in college females. A biased interactions treatment. *Behavior Modification, 7*, 611–623.

Hallam, R. S. (1978). Agoraphobia: A critical review of the concept. *British Journal of Psychiatry, 133*, 314–319.

Hamilton, M. (1959). The assessment of anxiety states by rating. *British Journal of Medical Psychology, 32*, 50–55.

Hamilton, M. (1960). A rating scale for depression. *Journal of Neurology, Neurosurgery, and Psychiatry, 23*, 56–62.

Hamm, A. O., Globisch, J., Cuthbert, B. N., & Vaitl, D. (1991). Startle reflex modulation in simple phobics and normals. *Psychophysiology.* (Abstract)

Hayes, S. C. (1987). A contextual approach to therapeutic change. In N. Jacobson (Ed.), *Psychotherapists in clinical practice: Cognitive and behavioral perspectives* (pp. 327–387). New York: Guilford.

Haynes, S. N., & Uchigakiuchi, P. (1993). Incorporating personality trait measures in behavioral assessment: Nuts in a fruitcake or raisins in a Mai Tai? *Behavior Modification, 17*, 72–92.

Heimberg, R. G., Hope, D. A., Dodge, C. S., & Becker, R. E. (1990). DSM-III-R subtypes of social phobia: Comparison of generalized social phobics and public speaking phobics. *Journal of Nervous and Mental Disease, 178*, 172–179.

Helzer, J. E., Robins, L. N., McEvoy, M. A., Spitznagel, E. L., Stoltzman, R. K., Farmer, A., & Brockington, I. F. (1985). A comparison of clinical and diagnostic interview schedule diagnoses: Physician reexamination of lay-interviewed cases in the general population. *Archives of General Psychiatry, 42*, 657–666.

Hersen, M., & Turner, S. M. (1985). *Diagnostic interviewing*. New York: Plenum.

Hodgson, R. J., & Rachman, S. (1977). Obsessional-compulsive complaints. *Behaviour Research and Therapy, 15*, 389–395.

Hoffart, A. (1995). A comparison of cognitive and guided mastery therapy of agoraphobia. *Behaviour Research and Therapy, 33*, 423–434.

Hollandsworth, J. G., Glazeski, R. C., Kirkland, K., Jones, G. E., & Van Norman, L. R. (1979). An analysis of the nature and effects of test anxiety: Cognitive, behavioral, and physiological components. *Cognitive Therapy and Research, 3*, 165–180.

Hope, D. A., & Heimberg, R. G. (1993). Social phobia and social anxiety. In D. H. Barlow (Ed.), *Clinical handbook of psychological disorders* (2nd ed.) (pp. 99–136). New York: Guilford.

Huber, J. W., & Altmeier, E. M. (1983). An investigation of the self-statement systems of phobic and nonphobic individuals. *Cognitive Therapy and Research, 7*, 355–362.

Husek, T. R., & Alexander, S. (1963). The effectiveness of the Anxiety Differential in examination stress situations. *Educational and Psychological Measurement, 23*, 309–318.

Jennings, J. R., Stringfellow, J. C., & Graham, M. (1974). A comparison of the statistical distributions of beat-by-beat heart rate and heart period. *Psychophysiology, 11*, 207–210.

Johnson, B., Mayberry, W. E., & McGlynn, F. D. (1990). Exploratory factor analysis of a sixty-item questionnaire concerned with fear of dentistry. *Journal of Behavior Therapy and Experimental Psychiatry, 21*, 199–203.

Kelly, D., & Walter, C. (1968). The relationship between clinical diagnosis and anxiety assessed by forearm blood flow and other measurements. *British Journal of Psychiatry, 114*, 611–626.

Klein, D. F. (1981). Anxiety reconceptualized. In D. F. Klein & J. Rabkin (Eds.), *Anxiety: New research and changing concepts* (pp. 235–265). New York: Raven.

Klein, D. F. (1986). Anxiety reconceptualized. In D. F. Klein (Ed.), *Anxiety* (pp. 1–35). New York: Karger.

Kleinknecht, R. A., Klepac, R. K., & Alexander, L. D. (1973). Origins and characteristics of fear of dentistry. *Journal of the American Dental Association, 86*, 842–848.

Kleinknecht, R, A., Thorndike, R. M., McGlynn, F. D., & Harkavy, J. (1984). Factor analysis of the Dental Fear Survey with cross validation. *Journal of the American Dental Association, 108*, 59–61.

Koskal, F., & Power, K. G. (1990). Four Systems Anxiety Questionnaire (FSAQ): A self-report measure of somatic, cognitive, behavioral, and feeling components. *Journal of Personality Assessment, 54*, 534–545.

Lacey, J. L. (1950). Individual differences in somatic

response patterns. *Journal of Comparative and Physiological Psychology, 43*, 338–350.

Lacey, J. L. (1967). Somatic response patterning and stress: Some revisions on activation theory. In M. H. Appey & R. Trumbull (Eds.), *Psychological stress: Issues in research* (pp. 14–37). New York: Appleton-Century-Crofts.

Lande, S. D. (1981). Physiological and subjective meaning of anxiety during flooding. *Behaviour Research and Therapy, 18*, 162–163.

Lang, P. J. (1968). Fear reduction and fear behavior: Problems in treating a construct. In J. M. Schlein (Ed.), *Research in psychotherapy* (Vol. 3) (pp. 90–103). Washington, DC: American Psychological Association.

Lang, P. J. (1979). A bio-informational theory of emotional imagery. *Psychophysiology, 16*, 495–512.

Lang, P. J. (1980). Behavioral treatment and bio-behavioral assessment: Computer applications. In J. B. Sidowski, J. H. Johnson, & T. A. Williams (Eds.), *Technology in mental health care delivery systems* (pp. 119–137). Norwood, NJ: Ablex.

Lang, P. J. (1985). The cognitive psychophysiology of emotion: Fear and anxiety. In A. H. Tuma & J. D. Maser (Eds.), *Anxiety and the anxiety disorders* (pp. 131–170). Hillsdale, NJ: Lawrence Erlbaum.

Lang, P. J. (1995). The emotion probe: Studies of motivation and attention. *American Psychologist, 50*, 372–385.

Lang, P. J., & Lazovik, A. D. (1963). Experimental desensitization of a phobia. *Journal of Abnormal and Social Psychology, 66*, 519–525.

Lee, C. (1984). Efficacy expectations and outcome expectations as predictors of performance in a snake handling task. *Cognitive Therapy and Research, 8*, 509–516.

Lick, J. R., & Unger, T. E. (1977). The external validity of behavioral fear assessment: The problem of generalizing from the laboratory to the natural environment. *Behavior Modification, 1*, 283–306.

Liebowitz, M. R., Gorman, D. J., Fyer, A. J., & Klein, D. F. (1985). Social phobia: Review of a neglected anxiety disorder. *Archives of General Psychiatry, 42*, 729–736.

Lindsley, D. B. (1951). Emotion. In S. S. Stevens (Ed.), *Handbook of experimental psychology* (pp. 473–516). New York: Wiley.

Lipschitz, A. (1988). Diagnosis and classification of anxiety disorders. In C. G. Last & M. Hersen (Eds.), *Handbook of anxiety disorders* (pp. 41–65). New York: Pergamon.

Lovibond, S. H., & Lovibond, P. F. (1992). *Self-report scales (DASS) for the differentiation and measurement of depression, anxiety, and stress*. Unpublished manuscript.

Marchetti, A., McGlynn, F. D., & Patterson, A. S. (1977). Effects of cue-controlled relaxation, a placebo treatment, and no treatment on changes in self-reported and psychophysiological indices of test anxiety among college students. *Behavior Modification, 1*, 47–72.

Marks, I. M. (1969). *Fears and phobias*. London: Heinemann.

Marks, I. M. (1975). Behavioral treatments of phobic and obsessive-compulsive disorders: A critical appraisal. In M. Hersen, R. M. Eisler, & P. M. Miller (Eds.), *Progress in behavior modification* (Vol. 1) (pp. 66–143). New York: McGraw-Hill.

Marks, I. M. (1978). *Living with fear*. New York: McGraw-Hill.

Marks, I. M., Hallam, R. S., Connelly, J., & Philpott, R. (1977). *Nursing in behavioral psychotherapy*. London: Royal College of Nursing of the United Kingdom.

Marks, I. M., & Mathews, A. M. (1979). Brief standard self-rating scale for phobic patients. *Behaviour Research and Therapy, 17*, 263–267.

Marshall, W. L. (1985). The effects of variable exposure in flooding therapy. *Behavior Therapy, 16*, 117–135.

Marshall, W. L., Cooper, C., & Parker, L. (1979). *Skills training and anxiety management in producing effective public speakers*. Paper presented at the 13th Annual Convention of the Association for Advancement of Behavior Therapy, San Francisco.

Martzke, J. S., Andersen, B. L., & Cacioppo, J. T. (1987). Cognitive assessment of anxiety disorders. In L. Michelson & L. Ascher (Eds.), *Anxiety and stress disorders: Cognitive-behavioral assessment and treatment* (pp. 62–88). New York: Guilford.

Mathews, A. M., & Gelder, M. G. (1969). Psychophysiological investigations of brief relaxation training. *Journal of Psychosomatic Research, 13*, 1–12.

Mathews, A. M., Gelder, M. G., & Johnston, D. W. (1981). *Agoraphobia: Nature and treatment*. London: Tavistock.

Mattick, R. P., & Clarke, J. C. (1989). *Development and validation of measures of social phobia scrutiny fear and social interaction anxiety*. Unpublished manuscript.

Mattick, R. P., & Peters, L. (1988). Treatment of severe social phobia: Effects of guided exposure with and without cognitive restructuring. *Journal of Consulting and Clinical Psychology, 56*, 251–260.

McGlynn, F. D., McNeil, D. W., Gallagher, S. L., & Vrana, S. (1987). Factor structure, stability, and internal consistency of the Dental Fear Survey. *Behavioral Assessment, 9,* 57–66.

McGlynn, F. D., Moore, P. M., Rose, M. P., & Lazarte, A. (1995). Effects of relaxation training on fear and arousal during *in vivo* exposure to a caged snake among DSM-III-R simple (snake) phobics. *Journal of Behavior Therapy and Experimental Psychiatry, 26,* 1–8.

McGlynn, F. D., Patterson, A. S., Marchetti, A., & Giesen, M. (1980). Heterosexual anxiety: Stable multichannel assessment for therapy outcome research. *Journal of Behavioral Assessment, 2,* 123–134.

McGlynn, F. D., Rose, M. P., & Lazarte, A. (1994). Control and attention during exposure influence arousal and fear among insect phobics. *Behavior Modification, 18,* 371–388.

McGlynn, F. D., & Vopat, T. (1994). Simple phobia. In C. G. Last & M. Hersen (Eds.), *Adult behavior therapy casebook* (pp. 139–152). New York: Plenum.

McGuinness, D. (1973). Cardiovascular responses during habituation and mental activity in anxious men and women. *Biological Psychology, 1,* 115–123.

Mehrabian, A., & Russell, J. A. (1974). *An approach to environmental psychology.* Cambridge, MA: MIT Press.

Mersch, P. P. A., Emmelkamp, P. M. G., Bogels, S. M., & Van Der Sleen, J. (1989). Individual response patterns and the effects of behavioral and cognitive interventions. *Behaviour Research and Therapy, 27,* 421–434.

Meyer, T. J., Miller, M. L., Metzger, R. L., & Borkovec, T. D. (1990). Development and validation of the Penn State Worry Questionnaire. *Behaviour Research and Therapy, 28,* 487–495.

Miller, G. A., Levin, D. N., Kozak, M. J., Cook, E. W. III, McLean, A., & Lang, P. J. (1987). Individual differences in emotional imagery. *Cognition and Emotion, 1,* 367–390.

Montgomery, G. K. (1977). Effects of performance evaluation and anxiety on cardiac responses in anticipation of difficult problem solving. *Psychophysiology, 14,* 251–257.

Mowrer, O. H. (1939). A stimulus-response analysis of anxiety and its role as a reinforcing agent. *Psychological Review, 46,* 553–565.

Nelson, R. O. (1977). Methodological issues in assessment via self-monitoring. In J. D. Cone & R. P. Hawkins (Eds.), *Behavioral assessment: New directions in clinical psychology* (pp. 217–240). New York: Brunner/Mazel.

Nelson, R. O., & Hayes, S. C. (1979). Some current dimensions of behavioral assessment. *Behavioral Assessment, 1,* 1–6.

Nietzel, M. T., Bernstein, D. A., & Russell, R. L. (1988). Assessment of anxiety and fear. In A. S. Bellack & M. Hersen (Eds.). *Behavioral assessment: A practical handbook* (3rd ed.) (pp. 280–312). New York: Pergamon.

Papillo, J. F., Murphy, P. M., & Gorman, J. M. (1988). Psychophysiology. In C. G. Last & M. Hersen (Eds.), *Handbook of anxiety disorders* (pp. 217–250). New York: Pergamon.

Papillo, J. F., Pijacki, R., & Tursky, B. (1984). A comprehensive software package for the management of psychophysiological experimentation. *Psychophysiology, 21,* 159.

Paul, G. L. (1966). *Insight vs. desensitization: An experiment in anxiety reduction.* Stanford, CA: Stanford University Press.

Peterson, R. A., & Heilbronner, R. L. (1987). The Anxiety Sensitivity Index: Construct validity and factor analytic structure. *Journal of Anxiety Disorders, 1,* 117–121.

Rachman, S., & Hodgson, R. (1974). Synchrony and desynchrony in fear and avoidance. *Behaviour Research and Therapy, 12,* 311–318.

Rachman, S., & Hodgson, R. (1980). *Obsessions and compulsions.* Englewood Cliffs, NJ: Prentice-Hall.

Rapee, R. M., Craske, M. G., & Barlow, D. H. (1990). Subject described features of panic attacks using a new self-monitoring form. *Journal of Anxiety Disorders, 4,* 171–181.

Reiss, S., & McNally, R. J. (1985). The expectancy model of fear. In S. Reiss & R. R. Bootzin (Eds.), *Theoretical issues in behavior therapy* (pp. 107–121). New York: Academic Press.

Reiss, S., Peterson, R., Gursky, D., & McNally, R. (1986). Anxiety sensitivity, anxiety frequency, and the prediction of fearfulness. *Behaviour Research and Therapy, 24,* 1–8.

Riggs, D. S., & Foa, E. B. (1993). Obsessive compulsive disorder. In D. H. Barlow (Ed.), *Clinical handbook of psychological disorders* (2nd ed.) (pp. 189–239). New York: Guilford.

Sanavio, E. (1988). Obsessions and compulsions: The Padua Inventory. *Behaviour Research and Therapy, 26,* 169–177.

Sanderson, W. C., & Wetzler, S. (1990). Five percent carbon dioxide challenge: Valid analogue and marker of panic disorder? *Biological Psychiatry, 27,* 689–701.

Shear, M. K., & Fyer, M. R. (1988). Biological and psychopathological findings in panic disorder. In A. J. Frances & R. E. Hales (Eds.), *American Psychiatric Press Review* (Vol. 7) (pp. 29–53). Washington DC: American Psychiatric Press.

Siddle, D. A. T., Turpin, G., Spinks, J. A., & Stevenson, D. (1980). Peripheral measures. In H. M. van Praag, M. H. Lader, O. J. Rafelson, & E. J. Sacher (Eds.), *Handbook of biological psychiatry: Part II— Brain mechanisms and abnormal behavior-psychophysiology* (pp. 45–78). New York: Marcel Dekker.

Snowdon, J. (1980). A comparison of written and post-box forms of the Leyton Obsessional Inventory. *Psychological Medicine, 10,* 165–170.

Spielberger, C., Gorsuch, R., Lushene, R., Vagg, P., & Jacobs, G. (1983). *Manual for the State-Trait Anxiety Inventory.* Palo Alto, CA: Consulting Psychologists Press.

Spitzer, R. L., Williams, J. B. W., & Gibbon, M. (1987). *Structured Clinical Interview for DSM-III-R (SCID).* New York: New York Psychiatric Institute, Biometrics Research.

Stanley, M. A., Prather, R. C., Beck, G., Brown, T. C., Wagner, A. L., & Davis, M. L. (1993). Psychometric analyses of the Leyton Obsessional Inventory in patients with obsessive-compulsive and other anxiety disorders. *Psychological Assessment, 5,* 187–192.

Steketee, G. S. (1993). *Treatment of obsessive-compulsive disorder.* New York: Guilford.

Sternberger, L. G., & Burns, G. L. (1990a). Compulsive Activity Checklist and the Maudsley Obsessional-Compulsive Inventory: Psychometric properties of two measures of obsessive-compulsive disorder. *Behavior Therapy, 21,* 117–127.

Sternberger, L. G., & Burns, G. L. (1990b). Maudsley Obsessional-Compulsive Inventory: Obsessions and compulsions in a nonclinical sample. *Behaviour Research and Therapy, 28,* 337–340.

Taylor, C. B., Fried, L., & Kenardy, J. (1990). The use of a real-time computer diary for data acquisition and processing. *Behaviour Research and Therapy, 28,* 93–97.

Taylor, C. B., Sheikh, J., Agras, S., Roth, W. T., Margraf, J., Ehlers, A., Maddock, R. J., & Gossard, D. (1986). Ambulatory heart rate changes in patients with panic attacks. *American Journal of Psychiatry, 143,* 478–482.

Taylor, C. B., Telch, M. J., & Haavik, D. (1983). Ambulatory heart rate changes during panic attacks. *Journal of Psychosomatic Research, 17,* 1–6.

Taylor, F. K. (1966). *Psychopathology: Its causes and symptoms.* London: Butterworths.

Taylor, S. (1995). Anxiety sensitivity: Theoretical perspectives and recent findings. *Behaviour Research and Therapy, 33,* 243–258.

Taylor, S., Koch, W., & Crockett, D. J. (1991). Anxiety sensitivity, trait anxiety, and the anxiety disorders. *Journal of Anxiety Disorders, 6,* 293–311.

Telch, M. J., Sherman, M., & Lucas, J. (1989). Anxiety sensitivity: Unitary personality trait or domain specific appraisals? *Journal of Anxiety Disorders, 3,* 25–32.

Turner, S. M., & Beidel, D. C. (1988). *Treating obsessive-compulsive disorder.* New York: Pergamon.

Turner, S. M., Beidel, D. C., Dancu, C. V., & Stanley, M. A. (1989). An empirically derived inventory to measure social fears and anxiety: The Social Phobia Anxiety Inventory. *Psychological Assessment, 1,* 35–40.

Turner, S. M., Beidel, D. C., & Larkin, K. T. (1986). Situational determinants of social anxiety in clinic and non-clinic samples: Physiological and cognitive correlates. *Journal of Consulting and Clinical Psychology, 54,* 523–527.

Twentyman, C., Boland, T., & McFall, R. M. (1981). Heterosocial avoidance in college males: Four studies. *Behavior Modification, 5,* 523–552.

van Oppen, P. (1992). Obsessions and compulsions: Dimensional structure, reliability, convergent and divergent validity of the Padua Inventory. *Behaviour Research and Therapy, 30,* 631–637.

Walk, R. D. (1956). Self-ratings of fear in a fear-invoking situation. *Journal of Abnormal and Social Psychology, 52,* 171–178.

Waters, W. F., Bernard, B. A., & Buco, S. M. (1989). The Autonomic Nervous System Response Inventory (ANSRI): Prediction of psychophysiological response. *Journal of Psychosomatic Research, 33,* 347–361.

Waters, W. F., Cohen, R. A., Buco, S. M., & Dreger, R. M. (1984). An Autonomic Nervous System Response Inventory (ANSRI): Scaling, reliability, and cross validation. *Journal of Behavioral Medicine, 7,* 315–341.

Watson, D., & Friend, R. (1969). Measurement of social-evaluative anxiety. *Journal of Consulting and Clinical Psychology, 33,* 448–457.

White, B. V., & Gilden, E. F. (1937). "Cold pressor test" in tension and anxiety: A cardiochronographic study. *Archives of Neurological Psychiatry, 38,* 964–984.

Williams, S. L. (1987). On anxiety and phobia. *Journal of Anxiety Disorders, 1,* 161–180.

Williams, S. L. (1988). Height avoidance test. In M. Hersen & A. S. Bellack (Eds.), *Dictionary of behavioral assessment techniques* (pp. 242–243). New York: Pergamon.

Williams, S. L. (1990). Guided mastery treatment of agoraphobia: Beyond stimulus exposure. In M. Hersen, R. M. Eisler, & P. M. Miller (Eds.), *Progress in behavior modification* (Vol. 26) (pp. 89–121). Newbury Park, CA: Sage.

Williams, S. L., Turner, S. M., & Peer, D. F. (1985). Guided mastery and performance desensitization treatments for severe acrophobia. *Journal of Consulting and Clinical Psychology, 53,* 237–247.

Williams, S. L., & Watson, N. (1985). Perceived danger and perceived self-efficacy as cognitive determinants of acrophobic behavior. *Behavior Therapy, 16,* 136–146.

Wing, J. K., Cooper, J. E., & Sartorius, N. (1974). *The measurement and classification of psychiatric symptoms.* Cambridge: Cambridge University Press.

Wolpe, J. (1958). *Psychotherapy by reciprocal inhibition.* Stanford, CA: Stanford University Press.

Wolpe, J. (1973). *The practice of behavior therapy* (2nd ed.). New York: Pergamon.

Wolpe, J. (1990). *The practice of behavior therapy* (4th ed.). New York: Pergamon.

Wolpe, J., & Lang, P. J. (1964). A fear survey schedule for use in behavior therapy. *Behaviour Research and Therapy, 2,* 27–30.

CHAPTER 10

ASSESSMENT OF DEPRESSION

Jacqueline B. Persons
Center for Cognitive Therapy, Oakland, CA

David M. Fresco
University of North Carolina, Chapel Hill

This chapter describes strategies for assessing depression. We focus on the assessment needs of the clinician who is utilizing cognitive-behavioral theories to guide his or her thinking and treatment. We present a theory-driven approach, where assessment decisions are dictated by the clinician's nomothetic and idiographic theories about the case. After discussing some conceptual issues, we review the most important nomothetic diathesis-stress theories of depression and we describe the measures currently available to measure the constructs of those theories. We also describe methods for obtaining a diagnosis. We conclude with a case presentation that illustrates the use of some of the methods we describe.

MAKING ASSESSMENT DECISIONS

The term *depression* can refer to a mood state, a set of symptoms, or a syndrome. Each of these terms has been defined in many ways (see Rehm [1988] for a good discussion of this point). The heterogeneity of symptoms seen in depressed patients also stems from the high rates of psychiatric, medical, and psychosocial comorbidity seen in these patients.

Because of this heterogeneity, dozens of measures have been developed for assessing the various aspects of depression. As a result, the assessor cannot simply administer a comprehensive battery; he or she must make choices. These choices are best guided by the purpose of the assessment (Hayes, Nelson, & Jarrett, 1987). In particular, the assessment procedures undertaken depend on the hypothesis being tested.

In the treatment setting, the hypothesis being tested is essentially "Treatment interventions X, Y, and Z will be effective in alleviating this individual's depressive symptoms." Thus, the therapist is functioning as a scientist, using a hypothesis-testing approach, even when treating a single case (Barlow, Hayes, & Nelson, 1984).

The results of the assessment assist the clinician in making treatment decisions. At the same time, the types of assessments carried out are often a function of the treatment the clinician expects to carry out—or at least the theoretical model underpinning the clinician's thinking about treatment. Thus, assessment and treatment are intertwined.

The treatment plan is often based on the clinician's hypothesis about the nature of the mechanisms causing and/or maintaining the patient's depressive symptoms. This hypothesis, stated idiographically, is the case conceptualization, or case formulation. The idiographic formulation is generally derived from a nomothetic theory.

IDIOGRAPHIC VERSUS NOMOTHETIC ASSESSMENT

The term *nomothetic* derives from the Greek word *nomos,* which means "law," and the term *idiographic* derives from the Greek word *idios,* which means "one's own, private" (Cone, 1986). Thus, *nomothetic assessment* refers to the search for general laws that are applicable to large numbers of subjects, and *idiographic assessment* refers to the search for idiosyncratic aspects of a specific person.

The cognitive-behavior (CB) therapist uses both nomothetic and idiographic assessment measures. The CB therapist uses a nomothetic theory (e.g., hopelessness theory or Beck's cognitive theory) to provide a general framework for an idiographic conceptualization of the particular case at hand. Certain widely used nomothetic categories and measures such as the *DSM-IV* and the Beck Depression Inventory (BDI) provide a useful point of contact with the literature and other clinicians.

However, the treatment process, and CB treatment in particular, requires assessment of the idiosyncratic aspects of the patient's depression. What particular symptoms does *this* depressed patient experience? As one of our patients (Mr. Smith) recently pointed out, the BDI does not do a good job of assessing his depression because when he's depressed he eats *more* and sleeps *more*; these symptoms do not appear on the BDI. Another type of interplay between nomothetic and idiographic arises from the fact that an idiographic assessment of a particular patient's depression might involve use of a nomothetic instrument that assesses a particular component (e.g., behavioral passivity) of

depressive symptomatology that particularly captures a particular patient's depression.

Because assessment choices are guided by the clinician's nomothetic theories, we begin with a brief description of current cognitive-behavioral theories of depression.

DIATHESIS-STRESS THEORIES OF DEPRESSION

Within the cognitive-behavioral tradition, several diathesis-stress theories have been offered. These theories stand together conceptually by proposing that an individual's risk for depression stems from the events that occur in his or her life. Through their experiences, individuals acquire a vulnerability to depression (the *diathesis)* that can be activated in the presence of new life stress. Following is a brief description of three diathesis-stress theories.

Beck's Theory of Depression

Beck's (1967, 1976) Cognitive Theory of Depression proposes that individuals who have negative and distorted views of the self, world, and future are at increased risk for depression when life stress occurs. Beck (1967, 1976) views this "negative cognitive triad" as dysfunctional attitudes or schema—organized, enduring representations of knowledge and experience, generally formed in childhood, that guide the processing of current situational information.

Beck (1983) expands his cognitive theory by identifying two dispositional/personality variables, *sociotropy* and *autonomy*, that serve as diatheses for depression when life stress occurs. *Sociotropy* is defined as a set of beliefs, attitudes, and concerns located in the individual's interpersonal and emotional domain. These individuals are at risk for depression when they face stressful interpersonal events such as a failed romantic relationship (Fresco, Craighead, & Koons, 1994b; Hammen, Ellicott, & Gitlin, 1992; Robins, 1990). Beck (1983) states that the sociotropic individual tends to experience specific depressive symptoms, including sadness, loneliness, anxious depressive symptoms, crying, and labile mood. *Autonomy* refers to a set of beliefs, attitudes, and concerns for one's self-investment and achievement.

Highly autonomous individuals are at risk for depression when they face stressful achievement events such as losing a job. Beck (1983) predicts that the autonomous depressed patient experiences certain specific symptoms, including unremitting anhedonia that is independent of good and bad events, inhibited crying, avoidance of others to maintain autonomy, and rejection of help from others. Although studies have shown that autonomous individuals experience more achievement events than nonautonomous subjects (Robins, 1990), no study has demonstrated an interaction of autonomy and achievement events either prospectively (Fresco et al., 1994b; Robins & Block, 1988; Robins, Hayes, Block, & Kramer, 1995) or cross-sectionally (Robins, 1990). Studies of Beck's (1983) symptom specificity hypothesis have enjoyed mixed success (Persons, Burns, Perloff, & Miranda, 1993; Persons, Miranda, & Perloff, 1991; Robins et al., 1995). Many of the negative findings have prompted researchers to refine the assessment devices (Clark & Beck, 1991; Robins & Luten, 1991). We describe the various assessment techniques later.

Helplessness/Hopelessness Theories

In Seligman's (1975) Learned Helplessness Theory and its two major revisions, the Reformulated Learned Helplessness Theory (RLH; Abramson, Seligman, & Teasdale, 1978) and the Hopelessness Theory of Depression (HT; Abramson, Metalsky, & Alloy, 1989), individuals acquire a vulnerability to depression following uncontrollable (Seligman, 1975) or negative life events (Abramson et al., 1978, 1989).

Abramson and associates (1978) incorporated aspects of attribution theory to define the diathesis for depression as an internal, stable, and global attributional style for negative events. The internal-external dimension refers to whether outcomes are attributed to the self or to factors outside the self and was used to explain changes in self-esteem. According to the theory, depressives who attribute the occurrence of bad events internally and good events externally experience a drop in self-esteem. The stability of attributions relates to perceptions that the causes of events are recurrent or long lived. Attributing outcomes to stable causes leads to an expectation that the causes will be present again in the future. This dimension accounts for the chronicity of the depression. Global attributions involve the belief that causes of a particular outcome occur in many areas of one's life rather than being limited to the specific circumstances surrounding the event.

Empirical tests of RLH demonstrate generally positive findings (Robins, 1988; Sweeney, Anderson, & Bailey, 1986). However, criticisms have surfaced—questioning whether attributional style is specific to depression (Hollon, Kendall, & Lumry, 1986) and whether it is a trait-like, dispositional variable (Barnett & Gotlib, 1988; Coyne & Gotlib, 1983).

The revisions presented by Abramson and associates (1989) in their Hopelessness Theory require changes to the measurement of the cognitive diathesis. The researchers retain the attributional dimensions of stability and globality and introduce two additional dimensions: the inferred consequences that negative events have for the sense of self and sense for the future. We discuss several approaches to the assessment of attributional style later.

Lewinsohn's Behavioral Model of Depression

The model of depression that remains most closely tied to traditional learning theory has been offered by Lewinsohn (1974a, 1974b). At the heart of Lewinsohn's model is the observation that depressed individuals lack or have lost the ability to obtain positive reinforcers. Lewinsohn (1974b) notes that the amount of positive reinforcement in one's life results from (1) the number and range of stimuli that a person find reinforcing, (2) the availability of reinforcers, and (3) the individual's skill (especially social skills) in obtaining reinforcers. Life events and stressors can lead to changes in any of these factors. Until individuals again learn to obtain positive reinforcement, they will be inactive, withdrawn, and dysphoric.

Two lines of evidence support the relationship between social skills and depression. First, Lewinsohn, Sullivan and Grosscup (1980) have shown that both depressed and nondepressed individuals who acquired new social skills experienced fewer bad events and more good events—and also experienced improvements in mood. Similarly, several researchers have shown that depressed individuals are less successful in social interactions than nondepressed controls (Gotlib & Robinson, 1982; Youngren & Lewinsohn, 1980) and may even possess an aversive behavioral style that initially elicits support but ultimately leads to rejection (Coyne, 1976a, 1976b; Joiner, Alfano, & Metalsky, 1992).

From Nomothetic to Idiographic

The diathesis-stress framework provides the scientist-practitioner with a compelling, empirically validated approach to understanding depression. All of the theories just described identify a *skills deficit* or *cognitive vulnerability* that makes individuals prone to *depressive symptoms* when *life stress* occurs. These vulnerabilities have their origins in the individual's learning history. The diathesis-stress theories have led directly to the development of cognitive and behavioral interventions that have been shown to reduce depressive symptoms (AHCPR, 1993) and that may reduce the risk of future depression (DeRubeis, Evans, Hollon, Garvey, Grove, & Tuason, 1990).

Therefore, we use the diathesis-stress framework to outline a strategy for assessing depression. To translate the general nomothetic model into an idiographic case conceptualization, the CB therapist must assess the *specific* life events that activate this individual's *particular* diatheses to produce the *particular* set of depressive symptoms the patient is experiencing, as well as information about the *particular* early experiences that contributed to the formation of the diatheses.

ASSESSMENT FOR TREATMENT PURPOSES

Because the CB therapist is using a diathesis-stress model, he or she needs methods for assessing the patient's depressive symptoms, the cognitive or behavioral diatheses, the current life events that appear to activate the diatheses, and the past life events that are likely to have caused the diathesis. Here, review measures for assessing these constructs.

We also review methods for obtaining a diagnosis for depressed patients. Although cognitive-behavioral theories are not stated in diagnostic terms, use of standard psychiatric nomenclature facilitates communication between patient and clinician, between patients and their families, among clinicians, with insurance companies, and provides a point of contact with the research literature.

We do not extensively review assessment of many other constructs and phenomena frequently seen in depressed patients and useful to know about in order to make a comprehensive treatment plan. Depressed patients frequently have many other difficulties and disorders, including psychiatric disorders (e.g., substance abuse, anxiety disorders, and personality disorders), medical problems (e.g., diabetes, hypertension, obesity, and AIDS), and psychosocial problems (e.g., interpersonal problems, work difficulties, financial stresses, and legal difficulties).

From a diathesis-stress perspective, a depressed patient's coexisting symptoms and problems may play the role of activating life events or stressors. For example, untreated panic and agoraphobia may lead to social isolation and a reduction in interpersonal reinforcers, which may lead in turn to depression. Sometimes causal arrows (Haynes, 1992; Haynes & O'Brien, 1990) appear to go in both directions. For example, depressive symptoms may lead to poor self-care; which may lead to complications due to diabetes; which may lead to losses of functioning, reductions in reinforcers, and depression. Or, a wife's depressive symptoms may contribute to communication difficulties with her husband; as a result, he withdraws, exacerbating her depressive symptoms. Medical problems and/or the medications used to treat them may lead to depressive symptoms via biological and/or psychological routes.

To obtain a useful conceptualization of the case and to make an adequate treatment plan for any depressed patient, we recommend a comprehensive assessment of coexisting psychiatric, medical, and psychosocial difficulties (Nezu & Nezu, 1993; Persons, 1989, 1992; Turkat, 1985). Effective treatment also requires assessment of the patient's strengths and resources (Evans, 1993; Surber, 1994). Although quite important, particularly to the cognitive-behavior therapist, we also do not discuss the assessment of treatment goals (Kiresuk & Sherman, 1968; Mintz & Kiesler, 1982). We also do not discuss the assessment of suicidality, which has been discussed in detail elsewhere (e.g., see Linehan, 1981).

In addition to assessing multiple domains, assessment across multiple time periods is also needed. Treatment is a hypothesis-testing process that is constantly evaluated by ongoing assessment (Barlow et al., 1984). The initial treatment plan is determined by the therapist's hypothesis about the mechanisms that cause and maintain the presenting symptoms. Ongoing assessment of progress provides data that are useful in evaluating the utility of the formulation (AHCPR, 1993; Kazdin, 1993). Lack of treatment progress suggests that the formulation needs revision. Thus, many of the measures described here are intended for repeated assessment of overall symptoms and of progress toward accomplishing treatment goals.

DIAGNOSIS

The structured clinical interview provides the scientist-practitioner with a reliable and valid means to assess the lifetime and current diagnostic histories of patients as well as the presence and severity of symptoms. In this section, we briefly describe the features and merits of two structured diagnostic interviews: the Structured Clinical Interview for *DSM-IV* (SCID; First, Spitzer, Gibbon, & Williams, 1995) and the Anxiety Disorders Interview Schedule for *DSM-IV* (ADIS-IV; Brown, Di Nardo, & Barlow, 1994). Although the ADIS has been designed primarily for the anxiety disorders, it has sections to assess the diagnostic categories and symptoms that most commonly co-occur with anxiety—notably the depressive disorders.

The SCID (First et al., 1995) is the instrument that is most suited to the clinician who needs to confirm the presence of a *DSM-IV* diagnosis or resolve

issues of differential diagnosis. The research version of the Axis I SCID takes between 60 and 90 minutes to administer. However, the SCID for *DSM-IV* now includes a clinician version (SCID-CV) that is a shortened version of the full *DSM-IV* SCID (First et al., 1995). It differs from the research version by excluding probes about diagnostic subtypes and other specifiers. The SCID for *DSM-IV* is relatively new, but previous versions of the SCID have enjoyed impressive reliability and validity (Spitzer, Williams, Gibbon, & First, 1992).

The SCID was fashioned after the traditional interview in which clinicians probed their clients in a manner that allowed for several diagnostic hypotheses to be considered and tested simultaneously. Each section begins with a yes/no probe followed by queries that ask for elaborations. If the probe is not answered with a yes, the interviewer skips to the following section. If the screen is met, the interviewer continues in the section until a diagnosis is earned or until a criterial item does not meet clinical significance. This strategy has two main advantages: (1) diagnostic decisions are known to the interviewer during the interview and (2) interviews are shorter because irrelevant sections are not exhaustively probed. However, the SCID may not be the most effective method of assessing symptom levels over time or over the course of a therapy. Self-report measures of depressive symptoms, such as the Beck Depression Inventory (BDI; Beck, Rush, Shaw, & Emery, 1979), represent a useful compliment to the SCID when a clinician needs to understand the diagnostic history at intake and also needs a repeated measure of syndromal depression over the course of therapy.

The SCID is the successor to two other well-known approaches to diagnostic assessment: the Schedule for Affective Disorders and Schizophrenia (SADS; Endicott & Spitzer, 1978) and the NIMH Diagnostic Interview Schedule (DIS; Robins, Helzer, Croughan, & Ratcliff, 1981). Neither the SADS nor the DIS have been updated for *DSM-IV* criteria. Further, both of these interviews share a logical strategy (Spitzer et al., 1992) to arrive at a diagnosis that makes them less useful to the clinician. For both interviews, all diagnostic decisions are made by hand or by computer after all interview data are collected. Thus, interviews can become lengthy since all items are asked. Interviewers are discouraged from obtaining additional information for fear of violating the standardized administration of the instrument. For these reasons, the SCID remains the structured interview that best serves the scientist-practitioner in need of assessing the presence of *DSM-IV* diagnoses.

The ADIS-IV (Di Nardo et al., 1994) is another structured interview updated for *DSM-IV* that permits the clinician to make differential diagnoses of the Axis I disorders (e.g., unipolar and bipolar depression, somatoform disorders, and substance use disorders) that commonly co-occur with anxiety as well as Mixed Anxiety-Depressive Disorder. Similar to the SCID, the ADIS takes roughly the same amount of time to administer. Many sections of the ADIS end with optional research-oriented probes that can be omitted to make the ADIS a briefer interview.

Perhaps the greatest advantage of the ADIS-IV for the clinician (over the SCID) is the inclusion of probes for assessing both impairment and the client's strengths. In addition, the ADIS-IV includes probes for assessing etiological factors and situational antecedents in each diagnostic session. The ADIS-IV-L includes sections for probing about the lifetime diagnostic histories of anxiety, affective, somatoform, and substance use disorders (ADIS-IV-L; Di Nardo, Brown, & Barlow, 1994). Additionally, the ADIS-IV-L adopts a "diagnostic time line" approach to assist the clinician in tracking the onset, remission, and temporal ordering of diagnoses. Although the ADIS-IV and ADIS-IV-L are relatively new, their predecessors have demonstrated strong reliability (Di Nardo et al., 1993).

In sum, we recommend two structured diagnostic interviews to the scientist-practitioner: the SCID for *DSM-IV* and the ADIS-IV. As we stated earlier, diagnostic assessment is not central to the diathesis-stress model. However, it is useful to the clinician when communicating with other clinicians, with insurance companies, with patients, and with the patients' families. Perhaps most important, diagnostic information allows the clinician to make use of and to contribute to the research literature, which (for better or worse) is frequently organized around the diagnostic nomenclature.

OVERALL SYMPTOMS OF DEPRESSION

Several nomothetic self-report instruments assess the presence and severity of a broad range of depressive symptoms. Clinician-rated measures have also been developed for assessing depressive symptoms, most notably the Hamilton Rating Scale for Depression (HRSD; Hamilton, 1960). We focus on self-report measures because they are most useful to the clinician, particularly when repeated assessments are conducted.

The Beck Depression Inventory

Initially developed as a clinician's rating scale (Beck, Ward, Mendelson, Mock, & Erbaugh, 1961), the Beck Depression Inventory (BDI) was revised in 1971 for use as a self-report instrument and has become one of the most widely used measures of depression in both psychiatric (Piotrowski, Sherry, & Keller, 1985) and nonpsychiatric populations (Steer, Beck, & Garrison, 1986). In its self-report form, the BDI (Beck, Rush, Shaw, & Emery, 1979) is a 21-item instrument that broadly assesses the symptoms of depression, including the affective, cognitive, behavioral, somatic, and motivational components as well as suicidal wishes. Notably absent from the BDI are items that measure psychomotor agitation, increased appetite, and hypersomnia—all included as symptoms of depression in the *DSM-IV*.

The patient's scores on each item of the BDI are generally summed to provide an overall index of depression that can be compared to cut-off scores. Recently, Beck, Steer, and Garbin (1988) conducted a meta-analytic study of the BDI and reported the mean coefficient alpha across 25 years of psychiatric studies to be 0.86 in studies of psychiatric populations. The criterion validity across studies that also administered the HRSD was also high ($r = 0.73$ in psychiatric samples), as were correlations with other criterion measures of depression such as the Zung (1965), MMPI-D, and MAACL-D (Zuckerman & Lubin, 1965). Beck and Beck (1972) developed a 13-item version of the BDI that has demonstrated a strong correlation with its longer predecessor ($r = 0.96$).

Other Measures

The Center for Epidemiological Studies' Depression Scale (CES-D; Radloff, 1977) resembles the BDI by inquiring about the frequency and severity of 20 depressive symptoms. The CES-D has been used extensively to assess community samples (Boyd, Weissman, Thompson, & Myers, 1982; Roberts & Vernon, 1983), ethnic minorities (Cho, Moscicki, Narrow, & Rae, 1993), the elderly (Mahard, 1988; Orme, Reis, & Herz, 1986), and adolescents (Garrison, Addy, Jackson, & McKeown, 1991). CES-D items tend to measure the affective component of the depressive syndrome more heavily than the other symptom areas (Rehm, 1988).

The MMPI-D scale (Hathaway & McKinley, 1951) represents 60 items from the larger Minnesota Multiphasic Personality Inventory (Hathaway & McKinley, 1942). As with the other items of the MMPI, the D scale contains obvious (face-valid) items as well subtle items (e.g., "I enjoy playing drop the handkerchief") that are used because they contribute to a scale score that discriminates depressed subjects from nondepressed subjects. The MMPI and the MMPI-D are supported by extensive reliability and validity data. However, the MMPI-D is less useful to the clinician than other similar measures because of its use of nonface-valid items.

Idiographic Measurement of Depressive Symptoms

Different individuals have different symptoms of depression. As a result, nomothetic measures do not always provide a sensitive measure of a particular patient's depressive symptoms. Sometimes, as in the case of Mr. Smith, the patient described earlier who sleeps and eats more when he is depressed, a useful idiographic measure can be created by simply modifying a nomothetic measure like the Beck Depression Inventory. In Mr. Smith's case, items could be added to the BDI to assess increased sleep and eating, and the insomnia and anorexia items could be deleted. Although the score on Mr. Smith's individualized BDI does not permit between-subject comparisons, it does provide a

useful measure for assessing *Mr. Smith's* progress in treatment.

Another idiographic strategy for assessing depressive symptoms is to use measures of one or two of the components of depressive symptomatology (mood, cognitions, behaviors, or somatic symptoms) that are particularly prominent or meaningful for the patient in question, as described next.

SPECIFIC COMPONENTS OF DEPRESSIVE SYMPTOMATOLOGY

Cognitive-behavior therapists commonly view depression as composed of three primary components (mood, behavior, and cognitions) and sometimes a fourth (somatic symptoms). We describe methods for assessing mood, behavior, and cognitions.

Mood

The Multiple Affect Adjective Checklist (MAACL; Zuckerman & Lubin, 1965) is a self-report measure that asks respondents to endorse adjectives describing their present mood state. The MAACL consists of 132 adjectives yielding three negative affect scales: depression (40 adjectives), anxiety (21 adjectives), and hostility (28 adjectives) plus 39 neutral filler adjectives. The three scales are comprised of both positive and negative affect words. Scores are computed by summing the number of negative adjectives endorsed (e.g., *alone, blue, hopeless, suffering*) with the number of positive adjectives not endorsed (e.g., *active, alive, enthusiastic*). That is, a mood state consists of the presence of negative affect plus the absence of positive affect. Recently, the MAACL underwent revision to restandardize the items and to add two new scales: positive affect and sensation seeking (MAACL-R, Zuckerman, Lubin, & Rinck, 1983). In either form, the MAACL is an easily administered, quick means of assessing affect.

The Positive Affect and Negative Affect Scales (PANAS; Watson, Clark, & Tellegen, 1988) is another self-report measure of current mood. Adjectives assess both positive affect (e.g., *interested, alert, strong*) and negative affect (e.g., *distressed, upset, irritable, nervous*). Unlike the

MAACL, positive affect (PA) and negative affect (NA) are treated as orthogonal, unipolar scales that cut across the syndromes of depression and anxiety (Watson, Clark, & Carey, 1988). The PANAS has also been shown to be a useful measure across time. Watson (1988) has shown that changes in NA predict changes in physical complaints and perceived stress, whereas changes in PA predict changes in social activity and response initiation.

The Visual Analogue Scale (VAS; Aitken, 1969) is a useful measure of mood in clinical practice because it is easy to administer and can be adapted idiographically to any mood state. This approach allows for the assessment of idiosyncratic states that may have special meaning for a patient (e.g., emptiness, fogginess, boredom). The VAS asks the question, "How is your mood right now?" Subjects respond by making a mark on a 100-mm line with anchors at the left ("worst") and right ("best"). The score is the distance in millimeters from the left of the line. An adaptation of the VAS substitutes a 100-item or 10-item scale on which the patient verbally reports the intensity of his or her mood state. A scale such as this can be useful for assessing mood state within the session or on a daily or weekly basis, or for assessing mood shifts during a therapy session (Persons & Burns, 1985; see its use on the Daily Record of Dysfunctional Thoughts in Beck, Rush, Shaw, & Emery, 1979).

Behavior

With its origins in the single-subject design paradigm from both experimental (Ferster & Skinner, 1957) and clinical settings (Wilson & O'Leary, 1980) and its emphasis on observable events and situational determinants of behavior, the idiographic assessment of behavior has a strong historical foundation.

Self-monitoring is a hallmark technique that emerged from traditional behavioral assessment. Kazdin (1974) describes self-monitoring as the process of observing and recording one's own overt and covert behaviors. Teaching a client to collect data on her or his behavior can be useful when defining the client's problems, changing the frequency of desired or undesired behaviors, and evaluating the progress of therapy. Thoresen and Mahoney (1974) describe self-monitoring as occurring in five steps: discriminating a response, recording a response, charting a response, displaying data, and analyzing data. Although we introduce the technique of self-monitoring in this section on the behavioral component of depression, the technique can be easily adapted for the assessment of other parts of the depressive syndrome. Linehan (1993) has blended aspects of Zen meditation and self-monitoring into a powerful and comprehensive technique that she calls "mindfulness." Clients who master Linehan's (1993) mindfulness techniques can gain a better understanding of the interplay between mood, cognition, and behavior.

Idiographic assessment of the depressed patient's activities, which are often sparse and unsatisfying, can be done with the Weekly Activity Schedule, presented in Beck and colleagues (1979, p. 122). The Activity Schedule is a sheet of paper divided into one-hour blocks beginning at 9 A.M. and ending at midnight, with a separate column for each day of the week. Beck and colleagues (1979) recommend that depressed patients complete an activity schedule describing their use of time, on an hour-by-hour basis, between the first and second therapy sessions of the standardized cognitive therapy for depression protocol described in Beck and associates (1979). Although an hour-by-hour catalog is not always necessary, certainly the Activity Schedule does provide the clinician with a useful measure of the patient's activities.

The Pleasant Events Schedule (PES), developed by Lewinsohn and published in Lewinsohn, Muñoz, Youngren, and Zeiss (1978), is a nomothetic measure of behavior. The PES is a 320-item self-report scale listing pleasant events. For each event, the patient is asked to rate the frequency and the pleasantness of the event on a 0 to 2 scale. The PES provides useful information about the depressed patient's behaviors and leads to obvious intervention suggestions.

Other behavioral measures can also be useful in treatment planning for a depressed patient. For some patients, as Lewinsohn's model emphasizes, a measure of social skills is needed (see Chapter 11 of this book). Role-play strategies can be useful in assessing assertiveness and other interpersonal difficulties. As Kohlenberg and Tsai (1991) and many others point out, observation of the patient's inter-actions with the therapist provides important *in vivo* assessments of interpersonal difficulties that probably occur outside the therapy session as well.

Cognitions

Automatic thoughts, or the "stream of conscious-ness" self-statements made by depressed individu-als, are believed to play a role in the onset (Abramson et al., 1989) and maintenance (Beck, 1976; Beck et al., 1979) of depression. They covary with the presence or absence of depressive mood (Hollon et al., 1986) and offer the clinician a rich source of information (Beck et al., 1979).

The Automatic Thoughts Questionnaire-Neg-ative (ATQ-N; Hollon & Kendall, 1980) is a 30-item self-report instrument designed to measure the frequency of negative self-statements described in Beck's (1967, 1976) theory of depression. Items such as "I'm no good," "Why can't I ever succeed?" and "I've let people down" represent the negative thoughts about the self that Beck (1967, 1976) describes as part of the cognitive triad. The ATQ-N has demonstrated excellent psychometric prop-erties, specificity to depression, and sensitivity to changes in mood state (Dobson & Breiter, 1983; Hill, Oei, & Hill, 1989; Hollon & Kendall, 1980; Hollon et al., 1986).

Ingram and Wisnicki (1988) developed the Au-tomatic Thoughts Questionnaire-Positive (ATQ-P), a 30-item questionnaire that inquires about the frequency of positive automatic thoughts such as "I am respected by my peers," "I'm proud of my ac-complishments," and "My life is running smoothly." The ATQ-P enjoys excellent psycho-metric properties ($a = .94$) and has been successful in discriminating between depressed and nonde-pressed subjects (Burgess & Haaga, 1994; Ingram et al., 1990).

Later, we describe several in-session tech-niques to assess negative self-statements. How-ever, these techniques assume that clients have access to their automatic thoughts and can reliably report them. For the client who is not practiced in identifying self-statements, measures such as the ATQ can help clients obtain information about the content and number of their automatic thoughts. Repeated administration of the ATQ can serve as a useful measure of treatment progress.

A useful first strategy in the idiographic assessment of cognitions is the simple counting of negative thoughts or thoughts that follow a partic-ular theme. Burns (1980) suggests using a golf stroke counter for this purpose. To test the hypoth-esis that her concerns followed a theme of feeling unsupported and alone, one of our patients recently kept a log of thoughts that followed that theme. A count of negative thoughts can serve as a useful marker of treatment progress. A count of suicidal thoughts or another type of thought (e.g., recurrent thoughts about a medical problem) can also be clinically useful.

The Thought Record (see Figure 10.1), de-scribed in Persons (1989), provides an idiographic method for assessing automatic thoughts that leads directly to intervention in the therapy session. The columns of the Thought Record are Situation, Emo-tion, Behavior, Thoughts, and Responses. The Thought Record thus captures the key features of the diathesis-stress model: situation, cognitions, and emotional reaction. The Thought Record is based on and includes all key features of the Daily Record of Dysfunctional Thoughts published in Beck and associates (1979); it differs from the Daily Record of Dysfunctional Thoughts in that it has a column for behavior, which makes it possible to show how cognitions, mood, and behavior are re-lated. Patients can be asked to record, over the course of a week, a Thought Record for one or two or more problematic situations. A review of several records often reveals repeated themes that appear across situational variations and point to underlying diatheses.

Specialized cognitive measures such as Beck's Hopelessness Scale (Beck, Weissman, Lester, & Trexler, 1974) and Linehan's Reasons for Living Scale (published in Corcoran & Fischer, 1987) can also be quite useful clinically. Beck, Steer, Kovacs, and Garrison (1985) reported, in a study of 207 sui-cidal patients, that the Hopelessness Scale was a strong predictor of completed suicides. Certainly, cognitions about suicide rate high priority and can be assessed with Beck's Scale for Suicide Ideation (Beck, Kovacs, & Weissman, 1979).

Figure 10.1 The Thought Record: A procedure for assessing automatic thoughts

DATE	SITUATION (EVENT, MEMORY, ATTEMPT TO DO SOMETHING, ETC.)	BEHAVIOR(S)	EMOTIONS	THOUGHTS	RESPONSES

THE DIATHESIS

Assessing the diathesis is important for several reasons. According to the diathesis-stress theories, patients remain vulnerable to depression relapse when treatments address only overt symptoms and problems while overlooking the underlying diathesis. Consequently, these patients tend to experience new bouts of depression following events that reactivate their diathesis. In addition, Persons (1989) argues that information about the diathesis helps the therapist set good treatment goals, choose helpful interventions, manage homework, minimize noncompliance, and bolster the patient/therapist relationship.

We describe both nomothetic and idiographic assessment techniques that measure the diatheses described in Beck's (1967, 1976, 1983) Theory and Helplessness Theory (Abramson et al., 1978, 1989).

Beck's Theory

The Dysfunctional Attitude Scale (DAS; Weissman & Beck, 1978) consists of two 40-item, factor analytically derived questionnaires that tap into the depressed person's unrealistic, distorted, and illogical beliefs about the self, world, and future. Form A of the DAS is the more widely used of the two measures. Weissman and Beck (1978) report excellent internal consistencies ($\alpha \geq .90$) across several samples. Two criticisms of the DAS have been raised. First, Hollon and associates (1986) reported that DAS scores were elevated in nondepressed psychiatric populations (such as schizophrenic patients and those with bipolar illness), suggesting that these cognitions are not specific to unipolar depression. Second, many studies have found that DAS scores of remitted depressed subjects were not different from a nonpsychiatric control group—suggesting that dysfunctional attitudes are mood-state dependent rather than a stable mode of perceiving the world.

Two separate explanations that account for these findings have been offered by Alloy, Albright, Fresco, and Whitehouse (1995) and Persons and Miranda (1992). Alloy and colleagues (1992) point out that many of the studies showing instability of cognitive style scores used psychiatric samples who received treatment or employed a cross-sectional design that makes direction of causality difficult to determine. Alternatively, Persons and Miranda (1992) proposed the mood-state hypothesis to account for them. The mood-state hypothesis states that the beliefs are stable in vulnerable individuals, but they are accessible only during negative mood states.

Weissman and Beck (1978) designed the DAS to broadly cover the dysfunctional attitudes held by depressed individuals described by Beck's (1967, 1976) Cognitive Theory of Depression. However, other researchers have successfully identified scales labeled *Approval by Others* and *Performance Evaluation* that correspond to Beck's (1983) cognitive/personality constructs of sociotropy and autonomy (Cane, Olinger, Gotlib, & Kuiper, 1986; Rude & Burnham, 1993).

The Sociotropy-Autonomy Scale (SAS; Beck, Epstein, Harrison, & Emery, 1983), a 60-item self-report measure, is the first instrument designed specifically to measure the interpersonal and achievement concerns of depressed subjects based on Beck's (1983) theory. Across many studies, both scales have demonstrated strong internal consistencies (sociotropy, $.82 \leq \alpha$ .93; autonomy, $.80 \leq \alpha$ .88), yet weak autonomy findings have prompted researchers to undertake revisions of the SAS (Clark & Beck, 1991; Robins & Luten, 1991).

Robins, Ladd, Welkowitz, Blaney, Diaz, and Kutcher (1993) reworked and dropped items from the original SAS to produce the Personal Style Inventory II, a 48-item self-report measure with two internally consistent scales (sociotropy, $\alpha = .88$; autonomy, $\alpha = 86$) that are relatively orthogonal ($r = .18$).

The Clark and Beck (1991) revision of the SAS involved adding to and reworking of the original 60 items to produce a scale of 74 items. The Sociotropy Scale remains relatively unchanged. In the validation study of the revised SAS, the Sociotropy Scale served as a predictor of both levels of depression and levels of anxiety. The Autonomy Scale ($\alpha = .87$) has been relabeled Solitude/Interpersonal Insensitivity to reflect the content of its items. In the same validation study, this new Solitude Factor served as a strong predictor of levels of depression but not anxiety. Two additional factors emerged from the remaining Autonomy items. Clark and Beck (1991) call these factors *independence* and *individualistic achievement*—neither of

the new scales demonstrated any relationship to depressive or anxious symptoms.

Helplessness Theory

The Attributional Style Questionnaire (ASQ; Peterson, Semmel, von Baeyer, Abramson, Metalsky, & Seligman, 1982; Seligman, Abramson, Semmel, & von Baeyer, 1979) is a self-report inventory that assesses attributions for 6 positive and 6 negative hypothetical events along the dimensions of internality, stability, and globality. The 12 events can be further divided into categories of achievement and interpersonal. Subjects respond by reporting the major cause for each hypothetical event and then rating the causes along the attributional dimensions. Positive and negative event composite scores can then be derived by summing across the internality, stability, and globality dimensions for the 6 positive and 6 negative events separately. Each dimension is scored on a 1 to 7 Likert-type scale, with the higher end representing a response endorsing internal, global, or stable causes, and the lower end representing external, specific, and unstable causes.

Generally, a Composite Negative (CN) score is computed by summing the values of the 18 internal, stable, and global items for the negative events. A similar Composite Positive (CP) score from the positive hypothetical event items is also computed. Alloy, Kayne, Romer, and Crocker (1995) have found modest internal consistencies for the individual dimensions but the composite scores have a more respectable Chronbach alpha score ($\alpha = .83$ for CP; $\alpha = .84$ for CN). Similarly, test-retest correlations with an interval of four weeks were good: $r = .81$ for the positive event composite score and $r = .73$ for the negative event composite score.

Despite robust positive findings, especially between CN and depression (Sweeney, Anderson, & Bailey, 1986), critics of the cognitive diathesis-stress theories suggest that negative attributional style is neither specific to depression nor stable over time (Barnett & Gotlib, 1988; Coyne & Gotlib, 1983; Hollon et al., 1986). In an effort to improve measurement of attributional style and to acknowledge theoretical uncertainty about attributional style for good events, Peterson and Villanova (1988) dropped the 6 hypothetical good events and added 18 hypothetical bad events to produce a broader, more internally consistent measure of negative attributional style.

Similarly, Metalsky (Abramson & Metalsky, 1986; Metalsky, Halberstadt, & Abramson, 1987) has undertaken revisions to the original ASQ to produce a more reliable measure of attributional style and to include revisions based on Hopelessness Theory (HT; Abramson et al., 1989). As noted above, HT identifies three separate diatheses related to the attributions and inferences that individuals make about negative events in their lives: the *attributional* (or generality) *diathesis* (e.g., stable and global attributions for negative events); the *self-diathesis* (e.g., a generalized tendency to make negative inferences about the self when negative events occur); and the *consequences diathesis* (e.g., a generalized tendency to make negative inferences about the future when negative events occur). Metalsky and Joiner (1992) provide initial psychometric and empirical support for all three scales by demonstrating diathesis-stress interactions between negative life events and generality ($\alpha = .87$), self ($\alpha = .91$), and consequences ($\alpha = .89$) to predict depression but not anxiety.

The ASQ provides a quick means of assessing attributional style, but obtaining a completed self-report measure represents an obstacle in some settings. Consequently, Peterson and Seligman (Peterson, 1992; Peterson, Schulman, Castellon, & Seligman, 1992; Peterson & Seligman, 1984) developed a technique for assessing individuals' spontaneous attributions about *real-life good and bad events*. The Content Analysis of Verbatim Explanation (CAVE) extracts event statements and attributions from verbatim passages and rates the extracted material for internality, stability, and globality. Although the efficacy of the CAVE technique has been demonstrated in depressed patients (Peterson, Luborsky, & Seligman, 1983; Peterson & Seligman, 1984), some questions remain about the relationship between attributional style scores obtained with the ASQ and the CAVE (Fresco, Craighead, & Koons, 1994a; Peterson, Bettes, & Seligman,

1985; Schulman, Castellon, & Seligman, 1989). Efforts are underway to adapt the CAVE technique for use as a clinical assessment tool (Fresco, Craighead, Sampson, Watt, & Koons, 1995).

Idiographic Assessment of the Diathesis

Idiographic assessment of patients' cognitive diatheses can be done in several ways. A frequently repeated automatic thought, particularly if it is one about the self or others (e.g., "I can't do it") seems likely to reflect the patient's guiding schemas. The *downward arrow* technique, described by David Burns (1980), can be helpful in obtaining information about schemas or core beliefs. To use the downward arrow technique, begin with a Thought Record that lists several automatic thoughts arising in a problematic situation. Pinpoint any thought, particularly one that might be true (e.g., "If I ask her to return the money I loaned her, she might get upset and angry"). Then ask the patient, "Imagine that happened; why would that be upsetting to you?" When the patient responds, ask the question again two or three or four times, until the patient's concerns appear to "bottom out"—the patient can't think of anything worse. The last thought or two in this sort of a downward stream seems to reflect patients' central concerns and views of self, others, and future. In the case of the patient who began with the thought, "If I ask her to return the money I loaned her, she might get upset and angry," the stream of thoughts following it was: "I wouldn't be able to handle it," "She'd get upset and it would be my fault," "I'd lose a friend," "I'd be alone." Thus, this patient's central view of herself seems to be that she is inept, and her view of others is that they are angry, attacking, and rejecting.

Information about core schemas can also be obtained through a review of several Thought Records that describe problematic situations and list automatic thoughts. A review of several records can often reveal a theme that occurs repeatedly and appears to have a certain cross-situational stability. Similarly, an oft-repeated automatic thought (e.g., "I can't do it") seems likely to reflect salient, important schemas.

Although the downward arrow and the "look for the theme" method of assessing schemas are probably widely used by clinicians, we are not aware of any data examining the reliability or validity of these methods of schema assessment.

LIFE EVENTS

The diathesis-stress theories point to the need for assessment of two types of life events: current situations and events that seem to play a role in activating diatheses to produce symptoms, and early life events that may have played a role in causing the diatheses. Important early life events can include major acute traumas (e.g., deaths or incidents of physical or sexual abuse) that may have occurred only once or twice or chronic, grinding kinds of events (e.g., daily criticism).

Researchers, drawing on the cognitive diathesis-stress theories, argue that individuals at risk for depression suffer from information processing biases in the way they gather information about their environments. Traditional life stress assessment (e.g., self-report scales) did not separate subjective distress ratings from measures of the hypothesized diathesis. To address this potential bias, Brown and Harris (Brown, Bifulco, Harris, & Bridge, 1986; Brown, Bifulco, & Harris, 1987; Brown & Harris, 1978; Brown, Harris, & Peto, 1973) and Monroe (Monroe, 1982a, 1982b, 1983; Monroe & Roberts, 1990; Monroe & Simons, 1991) pioneered the development of a system of structured life stress interviews. The appeal of these interview schemes is that the impact of life events can be derived by carefully probing for idiosyncratic, objective factors about particular events to see how they influence an individual's life. The protocol provides interviewers with a standard, default set of probes for each event to assist in arriving at an objective impact rating.

Although learning these life stress interview protocols may not be practical for clinicians, this work provides important suggestions for adaptation to clinical settings. First, clinicians should not rely completely on the subjective distress reported by clients. Rather, clinicians should probe their clients for objective details about the events. If a client describes the event in a way that reveals

significant cognitive distortion or magnification of the impact, this provides important information for the clinician about hypothesized underlying diatheses that can become the focus of treatment.

Clinicians may find self-report inventories of life stress more useful than interview methods. Three self-report inventories of life stress, used mostly in research settings, may be useful to clinicians. The Life Experiences Survey (LES; Sarason, Johnson, & Siegel, 1978) and the Social Readjustment Rating Scale (SRRS; Holmes & Rahe, 1967) are inventories of major life events, and the Hassles and Uplifts Scales (Kanner, Coyne, Shaeffer, & Lazarus, 1981) provide a list of daily bad and good happenings. The mention of important events in clients' lives will often emerge during routine interviewing. However, some clients may benefit from a list of items, such as these self-report inventories, that prompts their recall of important events.

Case Example

Jane was a 30-year-old single White woman who worked as a supervisor for an office supply business and lived with her boyfriend. Her presenting complaint was, "I'm stressed out at work, but it's really home problems that bring me in." Depressive symptoms were a prominent feature of Jane's clinical picture and we focus on them here. We describe the assessment methods the therapist (JBP) used to develop an idiographic formulation, based on the diathesis-stress model, of Jane's case.

Depressive Symptoms. When the initial interview revealed many depressive symptoms, the therapist asked Jane to complete a Beck Depression Inventory (BDI) and bring it to the next session. On the BDI, Jane had endorsed symptoms of sadness, lack of enjoyment, feeling discouraged about the future, guilt, feeling disgusted with herself, irritability, difficulty making decisions, difficulty getting things done, feeling old and unattractive, fatigue, insomnia, loss of libido, worry about physical problems, and suicidal thoughts that Jane described as "fleeting." Her BDI score was 22.

The therapist explained to Jane that she appeared to be clinically depressed and suggested that she complete a BDI each week so that her progress in treatment could be monitored. The therapist kept a clipboard and a supply of inventories in her waiting room. Jane was asked to come to her session five minutes early so she could complete a BDI for use in the session. She was able to do this task prior to most sessions.

Behavioral Component. The initial clinical interview revealed that the most prominent component of Jane's depression was behavioral. Jane reported that she typically came home from work and collapsed on the couch—eating dinner some nights and simply snacking others—and that she did almost nothing on weekends. When this information came out in the interview, the therapist asked Jane to complete a Weekly Activity Schedule (Beck et al., 1979). It indicated that Jane routinely slept until noon on weekends, then spent hours drinking coffee while reading the paper. Her Activity Schedule showed almost no social or pleasurable activities. Information obtained from the Activity Schedule formed the basis of interventions designed to increase Jane's activity level. She was receptive to this line of work and made some immediate changes—adding some social activities and structuring her day to make her weekend mornings more productive.

Another behavioral aspect of Jane's depression was her unassertiveness. For example, Jane reported that she frequently loaned money to friends and family then felt unable to ask for its return. She also expressed difficulty in disciplining subordinates at work or refusing their requests for special accommodations. To obtain some objective measurement of Jane's assertiveness difficulties, the therapist asked her to complete the Assertion Inventory (AI; Gambrill & Richey, 1975), a 40-item scale measuring degree of discomfort with assertion and response probability of engaging in assertive behaviors. This measure is supported by strong reliability and validity data (Corcoran & Fischer, 1987). Jane's initial scores on the AI indicated that she typically approached situations in an "unassertive" manner (as opposed to "assertive," "anxious performer," or "doesn't care").

The Thought Record (see Figure 10.1) provided a detailed idiographic assessment of the situational, behavioral, and cognitive components of Jane's lack of assertiveness. For example, in a typ-ical Thought Record, Jane reported she avoided speaking assertively to a subordinate who was arriving late to work. When Jane listed the automatic thoughts that she felt inhibited her from speaking up in this situation, she reported the thoughts: "He'll be angry at me," "It will create bad morale at the office," "I don't know how to handle this situation," and "If I were a good manager, I would handle this situation so that he wouldn't get angry at me." Getting these thoughts out on the table led directly to cognitive restructuring interventions. To test out Jane's hypothesis that she didn't know how to handle the situation, the therapist initiated a role-play in which Jane demonstrated how she would speak to her subordinate (an *in vivo* behavioral assessment). The demonstration made it clear to both the therapist and to Jane that her interpersonal skills in this situation were excellent and that Jane's view of herself as not knowing how to handle the situation was distorted.

Cognitive Diathesis. Jane completed the Dysfunctional Attitude Scale (DAS-A; Weissman & Beck, 1978) after the first session. It showed she had significant numbers of distorted beliefs and cognitions; her score was 142 (each item was scored on a 1 to 7 scale). Items reflecting distortions indicated problems in both the achievement ("If I cannot do something really well, there is little point in doing it at all") and interpersonal ("I nearly always try to avoid conflicts, arguments, or fights with my partner") domains.

Jane's core beliefs were also assessed idiographically using Thought Records and the downward arrow technique (which was illustrated earlier). These methods revealed a few beliefs that occurred repeatedly across many problematic situations. Jane often expressed the beliefs "I'm inadequate, inept, and helpless" and "I am responsible for others," as well as "Others are critical and attacking" and "Others are weak and helpless."

Activating Life Events. No formal measure was used to assess activating life events. Instead, the therapist asked, in detail, for this information, during an early interview. Jane reported several events, including the recent marriage of a close friend. This event both reminded her that her own relationship was not moving ahead and activated her beliefs of "I'm inadequate, I'm helpless, I can't cope."

Although she initially stated that it was her chief concern, Jane spent surprisingly little time talking about difficulties in her romantic relationship. The therapist hypothesized that it was an *in vivo* example of what proved to be Jane's chronic passivity and avoidance behavior. When discussing her romantic relationship, Jane mentioned that her boyfriend was working part time at a job that was far below his abilities. Jane felt hopeless about the future of their relationship, which had dragged on this way for years.

Significant Early Events. Significant early events were also assessed via the clinical interview. When assessing significant early events in an interview, we recommend asking the patient to describe specific events in detail, rather than simply providing a general overview. We have found specific event descriptions to be much more useful and informative than general descriptions.

A review of Jane's family history yielded information about the origins of her views of herself (i.e., not measuring up) and her views of others (i.e., as attacking and helpless). Jane's father was a harsh, critical, and self-centered alcoholic who was prone to irrational, angry outbursts over minor events. For example, there were times when he would fly into a rage if Jane came home from school a few minutes early or late. Her mother was passive, weak, and helpless—avoiding confrontation whenever possible. For example, when Jane's father was attacking her, her mother was likely to scurry into the kitchen to avoid the scene. Jane had five brothers and sisters. As a child, she adopted a care-giving role in the family. For example, if one of her siblings dropped a piece of food on the floor, Jane would step forward to distract her father in hopes of preventing him from flying into a rage.

Course of Treatment. Jane's treatment was an unusually long one, due in part to the multiplicity of her difficulties, not all of which were described here. She worked in therapy for 90 sessions over two years. The therapist kept a graph of weekly BDI scores that proved invaluable in monitoring and making adjustments over the course of this long treatment (see Figure 10.2).

At the beginning of treatment, Jane made quick progress on her behavioral inactivity, beginning by scheduling events with her friends to get herself up and about in the morning on weekends; she knew that if she did this, she had a more active day. Her depressive symptoms remitted gradually (see Figure 10.2).

At about session 20, Jane had a major setback when she decided to break off the relationship with her boyfriend yet felt too guilty and frightened to do so. She backed off from that decision, continued working on her depression, and made some progress. For many weeks, her BDI score consistently remained in the 10 to 15 range.

At about session 40, her BDI score jumped up again. To understand this increase, Jane and the therapist reviewed recent events and situations—searching for situations or circumstances that might have activated Jane's symptoms. Still, the reasons for this setback remained unclear. At this point, the therapist initiated a reformulation of the case and a review of the treatment plan, as Jane's progress seemed stalled, as the graph of BDI scores clearly showed.

The therapist recommended, and Jane agreed, to a medication consult. Around session 43, Jane began taking Zoloft (Sertraline); her depressive symptoms seemed to show a clear drop about one month later (see Figure 10.2), suggesting that she had responded to the drug.

Near the end of treatment, as Jane began feeling better, she followed through with her plans to break off the relationship with her boyfriend. She also resumed driving (she had stopped many years previously, following an accident, fearing "I'll be inept"). Jane's progress in overcoming her depressive symptoms is reflected in Figure 10.2; weekly BDI scores were discontinued before the end of treatment because Jane's depressive symptoms had remitted.

At post treatment, Jane completed the BDI, the DAS, and the Assertiveness Inventory. Her BDI was 10, indicating her depressive symptoms had largely remitted, though she remained somewhat dysthymic. Her DAS score was 104, suggesting a significant reduction in her reported dysfunctional beliefs. Part of this reduction, however, is likely due to the change in Jane's mood state—since a body of research has shown that mood influences re-

Figure 10.2 Weekly Beck Depression Inventory (BDI) scores for the case example "Jane." Note that the BDI was discontinued prior to the termination of treatment.

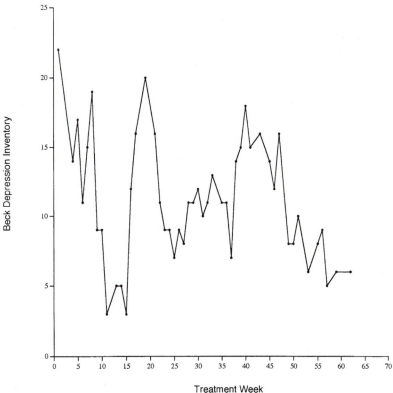

ported dysfunctional attitudes (Persons & Miranda, 1992). To test this hypothesis, we would ask Jane to agree to a negative mood induction before completing the posttreatment DAS. Jane's scores on the AI indicated that she made gains in this area as well.

Jane has agreed to a follow-up assessment six months after ending her treatment. At that time, she will meet with the therapist, who will assess her depressive symptoms, other difficulties, and recent life events in an interview. Jane will also complete a BDI, the DAS, and the AI.

SUMMARY

In this chapter we describe an approach to the assessment of depression that is informed by empirically validated cognitive-behavioral theories of depression, yet remains useful in clinical settings.

Our approach asks the clinician to adopt a cognitive-behavioral diathesis-stress framework to guide the case formulation and ongoing hypothesis testing that occurs during therapy. With the exception of instruments that help clinicians detect the presence of a depression diagnosis, we focus on measures that assess depression from the perspective of the cognitive diathesis-stress theories. Thus, we describe instruments that measure the overall symptom profile of depression as well as its cognitive, behavioral, and mood components; life events; and the underlying cognitive diathesis. Although the diathesis-stress theories are nomothetic theories, assessment of clinical cases is idiographic, and therefore we discuss the adaptation of nomothetic measures to idiographic cases.

This chapter focuses on assessment of depression, not assessment of the depressed patient. Assessment of the depressed patient typically requires assessment of many domains not addressed here, including comorbid Axis I, Axis II, and Axis III disorders and problems, as well as the psychosocial difficulties typically seen in depressed patients. It is also useful to assess a depressed patient's strengths and resources. Information from all of these areas helps a clinician identify target symptoms and develop treatment goals. Thus, a complete discussion of the assessment of the depressed patient requires an entire book—a book that includes material presented in many of the other chapters of this text.

REFERENCES

Abramson, L. Y., & Metalsky, G. I. (1986). *The Cognitive Style Questionnaire: Measurement of negative cognitive styles about self and consequences.* Unpublished manuscript, University of Wisconsin, Madison.

Abramson, L. Y., Metalsky, G. I., & Alloy, L. B. (1989). Hopelessness depression: A theory-based subtype of depression. *Psychological Review, 96*, 358–372.

Abramson, L. Y., Seligman, M. E. P., & Teasdale, J. D. (1978). Learned helplessness in humans: Critique and reformulation. *Journal of Abnormal Psychology, 87*, 49–74.

Agency for Health Care Policy and Research, U.S. Public Health Service. (1993). *Clinical Practice Guideline Number 5. Depression in Primary Care: Volume 2. Treatment of Major Depression.* Rockville, MD: Author.

Aitken, R. C. B. (1969). Measurement of feelings using visual analogue scales. *Proceedings of the Royal Society of Medicine, 62*, 989–993.

Alloy, L. B., Albright, J. S., Fresco, D. M., & Whitehouse, W. G. (1995) *Stability of cognitive styles across the mood swings of DSM-III cyclothymics, dysthymics, and hypomanics: A longitudinal study in college students.* Unpublished manuscript, Temple University, Philadelphia.

Alloy, L. B., Kayne, N. T., Romer, D., & Crocker, J. (1995) *Predicting depression and elation reactions in the classroom: A test of an attributional diathesis-stress theory of depression.* Manuscript under review, Temple University, Philadelphia.

American Psychiatric Association. (1987). *Diagnostic and statistical manual of mental disorders* (3rd ed., rev.). Washington, DC: Author.

American Psychiatric Association. (1993). Practice guideline for Major Depressive Disorder in adults. *The American Journal of Psychiatry, 150*, Supplement.

American Psychiatric Association. (1994). *Diagnostic and statistical manual of mental disorders* (4th ed.). Washington, DC: Author.

Barlow, D. H., Hayes, S. C., & Nelson, R. O. (1984). *The scientist-practitioner: Research and accountability in clinical and educational settings.* New York: Pergamon.

Barnett, P. A., & Gotlib, I. H. (1988). Psychosocial functioning and depression: Distinguishing among antecedents, concomitants, and consequences. *Psychological Bulletin, 104*, 97–126.

Beck, A. T. (1967). *Depression: Clinical, experimental, and theoretical aspects.* New York: Hoeber.

Beck, A. T. (1976). *Cognitive therapy and the emotional disorders.* New York: International Universities Press.

Beck, A. T. (1983). Cognitive therapy of depression: New Perspectives. In P. J. Clayton & J. E. Barrett (Eds.), *Treatment of depression: Old controversies and new approaches* (pp. 265–290). New York: Raven.

Beck, A. T., & Beck, R. W. (1972). Screening depressed patients in family practice: A rapid technique. *Postgraduate Medicine, 52*, 81–85.

Beck, A. T., Epstein, N., Harrison, R., & Emery, G. (1983) *Development of the Sociotropy-Autonomy Scale: A measure of personality factors in psychopathology.* Unpublished manuscript, University of Pennsylvania.

Beck, A. T., Kovacs, M., & Weissman, A. (1979). Assessment of suicidal intention: The Scale for Suicide Ideation. *Journal of Consulting and Clinical Psychology, 47*, 343–352.

Beck, A. T., Rush, A. J., Shaw, B. F., & Emery, G. (1979). *Cognitive therapy of depression.* New York: Guilford.

Beck, A. T., Steer, R. A., & Garbin, M. G. (1988). Psychometric properties of the Beck Depression Inventory: Twenty-five years of evaluation. *Clinical Psychology Review, 8*, 77–100.

Beck, A. T., Steer, R. A., Kovacs, M., & Garrison, B. (1985). Hopelessness and eventual suicide: A 10-year prospective study of patients hospitalized with suicidal ideation. *American Journal of Psychiatry, 142*, 559–563.

Beck, A. T., Ward, C. H., Mendelson, M., Mock, J., & Erbaugh, J. (1961). An inventory for measuring depression. *Archives of General Psychiatry, 4*, 53–63.

Beck, A. T., Weissman, A., Lester, D., & Trexler, L. (1974). The measurement of pessimism: The Hopelessness Scale. *Journal of Consulting and Clinical Psychology, 42,* 861–865.

Boyd, J. H., Weissman, M. M., Thompson, W. D., & Myers, J. K. (1982). Screening for depression in a community sample: Understanding the discrepancies between depression syndrome and diagnostic scales. *Archives of General Psychiatry, 39,* 1195–1200.

Brown, G. W., Bifulco, A., & Harris, T. O. (1987). Life events, vulnerability and onset of depression: Some refinements. *British Journal of Psychiatry, 150.*

Brown, G. W., Bifulco, A., Harris, T., & Bridge, L. (1986). Life stress, chronic subclinical symptoms and vulnerability to clinical depression. *Journal of Affective Disorders, 11,* 1–19.

Brown, G. W., & Harris, T. (1978). *Social origins of depression.* New York: The Free Press.

Brown, G. W., Harris, T. O., & Peto, J. (1973). Life events and psychiatric disorders: II. Nature of causal link. *Psychological Medicine, 3,* 159–176.

Brown, T. A., Di Nardo, P. A., & Barlow, D. H. (1994). *Anxiety Disorders Interview Schedule for DSM-IV: (ADIS-IV).* Albany, NY: Graywind.

Burgess, E., & Haaga, D. A. F. (1994). The Positive Automatic Thoughts Questionnaire (ATQ-P) and the Automatic Thoughts Questionnaire–Revised (ATQ–RP): Equivalent measures of positive thinking. *Cognitive Therapy & Research, 18,* 15–23.

Burns, D. D. (1980). *Feeling good: The new mood therapy.* New York: William Morrow.

Cane, D. B., Olinger, L. J., Gotlib, I. H., & Kuiper, N. A. (1986). Factor structure of the Dysfunctional Attitude Scale in a student population. *Journal of Clinical Psychology, 42,* 307–309.

Cho, M. J., Moscicki, E. K., Narrow, W. E., & Rae, D. S. (1993). Concordance between two measures of depression in the Hispanic Health and Nutrition Examination Survey. *Social Psychiatry & Psychiatric Epidemiology, 28,* 156–163.

Clark, D. A., & Beck, A. T. (1991). Personality factors in dysphoria: A psychometric refinement of Beck's Sociotropy-Autonomy Scale. *Journal of Psychopathology & Behavioral Assessment, 13,* 369–388.

Cone, J. D. (1986). Idiographic, nomothetic, and related perspectives in behavioral assessment. In R. O. Nelson & S. C. Hayes (Eds.), *Conceptual foundations of behavioral assessment* (pp. 111–128). New York: Guilford.

Corcoran, K., & Fischer, J. (1987). *Measures for clinical practice: A sourcebook.* New York: Free Press.

Coyne, J. C. (1976a). Depression and the response of others. *Dissertation Abstracts International, 36,* 5785.

Coyne, J. C. (1976b). Toward an interactional description of depression. *Psychiatry, 39,* 28–40.

Coyne, J. C., & Gotlib, I. H. (1983). The role of cognition in depression: A critical appraisal. *Psychological Bulletin, 94,* 472–505.

DeRubeis, R. J., Evans, M. D., Hollon, S. D., Garvey, M. J., Grove, W. M., & Tuason, V. B. (1990). How does cognitive therapy work? Cognitive change and symptom change in cognitive therapy and pharmacotherapy for depression. *Journal of Consulting & Clinical Psychology, 58,* 862–869.

Di Nardo, P. A., Brown, T. A., & Barlow, D. H. (1994). *Anxiety Disorders Interview Schedule for DSM-IV: Lifetime Version (ADIS-IV-L).* Albany, NY: Graywind.

Di Nardo, P. A., Moras, K., Barlow, D. H., Rapee, R. M., & Brown, T. A. (1993). Reliability of DSM-IIIR anxiety disorder categories using the Anxiety Disorders Interview Schedule-Revised. *Archives of General Psychiatry, 50,* 251–256.

Dobson, K. S., & Breiter, H. J. (1983). Cognitive assessment of depression: Reliability and validity of three measures. *Journal of Abnormal Psychology, 92,* 107–109.

Endicott, J., & Spitzer, R. L. (1978). A diagnostic interview: The schedule for affective disorders and schizophrenia. *Archives of General Psychiatry, 35,* 837–844.

Evans, I. M. (1993). Constructional perspectives in clinical assessment. *Psychological Assessment, 5,* 264–272.

Ferster, C. B., & Skinner, B. F. (1957). *Schedules of reinforcement.* New York: Appleton-Century-Crofts.

First, M. B., Gibbon, M., Spitzer, R. L., & Williams, J. B. W. (1995). *User's Guide for the Structured Clinical Interview for DSM-IV Axis I Disorders.* New York: Biometrics Research.

First, M. B., Spitzer, R. L., Gibbon, M., & Williams, J. B. W. (1995). Structured CLinical Interview for DSM-IV Axis I Disorders—Patient Edition (SCID-I/P, Version 2.0). New York: Biometrics Research Department, New York State Psychiatric Institute.

Fresco, D. M., Craighead, L. W., & Koons, A. N. (1994a, November). *A comparison of two techniques for measuring attributional style: How the ASQ and the CAVE relate to each other and to depression.* A poster presented at the annual meeting of the Association for the Advancement of Behavior Therapy, San Diego.

Fresco, D. M., Craighead, L. W., & Koons, A. N. (1994b, September). *Two approaches to the comorbidity of depression and anxiety: Comparing attributional style to sociotropy and autonomy.* A poster presented at the annual meeting of the Society for Research in Psychopathology, Coral Gables.

Fresco, D. M., Craighead, L. W., Sampson, W. S., Watt, N. & Koons, A. N. (1995, November). The Content Analysis of Verbatim Explanations technique: Applications within psychopathology research and therapy process. In D. M. Fresco & S. L. Sayers (Chairs), *Beyond the questionnaire: Broadening the behavioral and cognitive sciences with content analysis techniques*. A paper presented at the annual meeting of the Association for the Advancement of Behavior Therapy, Washington, DC.

Gambrill, E. D., & Richey, C. A. (1975). An assertion inventory for use in assessment and research. *Behavior Therapy, 6,* 550–561.

Garrison, C. Z., Addy, C. L., Jackson, K. L., & McKeown, R. E. (1991). The CES-D as a screen for depression and other psychiatric disorders in adolescents. *Journal of the American Academy of Child & Adolescent Psychiatry, 30,* 636–641.

Gotlib, I. H., & Robinson, L. A. (1982). Responses to depressed individuals: Discrepancies between self-report and observer-rated behavior. *Journal of Abnormal Psychology, 91,* 231–240.

Hamilton, M. (1960). A rating scale for depression. *Journal of Neurology, Neurosurgery, and Psychiatry, 23,* 56–62.

Hammen, C., Ellicott, A., & Gitlin, M. J. (1992). Stressors and sociotropy/autonomy: A longitudinal study of their relationship to the course of bipolar disorder. Special Issue: Cognitive vulnerability to psychological dysfunction. *Cognitive Therapy & Research, 16,* 409–418.

Hathaway, S. R., & McKinley, J. C. (1942). A multiphasic personality schedule (Minnesota): III. The measurement of symptomatic depression. *Journal of Psychology, 14,* 73–84.

Hathaway, S. R., & McKinley, J. C. (1951). *MMPI manual* (rev. ed.). New York: Psychological Corp.

Hayes, S. C., Nelson, R. O., & Jarrett, R. B. (1987). The treatment utility of assessment: A functional approach to evaluating assessment quality. *American Psychologist, 42,* 963–974.

Haynes, S. N. (1992). *Models of causality in psychopathology: Toward dynamic, synthetic and nonlinear models of behavior disorders*. New York: Macmillan.

Haynes, S. N., & O'Brien, W. H. (1990). Functional analysis in behavior therapy. *Clinical Psychology Review, 10,* 649–668.

Hill, C. V., Oei, T. P., & Hill, M. A. (1989). An empirical investigation of the specificity and sensitivity of the Automatic Thoughts Questionnaire and Dysfunctional Attitudes Scale. *Journal of Psychopathology & Behavioral Assessment, 11,* 291–311.

Hollon, S. D., & Kendall, P. C. (1980). Cognitive self-statements in depression: Development of an automatic thoughts questionnaire. *Cognitive Therapy & Research, 4,* 383–395.

Hollon, S. D., Kendall, P. C., & Lumry, A. (1986). Specificity of depressotypic cognitions in clinical depression. *Journal of Abnormal Psychology, 95,* 52–59.

Holmes, T. H., & Rahe, R. H. (1967). The Social Readjustment Rating Scale. *Journal of Psychosomatic Research, 11,* 213–218.

Ingram, R. E., Slater, M. A., Atkinson, J. H., & Scott, W. (1990). Positive automatic cognition in major affective disorder. *Psychological Assessment, 2,* 209–211.

Ingram, R. E., & Wisnicki, K. S. (1988). Assessment of positive automatic cognition. *Journal of Consulting & Clinical Psychology, 56,* 898–902.

Joiner, T. E., Alfano, M. S., & Metalsky, G. I. (1992). When depression breeds contempt: Reassurance seeking, self-esteem, and rejection of depressed college students by their roommates. *Journal of Abnormal Psychology, 101,* 165–173.

Kanner, R. D., Coyne, J. C., Shaeffer, C., & Lazarus, R. J. (1981). Comparison of two modes of stress management: Daily hassles and uplifts versus major life events. *Journal of Behavioral Medicine, 4,* 1–39.

Kazdin, A. E. (1974). Self-monitoring and behavior change. In M. J. Mahoney & C. E. Thoresen (Eds.), *Self-control: Power to the person*. Monterey, CA: Brooks/Cole.

Kazdin, A. E. (1993). Evaluation in clinical practice: Clinically sensitive and systematic methods of treatment delivery. *Behavior Therapy, 24,* 11–45.

Kiresuk, T. J., & Sherman, R. E. (1968). Goal Attainment Scaling: A general method for evaluating comprehensive community mental health programs. *Community Mental Health Journal, 4,* 443–453.

Kohlenberg, R. J., & Tsai, M. (1991). *Functional analytic psychotherapy: Creating intense and curative therapeutic relationships*. New York: Plenum.

Kulka, R. A., Schlenger, W. E., Fairbank, J. A., Hough, R. L., Jordon, B. K., Marmar, C. R., Weiss, D. S., & Grady, D. A. (1990). *Trauma and the Vietnam War Generation: Report of findings from the National Vietnam Veterans Readjustment Study: Bruner/Mazel Psychosocial Stress Series No. 18*. New York: Bruner/Mazel.

Lewinsohn, P. M. (1974a). A behavioral approach to depression. In R. J. Friedman & M. M. Katz (Eds.), *The psychology of depression: Contemporary theory and research.* New York: Wiley.

Lewinsohn, P. M. (1974b). Clinical and theoretical aspects of depression. In K. S. Calhoun, H. E. Adams, & K. M. Mitchell (Eds.), *Innovative treatment methods of psychopathology.* New York: Wiley.

Lewinsohn, P. M., Muñoz, R. F., Youngren, M. A., & Zeiss, A. M. (1978). *Control your depression.* Englewood Cliffs, NJ: Prentice-Hall.

Lewinsohn, P. M., Sullivan, J. M., & Grosscup, S. J. (1980). Changing reinforcing events: An approach to the treatment of depression. *Psychotherapy: Theory, Research & Practice, 17,* 322–334.

Linehan, M. M. (1981). A social-behavioral analysis of suicide and parasuicide: Implications for clinical assessment and treatment. In H. Glazer & J. Clarkin (Eds.), *Depression: Behavioral and directive intervention strategies* (pp. 229–294). New York: Brunner/Mazel.

Linehan, M. M. (1993). *Cognitive-behavioral treatment of borderline personality disorder.* New York: Guilford.

Mahard, R. E. (1988). The CES-D as a measure of depressive mood in the elderly Puerto Rican population. *Journals of Gerontology, 43,* 24.

Metalsky, G. I., Halberstadt, L. J., & Abramson, L. Y. (1987). Vulnerability to depressive mood reactions: Toward a more powerful test of the diathesis-stress and causal mediation components of the reformulated theory of depression. *Journal of Personality and Social Psychology, 52,* 386–393.

Metalsky, G. I., & Joiner, T. E. (1992). Vulnerability to depressive symptomatology: A prospective test of the diathesis-stress and causal mediation components of the hopelessness theory of depression. *Journal of Personality & Social Psychology, 63,* 667–675.

Mintz, J., & Kiesler, D. J. (1982). Individualized measures of psychotherapy outcome. In P. C. Kendall & J. N. Butcher (Eds.), *Handbook of research methods in clinical psychology* (pp. 491–534). New York: Wiley.

Monroe, S. M. (1982a). Assessment of life events: Retrospective vs. concurrent strategies. *Archives of General Psychiatry, 39,* 606–610.

Monroe, S. M. (1982b). Life events assessment: Current practices, emerging trends. *Clinical Psychology Review, 2,* 435–453.

Monroe, S. M. (1983). Major and minor life events as predictors of psychological distress: Further issues and findings. *Journal of Behavioral Medicine, 6,* 189–205.

Monroe, S. M., & Roberts, J. E. (1990). Conceptualizing and measuring life stress: Problems, principles, procedures, progress. Special Issue: II–IV. Advances in measuring life stress. *Stress Medicine, 6,* 209–216.

Monroe, S. M., & Simons, A. D. (1991). Diathesis-stress theories in the context of life stress research: Implications for the depressive disorders. *Psychological Bulletin, 110,* 406–425.

Nezu, A. M., & Nezu, C. M. (1993). Identifying and selecting target problems for clinical interventions: A problem-solving model. *Psychological Assessment, 5,* 254–263.

Orme, J. G., Reis, J., & Herz, E. J. (1986). Factorial and discrimanant validity of the Center for Epidemiological Studies Depression (CES-D) scale. *Journal of Clinical Psychology, 42,* 28–33.

Persons, J. B. (1989). *Cognitive therapy in practice: A case formulation approach.* New York: Norton.

Persons, J. B. (1992). The patient with multiple problems. In A. Freeman & F. Dattilio (Eds.), *Casebook of cognitive-behavior therapy* (pp. 241–247). New York: Plenum.

Persons, J. B., & Burns, D. D. (1985). Mechanisms of action of cognitive therapy: The relative contributions of technical and interpersonal interventions. *Cognitive Therapy and Research, 9,* 539–551.

Persons, J. B., Burns, D. D., Perloff, J. M., & Miranda, J. (1993). Relationships between symptoms of depression and anxiety and dysfunctional beliefs about achievement and attachment. *Journal of Abnormal Psychology, 102,* 518–524.

Persons, J. B., & Miranda, J. (1992). Cognitive theories of vulnerability to depression: Reconciling negative evidence. *Cognitive Therapy and Research, 16,* 485–502.

Persons, J. B., Miranda, J., & Perloff, J. M. (1991). Relationships between depressive symptoms and cognitive vulnerabilities of achievement and dependency. *Cognitive Therapy & Research, 15,* 221–235.

Peterson, C. (1992). Explanatory style. In C. P. Smith (Eds.), *Handbook of thematic content analysis* (pp. 376–382). New York: Cambridge University Press.

Peterson, C., Bettes, B. A., & Seligman, M. E. (1985). Depressive symptoms and unprompted causal attributions: Content analysis. *Behaviour Research & Therapy, 23,* 379–382.

Peterson, C., Luborsky, L., & Seligman, M. E. (1983). Attributions and depressive mood shifts: A case study using the symptom-context model. *Journal of*

Abnormal Psychology, 92, 96–103.

Peterson, C., Schulman, P., Castellon, C., & Seligman, M. E. P. (1992). The explanatory style scoring manual. In C. P. Smith (Eds.), *Handbook of thematic content analysis* (pp. 383–392). New York: Cambridge University Press.

Peterson, C., & Seligman, M. E. P. (1984) *Content analysis of verbatim explanations: The CAVE technique for assessing explanatory style*. Unpublished manuscript, University of Pennsylvania.

Peterson, C., Semmel, A., von Baeyer, C., Abramson, L. Y., Metalsky, G. I., & Seligman, M. E. P. (1982). The Attributional Style Questionnaire. *Cognitive Therapy & Research, 6*, 287–300.

Peterson, C., & Villanova, P. (1988). An Expanded Attributional Style Questionnaire. *Journal of Abnormal Psychology, 97*, 87–89.

Piotrowski, C., Sherry, D., & Keller, J. W. (1985). Psychodiagnostic test usage: A survey of the Society for Personality Assessment. *Journal of Personality Assessment, 49*, 115–119.

Radloff, L. S. (1977). The CES-D Scale: A self-report depression scale for research in the general population. *Applied Psychological Measurement, 1*, 385–401.

Rehm, L. P. (1988). Assessment of depression. In A. S. Bellack & M. Hersen (Eds.), *Behavioral assessment: A practical guide* (pp. 313–364). New York: Pergamon.

Roberts, R. E., & Vernon, S. W. (1983). The Center for Epidemiological Studies Depression Scale: Its use in a community sample. *American Journal of Psychiatry, 140*, 41–46.

Robins, C. J. (1988). Attributions and depression: Why is the literature so inconsistent? *Journal of Personality & Social Psychology, 54*, 880–889.

Robins, C. J. (1990). Congruence of personality and life events in depression. *Journal of Abnormal Psychology, 99*, 393–397.

Robins, C. J., & Block, P. (1988). Personal vulnerability, life events, and depressive symptoms: A test of a specific interactional model. *Journal of Personality & Social Psychology, 54*, 847–852.

Robins, C. J., Hayes, A. M., Block, P., & Kramer, R. J. (1995). Interpersonal and achievement concerns and the depressive vulnerability and symptom specificity hypotheses: A prospective study. *Cognitive Therapy & Research, 19*, 1–20.

Robins, C. J., Ladd, J., Welkowitz, J., Blaney, P. H., Diaz, R., & Kutcher, G. (1993). *The Personal Style Inventory: Preliminary validation studies of new measures of sociotropy and autonomy*. Unpub-

lished manuscript, Duke University Medical Center, Durham, NC.

Robins, C. J., & Luten, A. G. (1991). Sociotropy and autonomy: Differential patterns of clinical presentation in unipolar depression. *Journal of Abnormal Psychology, 100*, 74–77.

Robins, L. N., Helzer, J. E., Croughan, J. L., & Ratcliff, K. S. (1981). National Institute of Mental Health diagnostic interview schedule: Its history, characteristics, and validity. *Archives of General Psychiatry, 38*, 381–389.

Rude, S. S., & Burnham, B. L. (1993). Do interpersonal and achievement vulnerabilities interact with congruent events to predict depression? Comparison of DEQ, SAS, DAS, and combined scales. *Cognitive Therapy & Research, 17*, 531–548.

Sarason, I. G., Johnson, J. H., & Siegel, J. M. (1978). Assessing the impact of life changes: Development of the Life Experiences Survey. *Journal of Consulting and Clinical Psychology, 46*, 932–946.

Schulman, P., Castellon, C., & Seligman, M. E. (1989). Assessing explanatory style: The content analysis of verbatim explanations and the Attributional Style Questionnaire. *Behaviour Research and Therapy, 27*, 505–512.

Seligman, M. E., Abramson, L. Y., Semmel, A., & von Baeyer, C. (1979). Depressive attributional style. *Journal of Abnormal Psychology, 88*, 242–247.

Seligman, M. E. P. (1975). *Helplessness: On depression, development, and death*. San Francisco: W. H. Freeman.

Spitzer, R. L., Williams, J. B., Gibbon, M., & First, M. B. (1992). The Structured Clinical Interview for DSM-III-R (SCID). I: History, rationale, and description. *Archives of General Psychiatry, 49*, 624–629.

Steer, R. A., Beck, A. T., & Garrison, B. (1986). Applications of the Beck Depression Inventory. In N. Sartorius & T. A. Ban (Eds.), *Assessment of depression* (pp. 121–142). Geneva: World Health Organization.

Surber, R. W. (Ed.). (1994). *Clinical case management: A guide to comprehensive treatment of serious mental illness*. Thousand Oaks, CA: Sage.

Sweeney, P. D., Anderson, K., & Bailey, S. (1986). Attributional style in depression: A meta-analytic review. *Journal of Personality & Social Psychology, 50*, 974–991.

Thoresen, C. E., & Mahoney, M. J. (1974). *Behavioral self-control*. New York: Holt, Rinehart and Winston.

Turkat, I. D. (Ed.). (1985). *Behavioral case formulation*. New York: Plenum.

Watson, D. (1988). Intraindividual and interindividual analyses of positive and negative affect: Their relation to health complaints, perceived stress, and daily activities. *Journal of Personality & Social Psychology, 54,* 1020–1030.

Watson, D., Clark, L. A., & Carey, G. (1988). Positive and negative affectivity and their relation to anxiety and depressive disorders. *Journal of Abnormal Psychology, 97,* 346–353.

Watson, D., Clark, L. A., & Tellegen, A. (1988). Development and validation of brief measures of positive and negative affect: The PANAS scales. *Journal of Personality & Social Psychology, 54,* 1063–1070.

Weissman, A., & Beck, A. T. (1978, November). *Development and validation of the dysfunctional attitudes scale.* A paper presented at the annual meeting of the Association for the Advancement of Behavior Therapy, Chicago.

Wilson, G. T., & O'Leary, K. D. (1980). *Principles of behavior therapy.* Englewood Cliffs, NJ: Prentice-Hall.

Youngren, M. A., & Lewinsohn, P. M. (1980). The functional relation between depression and problematic interpersonal behavior. *Journal of Abnormal Psychology, 89,* 333–341.

Zuckerman, M., & Lubin, B. (1965). *Manual for the multiple affective adjective checklist.* San Diego: Educational and Industrial Testing Service.

Zuckerman, M., Lubin, B., & Rinck, C. M. (1983). Construction of new scales for the Multiple Affect Adjective Check List. *Journal of Behavioral Assessment, 5,* 119–129.

Zung, W. W. K. (1965). A self-rating depression scale. *Archives of General Psychiatry, 12,* 63–70.

CHAPTER 11

ASSESSMENT OF SOCIAL SKILLS

Valerie J. Meier
Debra A. Hope
University of Nebraska–Lincoln

Difficulties in social interactions are common among those who seek mental health services. Therefore, it is not surprising that hypothesized deficits in social skills have been associated with many psychosexual problems, including depression, chemical dependency, schizophrenia, social phobia, personality disorders, sexual dysfunction, marital discord, excessive anger, and developmental disabilities. Skills deficits have been attributed to the lack of appropriately skilled models, cognitive deficits, and even innate potential (Trower, Bryant, Argyle, & Marziller, 1978). Regardless of the specific etiology, difficulties in social interactions are presumed to result in difficulties in interpersonal relationships and thus lead to lower levels of psychological adjustment and functioning.

The topic of social skills began to receive considerable attention during the 1970s. Theories, observational procedures, and measurement scales were developed and tested. Many of these original works continue to dominate the field of social skills. This chapter will review these original works as well as more recently developed theories

and methods. In addition, specific methods for assessing social skills will be reviewed. These methods include clinical interviews, self-monitoring, behavioral observation, and self-report questionnaires. A clinical case summary will be used to demonstrate how these methods may be applied in research or clinical settings.

DEFINING SOCIAL SKILLS

The first task facing the clinician or researcher who wishes to assess social skills is to define exactly what is meant by *social skills*. Twenty-five years of research have revealed this task is more difficult than it first appears. In 1980, veteran social skills expert Curran and his colleague (Curran & Mariotto, 1980) stated, "We seem to have less trouble changing social skills than defining and measuring them. . . . Everyone is going around conducting social skills training while no one seems to agree upon just what it is we are training or how we should measure it" (p. 2). In the previous edition of this volume, Becker and Heimberg (1988) declined to define the central construct in their chapter on assessment of social skills. As will be seen here, each of the primary theoretical models in the area offer somewhat different conceptualizations of "social skills," suggesting little consensus exists even now.

Liberman's Theory of Social Skills

Liberman (1982) defined social skills as "the everyday conversations, encounters, and relationships that people have with each other. Social skills include the ability to give and obtain information, and to express and exchange attitudes, opinions, and feelings. Thus, a major function of social skills is to subserve interpersonal interactions" (p. 63). According to Liberman, most interpersonal interactions can be categorized as instrumental or social-emotional based on their functions. Within the *instrumental* category are those skills required for gaining information or services in order to satisfy one's physical, material, and financial well-being. For example, returning a purchased item, asking a physician questions about illness and medications, and asking for directions represent instrumental interactions. *Social-emotional* interactions are those that serve to initiate and maintain relationships. Asking another how he or she feels, sharing feelings with another, and engaging in small talk are types of social-emotional interactions.

According to Liberman (1982), social skills can be considered from three perspectives: topographical, functional, and information processing. The *topographical* approach represents the traditional approach to social skills, in that it emphasizes specific verbal and nonverbal behaviors, such as duration of speech, smiling, eye contact, and posture. In contrast, the *functional* view defines social skills in terms of the outcome of social interactions. Thus, if a person is able to satisfy material, physical, and social needs without violating the rights of others, he or she is considered to be socially skilled. The *information-processing* model of social skills assessment emphasizes an individual's ability to attend to, receive, and process cues from others (gestures, facial expression, etc.), generate alternative responses, decide on a response, and then implement it. Thus, this view takes a more cognitive

approach to understanding socially skilled behavior. Information processing influences behavior that may itself be viewed topographically or functionally. Taken together, these three categories provide a multidimensional assessment of social skills.

Trower's Theory of Social Skills

An alternative information-processing approach was proposed by Trower and colleagues (1978), who describe a socially unskilled person as one who appears "annoying, unforthcoming, uninteresting, cold, destructive, bad-tempered, isolated or inept, and . . . generally unrewarding to others" (p. 2). According to their social skills model, individuals are motivated by social goals—to make friends, to exchange information, and so on. The achievement of social goals provides affiliation, achievement, and other positive reinforcers. Complex sequences of interpersonal behavior are believed to be consciously planned, whereas shorter simpler sequences or behaviors are viewed as habitual in nature.

In social situations, according to Trower and colleagues (1978), the individual must perceive and attend to cues from others, including facial expressions, posture, and voice tone. Based on these perceptions and the individual's own unique motives and goals, alternative actions are generated, decided on, and acted out motorically. Throughout the whole process, a feedback system is in operation, continually evaluating the effect of executed behaviors on other people and making changes in that behavior based on its findings. Deficits in social skills may occur at any part of this process. When either the goals or the plans are absent, contradictory, or suppressed for some reason (i.e., psychopathology, learning history), a disturbance in social skill results. Difficulties may also arise when the individual misperceives cues from the environment. Additional sources of social skill deficits include faulty translation processes (inadequate ability to generate alternatives and decide among them), limited motor responses (facial expression, voice volume, tone, etc.), and an unrealistic or faulty feedback system.

Defining what one means by social skills is important because the definition will influence choices about assessment and intervention procedures. For example, if one believes that poor or insufficient motor responses are at the basis of social skills difficulties, then a topographical approach will be taken. Assessment will focus on specific behaviors (e.g., eye contact, gesturing), and training will involve instruction and practice in carrying out an appropriate level of such behaviors. If one believes that social skills are defined by their instrumental or social-emotional function, assessment will focus on the outcome of social interactions. Subsequent social skills training will emphasize socially appropriate means of obtaining desired outcomes. Finally, if one takes the information-processing approach, assessment and training will include one's perception of events, one's ability to generate and choose from alternatives, and one's specific behavior in social situations. This chapter will review techniques that are applicable to all of these differing approaches to social skills assessment. Before continuing, however, it is necessary to make a distinction between competence and social skill.

Competence versus Skill

McFall (1982) emphasized the importance of distinguishing between social competence and social skill. *Competence* refers to an evaluation of the quality or adequacy of a person's performance in a particular task. Thus, a person is said to have performed competently if the performance has been judged so on the basis of someone's criteria. Because competency is an evaluative judgment, it is subject to error and bias on the part of the judge. In addition, evaluations of competence may be influenced by the characteristics of the performer (e.g., age, gender, ethnicity). Even so, judgments of competency imply performance consistency. If a person is judged to perform competently at a task, it is likely he or she will perform competently at that same task in the future. *Skill*, on the other hand, refers to the specific abilities necessary to perform competently. A person who performs incompetently may have either a limited number of skills in his or her behavioral repertoire or possess skills that are not adequate for a competent performance.

Trait Model versus Situational Specificity

Social skills have been considered by some to represent trait-like dispositions to behave in relatively stable patterns across a variety of situations. According to this trait model, social behavior is cross-situational. That is, an individual's behavior in one situation is believed to be similar to his or her behavior in a similar situation. However, evidence has been accruing that supports a situationally specific view of social skill that contends that social behavior consists of specific, learned responses in specific situations. While an individual may perform in a particular way in one situation, it is not assumed that his or her behavior will be similar in another. For example, Eisler, Hersen, Miller, and Blanchard (1975) found that subject responses differed depending on the gender of the role-play partner. When the partner was male, male subjects complied with requests. However, when the partner was female, male subjects were more likely to ask their female partners to change their behavior.

The situationally specific view of social skill has been emphasized in the behavioral model. However, even behaviorists may inadvertently support the trait model. McFall (1982) argues that the cross-situational assumption is evident in the emphasis on total scores for many social skills assessment questionnaires. Furthermore, if the trait model of social skills is valid, contends McFall (1982), then measures of social skill should possess certain psychometric properties. Specifically, individual items should be highly correlated with each other as well as highly correlated with the total score, questionnaires should exhibit good split-half and test-retest reliability, measures should be amenable to factor analysis, and scores should predict a subject's performance in the natural environment. Although McFall argues that this has not been the case, other researchers report reasonably good psychometric properties in these scales (Beck & Heimberg, 1983).

Although some evidence supports the trait model of social skills, a good behaviorist cannot assume that a client's behavior will remain the same from one situation to the next. Client factors (e.g., fatigue, motivation) and situational factors (e.g., time of day, relationship to the other people present) will combine to differentially affect a client's behavior from one context to the next. For example, a client may be more willing to say no to family members than to employers in general, but in the right circumstances may decline employers as well.

Comment

Although differences in the conceptualization and definition of social skills exist, commonalities are apparent. Researchers and theorists alike tend to agree that social skill is comprised of a group of behaviors that enable an individual to effectively engage in, maintain, and succeed in social interactions. These behaviors include the expression of both positive and negative emotions; facial expressions; the tone, volume, and speed of verbal expressions; posture; and appropriate content (Eisler, Miller, & Hersen, 1973; Hargie, Saunders, & Dickson, 1994; Wolpe & Lazarus, 1966).

Factors operating within an environment may serve to elicit or maintain problematic behaviors. As a result, behavior may change from one environment to another. Thus, a behavioral approach to social skills assessment, like any behavioral analysis, will emphasize the situationally specific nature of social skill. The assessment techniques described in this chapter are based on the assumption of situational specificity.

ASSESSING SOCIAL SKILLS

Assessing social skills can be a complex and confusing process. Most clients present to mental health professionals reporting problems with relationships, depression, and/or anxiety. Only occasionally do clients arrive at a clinician's office complaining of deficits in social skills. Many clients are unaware that improvements in their social skills might positively affect their overall functioning. Therefore, it is incumbent on the clinician to consider whether a client's social skills might be insufficient to meet the demands of his or her daily life.

Several cues should prompt further assessment of social skills.

1. The clinician may develop a subjective impression that the client's interpersonal behavior is inappropriate or awkward during initial telephone and face-to-face contact. For example, the clinician may notice that the client frequently interrupts him or her, makes too little or too much eye contact, self-discloses excessively for a first session, speaks only if asked a direct question, or displays overly aggressive or unassertive behavior. However, interacting with a clinician is a novel, sometimes threatening, situation for many people. Thus, the clinician must be careful not to overinterpret problematic behavior without further assessment.

2. The clinician may notice that interactions with the receptionists, family members, or other clients in the waiting area are awkward or problematic.

3. Further assessment of social skills should be considered if the client reports difficulties in interpersonal relationships with their family, co-workers, supervisors, and neighbors, among others.

As noted above, in these situations, the client may not directly indicate a lack of skill but instead may be distressed about the outcome of such interactions (e.g., Liberman's "functional" approach).

Before continuing, it is important to acknowledge a distinction that has traditionally been made between a social skills deficit and a performance deficit. A *skills deficit* is believed to be present if a client does not possess the skills necessary for successful social interactions. In other words, the client with a skills deficit does not have the behavioral repertoire required for socially skillful behavior. A *performance deficit* is believed to exist when a client possesses the skills necessary for successful interactions but is inhibited from performing adequately in certain situations. Any number of factors may inhibit socially skilled behavior, including expectations of negative consequences, anxiety, and past punishment, among others.

The distinction between skills and performance deficits is plausible from a strictly behavioral perspective. However, as noted earlier, contemporary theories of social skill include a cognitive perspective. For example, anxiety may inhibit skilled performance. If such anxiety occurs as a result of biased information processing, as is the case with many social phobics (Hope, Rapee, Heimberg, & Dombeck, 1990), then the poor performance would be considered a cognitive skills deficit per Liberman and Trower's theories, as described earlier.

In addition, a client's skilled performance may be inhibited due to factors other than cognitive skills. For example, a battered woman may choose not to assert herself because she has learned that such behavior results in negative consequences (e.g., a beating). If her lack of assertion occurs only in the presence of the abusive partner, a skills deficit does not exist. In this case, the "performance deficit" is really not a deficit at all. Instead, the behavioral inhibition is quite skilled in that it is a learned response to a potentially dangerous situation. However, if her unassertiveness generalizes to nonthreatening individuals, then a skills deficit is evident.

Clearly, understanding complexities of a client's dysfunction in social situations represents a complex process. The clinician needs to consider potential cognitive biases and environmental contingencies as well as more traditional notions of social skill (e.g., poor eye contact, inappropriate self-disclosure) that may influence social performance. However, we will focus primarily on the behavioral skills that are often best remediated with social skills training (e.g., Stravynski, Marks, & Yule, 1982).

The behavioral approach to assessment of social skill involves observing the client's overt behavior as well as measuring his or her subjective experience. It is generally recommended that the assessment battery include, at a minimum, a clinical interview and an observational assessment. In addition, self-monitoring assignments and self-report questionnaires may provide useful information to the clinician. Each of these assessment methods will be reviewed in detail.

Clinical Interviews

If the clinician decides, based on his or her impressions and observations of a client, that a social skills assessment should be completed, the first step in that assessment process is a targeted clinical interview. A general outline for such an interview appears in Figure 11.1 The primary purpose of this interview is to identify situations in which the client experiences difficulty. Other assessment procedures, particularly behavioral observation, can then be used to determine the exact nature of the difficulties once the situations have been identified. The clinical interview also provides an analysis of the contingencies operating in the client's environment that may serve to maintain problematic behaviors (see Chapter 4 in this book for further information). As in nearly any clinical situation, an atmosphere of warmth and empathy will facilitate self-disclosure and allow the client to describe interactions that may have been embarrassing or humiliating.

The clinical interview should begin with a history of the client's social activity and functioning. This history serves two primary purposes. First, understanding how a client's social functioning may have changed (or not changed) over time helps identify important environmental influences and may yield clues about the specific deficits. For example, someone with poor assertiveness skills may initially function adequately in a new work situation; however, interpersonal difficulties may develop later as the person resents completing duties outside of assigned job responsibilities but has been unable to decline requests for extra work. Second, gathering information about childhood and adolescent socialization may yield information about whether the individual achieved normal developmental milestones, such as dating in high school. Understanding the extent and chronicity of interpersonal difficulties early in life may suggest whether basic social skills (e.g., choosing appropriate conversation topics) were never part of the person's repertoire or whether such skills were previously available but are currently inhibited for some reason.

The history of social functioning should emphasize the number and types of friendships and romantic relationships in childhood, adolescence, and adulthood; the nature and closeness of these relationships; and involvement in structured social activities such as sports or clubs. The historical portion of the clinical interview need not be greatly detailed, as the quality of retrospective self-report data are limited and superior assessment proce-

Figure 11.1   Outline of a typical social-skills assessment interview

---

A. Obtain a history of social functioning from the client.
   Goal: To identify recurrent themes and problems

   Ask about:
   1. The number of friends the client had in childhood, adolescence, and adulthood
   2. The nature and closeness of such friendships
   3. The client's dating history, most notably the number, frequency, and success
      of romantic relationships
   4. The client's involvement in social clubs or activities

B. Ask client to describe the kinds of social situations and relationships he or she finds
   difficult.
   Goal: To specify difficult social situations

   1. Be sure to cover the following situations if the client does not specify them:
      a. work or school
      b. at home
      c. pubic places (stores, buses, airplanes, etc.)
      d. recreational settings (parties, sports events, etc.)
      e. dating and sex-related situations
   2. For each situation described, ask the client to describe how he or she interacts
      with the following people of both the same and the opposite sex:
      a. friends
      b. bosses
      c. co-workers
      d. professionals (doctors, lawyers, etc.),
      e. service providers (salespeople, restaurant staff, mail clerks, delivery
         persons, mechanics, landlords, etc.)
      f. spouse, boyfriend or girlfriend
      g. in-laws
      h. children
      i. neighbors
   3. For each situation identified:
      a. Ask the client to describe what happened the last time he or she was in that
         situation. What did the client say? What did the client do? What did others
         say and do?
      b. Determine what happened immediately before the situation occurred.
      c. Determine what happened immediately afterward.
      d. Explore the client's motives in that particular situation. What was the
         client's goal?
      e. Ask the client to rate his or her performance on a 0 (extremely poor) to 100
         (extremely good) scale.
      f. Ask the client to describe what he or she may have done differently in that
         situation. If the client has difficulty with this question, ask how he or she
         would imagine a person with no social problems would behave in such
         situations.
      g. Ask the client how often such situations arise in his or her daily life.

C. Ask the client to rank-order the identified situations in terms of their difficulty.
   Goal: To identify a starting point for assessment and/or treatment

dures are available to assess *current* social functioning (the focus of any intervention for social skill deficits).

As shown in Figure 11.1, the next step in the clinical interview for assessment of social skills is to develop a detailed description of the situations the individual finds problematic. To assure that the full range of potentially problematic situations is assessed, the clinician should inquire about various social situations and assess the client's behavior within such contexts. Becker, Heimberg, and Bellack (1987) provide a useful checklist of human characteristics, situational factors, and types of assertion to be covered in the clinical interview. Within the human characteristics area, clients should be asked specifically about their relationships with friends, bosses or supervisors, professionals, salespeople, co-workers, in-laws, children, and significant others. Clients should also be asked about their performance in various situations such as work, school, public places, transportation systems, communication systems, and recreational settings. Finally, the clinician should inquire specifically whether clients have difficulty with positive assertion (e.g., making requests, complimenting others), negative assertion (e.g., refusals, confrontation), and conversations.

For each area identified as a problem, the client is asked to describe in detail the last time he or she engaged in that particular situation. For example, if the client expresses a lack of assertiveness when dealing with authority figures, ask for a detailed account of a recent example of this situation. As the client recounts the incident in detail, the clinician develops an understanding of the client's perception of events. For each situation the client identifies, it is helpful to obtain information about the following: (1) the client's goals and motives in the situation, (2) the client's plans and strategies for coping with problems and generating alternatives, (3) the client's interpretation of the events, and (4) the client's perception of his or her performance.

The interviewer must be alert to cues that indicate problems in the client's perception of events because such deficits may impair social performance, as suggested by both Trower and Liberman's theories. Some clients may be able to generate a list of alternative responses but suffer from an inability to select from them. Still others may not respond appropriately based on a faulty perception of the behavior's utility. They may judge a response as too risky or costly, and thus decide not to execute it.

Throughout the interview process, the clinician is advised to assess the relevance of the social situations discussed. If the client is not likely to be placed in certain situations, it is a waste of both time and money to pursue them when more salient situations may exist. The clinician or researcher may also wish to speak with the client's significant others. In some cases, significant others may provide a more objective assessment of the client's problem than the client can. This information may be particularly valuable when the client suffers from a developmental disability or a chronic and severe mental illness. Given that they interact with the client in the client's natural environment, significant others can provide an evaluation of the client's behavior as it occurs *in vivo*. However, significant others are subject to the same biases and distortions as are clients (McFall, 1982). They may have a variety of reasons to portray the subject in particular ways. As such, their report must be considered in combination with other sources of data.

Validity of Clinical Interviews for Assessing Social Skill

Unfortunately, little is known about the validity of clinical interviews for the assessment of social skills. The well-established limitations of self-report may be particularly problematic in this situation because misperceiving the interpersonal behavior of oneself and others is itself a common component of deficits in social skill. Although interviews with significant others may provide another perspective of the client's social skill, as noted earlier, these are potentially biased as well (McFall, 1982).

In one of the few studies to address the problem of self-report of interpersonal behavior, Bellack, Hersen, and Turner (1979) found little correspondence between statements subjects made about their own reactions and the actual behavior during role-played assessments. However, the subjects' behavior *in vivo* and their self-report during a clinical interview were more consistent, leading the authors to conclude that self-report was a better predictor of behavior in the natural setting than it was of behavior in a role-play. Thus, this study offers some support for the validity of clinical interviews for assessment of social skill. However, it is probably most appropriate to use the clinical interview to screen for potentially problematic situations that can then be further examined with other methods such as behavioral observation. As always, seeking converging evidence from multiple sources represents the most prudent assessment strategy.

Behavioral Observation

Although interviews provide valuable data for assessing social skill, a complete understanding of social functioning requires direct observation of the client's actual behavior in a variety of situations. Because the data obtained from observational assessments guide treatment decisions (Bellack, Hersen, & Turner, 1979), the careful design of a behavioral assessment is paramount. Poorly designed observations may yield inaccurate assessment data resulting in the erroneous selection of interventions and in the misguided application of social skills training techniques (Wessberg et al., 1979). Designing observational assessment requires decisions regarding the settings in which observation will occur, the observational format, instructions given to the subject, the physical environment, the confederate's behavior, level of measurement, and the use of video recording. Each of these decision points will be discussed next.

Conducting a Behavioral Assessment of Social Skills

The first decision the clinician must make is whether the assessment should occur in a naturalistic, contrived, or controlled setting (Curran & Mariotto, 1980). The advantages and disadvantages of each of these will be outlined.

Naturalistic Settings

Observations of the client's behavior may be made as the behaviors occur *in vivo* (in the natural environment). A client interacting with his or her spouse or a chronically mentally ill individual interacting with family members are both examples of common situations in which social skill deficits are apparent. Observing these interactions in the home allows the clinician to directly observe the antecedents and consequences present in the environment that may influence the client's behavior. Naturalistic observation may be particularly useful when the behavior of interest occurs only in certain settings (e.g., the classroom). Unfortunately, naturalistic observation is not feasible in all situations (Bellack, Hersen, & Turner, 1979) due to ethical concerns about confidentiality and consent and practical considerations of time and money. Ethical standards require that informed consent be obtained from all parties involved if the nature of the interaction may cause discomfort in others (e.g., asking for a date, confrontation, etc.). Fortunately, with some creativity, clinicians may be able to design a naturalistic observation that avoids these difficulties. For example, an unassertive client may be discretely observed returning a purchased item at a customer service counter, asking directions of store clerks, or making a necessary phone call.

Contrived Settings

Contrived situations are those in which a social interaction occurs between the client and a confederate but the client is unaware of the contrived nature of the situation until the interaction has been completed. For example, Wessberg and associates (1979) observed subjects' behavior with a trained confederate as it occurred during an imposed waiting period. Because contrived situations require deception on the part of the clinician, they would rarely be appropriate in clinical practice. In research settings, contrived situations may be used with appropriate safeguards such as informed consent. Designing observations in contrived situations presents the same challenges as in controlled settings (described next).

Controlled Settings

Observations in controlled settings, commonly called role-plays, are those in which the client engages in a staged interaction with either the clinician, a confederate, or a significant other. This is the most common method for obtaining behavioral data in the literature on social skills. Typically, a scene is presented to the client followed by a prompt from the role-play partner. The client responds to the prompt and the interaction proceeds. Typical scenarios include introducing oneself, asking for dates, giving and receiving compliments, refusing requests, and expressing positive and negative emotions (Eisler, Miller, & Hersen, 1973; Masters, Burish, Hollon, & Rimm, 1987; Mueser, Valenti-Hein, & Yarnold, 1987). Role-play assessment offers many advantages. Not only does it avoid the ethical concerns of confidentiality and consent that are associated with naturalistic and contrived observation, it provides an opportunity to elicit and observe behaviors that occur in low frequencies (Curran & Mariotto, 1980; Torgrud & Holborn, 1992). For example, assessing how a client responds to negative feedback from a supervisor requires that the supervisor engage in behavior that may be infrequent and unpredictable and thus unavailable for naturalistic assessment. Role-playing this situation is relatively straightforward.

Role-Play Format. Role-plays can take various forms. They may involve the presentation of a single prompt or an extended interaction (Galassi & Galassi, 1976), be either idiographically determined or standardized, and the stimulus may be live or audio/videotaped. As will be seen, determining the format to employ will depend on the client's level of functioning and the nature of the situation being assessed.

The single-prompt role-play involves the confederate delivering a single prompt and the client making a single response. The single prompt may be delivered via a live confederate or via audio/videotape. Extended role-plays, which involve multiple exchanges between partners, more closely approximate normal interactions. Galassi and Galassi (1976) studied the effects of stimulus presentation (audiotaped versus live confederate) and the number of stimulus statements (single prompt versus extended interaction) on the assertive behavior of unassertive college students. Subjects were randomly assigned to one of four conditions: audiotaped single-prompt role-play, audiotaped multiple-prompt role-play, live single-prompt role-play, and a live multiple-prompt role-play. Although the

audiotaped conditions resulted in lower subjective anxiety than live interactions, and single-prompt role-plays yielded longer responses than multiple-prompt role-plays, neither presentation format nor number of prompts was related to assertiveness. However, it should be noted that the assertiveness measure was somewhat limited.

Despite Galassi and Galassi's findings, the single-prompt format appears to have a number of limitations. Clients who lack the ability to maintain conversations may not be identified with single-prompt assessment. Although the client's initial response may be adequate, subsequent responses to an uncooperative partner may not. Based on these limitations, Bellack (1983) has stated that use of single-prompt role-plays in the assessment of social skills is no longer justified. However, with lowest functioning clients with limited attentional resources, only single-prompt role-plays may be realistically completed.

In addition to single-prompt and multiple-prompt role-plays, clinicians may choose between standardized and idiographically designed role-plays. One of the more extensively used standardized role-play assessments is the Behavioral Assertiveness Test-Revised (BAT-R) developed by Eisler and associates (1975). This assessment requires subjects to respond to 32 situations, half of which involve positive assertion skills (e.g., giving praise), the other half requiring negative assertion skills (e.g., expression of displeasure, refusal skills). The scenes also differ in terms of familiarity with the role-play partner. For half of the scenes, the subject is instructed to interact with a person whom they know well, whereas the other half of the scenes depict a person whom the subject does not know. The role-play partners are played by both male and female confederates. Following instructions to the subject to behave as he or she typically behaves in such situations, a brief scene is narrated, and a prompt is delivered to the subject by the role-play confederate. The following is an example of a male-positive-familiar situation (p. 332): "Narrator: 'You have been working on a difficult job all week, your boss comes over with a smile on his face.' Your boss says, 'That's a very good job you have done; I'm going to give you a raise next week.'" All role-plays are videotaped and later coded for several behavioral components (e.g., duration of eye contact, response latency, praise, smiles) as well as for overall assertiveness.

The Assessment of Interpersonal Problem Solving Skills (AIPSS),[1] developed by Donahoe and colleagues (Donahoe et al., 1990), uses video-taped sequences combined with role-plays to assess social skills. Clients watch 13 videotaped interactions, 10 of which involve interpersonal problems and 3 control situations. Clients are instructed to identify with one of the actors and are asked several questions about each video scene in order to assess receiving, processing, and sending skills. They are asked whether there is a problem in the scene and, if so, to identify it (receiving skills). To assess their processing skills, clients are asked to describe how they would respond in that situation. Sending skills are assessed by asking clients to role-play their responses. Role-plays are videotaped and later coded for content, performance, and overall quality by two raters using a scoring manual (Donahoe, Carter, Bloem, & Leff, 1984). The AIPSS has been reported to have reasonable test-retest reliability and internal consistency (Donahoe et al., 1990).

Although standardized role-plays such as the BAT-R and AIPSS have the advantage of already being prepared and they cover a broad range of situations, research suggests that idiographically designed role-plays may enhance the external validity of the assessment (Chiauzzi, Heimberg, Becker, & Gansler, 1985; Torgrud & Holborn, 1992). Furthermore, the situations in which the client experiences difficulty are often idiosyncratic. For example, if a cocktail waitress wants to set limits with overly friendly customers, specific role-plays that target this situation must be developed by the clinician. The thorough functional analysis, described earlier in the section on clinical interviewing, will provide the necessary information to adequately design one or more role-plays that are both relevant to the client's concerns and likely to elicit the target behaviors.

Setting the Stage for the Role-Play. Maximizing the the external validity of role-played assessment requires consideration of the effect of environmental stimuli, the setting, and confederate characteristics on the client's behavior (Torgrud & Holborn, 1992). Relevant stimuli may include the formality of the setting, confederate gender and clothing, and positioning (standing vs. sitting). Including props, such as a cup of water to represent a drink at a party, may make the situation more realistic. Careful questioning of the client regarding these factors will enable the clinician to identify the most important stimuli and include them in the role-play.

Instructions to Subjects. Instructions given to clients may directly affect their behavior in role-played behavioral assessment situations and, consequently, affect the external validity of the assessment (Liberman, 1982; Nietzel & Bernstein, 1976; Torgrud & Holborn, 1992). Clients can be asked to perform as they typically do, perform as best they can, or perform as they think socially skilled people perform. Nietzel and Bernstein (1976) found that subjects who were asked to respond as they normally would had significantly lower scores on measures of assertion than did those subjects who were asked to perform assertively.

The reactive nature of the role-play situation may also elicit more skillful behavior than typically observed (Torgrud & Holborn, 1992; Wessberg et al., 1979). In their attempt to estimate the ecological validity of role-play assessments, Wessberg and colleagues (1979) asked 45 male undergraduates to participate in two role-played interactions with a female confederate. Following each role-play, a bogus waiting period of three minutes was imposed, which provided an opportunity for the subject to interact with a female confederate if he chose to do so. Significant differences were obtained on global measures of skill made by six trained judges, with role-play behavior being rated as more skilled than the interactions during the waiting intervals. However, subjects rated the waiting periods as being significantly more naturalistic than the role-played situations. In addition, subjects indicated their performance in the role-play was not representative of their behavior in everyday life. Thus, role-plays may not always provide a representative assessment of an individual's behavior as it occurs in the natural setting. However, if the person performs appropriately and skillfully within the role-play situation, the researcher or clinician may ask whether this behavior is typical of behavior in natural settings. If the behavior is not typical, the role-play may be redesigned to better reflect the naturalistic situation. The cognitive and situational factors that preclude the person from enacting the socially skilled behavior can also be explored.

Instructions to Confederates or Collaterals. Due to the nature of observational assessment, it is helpful to procure confederates to act as role-play partners. In research settings, confederates are typically undergraduate or graduate research assistants. However, in clinical settings, the clinician or a clerical staffperson may have to perform the confederate role. Sometimes family members can serve as role-play partners. Either way, variations in confederate behavior will affect client responses (Torgrud & Holborn, 1992), so confederates must be instructed carefully to yield the desired outcome.

For example, in situations requiring refusal assertion, confederates can be instructed to be insistent, refusing to take no for an answer. When assessing conversation skills, confederates should receive instructions regarding how friendly to be and how much to facilitate a smooth conversation. Although social decorum will motivate the socially skilled confederate to help ease an awkward interaction, in an observational assessment of social skill, it may be more appropriate to test the client's ability to handle a difficult situation. Thus, the confederate may need specific instructions, such as to count to five before breaking a silent interlude. If family members are participating in the role-play, they may be instructed to respond as best they can, as they typically would at home, or as they have observed others responding to the client.

Video Recording. Advances in video technology have increased the viability of behavioral observation as a key component in the assessment of social skills. Videotaping interactions maximizes the flexibility of observational coding because ratings of social skill do not have to be made at the time of the interaction. For example, observers can code the role-play for one particular behavior, rewind the tape, and then code for another behavior. Videotaping also eases the burden of obtaining inter-

rater reliability if all raters need not be present at the original assessment session.

Video recording has disadvantages, as well. Viewing subtle nuances in behavior (e.g., eye contact, facial expression) as well as more gross elements (e.g., posture) may require multiple cameras or special lenses. In addition, technical difficulties may result in missing or incomprehensible segments. Many of these latter problems can be avoided with proper training of camera operators. In addition to these technical problems, it seems likely that the knowledge one is being videotaped may affect the behavior of interest, possibly by increasing anxiety or self-consciousness. However, reactivity of videotaping has not been investigated and may be decreasing as video cameras become more commonplace.

In one of the few studies to compare live and videotaped observation, Eisler, Hersen, and Agras (1973) examined the inter-rater reliability of observations of married couples. Four trained observers rate the occurrence of looking and smiling behaviors. Percent agreement among observer pairs was equally good for either the live or videotaped conditions. However, it is not clear whether inter-rater agreement was high between the two conditions.

All things considered, the advantages of videotaping observational assessment clearly outweigh the disadvantages in a research setting. For clinical work outside the research context, videotaping would enhance the quality and quantity of the information available to the clinician. Given a choice between only live observation versus omitting the direct observation component of the assessment battery, the former is definitely preferable.

Coding and Interpreting the Data

In order to quantify a client's performance in an observed interaction, molar, molecular, and self-ratings may be made. *Molar ratings* refer to judgments of global characteristics such as skillfulness, appropriateness, and effectiveness. *Molecular ratings*, on the other hand, refer to quantifying specific behaviors such as gesturing, smiling, and gaze. Finally, *self-ratings* are the clients' own quantified impressions of their performance.

Molar Ratings

Molar ratings of behavior provide a measure of the social impact the subject has on others in the environment (Bellack, 1983), and typically consist of a single, global rating of the person's overall social skill. Observers can either be trained with partially defined criteria or asked simply for their impressions (Curran & Mariotto, 1980). For example, Wessberg and associates (1979) trained six undergraduates to attend to specific behaviors denoting social skill (presenting compliments, maintaining the conversation in a timely manner, and smiling). They then made molar ratings on a 0 (not at all skillful) to 7 (extremely skillful) scale. Pairs of raters were highly reliable with each other (reliability = 0.85) on 35 practice tapes and on the actual study tapes (reliability = 0.72 to 0.87).

Reliable molar ratings can also be made by untrained observers. In an effort to maximize the social validity of the ratings, Hope and colleagues (Hope & Heimberg, 1988; Hope, Heimberg, & Bruch, 1995) asked six observers (typically undergraduate research assistants) to evaluate subjects in videotaped role-plays as though they had observed them in a naturally occurring situation. The ratings were made on a 0 (extremely unskilled or inappropriate) to 100 (highly skilled performance) scale. The only training raters received consisted of an explanation of the scale anchor points and practice ratings of three videotaped role-plays that were used to set anchors for highly skilled, highly unskilled, and moderately skilled behavior. No feedback was given on these initial ratings, however. Despite the lack of training, inter-rater agreement was high in two separate studies (Spearman-Brown $r = 0.88$ and 0.91), suggesting a consensus among raters of what constituted socially skilled performance in the role-plays.

Molecular Ratings

Molecular ratings of social interactions require highly trained observers to code for the occurrence of specific verbal and nonverbal behaviors. Typical behaviors include eye contact, response duration, speech latency, head movement/nods, gesturing, facial expressions, requests, compliments, and refusals. A time-sampling procedure is usually used to measure the frequency, duration, occurrence/nonoccurrence of these behaviors during brief intervals (usually about 15 seconds). With extensive training, excellent inter-rater reliability can be achieved (Bellack, Hersen, & Turner, 1979; Curran & Mariotto, 1980).

Which of the myriad of verbal and nonverbal behaviors that one chooses to rate depends on a number of factors, including one's definition of social skill, the particular context, the purpose of the ratings, and the quality of the videotape. For example, making or refusing a request would definitely be rated in an assertion situation but may not be included for dating scenarios. Thus, the most difficult question is not which behaviors to rate, but how to define the behaviors. Unfortunately, there are no standardized operational definitions of the molecular elements of social skill. A brief review of the controversy over how to define "eye contact" will be used to illustrate this point.

Bellack (1983) has suggested that the term *eye contact* is misleading because observers are unable to accurately detect whether direct eye contact is indeed occurring between two people. As an alternative, Bellack recommends that the label *gaze* be used, but cautions that accurate measurement remains difficult. However, when Caballo and Buela (1988) defined *gaze* as "looking directly at the other person's *face*," they achieved excellent inter-rater reliability (shortest observation (sec)/longest observation (sec) = 0.95). Similarly, Eisler, Miller, and Hersen (1973) measured *duration of looking* and obtained reliability (Pearson correlations) in the 0.96 to 0.99 range.

Even when reliable, operational definitions have been developed, molecular ratings have been subject to the criticism that their rigidity may result in misleading findings (Bellack, 1983). For example, sometimes an intermediate range of a behavior is preferable to either low or high frequencies of occurrence, as is the case for the individual who either stares too intently or does not establish eye contact at all (Bellack, 1983; Curran & Mariotto, 1980). Although measurement of the overall frequency or duration of gaze may be reliable, it is not a valid measure of social skill in this example.

Scales that detect even moderate differences in performance may provide a more sensitive measure than frequency and duration ratings. A Likert scale in which the anchors represent extreme levels of the behavior (0 = no eye contact to 5 = unbroken eye contact) with middle ratings reflecting the highest social skill may be used. Another solution to the rigid nature of frequency and duration measures is the system developed by Trower and associates (1978). They organized 29 specific behaviors into three categories: voice quality, nonverbal, and conversation. The category *voice quality* contains ratings of volume, tone, pitch, clarity, pace, and speech disturbances. *Nonverbal* ratings include proximity, orientation, appearance, face, gaze, posture tonus, posture position, gesture, and autistic gesture (self-manipulative behavior). The *conversation* category includes ratings of length, generality, formality, variety, humor, nonverbal "grammar," feedback, meshing, turn taking, question asking, assertive routines, public behavior, and situation-specific routines. For each specific behavior listed, a rating scale is provided. For example, the item *gaze* is rated by choosing one of the following alternatives (pp. 149–150):

0   Normal gaze frequency and pattern.
1(a) Tends to avoid looking, but no negative impression.
1(b) Tends to look too much, but no negative impression.
2(a) Looks too little. Negative impression.
2(b) Looks too much. Negative impression.
3(a) Abnormally infrequent looking. Unrewarding.
3(b) Abnormally frequent looking. Unpleasant.
4(a) Completely avoids looking. Very unrewarding.
4(b) Stares continually. Very unpleasant.

Thus, a higher score on this item is indicative of inappropriate eye contact, regardless of whether the eye contact is insufficient or excessive. Not surprisingly, inter-rater reliability for this type of scale can be high, particularly when the definitions have behavioral anchors (Bellack, 1983).

Training Observers

With the exception of Hope and colleagues' consensus molar ratings, training observers to make accurate judgments can be a formidable task. Carefully written operational definitions represent the first step toward ensuring discriminations among behaviors. Next, observers should view videotaped examples of the behaviors of interest to illustrate the operational definitions. Then the observers should alternate rating practice videotapes and discussing discrepancies until they meet an agreed upon criterion for inter-rater agreement with an expert or criterion rater. Care must be taken that observers do not discuss the assessments, nor rate videotapes in close proximity to avoid artificial inflation of reliability statistics. Frequent checks against a criterion rater are recommended throughout the rating process to prevent observer drift and resolve questions or discrepancies among raters.

Validity of Molar and Molecular Ratings

Researchers have questioned the relationship between molecular behaviors and the concept of social skill (McFall, 1982). It is unclear whether the rate of gesturing or head nodding is directly equivalent to a measure of skill in social situations. Some argue it is not. However, data have been reported that suggest molecular behaviors are indeed related to social skill. For example, Pachman, Foy, Massey, and Eisler (1978) found eye contact, response duration, requests for change, and compliance to be significantly correlated with global ratings of assertion. Eisler, Miller, and Hersen (1973) also found response latency, loudness of speech, compliance, and requests for new behavior to be correlated with global ratings of assertion.

In his review of the literature, Calvert (1988) raised questions about the validity of molar ratings of social skill when he concluded that studies have consistently found that physically attractive individuals are viewed as highly socially skilled and vice versa. Although attractive people may exhibit better social skills, presumably because they have more opportunities to practice, raters may demonstrate a positive bias for attractive people. For example, Hope and Mindell (1994) reported that, when a confederate performed skillfully, the same behavior was rated as more skilled when she was attractive than when she was unattractive. However, when she performed poorly, attractiveness did not affect the social skills rating. Nelson and colleagues (Nelson, Hayes, Felton, & Jarrett, 1985) also found that observers tended to rate socially skilled clients as more attractive than their unskilled peers.

Self-Ratings

It is often informative to have clients give subjective ratings of either specific components of social skill or of their overall performance. Because many clients will consider the top rating to equal perfect social performance, it is essential for the clinician to understand how the client is using the self-rating scale. For example, 7 on a 0 to 7 scale of overall social skills could be anchored with the descriptor "as well as the average person would do" to avoid unattainable standards of perfection.

It should be noted that clients are often poor judges of the quality of their own performance (Alden & Wallace, 1995; Hope et al., 1995; Rapee & Lim, 1992), particularly for more global ratings. When compared to experimenters' ratings, subjects have been found to rate themselves as having poorer social skills whether they rated their performance *in vivo* or on videotape (Nelson et al., 1985). Therefore, one should always include some type of observer rating in addition to self-ratings. Understanding how a particular client's self-assessment compares with objective observers will assist the clinician in interpreting accounts of social interactions outside of the therapy room. Inaccurate self-assessment may be an important problem to be targeted in treatment, as well.

Conclusion

Molar, molecular, and self-ratings of social skill each have relative strengths and weaknesses. Molecular ratings are essential for the standard social skill training interventions that involve feedback and rehearsal of specific behaviors. However, molar ratings are needed to determine whether the individual components fit together in a functional "Gestalt." Identifying and resolving discrepancies

between self and others' perceptions may ultimately be important for maintenance and generalization of any treatment success. Therefore, in order to maximize the utility of observational assessment data, it is best to seek convergence between molar, molecular, and self-ratings rather than to rely on any one type.

Validity of Role-Play Assessments

Role-play assessments are considered to be superior to paper-and-pencil measures because they provide an opportunity to actually observe a sample of the person's behavior. However, the validity of role-plays is based on the assumption that the behavior observed in a role-play is representative of behavior as it occurs *in vivo*. Unfortunately, an infinite number of variables that might impact behavior exist within a given setting, making it difficult to match role-play and *in vivo* situations. As will be seen here, studies examining the generalizability, or external validity, of role-played assessments of social skill have yielded conflicting results.

Bellack, Hersen, and Lamparski (1979) compared molar and molecular ratings of social skill obtained from role-played interactions and naturalistic observation. Some 39 male and 39 female college students participated in 20 single-prompt videotaped role-plays with an opposite-sex experimenter. Subjects returned approximately one week later, at which time they engaged in a staged five-minute waiting period, during which a confederate posed as another subject also waiting for the experimenter. Overall, the authors found moderate correlations between role-played and naturalistic behavior for female subjects. For male subjects, however, few significant correlations were found, leading the authors conclude, "The number of significantly correlated behaviors does not suggest a consistent relationship between the situations" (p. 341).

In another study with psychiatric patients, Bellack, Hersen, and Turner (1979) staged ostensibly naturalistic interactions in which a confederate approached the patients and presented one of six situations over a 10-day period. Three of the situations were positive in nature (a compliment on appearance, a compliment on the patient's progress during hospitalization, and an offer to fetch something from the hospital's canteen), and the other three involved negative incidents (telling the subject he or she was in an off-limits area, asking for an unreasonable favor, and telling the subject he or she had an overdue book from the hospital library). Following the six naturalistic situations, the subjects participated in 12 role-play scenarios, half of which were identical to the naturalistic situations. During the structured interview, subjects were asked how they would respond to similar situations. Naturalistic and role-played interactions were coded for eye contact, response latency, smiles, expression of praise and appreciation (positive scenes), requests for new behavior, and compliance with the confederate's requests (negative scenes). Although some of the correlations between role-play and naturalistic behaviors were statistically significant for similar situations, Bellack, Hersen, and Turner (1979) caution that the correlations were modest, at best, and offered little support for the external validity of role-play assessments.

Gorecki, Dickson, Anderson, and Jones (1981) assigned subjects to either a role-played or a contrived *in vivo* situation that was identical to the role-play scenarios. Subjects completed the Conflict Resolution Inventory, which measures responses to refusal situations, and the Assertive Self Statement Test, which measures the degree to which subjects think negative thoughts while engaged in assertive situations. In addition, judges rated the subjects' behavior for assertive content, affect, request for new behavior, response duration, and speech disturbances. Results indicated subjects behaved more skillfully during the role-played interactions than during the contrived *in vivo* situations. Furthermore, little correspondence was found between subjects' self-report of assertive behavior and that observed *in vivo*.

In contrast to the rather disappointing findings regarding the validity of role-plays reported by Bellack and colleagues and Gorecki and colleagues, two studies have yielded more promising results. Wessberg and associates (1979) found significant correlations between ratings of role-played behavior and behavior observed during a bogus waiting period. Although subjects behaved more skillfully during role-played interactions than during the unobtrusively observed waiting period, judges rank-ordered subjects on measures of anxiety and skill similarly across the two conditions. Ratings of anxiety and skill correlated between the role-play and waiting room assessment at $r = 0.68$ and $r = 0.62$, respectively.

Using a rather clever design, St. Lawrence, Kirksey, and Moore (1983) also found support for the external validity of role-play assessments. They assigned 40 female subjects to either a role-played or naturalistic condition in which subjects were unaware of the contrived nature of the interaction. In each condition, an experimenter told the subjects that they would not be receiving extra credit for their participation because a second subject had not arrived. If the subject protested, the experimenter initiated a series of requests ranging from demanding ("Can I reschedule you to come back Saturday morning at 8 AM, although I can't guarantee you will get the credit then?") (1983, p. 28) to least demanding ("If I go ahead and give you the credit now, will you fill out one more short questionnaire?") (1983, p. 28). Responses were videotaped and later rated for eye contact, speech latency, speech duration, number of requests refused, and overall assertion. The authors found no significant differences in subject behavior as observed during the role-play or naturalistic situation, leading them to conclude, "The current findings suggest that role play procedures may be a valid representation of naturalistic behavior" (1983, p. 32).

Given the extensive use of role-plays to assess social skill, empirical evidence for the external validity is surprisingly limited and perhaps somewhat stronger for women than for men (Bellack, Hersen, & Lamparski, 1979; St. Lawrence et al., 1983). In general, behavior observed in role-plays has not been found to be representative of that observed in *in vivo* situations; individuals are usually more skilled during role-plays than during naturalistic interactions. Bellack, Hersen, and Turner (1979) offer several explanations to account for the low external validity of role-played interactions. They suggest that subjects may behave more skillfully in role-play assessments due to the absence of negative consequences. Subjects know they will not be fired from a job or lose a close relationship, for example, as a result of their role-played performance. In addition, subjects may have difficulty playing a role in a controlled setting, as they sometimes report that the role-play did not feel "real" for them. Therefore, to increase the external validity of role-played assessments, it is best to make the assessment as similar to *in vivo* situations as possible.

Self-Monitoring

Self-monitoring can be another source of data for the clinician who is assessing social skill. Typically assigned as homework, the client is instructed to be alert to certain situations or events that usually cause difficulty. In this manner, frequency with which target situations occur in the natural environment can be obtained. A monitoring form or log is usually provided on which the client records information of interest (see Figure 11. 2). Clients can be asked to provide the date and time of the interaction, a brief description of the interac-

tion, the outcome, and their cognitions regarding the event, and to rate their subjective impression of their performance on a 0 to 100 scale with realistic anchor points.

Of course, the reactive nature of self-monitoring must be considered when utilizing such data. The client's behavior may change as a result of self-monitoring, typically in the desired direction (Masters et al., 1987). Thus, although reactivity may adversely affect the validity of self-monitoring, it may provide therapeutic benefits. In addition to the problem of reactivity, clients may selectively attend to either overly positive or overly negative aspects of the targeted behavior. In addition, poor memory on the part of the client may result in missing data. Even so, self-monitoring has been found to correspond with scores obtained on self-report measures and observer ratings of anxiety (Royce & Arkowitz, 1978; Twentyman & McFall, 1975).

Regardless of the influence of reactivity, memory, and attention, self-monitoring has many benefits. Data can be collected for the frequency with

Figure 11.2 Example of typical self-monitoring form

DATE, TIME	WHAT WAS THE SITUATION?	WHAT DID YOU DO?	WHAT WAS THE RESULT?	WHAT WAS YOUR GOAL?	DID YOU MEET YOUR GOAL? (Y/N)	PERFORMANCE RATING 0–100

which certain situations arise and the clients' subjective impression of the events. Self-monitoring also enables clients involved in their own treatment and provides an idiographic measure with which to monitor change.

Self-Report Questionnaires

Numerous self-report questionnaires have been developed over the years specifically addressing components of social skill. Although most of the questionnaires focus on assertion skills, others are available for heterosocial dating skills and friendliness. Single items on these questionnaires typically describe a specific social situation or event that are then tallied into an overall score. This practice has been criticized because it obscures the oftentimes situationally specific nature of social skills (McFall, 1982). Nonetheless, self-report questionnaires can provide data as to clients' attitudes and reactions to listed events and situations with relatively little demand on the clinician's time. Of course, self-report data are subject to demand characteristics and biases on the part of the client.

Because deficits in social skill can occur in individuals with a wide variety of backgrounds and presenting problems, concern has arisen regarding the reading level of self-report measures of social skill. As will be discussed, most measures were developed with college students. Andrasik, Heimberg, Edlund, and Blankenberg (1981) rated the reading level of 11 commonly used assertion questionnaires. In general, directions contained in the inventories required at least a high school reading level, whereas the actual items themselves required reading levels ranging from the 7th to 12th grades. In addition, the length of the scale and the complexity of response alternatives may decrease the validity of the responses with some clients. Given these concerns, Andrasik and colleagues suggested careful attention be paid to the client's ability to read and comprehend the inventories before their administration.

Due to the number of questionnaires that have been developed, a thorough review is not possible (see Beck & Heimberg [1983] for an excellent review). Thus, only a few of the more commonly used and well-researched questionnaires will be described here. These measures focus mainly on assertion in various contexts and situations.

Rathus Assertiveness Schedule (RAS)

The Rathus Assertiveness Schedule is probably the most well-known self-report measure of assertion. Developed by Rathus (1973), it contains 30 items that are rated on a scale from +3 ("Very characteristic of me, extremely descriptive") to –3 ("Very uncharacteristic of me, extremely nondescriptive"). Items describe various actions and beliefs related to assertive situations (e.g., "Most people seem to be more aggressive and assertive than I am" and "I enjoy starting conversations with new acquaintances and strangers"). The RAS is easy to administer and score, and norms are provided based on a sample of 68 undergraduate students. RAS scores were found to correlate significantly ($rs \geq 0.32$) with observer ratings of assertiveness. Split-half reliability was reported to be 0.77; test-retest reliability, obtained over an eight-week interval, was reported to be 0.78. Heimberg and Harrison (1980) administered the RAS to criminal offenders and found test-retest reliability of 0.80 and split-half reliability (over 11 to 15 days) of 0.80.

The RAS was revised by McCormick (Simple RAS; 1984) for use with individuals with poor reading skills and has been found to correlate with the original RAS at 0.90. Gustafson (1992) translated the RAS into Swedish and shortened it by six items. The Swedish version was found to have a Cronbach alpha of 0.82, a split-half reliability of 0.85, and correlated highly with the original version ($r = 0.94$). The RAS is sensitive to therapeutic change (Blanchard, Turner, Eschette, & Coury, 1977; Rathus, 1973).

Wolpe-Lazarus Assertiveness Schedule (WLAS)

The WLAS was originally published in Wolpe and Lazarus's 1966 text, *Behavior Therapy Techniques: A Guide to the Treatment of Neuroses*. It consists of 30 yes/no questions covering request, refusal, and positive expression skills. Despite the authors' suggestion to discuss the items with clients as part of an interview, Hersen and colleagues (1979) noted that the list was frequently used as a paper-and-pencil questionnaire, despite the fact that its British wording might be inaccessible for Americans (e.g. "If you arrived late at a meeting, would you rather stand than go to a front seat which could only be secured with a fair degree of conspicuousness?") and lack of psychometric data. Hersen and associates (1979) administered a revised version of the WLAS, in which British wording was replaced with American phrases, to a group of 257 psychiatric inpatients. The scale was found to have overall split-half and test-retest (one-week interval) reliability coefficients of 0.784 and 0.653, respectively. No significant sex differences were found. Although the WLAS differentiated between high- and low-assertion subjects (as determined by molar ratings) in previous studies (e.g., Eisler et al.,1975), it was not found to differentiate among subjects in this sample who were classified as having exhibited high or low assertion based on an overall rating of social skill. Thus, the external validity of the measure has yet to be unequivocally demonstrated.

Assertion Inventory (AI)

The AI, developed by Gambrill and Richey (1975), is a 40-item instrument that is useful for categorizing clients in terms of their overall assertiveness level. Scores are calculated based on the respondent's discomfort with assertion and probability of responding in an assertive manner. The number of items circled indicates those assertion situations in which the respondent has difficulty. Based on his or her scores on the discomfort scale and the response probability scale, the respondent is characterized as either "unassertive," "assertive," "anxious performer," or "doesn't care." The original study provided norms on college student samples and test-retest reliability is good (0.87 for the discomfort scale, 0.81 for the response probability scale).

The AI has commonly been used in research settings to differentiate between low- and high-assertive subjects. Pitcher and Meikle (1980) classified subjects as high, moderate, or low in assertion using the AI. Those subjects falling into the "high assertion" category were more assertive (expressed appreciation and praise, made requests and refusals more often) in a role-play than low-assertive subjects. The "moderate" group's role-play performance was similar to the "low" group, except that those with moderate assertion offered more praise and displayed more verbal aggression. Results of this study offer support for the concurrent validity of the AI.

Assertiveness Self-Report Inventory (ASRI)

The ASRI, developed by Herzberger, Chan, and Katz (1984), contains 25 items to which the respondent answers true or false. These items were chosen from a larger pool of potential items used in a preliminary study. Although the scale focuses heavily on the expression of negative feelings (e.g., "When my date has acted rudely at a party, I don't hesitate to let him/her know I don't like it"), several items refer to the expression of positive feelings (e.g., "After eating an excellent meal at a restaurant, I do not hesitate to compliment the chef"). Items are also included that assess the respondent's comfort in speaking in front of groups (e.g., "I feel comfortable engaging in discussions in a group" and "I would feel self-conscious asking a question in a large lecture class"). The measure is easy to administer and score, and Herzberger and colleagues provide norms based on a sample of 268 college students.

Test-retest reliability over a five-week interval was 0.81. The measure also appears to have convergent validity; ASRI scores correlated with the Rathus Assertiveness Schedule at $r = 0.70$. Assertiveness, as measured by the ASRI, was independent of aggression, providing support for the discriminant validity of the measure (Herzberger et al., 1984). In order to assess the criterion-related validity of the ASRI, Herzberger and associates (1984) asked subjects who completed the ASRI to return one month later for a separate assessment. Subjects were asked what they would do in response to six situations requiring assertion. Responses were coded for the degree of assertion and ratings were summed across the six scenarios to provide an overall score. The ASRI scores correlated significantly with the overall score obtained by the second assessment ($r = 0.67$).

Assertion Self-Statement Test-Revised (ASST-R)

The ASST, originally developed by Schwartz and Gottman (1976), was revised by Heimberg, Chiauzzi, Becker, and Madrazo-Peterson (1983), who reduced it from 32 to 24 items. The ASST-R assesses the frequency with which the respondent thinks positive (e.g., "I was thinking that I could benefit by expressing myself") or negative (e.g. "I was thinking that I would become embarrassed if I let my feelings be known") thoughts while engaged in assertive interactions. The respondent answers using a scale from 1 ("hardly ever had the thought") to 5 ("often had the thought"), resulting in scores on positive and negative dimensions. The measure is simple to administer and score and it provides a thorough assessment of the cognitions that may occur during situations requiring assertive action.

Negative self-statement scores on the ASST-R discriminated among subjects who were classified as either low or high in assertion based on WLAS scores (Heimberg et al., 1983). Reliability data are not provided by Heimberg and colleagues (1983) but an internal consistency coefficient of 0.78 was found for the original version (Bruch, Haase, & Purcell, 1984). A study by Gorecki and colleagues (1981) found correspondence between scores obtained on the ASST and behavior obtained in role-played situations, providing some support for the external validity of the measure. Those subjects who displayed assertive behavior reported more positive self-statements and fewer negative self-statements than did those who displayed unassertive behavior. However, this result did not hold for behavior observed *in vivo*. Although self-statements did not significantly correlate with behavior observed during a role-played assessment of refusal assertion, negative self-statements were associated with lower assertiveness on the Conflict Resolution Inventory (described next) and the Assertion Inventory (Pitcher & Meikle, 1980).

Conflict Resolution Inventory (CRI)

The CRI, developed by McFall and Lillesand (1971), contains 35 items that yield assertion and nonassertion scores. The items cover specific refusal situations, which are rated on a 5-point scale ranging from "refusing with no discomfort" to "acceptance of the request." An additional 8 items are included, which cover global assertion dimensions, such as "difficulty saying no." According to Beck and Heimberg (1983), the CRI is the most widely used assertion inventory due to its careful construction and focus on a single response class of assertion.

Galassi, Galassi, and Westefeld (1978) administered the CRI to 200 college students and found test-retest reliabilities (over a three-week interval) of 0.83 for the assertion score and 0.70 for the nonassertion score. Frisch and Higgins (1986) examined the correspondence between CRI scores in both contrived and *in vivo* observational assessment. Surprisingly, CRI scores did not correlate with global ratings of assertive behavior as observed during either a role-played or unobtrusive *in vivo* assessment, raising questions concerning the CRI's external validity. Frisch (1988) has also expressed concern that the CRI may be unduly influenced by social desirability.

Dating and Assertion Questionnaire (DAQ)

This measure, developed by Levenson and Gottman (1978), contains 18 items, half of which deal with dating situations, the other half with a variety of assertive situations. The questionnaire is clearly designed with college students in mind, although it has the potential to be useful for any single person for whom dating skills are an issue. Administration and scoring is relatively simple. Normative data are available on a sample of 92 college students with self-reported difficulties in dating and assertion situations. Test-retest reliability based on a two-week interval was found to be 0.71 and on a six-week interval was found to be 0.62. Internal consistency coefficients (Cronbach's alpha) were reported to be 0.92 for the dating items and 0.85 for the assertion items. Subjects responding to a social skills training advertisement were found to have significantly higher scores on both the dating and assertion items, as compared to normals, providing minimal support for the discriminant validity of the measures.

Comment

Seven of the more commonly used self-report questionnaires in the assessment of social skills were reviewed here. In general, these scales have adequate test-retest reliability. In addition, several of the scales have been shown to have reasonable concurrent and/or external validity. The DAQ and the ASRI are particularly useful with college students presenting with dating and assertion difficulties. The RAS, AI, and CRI cover assertion situations that are applicable to a broader adult population than the DAQ and ASRI. In addition, McCormick's (1984) simpler version of the RAS is appropriate for adolescents as well as adults. If the clinician is interested in the client's cognitive processes, the ASST-R would be an appropriate measure to include, since it assesses self-statements in relation to assertiveness. Although well known, the original WLAS was developed as a clinical interview and does not have any standardized scoring system. If using the WLAS as part of the assessment protocol, it would be wise to include at least one other self-report measure.

CASE EXAMPLE

David, a 36-year-old Caucasian male, was employed in the shipping department at a small company. He had been single for several years and wished to begin dating again. However, the prospect of dating caused him great anxiety because he believed he lacked the skills to make a positive impression. As a result, he avoided dating altogether. David responded to a newspaper advertisement recruiting socially phobic individuals to participate in a 12-week group cognitive-behavioral treatment study. Following an initial phone screening, David was interviewed using the Anxiety Disorders Interview Schedule-Revised (DiNardo & Barlow, 1988). David met criteria for Social Phobia, nongeneralized (dating fears only). He was given an ADIS-R clinician's severity rating of 6 on a 0 to 8 scale, where higher numbers indicate greater severity. His Axis V global severity rating of for both past and present functioning was 45. No other diagnoses were given.

David was asked to identify those social situations that caused him the greatest difficulty. For each situation, he was asked to rate the amount of fear each situation caused him on a 0 (no fear) to 100 (extreme fear) scale. David was also asked to rate the extent of his avoidance of each situation on a 0 (never avoid) to 100 (always avoid) scale. The 10 situations that caused him the most difficulty were then ordered in terms of anxiety and avoidance to form a fear hierarchy. The 6 most relevant situations for purposes here are presented in Table 11.1.

In order to observe his behavior directly, David was asked to engage in a four-minute, idiographically designed role-play with a trained undergraduate research assistant acting as a role-play partner. He was instructed to initiate and maintain a conversation with a woman whom he did not know. The role-played assessment was videotaped and later coded for a variety of molecular behaviors, including smiling, laughing, gaze aversion, head nods/shakes, gestures, body shifts, self-manipulations with hands, arm movement, and walking or pacing. The four-minute role-play was coded using a 10-second on/10-second off recording interval. This resulted in 12 observed 10-second intervals for which the occurrence of behaviors was recorded. The data are presented in Table 11.2. The observation revealed David gestured at least once during each recording interval. The frequency of David's

Table 11.1 David's Hierarchy of Feared Social Situations

SITUATION	FEAR RATING	AVOIDANCE RATING
Dating/Relationship Assertion		
1. Asking a woman out on a date	75	90
2. Breaking off a relationship	60	85
3. Being assertive, saying no	60	70
Conversations		
1. Going out on a first date	30	0
2. Going to a party where I don't know many people	30	0
3. Starting a conversation with a stranger	20	50

Note: Fear and avoidance are rated on 0–100 scales, with higher numbers indicating greater fear or avoidance.

Table 11.2 Behaviors observed during role-play assessment

BEHAVIOR	% OF INTERVALS IN WHICH BEHAVIOR OCCURRED
Smiling	41.7
Laughing	16.7
Gaze aversion	75.0
Head nods/shakes	8.3
Arm movement	8.3
Gesturing	100.0
Self-manipulation with hands	16.7
Arms crossed0	0
Body shifts/rocking	16.7
Walking/pacing	0
Global Rating of Performance (0–100):	50

gesturing, combined with self-manipulation with his hands (e.g., playing with hair, scratching head) was high, and suggested nervousness on his part. In addition, David's rate of gaze aversion was high enough to be considered inappropriate. All other behaviors occurred at an appropriate frequency. The overall global rating of his performance in the role-play, on a 0 to 100 scale, was 50. This score suggests fairly poor performance, especially given that a rating of 100 was anchored with the descriptor: "Good/as well as anyone could do."

In order to assess his cognitions, David was asked to list his thoughts as they occurred before and during his role-play. Before the role-play began, David's thoughts primarily consisted of self-instructions to act skillfully and appropriately (e.g., "I hope I don't say anything stupid. I've got to remember to let her talk. I've got to listen and not have my mind race"). He apparently did not believe he performed adequately, as his post–role-play thoughts were related to his excessive verbal behavior (e.g., "I talked too fast. I talked too much").

The treatment protocol included role-played exposures to feared heterosocial interactions and thus provided further opportunity for informal observation of David's social skills. During easier role-plays, David performed skillfully, asking and answering questions in a polite and friendly manner. However, as interactions became less superficial (e.g., sharing personal information appropriate to a second date), his performance suffered. David

asked too many questions and did not stop speaking long enough to allow the other person time to answer. He interrupted his role-play partners and cut them off in midsentence. It is worth noting that these are exactly the behaviors he reported being concerned about in the thoughts he listed before and after the initial role-play assessment.

This case illustrates the importance of multimodal assessment across situations. The molecular ratings of the initial assessment role-play indicated some anxious behaviors and poor eye contact, with the overall rating indicating moderately poor performance. However, in this case, the client's self-analysis of his social skill provided more information than was available from the single role-play. As indicated in the later treatment role-plays, David's behavior deteriorated under certain conditions. Without the limitations of a research protocol, it would have been advisable to attend to David's self-reported thoughts after the first role-play and use that information to develop one or more additional role-plays to further delineate the situations in which his skills were more and less appropriate.

SUMMARY

Although differences in theories of social skill exist, many commonalities are present. It is generally agreed that the concept of *social skill* encompasses those skills that enable an individual to effectively and appropriately engage in social interactions. Social skills can be defined in terms of their topography (specific verbal and nonverbal behaviors) and function (outcome), or from an information-processing perspective that focuses on an individual's ability to attend to and process cues from the environment. Within behaviorism, an emphasis has been placed on the situationally specific nature of social skills. That is, social skills are believed to consist of specific, learned responses in specific situations. When assessing social skills, it cannot be assumed that behavior observed in one situation will be generalized to the next.

The behavioral approach to social skills assessment involves both direct observation of client behavior and measurement of the client's subjective experiences. A clinical interview serves as the starting point in the assessment procedure because it allows the clinician to identify the situations in which the client experiences difficulty. Following the interview assessment, direct observation may occur in the form of naturalistic interactions or contrived or controlled role-play scenarios. Although questions have arisen as to the external validity of role-play assessments, role-plays represent the best means by which a clinician can gather observational data. Self-monitoring, self-ratings of performance, and self-report questionnaires provide an assessment of the client's subjective experiences. These strategies are easily employed in clinical settings and, taken together, provide a comprehensive assessment of social skills.

ENDNOTE

1. The authors wish to acknowledge Brett Buican for his contribution to the section describing the AIPSS.

REFERENCES

Alden, L. E., & Wallace, S. T. (1995). Social phobia and social appraisal in successful and unsuccessful social interactions. *Behaviour Research and Therapy, 33*, 497–505.

Andrasik, F., Heimberg, R. G., Edlund, S. R., & Blankenberg, R. (1981). Assessing the readability levels of self-report assertion inventories. *Journal of Consulting and Clinical Psychology, 49*, 142–144.

Beck, J. G., & Heimberg, R. G. (1983). Self-report assessment of assertive behavior. *Behavior Modification, 7*, 451–487.

Becker, R. E., & Heimberg, R. G. (1988). Assessment of social skills. In A. S. Bellack & M. Hersen (Eds.), *Behavioral assessment: A practical handbook* (3rd ed.) (pp. 365–395). New York: Pergamon.

Becker, R. E., Heimberg, R. G., and Bellack, A. S. (1987). *Social skills training treatment for depression*. Elmsford, NY: Pergamon.

Bellack, A. S. (1983). Recurrent problems in the behavioral assessment of social skill. *Behavior Research and Therapy, 21*, 29–41.

Bellack, A. S., Hersen, M., & Lamparski, D. (1979). Role-play tests for assessing social skills: Are they valid? Are they useful? *Journal of Consulting and Clinical Psychology, 47*, 335–342.

Bellack, A. S., Hersen, M., & Turner, S.M. (1979). The relationship of role playing and knowledge of appropriate behavior to assertion in the natural environment. *Journal of Consulting and Clinical Psychology, 47*, 670–678.

Blanchard, E. B., Turner, J., Eschette, N., & Coury, V. M. (1977). Assertiveness training for dental students. *Journal of Dental Education, 41*, 206–208.

Bruch, M. A., Haase, R. F., & Purcell, M. J. (1984). Content dimensions of self-statements in assertive situations: A factor analysis of two measures. *Cognitive Therapy and Research, 8*, 173–186.

Caballo, V. E., & Buela, G. (1988). Molar/molecular assessment in an analogue situation: Relationships among several measures and validation of a behavioral assessment instrument. *Perceptual and Motor Skills, 67*, 591–602.

Calvert, J. D. (1988). Physical attractiveness: A review and reevaluation of its role in social skill research. *Behavioral Assessment, 10*, 29–42.

Chiauzzi, E. J., Heimberg, R. G., Becker, R. E., & Gansler, D. (1985). Personalized versus standard role plays in the assessment of depressed patients' social skill. *Journal of Psychopathology and Behavioral Assessment, 7*, 121–133.

Curran, J. P., & Mariotto, M. J. (1980). A conceptual structure for the assessment of social skills. *Progress in Behavior Modification, 10*, 1–37.

DiNardo, P. A., & Barlow, D. H. (1988). *Anxiety disorders interview schedule-revised (ADIS-R)*. Albany, NY: Graywind.

Donahoe, C. P., Carter, M. J., Bloem, W. D., Hirsch, G. L., Laasi, N., & Wallace, C. J. (1990). Assessment of interpersonal problem-solving skills. *Psychiatry, 53*, 329–339.

Donahoe, C. P., Carter, M. J., Bloem, W. D., & Leff, G. Y. (1984). *Assessment of interpersonal problem-solving skills*. Unpublished test manual, West Los Angeles Veterans Affairs Medical Center.

Eisler, R. M., Hersen, M., & Agras, W. S. (1973). Videotape: A method for the controlled observation of nonverbal interpersonal behavior. *Behavior Therapy, 4*, 420–425.

Eisler, R. M., Hersen, M., Miller, P. M., & Blanchard, E. B. (1975). Situational determinants of assertive behaviors. *Journal of Consulting and Clinical Psychology, 43*, 330–340.

Eisler, R. M., Miller, P., & Hersen, M. (1973). Components of assertive behavior. *Journal of Clinical Psychology, 29*, 295–299.

Frisch, M. B. (1988). Social-desirability responding in the assessment of social skill and anxiety. *Psychological Reports, 63*, 763–766.

Frisch, M. B., & Higgins, R. L. (1986). Instructional demand effects and the correspondence among role-play, self-report, and naturalistic measures of social skill. *Behavioral Assessment, 8*, 221–236.

Galassi, J. P., Galassi, M. D., & Westefeld, J. S. (1978). The Conflict Resolution Inventory: Psychometric data. *Psychological Reports, 42*, 492–494.

Galassi, M. D., & Galassi, J. P. (1976). The effects of role-playing variations on the assessment of assertive behavior. *Behavior Therapy, 7*, 343–347.

Gambrill, E. D., & Richey, C. A. (1975). An assertion inventory for use in assessment and research. *Behavior Therapy, 6*, 550–561.

Gorecki, P. R., Dickson, A. L., Anderson, H. N., & Jones, G. E. (1981). Relationship between contrived *in vivo* and role-play assertive behavior. *Journal of Clinical Psychology, 37*, 104–107.

Gustafson, R. (1992). A Swedish psychometric test of the Rathus Assertiveness Schedule. *Psychological Reports, 71*, 479–482.

Hargie, O., Saunders, C., & Dickson, D. (1994). *Social skills in interpersonal communication* (3rd ed.). New York: Routledge.

Heimberg, R. G., Chiauzzi, E. J., Becker, R. E., & Madrazo-Peterson, R. (1983). Cognitive mediation of assertive behavior: An analysis of the self-statement patterns of college students, psychiatric patients, and normal adults. *Cognitive Therapy and Research, 7*, 455–464.

Heimberg, R. G., & Harrison, D. F. (1980). Use of the Rathus Assertiveness Schedule with criminal offenders: A question of questions. *Behavior Therapy, 11*, 278–281.

Hersen, M., Bellack, A. S., Turner, S. M., Williams, M. T., Harper, K., & Watts, J. G. (1979). Psychometric Properties of the Wolpe-Lazarus Assertiveness Scale. *Behaviour Research & Therapy, 17*, 63–69.

Herzberger, S. D., Chan, E., & Katz, J. (1984). The development of an assertiveness self-report inventory. *Journal of Personality Assessment, 48*, 317–323.

Hope, D. A., & Heimberg, R. G. (1988). Public and private self-consciousness and social phobia. *Journal of Personality Assessment, 52*, 626–639.

Hope, D. A., Heimberg, R. G., & Bruch, M. A. (1995). Dismantling cognitive-behavioral group therapy for social phobia. *Behaviour Research and Therapy, 33*, 637–650.

Hope, D. A., & Mindell, J. A. (1994). Global social skill ratings: Measures of social behavior or physical attractiveness? *Behaviour Research and Therapy, 32*, 463–469.

Hope, D. A., Rapee, R. M., Heimberg, R. G., & Dombeck, M. J. (1990). Representations of the self in social phobia: Vulnerability to social threat. *Cognitive Therapy and Research, 14*, 177–189.

Levenson, R. W., & Gottman, J. M. (1978). Toward the assessment of social competence. *Journal of Consulting and Clinical Psychology, 46*, 453–462.

Liberman, R. P. (1982). Assessment of social skills. *Schizophrenia Bulletin, 8*, 62–83.

Masters, J. C., Burish, T. G., Hollon, S. D., Rimm, D. C. (1987). *Behavior therapy: Techniques and empirical findings* (3rd ed.). New York: Harcourt Brace Jovanovich.

McCormick, I. A. (1984). A simple version of the Rathus Assertiveness Schedule. *Behavioral Assessment, 7*, 95–99.

McFall, R. M. (1982). A review and reformulation of the concept of social skills. *Journal of Behavioral Assessment, 4*, 1–33.

McFall, R. M., & Lillesand, D. B. (1971). Behavioral rehearsal with modeling and coaching in assertion training. *Journal of Abnormal Psychology, 77*, 313–323.

Mueser, K. T., Valenti-Hein, D., & Yarnold, P. R. (1987). Dating-skills groups for the developmentally disabled: Social skills and problem-solving versus relaxation training. *Behavior Modification, 11*, 200–228.

Neitzel, M. T., & Bernstein, D. A. (1976). Effects of instructionally mediated demand on the behavioral assessment of assertiveness. *Journal of Consulting and Clinical Psychology, 44*, 500.

Nelson, R. O., Hayes, S. C., Felton, J. L., & Jarrett, R. B. (1985). A comparison of data produced by different behavioral assessment techniques with implications for models of social skills inadequacy. *Behaviour Research and Therapy, 23*, 1–11.

Pachman, J. S., Foy, D. W., Massey, F., & Eisler, R. M. (1978). A factor analysis of assertive behaviors. *Journal of Consulting and Clinical Psychology, 46*, 347.

Pitcher, S. W., & Meikle, S. (1980). The topography of assertive behavior in positive and negative situations. *Behavior Therapy, 11*, 532–547.

Rapee, R. M., & Lim, L. (1992). Discrepancy between self- and observer ratings of performance in social phobics. *Journal of Abnormal Psychology, 101*, 728–731.

Rathus, S. A. (1973). A 30-item schedule for assessing assertive behavior. *Behavior Therapy, 4*, 398–406.

Royce, W. S., & Arkowitz, H. (1978). Multimodal evaluation of practice interactions as treatment for social isolation. *Journal of Consulting and Clinical Psychology, 46*, 239–245.

St. Lawrence, J. S., Kirksey, W. A., & Moore, T. (1983). External validity of role play assessment of assertive behavior. *Journal of Behavioral Assessment, 5,* 25–34.

Schwartz, R. M., & Gottman, J. M. (1976). Toward a task analysis of assertive behavior. *Journal of Consulting and Clinical Psychology, 44,* 910–920.

Stravynski, A., Marks, I., & Yule, W. (1982). Social skills problems in neurotic outpatients: Social skills training with and without cognitive modification. *Archives of General Psychiatry, 39,* 1378–1385.

Torgrud, L. J., & Holborn, S. W. (1992). Developing externally valid role-play for assessment of social skills: A behavior analytic perspective. *Behavioral Assessment, 14,* 245–277.

Trower, P., Bryant, B., Argyle, M., & Marzillier, J. (1978). *Social skills and mental health.* Pittsburgh: University of Pittsburgh Press.

Twentyman, C. T., & McFall, R. M. (1975). Behavioral training of social skills in shy males. *Journal of Consulting and Clinical Psychology, 43,* 384–395.

Wessberg, H. W., Mariotto, M. J., Conger, A. J., Conger, J. C., & Farrell, A. D. (1979). The ecological validity of role plays for assessing heterosocial anxiety and skill of male college students. *Journal of Consulting and Clinical Psychology, 47,* 525–535.

Wolpe, J., & Lazarus, A. A. (1966). *Behavior therapy techniques: A guide to the treatment for neuroses.* New York: Pergamon.

CHAPTER 12

ASSESSMENT OF HEALTH-RELATED DISORDERS

Donald A. Williamson
Staci Veron-Guidry
Karla Kiper
Louisiana State University

Over the past 20 years, behavioral research related to health and illness has grown at an enormous rate. One outcome of this research effort has been the development of a diverse set of procedures for evaluating behavioral, biological, cognitive, and emotional factors associated with many health-related problems. These assessment procedures utilize diverse methodologies, including direct behavioral observation, self-report inventories, physiological assessment, self-monitoring, and structured interviews. These assessment procedures have been developed for a variety of purposes, including diagnosis, assessment of severity, treatment planning, and measurement of treatment outcome.

In this chapter, we review nine health-related disorders: obesity and eating disorders, cardiovascular disease, headache, chronic pain, diabetes mellitus, acquired immune deficiency syndrome (AIDS), asthma, cancer, and sleep disturbances. These problems were selected because behavioral assessment research with these disorders is most highly developed in terms of diversity of procedures and sophistication of psychometric research.

Each section focuses on one health problem and reviews relevant research related to behavioral assessment procedures for diagnosis and treatment planning for that health-related disorder. Most of the diagnostic procedures can be used to define severity of the illness and can also be used for evaluation of treatment outcome.

OBESITY AND EATING DISORDERS

Description

Obesity is defined by excessive adipose tissue (body fat). There has been considerable controversy about the best method for operationally defining clinically significant obesity (Bray, 1992). In recent years, clinical researchers have begun to define adiposity using the Body Mass Index (BMI), which is defined as weight/height^2, where body weight is measured in kilograms and height is measured in meters (Bray, 1992; Kuczmarski, 1992). This index is highly correlated with more time-consuming and expensive methods for estimating body fat (e.g., body impedance, underwater weighing, or dual photon absorbitometry) (Bray, 1992).

Normative tables for BMI have been developed for different ages and genders. For adults, a BMI between 20 and 25 is normal and is not associated with significant health risks. A BMI between 25 and 30 is associated with a low health risk; a BMI of 30 to 40 is associated with a moderate to high risk; and a BMI above 40 is associated with very high risk for illness (Bray, 1992). Medical disorders associated with increased BMI are cardiovascular disease, diabetes mellitus, gall bladder disease, digestive diseases, sleep apnea, and pulmonary disease. Recent studies of the prevalence of obesity (Kuczmarski, 1992) have found that approximately 25% of adults in the United States are overweight (BMI > 27.3 for women and 27.8 for men) and approximately 9% are severely overweight (BMI > 32.3 for women and 31.1 for men). From these statistics, it is clear that obesity is a very significant threat to the health of our population.

Anorexia and bulimia nervosa are psychiatric disorders with disturbed patterns of eating, fear of fatness, and body image disturbances as central problems. Persons diagnosed with anorexia nervosa are significantly underweight and refuse to gain weight because of feelings of fatness (American Psychiatric Association, 1994). Two subtypes of anorexia nervosa have been identified: those who use restrictive eating to manage fears of weight gain and those who also binge and/or purge. Persons diagnosed with bulimia nervosa are generally in the normal range of body weight. The essential feature of bulimia nervosa is episodic binge eating. Bulimics who binge and purge are described as the purging subtype, whereas those who do not purge are described as nonpurging subtype (American Psychiatric Association, 1994).

Approximately 90% of persons diagnosed with anorexia or bulimia nervosa are female. Prevalence rates for these eating disorders are about 1% to 3% of adolescent and young adult females. Age of onset is generally during adolescence or early adult life. Health-related problems associated with anorexia and bulimia nervosa include anemia, dehydration, sinus bradycardia, hypotension, lowered resting metabolic rate, loss of bone mineral density, erosion of dental enamel, and gastric rupture (American Psychiatric Association, 1994; Williamson, Davis, & Ruggiero, 1987).

Another eating disorder that has drawn recent interest from researchers is binge eating disorder (American Psychiatric Association, 1994). Binge eating disorder is characterized by episodic binge eating with an absence of compensatory behavior to control body weight. Most persons diagnosed with binge eating disorder are significantly overweight, which places them at risk for the many medical problems associated with morbid obesity. Studies of persons seeking weight loss treatment have found that approximately 30% of these individuals can be diagnosed with binge eating disorder.

Assessment for Diagnosis

Two structured interviews have been developed for the assessment of eating disorder symptoms: Eating Disorder Examination (EDE) and Interview for Diagnosis of Eating Disorders (IDED). The EDE, which has undergone 12 revisions (Fairburn & Cooper, 1993), was originally developed as a measure of symptom severity and as a treatment outcome measure. It has been adapted for use as a diagnostic instrument. The reliability and validity of the EDE is well established (Fairburn & Cooper, 1993). The IDED was developed primarily for diagnosis of the eating disorders (Williamson, 1990). It has undergone 4 revisions and the current version of the IDED uses *DSM-IV* (American Psychiatric Association, 1994) diagnostic criteria for establishing diagnoses for anorexia nervosa, bulimia nervosa, and binge eating disorder. Reliability and validity of the IDED are well established (Williamson, Anderson, & Gleaves, in press).

Many self-report inventories have been developed for the assessment of the various symptoms of the eating disorders (e.g., eating behaviors, attitudes, and body image). A complete review of these measures is beyond the scope of this chapter; the interested reader should refer to several recent books on the topic (Allison, 1995; Thompson, in press; Williamson, 1990). Commonly used self-report inventories with strong psychometric properties include: (1) Bulimia Test-Revised (Thelen, Farmer, Wonderlich, & Smith, 1991), (2) Eating

Attitudes Test (Garner & Garfinkel, 1979), (3) Eating Disorder Inventory-2 (Garner, 1991), and (4) Body Shape Questionnaire (Cooper, Taylor, Cooper, & Fairburn, 1987). Many methods for measuring body image have been developed (Thompson, in press), but one method that is especially time efficient is the Body Image Assessment (Williamson, Davis, Bennett, Goreczny, & Gleaves, 1989). Two common methods for measuring eating behavior have been self-monitoring of binge eating and purging (Schlundt, 1995) and use of food frequency questionnaires (Wolper, Heshka, & Heymsfield, 1995). Williamson, Prather, McKenzie, and Blouin (1990) demonstrated that by using combinations of behavioral assessment methods, patients with different types of eating disorders could be reliably differentiated.

Assessment for Treatment Planning

Most of the methods for assessment of diagnosis can also be used for treatment planning and diagnosis. Recent factor-analytic studies (Gleaves & Eberenz, 1993; Gleaves, Williamson, & Barker, 1993; Tobin, Johnson, Steinberg, Staats, & Dennis, 1991) have reported four dimensions that should be assessed when planning treatment: (1) negative affect and personality disorders, (2) dietary restraint, (3) bulimic behavior, and (4) body image. Treatment programs can be individualized by assessing the severity of each of these dimensions and developing interventions that focus on the most significant problems associated with each individual. Treatment outcome has been evaluated most frequently using self-reported frequency of binge eating and purging (Williamson, Anderson, & Gleaves, in press). There is need for a standardized and validated treatment outcome measure that samples the behavior, emotions, and so on associated with the four dimensions identified by factor-analytic studies.

CARDIOVASCULAR DISEASE

Description

Cardiovascular disease refers to diseases affecting the heart or vascular system (e.g., heart attacks,

strokes, or atherosclerosis). Behavioral assessment related to cardiovascular disease generally focuses on behavioral and biological risk factors, including (1) obesity, (2) cigarette smoking, (3) Type A behavior pattern, (4) hypertension, and (5) cholesterol.

Assessment for Diagnosis

The diagnosis of cardiovascular disease requires intensive medical evaluation. Assessment of risk factors associated with obesity can utilize the methods described in the previous section. Biological assays for the constituents of tobacco (i.e., nicotine, cotinine, and carbon monoxide) have been validated as indices of recent tobacco consumption (Henningfield & Obarzanek, 1992). Indirect methods for measuring tobacco consumption include questionnaires that assess frequency and duration of smoking, self-monitoring of smoking, and counting cigarette butts (Henningfield & Obarzanek, 1992). Type A behavior pattern is associated with aggressive and competitive traits. This behavior pattern can be measured by interview (Rosenman, 1978) or by self-report inventory (e.g., the Jenkins Activity Survey) (Jenkins, Rosenman, & Friedman, 1967) or the Framingham Type A Scale (Haynes, Feinleib, Levine, Scotch, & Kannel, 1980). Hypertension is most commonly measured using a sphygmomanometer, inflatable cuff, and stethoscope. Hypertension is generally defined as systolic blood pressure above 160 mmHg and diastolic blood pressure above 95 mmHg. Cholesterol and serum lipids are typically measured using biochemical assays of blood serum.

Assessment for Treatment Planning

Individualized treatment plans can be based on the presence of one or more biobehavioral risk factors for cardiovascular disease. Most treatment programs will be designed to prevent heart attacks or strokes. The most common treatment approaches will include (1) biofeedback/relaxation training, (2) weight reduction strategies, (3) programs for reduction of Type A behavior, (4) smoking cessation programs, and (5) exercise enhancement programs (Williamson & Sebastian, 1994). Treatment outcome can be monitored by measurement of biobehavioral risk factors.

HEADACHE

Description

Headaches are one of the most common patient complaints; it is estimated that more than 35 million Americans experience recurrent headaches (Swartz, 1994). It has been estimated that about 91% of men and 96% of women experience some type of headache at least once a year, with migraine headaches occurring in about 6% of men and 18% of women (Silberstein & Lipton, 1993). Women between the ages of 30 and 49 years and from lower socioeconomic status are at higher risk for having migraine headaches (Stewart, Lipton, Celentano, & Reed, 1992).

Migraine headaches have two phases: a prodromal phase, during which there is intracranial vasoconstriction, followed by the headache phase, during which there is rebound vasodilation. Migraine headache is described as unilateral, pulsating pain, which often develops a more generalized locus of pain. Nausea, vomiting, fatigue, and photophobia (a sensitivity to bright lights) are commonly reported symptoms in association with migraine headaches. Two types of migraine headaches can be distinguished: common and classic, with the primary differentiation being the occurrence of clear prodromal symptoms with classic migraines, and the absence of prodromal symptoms in common migraine headache (Silberstein & Lipton, 1993).

Muscle contraction headaches are characterized by bilateral, constant pain commonly reported in the forehead, neck, and shoulders. Prodromal symptoms (nausea, vomiting, and photophobia) are not associated with muscle contraction headaches. Combined headaches, or mixed headaches, involve symptoms of both migraine and muscle contraction headaches, or the occurrence of two distinct types of headache (Blanchard & Andrasik, 1985). Recent research has provided evidence that migraine and muscle contraction headaches are not discrete syndromes but rather form a continuum of headache, ranging from muscle contraction to migraine (Nelson, 1994).

Assessment for Diagnosis

A structured interview is recommended for the diagnosis of headache. Blanchard and Andrasik (1985) developed a semistructured interview format for headache diagnosis. In conducting an interview for the diagnosis of headache, it is important that the clinician identify antecedents for the headache, behaviors that occur during the headache, and consequences of the headache (e.g., the reaction of family members or the inability to perform routine activities). From this information, the potential maintenance of headaches by positive or negative reinforcement can be ascertained. In the interview, it is very important to identify the frequency and duration of headaches and the presence of a family history of headache.

An example of a simple method for grading severity of a headache is the Chronic Pain Index, which assumes that a continuum of pain intensity and disability is the underlying dimension of severity. Along this continuum, lower levels of severity are differentiated by pain intensity and higher levels by interference with function (Von Korff, Stewart, & Lipton, 1994).

A complete physical examination should be conducted to rule out organic etiology for headaches. Additionally, psychological factors may be a primary cause of recurring headaches. Research has shown that patients who experience headaches are more neurotic, depressed, and anxious than patients who do not have headaches (Elwan, El, Mohamed, Elwan, & Helmi, 1993). However, Holroyd, France, Nash, and Hursey (1993) found that psychological symptoms were elevated in subjects with headaches if they were experiencing a headache at the time of the assessment, which raises the possibility that pain state at the time of assessment should be controlled to obtain an accurate evaluation of psychological factors.

Assessment for Treatment Planning

An effective treatment plan is based on a thorough assessment of the type, frequency, and duration of a patient's headache. Identification of headache antecedents allows the clinician to implement effective stimulus control procedures. Progressive muscle relaxation (Jacobson, 1938) and biofeedback (Williamson, 1981) are common behavioral treatments for headache. Relaxation training has been shown to have superior long-term treatment effects for tension headache when compared to EMG biofeedback, though for migraineurs, both relaxation training and skin temperature biofeedback seem to be equivalent for long-term efficacy (Blanchard, 1987). Treatment outcome can be evaluated using self-monitoring procedures as well as objective measures of concomitant psychological symptoms. Evaluations of nonpharmacologic treatment of chronic headaches have shown that anxiety, depression, and somatic complaints were reduced following successful treatment (Blanchard, Steffek, & Jaccard, 1991).

CHRONIC PAIN

Description

Chronic pain is described as pain that persists for at least six months that is not the result of malignant disease. The pain is often of severe intensity, possibly causing disability, and is usually the result of trauma, physical injury, or a physical disorder.

A patient's self-report of the experience of pain is subjective; therefore, there are many problems associated with the assessment and diagnosis of chronic pain. Clinicians must depend on the patient's self-report of the intensity, description, and location of the pain (Turk, Wack, & Kerns, 1985). A single rating of pain intensity has not yet been found to be valid. However, a composite pain intensity score calculated from an average of several ratings of pain can increase reliability and validity (Jensen & McFarland, 1993).

Assessment for Diagnosis

Several assessment measures are commonly used in the evaluation of patients with chronic pain. The West Haven–Yale Multidimensional Pain Inventory (MPI) has been shown to be a reliable and valid measure of the cognitive, behavioral, and affective dimensions of pain (Walter & Brannon, 1991). Other tests that are often used in the assessment of chronic pain patients include the Symptom Check-list-90-Revised (Derogatis, 1977), the McGill Pain Questionnaire (Melzack, 1975), and the Health Index (Sterbach, Wolf, Murphy, & Akeson, 1973). The Functional Interference Estimate (FIE) self-report scale is designed to measure functional impairment associated with chronic pain (Toomey, Mann, Hernandez, & Abashian, 1993). These questionnaires measure personality variables and focus on the report of pain symptoms.

Varying levels of psychopathology are identified among chronic pain patients. Individuals with chronic pain who are diagnosed with major depression or dysthymia have been found to have higher scores on the Cognitive Errors Questionnaire than nondepressed patients and normal controls (Smith, O'Keefe, & Christensen, 1994). The affective component of pain is usually a combination of anger, fear, and sadness (Fernandez & Milburn, 1994). These research findings indicate the need for a broad assessment of cognitions and specific emotions that are associated with pain.

Assessment for Treatment Planning

Fordyce, Fowler, Lehmann, Delateur, Sand, and Trieschmann (1973) developed an assessment paradigm that monitors the time that a patient spends walking, sitting, and standing. Direct observations of chronic pain patients and observations by family members and peers provide additional data for a functional analysis of pain behaviors (Fordyce, 1976). Overt expressions of pain and distress (i.e., grimacing, rubbing, bracing) can be quantified (Keefe & Block, 1982), providing goals for treatment. Treatment planning includes extinguishing pain behaviors and promoting well behaviors (behaviors that are incompatible with pain, such as exercise and work) (Fordyce, 1976). Relaxation training and biofeedback are often used with chronic pain patients if elevated muscle tension is found to exacerbate and/or maintain pain (Turk & Rudy, 1990). Cognitive restructuring can be used to modify cognitive errors that function to intensify the disability associated with chronic pain (Keefe & Williams, 1989). Self-monitoring of pain, as well as repeated assessments of pain behaviors and related psychological variables, are essential for effective pain treatment.

DIABETES MELLITUS

Description

Diabetes mellitus is a metabolic disorder that is caused by either ineffective production or ineffective utilization of insulin, a hormone which is secreted by the pancreas. There are two types of diabetes mellitus. Insulin-dependent diabetes mellitus (IDDM) usually develops during childhood and requires daily insulin injections (Surwit, Feinglos, & Scovern, 1983). Non-insulin-dependent diabetes mellitus (NIDDM) usually has an onset after age 40 in overweight individuals. For NIDDM patients, the disorder can often be controlled with the use of oral hypoglycemia medications and diet modification (Surwit et al., 1983).

Assessment for Diagnosis

A medical diagnosis of diabetes is always required. Various psychological problems such as noncompliance with self-care regimen, adjustment problems related to diagnosis of a chronic disease, and deficits in problem solving and stress management may complicate the management of diabetes. Given the importance of diet and maintenance of a normal body weight for effective management of diabetes, the assessment of diet and identification of disordered eating patterns are necessary. Approaches for the assessment of obesity and eating disorders were discussed in an earlier section of this chapter.

Assessment of problem-solving skills and social support may be important because diabetic individuals who have higher perceived support from friends and who use problem-solving coping strategies have been found to be healthier, whereas individuals with a wish-fulfillment coping style tend to be less healthy (Kvam & Lyons, 1991).

An assessment of the presence of depressive symptoms should be conducted with diabetic patients. Individuals with complications from diabetes have been found to score significantly higher on depression inventories than both individuals without diabetic complications and those without diabetes. Also, symptoms of sexual dysfunction have been significantly correlated with symptoms of depression in diabetic women but not in diabetic men (Leedom, Meehan, Procci, & Ziedler, 1991).

Assessment for Treatment Planning

Self-monitoring is used with diabetic patients in order to identify and target maladaptive behaviors related to the management of diabetes, including diet, exercise, and regular health care. Assessment of the relationship between stress and management of diabetes can have important treatment implications. Biofeedback-assisted relaxation to reduce stress and for control of blood glucose levels has been shown to be an effective treatment approach for some diabetic patients (Bailey, Good, & McGrady, 1990). Additional components of a treatment plan may be increasing problem-solving skills and assertiveness in social situations that will help a diabetic patient to adhere to a self-care regimen.

ACQUIRED IMMUNE DEFICIENCY SYNDROME (AIDS)

Description

Acquired immune deficiency syndrome (AIDS) is a disease that impairs the ability of one's body to fight disease. AIDS develops in individuals infected with the human immunodeficiency virus (HIV). HIV is spread by unprotected sexual contact with an infected person, by intravenous drug use with contaminated needles or syringes, by receiving blood transfusions of infected blood products, and from an infected mother to her baby (Gong, 1986). AIDS patients become more susceptible to opportunistic infections, which are commonly found in the environment but are detrimental only to individuals with weak immune systems.

Assessment for Diagnosis

A diagnosis of AIDS should be considered in patients under the age of 60 who develop recurrent and/or unusual infections (Gong, 1986). Cleary, Fowler, Weismann, and Massagli (1993) presented a set of scales used for assessing the symptoms and level of functioning of persons infected with HIV. These researchers reported that psychological well-being and perceived health status were the strongest correlates of life satisfaction. Among HIV-infected individuals, organic, mood, adjustment, and personality disorders have been found to be common psychiatric diagnoses (Ellis, Collis, & King, 1994), and many AIDS patients are diagnosed with nonalcohol psychoactive substance abuse. Assessment for cognitive impairment should include a basic screening or a thorough neuropsychological evaluation in order to identify symptoms of HIV-related dementia or other memory and attention disorders.

Assessment for Treatment Planning

Patients who have been diagnosed with AIDS often experience significant anxiety; therefore, anxiety management and the development of effective coping strategies are often an integral part of behavioral interventions with AIDS patients (Taylor, Kemeny, Schneider, & Aspinwall, 1993). Two types of coping skills can be distinguished: problem-focused coping and emotion-focused coping (Lazarus & Folkman, 1984). The focus of problem-focused coping is to facilitate the patient's attempts to actively manage a stressful situation, whereas emotion-focused coping relates to the emotional consequences of a stressful event (i.e., a diagnosis of AIDS).

Research has shown that avoidant coping strategies are generally not effective for management of chronic stressors (e.g., Suls & Fletcher, 1985). Common avoidant coping strategies of AIDS patients include overeating and substance abuse (Taylor, Kemeny, Schneider, & Aspinwall, 1993), which can further increase depression and feelings of hopelessness. Therefore, behavioral treatment with AIDS patients often involves identification of maladaptive coping patterns, depressive symptoms, feelings of hopelessness, and suicidal ideation. For example, treatment planning may include behavioral contracting to decrease maladaptive coping strategies, cognitive restructuring of dysfunctional thinking, and modification of high-risk behaviors (e.g., unprotected sex and sharing needles for intravenous drug use).

An important component of a treatment plan for AIDS patients is the implementation of AIDS risk-behavior change (e.g., Coates, 1990), targeting primary risk factors such as engaging in unprotected sex or sharing needles or syringes for intravenous drug use. Fisher and Fisher (1992) have proposed that three key components of AIDS risk

reduction are information about AIDS, motivation to reduce AIDS risk behavior, and the behavioral skills for performing specific preventive acts. Role-playing can be useful in increasing a patient's self-efficacy and likelihood of avoiding high-risk situations. For a complete discussion of this model of AIDS risk-behavior change, the reader is referred to Fisher and Fisher (1993).

Patients with AIDS often have neuropsychiatric disorders concurrent with complications of the physical disease. Therefore, it is important that clinicians be able to distinguish any central nervous system disturbances caused by AIDS from those psychological problems that are exacerbated by the social impact of having AIDS (Ostrow, Grant, & Atkinson, 1988).

ASTHMA

Description

Asthma is characterized by airflow obstruction caused by hyperesponsiveness of the large and small airways of the lungs. The prominent clinical manifestations of asthma include wheezing, coughing, and shortness of breath. Attacks may be of sufficient severity to impair normal daily activities such as walking and talking (Cluss & Fireman, 1985; Hayes & Fitzgerald, 1993). The specific etiology of asthma is unknown. However, asthma has been associated with familial, infectious, allergenic, and psychosocial factors (Asthma–United States, 1995). Asthma attacks brought on by allergic stimuli are often referred to as *extrinsic asthma*, whereas *intrinsic asthma* describes asthma attacks that where no allergens or infections are identified (Cluss & Fireman, 1985).

Prevalence studies have found that incidence and mortality associated with asthma increased in the United States and other countries during the 1980s (Weiss & Wagener, 1990). Approximately 10 million Americans suffer from asthma. The Centers for Disease Control (CDC) estimated that the prevalence of self-reported asthma increased 42% from 34.7 per 1,000 to 49.4 per 1,000 during the years 1982 through 1992. The same CDC report indicated that the annual age-adjusted death rate associated with asthma increased from 13.4 per 1 million to 18.8 per 1 million during 1982 through 1991, a 40% increase (Asthma–United States, 1995).

Assessment for Diagnosis

A complete medical evaluation is essential for a diagnosis of asthma. Medical diagnosis is based on patient report of symptoms and measurement of peak lung airflow using a spirometer. Assessment of the history of asthma symptoms typically includes patient report of the onset, duration, frequency, and severity of symptoms and attacks. It is important to note during the patient's report of symptoms any seasonal or diurnal changes in the frequency and severity of attacks, as well as any environmental factors that may provoke asthma attacks (e.g., dust, foods, beverages, drugs, plants, and animals). Finally, it is important to assess the impact of physical activity, exercise, and stress on asthma symptoms for the patient (Hayes & Fitzgerald, 1993).

Objective self-report measures to assess individual responding to asthma symptoms have been developed. The Asthma Symptom Checklist (ASC) assesses five symptom groups: (1) panic-fear, (2) irritability, (3) fatigue, (4) airway obstruction, and (5) hyperventilation-hypocapnia (Kinsman, Dahlem, Spector, & Staudenmayer, 1977). The Asthma Problem Behavior Checklist (APBC) assesses problem behavior patterns that may exacerbate asthma symptoms and maintain asthma attacks (e.g., potential reinforcers and the responses of family members to the asthma patient) (Creer, Marion, & Creer, 1983). More recently, the Asthma Symptom Profile (ASP) (Leher, Hochron, Isenberg, & Rausch, 1993) was developed to assess changes in the intensity, unpleasantness, and quality of asthma symptoms.

Assessment for Treatment Planning

Assessment for treatment planning should include identification of environmental factors that trigger asthma attacks (e.g., persons, places, stressful experiences) and reinforcers that might maintain asthma attacks (e.g., relief from occupational responsibilities or aversive situations) (Creer, 1982). It is very important to assess the level of daily stress and emotional reaction to stress by the asthma patient. Reactions by family members to the asthma patient are also important to note, since they may inadvertently worsen the severity of an asthma attack by increasing the arousal of the asthma patient or maintain asthma attacks by reinforcing illness behavior (Klinnert, Mrazek, & Mrazek, 1994). Compliance with medical treatment for asthma (medications, diet, activity level) is another important area to assess during the behavioral interview. Treatment outcome may be assessed using self-report inventories and daily self-monitoring of frequency and severity of asthma attacks. In addition, monitoring the number of days missed from school or work and the frequency of visits to the hospital or clinic for emergency care may be targeted during treatment and used to evaluate treatment outcome.

CANCER

Description

In 1990, over 500,000 Americans died from cancer. Cancer has been one of the 10 leading causes of death in the United States for some time. The root causes of cancer have often been identified as a combination of in-born/genetic and external factors, including tobacco use, diet patterns, contact with infectious agents, and exposure to carcinogens in the environment. In an analysis of the causes of death in the United States, the most common external factors that contribute to death were factors associated with cancer: tobacco, diet, exercise levels, and toxic agents (McGinnis & Foege, 1993).

It is estimated that tobacco contributes from 11% to 30% of all cancer deaths, particularly cancers of the lung, esophagus, oral cavity, pancreas, kidney, and bladder (Rothenberg, Nasca, Mikl, Burnett, & Reynolds, 1987). As of 1989, the U.S. Department of Health and Human Services (USDHHS) identified smoking as the leading cause of cancer deaths in the United States (USDHHS, 1989). Alcohol consumption may potentiate the effects of smoking and may increase risk for esophageal, laryngeal, and oral cancers (USDHHS, 1982). Dietary factors have been associated with colon and breast cancer (USDHHS, 1988), and inadequate physical activity has been identified as a risk factor for colon cancer (Powell, Caspersen, Hoplan, & Ford, 1989).

Obesity has also been identified as a significant risk factor in certain types of cancer and is seen as a manifestation of the connection between diet and activity patterns (McGinnis, & Foege, 1993). In an extensive analysis of risk factors for cancer, 35% of all cancer deaths are estimated to be related to diet (Doll & Peto, 1981). It has been suggested that a 50% decrease in the consumption of animal fats might produce a proportionate decrease in colon cancer risk (Henderson, Ross, & Pike, 1991).

Assessment for Diagnosis

Patients diagnosed with cancer may experience psychological problems associated with the diagnosis and treatment. It is important to identify any areas that may affect how well the patient complies and copes with treatment. Common problems associated with cancer diagnosis include depression, anxiety, and sleep problems. These problems may be assessed with psychological measures of general psychopathology such as the Minnesota Multiphasic Personality Inventory-2 (Butcher, 1989) as well as Symptom Checklist-90-Revised (Derogatis, 1983). Specific syndrome checklists such as the Beck Depression Inventory (Beck, Ward, Mendelson, Mock & Erbaugh, 1961) and the State-Trait Anxiety Inventory (Spielberger, Gorsuch, & Lushene, 1970) may also be employed. It is highly important to assess common problem areas associated with cancer treatment that may affect compliance. These problems include sexual dysfunction, pain, nausea, and vomiting. The McGill Pain Questionnaire (Melzack, 1975), and the Morrow Assessment of Nausea and Emesis (Morrow, 1984) have both been used to assess levels of pain associated with cancer treatment.

Assessment for Treatment Planning

Assessment of the cancer patient during treatment can focus on monitoring specific behaviors targeted for change, compliance with cancer treatment, as well as specific and general stressors associated with cancer diagnosis and treatment. Compliance with medical treatment (taking medications, attending chemotherapy sessions) is an important factor to assess on an ongoing basis via patient self-monitoring or interviews, given the evidence that noncompliance with medical treatment is common, especially when that treatment is complex or involving multiple phases (Gerber & Nehemkis, 1986). Problems commonly associated with cancer treatment, such as pain and nausea, can negatively affect compliance with cancer treatment. Careful assessment of the antecedents, frequency, and severity of problems such as nausea is helpful in successfully implementing relaxation or desensitization training to reduce the impact of these problems.

A second area of potential ongoing assessment in cancer treatment involves monitoring patient progress toward changing those behaviors that may increase their chances of surviving cancer. Cessation of cigarette smoking or alcohol use, weight loss and dietary changes for obese patients, and incorporation of physical exercise into lifestyle have all been recognized as having significant potential to enhance cancer survival and to prevent further chronic disease (Brantley & Garrett, 1993).

SLEEP DISTURBANCES

Description

The *Diagnostic and Statistical Manual of Mental Disorders (DSM-IV*; American Psychiatric Association, 1994) describes four major categories of sleep disturbances based on the etiology of the disturbance: (1) Primary Sleep Disorders, (2) Sleep Disorder Related to another Mental Disorder, (3) Sleep Disorder Due to a General Medical Condition, and (4) Substance-Induced Sleep Disorder. Primary Sleep Disorders may involve problems in the amount, timing, or quality of sleep (dyssomnias), or with the activation of autonomic, motor, or cognitive processes during sleep or the transition between sleep and wakefulness. Population surveys indicate that some 30% to 40% of the general adult population experience insomnia during a one-year period. Up to 60% of night workers experience sleep problems related to shift work, and between 1% to 10% of the general adult population report difficulties with sleep due to breathing problems (American Psychiatric Association, 1994).

Assessment for Diagnosis

Medical evaluation, including physical examination and drug history, is critical for accurate diagnosis of sleep disorders. In addition, a comprehensive psychiatric and sleep history also provides important information for diagnosis and treatment planning. The clinical interview with the patient should determine the exact nature of the sleep difficulty (e.g., falling asleep vs. staying asleep). It is helpful to note onset and duration of sleep difficulties as well as relevant life events that may have happened before the sleep problems began. Comprehensive evaluation of sleep parameters should gather data regarding the patient's sleep/wake schedule, including time spent in bed during a typical night, frequency and duration of daytime napping, and any variability in the sleep/wake schedule (e.g., weekday vs. weekend).

Other factors to assess include medication use, caffeine/nicotine use, exercise habits, and practices that are compatible with good sleep or sleep hygiene (e.g., going to bed and waking up at the same time every day) (Hauri, 1992). Finally, the clinical interview should assess antecedents and consequences of sleep difficulties—events that typically precede sleep difficulties, consequences of sleep problems, and how the patient responds or copes with sleep problems.

Several objective self-report measures have been developed. The Sleep History Questionnaire (Lacks, 1987) and the Sleep Impairment Index (Morin, 1993) are global measures of sleep dysfunction that allow the patient to report on the nature and severity of his or her sleep difficulties. The Pittsburgh Sleep Quality Index (PSQI; Buysse, Reynolds, Monk, Berman, & Kupfer, 1989) is a 19-item questionnaire that assesses sleep quality over a one-month period. The PSQI yields seven factor scores (sleep quality, sleep-onset latency, efficiency, duration of sleep, disturbances, use of medication, and daytime dysfunction) and one global score of sleep quality. The Sleep Behavior Self-Rating Scale (Kazarian, Howe, & Csapo, 1979) is

a 24-item questionnaire that assesses the frequency of sleep-incompatible practices and discriminates well between poor and good sleepers. The Sleep Hygiene Awareness and Practice Scale (Lacks & Rotert, 1986) assesses beliefs about the beneficial or negative effects of certain foods, beverages, drugs, and activities, and can provide useful data about the patient's sleep hygiene practices.

Nocturnal polysomnography is widely considered to provide the most comprehensive assessment of sleep problems. Polysomnography involves all-night electronic monitoring of sleep parameters that yields information about sleep stages. Nocturnal polysomnography can be very helpful in determination of any discrepancy between the patient's self-report and actual sleep difficulties, especially when insomnia and daytime sleepiness are the patient's chief complaints (Morin, 1993).

Assessment for Treatment Planning

Treatment for sleep problems often involves modification of specific environmental, behavioral, and emotional factors that contribute to the sleep disturbance. Behavioral interviewing and patient self-monitoring are useful ways to assess potential environmental or lifestyle factors that may initiate or maintain sleep problems and that can be targeted for change. Patient self-monitoring of bedtime, waking time, total hours spent in bed, number of awakenings during sleep, and quality of sleep via Sleep Diaries has been established as a useful, low-cost method for determining the severity of a patient's sleep problem. Sleep Diaries may also make patients more aware of their own sleep patterns (Morin, 1993).

Screening for psychopathology via measures of general psychopathology such as the Symptom Checklist-90-Revised (Derogatis, 1983) as well as depression and anxiety via the Beck Depression Inventory (Beck, Ward, Mendelson, Mock, & Erbaugh, 1961) and the State-Trait (Spielberger, Gorsuch, & Lushene, 1970) is important. Sleep disorders, especially insomnia, have been associated with a number of psychiatric disorders that may warrant further assessment and treatment of these problems (Ware & Morewitz, 1991).

Case Example

Presenting Problems. Dottie was a 46-year-old African American woman referred for evaluation of obesity and binge eating. At the time of assessment, she weighed 299 pounds, with a height of 5 feet, 5 inches. Her body mass index was calculated to be 49.9, which placed her in the range of extreme risk for medical problems. In addition to obesity, she was found to be hypertensive and diabetic. She had recently injured her back in an accident and her physician had advised weight loss before progressing to more intensive therapy for the pain she was experiencing.

History of Problems. Dottie grew up in a rural community where she and her family worked on a farm. She was never significantly overweight throughout childhood and adolescence. She had no significant medical problems as a child. Her mother and grandmother were obese and her father was slightly overweight. Her mother was still alive and was a non-insulin-dependent diabetic. Dottie graduated from high school and from nursing school with an R.N. degree. At the time of graduation, Dottie weighed approximately 145 pounds. She married when she was 22 years old and had three children over the next seven years. During this period, she gained about 50 pounds during each pregnancy and retained about 30 pounds after each delivery.

By the time Dottie was 30 years old, she weighed about 235 pounds. She was divorced from her husband at age 34 and reported a period of mild depression and loneliness over the next few years. She tried numerous commercial and noncommercial diets and always lost 10 to 20 pounds, but quickly regained the weight. She was employed as a nurse during her 20s and 30s. Her three children grew up with only minimal problems. Between the ages of 30 and 46 years, she gradually gained to a highest weight level of 310 pounds. When she was 44 years old, she experienced a fall at work and began to complain of back pain. At age 45, she was diagnosed with diabetes and hypertension. Just prior to this evaluation, she had taken a medical leave of absence from her job and was considering early retirement. She appeared to be highly motivated for medical and psychological treatment.

Behavioral Assessment. Dottie was interviewed using the Interview for Diagnosis of Eating Disorders-IV. The interview found that Dottie was engaging in episodes of binge eating almost every day. She worked the night shift and tried to refrain from eating during work, though she often snacked from vending machines. When she came home from work, she was usually tired, hungry, and unable to sleep. She found that if she ate large quantities of food, she could sleep well. Dietary and behavioral assessment indicated that she routinely consumed over 3,000 kcal/day and that over two-thirds of her caloric consumption occurred after 5:00 P.M. Results of self-report inventories confirmed the presence of significant binge eating (BULIT-R = 123) and low dietary restraint (TFEQ Restraint = 5). A Beck Depression Score of 22 indicated that she was mildly depressed. Food Frequency Questionnaire data suggested a diet high in dietary fat and carbohydrates.

Treatment Recommendations. Dottie was diagnosed with Binge Eating Disorder and mild depression. She was referred to a long-term outpatient treatment program that specialized in the treatment of these problems. She was prescribed fluoxetine and attended an outpatient cognitive-behavior therapy program for Binge Eating Disorder. Following successful reduction of binge eating and depression, she would be transferred to a weight management component of the program.

SUMMARY

Behavioral assessment methods for health-related disorders have been the focus of an extensive research effort over the past 20 years. During this period, many different assessment procedures have been devised and many of these methods have been tested in rigorous tests of reliability and validity.

The challenges of the future will be to (1) develop assessment procedures that lead directly to cost-effective treatment and (2) develop relatively straightforward methods for evaluating treatment outcome. We are currently in the midst of a revolution in health care. If behavioral assessment is to make a lasting mark, we must integrate assessment methods into an integrated continuum of care that upholds quality yet reduces the overall cost of care.

REFERENCES

Allison, D. B. (1995). *Handbook of assessment methods for eating behaviors and weight-related problems: Measures, theory, and research.* Thousand Oaks, CA: Sage.

American Psychiatric Association. (1994). *Diagnostic and statistical manual of mental disorders* (4th ed.). Washington, DC: Author.

Asthma–United States, 1982–1992. (1995, February). *Journal of the American Medical Association.* pp. 451–452.

Bailey, B. K., Good, M., & McGrady, A. (1990). Clinical observations on behavioral treatment of a patient with insulin-dependent diabetes mellitus. *Biofeedback and Self-Regulation. 15*, 7–13.

Beck, A. T., Ward, C. H., Mendelson, M., Mock, J., & Erbaugh, J. (1961). An inventory for measuring depression. *Archives of General Psychiatry, 4*, 561–571.

Blanchard, E. B. (1987). Long-term effects of behavioral treatment of chronic headache. *Behavior Therapy, 18*, 375–385.

Blanchard, E. B., & Andrasik, F. (1985). *Management of chronic headaches: A Psychological approach.* Elmsford, NY: Pergamon.

Blanchard, E. B., Steffek, B. D., & Jaccard, J. (1991). Psychological changes accompanying non-pharmacologic treatment of chronic headache: The effects of outcome. *Headache, 31*, 249–253.

Brantley, P. J., & Garrett, V. D. (1993). Psychobiological approaches to health and disease. In P. B. Sutker & H. A. Adams (Eds.), *Comprehensive handbook of psychopathology* (2nd ed.) (pp. 647–670). New York: Plenum.

Bray, G. A. (1992). Pathophysiology of obesity. *American Journal of Clinical Nutrition, 55*, 4885–4945.

Butcher, J. N. (1989). *Minnesota Multiphasic Personality Inventory-2, User's Guide, the Minnesota report: Adult Clinical System.* Minneapolis: National Computer Systems.

Buysse, D. J., Reynolds, C. F., Monk, T. H., Berman, S. R., & Kupfer, D. J. (1989). The Pittsburg Sleep Quality Index: A new instrument for psychiatric practice and research. *Psychiatry Research, 28*, 193–213.

Cleary, P. D., Fowler, F. J., Weismann, J., & Massagli, M. P. (1993). Health-related quality of life in persons with acquired immune deficiency syndrome. *Medical care, 31*, 569–580.

Cluss, P. & Fireman, P. (1985). Recent trends in asthma research. *Annals of Behavioral Medicine, 7*, 11–16.

Coates, T. J. (1990). Strategies for modifying sexual behavior for primary and secondary prevention of HIV disease. *Journal of Consulting and Clinical Psychology, 58*, 57–69.

Cooper, P. J., Taylor, M. J., Cooper, Z., & Fairburn, C. G. (1987). Development and validation of the Body Shape Questionnaire. *International Journal of Eating Disorders, 6*, 485–494.

Creer,. T. (1982). Asthma. *Journal of Consulting and Clinical Psychology, 50*, 912–921.

Creer, T., Marion, T., & Creer, P. (1983). Asthma Problem Behavior Checklist: Parental perceptions of the behavior of asthmatic children. *Journal of Asthma, 20*, 97–104.

Derogatis, L. (1977). *Manual for the Symptom Checklist-90, Revised.* Baltimore: John Hopkins University School of Medicine.

Derogatis, L. (1983). *SCL-90-R Manual-II.* Towson, MD: Clinical Psychometric Research.

Doll, R., & Peto, R. (1981). *The causes of cancer: Quantitative estimates of avoidable risks of cancer in the United States today.* New York: Oxford University Press.

Ellis, D., Collis, I., & King, M. (1994). A controlled comparison of HIV and general medical referrals to a liaison psychiatry service. *AIDS Care, 6.* 69–76.

Elwan, O. H., El, T., Mohamed, S., Elwan, F., & Helmi, A. A. (1993). Headache: Psychometric and hormonal assessment. *Headache Quarterly 4*, 343–349.

Fairburn, C. G., & Cooper, Z. (1993). The eating disorder examination (12th ed.). In C. G. Fairburn & G. T. Wilson (Eds.), *Binge eating: Nature, assessment, and treatment* (pp. 317–360). New York: Guilford.

Fernandez, E., & Milburn, T. W. (1994). Sensory and affective predictors of overall pain and emotions associated with affective pain. *Clinical Journal of Pain, 10*, 3–9.

Fisher, J. D., & Fisher, W. A. (1992). Changing AIDS risk behavior. *Psychological Bulletin, 111*, 454–474.

Fisher, W. A., & Fisher, J. D. (1993). A general social psychological model for changing AIDS risk behavior. In J. B. Pryor and G. D. Reeder (Eds.), *The social psychology of HIV infection* (pp. 127–153). Hillsdale, NJ: Lawrence Erlbaum.

Fordyce, W. E. (1976). *Behavioral methods for chronic pain and illness.* St. Louis: C. V. Mosby.

Fordyce, W. E., Fowler, R. S., Lehmann, J. R., Delateur,

B. J., Sand, P. L., & Trieschmann, R. B. (1973). Operant conditioning in the treatment of chronic pain. *Archives of Physical Medicine and Rehabilitation, 54*, 399–408.

Garner, D. M. (1991). *Eating Disorder Inventory-2 manual*. Odessa, FL: Psychological Assessment Resources.

Garner, D. M., & Garfinkel, P. E. (1979). The Eating Attitudes Test: An index of the symptoms of anorexia nervosa. *Psychological Medicine, 9*, 273–279.

Gerber, K. E., & Nehemkis, A. M. (1986). *Compliance: The dilemma of the chronically ill*. New York: Springer.

Gleaves, D. H., & Eberenz, K. (1993). Psychopathology of anorexia nervosa: A factor analytic investigation. *Journal of Psychopathology and Behavioral Assessment, 15*, 141–152.

Gleaves, D. H., Williamson, D. A., & Barker, S. E. (1993). Confirmatory factor analysis of a multidimensional model of bulimia nervosa. *Journal of Abnormal Psychology, 102* (1), 173–176.

Gong, V. (1986). Facts and fallacies: An AIDS overview. In V. Gong & N. Rudnick (Eds.), *AIDS: Fact and issues* (pp. 3–14). New Brunswick, NJ: Rutgers University Press.

Hauri, P. (1992). *Current concepts: The sleep disorders*. Kalamazoo, MI: Upjohn.

Hayes, J. P., & Fitzgerald, M. X. (1993). Modern management of asthma in adults. *Quarterly Journal of Medicine, 86*, 693–696.

Haynes, S., Feinleib, M., Levine, S., Scotch, N., & Kannel, W. (1980). The relationship of psychosocial factors to coronary heart disease in the Framingham Study. III. Eight-year incidence of coronary heart disease. *American Journal of Epidemiology, III*, 37–58.

Henderson, B. E., Ross, R. H., & Pike, M. C. (1991). Toward the primary prevention of cancer. *Science, 254*, 1131–1138.

Henningfield, J. E., & Obarzanek, E. (1992). Task Force 2: Methods of assessment, strategies for research. *Health Psychology, 11* (supplement), 10–16.

Holroyd, K. A., France, J. L., Nash, J. M., & Hursey, K. G. (1993). Pain state as artifact in the psychological assessment of recurrent headache sufferers. *Pain, 53,* 229–235.

Jacobson, E. (1938). *Progressive relaxation*. Chicago: University of Chicago Press.

Jenkins, C., Rosenman, R., & Friedman, M. (1967). Development of an objective psychological test for the determination of the coronary-prone behavior pattern in employed men. *Journal of Chronic Diseases, 20*, 371–379.

Jensen, M. P., & McFarland, C. A. (1993). Increasing the reliability and validity of pain intensity measurement in chronic pain patients. *Pain, 55*, 195–203.

Kazarian, S. S., Howe, M. G., & Csapo, K. G. (1979). Development of the Sleep Behavior Self-Rating Scale. *Behavior Therapy, 10*, 412–417.

Keefe, F, J., & Block, A. R. (1982). Development of an observation method for assessing pain behavior in chronic low back pain patients. *Behavior Therapy, 13*, 363–375.

Keefe, F. J., & Williams, D. A. (1989). New directions in pain assessment and treatment. *Clinical Psychology Review, 9*, 549–568.

Kinsman, R., Dahlem, N., Spector, S., & Staudenmayer, H. (1977). Observations on subjective symptomatology, coping behavior and medical decisions in asthma. *Psychosomatic Medicine, 35*, 250–267.

Klinnert, M. D., Mrazek, P. J., & Mrazek, D. A. (1994). Early asthma onset: The interaction between family stressors and adaptive parenting. *Psychiatry-Interpersonal and Biological Processes, 57*, 51–61.

Kuczmarski, R. J. (1992). Prevalence of overweight and weight gain in the United States. *American Journal of Clinical Nutrition, 55*, 4955–5025.

Kvam, S. H., & Lyons, J. S. (1991). Assessment of coping strategies, social support, and general health status in individuals with diabetes mellitus. *Psychological Reports, 68*, 623–632.

Lacks, P. (1987). *Behavioral-treatment for persistent insomnia*. New York: Pergamon.

Lacks, P., & Rotert M. (1986). Knowledge and practice of sleep hygiene techniques in insomniacs and poor sleepers. *Behavior Research and Therapy, 24*, 365–368.

Lazarus, R. S., & Folkman, S. (1984). *Stress, appraisal, and coping*. New York: Springer.

Leedom, L., Meehan, W. P., Procci, W., & Ziedler, A. (1991). Symptoms of depression in patients with Type II diabetes mellitus. *Psychosomatics, 32*, 280–286.

Leher, P. M., Hochron, S. M., Isenberg, S. & Rausch, L. (1993). The Asthma Symptom Profile: A psychophysically based scale for assessment of asthma symptoms. *Journal of Psychosomatic Research, 37*, 515–521.

McGinnis, J. M., & Foege, W. H. (1993). Actual causes of death in the United States. *Journal of the American Medical Association, 270*, 2207–2212.

Melzack, R. (1975). The McGill Pain Questionnaire: Major properties and scoring methods. *Pain, 1*, 277–299.

Morin, C. (1993). *Insomnia: Psychological assessment and management*. New York: Guilford.

Morrow, G. (1984). The assessment of nausea and vomiting. *Cancer, 105*, 2267–2280.

Nelson, C. F. (1994). The tension headache, migraine headache continuum: A hypothesis. *Journal of Manipulative and Physiological Therapeutics, 17*, 156–167.

Ostrow, D., Grant, I., & Atkinson, J. H. (1988). Assessment and management of the AIDS patient with neuropsychiatric disturbances. *Journal of Clinical Psychiatry, 49*, 14–22.

Powell, H. E., Caspersen, C. J., Hoplan, J. P., & Ford, E. S. (1989). Physical activity and chronic diseases. *American Journal of Clinical Nutrition, 49*, 999–1006.

Rosenman, R. (1978). The interview method of assessment of the coronary-prone behavior pattern. In T. Dembroski, S. Weiss, J. Shields, S. Haynes, & M. Feinleib (Eds.), *Coronary-prone behavior* (pp. 55–69). New York: Springer-Verlag.

Rothenberg, R., Nasca, P., Mikl, J., Burnett, W., & Reynolds, B. (1987). Cancer. *American Journal of Preventive Medicine 3*. 30–42.

Schlundt, D. G. (1995). Assessment of specific eating behaviors and eating style. In D. B. Allison (Ed.), *Handbook of assessment methods for eating behaviors and weight-related Problems: Measures, theory, and research* (pp. 241–302). Thousand Oaks, CA: Sage.

Silberstein, S. D., & Lipton, R. B. (1993). Epidemiology of migraine. *Neuroepidemiology, 12*, 179–194.

Smith, T. W., O'Keefe, J. L., & Christensen, A. J. (1994). cognitive distortion and depression in chronic pain: Associations with diagnosed disorders. *Journal of Consulting and Clinical Psychology, 62*, 195–198.

Spielberger, C. D., Gorsuch, R. L., & Lushene, R. E. (1970). *Manual for the State-Trait Anxiety Inventory*. Palo Alto, CA: Consulting Psychologists Press.

Sterbach, R. A., Wolf, S. R., Murphy, R. W., & Akeson, W. H. (1973). Traits of pain patients: The low back "loser." *Psychosomatics, 14*, 226–229.

Stewart, W. F., Lipton, R. B., Celentano, D. D., & Reed, M. L. (1992). Prevalence of migraine headache in the United States: Relation to age, income, race and other sociodemographic factors. *JAMA, 267*, 64–69.

Suls, J., & Fletcher, B. (1985). The relative efficacy of avoidant and nonavoidant coping strategies: A meta-analysis. *Health Psychology, 4*, 249–288.

Surwit, R., Feinglos, M., & Scovern, A. (1983). Diabetes and behavior: A paradigm for health psychology. *American Psychologist, 38*, 255–262.

Swartz, M. H. (1994). Headache. In M. H. Swartz (Ed.), *Textbook of Physical diagnosis—History and examination* (pp. 447–448). Philadelphia: W. B. Saunders.

Taylor, S. E., Kemeny, M. E., Schneider, S. G., & Aspinwall, G. (1993). Coping with the threat of AIDS. In J. B. Pryor & G. D. Reeder (Eds.), *The social Psychology of HIV infection* (pp. 305–332). Hillsdale, NJ: Lawrence Erlbaum.

Thelen, M. H., Farmer, J., Wonderlich, S., & Smith, M. (1991). A revision of the Bulimia Test: The BULIT-R. *Psychological Assessment, 3*, 119–124.

Thompson, J. K. (in press). *Body image, eating disorders, and obesity: A Practical guide to assessment and treatment*. Washington, DC: American Psychological Association Books.

Tobin, D. L., Johnson, C., Steinberg, S., Staats, M., & Dennis, A. B. (1991). Multifactorial assessment of bulimia nervosa. *Journal of Abnormal Psychology, 100*, 14–21.

Toomey, T. C., Mann, J. D., Hernandez, J. T., & Abashian, S. W. (1993). Psychometric characteristics of a brief measure of pain-related functional impairment. *Archives of Physical Medicine and Rehabilitation, 74*, 1305–1308.

Turk, D. C., & Rudy, T. E. (1990). Pain. In A. S. Bellack, M. Hersen, & A. E. Kazdin (Eds.), *International handbook of behavior modification and therapy* (pp. 399–413). New York: Plenum.

Turk, D. C., Wack, J. T., & Kerns, R. D. (1985). An empirical examination of the "pain-behavior" construct. *Journal of Behavioral Medicine, 8*. 119–130.

United States Department of Health and Human Services. (1982). *The health consequences of smoking: Cancer. A report of the surgeon general*. Washington, DC: Government Printing Office.

United States Department of Health and Human services. (1988). *The health consequences of smoking: Nicotine addiction. A the surgeon general*. Washington, DC: Government Printing Office.

United States Department of Health and Human Services. (1989). *Reducing the health consequences of smoking: 25 years of progress. A report of the surgeon general*. Washington, DC: Government Printing Office.

Von Korff, M., Stewart, W. F., & Lipton, R. B. (1994). Assessing headache severity: New directions. *Neurology, 44*, 40–46.

Walter, L., & Brannon, L. (1991). A cluster analysis of the Multidimensional Pain Inventory. *Headache, 31*, 476–479.

Ware, J. C., & Morewitz, J. (1991). Diagnosis and treatment of insomnia and depression. *Journal of Clinical Psychiatry, 52*, 55–60.

Weiss, K. B., & Wagener, D. K. (1990). Changing patterns of asthma mortality: Identifying target populations at high risk. *Journal of the American Medical Association, 264*, 1683–1687.

Williamson, D. A. (1981). Behavioral treatment of migraine and muscle-contraction headaches: outcome and theoretical explanations. In M. Hersen, R. Eisler, & P. Miller (Eds.), *Progress in behavior modification* (Vol. 11) (pp. 163–201). New York: Academic.

Williamson, D. A. (1990). *Assessment of eating disorders:, Obesity-anorexia. and bulimia nervosa*. New York: Pergamon.

Williamson, D. A., Anderson, D. A., & Gleaves, D. H. (in press). Anorexia and bulimia nervosa: Structured interview methodologies and psychological assessment. In K. Thompson (Ed.), *Body image, eating disorders, and obesity: A practical guide for assessment and treatment*. Washington, DC: American Psychological Association Books.

Williamson, D. A., Davis, C. J., Bennett, S. M., Goreczny, A. J., & Gleaves, D. H. (1989). Development of a simple procedure for assessing body image disturbances. *Behavioral Assessment, 11*, 433–446.

Williamson, D. A., Davis, C. J., & Ruggiero, L. (1987). Eating disorders. In R. L. Morrison & A. S. Bellack (Eds.), *Medical factors and psychological disorders: A handbook for psychologists* (pp. 351–370). New York: Plenum.

Williamson, D. A., Prather, R. C., McKenzie, S. J., & Blouin, D. C. (1990). Behavioral assessment procedures can differentiate bulimia nervosa, compulsive overeater, obese, and normal subjects. *Behavioral Assessment, 12*, 239–252.

Williamson, D. A., & Sebastian, S. B. (1994). Psychophysiological disorders. In M. Hersen & R. T. Ammerman (Eds.), *Handbook of Prescriptive treatments for adults* (pp. 423–442). New York: Plenum.

Wolper, C., Heshka, S., & Heymsfield, S. B. (1995). Measuring food intake: An overview. In D. B. Allison (Ed.), *Handbook of assessment methods for eating-behaviors and weight-related problems: Measures, theory, and research* (pp. 215–240). Thousand Oaks, CA: Sage.

CHAPTER 13

ASSESSMENT OF APPETITIVE DISORDERS
STATUS OF EMPIRICAL METHODS IN ALCOHOL, TOBACCO, AND OTHER DRUG USE

Robert G. Rychtarik
Neil B. McGillicuddy
Research Institute on Addictions, Buffalo, NY

Appropriate treatment planning for appetitive or substance use disorders requires behavioral assessment along several areas of an individual's functioning, including the substance use itself, motivation to change, psychiatric comorbidity, cognitive functioning, marital functioning, vocational functioning, and intrapersonal adjustment. Assessment methods in a number of areas related to these domains are covered elsewhere in this book. Also, a comprehensive clinically oriented review of methods for assessing appetitive disorders across several domains recently has appeared in the literature (Sobell, Toneatto, & Sobell, 1994). This chapter will focus on assessment of actual alcohol, tobacco (smoking), and other drug use behavior or physiological indicants of it. Direct behavioral observation methods of substance use, which are primarily limited to laboratory and field research settings, will not be discussed.

GENERAL ISSUES

An individual's own verbal or written report of the frequency and quantity of recent or past alcohol, tobacco, or other drug use remains the method of choice for assessing substance use behavior. The relative ease and low cost of administering self-report measures, as well as the absence of any viable alternative for assessing substance use over long periods, has led to their widespread use in clinical settings and in epidemiological, marketing, and treatment outcome research. This heavy reliance on self-report measures, however, has occurred in the face of much debate and controversy. At the root of the controversy are three main issues.

The first issue centers on the extent to which individuals can and do give accurate reports of their substance use behavior. Given (1) the social stigma attached to alcoholism, (2) the increasing social sanctions against smoking, (3) the illegality of most other drug use, and (4) the increased monitoring of drug use in the workplace and other settings, it is not surprising that some inaccurate reporting of substance use would occur. A second troubling issue about self-report measures is that (with the exception of self-monitoring methods) they rely heavily on retrospective reports of substance use. These retrospective methods introduce the potential for additional random error due to the passage of time and other factors associated with inaccurate recall. Finally, as will be seen in the following sections, the third problem is that there is no "gold standard" in either alcohol, tobacco, or other drug use upon which to fully judge the accuracy of self-report data.

Problems posed by self-report methods and the controversy surrounding them have spawned several discussion articles and methodological reviews over the past decade in alcohol (Babor, Stephens, & Marlatt, 1987; Litten & Allen, 1992; Maisto & Connors, 1992; Midanik, 1988; O'Farrell & Maisto, 1987), tobacco (Kozlowski & Heatherton, 1990; Patrick et al., 1994; Velicer, Prochaska, Rossi, & Snow, 1992), and other drug use (Babor, Brown, & Del Boca, 1990; Harrell, 1988; Magura, Goldsmith, Casriel, Goldstein, & Lipton, 1987; Maisto, McKay, & Connors, 1990). As will be seen in the following sections, there is a general consensus among reviews of the literature in this area. Yet, our understanding of factors influencing self-report data collection methods remains limited.

ALCOHOL USE ASSESSMENT

Self-Report Methods

There are four primary methods for obtaining data about self-reported drinking: (1) the quantity-frequency method (Armor & Polich, 1982; Cahalan & Room, 1974), (2) the time-line follow-back method (Sobell & Sobell, 1992), (3) self-monitoring/diary methods (Flegal, 1991; Sobell, Bogardis, Schuller, Leo, & Sobell, 1989), and (4) the Life-Time Drinking History method (Chaikelson, Arbuckle, Lapidus, & Gold, 1994; Skinner & Sheu, 1982). With the exception of self-monitoring and diary methods, all of these typically are administered in either

a structured interview or questionnaire format and are retrospective in nature.

The *quantity-frequency method* focuses on an individual's *typical* drinking pattern over the period of time covered. The individual is asked to estimate the number of days in the time period during which he or she consumed beer, wine, or liquor. The number of days in which each of the respective beverages was consumed also is recorded, and, for each beverage, the individual is asked to report the typical amount of beverage (e.g., beer) consumed on days that beverage was used. Variations on the quantity-frequency method also may include questions as to the number of drinking days when drinking was above or below certain predetermined levels (e.g., heavy days, light days). Questionnaire applications of the quantity-frequency method also frequently will provide the respondent with a multiple-choice format with respect to beverage frequency and amount of a beverage consumed on a typical day (e.g., Embree & Whitehead, 1993).

Major variables derived from the quantity-frequency method include (1) number or proportion of days drinking or abstinent over the period; (2) total quantity index representing the total amount of alcohol consumed converted to absolute alcohol (i.e., ethanol) units, (3) typical quantity index representing the typical amount of absolute alcohol consumed on a drinking day (i.e., total absolute alcohol during the period divided by the total number of days drinking); and (4) a quantity-frequency index (QFI) that represents the typical amount of absolute alcohol consumed per day over the period (i.e., total amount of absolute alcohol consumed divided by the total number of drinking and nondrinking days in the period).

The *time-line follow-back method* presents the respondent with a calendar of the time period under study. The respondent then is asked to reconstruct in detail his or her drinking by indicating the amount of beer, wine, or liquor consumed on *each day* of the calendar period covered. Holidays and dates of personally significant events (e.g., birthdays) and days incarcerated or hospitalized are used as anchor points to assist in recall. Major variables derived from the time-line method typically include (1) number of days drinking or abstinent over the period; (2) number of days in different drinking dispositions (e.g., light drinking days, heavy drinking days); (3) average amount of absolute alcohol consumed on drinking days (typically expressed in Standard Drink Units: 1 Standard Drink = .5 ounce of absolute alcohol); and (4) number of days in involuntary drinking dispositions (e.g., incarcerated, hospitalized). Recent variations of the time-line method include the Form 90 interview (Miller & Del Boca, 1994) and the Retrospective Drinking Diary (Redmond, Sanson-Fisher, Wilkinson, Fahey, & Gibberd, 1987).

Self-monitoring/prospective diary methods have been used less frequently in the alcohol field relative to quantity-frequency and time-line methods. Although several variants exist, the self-monitoring method provides the respondent with forms or a diary in which to record the type and amount of alcoholic beverages consumed on a daily basis over a one-week period. In addition, respondents often are asked to indicate the start and stop times of their drinking episodes. Drinking diaries in research settings frequently have been imbedded within more general Activity Diaries or Dietary Diaries. When used in clinical settings, the individual also may be asked to record other events that may have happened before and after drinking to assist the therapist with a functional analysis of the individual's drinking and precipitants to relapse. The usual measures derived from the diary are number of drinking days over the period and mean quantity of alcohol consumption per day.

The *Life-Time Drinking History* (LDH; Skinner & Sheu, 1982) is an interview method designed to examine the pattern of alcohol consumption over an individual's lifetime from first drink to very recent consumption. Usually administered via interview, the interviewer starts with the first year of the respondent's life in which she or he drank at least one standard drink per month. The interviewer then chronologically traces the individual's alcohol consumption from first regular drinking to the present and identifies different phases of drinking. For each phase, frequency of drinking, typical amount consumed, maximum amount per occasion, types of beverage, style of drinking, and life events that mark a change in drinking pattern are recorded. A recent variation of the LDH is the Concordia Lifetime Drinking Questionnaire (Chaikelson et al., 1994).

Selection of a self-report method depends largely on the questions to be answered and the time and resources available. If one's goal is to examine the pattern of drinking, detect relapses or time to relapse, and identify particularly heavy drinking episodes, then the time-line procedure is optimal. The time-line procedure, however, takes twice as long to administer as the quantity-frequency method and may not be feasible in some settings or agreeable to some participants. If the goal is to obtain a general assessment of alcohol consumption, then the Quantity-Frequency method may be adequate. The diary method, although not applicable for collecting baseline drinking, may be helpful in the clinical setting to identify precipitants to a slip or relapse. In order to collect adequate group data, however, the diary demands a high level of compliance among participants, an initial time commitment for training in diary use, and frequent repeated prompting of participants to complete diary materials. Also in the research setting, self-monitoring itself may be reactive, hence reducing drinking behavior independent of other factors.

Reliability of Self-Reported Drinking Methods

There is a growing body of literature indicating that alcoholics move in and out of different drinking dispositions across time (Polich, Armor, & Braiker, 1980; Watson & Pucel, 1985). Thus, drinking behavior assessed during one brief interval (e.g., the last 30 days) may not be a reliable measure of drinking behavior over longer periods. For example, drinking behavior collected for the 30 days before treatment has been reported to be higher than usual among inpatients in one study (Cooper, Sobell, Maisto, & Sobell, 1980) and lower than usual among outpatients in another (McCrady, Duclos, Dubrekuil, Stout, & Fisher-Nelson, 1984). Similarly, posttreatment periods of abstention of less than 3 months have not been found to be representative of stable abstention over longer periods (Polich et al., 1980). Thus, 6- and preferably 12-month pretreatment and posttreatment assessment timeframes are recommended in outcome research to obtain more representative drinking indices. Also, specific drinking measures should be adjusted for excessive hospitalizations or incarcerations, which could positively bias abstinence outcome results.

Test-retest reliabilities have been found to be quite high for quantity-frequency (Babor et al., 1987) and time-line-follow-back procedures (Sobell, Sobell, Leo, & Cancilla, 1988), and moderate to high for life-time drinking history methods (Chaikelson et al., 1994; Sobell, Sobell, Riley et al., 1988). Such consistency also appears applicable across a wide range of treatment and nontreatment populations (Babor et al., 1987; Sobell, Sobell, Leo et al., 1988). Differences in the extent of self-report test-retest discrepancies, however, have been reported for certain methods, groups, and variables (e.g., Maisto, Sobell, Cooper, & Sobell, 1979; Skinner & Sheu, 1982).

Emhart, Morrow-Tlucak, Sokol, and Martier (1988) found relatively good long-term test-retest reliability (.67) between reports of drinking among women during pregnancy and retrospective reports for the same period over four years later. However, they noted that 41% of the group reported higher retrospective drinking during their pregnancy than they did at the time of pregnancy. Furthermore, the retrospective retest index was more highly correlated with alcohol severity scores and alcohol-related craniofacial anomalies in the child than was the in-pregnancy index. This latter finding suggests that the retrospective report may have been the more valid drinking index in this population.

The finding that every study has at least some individuals with marked test-retest discrepancies has led recent investigations away from studying whether individuals are consistent in their reports and toward examining what factors predict consistent or inconsistent reporting (Toneatto, Sobell, & Sobell, 1992). Although more study in this area is required, there is some converging evidence to suggest that individuals with more severe drinking problems or who have higher levels of alcohol consumption are more likely to give discrepant reports in test-retest analyses. Maisto and associates (1979) found a higher level of discrepancy among inpatients (presumably a more severely impaired group) than outpatients. Emhart and associates (1988) found underreporters to have had higher alcohol severity scores at both pregnancy and at the

retest. Finally, Toneatto and associates (1992) found a higher level of test-retest discrepancies in a five-year adaptation of the Life-Time Drinking History among individuals who had higher reports of amount, frequency, and number of drinking phases at the initial testing.

Considerable consistency between *different* self-report methods also has been reported. Moderate to high levels of agreement have been found between the quantity-frequency method and the time-line or related procedures (Maisto, Sobell, Cooper, & Sobell, 1982; O'Hare, 1991; Sobell, Cellucci, Nirenberg, & Sobell 1982). Prospective diary procedures, particularly when administered on several occasions over time, also have shown good agreement with quantity-frequency methods (Flegal, 1991; Hilton, 1989). In fact, some data suggest that prospective diaries yield higher consumption levels when compared to quantity-frequency or time-line methods (e.g., O'Hare, 1991; Redman et al., 1987; Tucker, Vuchinich, Harris, Gavornik, & Rudd, 1991). The diary, however, because of its relatively short assessment window, appears less sensitive to detecting individuals who drink a particular beverage infrequently or drink small amounts of a beverage over a long period (Flegal, 1991).

Validity of Self-Report Drinking

Despite some lingering controversy, there is a growing consensus that, as a group, alcoholics' and other individuals' reports of drinking are quite accurate across various self-report methods. The primary validity criteria against which self-reports have been compared are the corresponding report of a collateral (i.e., a spouse, family member, friend, etc.) and the result of a biochemical measure indicative of drinking (e.g., blood alcohol concentration). As will be briefly discussed here and in other sections, however, these criteria have their own limitations.

Collateral reports have been the most frequently used method for assessing accuracy of self-reported drinking. Reviews of the literature in this area have consistently indicated that, with few exceptions (Fuller, Lee, & Gordis, 1988), self-reported drinking across a range of methods and a wide range of clinical and nonclinical populations shows overall good agreement with collateral reports (see Maisto & Connors, 1992). When lower validity coefficients have been reported, they appear to be associated with behaviors that may be less obvious to the collateral. For example, it is more difficult for collaterals to accurately report the *amount* of alcohol an individual consumed on drinking days. Collateral reports of respondent drinking also appear to be lowered when the collateral is required to report drinking over a long period of time (e.g., one year).

As with reliability, a considerable amount of individual respondent-collateral pair discrepancy occurs in nearly every study in this area. This intersubject variability poses few problems for group research designs. However, it could pose significant problems for research on factors influencing individual drinking patterns over time and for clinical assessment of individual clients (Tucker et al., 1991). Little attention has been given to identifying characteristics of individual pairs for whom discrepancies are large. In one recent report (Graham & Jackson, 1993), discrepancies among a community sample appeared to increase with greater levels of consumption—a finding consistent with that found for reliability. The study also reported higher absolute discrepancies for male subjects than female subjects. Also, for male subjects, lower levels of discrepancies were associated with the spouse serving as a collateral, whereas no relationship between collateral type and discrepancy level was found for female subjects. Additional research on parameters of respondent-collateral pair discrepancies is needed.

Finally, a consistent finding is that individuals in treatment populations who have been drinking recently (i.e., blood alcohol concentration [BAC] > .00%) tend to give inaccurate reports of the level of their drinking (Orrego, Blendis, Blake, Kapur, & Israel, 1979; Polich, 1982; Sobell, Sobell, & Vander-Spek, 1979). In fact, underreporting of *amount* consumed in the last 24 hours among these recent drinkers has been reported as high as 35% when compared to blood alcohol concentration measures. Among individuals who report abstinence, however, very few are found with positive blood alcohol levels. As a general rule, self-reports of alcohol use should, if at all possible, be obtained when the respondent has a BAC of .00%.

Biochemical Measures of Alcohol Use

Blood Alcohol Concentration (BAC)

The most widely known biochemical measure of alcohol consumption is blood alcohol concentration. BAC typically is represented as a percentage of ethyl alcohol to blood volume. Although BAC can be measured directly in blood, urine, or saliva, it is most frequently measured using a breath analysis procedure. In this procedure, the individual is asked to provide a small sample of air by blowing into a device that measures the content of alcohol expired by the lungs.

Instruments for assessing BAC range from those with less precise measurement of whether an individual's BAC is above legal limits, to sophisticated machines that provide accuracy to plus or minus .01%. However, alcohol is metabolized in the body at the rate of approximately one ounce per hour. Thus, since alcohol leaves the system relatively quickly, breath analysis procedures are sensitive to consumption of large amounts of alcohol for a period of only 24 hours. Heavy drinking that occurred two to three days prior to the breath test would not be detected. A client in a treatment program could, therefore, pace his or her drinking so as not to be detected during regularly scheduled appointments. Random breath testing is obviously one solution to this problem, but such random probes require considerable staff time and may be impractical in clinical settings. Breath test readings at outpatient appointments have been used as treatment outcome measures, but they are limited by their ability to detect only recent drinking.

BAC assessment is a particularly useful method of ensuring that an individual is sober upon presenting for a clinical session or prior to administration of in-person self-report measures. The clinical value of breath testing in these circumstances is highlighted by findings that even clinical staff judgments are not very accurate in identifying clients presenting with positive BACs (Sobell et al., 1979).

An alternative method for measuring alcohol in the body is the use of a sweat patch or transdermal ethanol sensor to detect alcohol expired through the skin (Phillips, 1992; Swift & Swette, 1992). The most sophisticated of these methods, the transdermal ethanol sensor, uses a modification of technology found in advanced breathalyzers. Attached via adhesives to the skin, the sensor oxidizes ethanol expired from the skin and generates electrical current in proportion to the concentration of ethanol expired. Using such a device, alcohol consumption can be monitored continuously anywhere from eight days to two weeks. Preliminary data on this device appear promising, but the device is only experimental in nature, requires further development, and its practicality in clinical settings remains to be seen.

Blood Chemistry Measures

The most active research into alcohol consumption measures over the last 10 years has been in the identification of biological markers of heavy alcohol consumption. Interest in this area has been fueled by (1) continuing concerns over the heavy reliance on self-report measures, (2) the need for objective markers of alcohol abuse that are sensitive (unlike BAC) to more than just very recent drinking, and (3) interest in the identification of alcoholics or early stage problem drinkers who are not yet seeking help. Several potential markers or combinations of markers for alcohol abuse have been proposed (see Cushman, 1992; Rosman & Lieber, 1992). Two tests that have received much of the attention are gamma-glutamyl transpeptidase (GGT) and carbohydrate deficient transferrin (CDT). These tests often are evaluated with respect to their sensitivity and specificity. Sensitivity is the proportion of individuals engaging in alcohol abuse accurately identified as such by the test (i.e., have an abnormal or positive test). Specificity, on the other hand, is the proportion of those *not* abusing alcohol accurately classified as such.

GGT is a liver enzyme normally found at low levels in the bloodstream. It appears to be significantly elevated by heavy alcohol consumption and ordinarily requires two to six weeks to return to normal upon cessation of drinking. As such, it is thought to provide an indirect index of heavy drinking in the recent past. It also is usually readily available from commercial laboratory blood test panels. Correlations between recent alcohol consumption and GGT levels, however, have not always been significant (e.g., Poikolainen, Karkkainen, & Pikkarainen, 1985) and when they have been significant, they have been relatively low (see Cushman, 1992). As a marker for either presence or absence of alcohol abuse, GGT also appears to lack sensitivity. Although the proportion of alcoholics correctly identified by GGT is relatively high among hospitalized individuals with manifest liver disease (sensitivities .75 to .92), the proportion of alcoholics accurately identified by GGT is relatively low among outpatients (.46 to .60) and even lower among community samples (.13 to .50).

Importantly, concomitant drug use (e.g., cocaine) has been shown to *reduce* GGT to normal levels among combined alcohol and drug abusers, thus accounting for some false negatives. False positives can result from certain physical conditions (e.g., pancreatitis, nonalcoholic liver disease) and medications (e.g., anticonvulsants) independent of drinking. Thus, several factors need to be considered in evaluating the adequacy of GGT for detecting alcohol abuse in a particular individual. Once elevated by heavy drinking, however, GGT often does show marked reductions in level over time with abstinence. Establishment of individual baseline levels of GGT and subsequent repeat testing can be helpful in some individuals for corroborating self-report of abstinence or heavy drinking. Of course, blood collection for GGT and other blood markers is invasive and some individuals may be highly disagreeable to repeat assessments.

Transferrin is a protein in blood serum responsible for transporting iron. For reasons not yet totally understood, individuals who consume large amounts of alcohol develop an altered form of transferrin, which lacks the typical carbohydrates in its chemical structure—hence the name Carbohydrate *Deficient* Transferrin (CDT). As with GGT, elevations of CDT, or an increased ratio of CDT to normal transferrin, may be indicative of heavy drinking in the recent past (e.g., the last three to four weeks). Recent reviews of biochemical markers for harmful alcohol consumption conclude that CDT is the best marker of alcohol consumption available at this time (Mihas & Tavassoli, 1992; Stibler, 1991). Indeed, sensitivities and specificities in the .90 range have been reported in some studies of this measure. Also, unlike GGT, CDT values appear to be little influenced by other physical conditions.

As Allen, Litten, Anton, and Cross (1994) note, however, CDT is not a perfect marker. It has been found to have high sensitivity and high specificity when heavily drinking alcoholics are compared with abstainers or light drinkers. However, among more heterogeneous groups of drinkers, its sensitivity in detecting high-level drinkers is lowered. Also, CDT has not been found to be a good marker for heavy alcohol consumption among women (Allen et al., 1994; Gronbaek, Henriksen, & Becker, 1995). As with GGT, however, CDT may be helpful in the clinical monitoring of alcoholics to detect relapse. At the present time, CDT is not a routine laboratory test, and despite availability of a commercial laboratory test kit, it remains expensive.

TOBACCO USE ASSESSMENT (SMOKING)

Self-Report Methods

Self-reported tobacco use typically is assessed with either (1) self-administered questionnaires (e.g., Diguisto & Bird, 1995), (2) structured in-person interviews (e.g., Wagenknecht et al., 1990), or (3) self-monitoring of cigarette use (e.g., Shiffman, 1988). In questionnaire and interview formats, items assessing tobacco use typically focus on whether the respondent has smoked over a specified period (i.e., last 24 hours, last 7 days, last 30 days, etc.), length of abstinence from tobacco use, time to first relapse to smoking, number of cigarettes (or packs of cigarettes) smoked per day, and the time until the first cigarette upon waking in the morning. Questions may be worded in either open-ended, closed-ended, or multiple-choice format. Additional questions also may include the cigarette brand and the specific tar and nicotine content of the cigarettes used. Measures of tobacco use derived from these self-report questionnaires include the point prevalence smoking status over the time period assessed (e.g., 7 days), length of continuous abstinence, and/or the rate of smoking (e.g., cigarettes per day).

Self-monitoring methods usually rely on the individual to record each cigarette as it is smoked, using either paper, mechanical, or electronic counters. As in alcohol use assessment, the individual also may be asked to record the setting, precipitants, and consequences of smoking (see Shiffman, 1988). Measures derived from self-monitoring methods often include those similarly derived from questionnaire and interview formats.

As in alcohol use assessment, the method and measures used depend largely on the purpose of the assessment (see Velicer et al., 1992). Questionnaire methods are particularly useful in large sample studies in which it is common for investigators to send materials via the mail. Self-monitoring methods, on the other hand, can be particularly useful in the clinical setting for conducting a functional analysis of tobacco use behavior. Self-monitoring methods in the smoking area, however, suffer from many of the same problems noted in the use of self-monitoring of alcohol use. More importantly, self-monitoring of smoking behavior may be reactive (King, Scott, & Prue, 1984) and the effort required of the client may contribute to an increased likelihood of early dropout (Moss, Prue, Lomax, & Martin, 1982).

Reliability of Self-Reported Smoking

As with other substance use/abuse, smoking often is a chronic, relapsing condition (Hunt, Barnett, & Branch, 1971). Thus, the time period over which smoking is assessed becomes particularly relevant in evaluation of smoking cessation programs or in evaluation of the health effects of smoking behavior. Importantly, the most widely used point prevalence abstinence period is a seven-day interval (Lichtenstein & Glasgow, 1992). The seven-day point prevalence measure has been chosen because smoking during this time period can be validated using biochemical markers (discussed later). Point prevalence abstinence from smoking reported over such a short time period, however, may not be representative of tobacco abstinence over longer periods or provide an adequate estimation of abstinence to assess the health benefits of smoking cessation. Furthermore, among active smokers, self-reported cigarette consumption can be quite unstable across relatively small time intervals (Anderson, Bright, & Snider, 1979). Repeated point prevalence and continuous abstinence measures over extended periods are recommended (Lichtenstein & Glasgow, 1992).

There are relatively few reports of the test-retest reliability of smoking measures (Kozlowski & Heatherton, 1990). Fox, Sexton, Hebel, and Thompson (1989) reported 71% to 74% exact agreement in prepregnancy smoking categories among pregnant smokers over an interval of approximately 4.5 months, with Kappa coefficients in the .56 to .61 range. Higher estimates of agreement over longer periods of time have been reported when smoking status (smoking or not) and broader classification of smoking rates have been used. In a sample of 87 subjects, Krall, Valadian, Dwyer, and Gardner (1989) found that 90% and 86% were able to correctly recall whether they were smoking or not 20 years and 32 years earlier, respectively. Recall of cigarettes consumed per day using a broad categorical system was 74% and 57% for the two respective time periods. Importantly, current smoking status can bias recall, with estimates of prior smoking often most similar to current smoking levels.

Validity of Self-Report Smoking

Self-reports of point prevalence smoking, as a general rule, have been found to be quite valid. In a recent meta-analysis of self-report smoking studies using biochemical measures for verification, Patrick and colleagues (1994) found an overall average self-report sensitivity of 87.5 and an average specificity of 89.2. Despite these high validity coefficients, however, a high degree of across-study variability also exists in this line of research, and deception rates of up to 18% have been reported (Jarvis, Tunstall-Pedoe, Feyerabend, Vesey, & Saloojee, 1987).

Association between number of cigarettes smoked per day and biochemical measures has not been as strong as that for point prevalence estimates. This finding partially may result from a ceiling effect in biochemical measures beyond a certain number of cigarettes smoked. Support for the validity of rate measures comes from their positive association with disease risk (Vesey, 1981). However, rate measures in the absence of tar and nicotine content of cigarettes may not be the best indicators of individual health risk behavior. Unfortunately, self-reports of cigarette brand and tar and nicotine content have not been found to be particularly valid (Peach, Shah, & Morris, 1986). Requiring the smoker to bring in an empty pack is a better way of assessing tar and nicotine content.

Collateral reports of an individual's smoking behavior have been used less frequently in the smoking literature when compared to the alcohol assessment literature. This may stem, in part, from the wider use and higher sensitivity and specificity of biochemical measures to verify self-reported smoking. Nevertheless, when collaterals have been used, there appears to be fairly good agreement between subject and collateral in accurately identifying smoking status (McLaughlin, Dietz, Mehl, & Blot, 1987; Ossip-Klein et al., 1991). As in the alcohol area, collaterals have more difficulty reporting specific information such as the number of cigarettes per day. In fact, Kozlowski and Heatherton (1990) conclude that collateral reports may best be used to establish an individual's smoking status and may not be useful for verifying cigarettes smoked per day.

As in the alcohol measurement area, there have been increasing efforts to identify those parameters that account for variability in the accuracy of self-reports across studies. Patrick and associates (1994), in their meta-analysis of self-report smoking studies, examined a number of different parameters that could account for between-study differences in correspondence between self-report and biochemical measures. Although their results require caution in interpretation, they do provide direction for future study in this area. In these analyses, studies using interviewer-administered questionnaires were found to identify more of the smokers correctly and identify the nonsmokers more accurately than self-administered questionnaires. The self-reported smoking of student samples also appeared to have lower sensitivity than general population samples—possibly because it is illegal for minors to smoke in most states and/or minors may still be in an experimental stage and not label themselves as smokers. Finally, self-reports from subjects in smoking intervention studies were found to have lower sensitivity and specificity than subjects in general observational research. This latter finding may be attributed to the higher demands to report no smoking following smoking intervention programs.

It is important to note that Patrick and associates (1994) also found a large amount of between-study variability in sensitivity and specificity of self-report smoking that could not be accounted for by study and population parameters they assessed. As in the alcohol use assessment area, further research identifying parameters influencing smoking self-report measures is needed. Along these lines, Bauman and Ennett (1994) found that much of the difference in tobacco use commonly reported between Black and White adolescents can be accounted for by Black/White differences in self-report validity. In particular, Black adolescents were found more likely than White adolescents to underreport cigarette and tobacco use, whereas White adolescents were found to engage in more overreporting. Other research suggests that adolescents who are more rebellious and higher in deviance may be prone to overreport smoking behavior (Palmer, Dwyer, & Semmer, 1994). Thus, validity of self-reported smoking and the nature of discrepancies may very well depend on the characteristics of the population sampled.

Biochemical Measures of Smoking

Biochemical measures of smoking have become commonly used in smoking research. In fact, few smoking intervention studies are published without use of biochemical measures. The three most commonly used biochemical markers in this area are carbon monoxide (CO), cotinine, and thiocyanate (SCN).

Carbon monoxide is a gas present in high concentrations in cigarette smoke and is rapidly absorbed into the bloodstream. It can be measured either as carboxyhemoglobin in the blood or can be assessed directly and most easily in expired air using measuring instruments that are easy to use and require no special laboratory procedures. Sensitivities of 80% to 85% and specificities of 84% to 98% have been reported using CO (Velicer et al., 1992). Unfortunately, CO has a relatively brief half-life of four to five hours and is influenced by the daily pattern of smoking (Benowitz, 1983). Thus, CO can detect only recent smoking behavior and has not been found to be very sensitive to light smoking, as may be found in adolescents. CO levels also can be elevated from sources other than smoking. These sources include industrial pollution and exposure to the smoke of others. Although other measures appear to offer more consistent levels of sensitivity and specificity, CO measurement is simple and relatively inexpensive. Hence, it is still commonly used in smoking research.

Hydrogen cyanide, also present in high concentrations in cigarette smoke, is a toxic gas rapidly broken down by the liver into thiocyanate (SCN). It is most commonly assessed through use of saliva samples, although its presence in blood and urine also can be measured. Initially, SCN was viewed as an optimal marker for more than very recent smoking due to its relatively long half-life of 10 to 14 days. Unfortunately, like CO, it has low sensitivity to light smoking. Also, levels of SCN can be increased to the levels attained by smokers by several food products containing naturally occurring SCN or related substances (e.g., broccoli, cauliflower, almonds). As a result, the potential for false positives may be high, and thus specificity relatively low. An additional disadvantage of SCN is the sophisticated equipment and cost required for SCN measurement. There is some convergence in the smoking area against the further use of SCN as a marker for smoking (Lichtenstein & Glasgow, 1992; Velicer et al., 1992).

Although nicotine is one of the primary components of tobacco, it cannot easily be used as a marker for smoking due to its very short half-life of 30 minutes (e.g., Langone & Van Vunakis, 1975). Instead, cotinine, a direct metabolite of nicotine, can be measured in saliva, blood, and urine and has a half-life that ranges from 15 to 40 hours. Because it is a direct metabolite of nicotine and is not influenced by other factors, its sensitivity and specificity have typically been very high (90% to 98%). Also, unlike other biochemical tobacco measures, cotinine can detect smokeless tobacco use. In fact, in summarizing the literature comparing different biochemical markers for smoking, Velicer and associates (1992) describe cotinine as the measure of choice for smoking detection. Also, a recent meta-analysis of the literature suggests that cotinine as measured in blood plasma may have higher specificity than other biochemical measures (including cotinine measured in saliva; Patrick et al., 1994). A disadvantage of cotinine, however, is that it is more expensive to assess than CO. Also, cotinine is an inappropriate marker for smoking when nicotine-replacement treatments (e.g., nicotine gum, nicotine patch) are used, since these interventions themselves elevate cotinine levels.

ASSESSMENT OF OTHER DRUG USE

Self-Report Methods

Similar to self-reported smoking, self-reported illicit drug use typically has been assessed using standardized questionnaires (e.g., Harrison, Haaga, & Richards, 1993; Weatherby et al., 1994) or structured in-person interviews (e.g., Anglin, Hser, & Chou, 1993; Maisto & Connors, 1990; Maisto, Sobell, & Sobell, 1983; McElrath, 1994). The timeline procedure also recently has been adapted for collection of drug use reports (Ehrman & Robbins, 1994). These methods typically query the respondent on use of each of several specific drug classes over the assessment period. For each drug category for which use is reported, follow-up items assess frequency of use (e.g., number of days), typical amount and mode of administration (e.g., oral, nasal, intravenous), period of time since use started, and number of days of multiple substance use. Such questioning is facilitated by defining each drug category and providing examples of common drug street names. Drug categories frequently assessed include

Cannabis (e.g., marijuana, hashish, pot, joints)
Crack cocaine (e.g., rock)
Cocaine other than crack (e.g., blow)
Heroin (e.g., horse, smack, skag)
Heroin and cocaine mixed together (e.g., speedball)
Nonprescription methadone

Other opiates (e.g., morphine, demerol, codeine)
Amphetamines (e.g., speed, uppers, bennies, whizz, poppers)
Barbiturates (e.g., downers)
LSD (e.g., acid)
PCP (e.g., angel dust)
Other hallucinogens (e.g., mushrooms)
Inhalants (e.g., glue, petrol, solvents)
Any other drugs

The specific drug category and drugs assessed, of course, vary with the particular aims of the assessment.

Reliability of Self-Reported Drug Use

Test-retest reliability reported for measures of both point prevalence (use/nonuse) and frequency of specific drugs has varied but generally has been acceptable, even after long-term test-retest intervals (Anglin et al., 1993; Bailey, Flewelling, & Rachal, 1992; Ehrmann & Robbins, 1994; Harrison et al., 1993; McElrath, 1994; Pedersen, 1990). As with alcohol use, however, exceptions do occur. For example, lower levels of both short-term and long-term point prevalence test-retest reliability for marijuana use have been reported among prisoner (McElrath, 1994) and treatment populations (Anglin et al., 1993), respectively. Parameters accounting for test-retest variability among drugs of abuse and between specific populations, however, have not been thoroughly explored.

Validity of Self-Reported Drug Use

Self-reports of drug use generally have been found to have moderate to good levels of validity, although the quality of studies has varied and inter-study findings have been quite variable (for a review of earlier studies, see Maisto et al., 1990). Some of this variability may result from limitations of biochemical markers of drug use (discussed later), which frequently have been used as the standard against which self-reports are compared. Using self-report with biochemical comparisons, numerous studies have examined the validity of drug use self-reports for diverse populations, including arrestees (e.g., McElrath, 1994), past and present drug treatment clients (e.g., Magura, et al., 1987), street addicts (e.g., Wish, Johnson, Strug, Chedekel, & Lipton, 1983), adolescents (e.g., Needle, Jou, & Su, 1989) and pregnant women (e.g., Christmas et al., 1992; Zuckerman, Amaro, & Cabral, 1989).

Taken together, studies in this area suggest that accuracy of self-reported drug use can vary markedly with type of population studied, type and pattern of drug use, and time and measurement procedures used (Hubbard, Eckerman, & Rachal, 1977). Although clear patterns are difficult to discern among these studies, it does seem clear that groups for whom sanctions against drug use are perceived as high have overall lower levels of valid reporting. For example, relatively low point prevalence drug use validity has been reported among juvenile arrestees (Fendrich & Xu, 1994). Another report found that, among pregnant women with positive urine tests for cocaine, 20% to 35% actually denied cocaine use (Zuckerman et al., 1989). Rate of underreporting among incarcerated individuals has been positively associated with such factors as severity of arrest charge and prior drug arrests, and has been found to be more prevalent for the period immediately preceding arrest (see Magura, 1987). Sherman and Bigelow (1992) found a significant increase in underreporting among opiate addicts from pretreatment (1%) to four weeks into treatment (10%)—possibly reflecting fear of sanctions as one continues in a treatment program.

Relative to other drugs, somewhat lower levels of accuracy have been reported for marijuana self-reports (e.g., Brown et al., 1992) and higher accuracy levels found for reports of opiate use (e.g., Magura et al., 1987; Mieczkowski, 1990; Falck, Siegal, Forney, Wang, & Carlson, 1992). This pattern, however, has not been consistently found across studies. Somewhat more consistent is the finding that higher (and more accurate) levels of substance use are reported on privately completed questionnaires as compared to in-person interviews (Brown et al., 1992; McElrath, 1994; Turner, Lester, & Devore, 1992).

When collateral reports have been used as the criterion upon which to compare drug use self-reports, an adequate to high rate of agreement in point prevalence and frequency of drug use has been found (e.g., Darke, Heather, Hall, Ward, & Wodak, 1991; Hoffman & Ninonuevo, 1994; Rounsaville, Kleber, Wilber, Rosenberger, & Rosenberger, 1981; Stephens, Roffman, & Simpson, 1994). As was also true in both the alcohol and smoking literature, however, collaterals tend to underestimate extent of addiction, due to a lack of specific information about the individual's drug use behavior.

Biochemical Measures of Drug Use

As drugs metabolize, a high proportion of their metabolites exits the body in urine. Consequently, urinalysis has become the most common biochemical method for identifying drug use. Testing of urine for drugs typically is a two-tier process readily available in most commercial laboratories. First, an initial screening test (usually an immunoassay) is completed on the urine sample to test for evidence of drug use. Second, should the urine test be positive for one or more drugs, a second, more rigorous, confirmatory testing method (gas chromatography-mass spectrophotometry) is used on the same sample. Detailed discussion of urine testing methods is beyond the scope of this chapter (for more detail, see Bigger, 1979; Schwartz, 1988). Some understanding of the two primary methods of analysis and their strengths and weaknesses, however, is important.

Immunoassay is the most common method for initial screening of urine for drugs. This method is designed to identify drug classes (e.g., opiates), and not individual drugs. Advantages of immunoassay techniques include their relatively low cost and ease of use in laboratory settings, their provision of information about the *quantity* of drug present in the urine, and their ability to detect even small amounts of drugs (e.g., Schwartz, 1988; Willette, 1991). Immunoassays, however, frequently result in false positives (discussed later), their specificity for individual drug detection is low, and they can only be conducted on one drug class at a time (e.g., Kapur, 1993; Schwartz, 1988). Hence, immunoassays are used only as an initial step in the urine testing process.

The most commonly used method for confirming positive immunoassay findings is gas chromatography-mass spectrometry (GC/MS). GC/MS is a highly sensitive and specific testing method that can detect a single metabolite of a given drug. In fact, GC/MS is considered the "gold standard" of urine screen tests (Lehrer, 1990; Schwartz, 1988). Government guidelines for drug testing in the workplace require confirmation of positive immunoassay techniques by GC/MS, and its use as a confirmatory method is recommended by the National Institute on Drug Abuse (NIDA; 1988). The importance of this second, confirmatory test is evident in findings that 21% to 35% of specimens testing positive under immunoassay procedures may not be confirmed by GC/MS methods (e.g., McGuffey & Mullins, 1994; Schwartz, 1988). GC/MS, however, is an extremely expensive test that requires a high degree of technical skill, making its use as an initial screening device prohibitive in many settings.

As with biochemical tests for alcohol and tobacco use, urine drug tests, with the exception of those for marijuana, can detect only fairly recent drug use. For example, urine tests for amphetamines have a window of detection (WOD) of 1 to 2 days; opiates, 2 to 4 days; cocaine, 2 to 5 days; and marijuana, 10 to 77 days (Bigger, 1979; Lafolie, & Beck, 1994; Lafolie, Beck, & Hjemdahl, 1994; Sarvela, 1990). The wide WOD for marijuana use may have advantages, but it poses problems as well. For example, a heavy marijuana smoker who stopped use 40 days ago could still test positive for the drug and have a relapse falsely assumed (Coombs, 1991). The level of marijuana metabolite could be compared between testings to detect a continued decrease in its presence, although release of the metabolite may be quite unstable. Hence, knowledge of the WOD for respective drugs is important in interpreting results of urine drug tests in treatment and other settings.

Beyond the high false-positive rate attributed to immunoassay methods, false positives remain a concern in the drug testing area. Specifically, several different foods and medications have the potential to result in false positives for various drug groups, including poppy seeds for codeine or morphine; antihistamines and antidiarrheals for opiates; some cold and other over-the-counter preparations for amphetamines or PCP; and eye drops for cannabinoids (e.g., Colbert, 1994; McGuffie & Mullins, 1994, Potter & Orfali, 1990; Schwartz, 1988).

False negatives also can occur as a result of individuals adept at concealing their use of specific substances (e.g., Coombs, 1991). Among the methods individuals have used to attain false negatives are substitution of another individual's urine; substitution of apple juice or tea; dilution of the drug by large amounts of water or vinegar consumption; and addition of various adulterating products to the urine, including table salt, bleaches, or liquid soap (e.g., Coombs, 1991; Kapur, 1993; Schwarzhoff & Cody, 1993). A number of methods can help to detect or minimize the presence of adulterated samples. For example, small temperature strips attached to the collection cup can detect abnormal urine sample temperatures (a sign of contamination).

Hair Analysis

Given the limitations of urine drug tests, alternative biological sources of drug metabolites have been explored. Of particular interest over the last decade has been a steady accumulation of experimental data on the analysis of hair for trace elements and drugs (e.g., Henderson, 1993). The precise mechanism(s) by which drugs are incorporated into the hair are unknown, although one pathway may be through perspiration (e.g., Blank & Kidwell, 1993). As is true with urine specimens, analyses are generally conducted through immunoassays and GC/MS techniques (e.g., Cone, Darwin, & Wang, 1993; Mieczkowski & Newel, 1993). While most analyses have been conducted on hair samples from the top of the head, there also is preliminary evidence suggesting that beard (Nakahara, Takahashi, & Konamu, 1993) and arm hair (Cone et al., 1993) incorporate drugs as well.

Preliminary evidence also suggests that drugs are present in hair for lengthier periods than in urine (e.g., Cone et al., 1993; Magura, Freeman, Siddiqi, & Lipton, 1992; Polettini, Groppi, & Montagna, 1993). Because hair grows at approximately the rate of a half-inch per month, a two-inch strand of hair would provide a time record for analysis of four months. In addition to the lengthy WOD, hair analysis offers the following advantages: collection of a sample is difficult to manipulate or evade; collection is ordinarily less embarrassing than collecting urine; no special storage considerations are necessary; drugs appear in hair approximately within three to four days of use, corresponding to the period they are no longer detectable in urine; and if a test result is debated, retest on a comparable hair sample is easy to conduct. Importantly, hair analyses on "true positives" (as measured by self-report) are confirmed at rates of 88% to 100% for cocaine use (e.g., Baer, Baumgartner, Hill, & Blahd, 1991; Hindin et al., 1994; Magura et al., 1992; Mieczkowski, Barzelay, Gropper, & Wish, 1991).

Despite numerous potential advantages of hair analysis, a number of problems exist. Included among these are the high cost of each analysis, the potential to discriminate along racial lines (i.e., hair pigmentation in Blacks may retain higher drug concentration levels; Cone et al., 1993; Holden, 1990; Kidwell, 1993), and gender categories (i.e., against women, as men frequently have hair too short for analysis; Hindin et al., 1994). Hair analysis also has been found to have low sensitivity (e.g., Mieckowski & Newel, 1993), and specificity for marijuana use (e.g., Hindin et al., 1994) and one-time use of a substance is difficult to detect (e.g., Magura et al., 1992). Also, outside influences may produce either false positives or false negatives. For example, false positives may occur simply from passive exposure to drugs (e.g., Blank & Kidwell, 1993; Brewer, 1993; Chiarotti, 1993). False negatives may result from shampoo or hair conditioners (e.g., Bost, 1993; Welch, Sniegoski, Allgood, & Habram, 1993). Direct sunlight and heat also may impact metabolite concentrations in hair (Bost, 1993). Finally, other issues that need to be addressed include examination of the causes of inter-subject variability in the amount of time it takes for a drug to appear in hair, and in the amount of drug concentration observed when similar dosage of a drug is consumed (e.g., Henderson, 1993; Kintz, Cirimele, Edel, Jamey, & Mangin, 1994). Until such issues are resolved, hair analysis likely will be limited to the research setting.

Concluding Comment

As the discussion suggests, no single source (self-report, collateral, biochemical) may be adequate in all situations for obtaining accurate alcohol, tobacco, or other drug use data. A combination of self-report and other measures, however, has been shown to increase validity and may be optimal in increasing confidence in the characterization of an individual's substance use. Use of this multi-method approach is exemplified in the following case study.

Case Study

The client was a 58-year-old Black male with a ninth-grade education. He was a retired industrial plant worker who lived by himself in his own home where he had resided for 22 years. He reported his first drink at the age of 15 and first intoxication at 20 years of age. He reported that his father was a social drinker but that his mother was a heavy drinker and had several relatives on her side who had drinking problems. For several years prior to his retirement, he reported a pattern of heavy weekend (Friday/Saturday) drinking during which he would drink beer and hard liquor until he passed out. His drinking increased substantially upon retirement. He had been hospitalized for detoxification on two prior occasions and also had been in an inpatient treatment program in the prior year. He was referred for this current treatment episode by the county probation department following an assault charge stemming from a firearm incident when he was intoxicated.

In a complete diagnostic assessment, the client met *DSM-IV* criteria for alcohol dependence (with physiological dependence). No other Axis I psychiatric diagnoses were met. A functional analysis of his current drinking behavior revealed that his alcohol abuse was maintained by (1) boredom due to lack of leisure/recreational activities other than drinking, (2) a social network that reinforced heavy drinking (friends and fellow retired workers frequently came to his house to drink), and (3) a grief response to his son's death for which he had unrealistic beliefs that he somehow was responsible for the circumstances leading up to it. The client subsequently was scheduled for a seven-month treatment program, including a multifaceted 28-day primary phase of intensive outpatient treatment followed by six months of individual and group aftercare sessions. Treatment and aftercare goals focused on teaching the client to resist peer pressure to drink, to develop alternative leisure and recreational activities, and to cope in alternative ways with negative thoughts about his son's death and his feelings of responsibility for it.

The client exhibited a high level of individual and group session attendance throughout the primary phase of treatment. On his first and last individual counseling sessions, however, he presented with a BAC of .03 and reported consumption of four beers and two pints of whiskey the night before. In the aftercare phase of treatment, he attended the majority of his individual counseling sessions but had a poor showing at aftercare groups. At one individual appointment (during the fourth month) he presented with a BAC of .01 and reported drinking six beers and a half-pint of whiskey the previous night. This coincided closely with the time of termination of his probation status. The client continued to report improvement in his drinking and declined further treatment upon completion of the six-month aftercare phase.

At the time of screening, the client was administered a 12-month pretreatment drinking/drug use time line. In addition, a urine screening for drugs of abuse was conducted along with a blood chemistry work-up. The time line was repeated at the end of the primary treatment phase (for the 27-day primary treatment period) and at 90-day intervals up until 12 months had passed. All time lines were conducted by phone by a research assistant independent of the client's clinical care staff. In addition to time lines, a urine screening for drugs of abuse and a blood chemistry profile were obtained at the end of the primary treatment phase and at subsequent 6- and 12-month points. The client also consented to having the follow-up staff contact a close friend for use as a collateral. Telephone contacts for administration of the time line procedure were conducted at pretreatment, at the end of primary treatment, and at 3-, 6-, 9-, and 12-month follow-up points. In all assessment periods, the client and collateral reported no abuse of drugs other than alcohol. This was confirmed using immunoassay procedures on urine collected at all blood collection times.

Results of alcohol use assessments from the client's self-report, collateral report, and GGT across the pretreatment (90 days prior to screening), primary treatment (a 27-day period), and 90-day postprimary-care time periods are presented in Figure 13.1. In the 90 days prior to screening, the client was reporting drinking on 59% of the days. This was somewhat higher than the 41% of client drinking days reported by the collateral. The average number of standard drinks per drinking day during this period was reported by the client and collateral to be 6.23 and 7.95, respectively. The frequency and quantity of drinking at pretreatment also is confirmed in the GGT level of 186, which is considerably higher than the upper limit of the normal range (i.e., 60) of the reference sample used in the lab analyses.

A complete medical examination found no evidence of actual liver disease or other environmental source for this GGT elevation. During the 27-day primary treatment phase, as already noted, the client continued to engage in some drinking. However, both the client and collateral reported a significant reduction in the proportion of days drinking to 15%, and this reduction in drinking appeared to be confirmed by the descending GGT level. Client drinking days further decreased to 4% to 6% in the first three months posttreatment. However, at six months, there was a marked discrepancy between client and collateral with respect to drinking days. The client reported only 11% of the days drinking, whereas the collateral reported that the client was drinking on 97% of the days in the period. Frequency of drinking appeared to be further confirmed by the extremely high GGT level of 867 obtained at the six-month point.

Thus, in this case, the collateral report and GGT level appear to converge and confirm a significant relapse that the client is himself minimizing. The proportion of days drinking increased, based on the client's report, in the 90 days preceding the 9-month follow-up point. During the same period, the collateral reported a marked decrease in drinking days (from the prior period) to a level lower than that reported by the client. At the 12-month follow-up point, both subject and collateral were in agreement that the subject had nothing to drink in the previous 90 days. This appeared to be

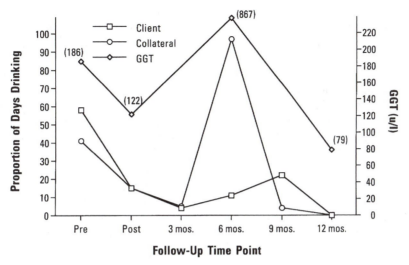

Figure 13.1 Client, collateral, and biochemical (GGT) assessment of client drinking over pretreatment, treatment, and posttreatment follow-up intervals

confirmed, in part, by a GGT level lower than any previously obtained.

In sum, this case demonstrates use of self-report, collateral report, and blood chemistry for assessing drinking before and following treatment. Inclusion of the collateral and GGT measures allowed for the detection of significantly more drinking in the client than would have been determined had reliance been placed on only the client's own drinking report. Although there appeared to be a fairly high correspondence in the current case between GGT level and proportion of days drinking, such correspondence is not found in all cases. Some individuals return to drinking without significant elevations in GGT. Also, as noted earlier, concurrent drug use can normalize GGT levels in combined alcohol/drug abusers. Establishing individual baseline levels of GGT is useful in assessing the value of this marker for detection of relapse in individual alcohol abusers.

Finally, it should be noted that had one simply relied on a one-time follow-up interval of 90 days prior to the 12-month follow-up point, our picture of the client's drinking would have been considerably different from the fluctuations seen in our continuous measurement of drinking days over the entire 12 months.

SUMMARY

Self-report methods, despite their many limitations, remain the primary method for assessment of alcohol, tobacco, and other drug use. Although biochemical markers have and continue to draw interest in this area, they remain limited by their relatively small windows of detection and/or lack of sensitivity and specificity. Research continues into intriguing biochemical methods of substance use detection, yet self-report methods are and will likely continue to be the main source of substance use assessment data.

For the most part, adequate levels of reliability and validity of these self-report methods have been found. There still remains, however, a high degree of inter-subject variability in both the reliability and validity of substance use measures. In light of the variability among individual subjects and some studies showing poorer reliability/validity, investigators in this area have moved away from trying to answer the question: "Is self-reported substance use reliable and valid?" Instead, they have begun to examine the parameters that influence the level of self-report reliability and validity. Reference to some initial findings in this area has been made throughout this chapter.

In examining parameters of self-report reliability and validity, one can view the question-and-answer approach in self-report methods as a complex social psychological process which *itself* can be studied. Drawing from general research on measurement of response and interviewer bias, Babor and colleagues (1987) have discussed several sources of bias in self-report drinking methods, and offer suggestions for reducing them. These suggestions, summarized here, apply to self-report tobacco and other drug use methods as well.

1. It is important to make clear to the respondent the purpose of the data collection process and to guarantee confidentiality/anonymity. In clinical settings, this may mean developing a trusting, collaborative relationship with the client by ensuring that reports of substance use will not result in termination from treatment or long harangues from the therapist. The importance of assuring confidentiality/anonymity is even more salient among illicit drug users, arrestees, and prison populations.

2. Careful wording of questions is important to make clear to the respondent the information requested. This can be facilitated by use of multiple questions and probe questions.

3. Training interviewers in standardized protocol and effective interview techniques canensure adequate administration of self-report measures.

4. Use of clear instructions, longer questions, aided recall (e.g., fixed response choices), memory aids, and bounded recall (i.e., reminding the individual of previous responses that may help present responding) can assist the respondent in remembering specific drinking episodes more accurately.

5. Motivation of the respondent can be increased by requesting a signed commitment agreement wherein the respondent pledges to work hard at providing accurate drinking/drug use information. Social reinforcement of careful thinking and recall on the part of the respondent during the interview or assessment process also can assist ineinsuring more accurate reports. The "bogus pipeline" procedure is another motivation enhancement procedure with possible application. In this procedure, the respondent is led to believe that some objective verification of her or his behavior will be available to the interviewer. With this knowledge, the respondent is believed less likely to provide inaccurate information. The deception involved in the bogus pipeline poses obvious ethical problems. Nevertheless, results of this line of research may have value since the use of breath testing, collateral interviewers, and biological tests themselves, although not "bogus," may serve to increase the accuracy of self-report measures using similar processes.

6. Incorporation of fictitious drug names in drug use questionnaires may assist in detection of inaccurate reports.

Empirical support for some of these procedures as directly applied to self-report substance use has begun to appear. For example, Hill, Dill, and Davenport (1988) found that an anonymity-assuring procedure was equally if not more effective in increasing self-reports of narcotic use among a college sample than was a bogus pipeline procedure. The positive effect of the bogus pipeline, however, was larger when anonymity was not guaranteed. The parameters under which bogus pipelines are effective in improving self-reported cigarette use also recently have been explored (see Auginis, Pierce, & Quigley, 1993).

As more knowledge of parameters affecting self-report measures of substance use becomes available, more judicious use of self-report, collateral report, and biochemical methods can be made. Velicer and associates (1992), for example, suggest that with current knowledge, biochemical measures of smoking may only be necessary in selected populations for whom lower self-report validity coefficients have been found. Nevertheless, until more is known about the mediators and moderators of self-report substance use methods, a multimethod approach to assessment that incorporates self-, collateral, and biochemical methods appears optimal at this time.

REFERENCES

Aguinis, H., Pierce, C. A., & Quigley, B. M. (1993). Conditions under which a bogus pipeline procedure enhances the validity of self-reported cigarette smoking: A meta-analytic review. *Journal of Applied Social Psychology, 23*, 352–373.

Aiken, L. S., & LoSciuto, L. A. (1985). Ex-addict vs. non-addict counselors' knowledge of clients' drug use. *International Journal of Addictions, 20*, 417–433.

Allen, J. P., Litten, R. Z., Anton, R., & Cross, G. M. (1994). Carbohydrate deficient transferrin as a measure of immoderate drinking: Remaining issues. *Alcoholism: Clinical and Experimental Research, 18*, 799–812.

Anderson, W. H., Bright, M., & Snider, H. L. (1979). Relation of smoking to cardiopulmonary disease. In S. L. Sullivan (Ed.), *Proceedings of the fifth workshop conference, Tobacco and Health Research Institute, University of Kentucky, November 1–2, 1979* (pp. 173–188). Lexington, KY: University of Kentucky Press.

Anglin, M. D., Hser, Y. I., & Chou, C. P. (1993). Reliability and validity of retrospective behavioral self-report by narcotics addicts. *Evaluation Review, 17*, 91–108.

Armor, D. J., & Polich, J. M. (1982). Measurement of alcohol consumption. In E. M. Pattison & E. Kaufman (Eds.), *Encyclopedic handbook of alcoholism* (pp. 72–80). New York: Gardner.

Babor, T. F., Brown, J., & Del Boca, F. K. (1990). Validity of self-reports in applied research on addictive behaviors: Fact or fiction? *Behavioral Assessment, 12*, 5–31.

Babor, T. F., Stephens, R. S., & Marlatt, G. A. (1987). Verbal report methods in clinical research on alcoholism: Response bias and its minimization. *Journal of Studies on Alcohol, 48*, 410–424.

Baer, J. D., Baumgartner, W. A., Hill, V. A., & Blahd, W. H. (1991). Hair analysis for the detection of drug use in pretrial, probation, and parole populations. *Federal Probation, 55*, 3–10.

Bailey, S. L., Flewelling, R. L., & Rachal, J. V. (1992). The characterization of inconsistencies in self-reports of alcohol and marijuana use in a longitudinal study of adolescents. *Journal of Studies on Alcohol, 53*, 636–647.

Bauman, K. E., & Ennett, S. E. (1994). Tobacco use by black and white adolescents: The validity of self-reports. *American Journal of Public Health, 84*, 394–398.

Benowitz, N. L. (1983). The use of biological fluid samples in assessing tobacco smoke consumption. *NIDA Research Monograph Series, 48*, 6–26.

Bigger, P. J. (1979). Urinalysis: Issues and applications. *Federal Probation, 43*, 23–37.

Blank, D. L., & Kidwell, D. A. (1993). External contamination of hair by cocaine: An issue in forensic interpretation. *Forensic Science International, 63*, 145–156.

Bost, R. O. (1993). Hair analysis—Perspectives and limits of a proposed forensic method of proof: A review. *Forensic Science International, 63*, 31–42.

Brewer, C. (1993). Hair analysis as a tool for monitoring and managing patients on methadone maintenance: A discussion. *Forensic Science International, 63*, 277–283.

Brown, J., Kranzler, H. R., & Del Boca, F. K. (1992). Self-reports by alcohol and drug abuse inpatients: Factors affecting reliability and validity. *British Journal of Addiction, 87*, 1013–1024.

Cahalan, D., & Room, R. (1974). *Problem drinking among American men*. New Brunswick, NJ: Rutgers Center of Alcohol Studies.

Chaikelson, J. S., Arbuckle, T. Y., Lapidus, S., & Gold, D. P. (1994). Measurement of lifetime alcohol consumption. *Journal of Studies on Alcohol, 55*, 133–140.

Chiarotti, M. (1993). Overview on extraction procedures. *Forensic Science International, 63*, 161–170.

Christmas, J. F., Knisely, J. S., Dawson, K. S., Dinsmoor, M. J., Weber, S. E., & Schnoll, S. H. (1992). Comparison of questionnaire screening and urine toxicology for detection of pregnancy complicated by substance use. *Obstetrics & Gynecology, 80*, 750–754.

Colbert, D. L. (1994). Drug abuse screening with immunoassays: Unexpected cross-reactivities and other pitfalls. *British Journal of Biomedical Science, 51*, 136–146.

Cone, E. J., Darwin, W. D., & Wang, W. L. (1993). The occurrence of cocaine, heroin and metabolites in hair of drug abusers. *Forensic Science International, 63*, 55–68.

Coombs, R. H. (1991). Drug testing as experienced by mandatory participants. In R. H. Coombs & L. J. West (Eds.), *Drug testing: Issues and options*, (pp. 202–214). New York: Oxford.

Cooper, A. M., Sobell, M. B., Maisto, S. A., & Sobell, L. C. (1980). Criterion intervals for pretreatment drinking measures in treatment evaluation. *Journal of Studies on Alcohol, 41*, 1186–1195.

Cushman, P., Jr. (1992). Blood and liver markers in the estimation of alcohol consumption. In R. Z. Litten & J. P. Allen (Eds.), *Measuring alcohol consumption; Psychosocial and biochemical methods* (pp. 135–147). Totowa, NJ: Humana Press.

Darke, S., Heather, N., Hall, W., Ward, J., & Wodak, A. (1991). Estimating drug consumption in opioid users: Reliability and validity of a 'recent use' episodes method. *British Journal of Addiction, 86,* 1311–1316.

Diguisto, E., & Bird, K. D. (1995). Matching smokers to treatment: Self-control versus social support. *Journal of Consulting and Clinical Psychology, 63,* 290–295.

Eckerman, W. C., Bates, J. D., Rachal, J. V., & Poole, W. K. (1971). *Drug usage and arrest charges.* Washington, DC: Bureau of Narcotics and Dangerous Drugs.

Ehrman, R. N., & Robbins, S. J. (1994). Reliability and validity of 6-month timeline reports of cocaine and heroin use in a methadone population. *Journal of Consulting and Clinical Psychology, 62,* 843–850.

Embree, B. G., & Whitehead, P. C. (1993). Validity and reliability of self-reported drinking behavior: Dealing with the problem of response bias. *Journal of Studies on Alcohol, 54,* 334–344.

Emhart, C. B., Morrow-Tlucak, M., Sokol, R. J., & Martier, S. (1988). Underreporting of alcohol use in pregnancy. *Alcoholism: Clinical and Experimental Research, 12,* 506–511.

Falck, R., Siegal, H., Forney, M. A., Wang, J., & Carlson, R. G. (1992). The validity of injection drug users self-reported use of opiates and cocaine. *The Journal of Drug Issues, 22,* 823–832.

Fendrich, M., & Xu, Y. (1994). The validity of drug use reports from juvenile arrestees. *The International Journal of the Addictions, 29,* 971–985.

Flegal, K. M. (1991). Agreement between two dietary methods in reported intake of beer, wine and liquor. *Journal of Studies on Alcohol, 52,* 174–179.

Fox, N. L., Sexton, M., Hebel, J. R., & Thompson, B. (1989). The reliability of self-reports of smoking and alcohol consumption by pregnant women. *Addictive Behaviors, 14,* 187–195.

Fuller, R. K., Lee, K. K., & Gordis, E. (1988). Validity of self-report in alcoholism research: Results of a Veterans Administration cooperative study. *Alcoholism: Clinical and Experimental Research, 12,* 201–205.

Graham, P., & Jackson, R. (1993). Primary versus proxy respondents: Comparability of questionnaire data on alcohol consumption. *American Journal of Epidemiology, 138,* 443–452.

Gronbaek, M., Henriksen, J. H., & Becker, U. (1995). Carbohydrate-deficient transferrin—A valid marker of alcoholism in population studies? Results from the Copenhagen city heart study. *Alcoholism: Clinical and Experimental Research, 19,* 457–461.

Harrell, A. V. (1988). Validation of self-report: The research record. In B. Rouse, N. Kozel, & L. G. Richard (Eds.), *Self-report methods of estimating drug use: Meeting current challenges to validity.* Rockville, MD: National Institute on Drug Abuse.

Harrison, E. R., Haaga, J., & Richards, T. (1993). Self-reported drug use data: What do they reveal? *American Journal of Drug and Alcohol Abuse, 19,* 423–441.

Henderson, G. L. (1993). Mechanisms of drug incorporation into hair. *Forensic Science International, 63,* 19–29.

Hill, P. C., Dill, C. A., & Davenport, E. C., Jr. (1988). A reexamination of the bogus pipeline. *Educational and Psychological Measurement, 48,* 587–601.

Hilton, M. E. (1989). A comparison of a prospective diary and two summary recall techniques for recording alcohol consumption. *British Journal of Addiction, 84,* 1085–1092.

Hindin, R., McCusker, J., Vickers-Lahti, M., Bigelow, C., Garfield, F., & Lewis, B. (1994). Radioimmunoassay of hair for determination of cocaine, heroin, and marijuana exposure: Comparison with self-report. *The International Journal of the Addictions, 29,* 771–789.

Hoffman, N. G., & Ninonuevo, F. G. (1994). Concurrent validation of substance abusers' self-reports against collateral information: Percentage agreement vs. K vs. Yule's Y. *Alcoholism: Clinical and Experimental Research, 18,* 231–237.

Holden, C. (1990). Hairy problems for new drug testing method. *Science, 249,* 1099–1100.

Hubbard, R. L., Eckerman, W. C., & Rachal, J. V. (1977). *Factors affecting the validity of self-reports of drug use: An overview.* Paper presented at the annual meeting of the American Statistical Association.

Hunt, W. A., Barnett, L. W., & Branch, L. G. (1971). Relapse rates in addiction programs. *Journal of Clinical Psychology, 27,* 455–456.

Jarvis, M., Tunstall-Pedoe, H., Feyerabend, C., Vesey, C., & Salloojee, Y. (1987). Comparison of tests used to distinguish smokers from nonsmokers. *American Journal of Public Health, 77,* 1435–1438.

Kapur, B. M. (1993). Drug-testing methods and clinical interpretations of test results. *Bulletin on Narcotics, 45,* 115–154.

Kidwell, D. A. (1993). Analysis of phenylcyclidine and cocaine in human hair by tandem mass spectrometry. *Journal of Forensic Science, 38,* 272–284.

King, A., Scott, R. R., & Prue, D. M. (1984). The reactive effects of assessing reported rates and alveolar carbon monoxide levels on smoking behavior. *Addictive Behaviors, 8,* 323–327.

Kintz, P., Cirimele, V., Edel, Y., Jamey, C., & Mangin,

P. (1994). Hair analysis for buprenorphine and its dealkylated metabolite by RIA and confirmation by LC/ECD. *Journal of Forensic Sciences, 39*, 1497–1503.

Kozlowski, L. T., & Heatherton, T. F. (1990). Self-report issues in cigarette smoking: State of the art and future directions. *Behavioral Assessment, 12*, 53–75.

Krall, E. A., Valadian, L., Dwyer, J. T., & Gardner, J. (1989). Accuracy of recalled smoking data. *American Journal of Public Health, 79*, 200–202.

Lafolie, P., & Beck, O. (1994). Deficient performance of drugs of abuse testing in Sweden: An external control study. *Scandinavian Journal of Clinical Laboratory Investigation, 54*, 251–256.

Lafolie, P., Beck, O., & Hjemdahl, P. (1994). Using relation between urinary cannabinoid and creatinine excretions to improve monitoring of abuser adherence to abstinence. *Clinical Chemistry, 40*, 170–171.

Langone, J. J., & Van Vunakis, H. (1975). Quantitation of cotinine in sera of smokers. *Research Communication in Chemical Pathology and Pharmacology, 10*, 21–28.

Lehrer, M. (1990). Application of gas chromatography/mass spectrometry instrument techniques to forensic urine drug testing. *Clinics in Laboratory Medicine, 10*, 271–288.

Lichtenstein, E., & Glasgow, R. E. (1992). Smoking cessation: What have we learned over the past decade? *Journal of Consulting and Clinical Psychology, 60*, 518–527.

Litten, R. Z., & Allen, J. P. (Eds.). (1992). *Measuring alcohol consumption; Psychosocial and biochemical methods*. Totowa, NJ: Humana Press.

Magura, S., Freeman, R. G., Siddiqi, Q., & Lipton, D. S. (1992). The validity of hair analysis for detecting cocaine and heroin use among addicts. *The International Journal of the Addictions, 27*, 51–69.

Magura, S., Goldsmith, D., Casriel, C., Goldstein, P.J., & Lipton, D. S. (1987). The validity of methadone clients' self-reported drug use. *The International Journal of the Addictions, 22*, 727–749.

Maisto, S. A., & Connors, G. J. (1990). Clinical diagnostic techniques and assessment tools in alcoholism research. *Alcohol Health and Research World, 14*, 232–238.

Maisto, S. A., & Connors, G. J. (1992). Using subject and collateral reports to measure alcohol consumption. In R. Z. Litten & J. P. Allen (Eds.), *Measuring alcohol consumption; Psychosocial and biochemical methods* (pp. 73–96). Totowa, NJ: Humana Press.

Maisto, S. A., McKay, J. R., & Connors, G. J. (1990). Self-report issues in substance abuse: State of the art and future directions. *Behavioral Assessment, 12*, 117–134.

Maisto, S. A., Sobell, M. B., Cooper, A. M., & Sobell, L. C. (1979). Test-retest reliability of retrospective self-reports in three populations of alcohol abusers. *Journal of Behavioral Assessment, 1*, 315–326.

Maisto, S. A., Sobell, L. C., Cooper, A. M., & Sobell, M. B. (1982). Comparison of two techniques to obtain retrospective reports of drinking behavior from alcohol abusers. *Addictive Behaviors, 7*, 33–38.

Maisto, S. A., Sobell, L. C., & Sobell, M. B. (1983). Corroboration of drug abusers' self-reports through the use of multiple data sources. *American Journal of Drug and Alcohol Abuse, 9*, 301–308.

Martin, G. W., Wilkinson, D. A., & Kapur, B. M. (1988) Validation of self-reported cannabis use by urine analysis. *Addictive Behaviors, 13*, 147–150.

McCrady, B. S., Duclos, S., Dubrekuil, E., Stout, R., & Fisher-Nelson, H. (1984). Stability of drinking prior to alcoholism treatment. *Addictive Behaviors, 9*, 329–333.

McElrath, K. (1994). A comparison of two methods for examining inmates' self-reported drug use. *The International Journal of the Addictions, 29*, 517–524.

McGuffey, E. C., & Mullins, B. A. (1994). Testing for drug abuse. *American Pharmacy, NS34*, 18.

McLaughlin, J. K., Dietz, M. S., Mehl, E. S., & Blot, W. J. (1987). Reliability of surrogate information on cigarette smoking by type of informant. *American Journal of Epidemiology, 126*, 144–146.

Midanik, L. T. (1988). Validity of self-reported alcohol use: A literature review and assessment. *British Journal of Addiction, 83*, 1019–1029.

Mieczkowski, T. (1990). The accuracy of self-reported drug use: An evaluation and analysis of new data. In R. Weisheit (Ed.), *Drugs, crime, and the criminal justice system* (pp. 275–302). Cincinnati: Anderson.

Mieczkowski, T., Barzelay, D., Gropper, B., & Wish, E. (1991). Concordance of three measures of cocaine use in an arrestee population: Hair, urine, and self-report. *The Journal of Psychoactive Drugs, 23*, 241–249.

Mieczkowski, T., & Newel, R. (1993). Comparing hair and urine assays for cocaine and marijuana. *Federal Probation, 57*, 59–67.

Mihas, A. A., & Tavassoli, M. (1992). Laboratory markers of ethanol intake and abuse: A critical appraisal. *American Journal of Medical Sciences, 303*, 415–428.

Miller, W. R., & Del Boca, F. K. (1994). Measurement of drinking behavior using the Form 90 family of instruments. *Journal of Studies on Alcohol,* (Supplement No. 12), 112–118.

Moss, R. A., Prue, D. M., Lomax, D., & Martin, J. E. (1982). Implications of self-monitoring for smoking treatment: Effects on adherence and session attendance. *Addictive Behaviors, 7,* 381–385.

Nakahara, Y., Takahashi, K., & Konuma, K. (1993). Hair analysis for drugs of abuse. VI. The excretion methoxyphenamine and methamphetamine into beards of human subjects. *Forensic Science International, 63,* 109–119.

National Institute on Drug Abuse. (1988). Mandatory guidelines for federal workplace drug testing programmes: Final guidelines. *Federal Register, 53* (69).

Needle, R. H., Jou, S. C., & Su, S. S. (1989). The impact of changing methods of data collection on the reliability of self-reported drug use of adolescents. *American Journal of Drug and Alcohol Abuse, 15,* 275–289.

O'Farrell, T. J., & Maisto, S. A. (1987). The utility of self-report and biological measures of alcohol consumption in alcoholism treatment outcome studies. *Advances in Behavior Research and Therapy, 9,* 91–125.

O'Hare, T. (1991). Measuring alcohol consumption: A comparison of the retrospective diary and the quantity-frequency methods in a college drinking survey. *Journal of Studies on Alcohol, 52,* 500–502.

Orrego, H., Blendis, L. M., Blake, J. E., Kapur, B. M., & Israel, Y. (1979). Reliability of assessment of alcohol intake based on personal interviews in a liver clinic. *Lancet, 2,* 1354–1356.

Ossip-Klein, D. J., Giovino, G. A., Megahed, N., Black, P. M., Emont, S. L., Stiggins, J., Shulman, E., & Moore, L. (1991). Effects of a smokers' hotline: Results of a 10-county self-help trial. *Journal of Consulting and Clinical Psychology, 59,* 325–332.

Page, W. F., Davies, J. E., Ladner, R. A., Alfasso, J., & Tennis, H. (1977). Urinalysis screened versus verbally reported drug use: The identification of discrepant groups. *The International Journal of the Addictions, 12,* 439–445.

Palmer, R. F., Dwyer, J. H., & Semmer, N. (1994). A measurement model of adolescent smoking. *Addictive Behaviors, 19,* 477–489.

Patrick, D. L., Cheadle, A., Thompson, D. C., Diehr, P., Koepsell, T., & Kinne, S. (1994). The validity of self-reported smoking: A review and meta-analysis. *American Journal of Public Health, 84,* 1086–1093.

Peach, H., Shah, D., & Morris, R. W. (1986). Validity of smokers' information about present and past cigarette brands—Implications for studies of the effects of falling tar yields of cigarettes on health. *Thorax, 41,* 203–207.

Pedersen, W. (1990). Reliability of drug use responses in a longitudinal study. *Scandinavian Journal of Psychology, 31,* 28–33.

Phillips, M. (1992). Measuring alcohol consumption by transdermal dosimetry. In R. Z. Litten & J. P. Allen (Eds.), *Measuring alcohol consumption; Psychosocial and biochemical methods* (pp. 183–187). Totowa, NJ: Humana Press.

Poikolainen, K., Karkkainen, P., & Pikkarainen, J. (1985). Correlations between biological markers and alcohol intake as measured by diary and questionnaire in men. *Journal of Studies on Alcohol, 46,* 383–387.

Polettini, A., Groppi, A., & Montagna, M. (1993). Rapid and highly selective GC/MS/MS detection of heroin and its metabolites in hair. *Forensic Science International, 63,* 217–225.

Polich, J. M. (1982). The validity of self-reports in alcoholism research. *Addictive Behaviors, 7,* 123–132.

Polich, J. M., Armor, D. J., & Braiker, M. B. (1980). Patterns of alcoholism over four years. *Journal of Studies on Alcohol, 41,* 397–416.

Potter, B. A., & Orfali, J. S. (1990). *Drug testing at work: A guide for employers and employees.* Berkeley, CA: Ronin Publishing.

Redman, S., Sanson-Fisher. R. W., Wielkinson, C., Fahey, P. P., & Gibberd, R. W. (1987). Agreement between two measures of alcohol consumption. *Journal of Studies on Alcohol, 48,* 104–108.

Rosenfeld, R., & Decker, S. (1992). Discrepant values, correlated measures: Cross-city and longitudinal comparisons of self reports and urine tests of cocaine use among arrestees. *Journal of Criminal Justice, 21,* 223–230.

Rosman, A. S., & Lieber, C. S. (1992). An overview of current and emerging markers of alcoholism. In R. Z. Litten & J. P. Allen (Eds.), *Measuring alcohol consumption; Psychosocial and biochemical methods* (pp. 99–134). Totowa, NJ: Humana Press.

Rounsaville, B. J., Kleber, H. D., Wilber, C., Rosenberger, D., & Rosenberger, P. (1981). Comparison of opiate addicts' reports of psychiatric history with reports of significant-other informants. *American Journal of Drug and Alcohol Abuse, 8,* 51–69.

Sarvela, P. D. (1990). Establishing drug use questionnaire concurrent validity: Methodological considerations. *Health Values, 14,* 48–55.

Schwartz, R. H. (1988). Urine testing in the detection of drugs of abuse. *Archives of Internal Medicine, 148,* 2407–2412.

Schwarzhoff, R., & Cody, J. F. (1993). The effects of adulterating agents on FPIA analysis of urine for drugs of abuse. *Journal of Analytical Toxicology, 17,* 14–17.

Sherman, M. F., & Bigelow, G. E. (1992). Validity of patients' self-reported drug use as a function of treatment status. *Drug and Alcohol Dependence, 30,* 1–11.

Shiffman, S. (1988). Smoking behavior: Behavioral assessment. In D. M. Donovan & G. A. Marlatt (Eds.), *Assessment of addictive behaviors* (pp. 139–188). New York: Guilford.

Skinner, H. A., & Sheu, W. J. (1982). Reliability of alcohol use indices; The lifetime drinking history and the MAST. *Journal of Studies on Alcohol, 43,* 1157–1170.

Sobell, L. C., Cellucci, T., Nirenberg, T. D., & Sobell, M. B. (1982). Do quantity-frequency data underestimate drinking-related health risks? *American Journal of Public Health, 72,* 823–828.

Sobell, L. C., & Sobell, M. B. (1992). Timeline follow-back: A technique for assessing self-reported alcohol consumption. In R. Z. Litten & J. P. Allen (Eds.), *Measuring alcohol consumption; Psychosocial and biochemical methods* (pp. 41–72). Totowa, NJ: Humana Press.

Sobell, L. C., Sobell, M. B., Leo, G. I., & Cancilla, A. (1988). Reliability of a timeline method: Assessing normal drinkers' reports of recent drinking and a comparative evaluation across several populations. *British Journal of Addictions, 83,* 393–402.

Sobell, L. C., Sobell, M. B., Riley, D. M., Schuller, R., Pavan, D. S., Cancilla, A., Klajner, F., & Leo, G. I. (1988). The reliability of alcohol abuser's self-reports of drinking and life events that occurred in the distant past. *Journal of Studies on Alcohol, 49,* 225–232.

Sobell, L. C., Toneatto, T., & Sobell, M. B. (1994). Behavioral assessment and treatment planning for alcohol, tobacco, and other drug problems: Current status with an emphasis on clinical applications. *Behavior Therapy, 25,* 533–580.

Sobell, M. B., Bogardis, J., Schuller, R., Leo, G. I., & Sobell, L. C. (1989). Is self-monitoring of alcohol consumption reactive? *Behavioral Assessment, 11,* 447–458.

Sobell, M. B., Sobell, L. C., & VanderSpek, R. (1979). Relationships among clinical judgment, self-report, and breath-analysis measures of intoxication in

alcoholics. *Journal of Consulting and Clinical Psychology, 47,* 204–206.

Stevens, R. S., Roffman, R. A., & Simpson, E. E. (1994). Treating adult marijuana dependence: A test of the relapse prevention model. *Journal of Consulting and Clinical Psychology, 62,* 92–99.

Stibler, H. (1991). Carbohydrate-deficient transferrin in serum: A new marker of potentially harmful alcohol consumption. *Review of Clinical Chemistry, 37,* 2029–2037.

Swift, R. M., & Swette, L. (1992). Assessment of ethanol consumption with a wearable electronic ethanol sensor/recorder. In R. Z. Litten & J. P. Allen (Eds.), *Measuring alcohol consumption; Psychosocial and biochemical methods* (pp. 189–202). Totowa, NJ: Humana Press.

Toneatto, T., Sobell, L. C., & Sobell, M. B. (1992). Predictors of alcohol abusers' inconsistent self-reports of their drinking and life events. *Alcoholism: Clinical and Experimental Research, 16,* 542–546.

Tucker, J. A., Vuchinich, R. E., Harris, C. B., Gavornik, M. G., & Rudd, E. J. (1991). Agreement between subject and collateral verbal reports of alcohol consumption in older adults. *Journal of Studies on Alcohol, 52,* 148–155.

Turner, C. F., Lessler, J. T., & Devore, J. (1992). Effects of mode of administration and wording on reporting of drug use. In C. F. Turner, J. T. Lessler, & J. C. Gfroerer (Eds.), *Survey measurement of drug use: Methodological studies.* Washington, DC: Government Printing Office.

Velicer, W. F., Prochaska, J. O., Rossi, J. S., & Snow, M. G. (1992). Assessing outcome in smoking cessation studies. *Psychological Bulletin, 111,* 23–41.

Vesey, C. J. (1981). Thiocyanate and cigarette consumption. In R. M. Greenhalgh (Ed.), *Smoking and arterial disease.* Bath, U.K.: Pitman Medical.

Wagenknecht, L. E., Cutter, G. R., Haley, N. J., Sidney, S., Manolio, T. A., Hughes, G. H., & Jacobs, D. R. (1990). Racial differences in serum cotinine levels among smokers in the coronary artery risk development in (young) adults study. *American Journal of Public Health, 80,* 1053–1056.

Watson, C. G., & Pucel, J. (1985). Consistency of post-treatment of alcoholics' drinking patterns. *Journal of Consulting and Clinical Psychology, 53,* 679–683.

Weatherby, N. L., Needle, R., Cesari, H., Booth, R., McCoy, C. B., Watters, J. K., Williams, M., & Chitwood, D. D. (1994). Validity of self-reported drug use among injection drug users and crack cocaine users recruited through street outreach. *Evaluation and Program Planning, 17*, 347–355.

Welch, M. J., Sniegoski, L. T., Allgood, C. C., & Habram, M. (1993). Hair analysis for drugs of abuse: Evaluation of analytical methods, environmental issues, and development of reference materials. *Journal of Analytical Toxicology, 17*, 389–398.

Willette, R. E. (1991). Techniques of reliable drug testing. In R. H. Coombs & L. J. West (Eds.), *Drug testing: Issues and options* (pp. 67–91). New York: Oxford.

Wish, E., Johnson, B., Strug, D., Chedekel, M., & Lipton, D. (1983). *Are urine tests good indicators of the validity of self-reports of drug use? It depends on the test.* New York: Narcotic and Drug Research, Inc.

Zuckerman, B., Amaro, H., & Cabral, H. (1989). Validity of self-reporting of marijuana and cocaine use among pregnant adolescents. *Journal of Pediatrics, 115*, 812–815.

CHAPTER 14

ASSESSMENT OF MARITAL DYSFUNCTION

Steven L. Sayers
David B. Sarwer
Allegheny University of the Health Sciences

Marital dysfunction presents a special challenge for behavioral assessment. In contrast to many of the other clinical problems in this volume, marital dysfunction entails two individuals as the focus of the assessment. In the behavioral assessment of an individual, the patient is often vague or selective in reporting his or her own behavior. With couples, however, these problems are compounded by the fact that spouses have a natural vested interest in how they report marital behavior to a clinician. This is compounded again by the fact that both spouses are reporting the same events to the clinician from divergent viewpoints, primarily because the spouses occupy different roles in the same interpersonal system they are describing. How can we deal with the influence that spouses' biases have when trying to utilize their reports about marital interaction? Unfortunately, the marital field has not advanced to the point where many of the measures take the bias of discordant spouses into account when using scores from self-report inventories to make statements about marital behavior.

In a related vein, in the marital assessment area there are several unresolved issues, including the question of how to understand "objective" coders' ratings of marital interaction in light of spouses' ratings of their own interactions. There has also been some disagreement among marital theorists regarding the reliance on observational data in examining the outcome of treatment, when purportedly the goal of marital therapy is to increase spouses' subjective assessments of satisfaction. These issues are substantive in that they could dramatically influence the way marital assessment data are collected and interpreted.

This chapter will address these theoretical issues and then provide some suggestions for conducting behavioral assessments of marital dysfunction. Practical issues in marital assessment will then be discussed, followed by a review of various assessment measures. Finally, a case description will illustrate the use of some of these issues.

THEORETICAL ISSUES IN MARITAL ASSESSMENT

What Are We Trying to Find? Idiographic and Nomothetic Vantage Points

The behavioral assessment process is a prototypical example of an idiographic approach to assessment and the understanding of human behavior. Consistent with this idea, most formulations of behavioral marital therapy (BMT) have emphasized that an individualized assessment and conceptualization of a couple's problems is necessary for successful treatment (Jacobson & Margolin, 1979; Baucom & Epstein, 1990). Perhaps because of its manualization of BMT in outcome studies, however, it can be criticized as a "one-size-fits-all" approach to treatment. The suggestion is that, as well-controlled tests of BMT have demonstrated the clinical usefulness of the therapy, the standard application of BMT in outcome research represents a nomothetic approach to the alleviation of marital dysfunction. A nomothetic approach to marital discord would rest on the assumption that the similarities of dissatisfied couples dictates that one should apply a standardized form of the treatment demonstrated to be effective.

Another way in which nomothetic concepts are "creeping in" on idiographic, behavioral conceptions of marital distress is through the development of typologies of marriage. At first glance, it may not seem evident how a classification system can fit comfortably with an idiographic approach to marital discord. Gottman (1993) has presented perhaps the first typology of marriage developed on the basis of observational data of couples' interactions. This typology is based on the balance of positivity and negativity in marital interaction. He proposes the idea that stably married couples exhibit positive to negative affect at a ratio of 5:1, whereas unstably married couples exhibit a ratio closer to 1:1. Gottman presents several subtypes of stable and unstable couples, suggesting that some couples maintain the 5:1 ratio through highly emotional engagement, whereas others maintain this balance through both conflict avoidance and fewer positive interactions.

Even though this typology implies great similarity between discordant couples, there may be idiographic elements of this conception of marital discord. For example, the kind of "negative" communication that spouses of one couple use may differ from another. The husband may criticize and invalidate his wife's concerns about finances, but only prompt a countercriticism from his wife when he states that she has negative motives. If restoring a balance of 5:1 in positive to negative behavior is indeed crucial to helping a specific couple, the clinician has to identify the specific kinds of behaviors that lead to negative cycles of interaction in that couple to effectively intervene.

What Should We Assess and How Can We Discover It?

Marital assessment from a behavioral perspective is typically a precursor to behavioral marital therapy. There are wide differences among behavioral conceptions of marital discord as well as the kind of data that should be gathered in the assessment process. Specifically, is marital discord due to communication and problem-solving skill deficits? Is it important to detect patterns of interaction, such as coercion, which is reflected by one spouse's use of aversive behavior (e.g., threats to leave) reinforced by the other partner's acquiescence (e.g., agreement to change) (Patterson & Reid, 1970)? Alternatively, it is possible to understand marital discord as resulting from a dysfunctional behavioral system (Weiss, 1980); the goal of behavioral assessment in this conception would be identifying constituent behaviors that create this problematic pattern of interaction. What does the existence of these differences in behavioral perspectives mean for behavioral assessment of marriage?

It is certainly possible for communication skills deficits to be important in the development of one couple's marital discord, whereas another's discord may be due to rigid, dysfunctional interactional patterns. It is important for the clinician to consider a broad range of the behavioral aspects of marital interaction. As described here, the starting place is the spouses' complaints, leading to an estimate of the basic frequency or probability of the specific behaviors described in the complaint. For example, one couple we have worked with had conflicts over the husband's purchase of compact discs. The first line of inquiry concerned the frequency of these conflicts—that is, when and where did they occur? Second, we assessed how often the husband bought CDs and how the wife monitored the purchases. This assessment process should then lead the astute assessor to examine behaviors that precede and follow each of the problem behaviors in a complaint, as well as the context of the problem.

Are these behaviors part of a longer pattern? Are they part of a more generalized pattern, in which there are multiple variants on this same theme? Have the spouses attempted a number of solutions, or do they persist with the same routinized responses? What are their problem-solving attempts like? Are the difficulties of one person, such as stably negative mood, determining his or her responses to conflicts when they arise? All of these questions should be considered when the clinician proceeds with assessment of the couple.

As the clinician proceeds to examine individual behaviors, sequential patterns of interaction, or entire systems, it is important for him or her to be conservative in reifying the concept of pattern or system. A high degree of inference can be destructive in understanding the couple. For example, it may seem quite plausible to the therapist that the conflicts a couple have over disciplining their children is a symptom of enmeshment with their families of origin. Do the data support such an interpretation? Are there more parsimonious explanations? The simple fact that the couple disagrees over discipline may indeed be related to beliefs developed in their family of origin. Is the clinician sure that he or she actually has the data necessary to incorporate the couple's problems into a larger system that includes in-laws, children, and families of origin? These more complex formulations of marital discord can have tremendous appeal on intellectual grounds, but may not provide a very practical guide for treating the couple.

Who Do We Believe? Insider and Outsider Perspectives in Marital Assessment

There are often differences between the perceptions of trained coders, or *outsiders*, and the perceptions of spouses, or *insiders*. These differences can be dramatic. The consensus between insiders' and outsiders' ratings of couples' interactions ranges from nonexistent to moderately high (Baucom & Adams, 1987). In addition, differences between spouses' reports of their own interactions can be substantial, with only a 40% to 50% level of interspousal agreement for specific marital behaviors. To ensure a valid assessment, it is useful to think about how one might interpret data from several sources, including each spouse's report of his or her own behavior and cognitions, report of his or her partner's behavior, and the therapists' observations of their interactions. It is crucial to the assessment process, then, to understand why these differences exist.

The first explanation for differences between spouses' and trained coders' ratings of marital interaction is that the methodology of the ratings sometimes differs. Birchler, Clopton, and Adams (1984) and Weiss (1984) compared spouses' ratings of their videotaped problem-solving interactions with trained coders' ratings. Unfortunately, the trained coders used the frequency-based Marital Interaction Coding System (MICS; Hops, Wills, Patterson, & Weiss, 1972), and the spouses used dimensional scales of subjective impact of their partners' communication behavior. This methodological difference makes it difficult to assess the degree of consensus between the spouses and objective coders.

Second, the fact that spouses have not been trained to be "objective" in their perceptions of marital interaction behavior limits the degree to which they would agree with trained coders. Two studies offer limited support for this idea (Birchler, Clopton, & Adams, 1984; Jacobson & Moore,

1981); the results of these studies suggest that distressed couples, in particular, may benefit from training. But even after 21 days of practice with a behavioral checklist, spouses still have only a 50% consensus level for observable marital events (Jacobson & Moore, 1981).

Other explanations of insider/outsider differences in perceptions of marital interaction are related to the couples' level of marital discord. One such explanation is the private messaging hypothesis (Gottman, 1979), which has received mixed empirical support. This hypothesis suggests that nondistressed couples have a private system of communication not shared by those outside the relationship; alternatively, distressed spouses are hypothesized not to have such a system.

Most of the available evidence does support the notion that nondiscordant spouses have greater consensus with their partners than do discordant spouses (Christensen & Nies, 1980; Christensen, Sullaway, & King, 1983; Elwood & Jacobson, 1982; Jacobson & Moore, 1981; Robinson & Price, 1980). There is inconsistent support for the other aspect of the private messaging hypothesis concerning nondiscordant spouses' decreased consensus with objective coders. Only some studies report this finding (Birchler, Clopton, & Adams, 1984; Notarius, Benson, Sloane, Vanzetti, & Hornyak, 1989), with other studies indicating that nondiscordant spouses show greater consensus with trained coders (Margolin, Hattem, John, & Yost, 1985; Robinson & Price, 1980). These inconsistencies are perhaps due to relatively small sample sizes in some of the studies.

Weiss (1980) introduced the concept of *sentiment override* as a way of understanding the influence of the spouses' primary sentiment (i.e., subjective satisfaction level) on their evaluations of their partner's interactional behavior. Sentiment override is simply the process of a spouse making inappropriate generalizations about the causes of the behavior, consistent with the sentiment in the marriage. Positive sentiment override seems to arise out of the societally related promise of noncontingent love and leads spouses to disregard their partner's negative behavior (Weiss, 1980). Negative sentiment override leads to negative attributions for negative behavior (e.g., "My partner is be-

having negatively to 'get even' for some previous fight").

There are several ways to resolve the potential problem of the spouses' biases in their reporting of relationship events. A relentless "search for the truth" in interviewing a couple is often in vain. Most of the time, the shared reality—or that which the spouses agree upon—is sufficient to understand how spouses behave with one another. Spouses rarely present many important factual discrepancies, thus preventing the assessor from understanding the couple. Second, the discrepancies spouses' report often represent different *interpretations* of the same behavior. For example, a husband who made a financial decision without consulting his wife might explain his behavior by saying he was trying to avoid a fight with his wife; the wife might believe that her husband does not respect her opinion. Further inquiry might reveal that these interpretations are useful in revealing the spouses' tendencies to focus only on negative events, as well as their beliefs about conflict and their roles in the marriage.

Resolving potential differences in insider/outsider perspectives of couples' interactional behavior requires that the clinician utilize both self-report and observational methods. When integrating these two sources of information, the clinician should account for the context of each type of assessment (clinician's office vs. home), the format of the assessment (clinician observed interaction vs. self-report checklist), and the interactional task (structured problem-solving task vs. spontaneous discussion). There will be few insider/outsider differences that remain once the clinician has considered all of these factors.

Developmental Aspects of Relationships

Increasingly, family theorists have stressed the importance of understanding the developmental aspects of family relationships (Fuller & Fincham, 1994; Heavey, Shenk, & Christensen, 1994). From a behavioral perspective, how can marital assessment benefit from considering the developmental course of the marital relationship?

First, there is evidence that the probability of divorce when a couple is dissatisfied differs among couples with marriages of different length. That is, the spouses' marital dissatisfaction may have different consequences and meanings depending on the developmental stage of the marriage (White & Booth, 1991). Second, it may be difficult to accurately gauge behavioral deficits, excesses, and skills of couples if they are currently in a transition or crisis. Understanding how the couple resolved previous crises, what skills they learned, and what changes they experienced in their interaction patterns enables the clinician to develop an effective treatment plan. Third, there may be general trends and experiences that are common across couples that help the clinician anticipate what a successful resolution to their crisis might be. For instance, it is important for a clinician to understand how a couple's interactional patterns might be altered to adjust to the arrival of their first child.

Although behavioral-developmental approaches to marriage are not yet fully explicated, recent theoretical outlines identify both transitional events and more continuous marital processes as important in understanding the relationship between marital development and marital conflict (Heavey, Shenk, & Christensen, 1994). An understanding of the effects of normative transitional events (e.g., birth of the first child) and nonnormative events (e.g., extended unemployment) can be very helpful to the clinician in probing for changes in couples' interactions or unstated beliefs about these events.

For example, what meaning does each of the spouses take from the decrease in intimacy after the birth of their first child? Have their beliefs about these changes led to changes in communication patterns? Several continuous or slow-changing aspects of marriage might also be considered when assessing couples. First, over the course of a marriage, couples often experience a slow shift from positive sentiment override (Weiss, 1980) and passionate love (Berscheid, 1983) to contentment (or even negative sentiment override in distressed couples). Where is the couple in this process? How long have they been experiencing consistently negative feelings that color their perceptions of one another? Is their decrease of passion normative for a relation-

ship of this longevity? The answers to such questions frame the context of the couple's current complaints and help the clinician to understand whether their current affect can be attributed to recent conflict or longer-term developmental processes.

PRACTICAL ISSUES IN MARITAL ASSESSMENT

Marital assessment is a broad concept that encompasses many different information gathering methods and that often occurs over a long period of time. An effective marital assessment involves more than simply collecting spouses' verbal responses to a series of questions. It also involves responses to questionnaires and actual observations of marital communication. However, it is equally important to assess the way spouses think about each other and their problems, as well as their predominant affective states. There are a number of issues to attend to in meeting these goals, including the reason for the assessment, the selection of the procedures used, and the practical nature of the different assessment modalities.

Why Are We Assessing This Couple? Reasons for Marital Assessment and the Implications for Assessment Strategies

There are at least two general reasons to assess a couple: to evaluate for treatment and treatment planning or to address research questions. This is an obvious and important distinction. Even if most or all of the assessments used in research protocols are relevant to understanding the couple's functioning, rarely are research protocols the most efficient way of obtaining this information. The assessments used in research protocols are driven by research questions and are typically too numerous for a couple paying for treatment to tolerate. Additionally, the large majority of studies using observational methods rely on data aggregated across couples (e.g., Notarius, Benson, Sloane, Vanzetti, & Hornyak, 1989) or use an index of contingencies between spouse's behaviors in each couple while still relying on group-level statistics (e.g., Sayers, Baucom, Sher, Weiss, & Heyman, 1991). Such strategies are unlikely to yield the kind of information necessary for the treatment of a particular couple.

On the other hand, assessment for the purpose of treatment planning is typically more individualized and relies more on spouses' self-report of their interactions. In this chapter, we will present examples of measures that can be used for research or clinical pursuits, but will emphasize discussion of clinical assessment methods. There are a number of other texts devoted to the assessment of marriage for research purposes, in particular using observational methodology (e.g, Gottman, 1979; Hahlweg & Jacobson, 1984; Jacob, 1987).

As alluded to in the discussion of nomothetic versus idiographic viewpoints, the relevance of the results of observational methods to the evaluation of behavior marital therapy has been hotly debated (Jacobson, 1985; Weiss & Frohman, 1985; Gottman, 1985). One of the arguments most relevant to this chapter is that observational coding systems do not directly tap the couple's problems when the couple does not indicate that communication is their primary concern. In addition, the coding categories in observational coding systems may not be particularly relevant to a specific couple, and the artificial nature of laboratory assessments limits the usefulness of a functional analysis based on this type of data.

On the other side of the argument, however, behavioral changes in communication are often seen as crucial to the success of behavioral treatment with couples (Weiss & Frohman, 1985). Despite the inability of most clinicians to make use of formal laboratory observational assessments, it is quite possible to use a more informal version of standard problem-solving assessments to gain important information about a couple's interactional style. How to conduct such informal assessments is discussed next.

The Process of Clinical Marital Assessment

Although it is important to continue marital assessment from the beginning to the end of the clinical work with a couple, the vast majority of assessment occurs in the initial two or three sessions. The first phase of assessment occurs in the clinical interview. Typically, the initial interview should cover at least two areas: (1) discussion of current relationship problems and goals for attending therapy and (2) the collection of a marital history (Baucom & Epstein, 1990; Jacobson & Margolin, 1979).

The discussion of current relationship problems should be relatively brief so that the first session is not dominated by contentiousness and negative affect. It is the therapist's first opportunity to begin shaping the spouses' in-session behavior so that all the pertinent information is gathered, and the spouses do not engage in unconstrained conflict in the presence of the therapist. The clinician can open with a review of the information already gained from telephone or referral contacts and can ask each of the spouses in turn for his or her primary concern and reason for being there. It is important to distinguish the couple's statements of current problems from their purposes for being there, and the latter question will highlight what each spouse hopes to gain from the sessions, whether attendance at the session resulted from coercion from one partner, and the overall level of hopefulness of each spouse.

Although this initial statement of the current problems and reasons for being in treatment is meant to be brief (i.e., 15 to 20 minutes), it allows the clinician to witness how the couple interacts around these problem issues. Do they name-call and point fingers? Does one partner become easily defensive or reticent? Do they attempt to control one another's interaction? Do they have readily apparent ideas about the cause of their current problems? The therapist should bring this initial phase of the session to a close by outlining the other areas he or she wishes to address. Couples usually consent to temporarily delaying the discussion of their presenting complaints if they see that the clinician has a systematic way of learning about them.

The gathering of the marital history should include a discussion of how the couple met, the nature and length of their courtship, and the circumstances around their engagement and marriage. The recollection of the early part of the couple's relationship is an opportune time to encourage the spouses to refocus on the positive qualities of the partner that attracted them ("What attracted you to him/her?"). This often takes some encouragement when the couple is particularly distressed, but if successful, it can produce an immediate positive shift in the predominant affect in the session. Because smiles and laughter may accompany the description of the couple's first days and months together, this review may serve as a reminder to the spouses of their capacity to enjoy each other. It can also ensure a less contentious recitation of the couple's history.

Also, discussion can reveal what factors contributed to the development of their relationship. Did the spouses' want their relationship to develop at different paces? How did they make the decision to get married? Any significant milestones that have occurred prior to the present time are also assessed, including births of children, moves, changes in employment status or jobs, and deaths of family members. In addition, the clinician should inquire about the nature of relationships with in-laws, other family members, and close friends in order to assess how the couple interacts with others. This assessment allows the clinician to begin to identify dysfunctional behaviors as part of a social context.

At this point in the initial session, the clinician should quickly review with spouses the major pieces of information covered in order to close the session and prepare them for the rest of the assessment. The therapist should note strengths of the couple, including the mere fact that they have initiated treatment. In addition, the therapist can note any functional marital behavior as a strength so as to encourage it in the future. For example, the therapist can note that one or both spouses are willing to allow that they have made some mistakes and that this focus on one's own behavior is important for the future process of change in the relationship. As in individual assessment, it is important to outline the basics of the behavioral approach to treatment, including the active role of each spouse in behavioral exercises.

Typically as part of the assessment process, couples are asked to complete selected questionnaires that provide the clinician with additional information regarding the thoughts and behaviors of the couple at the present time. Self-report measures can be given to a couple to complete prior to the first session, although most therapists would choose to have the spouses complete the forms between the first and second assessment sessions. For clinical purposes, the clinician should ask spouses to complete forms that would take less than an hour, so as to not immediately erode their commitment to treatment. These measures are reviewed in this chapter.

Additional sessions should accomplish several goals. These include a detailed review of the changes each spouse wants in the relationship, the spouses' current frequency and patterns of interaction, current stressors, spouses' marital cognitions and beliefs, and other individual history as appropriate. Also, the therapist should perform a relatively standardized communication assessment which provides an opportunity to make direct observations of the couple's communication style. The review of changes in the relationship desired could be accomplished through the detailed review of the spouse's responses to the Areas of Change Questionnaire (described later) on which the respondent indicates behaviors he or she wishes the partner to engage in at a different rate. For example, one item refers to the partner participating in decisions about money, and the respondent marks the form to indicate a desire for the partner to engage in this activity less or more (or in some degree of less or more).

Any form that covers a range of relationship behavior would suffice for the purpose of gaining an understanding of the spouses's desired interaction patterns. It is useful to cover these areas comprehensively but briefly, with an emphasis on the description of specific behaviors and with each spouse in turn. This allows both spouses to gain experience in using behaviorally specific language and enables each spouse to hear what specific behavior changes are desired by the partner.

The clinician can use the discussion of desired changes as an entree into an assessment of the couple's current interaction patterns. Of interest are the frequency of pleasurable interactions, the pattern and outcome of conflicts, the contexts that lead to conflicts, and other people who may have a role in the couple's problematic interactions (e.g., children, in-laws, friends). Of particular interest are the sequences of the behaviors involved in conflicts and the cognitions each spouse has about the conflict.

For example, how is the conflict initiated? What patterns of conflict are exhibited—is one spouse pursuing the conflict and the other attempting to withdraw? Do both spouses escalate until the point of aggression, after which one spouse acquiesces? Are arguments followed by several days of quiet resentment and anger while each spouse waits for the other to apologize? What attempts do the spouses make to resolve the conflict and what are the results? What expectations do the spouses have of one another in these situations? What would be an adequate resolution in the spouses' minds? It is important to use detailed questioning of both spouses in order to develop a reasonable consensus about the couple's typical pattern of conflict. There are several self-report forms described here that can help the clinician assess these areas.

Finally, the clinician should observe the spouses communicating with one another. Couples can be asked to discuss and attempt to resolve one or two areas of disagreement that currently exist in the relationship. It is most useful to identify and use topics of moderate levels of disagreement at this time, so as not to set the couple up for a potential failure experience. The purpose is not for the couple to be able to resolve the conflict, but for the clinician to observe their patterns of interaction. Familiarity with one or more of the microanalytic codings systems described in this chapter can provide a framework for understanding and tracking the problem-solving discussion (e.g., Marital Interaction Coding System [MICS], Weiss, 1992). Alternatively, several of these coding systems provide a similar degree of specificity concerning the types of behaviors falling into broad coding categories (e.g., MICS-Global; Weiss & Tolman, 1990). It is important that the clinician take care in handling this assessment method by explaining the rationale, preparing the couple to be stopped after a predetermined time (e.g., usually 10 minutes), and helping them deal with the aftermath of the discussion.

Any residual feelings that the spouses have at the conclusion of the discussion can be dealt with by mediating the discussion further, tabling the issue until later sessions, or redirecting the couple to consider the problem in the context of their entire relationship. At the conclusion of the discussion, the clinician also should ask the spouses to describe the subjective experience of the conversation and contrast it with typical conversations in the home. Furthermore, as part of the initiation of therapy, the therapist might use this opportunity to describe his or her conceptualization of the couple's difficulties and integrate any patterns observed during the observational assessment within that conceptualization.

It is important to recognize that ongoing assessment of the couple will help the clinician track changes throughout the therapy, including shifts in behavior and relationship satisfaction. Often this can be accomplished through a regular review of the couple's interaction during the week, including a report of the pleasant times spent together and a brief description of the conflictual interactions they had. In addition, the therapist can ask the spouses to complete a brief self-report measure of satisfaction prior to the session in order to gain a quick gauge of their relationship. By referring to this data collected over time, the therapist can gain a more detailed understanding of the factors that lead to deterioration or improvement in the couple's functioning.

Assessment Modalities

It is clear that behavioral assessment can use a variety of modalities, including the clinical interview, written self-report, and direct observation. Within each modality, the clinician can obtain information about several domains of the patient's functioning, including his or her specific complaints, behavior, mood and affect, cognitions, and the social context of the problems. It is important to recognize that, although many of the measures are targeted toward one domain or another, they inevitably provide some information about several domains. For example, a written log may be used to assess each spouse's interactional behavior, but inevitably the spouses' cognitions influence what behavior they report. In addition, a widely used measure such as the Dyadic Adjustment Scale not only assesses the overall satisfaction in the relationship but it also assesses the spouses' affectionate and conflict behavior. With these points in mind, we will review measures within each type of modality and identify the primary targets of the assessment method.

REVIEW OF MARITAL ASSESSMENT METHODS

Clinical Interview

Perhaps the most straightforward method of behavioral assessment involves the clinical interview. To assess interactional patterns, the interviewer takes an approach similar to that described in Chapter 4 of this book, by Sarwer and Sayers, regarding behavioral interviewing techniques. Essentially, the interviewer is assessing the sequences of interactional behaviors, which entails the antecedent-behavior-consequent chains of behavioral events, so that the interviewer can develop a functional analysis of the conflicts. The interviewer also tries to obtain specificity in the spouses' description of their interactions. That is, what does each spouse do and when? What are the conditions that give rise to the conflicts and what precipitates them? How often do these type of conflicts occur? The more specific and behavioral the spouses can be, the closer will be their description of these events.

Obtaining this information from two individuals can be a very complex process. The questioning of each spouse in turn, and asking the other spouse to wait momentarily to contribute his or her perspective, will be necessary to prevent a chaotic discussion. Acknowledging that it is common for each spouse to have a somewhat different memory of the event and to emphasize different details can help to preempt a conflictual behavioral interview with a couple.

When assessing cognitions and affect associated with a problem or conflict, the interviewer adopts a slightly different method. Because the interviewer is pursuing the subjective aspects of the situation, he or she encourages an increased self-focus, which is contrary to distressed spouses' tendencies to focus on the behavior of the partner. After obtaining a behavioral description of the event, this shift can be accomplished by asking,

"How did you end up feeling during and after that fight?" and "It sounds like you were angry about what happened, but what other kinds of feelings did you have? How long did they last?" This strategy can be pursued in the context of the assessment session at the time when spouses are interacting informally with each other, or more formally as part of a communication assessment or exercise.

Regarding cognitions, a great deal of research has been conducted concerning the role of attributions in marital discord with relatively fewer studies examining other types of cognitions (see Bradbury & Fincham, 1990). To address this need, Baucom, Epstein, Sayers, and Sher (1989) describe at least five cognitive factors relevant to marital discord.

1. Each partner has a degree of inaccuracy or bias in the *perceptions* to which his or her spouse attends. The primary example of this factor is selective attention, which is illustrated by a spouse's focus on his or her partner's negative behavior.

2. Each spouse makes *attributions* for marital behavior, such as, "She criticizes me because she is ignoring all the positive things I do."

3. Each spouse has *expectancies* for future behavior, including whether the partner will continue to behave angrily and whether he or she will attempt to leave the relationship.

4. Each partner has *assumptions* about men/women and relationships that influence behavior. An assumption can come in the form of scripts (e.g., how the spouses usually interact when a sexual encounter occurs) or personae (e.g., "My husband is self-centered").

5. Each partner has *standards* of behavior for both the relationship and the partner. A standard is a relatively stable belief about how a relationship or the spouse should be in order to be successful (e.g., "We should always be open and honest about how we feel"). These different types of cognitions are highly interrelated. Attributions about specific behavior are often formed as a result of assumptions a spouse has about a partner, such as when a spouse thinks, "He's just trying to manipulate me into giving in [because he is a selfish person but won't admit it]."

The interviewer can take an approach similar to the inquiry developed from models of individual cognitive therapy in order to assess the broad range of cognitions. One can ask about the spouse's thoughts and feelings about a problem situation, listing each of them. Many of the thoughts can be noted at that point as potential targets of restructuring or modification. Common examples of attributions and assumptions might be, "He's just getting back at me," "She just wants things her own way," and "She thinks I don't do anything around the house and doesn't appreciate how hard I work in my job." The clinician can elicit expectancies about a particular type of situation by asking, "What would you expect would happen then?" To assess how appropriate or accurate these thoughts are, the interviewer might inquire as to what the evidence is that things will continue to happen as they have.

The interviewer should recognize that assessing cognitions and affect without subsequent modification tends to intensify them and should prepare the spouses for this effect. An attempt should be made to provide an alternative viewpoint or scenario of the relationship by reminding them of their strengths. Furthermore, the spouses can be told that some of their more negative cognitions are part of their current distress rather than a prediction of the future of the relationship. As already noted, a review of more positive aspects of their history often helps spouses take the discussion of their current conflicts into perspective.

Self-Report Methods

Self-report measures constitute the majority of the discussion of assessment methods primarily because of the numerous measures available and the relative efficiency of the method. The review presented here is meant to be representative, rather than exhaustive, and includes measures with interesting or useful properties.

Marital Satisfaction and Affect

Marital satisfaction is one of the most frequently assessed areas of marital relationships. The Locke Wallace Marital Adjustment Test (MAT; Locke & Wallace, 1959) was at one time the most commonly used. A more current cousin of the MAT is the Dyadic Adjustment Scale (DAS; Spanier, 1976), a 32-item measure of general relationship satisfaction. Spanier (1976) identified four subscales of the DAS: Dyadic Cohesion, Dyadic Satisfaction, Dyadic Consensus, and Affectional Expression. However, more recent investigations of the DAS have failed to identify the four factors (see Margolin, Michelli, & Jacobson, 1988). Furthermore, both the MAT and DAS have been criticized on methodological and conceptual grounds, especially in that both measures seem to intertwine the assessment of conflict behavior in the measurement of sentiment or satisfaction (see Eddy, Heyman, & Weiss, 1991; Fincham & Bradbury, 1987). However, both measures are still considered acceptable for the assessment of overall adjustment in the relationship.

There are several other measures focusing primarily on satisfaction that are good alternatives to the MAT and the DAS. Snyder (1979) developed the Marital Satisfaction Inventory (MSI). This lengthy self-report questionnaire (280 items) has both a global satisfaction scale and nine subscales that assess other areas of the marriage, including communication, child rearing, and family history of distress. Its Global Distress Subscale is recommended for use as a primary treatment outcome measure for marital therapy (e.g., Whisman & Jacobson, 1992). The Marital Happiness Scale (Azrin, Naster, & Jones, 1973) and the Relationship Satisfaction Scale (RSAT; Burns & Sayers, 1992) have been recommended on psychometric and theoretical grounds (Heyman, Sayers, & Bellack, 1994). The Quality of Marriage Index (QMI; Norton, 1983) is another 6-item measure of satisfaction that is a broad and global measure of satisfaction. Many of these scales have advantages over the MAT, DAS, and MSI in that they are briefer, simpler, and may yield equally valuable information for clinical intervention. The RSAT and the QMI have been demonstrated to have good psychometric characteristics and are highly correlated with the more widely used DAS.

Mood and affect in marital interaction have not been as frequently investigated in a self-report format as other aspects of relationships. Although satisfaction and happiness with a partner are frequently assessed both formally and informally, more careful intricate assessment of mood and affect is often needed. The most important aspects of affect to be assessed appear to be (1) the degree of positive and negative emotions experienced by the spouses, (2) the awareness of the specific emotion experienced by spouses, (3) the ability of spouses to express affect adaptively, and (4) the presence of affect that interferes with one or both spouses' adaptive functioning (Baucom & Epstein, 1990).

There are several self-report strategies for measuring affect. First, the clinician can have each spouse track his or her affect as part of an exercise in recording his or her cognitions, perhaps using a form designed for that purpose. For example, the Daily Mood Log (Burns, 1989) or the Daily Record of Dysfunctional Thoughts or the Weekly Activities Schedule (Beck, Rush, Shaw, & Emery, 1979) can be used to track emotions or moods across a given week. The Anger Log (Neidig & Friedman, 1984) is another useful form for tracking incidents of anger, including precipitants, consequences of the angry behavior, and the cognitions regarding the incident. If a more standardized assessment of emotion is needed, the Positive Feelings Questionnaire (O'Leary, Fincham, & Turkewitz, 1983) is a questionnaire designed to assess affect experienced in a variety of situations and interactions, including affectionate physical contact. It has high internal consistency (Cronbach's alpha = .94), correlates moderately highly with the Marital Adjustment Test, and is sensitive to changes due to marital therapy (O'Leary & Arias, 1983).

Cognitions

As noted earlier, more studies have examined marital attributions than other types of cognitions, resulting in the greater availability of attributional measures. However, the Daily Record of Dysfunctional Thoughts (Beck et al., 1979) can be used to assess any type of spontaneously occurring thought about conflict situations. Through a careful inquiry, the interviewer can elicit a wide range of cognitions that underlie the spontaneous thoughts already produced. Another assessment method often used in research contexts to assess spontaneous attributions is called *thought listing*. This procedure requires spouses to report their thoughts about a spe-

cific situation or conflict by free recall, or in response to viewing a videotape sample of the couple's problem-solving communication. These thoughts can be recorded on audiotape using a "think-aloud" procedure or on written forms. Details of these procedures can be found in Halford and Sanders (1988), Holtzworth-Munroe and Jacobson (1988), and Sayers, Fresco, Kohn, and Sarwer (1995).

There are a variety of more structured measures to assess attributions made within a relationship. The Dyadic Attribution Inventory (DAI; Baucom, Sayers, & Duhe, 1989) is a 24-item self-report measure that assesses a partner's attributions for 12 positive and 12 negative hypothetical relationship events. Each event is rated on each of five causal attributional dimensions, including three that reflect the causal source (i.e., Self, Partner, Outside Circumstances) and two that reflect the stability or globality of that cause. For example, an attribution concerning the item "Your partner does not appear to be listening" might be "He is self-centered"; this cause might receive high ratings on the Partner, Stable, and Global dimensions with low ratings on Self and Outside Circumstances. The internal consistency of the dimensions within each positive and negative item set is high (coefficient alphas range from .71 to .88), and the attributional dimension scores for negative events are significantly correlated with marital satisfaction in theoretically expected ways (e.g., distressed spouses attribute negative behavior to the partner and see it as stable and global).

The Relationship Attribution Measure (RAM; Fincham & Bradbury, 1992) also assesses causal attributions using hypothetical events, but in addition it assesses responsibility attributions. Responsibility attributions indicate the extent to which the partner intentionally behaved negatively, was selfishly motivated, and was blameworthy for the event. The coefficient alphas for the subscales are high, ranging from .77 to .86. The scales are significantly correlated with marital satisfaction, with less favorable judgments of the partner (i.e., blame of the partner) being associated with lower marital satisfaction.

The Marital Attitude Survey (MAS; Pretzer, Epstein, & Fleming, 1992) is a measure that uses commonplace concepts in its subscales (i.e., lack of love), potentially rendering it more directly informative to the types of attributions dealt with in the treatment of marital discord. The six dimensions that focus on attributions are Attribution of Causality to Own Behavior, Attribution of Causality to Own Personality, Attribution of Causality to Spouse's Behavior, Attribution of Causality to Spouse's Personality, Attribution of Malicious Intent to Spouse, and Attribution of Lack of Love to Spouse. These dimensions have acceptable internal consistency, with most of the coefficient alphas ranging from .66 to .88; the first dimension (i.e, Own Behavior) is an exception, with alpha = .58. Of particular interest is the last dimension referring to the lack of love because of its high degree of relevance to cognitions that spouses often produce (e.g., "When things are rough between us it shows that my partner doesn't love me"). Whereas this is not a causal attributional dimension per se, one can clearly see how it may interfere with a spouse's cooperation and effort in treatment. Ratings high on each of these six attributional dimensions correlate negatively with marital satisfaction (Pretzer et al., 1992).

There are few measures of the other types of cognitions outlined by Baucom and associates (1989). One exception is the Relationship Beliefs Inventory (RBI; Eidelson & Epstein, 1982; Epstein & Eidelson, 1981), which assesses five dysfunctional ideas about marriage. Three subscales measure assumptions, including: (1) disagreements are destructive to a marital relationship, (2) relationships cannot be changed, and (3) differences between the sexes cause marital conflict. Two other subscales assess dysfunctional standards, including: (4) spouses should know each other's feelings and thoughts without asking, and 5) sexual perfectionism is necessary in a marriage. The subscales have adequate internal consistency and test-retest reliability (Emmelkamp, Krol, Sanderman, & Ruphan, 1987), and acceptance of these beliefs has been found to be negatively correlated with marital adjustment (Eidelson & Epstein, 1982). The RBI has been found to discriminate between distressed and nondistressed couples (Eidelson & Epstein, 1982), and its psychometric properties are compa-

rable for men and women (Bradbury & Fincham, 1993).

More recently, the Inventory of Specific Relationship Standards (ISRS; Baucom, Epstein, Rankin, & Burnett, 1996) was developed to assess a range of relationship standards. Relationship standards are assessed for three basic dimensions: (1) degree of individual boundaries in the relationship, (2) power/control in the relationship (i.e., the appropriateness of influencing one's partner and whose preferences should the decision reflect), and (3) the degree of investment in the relationship (i.e., through expressing affection as well as instrumental support). The results of an initial investigation suggested that the ISRS has adequate internal consistency (Baucom et al., 1996). Furthermore, this study showed that spouses who endorsed relationship-oriented standards (e.g., few boundaries, egalitarian decision making, high relationship investment) were more likely to have higher marital satisfaction. Surprisingly, the endorsement of relationship standards in a way suggesting an extreme level of belief (e.g., *always* or *never*) was positively correlated with relationship satisfaction. The ISRS provides some interesting new information about basic beliefs spouses have about how a relationship should be, but additional study is needed before this measure is clinically useful.

The Marital Agendas Protocol (MAP; Notarius & Vanzetti, 1983) is one of the few measures that taps expectancies in marriage. It assesses information about five areas regarding conflicts: (1) the intensity of the specific problem areas (e.g., money, in-laws), (2) the respondents' perceptions of the partner's view of these areas, (3) responsibility attributions, (4) expectations about resolving conflicts, and (5) importance of resolving the conflicts. Particularly relevant are the ratings concerning the spouses' expectations about resolving the conflicts. These efficacy expectations have been found to be moderately related to marital satisfaction (average $r = .57$) and minimally related to social desirability. However, the lack of extensive testing of the measure limits it to use as an idiographic clinical assessment tool.

The Marital Attitude Survey (discussed earlier) also has two additional subscales that assess expectancies. One subscale, Perceived Ability of the Couple to Change the Relationship, focuses on efficacy expectancies (Bandura, 1977). An example of this type of cognition includes, "We could improve the relationship if we tried." The subscale labeled Expectancy of Improvement in the Relationship taps outcome expectancies (Bandura, 1977). It is exemplified by the cognition, "I think that our relationship will get better in the future." These subscales have high internal consistency; the alpha coefficients are .87 and .89, for Ability to Change and Expectancy of Improvement, respectively. However, the meaning of the scales may be clear only for couples who are maritally distressed, in that nondistressed couples may not endorse items that indicate an expectation for improvement. The clinician using the MAS might inquire directly about expectancies to ensure a proper interpretation of the scores.

Several measures combine the assessment of interactional behavior with the systematic assessment of the spouses' cognitions. These measures include the Interaction Record Procedure, the Styles of Conflict Inventory, the Marital Agendas Protocol, and the Managing Affect and Differences Scale, and will be discussed here.

Communication and Interactional Behavior

One of the most straightforward strategies for the assessment of couples' communication and interactional behavior is the Interaction Record Procedure (Peterson, 1979). This procedure can produce the "raw" data of spouses' perceptions of their interactions in a relatively systematic way. The spouses are asked to describe in writing the most important event of the day, the conditions under which it took place, how it started, and then any subsequent behavior, events, thoughts, and feelings. The procedure can be used to produce a rich interactional record to be rated using a formal coding system, or it can be used clinically because of its efficiency in providing the clinician with sequences of meaningful exchanges. The clinician can direct the spouses to keep daily records of their interactions, describe a common interaction in order to examine their differential perceptions of

important events, and track changes in interactional patterns over time. Because of the nature of the task and instruction set, the method clearly assesses the cognitions and affect associated with the couple's ongoing interactional behavior.

The Spouse Observation Checklist (SOC; Weiss & Perry, 1979, 1983) was designed as an assessment measure for behavioral exchange. According to the behavioral exchange theory of marital satisfaction, the ratio of rewarding to punishing behaviors determines the level of satisfaction in the marriage. The SOC accesses behavioral performance in a natural setting and allows the therapist to identify behaviors in need of change. This lengthy questionnaire (408 items) is used by each spouse to track his or her partner's behavior on a daily basis over a period of time, typically for two weeks. The items are grouped into 12 categories, measuring both positive and negative behaviors in areas such as affection, communication, household management, and financial decision making. In addition, the partners rate their daily level of satisfaction with the relationship. It has been used to demonstrate that negative behavior strongly affects distressed spouses' satisfaction (e.g., Jacobson et al., 1980). As with all self-report measures of interaction, low reliability between spouses is potentially an issue to be examined when used in a clinical context (Weiss & Perry, 1983), but its length may make it an inefficient tool for clinical work.

The Cost-Benefit Analysis (CB; Weiss & Perry, 1983) is a derivative of the SOC and is an operationalization of social exchange theory. Partners rate both the perceived benefit and cost of performing 400 different behaviors. By comparing the responses, the therapist can identify conflict behaviors as well as good therapy behaviors. The CB can be used as an aid in functional analysis of behavior as well as to assist the therapist in the ordering of therapeutic interventions. Similar to the SOC, its length is its primary disadvantage.

Gelles and Straus (1988), among others, suggest that clinicians will vastly underdetect relationship aggression without systematic assess-ment. One of the most widely used measures of aggressive behaviors is the Conflict Tactics Scale (CTS,

Straus, 1979). It assess the frequency of 18 conflict behaviors ranging from constructive talk to verbal abuse and physical abuse. Gelles (1990) has offered several criticisms of the CTS, including that its hierarchy of abusive behaviors is not comprehensive, it ignores the context of the behavior, it does not measure the result of the behavior, and its one-year time frame may result in retrospective bias.

O'Leary and Murphy (1992) have made several recommendations concerning the assessment of relationship aggression. First, clinicians should use both a questionnaire like the CTS and an interview to assess aggression. Second, since aggression is typically underrepresented as a presenting problem, assessment of aggression should be conducted with all couples in treatment. Third, clinical sensitivity and awareness to the existence of spousal abuse is necessary for the effective therapist. Jouriles and O'Leary (1985) have also recommended that in case of discrepancies between partners' reports on the CTS, the clinician "accept" the report of more frequent or severe violence. The reader is referred to O'Leary and Murphy (1992) for more detailed information on the clinical assessment of spouse abuse.

Several self-report measures are available that provide the clinician with global information about the couple's communication. The Primary Communication Inventory (PCI; Navran, 1967) and the Marital Communication Inventory (MCI; Bienvenu, 1970) each provide a global index of a couple's communication skill; both correlate positively with indices of marital satisfaction. The global index from the PCI represents the frequency of discussion of a variety of topics, discussion in a range of situations, as well as items regarding the clarity of communication. The scale's author suggests a division of verbal and nonverbal communication on the scale, but this distinction has been challenged (Baucom & Adams, 1987; Beach & Arias, 1983).

The MCI assesses communication in terms of frequency of occurrence, but the items also assess expectations about communication (e.g., failing to express disagreement for fear the spouse will get angry) (Baucom & Adams, 1987). Based on several empirical investigations of the MCI, Schumm, Anderson, Race, Morris, Griffin, McCutchen, and Benigas (1983) suggested that it may contain up to

six subscales concerning communication (e.g., empathy, conflict management). The MCI total score, however, has an inconsistent association with observational measures of communication but is highly associated with various measures of marital satisfaction. As discussed earlier, the MAP (Notarius & Vanzetti, 1983) assesses the intensity of problems in five content areas. However, the scale does not assess specific behaviors that may lead to the conflicts. The PCI, MCI, and the MAP are perhaps most appropriately used to target problem areas; the specific communication about these areas can be further assessed through the Interaction Record Procedure or behavioral observation.

Self-report measures that assess interactional behavior in a much more detailed fashion include the Styles of Conflict Inventory, which uses a decidedly cognitive-behavioral approach (SCI; Metz, 1993). This measure not only provides spouses' self-report of their own behavior in response to a conflict situation but it also provides measures of perceptions of the conflicts regarding frequency, intensity, responsibility, and power. Thoughts and perceptions about the partner's behavior are also assessed. All 126 items have the same response categories using a 5-point Likert-type response format (i.e., "never" to "very often"). The publisher provides an analysis of the results, which presents a comparison of the responses of spouses within a couple, as well as a comparison of the results to a standardization sample. The measure has satisfactory reliability, and the validity evidence is supportive. Despite its strengths, however, the measure cannot substitute for a functional analysis of conflict situations because no information is provided about the sequence of behaviors during a conflict. The SCI is the best effort to date to assess differences in spouses' perceptions of conflict in a way that can help the clinician understand the contribution of these differences to the conflict itself.

Several other self-report measures of communication provide detailed assessments of couples' interactions and are worthy of consideration. The Communication Patterns Questionnaire (CPQ; Christensen, 1987, 1988) is an inventory designed to measure spouses' perceptions of specific patterns of interaction. Separate items assess perceptions of the spouses' communication at the onset of a conflict, during a conflict, and after a conflict. Of particular interest are subscales that tap the demand-withdraw pattern of interaction, in which one spouse attempts to engage (or "pressure") the other spouse to address the conflict, while the other spouse attempts to withdraw or avoid the conflict. The evidence for the reliability and validity of the subscales is good (Christensen, 1987; Christensen & Shenk, 1991). However, the "patterns" of interaction assessed in the scales' items do not indicate the actual sequence of behaviors, making the careful interview assessment of communication still essential.

The Interactional Behaviors and Patterns Questionnaire (IBPQ; Roberts & Leonard, 1992, 1994) assesses the frequency of four types of interactional sequences associated with engagement and avoidance behavior: Intimacy Avoidance, Conflict Avoidance, Angry Withdrawal, and Hostile Reciprocity. The measure is very promising because of high reliability estimates, supportive correlations with observational assessments of communication, and significant longitudinal predictions of marital satisfaction and stability.

The Responses to Conflict Questionnaire (RTC; Birchler & Fals-Stewart, 1994; Birchler, Fals-Stewart, & Schafer, 1994) is a very brief self-report checklist that assesses the likelihood of specific spouse behaviors during a conflict. Initial investigations suggest that it has good temporal stability, internal consistency, and validity, and is minimally associated with social desirability. Its items load onto an Active factor (e.g., hitting, yelling, complaining) and a Passive factor (e.g., sulking, ignoring). The RTC's principle asset is its brevity. It can be completed in less than five minutes, making it ideal for weekly completion at the time of the session.

The Managing Affect and Differences Scale (MADS; Arellano & Markman, 1995) was designed to measure specific communication behaviors and conflict management skills associated with marital satisfaction (e.g., validation of each other, negative escalation of the conflict). The measure consists of 12 subscales that have adequate internal consistency and significant associations with measures of relationship satisfaction, relationship efficacy, and problem intensity. Unfortunately, the initial presentation of the MADS was limited by a small sample size and poor associations with observed communication. Because of the specificity of the MADS subscales, further validation study may show that it is a useful gauge of change due to communication training.

Observational Methods

Observational methods have traditionally been viewed as the signature of behavioral assessment, but some cognitive-behaviorally oriented theorists have questioned the relevance of these methods to the clinical outcome of behavioral marital therapy (see Jacobson [1985] for a debate about this issue). The essential lesson one can take from this debate is the importance of attending to the nature of the information one wishes to take from the observational sessions, the type of tasks couples are asked to engage in, the settings in which they occur, and the nature of the ratings or observations made of the couple's communication. Each of these variables (discussed next) can influence heavily the usefulness of the information gathered. It should be noted that each coding system discussed here has its own strengths and limitations, and the selection of the coding system should take into account the researcher's or clinician's needs.

Discussion Tasks

A key issue in using observational methods to assess behavior is the type of discussion task used. Whether the couple is asked to talk about a real problem in their relationship or to express their positive feelings about an issue determines the type of discussion that ensues. One of the earliest types of discussion tasks used to assess couples is the revealed differences technique (Strodtbeck, 1951). In this task, spouses are interviewed separately to ascertain their preferred answer to questions of mutual interest (e.g., opinions about other families in their social group). The couple is then asked to resolve the difference in their answers. As an alternative to this technique, Olson and Ryder (1970) developed the Inventory of Marital Conflict, which presents vignettes of marital events. Conflict in this task is produced because the husband's and the wife's versions of the vignette each differ from the other. Other tasks have also been used, including "free conversation" (Birchler, Weiss, & Vincent, 1975), and discussions about a list of enjoyable activities (i.e., the "fun deck," Gottman, 1979). The Verbal Interaction Task (Guerney, 1977), is designed to tap emotional expressiveness skills and empathic listening skills. In this task, one spouse is asked to express his or her positive (or negative) feelings about an issue, and the partner is directed to try to "help" that spouse express his or her feelings.

The most frequently used discussion task in research contexts requires couples to attempt to resolve an actual relationship conflict in a specific period of time. Using this format the assessor identifies issues from the spouses' responses to an inventory, such as the Areas of Change Questionnaire or the Marital Agendas Protocol, and asks the spouses to try to resolve one of the issues in the time allotted. Through an initial dialogue with the spouses, the clinician helps the couple select an issue for the observed interaction that is of great enough importance to lead to a meaningful discussion, but not too sensitive so as to lead to an unusually silent or volatile discussion. Some researchers have selected the discussion topic so as to control which spouse's primary concern was being discussed. This conceivably alters whose investment is highest in the discussion, allowing an examination of the couple with each spouse in the "demand" or "pursuer" role (e.g., Heavey, Christensen, & Malamuth, 1995).

Usually the discussion tasks just described are implemented in an observational laboratory arranged as a living room or in a therapist's office as part of a clinical assessment. Most couples acknowledge the similarity between conflict discussions in these contexts and arguments they have at home, except that conflicts at home tend to be more intense and volatile. It is possible to conduct home observations of couples' interactions, either through a direct observation or electronic recording. Margolin, Burman, and John (1989) describe a method of having couples reenact their naturalistic conflicts for the assessor in the home. These interactions were videotaped for later coding, revealing significant differences in interactional behavior of the discordant couples, as compared to the nondiscordant couples. An alternative to this procedure that might be more feasible for clinical purposes is to have couples use a portable cassette recorder to audiotape their problem discussions at home. This may make it possible to conduct weekly assessments of the couple's conflictual communication.

Coding Systems

There are several sophisticated and complex microanalytic coding systems that can be used to assess communication patterns, all of which have received substantial support for their reliability and validity. The first is the Marital Interaction Coding System (MICS; Hops, Wills, Patterson, & Weiss, 1972; Weiss, 1992). The MICS is utilized with videotaped problem-solving discussions and taps 37 specific target behaviors in a two-person interaction. These behaviors fall into several categories: State codes (e.g., Attention), Form codes (e.g., Command), Nonverbal codes (e.g., Dysphoric Affect), and Content codes (e.g., Problem Description, Invalidation). The system can be used to examine rates of behavior as well as sequences of interactions within a couple. The primary asset of the MICS is the existence of more than 100 studies that have utilized the coding system; furthermore, the Oregon Marital Studies Program, under the direction of Robert Weiss, can (for a fee) provide coding services for investigators. However, most of the codes of the MICS are blends of affect and behavior (e.g., Criticize), with only a few of the codes defined strictly on the basis of affect (e.g., Smile/Laugh). Lack of this distinction in the definitions of the codes makes it difficult to examine interaction patterns of affect separately from the content of the behavior.

The Couples Interaction Scoring System (CISS; Gottman, 1979; Notarius & Markman, 1981) is another widely used coding system for videotaped interactions by the marital couple. Like the MICS, the CISS allows for the assessment of specific behaviors as well as patterns of behavior. The behaviors on the coding system include levels of agreement, mind reading, and problem solving as well some basic communication skills such as expressing affect and summarizing self and other's verbalizations. The CISS separates the coding of the content of each speaker's statements from the coding of the affect. This makes it possible to examine the unique contribution of affect patterns and content to marital distress.

Although not as widely used in this country, the Kategoriensystem fur Partnerschaftliche Interaktion (KPI; Hahlweg, Reisner, Kohli, Vollmer, Schindler, & Revenstorf, 1984) is another multidimensional coding system for verbal interaction. The system codes both speaker and listener skills, such as disclosure and acceptance, as well as nonverbal ratings of both face and body posture. It differs from the MICS and the CISS somewhat in that its primary goal is to assesses actual communication skills.

One broad limitation of observational coding systems that provide a separate coding for affect is that no differentiation is made between different affects, such as anger versus sadness. In response to the need for such a system, Gottman developed the Specific Affect Coding System (SPAFF; Gottman & Krokoff, 1989). Five negative affects are coded using the SPAFF: anger, disgust or contempt, sadness, fear, and whining. Five positive affects can also be coded using the SPAFF: affection, humor, interest, anticipation, and excitement or joy. The system has not received widespread use, but it is unique in its recognition that different affects can have different consequences for intimate interactions.

Although the coding systems discussed here provide a wealth of information about a couples' communication patterns, many clinicians may not have the time or resources to utilize these tools. The clinician may wish to use one of the global rating scales that includes assessment of problem-solving communication. Taken from the preceding research assessment tools, these measures include the Marital Interaction Coding System-Global (MICS-G; Weiss & Tolman, 1990), the Global Rapid Couples Interaction Scoring System (RCISS; Krokoff, Gottman, & Haas, 1989), the Interactional Dimensions Coding System (IDCS; Julien, Markman, &

Lindahl, 1989), the Marital Interaction Rating System (MIRS; Roberts & Krokoff, 1990), and the Georgia Marriage Q-Sort (Wampler & Halverson, 1990).

Case Study

The case of Bob and Jane presented moderate difficulty for behavioral assessment and is therefore an excellent case for discussion. Assessment was difficult for several reasons. First, although a great deal of data were obtained from the couple, there were important inconsistencies and contradictions in the spouses' reports of their problems. Second, the reporting of the couple's interaction was often biased because of the couple's conflict. Third, attention to major crises in the treatment made it difficult to obtain an ongoing assessment of the couple's interaction.

Bob and Jane participated in an assessment study of couples' communication and, after an initial assessment session, began treatment with the first author. As part of the study, they completed several self-report measures, Jane participated in a structured clinical diagnostic interview, and the couple participated in a videotaped problem-solving assessment. Furthermore, each spouse participated in a thought-listing procedure in which they viewed the videotape of their problem-solving interaction and then listed their thoughts at predetermined points throughout the viewing (see Sayers, Fresco, Kohn, & Sarwer, 1995).

The assessment seemed to portray a fairly clear picture of the couple's relationship. Both spouses scored in the discordant range on the Dyadic Adjustment Scale, indicated a desire for a significant amount of relationship change on the Areas of Change Questionnaire, and indicated a desire to begin treatment for marital problems. Neither spouse reported significant psychiatric distress. Bob reported on the Conflict Tactics Scale that Jane had hit and kicked him in the last year, and Jane reported that Bob had pushed or shoved her. Neither spouse acknowledged his or her own aggressive actions at the level reported by the other spouse. The primary issues the couple fought about were the intrusion of Bob's mother into the couple's decision making and Jane's complaint that Bob occasionally became abusive and controlling.

The observational and thought-listing assessment of a discussion about difficulties with Bob's mother revealed that Jane could be critical, demanding, and condescending during the problem discussion, while Bob withdrew, became defensive, and acknowledged guilt. This interaction pattern was also observed during therapy sessions. Jane was often wholly focused on Bob becoming more assertive with his mother, with very little acknowledgment that her own critical and demanding style might be altered in order to communicate better with Bob about this issue. Although Bob acknowledged that fault for their problems lay with him, he claimed that he had little freedom of action to better the situation.

The contradictions in the assessment information became apparent regarding issues of control and dominance. Was Bob as abusive and controlling as Jane reported, or was Jane as dominant as she appeared in the assessment? Jane openly described Bob as severely limiting her interaction with her friends, whereas Bob only acknowledged disapproving of her friends. It was difficult to reconcile Jane's powerful interpersonal presentation with the suggestion that she yielded easily at home. There was no indication that she ever anticipated Bob to threaten her physically, but at times when conflicts were high, she asserted that Bob had been continually emotionally abusive throughout their 14 years of marriage. During conflicts at home, she was able to command him to leave the house with no emotional or physical resistance from Bob. Other contradictions concerned Bob's reported "self-centeredness." Jane reported that Bob made decisions without any consultation with Jane. In some contexts, such as work-related decisions, this seemed to be a desire on Jane's part to control the relationship. Bob portrayed these instances as being innocent attempts to make decisions in the best interest of his family.

Many of the contradictions were resolved through repeated, careful behavioral interviewing of important conflict situations. For example, Bob did disapprove of Jane's friends, and, despite her controlling interpersonal style, her traditional view of her family role allowed this disapproval to con-

trol her behavior. Furthermore, time with her friends would leave child care in Bob's hands, which had often had a negative outcome in the past. Other contradictions in the report of the spouses were understood in light of each spouse's own relationship standards and assumptions. Bob had difficulty acknowledging that he occasionally had selfish motives for his behavior, leading to very biased reporting of actual behavioral events and difficulty recognizing instances of his demandingness. Jane's frequent complaint of emotional abuse and neglect was often fueled by Bob's inability to anticipate her needs, although she believed he should. It should be noted that during times of emotional crises, it was difficult to have each spouse set aside his or her emotional distress in order to relate the series of events that led to conflicts resulting from the couple's faulty assumptions. However, by carefully asking about specific interactional behaviors and understanding the reasons for error and bias of the sources, it was possible to achieve a clinically useful understanding of this couple's difficulties.

SUMMARY

This chapter began with a review of the issues one faces when attempting a behavioral assessment of marital discord. Behavioral assessment has traditionally been seen as an idiographic method. However, it is possible to acknowledge the nomothetic viewpoint that there are some similarities across discordant couples, while recognizing that a functional analysis of a specific couple's difficulties is the most effective way of formulating an effective treatment. The effective assessor understands that for some couples the source of difficulties include specific skills deficits, whereas other couples suffer from a complex dysfunctional interactional system. In any case, the formulation should be parsimonious and eschew a high level of inference.

It is necessary to integrate information from both self-report and observational methods because of the differences in the information these methods produce. Differences among assessment sources have a variety causes, including the context in which the information is gathered, the effects of spouses' sentiment about the marriage, and the influence of spouses' cognitions on their reporting.

Developmental aspects of the relationship should also be assessed because of the importance of recognizing the role of development transitions in the couple's current functioning.

Specific research questions usually dictate many decisions in marital assessment in a research context. Within the clinical context, several procedures should be used: (1) the assessment of initial complaints and the marital history; (2) self-report and interview assessment of specific problems, daily interactional behavior, and cognitions; and (3) observational assessment of marital communication. Although there are many self-report measures available, selection of these should be judicious because the use of too many questionnaires could erode some spouses' commitments to treatment. None of the available self-report forms provide sufficient information to eliminate the need for a detailed behavioral interview.

The case presented illustrates the problems inherent in obtaining information from two spouses who are in conflict with one another. The integration of information from several sources, with close attention to the spouses' cognitions, was crucial in developing a clear understanding of this couple's marital dysfunction.

REFERENCES

Arellano, C. M., & Markman, H. J. (1995). The Managing Affect and Differences Scale (MADS): A self-report measure assessing conflict management in couples. *Journal of Family Psychology, 9,* 319–334.

Azrin, N. H., Naster, B. J., & Jones, R. (1973). Reciprocity counseling: A rapid learning-based procedure for marital counseling. *Behaviour Research and Therapy, 11,* 365–372.

Bandura, A. (1977). *Social learning theory.* Englewood Cliffs, NJ: Prentice-Hall.

Baucom, D. H., & Adams, A. (1987). Assessing communication in marital interaction. In K. D. O'Leary (Ed.), *Assessment of marital discord* (pp. 139–182). Hillsdale, NJ: Lawrence Erlbaum.

Baucom, D. H., Bell, W. G., & Duke, A. G. (1982). *The measurement of couples' attributions for positive and negative dyadic interactions.* Paper presented at the 16th Annual Convention of the Association for Advancement of Behavior Therapy, Los Angeles.

Baucom, D. H., & Epstein, N. (1990). *Cognitive-behavioral marital therapy.* New York: Brunner/Mazel.

Baucom, D. H., Epstein, N., Rankin, L. A., & Burnett, C. K. (1996). Assessing relationship standards: The Inventory of Specific Relationship Standards. *Journal of Family Psychology, 10,* 72–88.

Baucom, D. H., Epstein, N., Sayers, S., & Sher, T. G. (1989). The role of cognitions in marital relationships: Definitional, methodological, and conceptual issues. *Journal of Consulting and Clinical Psychology, 57,* 31–38.

Baucom, D. H., Sayers, S. L., & Duhe, A. (1989). Marital attributions: Issues concerning attributional pattern and attributional style. *Journal of Personality and Social Psychology, 56,* 596–607.

Beach, S. R. H., & Arias, I. (1983). Assessment of perceptual discrepancy: Utility of the Primary Communication Inventory. *Family Process, 22,* 310–316.

Beck, A. T., Rush, A. J., Shaw, B. F., & Emery, G. (1979). *Cognitive therapy of depression.* New York: Guilford.

Berscheid, E. (1983). Emotion. In H. H. Kelley, E. Berscheid, A. Christensen, J. H. Harvey, T. L. Huston, G. Levinger, E. McClintock, L. A. Peplau, & D. Peterson (Eds.), *Close relationships* (pp. 110–168). New York: Freeman.

Bienvenu, M. J. (1970). Measurement of marital communication. *The Family Coordinator, 19,* 26–31.

Birchler, G. R., Clopton, P. L., & Adams, N. L. (1984). Marital conflict resolution: Factors influencing concordance between partners and trained coders. *American Journal of Family Therapy, 12,* 15–28.

Birchler, G. R., & Fals-Stewart, W. (1994). The Response to Conflict Scale: Psychometric properties. *Assessment, 1,* 335–334.

Birchler, G. R., Fals-Stewart, W., & Schafer, J. (1994). The Response to Conflict Scale: A brief measure of maladaptive marital conflict. *The Behavior Therapist, 17,* 68–69.

Birchler, G. R., Weiss, R. L., & Vincent, J. P. (1975). Multimethod analysis of social reinforcement exchange between maritally distressed and nondistressed spouse and stranger dyads. *Journal of Personality and Social Psychology, 31,* 349–360.

Bowman, M. L. (1990). Coping efforts and marital satisfaction: Measuring marital coping and its correlates. *Journal of Marriage and the Family, 52,* 463–474.

Bradbury, T. N., & Fincham, F. D. (1990). Attributions in marriage: Review and critique. *Psychological Bulletin, 1,* 3–33.

Bradbury, T. N., & Fincham, F. D. (1993). Assessing dysfunctional cognitions in marriage: A reconsideration of the Relationship Belief Inventory. *Psychological Assessment, 5,* 92–101.

Burns, D. D. (1989). *The feeling good handbook: Using the new mood therapy in everyday life.* New York: William Morrow.

Burns, D. D., & Sayers, S. L. (1992). *Development and validation of a brief relationship satisfaction scale.* Unpublished manuscript.

Christensen, A. (1987). Detection of conflict patterns in couples. In K. Hahlweg & M. J. Goldstein (Eds.), *Understanding major mental disorder: The contribution of family interaction research* (pp. 250–265). New York: Family Process Press.

Christensen, A. (1988). Dysfunctional interaction patterns in couples. In P. Noller & Fitzpatrick (Eds.), *Perspectives on marital interaction* (pp. 31–52). Clevedon, Avon, England: Multilingual Matters.

Christensen, A., & Nies, D. C. (1980). The Spouse Observation Checklist: Empirical analysis and critique. *The American Journal of Family Therapy, 8,* 69–79.

Christensen, A., & Shenk, J. L. (1991) Communication, conflict, and psychological distance in nondistressed, clinic, and divorcing couples. *Journal of Consulting and Clinical Psychology, 59,* 458–463.

Christensen, A., Sullaway, M., & King, C. E. (1983). Systematic error in behavioral reports of dyadic interaction: Egocentric bias and content effects. *Behavioral Assessment, 5,* 129–140.

Eddy, J. M., Heyman, R. E., & Weiss, R. L. (1991). An empirical evaluation of the Dyadic Adjustment Scale: Exploring the differences between marital "satisfaction" and "adjustment." *Behavioral Assessment, 13,* 199–220.

Eidelson, R. J., & Epstein, N. (1982). Cognitive and relationship maladjustment: Development of a measure of dysfunctional relationship beliefs. *Journal of Consulting and Clinical Psychology, 50,* 715–720.

Elwood, R. W., & Jacobson, N. S. (1982). Spouses' agreement in reporting their behavioral interactions: A clinical replication. *Journal of Consulting and Clinical Psychology, 50,* 783–784.

Emmelkamp, P. M., Krol, B., Sanderman, R., & Ruphan, M. (1987). The assessment of relationship beliefs in a marital context. *Personality and Individual Differences, 8,* 775–780.

Epstein, N., & Eidelson, R. J. (1981). Unrealistic beliefs of clinical couples: Their relationship to expectations, goals, and satisfaction. *American Journal of Family Therapy, 9,* 13–22.

Fincham, F. D., & Bradbury, T. N. (1987). The assessment of marital quality: A reevaluation. *Journal of Marriage and the Family, 49,* 797–809.

Fincham, F. D., & Bradbury, T. N. (1992). Assessing attributions in marriage: The Relationship Attribution Measure. *Journal of Personality and Social Psychology, 62,* 457–468.

Fuller, T. L., & Fincham, F. D. (1994). The marital life cycle: A developmental approach to the study of marital change. In L. L'Abate (Ed.), *Handbook of developmental family psychology and psychopathology* (pp. 60–82). New York: John Wiley & Sons.

Gelles, R. J. (1990). Methodological issues in the study of family violence. In G. R. Patterson (Ed.), *Depression and aggression in family interaction* (pp. 49–74). Hillsdale, NJ: Lawrence Erlbaum.

Gelles, R. J., & Straus, M. A. (1988). *Intimate violence: The causes and consequences of abuse in the American family.* New York: Touchstone/Simon & Schuster.

Gottman, J. M. (1979). *Marital interaction: Experimental investigations.* New York: Academic Press.

Gottman, J. M. (1985). Observational measures of behavior therapy outcome: A reply to Jacobson. *Behavioral Assessment, 7,* 317–322.

Gottman, J. M. (1993). The role of conflict engagement, escalation, and avoidance in marital interaction: A longitudinal view of five types of couples. *Journal of Consulting and Clinical Psychology, 61,* 6–15.

Gottman, J. M., & Krokoff, L. J. (1989). Marital interaction and satisfaction: A longitudinal view. *Journal of Consulting and Clinical Psychology, 57,* 47–52.

Guerney, B. G. (1977). *Relationship enhancement.* San Francisco: Jossey-Bass.

Hahlweg, K., & Jacobson, N. S. (1984). *Marital interaction: Analysis and modification.* New York: Guilford.

Hahlweg, K., Reisner, L., Kohli, G., Vollmer, M., Schindler, L., & Revenstorf, D. (1984). Development and validity of a new system to analyze interpersonal communication: Kategoriensystem fur partnerschaftliche interaktion. In K. Hahlweg & N. S. Jacobson (Eds.), *Marital interaction: Analysis and modification* (pp. 182–198). New York: Guilford.

Halford, W. K., & Sanders, R. M. (1988). Assessment of self statements during marital problem solving: A comparison of two methods. *Cognitive Therapy and Research, 12,* 515–530.

Heavey, C. L., Christensen, A., & Malamuth, N. M. (1995). The longitudinal impact of demand and withdrawal during marital conflict. *Journal of Consulting and Clinical Psychology, 63,* 797–801.

Heavey, C. L., Shenk, J. L., & Christensen, A. (1994). In

L. L'Abate (Ed.) *Handbook of developmental family psychology and psychopathology* (pp. 221–242). New York: John Wiley & Sons.

Heyman, R. E., Sayers, S. L., & Bellack, A. S. (1994). Global marital satisfaction versus marital adjustment: An empirical comparison of these measures. *Journal of Family Therapy, 8*, 432–446.

Holtzworth-Munroe, A., & Jacobson, N. S. (1988). Toward a methodology for coding spontaneous causal attributions: Preliminary results with married couples. *Journal of Social and Clinical Psychology, 7*, 101–112.

Hops, H., Wills, T. A., Patterson, G. R., & Weiss, R. L. (1972). *Marital interaction coding system*. Eugene, OR: University of Oregon and Oregon Research Institute.

Jacob, T. (1987). *Family interaction and psychopathology: Theories, methods, and findings*. New York: Plenum.

Jacobson, N. S. (1985). The role of observational measures in behavior therapy outcome research. *Behavioral Assessment, 7*, 297–308.

Jacobson, N. S., & Margolin, G. (1979). *Marital therapy: Strategies based on social learning and behavior exchange principles*. New York: Brunner/Mazel.

Jacobson, N. S., & Moore, D. (1981). Spouses as observers of the events in their relationship. *Journal of Consulting and Clinical Psychology, 49*, 269–277.

Jacobson, N. S., Waldron, H., & Moore, D. (1980). Toward a behavioral profile of marital distress. *Journal of Consulting and Clinical Psychology, 48*, 696–703.

Jouriles, E. N., & O'Leary, K. D. (1985). Interpersonal reliability of reports of marital violence. *Journal of Consulting and Clinical Psychology, 53*, 419–421.

Julien, D., Markman, H. J., & Lindahl, K. M. (1989). A comparison of a global and a microanalytic coding system: Implication for future trends in studying interactions. *Behavioral Assessment, 11*, 81–100.

Krokoff, L. J., Gottman, J. M., & Haas, S. D. (1989). Validation of a global rapid couples interaction scoring system. *Behavioral Assessment, 11*, 65–80.

Locke, H. J., & Wallace, K. M. (1959). Short marital adjustment and prediction tests: Their reliability and validity. *Marriage and Family Living, 21*, 251–255.

Margolin, G., Burman, B., & John, R. S. (1989). Home observations of marital couples reenacting naturalistic conflicts. *Behavioral Assessment, 11*, 101–118.

Margolin, G., Hattem, D., John, R. S., & Yost, K. (1985). Perceptual agreement between spouses and outside observers when coding themselves and a stranger dyad. *Behavioral Assessment, 7*, 235–247.

Margolin, G., Michelli, J., & Jacobson, N. (1988). Assessment of marital dysfunction. In A. S. Bellack & M. Hersen (Eds.), *Behavioral assessment: A practical handbook* (3rd ed.). New York: Pergamon.

Metz, M. E. (1993). *Manual for the Styles of Conflict Inventory*. Palo Alto, CA: Consulting Psychologists Press.

Navran, L. (1967). Communication and adjustment in marriage. *Family Process, 6*, 173–184.

Neidig, P. H., & Friedman, D. H. (1984). *Spouse abuse: A treatment program for couples.* Champaign, IL: Research Press.

Norton, R. (1983). Measuring marital quality: A critical look at the dependent variable. *Journal of Marriage and the Family, 45*, 141–151.

Notarius, C. I., Benson, P. R., Sloane, D., Vanzetti, N. A., & Hornyak, L. M. (1989). Exploring the interface between perception and behavior: An analysis of marital interaction in distressed and nondistressed couples. Special Issue: Coding marital interaction. *Behavioral Assessment, 11*, 39–64.

Notarius, C. I., & Markman, H. J. (1981). The Couples Interaction Scoring System. In E. E. Filsinger (Ed.), *Assessing marriage: New behavioral approaches* (pp. 112–127). Beverly Hills: Sage.

Notarius, C. I., & Vanzetti, N. A. (1983). The Marital Agendas Protocol. In E. E. Filsinger (Ed.), *Marriage and family assessment: A sourcebook for family therapy* (pp. 209–227). Beverly Hills: Sage.

O'Leary, K. D., & Arias, I. (1983). The influence of marital therapy on sexual satisfaction. *Journal of Sex and Marital Therapy, 9*, 171–181.

O'Leary, K. D., Fincham, F. D., & Turkewitz, H. (1983). Assessment of positive feelings toward spouse. *Journal of Consulting and Clinical Psychology, 51*, 949–951.

O'Leary, K. D. & Murphy, C. M. (1992). Clinical issues in the assessment of spouse abuse. In R. T. Ammerman & M. Hersen (Eds.), *Assessment of family violence: A clinical and legal sourcebook* (pp. 26–46). New York: Wiley.

O'Leary, K. D., Vivian, D., & Malone, J. (1992). Assessment of physical aggression against women in marriage: The need for multimodal assessment. *Behavioral Assessment, 14*, 5–14.

Olson, D. H., & Ryder, R. G. (1970). Inventory of marital conflicts (IMC): An interaction procedure. *Journal of Marriage and the Family*, 443–448.

Patterson, G. R., & Reid, J. B. (1970). Reciprocity and coercion: Two facets of social systems. In C. Neuringer & J. L. Michael (Eds.), *Behavior modifica-*

tion in clinical psychology. New York: Appleton-Century-Crofts.

Peterson, D. R. (1979). Assessing interpersonal relationships by means of interaction records. *Behavioral Assessment, 1*, 221–236.

Pretzer, J. L., Epstein, N., & Fleming, B. (1992). The Marital Attitude Survey: A measure of dysfunctional attitudes and expectancies. *Journal of Cognitive Psychotherapy, 5,* 131–148.

Roberts, L. J., & Krokoff, L. J. (1990). A time-series analysis of withdrawal, hostility, and displeasure in satisfied and dissatisfied marriages. *Journal of Marriage and the Family, 52,* 95–105.

Roberts, L. J., & Leonard, K. E. (1992). *Intimacy avoidance and conflict avoidance in early marriage: Predictors of relationship satisfaction.* Paper presented at the 26th Annual Convention of the Association for the Advancement of Behavior Therapy, Boston.

Roberts, L. J., & Leonard, K. E. (1994). *Spousal perceptions of withdrawal behaviors in the longitudinal prediction of marital adjustment and stability.* Paper presented at the 28th Annual Convention of the Association for Advancement of Behavior Therapy, San Diego.

Robinson, E. A., & Price, M. G. (1980). Pleasurable behavior in marital interaction: An observational study. *Journal of Consulting and Clinical Psychology, 48,* 117–118.

Sayers, S. L., Baucom, D. H., Sher, T. G., Weiss, R. L., & Heyman, R. E. (1991). Constructive engagement, behavioral marital therapy, and changes in marital satisfaction. *Behavioral Assessment, 13,* 25–49.

Sayers, S. L., Fresco, D. M., Kohn, & C., Sarwer, D. S. (1995, November), *Thought listing using free recall and videotape reconstruction: Content coding of cognitions and depressed-discordant wives.* Paper presented at the 29th Annual Meeting of the Association for the Advancement of Behavior Therapy, Washington, DC.

Schumm, W. R., Anderson, S. A., Race, G. S., Morris, J. E., Griffin, C. L., McCutchen, M. B., & Benigas, J. E. (1983). Construct validity of the Marital Communication Inventory. *Journal of Sex & Marital Therapy, 9,* 153–162.

Snyder, D. K. (1979). Multidimensional assessment of marital satisfaction. *Journal of Marriage and the Family, 41,* 121–131.

Spanier, G. B. (1976). Measuring dyadic adjustment: New scales for assessing the quality of marriage and similar dyads. *Journal of Marriage and the Family, 38,* 15–28.

Straus, M. A. (1979) Measuring intrafamily conflict and violence: The conflict tactics (CT) scales. *Journal of Marriage and the Family, 41,* 75–88.

Strodtbeck, F. L. (1951). Husband-wife interaction over revealed difference. *American Sociological Review, 16,* 468–473.

Wampler, K. S., & Halverson, C. F. (1990). The Georgia marriage Q-sort: An observational measure of marital functioning. *The American Journal of Family Therapy, 18,* 169–178.

Weider, G. B., & Weiss, R. L. (1980). Generalizability theory and the coding of marital interactions. *Journal of Consulting and Clinical Psychology, 48,* 469–477.

Weiss, R. L. (1980). Strategic behavioral marital therapy: Toward a model for assessment and intervention. In J. P. Vincent (Ed.), *Advances in family intervention, assessment and theory* (Vol. 1) (pp. 229–271). Greenwich, CT: JAI Press.

Weiss, R. L. (1984). Cognitive and behavioral measures of marital interaction. In K. Hahlweg & N. S. Jacobson (Eds.), *Marital interaction: Analysis and modification* (pp. 232–252). New York: Guilford.

Weiss, R. L. (1992). *The Marital Interaction Coding System-Version IV.* Eugene, OR: Oregon Marital Studies Program.

Weiss, R. L., & Frohman, P. E. (1985). Behavioral observation as outcome measures: Not through a glass darkly. *Behavioral Assessment, 7,* 309–316.

Weiss, R. L., & Perry, B. A. (1979). *Assessment and treatment of marital dysfunction.* Eugene, OR: Oregon Marital Studies Program.

Weiss, R. L., & Perry, B. A. (1983). The Spouse Observation Checklist: Development and clinical applications. In E. E. Filsinger (Ed.), *Marriage and family assessment: A sourcebook for family therapy* (pp. 65–84). Beverley Hills: Sage.

Weiss, R. L., & Tolman, A. O. (1990). The marital interaction coding system-global (MICS-G): A global companion to the MICS. *Behavioral Assessment, 12,* 271–294.

Whisman, M. A. & Jacobson, N. S. (1992). Change in marital adjustment following marital therapy: A comparison between two outcome measures. *Psychological Assessment: A Journal of Consulting and Clinical Psychology, 4,* 219–223.

White, L. K., & Booth, A. (1991). Divorce over the life-course: The role of marital unhappiness. *Journal of Family Issues, 12,* 5–21.

CHAPTER 15

ASSESSMENT OF SEXUAL DYSFUNCTION AND DEVIATION

Nathaniel McConaghy
University of New South Wales

With the increase in technological complexity and associated cost of procedures for assessing sexual dysfunctions and deviations, avoidance of unnecessary assessment has become more salient, and the reason for the use of any procedure should remain under constant scrutiny. Ideally for the clinician, only those assessments should be employed that provide information that will increase her or his ability to ensure the best outcome for the client at the least cost. This should result in the exclusion of assessments that have not been shown to reach this criterion, even though this results in income reduction. Of course, medico-legal considerations may at times require the use of assessments for additional purposes (e.g., providing evidence as to the validity of subjects' complaints where compensation is involved). Also, research requirements may necessitate inclusion of procedures such as those providing operationally defined diagnoses of established reliability or that conform to current ideology, to increase the likelihood of publication of findings.

THE CLINICAL INTERVIEW

The clinical interview remains the major form of assessment of sexual dysfunctions and deviations, as its flexibility allows it to serve a number of functions. It enables the clinician to determine whether, as Morganstern (1988) pointed out is often the case, the patient's reported problem is an expression of much more generalized emotional and relationship problems to which the highest treatment priority needs to be given. It also allows investigation of the possible presence of personality disorders, which are of major importance in determining the outcome of therapy of sexual disorders (McConaghy, 1993). If patients show sips of guilt, embarrassment, or reluctance to talk when particular topics are introduced, as of course is common with the investigation of their sexual attitudes and behaviors, the interviewer using a nonstructured approach can respond with encouragement and support and so elicit crucial information that may not be obtained using more structured assessments. Patients are unlikely to reveal such information unless the relationship established by the clinician is such that they are confident that this information will not be disclosed, deliberately or inadvertently, without their permission.

The clinical interview is usually initiated by asking patients the nature of their problem or why they have sought help, and responding only as much as is necessary to maintain the flow of information within reasonable limits of relevance. Patients' reasons for seeking treatment can include external pressures varying from obvious legal ones to subtle social ones, which may require intuitive detection. Only after assessing a woman's interaction with her partner may it become apparent that her complaint of failing to reach orgasm with intercourse does not reflect her dissatisfaction, but her partner's.

The reasons given for seeking treatment provide the initial information for assessing the patient's motivations, both conscious and unconscious. Assessors more strongly influenced by traditional behavioral assessment will require detailed information concerning the nature of the patient's problematic behaviors and the specific stimulus situations in which they occur. Assessors influenced by traditional psychiatric assessment will seek any past history of similar problems, other illnesses, previous treatment, childhood and adolescent relationships with parents and siblings, social and sexual relationships and practices (including coercive sexual acts carried out or experienced), sexual fantasies, educational and work history, and current domestic, social, sexual, and occupational situations (including the nature and extent of recreational interests and activities and use of recreational drugs and medications). Criminal history is investigated when relevant.

Voeller (1991) discussed the failure of most clinicians and researchers to inquire about heterosexual anal intercourse, a failure he attributed to their embarrassment concerning the topic. This would appear to apply to the even more common failure to inquire about oral-anal activities. The possibility of memory or intellectual impairment may require specific investigation. Severity of depression requires assessment if there is evidence

of reduced enjoyment of life events or of appetite or sleep disturbance.

As it provides the patient's final impression, the termination of the clinical interview is of major importance and adequate time must be left for this. When a treatment plan is proposed, the clinician should ensure that patients are fully aware of what it entails and why it (rather than alternatives) has been selected. Any reservations patients have concerning the plan should be fully dealt with so that following its discussion, they commit themselves either to accepting the plan or making a decision concerning this within the next week, possibly in consultation with the person who referred them.

The Structured Interview and Operational Diagnosis

It is becoming common practice in research publications to report that diagnoses of patients with schizophrenia or affective, psychoses were made using standardized interviews and operational diagnostic criteria. This does not appear to be the case in sexuality research. In none of the studies published from 1989 to 1994 in the *Archives of Sexual Behavior*, a major academic sexuality research journal, were structured interviews used to reach diagnoses. Walling, Andersen, and Johnson (1990), in a review of studies of hormonal replacement therapy, pointed out that though the most common sexual dysfunction noted was dyspareunia, a *DSM-III-R* definition was never cited.

Although clinicians may consider the flexibility of unstandardized interviews necessary to obtain the relevant information concerning sexual behaviors, the use of standardized diagnostic criteria would appear to carry no significant disadvantage, and the clear advantage would be that therapists would know the nature and severity of the symptoms of patients given a particular diagnosis in clinical and research communications. Neglect of the *DSM* diagnostic criteria of sexual disorders is probably due not to any aversion to the employment of standardized diagnostic criteria, but to the failure of those in the *DSM* to provide adequate operational definitions. This is most evident in their leaving major issues in diagnosis of dysfunctions to the clinician's judgment (McConaghy, in press), which will inevitably differ between clinicians.

In the *DSM-IV*, the sexual dysfunctions are divided into four major categories: desire disorders, arousal disorders, orgasmic disorders, and sexual pain disorders. All must be persistent or recurrent, as judged by the clinician, taking into account such factors as the age and experience of the subject, the frequency and chronicity of the symptom, subjective distress, and the effect on other areas of the subject's functioning. In the absence of criteria for taking these factors into account, these diagnostic categorizations must inevitably be unreliable.

In relation to hypoactive sexual desire disorder, *DSM-IV* states that the diagnosis must rely on clinical judgment based on the individual's characteristics, the interpersonal determinants, the life context, and the cultural setting. Sexual aversion disorder is defined as the aversion to and active avoidance of genital sexual contact, leaving it unclear whether the diagnosis can be applied to patients whose aversion is to having their breasts touched or to touching their partner's genitals, but not to having intercourse. Female sexual arousal disorder and male erectile and orgasmic disorders are not diagnosed if sexual stimulation is inadequate in focus, intensity, or duration—judgments again left to the clinician. Diagnosis of female orgasmic disorder requires the clinician's judgment that the woman's orgasmic capacity is less than would be reasonable for her age, sexual experience, and the adaquacy of sexual stimulation she receives. It is not stated whether the failure to reach orgasm under all conditions present in approximately 7% of women (McConaghy, 1993) is to be always considered a disorder. Premature ejaculation is defined as persistent or recurrent ejaculation with minimum stimulation before, or shortly after, penetration and before the person wishes it. In a sample of 110 heterosexual male undergraduates using what were considered the two most commonly used diagnostic criteria, seven minutes or less latency to ejaculation combined with 4 or less on the control scale, classified 24% as rapid ejaculators, whereas two minutes or less latency and little or no control classified none (Grenier & Byers, 1997).

A further problem with the *DSM-IV* classification of sexual disorders is that it ignores some disorders that are very common and very important in determining the sexual satisfaction of the middle-class couples who are the usual subjects of study. In an investigation of 100 predominantly White, well-educated, happily married couples, Frank, Andersen, and Rubinstein (1978) found evidence that what they termed sexual difficulties—problems resulting from the emotional tone of sexual relations—were more prevalent and important than dysfunctions (problems of performance). While 63% of the women and 40% of the men reported the presence of dysfunctions, 77% of the women and 50% of the men reported difficulties.

The problems most commonly reported by the women were inability to relax, too little foreplay before intercourse, disinterest, and the partner choosing an inconvenient time. Men identifiied attraction to persons other than their spouses, too little foreplay before intercourse, too little tenderness after intercourse, and the partner choosing an inconvenient time. In both men and women, reported sexual difficulties correlated more strongly with reduced sexual satisfaction than did reported dysfunctions. In men, the correlation between dysfunctions and reduced sexual satisfaction was insignificant.

Snyder and Berg (1983) found similar relationships in couples presenting with lack of sexual satisfaction. It did not correlate in women with the presence of dysfunctions, and in men only with the uncommon dysfunction of failure to ejaculate in intercourse. It correlated strongly in both sexes with the partner's lack of response to sexual requests and the frequency of intercourse being too low. From their nature, it would seem sexual difficulties result from poor communication in couples concerning their sexual wishes and needs, indicating the need to question patients concerning this during clinical interview, as well as assessing it when couples are interviewed jointly.

The term *paraphilia* was introduced in the *DSM-III-R* to replace the older term *sexual deviation,* as it emphasized that the deviation (*para*) lay in that to which the subject was attracted (*philia*)—namely, sexual objects or situations that were not part of normative arousal-activity patterns. Use of the term was retained in the *DSM-IV*, although it recognized that the sexual objects or situations in paraphilias are frequently part of a normative arousal-activity patterns; they are reported as *sexual fantasies* by a significant number, (possibly the majority) of normal subjects (McConaghy, 1993). In addition, evidence has been presented that many adolescents not only experience such attractions but express them in behaviors (Person, Terestman, Myers, Goldberg, & Salvadori, 1989; Templeman & Stinnett, 1991). The older term, *sexual deviation*, has the advantage of indicating no more than that the behaviors concerned deviate from those considered acceptable at the time. In the last few decades, masturbation and homosexuality have ceased to be regarded as deviant.

DSM-IV provides diagnostic criteria for exhibitionism, fetishism, frotteurism, pedophilia, sexual masochism, sexual sadism, transvestic fetishism, and voyeurism. Telephone scatologia (obscene phone calls), necrophilia (corpses), partialism (exclusive focus on part of the body), zoophilia (animals), coprophilia (feces), klismaphilia (enemas), and urophilia (urine) are listed as examples of paraphilias not otherwise specified.

The *DSM-IV* abandoned the widely clinically accepted terms *transvestism*, and *transsexualism*. The latter condition was included with cross-gender identification in children as gender identity disorder. There is a seeming paradox that gender identity disorder of childhood remains classified, unlike its adult expression as homosexuality (McConaghy & Silove, 1991). The *DSM-IV* states that gender identity disorder of childhood is not meant to describe a child's nonconformity to stereotypic sex-role behavior, as for example, in "tomboyishness" in girls or "sissyish" behavior in boys. Rather it represents a profound disturbance of the normal sense of identity with regard to maleness and femaleness.

Transvestism can be diagnosed in *DSM-IV* only as transvestic fetishism, a term that emphasizes the fetishistic aspect of the behavior. While in its discussion of the condition, *DSM-IV* points out that sexual arousal to cross-dressing diminishes or disappears in some individuals. In relation to the differential diagnosis of gender identity disorder, it states that transvestic fetishism occurs in heterosexual (or bisexual) men for whom the cross-dressing

behavior is for the purpose of sexual excitement. Consistent with the earlier statement, most adult transvestites do not cross-dress for sexual excitement, and indeed many prefer not to acknowledge any fetishistic aspect to their behavior (McConaghy, 1993).

The *DSM-IV* diagnosis of paraphilia requires both that the behavior, sexual urges, or fantasies have been present over a period of at least six months, and that they cause clinically significant distress or impairment in social, occupational, or other important areas of functioning. It does state that many individuals with these disorders assert that the behavior causes them no distress and that their only problem is social dysfunction as a result of the reaction of others to their behavior. However, investigations of the prevalence of child/adult sexual activity indicate that the majority of perpetrators have not been detected and so have not been detected, and so have not been exposed to the reaction of others. Some perpetrators who have been detected long after the offense appear to have shown no clinically significant distress or impairment in social, occupational, or other important areas of functioning. This would also appear true of many adult transvestites and subjects involved in sadism and masochism (McConaghy, 1993).

Some adult sex offenders against children report an isolated act without awareness of recurrent, intense sexually arousing fantasies or sexual urges concerning prepubescent children. Marshall and Eccles (1991) commented that many rapists, incest offenders, exhibitionists, and a substantial number of nonfamilial child molesters do not display or report deviant sexual preferences and yet they persistently engage in sexually offensive behaviors, so that most clinicians tend to ignore *DSM* diagnoses. They were also critical of Abel and Rouleau's (1990) recommendation that penile circumference responses (PCR) assessments should include the evaluation of all possible sexual deviations, based on their finding of a high incidence of multiple paraphilias among sex offenders. Marshall and Eccles pointed out that evaluation of the index offense could take up to six-hours, and to assess all possible paraphilias up to 21 in number would increase the time involvement enormously. In their experience, few exhibitionists and child molesters had additional paraphilias. Certainly, offenders who are repeatedly charged are usually charged with the same offense.

The sexual offense of sexual assault, which, along with child molestation, most commonly results in incarceration, is not classified in the *DSM-IV* as a paraphilia. The *DSM-III-R* classified as sadists those rapists who were considered to inflict suffering on the victims far in excess of that necessary to gain compliance and in whom the visible pain of the victim was sexually arousing. This was considered to. apply to less than 10% of rapists. The *DSM-III-R* further stated that some rapists were sexually aroused by coercing or forcing a nonconsenting person to engage in intercourse and could maintain sexual arousal while observing the victim's suffering, but, unlike persons with sexual sadism, they did not find the victim's suffering sexually amusing.

Knight and Prentky (1990) were unable to substantiate the existence of these subtle distinctions in sex offenders. The claim should not mislead assessors into regarding as markedly deviant or uncommon the presence of sexual, arousal in men to visual stimuli or fantasies of the infliction of pain or suffering on women (Crepault & Couture, 1980; Person, Terestman, Myers, Goldberg, & Salvadori, 1989) or in women to fantasies of their having pain or suffering inflicted upon themselves or of being raped (Hariton & Singer, 1974; Person et al., 1989). It would seem necessary to investigate the presence of such fantasies in victims of rape as the acknowledgment and management of these fantasies has been considered of importance in their recovery (McCombie & Arons, 1980).

The *DSM-IV* stated, in regard to sadists, that some act on their sadistic sexual urges with nonconsenting victims, possibly allowing the retention of the concept of sadistic rapists advanced in the *DSM-III-R*. It further states that usually the severity of sadistic acts increases over time, and, when severe, and especially when associated with antisocial personality disorder, individuals with sexual sadism may seriously injure or kill their victims. In fact, physical harm resulting from the activity of subjects who identify as masochists and sadists by joining clubs is rarely reported and most such subjects do not appear to show significant distress or impairment (McConaghy, 1993).

THE RESEARCH INTERVIEW

In addition to their use in diagnosis, structured interviews have been developed for researching sexual behavior. Knight and Prentky (1993) used the Developmental Interview, which lasted two to three hours and was based on several interview schedules, to study incarcerated sex offenders. It consisted of 541 questions and statements regarding the subject's family, developmental experiences, school experiences, and peer relations through childhood, and a lengthy section containing self-descriptive statements. It was programmed for computer administration, permitting considerable flexibility in formatting and presenting questions, allowing response-based branching so that follow-up questions could gather more detailed information about specific responses. In addition subjects completed an inventory administered in two sessions lasting 60 to 90 minutes, which was based on self-report inventories and focused especially on areas like sexual fantasies. Empirically validated Likert scales derived from the inventory were shown to have good test-retest reliability and high internal consistency.

Laumann, Gagnon, Michael, and Michaels (1994) pointed out the lack of empirical data concerning the importance in research interviews of matching the interviewer with the respondents on such variables as gender or race, of modes such as telephone versus face to face, and of contexts such as at home versus away from home where greater privacy could be guaranteed They noted that use of self-administered forms by mail required that the questions be self-explanatory, and that much prodding by follow-up requests was required to obtain an acceptable response rate. Self-administered forms combined with face-to-face interviewing, however, had been shown to produce somewhat higher rates of reporting socially undesirable behaviors, such as engaging in criminal acts. They used this mixed mode, combining face-to-face interviews to yield a high response rate and to ask more complex and detailed questions, with questionnaires concerning sexual experiences that were given to subjects to complete and place in "privacy envelopes" so that they were not seen by the interviewer. In regard to the gender of interviewers and respondents, they stated what slim evidence there was suggested it made no difference, or that women interviewers were preferable, and decided in relation to race that matching was unnecessary. Their conclusions were virtually identical with those reached by Catania and colleagues (1990a) in their extensive review of studies investigating measurement error and participation bias in studies of sexual behavior, suggesting subsequent research has not further clarified these issues.

Ostrow, Kessler, Stover, and Pequegnat (1993) pointed out that in investigating the sexual behavior of communities that might be difficult to access, there were both problems and benefits in using community members as interviewers. Though it could facilitate access, it might blunt honesty if the respondents felt that their confidentiality could be violated. This was consistent with the earlier statement of Catania and associates (1990b) that minority interviewers might be expected to have more success gaining access to minority respondents, but whether respondents would report sexual behavior more or less easily to someone of the same ethnicity is unknown.

Stevenson, De Moya, and Boruch (1993) considered the use of suitable informants experienced with the population was a must in ethnographic research, not only in identifying and obtaining the cooperation of appropriate subjects but also in the selection and development of questions to be asked. They pointed out that the history of distrust between investigators of sexual behavior of African Americans and the African American community could be a major stumbling block for AIDS researchers and advised such researchers to reduce this problem by such strategies as obtaining endorsement from respected African American leaders in advance. Stevenson and colleagues cited a study reporting that a proactive or initiating style was used by African American workers, and a reactive or more passive style was used by Hispanic and gay multiethnic workers. They considered that researchers of sexual behaviors might increase cultural fit by interviewing subjects in a cultural style that maximized disclosure. The failure to match interviewers and respondents for race in the investigation by Laumann and associates (1994) was highlighted by Lewontin (1995) in his trenchant criticism of their study. He commented satirically in relation to the

authors' recognition that race was an important variable organizing the pattern of social relationships, that "apparently being interviewed about your sex life is not part of social relationships" (p. 28).

Catania and colleagues (1990a) found that telephone surveys were rapidly becoming the mainstay of AIDS-related sexual behavioral assessment, though drug users and street youth were unlikely to have residential telephones. Depending on the sensitivity of the topic, measurement error might be less or greater than that with face-to-face interviews, but there were indications that socially undesirable behaviors would be less likely to be underreported in telephone interviews. Stevenson and colleagues (1993) pointed out the need to ensure both the confidentiality of data collected and the respondent's confidence concerning this protection.

An ethical issue in assessment of sexual behavior was raised by Croyle and Loftus (1993). If the concept of repression is valid and unpleasant memories are held below awareness to prevent experiencing anxiety, then application of techniques to enhance memory could provoke a renewed sense of loss and despair. They stated that although anecdotal reports from survey administrators indicate that questions upset respondents less often than many critics assume, there was a lack of good data on this issue. Kelly (1990) noted that feminists have opted for face-to-face interviews as the preferred research method, and it was accepted within the international research community as producing the most accurate findings at least in relation to prevalence of women's experiences of sexual violence from men. McConaghy (1993) pointed out the much higher prevalence of child sexual abuse reported by adult women in face-to-face interviews with women trained to probe for such experiences compared to other procedures. Kelly found that several of the women she interviewed in this way continued to be troubled by issues raised, so she remained a source of support for some time after the research was completed She pointed out that not all interviewers, feminist or otherwise, were willing or able to offer such ongoing support. She therefore questioned the endorsement of face-to-face, interviews, as they could bring to the surface previously suppressed distressing experiences. An impersonal questionnaire, on the other hand, could allow participants more control over their emotions and memories. At the same time, questionnaires set the research agenda in advance and offered the subjects no possibility for dialogue. As a feminist researcher, Kelly considered it desirable that subjects should be participants in, not merely objects of, research.

In a future study of the prevalence of child sexual abuse, Kelly (1990) planned to ask the young subjects what kind of responses they would want from those in a position to help and how they believed the questionnaire could be improved. The aim was to develop a questionnaire that young people could fill in without becoming distressed, and to conduct the assessment so that support was available for anyone who, as a consequence of participating, needed it. This latter aspect raised the issue of the possible ethical requirement of "action research" in investigations of sexual abuse, such as the need to put subjects in touch with lawyers or Women's Aid Refuges, or the establishment of support groups.

BEHAVIORAL INVENTORIES AND QUESTIONNAIRES

Behavioral inventories are particularly useful to researchers who wish to obtain data inexpensively from a number of subjects and in quantifiable form suitable for statistical analysis. Catania and colleagues (1990) concluded that in regard to data about which subjects have privacy concerns, current evidence suggested that self-administered questionnaires reduced measurement error compared to face-to-face interviews. People willing to complete the former but not volunteer for the latter were significantly less sexually self-disclosing than those willing to do both. Siegel, Krauss, and Karus (1994) found that gay men were more likely to report riskier behaviors on a self-administered questionnaire than in a subsequent face-to-face interview. However, of 100 51-year-old men who accepted being interviewed after having completed a questionnaire, 7 said at interview that they had erectile dysfunction more than occasionally, whereas none had reported this by questionnaire (Solstad & Hertoft, 1993).

Bolling and Voeller (1987) stated in regard to their findings that a quarter of American women occasionally engaged in anal intercourse, and about 10% did so regularly for pleasure. Most of the women only revealed this after repeated personal interviews and development of strong trust in the interviewer; it was unlikely to be revealed in standard medical or field interviews. In fact, such studies have revealed incidences not far below that reported by Bolling and Voeller (McConaghy, 1993). However, as Seidman and Rieder (1994) pointed out, in some of the few population studies that have investigated this behavior, there was a potential for confusion with rear-entry vaginal intercourse.

In studies in which subjects completed anonymous questionnaires, between 42% and 62% of male and 54% and 69% of female medical students who completed them over four years (McConaghy, 1987; McConaghy & Silove, 1991) and 18.9% of male twins on the Australian National Health and Medical Research Council Twin Registry (McConaghy, Buhrich, & Silove, 1994) reported awareness of some degree of homosexual feelings up to age 15. In face-to-face interviews, 6.2% of men and 4.5% of women reported ever experiencing such awareness (Laumann et al., 1994). Laumann and colleagues investigated a representative population sample, but the discrepancy seems sufficiently great to justify investigation of this and other sexual behaviors comparing face-to-face interviews with anonymous questionnaires. Seidman and Rieder (1994) reported that surveys found that 12% to 25% of American men have had at least one homosexual experience, but do not relate this marked variation to the mode of collection of the data.

Inventories completed by the subjects avoid the criticism that they have been influenced by the interviewer. However, the influence of the research context remains. AuBuchon and Calhoun (1985) found a negative relationship between menstruation and mood reported by women who were informed the study was to investigate a possible relationship between behavior and their menstrual cycles, which was not present in those women not so informed. The difference was attributed to social expectancy and demand characteristics of the experiment.

Few studies have investigated the test-retest reliability of questionnaire assessments of sexual behaviors. Saltzman, Stoddard, McCusker, Moon, and Mayer (1987) reported the responses of 116 homosexual men who completed retest questionnaires after 2 to 18 weeks. High reliability (Kappa values > .8) was found for demographic data, smoking history, and sexual orientation. Moderate reliability (Kappa values .41 to 6) was found for six-month number of steady and nonsteady partners and frequency of various sexual practices. The authors speculated social desirability effects could have been responsible for the shifts, which were toward more safe-sex behaviors. The subjects may have received HIV risk reduction education during or as a result of the initial visit, when blood was taken for HIV testing. Reliability did not correlate with length of intertest interval or reported changes in behaviors between the two tests. Catania and associates (1990b) misread the test-retest interval in the study as 2 to 18 months, and consequently found the results difficult to interpret, but still concluded they raised concerns about the stability of self-reported sexual behavior in such research.

Catania and colleagues (1990b) found in a two-week interval test-retest study of heterosexual college undergraduates that for frequency of vaginal intercourse six months previously, reliability was in the range of that reported by Saltzman and colleagues (r = .65); but for one month previously, it was high (r = .89). Catania and colleagues concluded that in assessing frequencies, one- or two-month estimates are probably optimal, whereas for numbers of sexual partners, the past year's contacts are more meaningful than the past months. Clark and Tifft (1966) retested 45 male sociology students prior to their undergoing a polygraph examination that the subjects believed would detect falsehoods. If the responses to the second questionnaire are accepted as valid, in the initial questionnaire percentages of over- and underreporting were nearly equal (15% and 17.5%) for vaginal intercourse; 15% underreported and 5% overreported homosexual contacts; and 30% underreported masturbation, 95% admitting it in their final responses.

Catania and associates (1990a) found no evidence of effects of order of sexual questions in self-administered questionnaires or face-to-face interviews, though they pointed out the studies were of college students and so the results may not be generalizable. They recommended beginning questionnaires with items that reflect a nonjudgmental view of the behaviors being investigated, adding that it may be a benefit that longer questions result, as they tend to produce higher levels of reporting than short questions on highly sensitive topics. Wiederman, Weis, and Allgeier (1994) found that fewer women responded to sexual questions in a telephone survey when they were prefaced by a general statement rather than one referring to public concern about AIDS. There was no difference for men. Catania and colleagues (1990a) pointed out the importance of subjects' motivation particularly for behaviors which require effort to recall or estimate, such as the varied sexual repertoires of subjects with large numbers of partners.

In the test-retest study of Coates, Soskolne, Calzavara, Read, Fanning, Shepherd, Klein, and Johnson (1986), the 26 homosexual men investigated reported a mean of over 1,000 lifetime male partners, ranging from 5 to over 9,000. Nevertheless, perhaps reflecting the short test-retest interval of 72 hours, the correlation coefficient for the reliability of these figures was 0.99. However, the correlation for the percentage of male partners with whom they had had sexual contact more than five times since 1978 was 0.24. Level of motivation is also of importance in relation to compliance with use of regular self-reporting by diary. Reading (1983) randomly allocated paid male volunteers to report their sexual behaviors either by interview after one and three months (n = 21); interviews after one, two, and three months (n = 18); or diary cards completed daily and returned every three days in addition to interviews at one, two, and three months (n = 29). Dropout occurred in 14%, 16%, and 34% of the three procedures, respectively. A further 3 dropped out prior to the first month with the last procedure, as they considered that completing diary cards caused potency difficulties.

The frequency of urges of pedophiles for sexual contact with children reported by daily diary cards did not differ in those receiving the male-sex-hormone-reducing chemical, medroxyprogesterone from those receiving placebo (Wincze, Bansal, & Malamud, 1986). This indicated the diary card assessment lacked validity. In addition to the clinical evidence of the efficacy of the chemical in reducing such urges (McConaghy, 1993), the reduction (to which they were blind) in sex offenders' testosterone levels produced by medroxyprogesterone, correlated highly with their global assessment by questionnaire of the degree of reduction of their deviant urges (McConaghy, Blaszczynski, & Kidson, 1988). Self-rated responses of patients treated for sexual deviations correlated highly ($r =.93$ and .96) with their self-rated expectancies of response following five days of treatment, indicating a high degree of reliability of such estimates (McConaghy, Armstrong, & Blaszczynski, 1985). A novel development of diary assessment, the Experience Sampling Method, was employed by Hillbrand and Waite (1994). The subject, a rapist, wore a beeper that signaled, at randomly generated, preprogrammed times, when he was instructed to enter his current activity, location, thought content, and mood. He reported a high frequency of sexual thoughts about women.

Patients' self-report of behaviors in inventories can of themselves produce changes in behaviors. LoPiccolo and Steger (1974) found the test-retest reliabilities of subjects' scores on the Sexual Interaction Inventory lower than hoped for. They related this to evidence that self-recording of sexual activity leads to marked changes in activity. If such inventories are to be used to assess response to treatment, they need to be administered sufficiently often prior to initiation of treatment for such reactivity to stabilize. Also subjects' behavior may change following cessation of their self-recording, so their final response to treatment cannot be judged from the final inventory.

Clinicians' assessments of behaviors on rating scales was found to be less sensitive than their global impressions, a difference attributed to narrowing of the clinicians' perspectives when forced to rate along specific dimensions (Paredes, Baumgold, Pugh, & Ragland, 1966). A similar narrowing could account for the failure of the Sexual Arousal Inventory, developed to discriminate sexually functional from dysfunctional women, to discriminate victims of sexual assault who, on clinical assessment, reported no sexual problems from those who reported one or more problems related to

the assault (Becker, Skinner, Abel, & Treacy, 1982). Reduction in sensitivity of subjects' self-ratings as compared with global assessment has also been noted. Women reported increased satisfaction in their sexual relationship with global assessment but decreased satisfaction when specific activities were measured by the Sexual Interaction Inventory (DeAmicis, Goldberg, LoPiccolo, Friedman, & Davies, 1984).

Failure of subjects' Kinsey ratings, termed *statistical*, to change following aversive therapy caused Birk, Huddleston, Miller, and Cohler (1971) to pay little attention to the significant changes in the subjects' global reports of sexual feelings and behaviors, termed *anecdotal*. They therefore overlooked the fact that following therapy, the subjects' ability to control their behavior had increased markedly without change in their sexual orientation (McConaghy, 1993). Feldman and MacCulloch (1971) made a similar error in assessing response to treatment. though stating that the Sexual Orientation Method (SOM) rating scale was not intended to supplant clinical interviews, they reported only subjects' SOM scores, and no global assessment of change in their feelings and behaviors. It is essential that rating scales used clinically or in research are established to measure all relevant aspects of behaviors before they are used in preference to clinical assessment

Wincze and Carey (1991) pointed out that behavioral inventories have not been widely used in clinical sexuality assessments. They cited Conte's (1983) suggestion that one reason was that many inventories were developed for specific research purposes and had limited clinical utility. They also pointed out that their use could be time consuming and inconvenient in a busy practice. Nevertheless, they stated they had used a number of self-report questionnaires in assessing patients with sexual dysfunctions, including the Sexual Interaction Inventory and the Derogatis Sexual Functioning Index, and suggested Conte's (1983) review and the compendium of Davis, Yarber, and Davis (1988) as sources for other measures that could be useful. Another valuable source is the *Dictionary of Behavioral Assessment Techniques* (Hersen & Bellack, 1988). An example of the limited clinical relevance of certain inventories noted by Conte (1983) was reported in a psychometric analysis of the Sexual Experience Scale of the Derogatis Sexual Functioning Inventory.

Andersen and Broffitt (1988) approved of its investigation of a wider range of sexual behaviors, including masturbation and anal activities, in comparison with other scales in view of the frequency with which their female subjects reported these activities. However, they found it was not able to identify women with sexual dysfunctions, which they considered due to its measuring the occurrence of sexual behaviors rather than their frequency. As an assessment of self-reported sexual behavior of sexually active heterosexual individuals, they considered a simple alternative could be self-reports of intercourse frequency, as they found this frequency to be stably reported by healthy subjects over four occasions at four monthly intervals. Rating scales must be sensitive to the appropriate behaviors of interest, but they can be too sensitive so that they exaggerate the degree of behavioral change that has occurred. Jacobson, Follette, and Revenstorf (1984) noted in relation to behavioral marital therapy that differences on scales of marital satisfaction of the group means of subjects who received active and placebo therapy could be highly statistically significant when the changes were clinically trivial. They recommended comparing treated subjects' individual scores with the norms of functionally well subjects on the same scales. With this procedure, the mean improvement rate with behavioral marital therapy was about 35%, considerably less than was generally believed (Jacobson, Follette, Revenstorf, Baucom, Hahlweg, & Margolin, 1984).

Rating scales can also produce misleading findings when the behaviors they are assessing are reified into entities. One widely used assessment of masculinity and femininity, the Bem Sex-Role Inventory (BSRI; Bem, 1974) requires subjects to indicate how well each of 60 masculine, feminine, and neutral personality traits describe them. The traits were those previously judged by undergraduates to be more desirable in U.S. society for one sex than for the other. Masculinity and femininity, as assessed on this inventory, has shown no consistent relationship with subjects' reported ratio of hetero-

sexual/homosexual feelings (McConaghy & Zarnir, 1995a). This finding supported the statement that masculinity and femininity are culturally defined attributes and have no demonstrable correlation with sexual orientation (Katchadourian, Lunde, & Trotter, 1979). In an alternative approach, masculinity and femininity were assessed by the degree subjects reported behaviors that are empirically demonstrated to be shown more often by members of one as compared to the other sex (i.e., sex-linked behaviors, such as interest in sports versus keeping one's room neat). Consistent relationships were found between female sex-linked behaviors and homosexual orientation in men (McConaghy, 1987). In women, BSRI-assessed masculinity (McConaghy & Zamir, 1995a) and exposure to excess male sex hormone levels in utero (McConaghy, 1993) were associated with male sex-linked behaviors.

Another aspect of masculinity and femininity that has been reified into a categorical entity is sexual or gender identity, first identified in relation to transsexualism (McConaghy, 1993). Since transsexuals were conceptualized as identifying totally as members of the biologically opposite sex, the possibility that sexual identity could be dimensional in nontranssexuals was not considered. In their investigation of girls exposed to increased levels of androgens in utero, Ehrhardt and Baker (1974) commented that 35% were undecided or thought that they might have chosen to be boys but that "none had a conflict with their female gender identity" (p. 43).

However, when subjects were given the opportunity to report their sexual identity dimensionally by rating the degree to which they ever feel uncertain of their identity as a member of their sex, their strength of identity as a member of their sex, and the strength to which they feel like a member of the opposite sex, their responses to these items correlated at most about .5 (McConaghy & Armstrong, 1983). The correlations were stronger in subjects who reported some awareness of homosexual feelings, these subjects reporting a greater degree of opposite sex identity. Some 59% of lesbian, 32% of bisexual, and 22% of heterosexual women answered affirmatively to the question, "As a child

I felt like a boy or a man" (Phillips & Over, 1995). Some male transvestites report a male identity when dressed as men and a female identity when dressed as women (Buhrich & McConaghy, 1977). It would appear that sexual identity should not be assessed as a categorical, unitary concept, particularly in subjects who do not belong to a minority.

Inventories are of value for the anonymous collection of data that subjects may not reveal if their identities were known (and that may require the interviewer to report if the identity of the subject was known). A questionnaire of this nature was introduced by Koss and Oros (1982), on which men reported sexually coercive behaviors only as perpetrators and women only as victims. Despite this sexist bias (McConaghy, Zamir, & Manicavasagar, 1993), it has been widely used to support the concept that rape is on a dimension of normal male behavior. Use of the questionnaire modified to allow men and women to report coercive behaviors as both perpetrators and victims demonstrated that the perpetration of sexual coercive acts from verbal persuasion to rape correlated with BSRI-assessed masculine behavior in both men and women (McConaghy & Zamir, 1995b).

Not all researchers have accepted that use of verbal pressure to obtain intercourse should be regarded as a form of sexual assault. Davis and Leitenberg (1987) rejecting the findings of a major study that did so. However, in the case of sexual assaults in the workplace or teaching institution, the use of economic or educational threats or promises by the harasser can be crucial to adjudication (Schneider, 1991). The randomized response technique was introduced to obtain nonanonymous self-reports of socially unacceptable behaviors. It was used by Finkelhor and Lewis (1988) in a phone survey to determine the number of child molesters in the general population. With this technique, subjects are asked two questions simultaneously (e.g., Have you ever sexually abused a child? and Do you rent the place where you live?). By independently determining the percent of subjects who rent, the percent of child molesters can be estimated from the percentage who answer yes to the combined questions if either was correct. Finkelhor and Lewis did not obtain consistent results, which they

attributed to the questions they used. Also, Catania and associates (1990a) cited studies where its use did not appear to enhance reporting. However, the technique seems worthy of further evaluation.

In relation to the obtaining of reliable data, Catania and colleagues (1990a) pointed out that it meant little if the behavior measured is a pale reflection of actual sexual behavior. Lewontin's (1995) major criticism of the study by Laurmann and colleagues (1994) was of the use of self-report to provide data concerning sexual behaviors. He focused on the finding that men reported 75% more sexual partners in the most recent five years than did women, whereas the average number of sex partners reported by men and women should, discounting homosexual partners, be equivalent. Laumann and colleagues (1994) attributed the discrepancy largely to men exaggerating or women understating the number of their partners, leading Lewontin to comment, "In the single case where one can actually test the truth, the investigators themselves think it most likely that people are telling themselves and others enormous lies" (p. 29).

However, the possibility that female prostitutes. "probably underrepresented" in the sample, could largely account for the difference could have been explored. Also, it would seem reasonable to balance this apparently negative finding with those supporting the validity of self-reports, such as: (1) the relationship between reported increase in safe-sex behaviors and the fall in prevalence of sexually transmitted diseases (McConaghy, 1993); (2) the prediction of HIV seroconversion from risk indices based on self-reported sexual behaviors (Catania et al., 1990b); (3) the strong correlations between men's reports of their sexual orientation and their penile volume responses, discussed subsequently; and (4) the strong correlations between the degree of reduction in sex offenders' deviant sexual urges and the medroxyprogesterone produced reduction in their levels of testosterone, to which they were blind (McConaghy, Blaszczynski, & Kidson, 1988).

Catania and associates (1990a) considered the frequently investigated correlations between partners' reports; of their sexual behaviors to be, at best, weak validity estimates that required validation against some objective index, though they were of interest in their own right as mutual perceptions. Catania and associates pointed out that such objective indices as have been employed (e.g., sexually transmitted disease rates, condom sales, urine analysis for sperm) did not achieve one-to-one correspondence with self-reports of sexual behavior and concluded that though such indices were useful, development of more exacting measures remains a major challenge.

BEHAVIORAL OBSERVATION

Observation of subjects' nonverbal behaviors is an important component in assessment by unstructured clinical interview. Observations of sexual behaviors either directly or by videotape were briefly popular in the more permissive climate of the 1970s (LoPiccolo, 1990), following the report of Masters and Johnson (1966) of their laboratory observations of the sexual responses of sexually functional men and women. LoPiccolo argued against the employment of such procedures with patients with sexual dysfunctions, considering that the effect of observation would make it unlikely that the behaviors observed would be similar to their private behaviors, that the procedure would be unacceptable to the majority of couples, and that it allowed the exploitation of patients by therapists. These objections would certainly apply to the "sexological exam," described by LoPiccolo, in which sex therapists stimulated the breasts and genitals of the opposite sex partner to assess and demonstrate physiological responsiveness.

However it would seem possible to provide adequate ethical safeguards to investigate the value of videotaped observational assessment of couples' sexual interactions. With the use of preliminary sessions to allow the couples to adjust to the procedure, their observed behavior could be sufficiently related to their private behavior to provide information of value. This is accepted to be the case with the observational assessment of nonsexual behaviors such as phobias as well as with the laboratory assessment of physiological evidence of sexual arousal, the clinical examination of the adequacy of penile erection occurring during sleep or produced by masturbation (recommended by Karacan [1978]

and Wasserman, Pollak, Spielman, and Weitzman [1980]), and the determination by surrogate sex therapists of the sexual activity of clients. It would seem that taboos concerning sexuality remain a significant obstacle to other potentially valuable observational assessments of sexual activity.

Maletzky (1980) introduced an observational assessment of exhibitionists, who were informed that experimental and unusual procedures would be employed. A comely actress unknown to the subjects placed herself in situations in which they had previously frequently offended to determine their response. The effeminate behavior of boys has also been assessed by observation. Clinicians using a one-way mirror noted the degree boys played with boys' and girls' toys (Rekers & Lovaas, 1974). Teachers (Kagan & Moss, 1962) and parents (Bates, Bentler, & Thompson, 1973) completed inventories of the effeminate behaviors shown by their pupils or sons. A quantification of the observed effeminate behavior of adult males was reported by Schatzberg, Westfall, Blumetti, and Birk (1975), but subsequently has not been widely used, possibly because of its complexity.

PHYSIOLOGICAL AND PHYSICAL ASSESSMENTS

Assessment of men's sexual arousal by measurement of their penile volume responses (PVRs) to erotic stimuli was introduced by Freund (1963). It classified correctly all of 65 men who reported relatively exclusive heterosexual feelings or behavior, and 48 of 58 men who reported relatively exclusive homosexual feelings or behavior. McConaghy (1967) introduced a simpler apparatus for measuring PVRs to a brief standardized presentation of 20 10-second segments of moving pictures, 10 of nude men and 10 of nude women presented alternately at one-minute intervals within a film of landscapes. It also classified correctly the majority of individuals who identified as predominantly heterosexual or homosexual. Bancroft, Jones, and Pullan (1966) assumed that a strain gauge that measured penile circumference (PC) would provide an equivalent measure of PV and reported its use to assess sexual arousal. Validation was not considered necessary. The results should have led to realization that PC responses (PCRs) were not equivalent to PV responses (PVRs). Reporting the PCRs of a pedophile, Bancroft and associates (1966) stated that to obtain the responses, some mental imagery was required and most PCRs occurred within five minutes of exposure to the stimulus. The duration of stimuli used to elicit PVRs by Freund and McConaghy was 13 and 10 seconds, respectively. Mental imagery was not required. This marked difference in the two responses went unnoticed.

Zuckerman in his widely cited review (1971) of physiological measures of sexual arousal unquestioningly accepted that PVRs and PCRs were identical, quoting results of studies using one or the other, without identifying which was used. He decided the use of PCRs was preferable on the grounds that the circumference gauge was easier to apply, simpler to calibrate, and did not stimulate as large an area of the penis. As it was generally accepted that PCRs and PVRs were equivalent, most workers other than Freund and McConaghy used PCRs. In an attempt to document differences between the measures, McConaghy (1974) compared PCRs and PVRs of individual subjects. It was reported that while the two responses could be reasonably equivalent, they could also be largely mirror-images. In the latter case, the initial penile tumescence or PVR increase was associated with a rapid elongation of the penis, such that the increase in blood flow to maintain the elongation was not sufficient to also maintain an increase in circumference, (the response measured by the PCR). The PVR increases were, therefore, paralleled by PCR decreases. As the initial stage of penile tumescence is more accurately assessed by PVRs than PCRs, this finding could account for the greater validity of PVRs in assessing sexual orientation. The initial stage may more accurately reflect sexual arousal, the later stage of tumescence possibly being more affected by variables reflecting haemodynarnic factors determining erections.

PVRs and PCRs continued to be treated as equivalent, even when after several years it was reported that for PCRs to correctly identify most individual heterosexual and homosexual men, it was necessary to use the more powerful erotic stimuli of moving films of men and women involved in homosexual activity, rather than of single male and female nudes (Sakheim, Barlow, Beck, & Abrahamson, 1985). By that time, PCRs to the latter stimuli had been adopted for use in single-case studies as the major outcome measure of change in individual subjects' heterosexual and homosexual feelings (McConaghy, 1993). The findings of these studies remain the only evidence that such widely used techniques as masturbatory satiation and aversive procedures modify deviant sexual arousal. They continue to be cited in this respect (Laws & Marshall, 1991), despite the demonstration of the lack of validity of PCRs to such stimuli as an outcome measure in individuals. When PCR assessment with use of the more powerful stimulus of movies of sexual activity failed to distinguish bisexual from homosexual men, Tollison, Adams, and Tollison (1979) questioned the existence of bisexuality, claiming there was, to that date, no physiological evidence for bisexual arousal except where this was a by-product of sexual reorientation therapy. In fact, two PVR assessments (Barr & McConaghy, 1971; McConaghy, 1978) had provided such evidence.

On the basis of early studies reporting that pedophiles and rapists could be identified from their PCRs to audio- or videotaped descriptions of sexual activities or pictures of male and female nudes of various ages (Abel, Barlow, Blanchard, & Guild, 1977; Barbaree, Marshall, & Lanthier, 1979; Quinsey, Steinman, Bergersen, & Holmes, 1975), these responses have become widely employed in diagnosis and assessment of change with treatment of these subjects. Despite subsequent studies showing inconsistent results (Murphy, Krisar, Stalgaitis, & Anderson, 1984; Nagayama Hall, Proctor, & Nelson, 1988), Quinsey and Earls (1990) concluded that the use of PCRs to distinguish individual sex offenders from nonoffenders remained central in most treatment programs in North America. However, they pointed out that normal men with no history of child molestation show sizable PCRs in response to slides of pubescent females; and that uncertainty existed concerning the ratio of subjects' PCRs to descriptions of coercive as opposed to consenting sexual activity which identified individual rapists from nonrapists.

Lalumiere and Quinsey (1994) reported that meta-analysis of the findings of selected studies investigating the PCRs of rapists demonstrated that the assessment did discriminate rapists from non-rapists, as groups. The fact that it was necessary to combine the responses of groups of rapists and groups of nonrapists by use of meta-analysis to obtain convincing statistical evidence that PCR assessment discriminated the two groups would seem to indicate it should be used to investigate groups, but not for individual clinical assessment. Nevertheless, the authors included that these results supported the use of the assessment to identify individual offenders' treatment needs and risk of recidivism. Statistical procedures should not be separated from the ethical consequences of their use. Meta-analysis appropriately employed provides convincing evidence of the specificity of weak effects (McConaghy, 1990). However, administering a treatment to which only a small percentage of subjects will respond specifically is not ethically equivalent to identifying as a sex offender someone who is not, or persisting with the use of aversive procedures on subjects so identified until they are able to modify their PCRs.

The validity of penile response assessment of sexual arousal is further compromised by the ability of subjects to modify their responses. Freund (1971) asked subjects to attempt to produce sexual arousal by using fantasies that would be erotic for them, when shown pictures of members of the non-preferred sex, and to attempt to diminish arousal to pictures of members of the preferred sex by imagining something disagreeable. Results were: 2 of 22 heterosexual men and 1 of 9 homosexual men tested for the first time, and 3 of 20 heterosexual and 5 of 15 homosexual men previously tested were able to produce PVRs, which misclassified them.

Laws and Rubin (1969) investigated four men who developed PCR-assessed full erections within 3 minutess to erotic films that lasted 10 to 12 minutes. All reduced their erections to the films by at least 50% when instructed to avoid getting an erection by any means except not watching the film. They were then asked to produce an erection by any means except manipulating themselves, without being shown any erotic stimuli. All were able to produce partial PCR measures of erections, which reached a momentary peak of about 30% of maximum erection in three subjects and 90% in

one. Latency of any increase in PCRs ranged from slightly less than 1 minute to 10 minutes. The markedly higher percentage of subjects able to modify PCRs as opposed to PVRs escaped notice, as did the striking latency difference. PVRs occurred and were assessed within 13 seconds.

Freund (1971) commented that the study did not "obey the rule of showing each picture for no more than a few seconds, to provoke only the minimal penis volume changes of which the subjects are often not aware" (p. 225), indicating he believed that the markedly longer duration of stimuli necessary for PCR assessment was likely to contribute to the greater ease with which these responses were consciously modified. With brief presentation of stimuli, Freund (1971) found that only 1 of 19 heterosexual pedophiles and none of 9 homosexual pedophiles were able to produce PVRs indicating a preference for adult females. In a recent study using 54-second presentations of stimuli, Winton (1998) found that 17 of 20 university students asked to cognitively elevate their PVRs to female children while suppressing PVRs to all other stimuli were able to fake a preference for female children or at least raise their level of arousal to that equivalent to their responses to women. Using visual and verbal stimuli of 28- and 46-second duration, Freund and Watson (1991) reported that PVRs indicative of a preference for minors were shown by 78.2% of sex offenders against at least 2 female children and 88.6% of offenders against at least 2 male children, compared with 19.4% of paid volunteers who claimed to be attracted to adult women, and 3.1% of sex offenders against female adults.

Freund and Watson considered that offenders against female adults were more suitable as control subjects than unselected paid volunteers. They suggested the latter were not likely to be concerned about the test outcome and did not pay enough attention to the stimuli. The possibility that sexually normal men were erotically more interested in children than offenders against adults was considered unlikely on the basis of a report that there was a high proportion (44%) of offenders against female children among rapists. The logic of this latter statement is difficult to follow. The offenders against women in their study were chosen on the basis that they had no known sex offense against a minor. If this was correct, it means they were, not similar to the rapists discussed in the report. If it was not, they were able to prevent their offenses against children being indicated in their PVRs assessment to a much greater extent than were the sex offenders against children. It would seem possible that many of the controls who showed PVR evidence of pedophilia were sexually aroused by children, though they did not necessarily express the arousal in behaviors.

Some 15% of male university students in the United States and Australia reported some likelihood of having sexual activity with a prepubertal child if they could do so without risk (Malamuth, 1989; McConaghy et al., 1993). Using subjects' PCRs to slides, Fedora, Reddon, Morrison, Fedora, Pascoe, and Yeudall (1992) reported a similar incidence of pedophilia in controls (18.3%). In all, 28% of the controls showed PCRs indicating the presence of a paraphilia; sadism, shown by 5%, was the most common form after pedophilia. The authors commented that during debriefing many of the 28% revealed nothing unusual about their fantasies, while others freely admitted to having deviant fantasies, which distressed some of them. The high percentage of subjects who report deviant fantasies has been discussed elsewhere (McConaghy, 1993).

The ability of some men, given sufficient time, to produce marked PCRs without exposure to erotic stimuli (Alford, Wedding, & Jones, 1983) could explain findings that homosexual men treated by regular exposure to pictures of women developed 80% to 100% PCR-assessed erections to the pictures (Barlow & Agras, 1973; McGrady, 1973), although they reported no increase in their heterosexual feelings. This finding also questions the validity of PCR assessment of individuals. It has been suggested that changes in PCRs; of sex offenders with treatment represents learning to increase voluntary control (Quinsey & Earls, 1990), consistent with failure of reduction in PCRs of treated child molesters to correlate with less recidivism (Marshall & Barbaree, 1988; Rice, Quinsey, & Harris, 1991). This suggestion was supported by demonstration that the PCRs of treated sex offenders indicated more deviant preference if, during the assessment, they carried out a semantic tracking task, which was assumed would reduce their ability to voluntarily control their penile responses (Proulx, Cote, & Achille, 1993).

Some questioning of the value of PCR assessments of individual sex offenders is emerging: "If behaviorists are to maintain [their] exaggerated faith in erectile measurements, they must solve the experimental riddle of demonstrating the relevance of changing such indices to the maintenance of offensive behavior and, particularly, to the issue of treatment benefits" (Marshal & Barbaree, 1990, p. 382). Also, ethical concerns are being expressed regarding the forcing of uninformed subjects to see or hear pornographic material, an issue contributing to the termination of the use of PCRs in prison treatment programs in Utah (Card & Dibble, 1995).

In view of the small number of women sex offenders, little attention has been given to the investigation of their genital physiological responses—such investigations in women being currently limited to laboratory studies of sexual arousal of the sexually functional and dysfunctional. Vaginal, clitoral, or labial blood flow changes in response to erotic stimuli are measured either by the associated temperature changes using a thermistor, or by vaginal color changes using a photoplethysmograph. Clitoral responses have also been assessed using a strain gauge.

Carmichael, Warburton, Dixen, and Davidson (1994) reported the anal electromyographic and photoplethysmographic responses accompanying orgasm in men and women. Rosen and Beck (1988) concluded that photoplethysmograph assessment of vaginal pulse amplitude (VPA) was the most widely used measure of arousal and the most sensitive in distinguishing the responses of groups of women to erotic as compared to nonerotic stimuli. Its correlation with subjectively assessed arousal, however, was insignificant in the majority of individuals studied.

The relationships between genital and subjectively assessed arousal appears weaker in women than men. Correlations between individual VPA responses and reported subjective arousal of eight lesbian women to erotic films varied from $r = .26$ to .89, the average for the group not being significant. The correlations of subjective arousal and PCRs of eight homosexual men who viewed the same films were $r = .62$ to $.98$, the average being significant (Wincze & Qualls, 1984). Hatch (1981) found no consistent reports of differences in physiologically assessed genital arousal to erotic stimuli of sexually functional and dysfunctional women, or of changes in the arousal of the dysfunctional women following treatment. However, Palace and Gorzalka (1990, 1992) provided convincing evidence that sexually dysfunctional women showed less vaginal blood volume (VBV) response and subjective arousal to erotic films, and that the inconsistencies of previous studies could be accounted for by such factors as differences in stimuli and assessment procedures, including the use of VPA rather than VBV; they considered the latter could be the more sensitive indicator of sexual arousal. Few significant correlations were found, however, between genital and subjective measures of sexual arousal.

The VBV of dysfunctional women increased to a level equivalent to those of functional women following false physiological feedback combined with preexposure to an arousal-evoking film, while their subjective sexual arousal was unchanged (Palace, 1995). Palace suggested generalized sympathetic arousal associated with anxiety, laughter, or exercise could facilitate genital sexual arousal. This raises the possibility that VBV could be in part determined by nonsexual stimuli, supported by the finding that the VBV of sexually functional women significantly decreased during exposure to anxiety-eliciting stimuli (Palace & Gorzalka, 1990). However, this finding was not replicated (Palace, 1995). If strategies combining physiological feedback and increasing autonomic arousal prove effective in improving the sexual responses of dysfunctional women, this could provide evidence that VBV is validly assessing specifically sexual responses, not more generalized genital haemodynamic responses. It should also lead to more attention being given the physiological assessment of genital arousal of sexually dysfunctional women.

Physical examination and laboratory assessments are required for men with hypoactive sexual desire and in those whose erectile disorder is not situational and hence not obviously psychogenically determined. Situational erectile disorder is that occurring with some but not other partners or

with all partners but not in private masturbation where no pressure to produce an erection is experienced. Physical examination is indicated to exclude such conditions as Peyronie's disease, and hypogonadism. Blood and urine screening is indicated to exclude diabetes, hyperprolactinaernia (raised levels of the pituitary hormone prolactin, HPRL), and thyroid dysfunction. Presumably reflecting differences in patient samples, the percentage of men with erectile dysfunction reported to show hormone abnormalities varies markedly between studies, as do the conclusions as to what hormone studies are clinically necessary.

Lehmann, Schopke, Brutsch, and Hauri (1994) found that only 17 of 107 men with erectile dysfunction showed hormonal adnormalities; testosterone was low in all 17 and only 3 of the 17 had additional hormonal abnormalities: all 3 showed increased prolactin levels. The authors conclied that only testosterone level need be measured in initial evaluation. Akpunonu, Mutgi, Federman, York, and Woldenberg (1994) considered rolactin estimation necessary only in patients who had low testosterone levels. They found that of 212 patients with erectile dysfunction, 51 had low testosterone levels and only 3 had elevated prolactin, 2 of whom had low testosterone levels. None of the 3 had pituitary tumors. Buvat, Lemaire, Buvat-Herbaut, Fourlinnie, Racadot, and Fossati (1985) examined 1,053 men consecutively referred for sexual dysfunctions without obvious organic causes (drugs, apparent endocrinopathies, diabetes, neuropathy, and arthritis). Only 10 (1%) of the 850 men diagnosed as having erectile dysfunction showed marked HPRL (above 35ng/ml), but 6 of the 10 showed radiologic evidence of a pituitary adenoma. Also, 5 of the 10 had testosterone levels within the normal range (3–10 ng/ml).

It would seem possible that failure to estimate prolactin levels and perhaps diabetes and thyroid dysfunction in men with erectile disorder or hypoactive sexual desire could have medico-legal consequences. This renders all the more disturbing the evidence that patients are reluctant to report and medical practitioners reluctant to inquire about the presence of sexual dysfunctions. Only 6 of 1,080 men attending a medical outpatient clinic were identified as having erectile disorder prior to a direct inquiry, which revealed its presence in 401 (Slag, Morley, Elson, Trence, Nelson, Nelson, Kinlaw, Beyer, Nuttall, & Shafer, 1983). Jones (1985) found the testosterone levels in men with erectile dysfunction under the age of 50 years to be almost invariably in the normal range in the absence of such signs of marked reduction as loss of libido, physical signs of regression of male hair pattern, gynecomastia (increased breast development) or small, soft testes.

Though Korenman, Morley, Mooradian, Davis, Kaiser, Silver, Viosca, and Garza (1990) found reduction of bioavailable testosterone due to secondary hypogonadism to be present in about 40% of men over the age of 50, they found no relation between the reduction and erectile disorder. These findings are consistent with the evidence that the level of testosterone to maintain erectile function is markedly below that necessary to maintain sexual interest (McConaghy, 1993). Nevertheless, testosterone levels are usually routinely investigated in men with nonsituational erectile disorder even though they do not show physical sips of hypogonadism.

Assessment of nocturnal penile tumescence (NPT) by PCR remains widely used in the differential diagnosis of psychogenic and organic erectile dysfunction in men. Wincze and Carey (1991) stated that its use, usually in a full sleep laboratory, has been considered the gold standard of differential diagnosis. They did not appear to be referring to the cost of the procedure, though they pointed out that it is well beyond the financial means of most clients. Thus clinicians might want to consider more affordable and perhaps more valid psychophysiological assessments.

Karacan (1978) recommended NPT assessment of erectile dysfunction on the basis that if men with erectile disorder showed erections during dream or rapid eye movement (REM) sleep similar to those of normal men, their dysfunction was due to a psychological, not an organic, cause. The procedure was conducted in a sleep laboratory on three consecutive nights. Men who showed erections on PCR were awakened on the third night for them to assess the fullness and to have the rigidity determined by the pressure necessary to produce buckling. Wasserman and coleagues (1980) pointed out

that the hypothesis that psychogenic could be distinguished from organic erectile dysfunction by NPT had not been tested by studies in which the two conditions were diagnosed by criteria independent of NPT assessment. Also, impaired NPT had been found in normally functioning men in response to psychogenic factors, in men with erectile disorder diagnosed on clinical grounds as psychogenic, and in elderly men who reported having erections adequate for intercourse.

Schiavi (1992) considered assessment of penile buckling to be impractical in older subjects because of rapid penile detumescence on testing. Thase, Reynolds, and Jennings (1988) found that 40% of depressed men showed reduction of duration of NPT corrected for diminished sleep time, in the same range as that of men with organic erectile disorder. The reduction was associated with erectile dysfunction within the depressive episode, and the authors speculated it assessed a reversible decrease in erectile capacity. However, Nofzinger, Thase, Reynolds, Frank, Jennings, Garamoni, Fasiczka, and Kupfer (1993) found that the NPT abnormalities of depressed men did not correlate with behavioral measures of sexual function, nor did they reverse in early remission. They suggested the abnormalities may be more trait than state indices of depression.

Schiavi, Fisher, White, Beers, and Szechter (1984) reported recovery of potency after psychotherapy in a man with primary erectile disorder who showed no episodes of full penile tumescence over five nights. Men with reduced testosterone levels due to hypogonadism or estrogen administration showed normal erectile responses to sexual films and fantasy (Kwan, VanMaasdam, & Davidson, 1985) but impaired NPT, suggesting different neurophysiological pathways may be involved in the production of NPT and of erections in sexual situations. In their recent critical evaluation of NPT assessment, Meisler and Carey (1990) considered a conservative appraisal to be that it may misdiagnose as many as 20% of the subjects investigated.

Because of this evidence that such factors as illness and pharmacological agents in addition to psychological conditions such as anxiety or depression associated with abnormalities of sleep were likely to disrupt NPT patterns, Schiavi (1992) suspected that NPT over three nights in a sleep laboratory should continue to be used where diagnostic uncertainty persisted. Cheaper alternatives should be employed only as screening devices, as they failed to provide information to identify sleep disorders and REM activity and were likely to lead to false diagnostic conclusions. The implication that experienced investigators could intuitively use such information to improve the validity of NPT assessment does not appear to have been tested empirically. NPT investigation is routine for medico-legal purposes in patients complaining of erectile disorder secondary to compensative accidents or injuries.

The cheaper alternatives to sleep laboratory assessment of NPT include assessing subjects' NPT in their own homes by placing around the penis a ring of stamps or a snap gauge that bursts if tumescence occurs, or using the Rigiscan portable monitoring instrument. This instrument continuously records the frequency, duration, and degree of NPT using two strain gauge loops, one placed at the base of the penis and one immediately behind the glans. The loops tighten periodically, indenting the penis and providing a measure of turgidity. However, though penile buckling force and observer ratings of erectile rigidity correlated well, both correlated poorly with Rigiscan assessment when base and tip rigidity exceeded 60% of the maximum, when the assessment failed to discriminate buckling forces between 450 and 900 grams. A buckling force of 550 grams was considered adequate for vaginal penetration (Allen, Smolev, Engel, & Brendler, 1993). It was concluded that exclusion of mild abnormalities in erectile function may not be possible using Rigiscan assessment, and when it exceeds 60% of the maximum, buckling force or observer assessment may be necessary.

In contrast to the belief of the 1970s that most cases of erectile disorder were entirely psychogenically determined (LoPiccolo, 1982), it is now generally accepted that organic factors, usually impairment in penile blood flow, commonly contribute to their etiology (Meuleman, Bemelmans, Doesburg, van Asten, Skotnicki, & Debruyne, 1992). This impairment is assessed by determination of the penile-brachial index (PBI), the ratio of the blood pressure in the penile arteries, commonly measured by Dop-

pler ultrasound probe, and conventionally measured blood-pressure in the brachial artery in the arm. A study of 48 healthy men and 55 men with peripheral arteriosclerotic disease, 32 of whom had erectile dysfunction, found that more than 90% of those with PBIs of 0.6 or less had erectile dysfunction; all healthy controls had PBIs of 0.7 or more (Metz & Bengtsson 1981).

However, 30% of those with arteriosclerotic disease with PBIs of 0.7 to 0.9 had erectile dysfunction, and it was emphasized that PBIs above 0.6 did not exclude vascular disease as a cause of erectile dysfunction. Only three healthy men and one with arteriosclerosis obtained PBIs of over 0.9, the level Gewertz and Zarins (1985) reported should indicate sufficient to maintain erection. The reliance of clinicians on NPT and PBI assessment in erectile dysfunction was questioned by Saypol, Peterson, Howards, and Yazel (1983). They reported close agreement between the diagnoses of the psychiatrist and urologist reached by clinical examination alone, and the diagnoses reached on the results of the patients' fasting blood sugar and testosterone levels and their PBI and NPT assessments. They suggested that expensive tests be reserved for patients in whom the psychiatrist and urologist disagree or cannot determine the diagnosis.

The pharmacological erection test is increasingly being used to assess penile vascular supply in erectile dysfunction. Vasodilating chemicals, papaverine alone or with phentolamine, prostaglandin El alone, or a mixture-of all three is injected into one of the cavernous sinuses of the subject's penis. McMahon (1994) considered the development of a rigid well-sustained erection within 10 minutes suggests no major vascular abnormality exists, and, as assessed by Rigiscan, a slow onset indicates the presence of some degree of arterial diseases and rapid detumescence suggests a venous leak. Pescatori, Hatzichristou, Namburi, and Goldstein (1994) concluded that a positive response indicated normal veno-occlusive function but was present in 19% of patients with evidence suggestive of arterial occlusive disease. If the subject does not develop an adequate erection following the injection, he may do so if he views an erotic video.

Lee, Sikka, Randrup, Villemarette, Baum, Hower, and Hellstrom (1993) report routinely showing such a video immediately after injection, considering it negates the anxiety factor inherent in testing. They found 17 of 20 healthy men with a mean age of 49 years obtained a full erection following 10 micrograms of prostaglandin El; the 3 who did not said they found the video somewhat offensive. Lee and colleagues advised that the physician should inquire about this possibility before using a video. Meuleman and associates (1992) emphasized the inhibiting effect of the test setting to account for their finding that even with the addition of manual stimulation in private, only 31 of 44 men (mean age 53 years) with normal erectile potency demonstrated a full erectile response following intracavernous injections of 12.5 milligrams of papaverine, a further 9 developing full erection after they left the test situation. ne subjects did not view an erotic video. In patients who filled to produce a full erectile response with the test, Meuleman and associates recommended prolongation of the observation period with addition of manual and/or visual stimulation. The higher percentage of men developing full erections during the test in the study by Lee and colleagues when visual stimulation was used routinely suggests this procedure is advisable with patients who accept it.

When the pharmacological erection test indicates the presence of vascular pathology, investigations are necessary to determine its nature, generally commencing with color Duplex Doppler ultrasonography to evaluate the cavernous arteries. If the equipment is available, this investigation is commonly carried out as part of the pharmacological erection test. Arterial response is assessed in the phase of highest arterial flow rate in the first five minutes after injection, by peak flow velocity, acceleration time, and dilatation of the cavernous arteries; venous leakage is assessed when arterial inflow and venous outflow are equal (Meuleman et al., 1992). These workers found only acceleration time significantly differentiated 44 men with normal erectile potency and 280 consecutive patients with erectile disorder. When test results are equivocal, venous leakage may be further assessed by infusion of saline into the corpora cavernosa after intracavernous injection of a vasodilating chemical fails to maintain an erection; the leakage can be visualized by injection of a contrast agent and serial radiography (Krysiewicz & Mellinger, 1989). If no impairment in the arterial or venous blood flow within the penis is demonstrated, investigation of the arteries providing this flow may be indicated, particularly if the subject has a history of pelvic trauma. As these tests increasingly require more expensive equipment and considerable experience in interpretation, the investigation of physical causes for erectile dysfunction is being taken over by urologists with an interest in its treatment.

Assessment of neurogenic factors producing erectile dysfunction is indicated if the patient has a history of diabetes, pelvic pathology, or radical prostatectomy or if physical examination reveals the absence of the cremasteric or bulbocavernosal reflex or reduced lower limb reflexes. McMahon (1994) found simple screening with a vibratory biothesiometer useful, but not the more complex procedures developed to investigate impairment of nerve transmission, such as the latency of bulbocavernosal reflex and the latency and form of cerebral potentials evoked by stimulation of the penis and the peroneal nerve. This is consistent with the finding that overall, men with erectile dysfunction who have diabetes or a history of neurological disturbance had significantly longer latency or absence of the first positive peak of penile cerebral-evoked responses than did those with nonneurogenic erectile dysfunction, but the discrimination of individual subjects was poor (Pickard, Powell, & Schofield, 1994). It was suggested that the test could be worthwhile clinically if objective evidence of penile sensory dysfunction was required. Its research use demonstrated that sensory neuropathy has a crucial role, whereas arterial disease is of secondary importance in the etiology of diabetic erectile dysfunction (Bemelmans, Meuleman, Doesburg, Notermans, & Debruyne, 1994).

Physical and laboratory examination of women with sexual dysfunctions are more rarely carried out. Though, as in men, it is necessary to exclude illness, medications, or substances as responsible for reduced sexual interest or ability to reach orgasm, the effects of neurological and vascular disease and of medications and drugs of abuse on the sexuality of women are much more poorly documented. Gynecological investigation is indicated when dyspareunia is present. Vaginal lesions, dermatitis, or infections are likely to be associated with pain on penetration, and inflammation or disease of the pelvic organs are likely to be associated with pain on deep penile thrusting. Hormone studies are rarely indicated in the routine investigation of sexually dysfunctional women, in the absence of indications of hormonal imbalance such as excessive hirsutism. The nature and significance of the influence of hormonal factors on the sexual interest and activity of women remains largely unestablished. Psychological variables, particularly the presence and nature of a relationship with a male partner, appear to be the major determinants, at least in heterosexual women who make up the majority of those studied (McConaghy, 1993). The significant hormonal fluctuations that occur throughout the menstrual cycle have not been demonstrated to be accompanied by consistent fluctuations in sexual behaviors.

Monitoring of serum testosterone levels is of value in evaluating the response of paraphilic men to androgen-reducing chemical therapy. Percentage reduction of the level from pretreatment levels was shown to correlate highly with subjects' reported degree of reduction of paraphilic urges when subjects and interviewer were unaware of the levels (McConaghy, Blaszczynski, & Kidson, 1988). Reduction to 30% of pretreatment level produced sufficient reduction in deviant arousal without impairing erectile responses in acceptable sexual activities.

The various brain mapping techniques developed over recent years have not as yet been extensively applied to the assessment of sexual behaviors. Emory, Williams, Cole, Amparo, and Meyer (1991) reported no difference in cross-sectional area of the corpus callosum of men and women or transsexuals of either sex; genetic males had a larger whole-brain cross-sectional area. Flor-Henry, Lang, Koles, and Frenzel found electroencephalographic differences in pedophiles maximally erotically aroused by children aged 6 to 12 years. A number of studies have reported differences in hypothalamic nuclei in men and women, in homosexual compared to heterosexual subjects, and in male-to-female transsexuals compared to control males (Swaab, Zhou, & Hofman, 1995).

Case Study

Mr. E. D., a 31-year-old man, was referred by a urologist, with a brief note stating that nocturnal penile tumescence done over three days consistently showed normal erections, which strongly suggested a psychogenic cause for his erection problem. When I commenced the assessment by stating this, he responded that although the urologist said the nocturnal penile tumescence test was normal, he did not get a full erection when given an intracavernous injection of prostaglandin. He believed that his problem commenced at age 15, when he put a rod down his penis and the next day developed torsion of the testis, which was surgically corrected. Since then, he believed that he did not get a normal erection, that he could penetrate but the head of the penis was never as large as it had been, and that he lost erection soon after penetration.

In my experience, patients who focus on the details of their erection, particularly if they spontaneously comment on this early in the interview, commonly have marked obsessive or paranoid personality traits that require the interviewer to be prepared to listen to such details and avoid any suggestion of scepticism. When I continued to adopt a listening attitude, conveying my readiness to sympathetically consider his point of view, Mr. E. D. revealed that despite the urologist's conclusion, he believed his problem was physical. He added, "I'm 31. I've paid an enormous price. When I first came out and was in love, I couldn't perform or talk about it. Two doctors will tell you that I had a paranoid episode but I don't think I did."

I interpreted these statements as reflecting his need for me to recognize the severity of his condition and remain concerned and not adopt a labeling approach to him, as previous doctors had done. When I asked why these doctors would say this, Mr. E. D. said that he did not want to talk about it, that he was involved in a political situation, and that people knew he was impotent and passive. This strengthened my impression that there could be paranoid aspects to his personality and I decided I should not confront his views nor explore issues he wished to avoid, at least until I had obtained his trust.

As an opportunity to express concern and at the same time to obtain further information about both his erectile problem and his personality I asked Mr. E. D. if he was currently in a relationship. He said he had not had a steady partner for four years. Their relationship had lasted a year and he believed he sabotaged it because he was the passive partner and he had the impression that his partner wanted him to be active. Since then, he had been active at times in casual relationships, but had not been able to ejaculate. He added, "I feel this is my Achilles heel. I don't make an impact on people, just as I can't penetrate. I'm passive in every sense of the word." This statement further strengthened my assessment that his management would require attention to a personality problem, as much as to erectile dysfunction.

To obtain further information about the severity of the personality disorder in areas that would not be challenging, I inquired about the patient's past history and his current work and social life. He was the only child of parents who divorced when he was age 6, when his father was institutionalized with a diagnosis of schizophrenia; he had not seen him since. Awareness of the increased risk of psychosis and schizotypal personality disorder in the children of schizophrenics further encouraged me to maintain an attitude of nonconfronting support. His relationship with his mother was and remained good. She remarried when he was 9 years old and he said he came to accept his stepfather, though he was never close to him. Otherwise, his childhood and educational experiences appeared to be uneventful and his employment history was one of stability. He currently had occupied an administrative position for five years. He shared a house with a male gay friend for over 12 months, went to the gym three times a week, and met friends at least weekly. These factors indicated that his personality disorder was not sufficiently great to prevent him from organizing significant areas of his life satisfactorily.

Asked about his drug usage, Mr. E. D. said he was self-destructive and had been spending a third of his income on alcohol. He added that to have intercourse with anyone, he had to be "out of it." This allowed me to begin asking about his sexual life. He had dated girls infrequently in adolescence, but had not attempted to initiate sexual activity because he thought he could not got an adequate erection. This fear also caused him not to initiate homosexual activity until six years previously, although he had decided in early adulthood that he was exclusively gay. He regularly had what he termed unsatisfactory sex in "back rooms" on Saturday nights, after binge drinking. Currently, he masturbated a few times a week and had morning erections adequate for penetration about twice a week. Asked about his masturbatory fantasies, he said he was reluctant to talk about them because he was ashamed of them. I attempted to reassure him that many men had very deviant sexual fantasies during masturbation or intercourse that could involve aggression or pedophilia. He then said that mainly he thought about unknown men inflicting bodily pain on him to the point of mutilation, and that in his sexual relationships he used similar fantasies to maintain arousal.

I then felt I could explore his earlier statement about the "political situation" in relation to his past experiences with psychiatrists, by asking about the previous therapy he had received. He had had psychotherapy for two years, which he terminated because of the political situation. In response to questioning, he was then prepared to elaborate on this as meaning he wasn't given the assurance of confidentiality that he required and that he was concerned that the gay community could be given information about his condition.

In preparing to terminate the interview, I then asked him what help he felt he needed. He replied that he needed a penile implant, that he was given no reason as to why he didn't get an erection with intracavernous injection, and that the rigidity of his erection during nocturnal penile tumescence was not 100%. In regard to the need for further physical assessments, he informed me he had had blood tests, including one for HIV. I told him I would discuss his concerns with the urologist, and, if necessary, obtain the record of the nocturnal penile tumescence test and discuss this with him. I pointed out that a penile implant would not produce any glans and that response to the initial intracavenous injection isn't always positive. If the evidence supported a diagnosis of psychogenic erectile disorder, but Mr. E. D. did not respond to psychotherapy, it should be possible to add the effective use of intracavernous injections to this, at least temporarily, in the expectation that he may not need these permanently.

Assessment of Mr. E. D. indicated the presence of paranoid personality traits that would constantly have to be kept in mind both in order to maintain him in therapy and in determining therapeutic options. Establishing a trusting relationship would seem to be the initial priority, which could possibly be aided by some focus on his guilt concerning his sadomasochistic fantasies, whereas early challenge of his conviction that his erectile problem was largely organic and any questioning of its severity would seem contraindicated. His alcohol intake and his commitment to safe sexual activities would also require monitoring.

SUMMARY

The unstructured interview as the major clinical assessment is described in this chapter. The lack of adequacy of operational definitions of the *DSM-IV* diagnostic criteria of sexual disorders is suggested to be the reason for their limited use, along with their failure to include clinically important behaviors. The lack of data concerning the features of research assessments likely to increase the validity of their findings and the value of behavioral inventories are discussed Behavioral observation is rarely employed in assessing sexual activities. Penile plethysmography continues to be used in the assessment and treatment of individual sex offenders despite the evidence that it can distinguish such offenders from normals as groups with reasonable consistency but it cannot distinguish them as individuals. Physiological assessment of vaginal blood volume changes have shown consistent differences between sexually functional and dysfunctional women. The physical and physiological assessment of male erectile dysfunction is reviewed and a case study of assessment of a man with paranoid personality features who complained of erectile dysfunction is reported.

REFERENCES

Abel, G. G., Barlow, D. H., Blanchard, E. B., & Guild, D. (1977). The components of rapists' sexual arousal. *Archives of General Psychiatry, 34*, 895–903.

Abel, G. G., & Rouleau, J. L. (1990). The nature and extent of sexual assault. In W. L. Marshall, D. R. Laws, & H. E. Barbaree (Eds.), *Handbook of sexual assault: Issues, theories, and treatment of the offender* (pp. 9–21). New York: Plenum.

Akpunonu, B. E., Mutgi A. B., Federman, D. J., York, J., & Woldenberg, L. S. (1994). Routine prolactin measurement is not necessary in the initial evaluation of male impotence. *Journal of General Internal Medicine, 9*, 336–338.

Alford, G. S., Wedding, D., & Jones, S. (1983). Faking "turn-ons" and "turn-offs." *Behavior Modification, 7*, 112–125.

Allen, R. P., Smolev, J. K., Engel, R. M., & Brendler, C. B. (1993). Comparison of Rigiscan and formal nocturnal penile tumescence testing. *Journal of Urology, 149*, 1265–1268.

Andersen, B. L., & Broffitt, B. (1988). Is there a reliable and valid self-report measure of sexual behavior? *Archives of Sexual Behavior, 17* 509–525.

AuBuchon, P. G., & Calhoun, K. S. (1985). Menstrual cycle symptomatology: The role of social expectancy and experimental demand characteristics. *Psychosomatic Medicine, 47*, 35–45.

Bancroft J., Jones, H. C., & Pullan, B. P. (1966). A simple transducer for measuring penile erections with comments on its use in the treatment of sexual disorders. *Behaviour Research and Therapy, 4*, 239–241.

Barbaree, H. E., Marshall, W. L., & Lanthier, R. D. (1979). Deviant sexual arousal in rapists. *Behaviour Research and Therapy, 17*, 215–222.

Barlow, D. H., & Agras, W. S. (1973). Fading to increase heterosexual responsiveness in homosexuals. *Journal of Applied Behavior Analysis, 6*, 355–366.

Barr, R. F., & McConaghy, N. (1971). Penile volume responses to appetitive and aversive stimuli in relation to sexual orientation and conditioning performance. *British Journal of Psychiatry, 119*, 377–383.

Bates, J. E., Bentler, P. M., & Thompson, S. K. (1973). Measurement of deviant gender development in boys. *Child Development, 44*, 591–598.

Baxter, D. J., Marshall, W. L., Davidson, P. R., & Malcolm, P. B. (1984). Deviant sexual behavior: Differentiating sex offenders by criminal and personal history, psychometric measures, and sexual response. *Criminal Justice and Behavior, 11*, 477–501.

Becker, J. V., Skinner, L. J., Abel, G. G., & Treacy, E. C. (1982). Incidence and types of sexual dysfunctions in rape and incest victims. *Journal of Sex and Marital Therapy, 8*, 65–74.

Bem, S. L. (1974). The measurement of psychological

androgyny. *Journal of Consulting and Clinical Psychology, 42*, 155–162.

Bemelmans, B. L, Meulernan, E. J., Doesburg, W. H, Notermans, S. L., & Debruyne, F. M. (1994). Erective dysfunction in diabetic men: The neurological factor revisited. *Journal of Urology, 151*, 884–889.

Birk, L., Huddleston, W., Miller, E., & Cohler, B. (1971). Avoidance conditioning for homosexuality. *Archives of General Psychiatry, 25*, 623–630.

Bolling, D. R., & Voeller, B. (1987). AIDS and heterosexual anal intercourse. *Journal of the American Medical Association, 258*, 474.

Buhrich, N., & McConaghy, N. (1977). The clinical syndromes of femmiphilic transvestism. *Archives of Sexual Behavior, 6*, 397–412.

Buvat, J., Lemaire, A., Buvat-Herbaut, M., Fourlinnie, J. C., Racadot, A., & Fossati, P. (1985). Hyperprolactinaernia and sexual function in men. *Hormone Research, 22*, 196–203.

Card, R. D., & Dibble, A. (1995). Predictive value of the Card/Farr-all stimuli in discriminating between gynephilic and pedophilic sexual offenders. *Sexual Abuse: A Journal of Research and Treatment, 7*, 129–14 1.

Carmichael, M. S., Warburton, V. L., Dixon, J., & Davidson, J. M. (1994). Relationships among cardiovascular, muscular, and oxytocin responses during human sexual activity. *Archives of Sexual Behavior, 23*, 59–79.

Catania, L. A., Gibson, D. R., Chitwood, D. D., & Coates, T. J. (1990a). Methodological problems in AIDS behavioral research: influences on measurement error and participation bias in studies of sexual behavior. *Psychological Bulletin, 108*, 339–362.

Catania, J. A., Gibson, D. R., Marin, B., Coates, T. J., & Greenblatt, R. M. (1990b). Response bias in assessing sexual behaviors relevant to HIV transmission. *Evaluation and Program Planning 13*, 19–29.

Chambless, D. L. (1985). Agoraphobia. In M. Hersen & A. S. Bellack (Eds.), *Handbook of clinical behavior therapy with adults* (pp. 49–87). New York: Plenum.

Clark, J. P., & Tifft, L. L. (1966). Polygraph and interview validation of self-reported deviant behavior. *American Sociological Review, 31*, 516–523.

Coates, R. A. Soskolne, C. L., Calzavara, L., Read, S. E., Fanning, M. M., Shepherd, F. A., Klein, M. M., & Johnson, J. K. (1986). The reliability of sexual histories on AID's-related research: Evaluation of an interview-administered questionnaire. *Canadian Journal of Public Health, 77*, 343–348.

Conte, H. R. (1983). Development and use of self-report techniques for assessing sexual functioning: A review and critique. *Archives of Sexual Behavior, 12*, 555–576.

Crepault, C., & Couture, M. (1980). Mens erotic fantasies. *Archives of Sexual Behavior, 9*, 565–581.

Croyle, R. T., & Loftus, E. F. (1993). Recollection in the kingdom of AIDS. In D. G. Ostrow & R. C. Kessler (Eds.), *Methodological issues in AIDS behavioral research* (pp. 163–180). New York: Plenum.

Davis, C. M., Yarber, W. L., & Davis, S. L. (1988). *Sexuality-related measures: A compendium*. Lake Mills, IA: Graphic Publishing.

Davis, G. E., & Leitenberg, H. (1987). Adolescent sex offenders. *Psychological Bulletin, 101*, 417–427.

DeAmicis, L. A., Goldberg, D. C., LoPiccolo, J., Friedman, J., & Davies, L. (1984). Three-year follow-up of couples evaluated for sexual dysfunction. *Journal of Sex and Marital Therapy, 10*, 215–228.

Ehrhardt, A. A., & Baker, S. W. (1974). Fetal androgens, human central nervous system differentiation, and behavior sex differences. In R. C. Friedman & R. M. Richart (Eds.), *Sex differences in behavior* (pp. 33–5 1). New York: Wiley.

Emory, L. E., Williams, D. H., Cole, C. M., Amparo, E. G., & Meyer, W. J. (1991). Anatomic variation of the corpus callosurm in persons with gender dysphoria. *Archives of Sexual Behavior, 20*, 409–417.

Fedora, O., Reddon, J. R., Morrison, J. W., Fedora, S. K., Pascoe, H., & Yeudall, L. T. (1992). Sadism and other paraphilias in normal controls and aggressive and nonaggressive sex offenders. *Archives of Sexual Behavior, 21*, 1–15.

Feldman, M. P., & MacCulloch, M. J. (1971). *Homosexual behavior: Therapy and assessment*. Oxford: Pergamon.

Finklehor, D., & Lewis, I. A. (1988). An epidemiologic approach to the study of child molestation. *Annals of the New York Academy of Sciences, 528*, 64–78.

Flor-Henry, P., Lang, R. A., Koles, Z. J., & Frenzel, R. R. (1991). Quantitive EEG studies of pedophilia. *International Journal of Psychophysiology, 10*, 253–258.

Frank, E., Anderson, B., & Rubinstein, D. (1978). Frequency of sexual dysfunction in "normal" couples. *New England Journal of Medicine, 229, 111–115*.

Freund, K. (1963). A laboratory method of diagnosing predominance of homo- or hetero-erotic interest in the male. *Behaviour Research and Therapy, 12*, 355–359.

Freund, K. (1971). A note on the use of the phallometric method of measuring mild sexual arousal in the male. *Behavior Therapy, 2*, 223–228.

Freund, K., & Watson, R. J. (1991). Assessment of the sensitivity and specificity of a phallometric test: an update of phallometric diagnosis of pedophilia. *Physiological Assessment: A Journal of Consulting and Clinical Psychology, 3*, 254–260.

Gewertz, B. L., & Zarins, C. K. (1985). Vasculogenic impotence. In R. T. Segraves & H. W. Schoenberg (Eds.), *Diagnosis and treatment of erectile disturbances* (pp. 105–413). New York: Plenum.

Grenier, G., & Byers, E. S. (1997). The relationship among ejaculatory control, ejaculatory latency, and attempts to prolong heterosexual intercourse: Trying to make a good thing better. *Archives of Sexual Behavior, 26*, 27–47.

Hariton, E. B., & Singer, J. L. (1974). Women's fantasies during sexual intercourse. *Journal of Consulting and Clinical Psychology, 42*, 313–322.

Hatch, J. P. (1981). Psychophysiological aspects of sexual dysfunction. *Archives of Sexual Behavior, 10*, 49–64.

Hersen, M., & Bellack, A. S. (1988). *Dictionary of behavioral assessment techniques*. New York: Pergamon.

Hillbrand, M., & Waite, B. M. (1994). The everyday experience of an institutionalized sex offender: An idiographic application of the experience sampling method. *Archives of Sexual Behavior, 23*, 453–463.

Jacobson, N. S., Follette, W. C., & Revenstorf, D. (1984). Psychotherapy outcome research: Methods for reporting variability and evaluating clinical significance. *Behavior Therapy, 15*, 336–352.

Jacobson, N. S., Follette, W. C., Revenstorf, D., Baucom, D. H., Hahlweg, K., & Margolin, G. (1984). Variability in outcome and clinical significance of behavioral marital therapy: A reanalysis of outcome data. *Journal of Consulting and Clinical Psychology, 53,* 497–504.

Jones, T. M. (1985). Hormonal considerations in the evaluation and treatment of erectile disorder. In R. T. Segraves & H. W. Schoenberg (Eds.), *Diagnosis and treatment of erectile disturbances* (pp. 115–158). New York: Plenum.

Kagan, J., & Moss, H. A. (1962) *Birth to maturity*. New York: Wiley & Sons.

Karacan, L (1978). Advances in the psychophysiological evaluation of male erectile impotence. in J. LoPiccolo & L. LoPiccolo (Eds.), *Handbook of sex therapy* (pp. 137–145). New York: Plenum.

Katchadourian, H. A., Lunde, D. T., & Trotter, R. (1979). *Human sexuality*. New York: Holt, Rinehart and Winston.

Kelly, L. (1990). Journeying in reverse: Possibilities and problems in feminist research on sexual violence. In L. Gelthorpe & A. Morris (Eds.), *Feminist perspective in criminology* (pp. 107–114). Bristol, PA: Open University Press.

Knight, R. A., & Prentky, R. A. (1990). Classifying sexual offenders. In W. L. Marshall, D. R. Laws, & H. E. Barbaree (Eds.), *Handbook of sexual assault* (pp. 23–52). New York: Plenum.

Knight, R. A., & Prentky, R. A. (1993). Exploring characteristics for classifying juvenile sex offenders. In H. E. Barbaree, W. L. Marshall, & S. M. Hudson (Eds.), *The juvenile sex offender* (pp. 45–83). New York: Guilford.

Korenman, S. G., Morley, J. E., Mooradian, A. D., Davis, S. S., Kaiser, F. E., Silver, A. J., Viosca, S. P., & Garza, D. (1990). Secondary hypogonadism in older men: Its relation to impotence. *Journal of Clinical Endocrinology and Metabolism, 71*, 963–968.

Krysiewicz, S., & Mellinger, B. C. (1989). The role of imaging in the diagnostic evaluation of impotence. *American Journal of Roentgenology, 153*, 1133–1139.

Kwan, M., VanMaasdam, J., & Davidson, J. M. (1985). Effects of estrogen treatment on sexual behavior in male-to-female transsexuals: experimental and clinical observations. *Archives of Sexual Behaviors, 14*, 29–40.

Lalumiere, M. L., & Quinsey, V. L. (1994). The discriminability of rapists from non-sex offenders using, phallometric measures A meta-analysis. *Criminal Justice and Behavior, 21*, 150–175.

Laumann, E. O., Gagnon, J. H., Michael, R. T., & Michaels, S. (1994). *The social organization of Sexuality*. Chicago: University of Chicago Press.

Laws, D. R., & Marshall, W. L. (1991). Masturbatory reconditioning with sexual deviates: An evaluative review. *Advances in Behavior Research and Therapy, 13*, 13–25.

Laws, D. R., & Rubin, H. H. (1969). Instructional control of an autonomic sexual response. *Journal of Applied Behavior Analysis, 2,* 93–99.

Lee, B., Sikka, S. C., Randrup, E. R., Villemarette, P., Baum, N., Hower, J. F., & Hellstrom, W. J. (1993). Standardization of penile blood flow parameters in normal men using intracavernous prostaglandin E1 and visual sexual stimulation. *Journal of Urology, 149*, 49–52.

Lehmann, K., Schopke, W., Brutsch, H. P., & Hauri, D. (1994). Which hormone determinations are necessary in the initial assessment of erectile dysfunction? *Schweizerische Rundschan fur Medizin Prazis, 83*, 1030–1033.

Lewontin, R. C. (1995). Sex, lies, and social science. *The New York Review*, April 20, 24–29.

LoPiccolo, J. (1982). Book review. *Archives of Sexual Behavior, 11*, 277–279.

LoPiccolo, J. (1990). Sexual dysfunction. In A. S. Bellack, M. Hersen, & A. E. Kazdin (Eds.), *International handbook of behavior therapy and modification* (2nd ed.) (pp. 547–564). New York: Plenum.

LoPiccolo, J., & Steger, J. C. (1974). The sexual interaction inventory: A new instrument for assessment of sexual dysfunction. *Archives of Sexual Behavior, 3*, 585–595.

Malamuth, N. M. (1989). The attraction to sexual aggression scale: Part two. *Journal of Sex Research, 26*, 324–354.

Maletzky, B. M. (1980). Assisted covert sensitization. In D. J. Cox & R. J. Daitzman (Eds.), *Exhibitionism: Description, assessment, and treatment* (pp. 289–293). New York: Garland STPM Press.

Marshall, W. L., & Barbaree, H. E. (1988). The long-term evaluation of a behavioral treatment program for child molesters. *Behaviour Research and Therapy, 26*, 499–511.

Marshall, W. L., & Barbaree, H. E. (1990). Outcome of comprehensive cognitive-behavioral treatment programs. In W. L. Marshall, D. R. Laws, & H. E. Barbaree (Eds.), *Handbook of sexual assault* (pp. 363–385). New York: Plenum.

Marshall, W. L., & Eccles, A. (1991). Issues in clinical practice with sex offenders. *Journal of Interpersonal Violence, 6*, 68–93.

Masters, W. H., & Johnson, V. E. (1966). *Human sexual response*. Boston: Little, Brown.

Mavissakalian, M., Blanchard, E. B., Abel, G. G., & Barlow, D. H. (1975). Responses to complex erotic stimuli in homosexual and heterosexual males. *British Journal of Psychiatry, 126*, 252–257.

McCombie, S. L., & Arons, J. H. (1980). Counselling rape victims. In S. L. McCombie (Ed.), *The rape crisis intervention handbook* (pp. 145–171). New York: Plenum.

McConaghy, N. (1967). Penile volume change to moving picture of male and female nudes in heterosexual and homosexual males. *Behavior Research and Therapy, 5*, 43–48.

McConaghy, N. (1978). Heterosexual experience, marital status and orientation of homosexual males. *Archives of Sexual Behavior, 7*, 575–581.

McConaghy, N. (1985). Psychosexual dysfunction. In M. Hersen & A. S. Bellack (Eds.), *Handbook of clinical behavior therapy with adults* (pp. 659–692). New York: Plenum.

McConaghy, N. (1987). Heterosexuality/homosexuality: Dichotomy or continuum. *Archives of Sexual Behavior, 16*, 413–426.

McConaghy, N. (1990). Can reliance be placed on a single meta-analysis? *Australian and New Zealand Journal of Psychiatry, 24*, 405–415.

McConaghy, N. (1993). *Sexual behavior: Problems and management*. New York: Plenum.

McConaghy, N. (in press). Sexual and gender identity disorders. In S. Turner & M. Hersen (Eds.), *Adult Psychopathology and Diagnosis* (3rd ed.). New York: Plenum Press.

McConaghy, N., & Armstrong, M. S. (1983). Sexual orientation and consistency of sexual identity. *Archives of Sexual Behavior, 12*, 317–327.

McConaghy, N., Armstrong, M. S., & Blaszczynski, A. (1985). Expectancy, covert sensitization and imaginal desensitization in compulsive sexuality. *Acta Psychiatrica Scandinavica, 72*, 176–187.

McConaghy, N., & Blaszczynski, A. (1991). Initial stages of validation by penile volume assessment that sexual orientation is distributed dimensionally. *Comprehensive Psychiatry, 32*, 52–58.

McConaghy, N., Blaszczynski, A., & Kidson, W. (1988). Treatment of sex offenders with imaginal desensitization and/or medroxyprogesterone. *Acta Psychiatrica Scandinavica, 77*, 199–206.

McConaghy, N., Buhrich, N., & Silove, D. (1994). Opposite sex-linked behaviors and homosexual feelings in the predominantly heterosexual male majority. *Archives of Sexual Behavior, 23*, 565–577.

McConaghy, N., & Silove, D. (1991). Opposite sex behaviors correlate with degree of homosexual feelings in the predominantly heterosexual. *Australian and New Zealand Journal of Psychiatry, 25*, 77–83.

McConaghy, N., & Zamir, R. (1995a). Sissiness, tomboyism, sex role, identity and orientation. *Australian and New Zealand Journal of Psychiatry, 29*, 278–283.

McConaghy, N., & Zamir, R. (1995b). Heterosexual and homosexual coercion, sexual orientation and sexual roles in medical students. *Archives of Sexual Behavior, 24*, 489–502.

McConaghy, N., Zamir, R., & Manicavasagar, V. (1993). Non-sexist sexual experiences survey and scale of attraction to sexual aggression. *Australian and New Zealand Journal of Psychiatry, 27*, 686–693.

McGrady, R. E. (1973). A forward-fading technique for increasing heterosexual responsiveness in male homosexuals. *Journal of Behavior Therapy and Experimental Psychiatry, 4*, 257–261.

McMahon, C. G. (1994). Management of impotence part ii: Diagnosis. *General Practitioner. CME Files, 2*, 83–85.

Meisler, A. W., & Carey, M. P. (1990). A critical reevaluation of nocturnal penile tumescence monitoring in the diagnosis of erectile disorder. *Journal of Nervous and Mental Disease, 178*, 78–89.

Metz, P., & Bengtsson, J. (1981). Penile blood pressure. *Scandinavian Journal of Urology and Nephrology, 15*, 161–164.

Meuleman, E. J. H., Bemelmans, B. L. H., Doesburg, W. H., van Asten, W. N. J. C., Skotnicki, S. H., & Debruyne F. M. J. (1992). Penile pharmacological duplex ultrasonography: A dose-effect study comparing papaverine, papaverine/phentolamine and prostaglandin El. *Journal of Urology, 148*, 63–66.

Morganstern, K. P. (1988). Behavioral interviewing. In M. Hersen & A. S. Bellack (Eds.), Behavioral assessment: a practical handbook (3rd. ed.) (pp. 86–118). New York: Pergamon.

Murphy, W. D., Krisar, J., Stalgaitis, S., & Anderson, K. (1984). The use of penile tumescence measures with incarcerated rapists: Further validity issues. *Archives of Sexual Behavior, 13*, 545–554.

Nagayama Hall, G. C., Proctor, W. C., & Nelson, G. M. (1988). Validity of physiological measures of pedophilic sexual arousal in a sexual offender population. *Journal of Consulting and clinical Psychology, 56*, 118–122.

Nofzinger, E. A., Thase, M. E., Reynolds, C. F., Frank, E., Jennings, J. R., Garamoni, G. L., Fasiczka, A. L., & Kupfer, D. J. (1993). Sexual function in depressed men— assessment by self-report, behavioral, and nocturnal penile tumescence measures before and after treatment with cognitive behavior therapy. *Archives of General Psychiatry, 50*, 24–30.

Ostrow, D. G., Kessler, R. C., Stover, E., & Pequegnat, W. (1993). Introduction: Design, measurement, and analysis issues in AIDS mental health. In D. G. Ostrow & R. C. Kessler (Eds.), *Methodological Issues in AIDS behavioral research* (pp. 1–16). New York: Plenum.

Palace, E. M. (1995). Modification of dysfunctional patterns of sexual response through autonomic arousal and false physiological feedback. *Journal of Consulting and Clinical Psychology, 63*, 604–615.

Palace, E. M., & Gorzalka, B. B. (1990). The enhancing effects of anxiety on arousal in sexually dysfunctional and functional women. *Journal of Abnormal Psychology, 99*, 403–411.

Palace, E. M., & Gorzalka, B. B. (1992). Differential patterns of arousal in sexually functional and dysfunctional women: Physiological and subjective components of sexual response. *Archives of Sexual Behavior, 21*, 135–159.

Paredes, A., Baumgold, J., Pugh, L. A., & Ragland, R. (1966). Clinical judgment in the assessment of psychopharmcological effects. *Journal of Nervous and Mental Disease, 142*, 153–160.

Person, E. S., Terestman, N., Myers, W. A., Goldberg, E. L., & Salvadori, C. (1989). Gender differences in sexual behaviors and fantasies in a college population. *Journal of Sex and Marital Therapy, 15*, 187–198.

Pescatori, E. S., Hatzichristou, D. G., Namburi, S., & Goldstein, I. (1994). Does a positive injection test always mean normal penile function? *Journal of Urology, 151*, 1209–1216.

Phillips, G., & Over, R. (1995). Differences between heterosexual, bisexual, and lesbian women in recalled childhood experiences. *Archives of Sexual Behavior, 24*, 1–20.

Pickard, R. S., Powell, P. H., & Schofield, I. S. (1994). Dorsal nerve conduction studies in investigation of impotence. *British Journal of Urology, 74*, 231–235.

Proulx, J., Cote, G., & Achille, P. A. (1993). Prevention of voluntary control of penile response in homosexual pedophiles during phallometric testing. *Journal of Sex Research, 30*, 140–147.

Proust, M. (1981). *Remembrance of things past* (Vol. 3). Tr. C. K. Scott Moncrieff, T. Kilmartin, A. Mayor. New York. Random House.

Quinsey, V. L., & Earls, C. M. (1990). The modification of sexual preferences. In W. L. Marshall, D. R. Laws & H. E. Barbaree (Eds.), *Handbook of sexual assault* (pp. 279–295). New York: Plenum.

Quinsey, V. L., Steinman, C. M., Bergersen, S. G., & Holmes, J. (1975). Penile circumference, skin conductance and ranking responses of child molesters and 'normals' to sexual and non-sexual visual stimuli. *Behavior Therapy, 6*, 213–219.

Reading, A. E. (1983). A comparison of the accuracy and reactivity of methods of monitoring male sexual behavior. *Journal of Behavioral Assessment, 5*, 11–23.

Rekers, G. A., & Lovaas, O. I. (1974). Behavioral treatment of deviant sex-role behavior in a male child. *Journal of Applied Behavior Analysis, 7*, 173–190.

Rice, M. E., Quinsey, V. L., & Harris, G. T. (1991). Sexual recidivism among child molesters released from a maximum security psychiatric institution. *Journal of Consulting and Clinic Psychology, 59*, 381–386.

Rosen, R. C., & Beck, J. G. (1988). *Patterns of sexual arousal*. New York: Guilford.

Sakheirn, D. K., Barlow, D. H., Beck, J. G., & Abrahamson, D. J. (1985). A comparison of male heterosexual and male homosexual patterns of sexual arousal. *Journal of Sex Research, 21*, 183–198.

Saltzman, S. P., Stoddard, A. M., McCusker, J., Moon, M. W., & Mayer, K. H. (1987). Reliability self-reported sexual behavior risk factors for HIV infection in homosexual men. *Public Health Reports, 102*, 692–697.

Saypol, D. C., Peterson, G. A., Howards, S. S., & Yazel, U. (1983). Impotence: Are the newer diagnostic methods a necessity. *Journal of Urology, 130*, 260–262.

Schatzberg, A. F., Westfall, M. P., Blumetti, A. B., & Birk, C. L. (1975). Effeminacy 1: A quantitative rating scale. *Archives of Sexual Behavior, 4*, 31–41.

Schiavi, R. C. (1992). Laboratory methods for evaluating erectile disorder. In R. C Rosen & S. R. Leiblum (Eds.), *Erectile disorders assessment and treatment* (pp. 141–170). New York: Guilford.

Schiavi, R. C., Fisher, C., White, D., Beers, P., & Szechter, R. (1984). Pituitary-gonadal function during sleep in men with erectile impotence and normal controls. *Psychosomatic Medicine, 46*, 239–254.

Schneider, B. E. (1991). Put up and shut up: Workplace sexual assaults. *Gender and Society, 5*, 533–548.

Seidman, S. N. & Reider, R. O. (1994). A review of sexual behavior in the United States. *American Journal of Pstchiatry, 151*, 330–341.

Siegel, K., Krauss, B., & Karus, D. (1994). Reporting recent sexual practices: Gay men's disclosure of HIV risk by questionnaire and interview. *Archives of Sexual Behavior, 23*, 217–234.

Slag, M. F., Morley, J. E., Elson, M. K., Trence, D. L., Nelson, C. J., Nelson, A. E., Kinlaw, W. B., Beyer, H. S., Nuttall, F. Q., & Shafer, R. B. (1983). Impotence in medical clinic outpatients. *Journal of the American Medical Association, 249*, 1736–1740.

Snyder, D. K., & Berg, P. (1983). Determinants of sexual dissatisfaction in sexually distressed couples. *Archives of Sexual Behavior, 12*, 237–246.

Solstad, K., & Hertoft, P. (1993). Frequency of sexual problems and sexual dysfunction in middle-aged Danish men. *Archives of Sexual Behavior, 22*, 51–58.

Stevenson, H. C., De Moya, D., & Boruch, F. R. (1993). Ethical issues and approaches in AIDS research. In D. G. Ostrow & R. C. Kessler (Eds.), *Methodological issues in AIDS behavioral research* (pp. 19–51). New York: Plenum.

Swaab, D. F., Zhou, J. N., & Hofman, M. A. (1995). *Sexual differentiation of the human hypothalamus*. Presented at the International Behavioral Development Symposium May 25–27, Minot State University, ND.

Templeman, T. L., & Stinnett, R. D. (1991). Patterns of sexual arousal and history in a "normal" sample of young men. *Archives of Sexual Behavior, 20*, 137–150.

Thase, M. E., Reynolds, C. F. III, & Jennings, J. R. (1988). Nocturnal penile tumescence is diminished in depressed men. *Biological Psychiatry, 24*, 33–46.

Tollison, C. D., Adams, H. E., & Tollison, J. W. (1979). Cognitive and physiological indices of sexual arousal in homosexual, bisexual, and heterosexual males. *Journal of Behavioral Assessment, 1*, 305–314.

Voeller, B. (1991). AIDS and heterosexual anal intercourse. *Archives of Sexual Behavior, 20*, 233–276.

Walling, M., Andersen, B. L., & Johnson, S. R. (1990). Hormonal replacement therapy for postmenopausal women: A review of sexual outcomes and related gynecologic effects. *Archives of Sexual Behavior, 19*, 119–137.

Wasserman, M. D., Pollak, C. P., Spielman, A. J., & Weitzman, E. J. (1980). Theoretical and technical problems in the measurement of nocturnal penile tumescence for the differential diagnosis of impotence. *Psychosomatic Medicine, 43*, 575–585.

Wiederman, M. W., Weis, D. L., & Allgeier, E. R. (1994). The effect of question preface on response rates to a telephone survey of sexual experience. *Archives of Sexual Behavior, 23*, 203–215.

Wincze, J. P., Bansal, S., & Malamud, M. (1986). Effects of medroxyprogesterone acetate on subjective arousal, arousal to erotic stimulation, and nocturnal penile tumescence in male sex offenders. *Archives of Sexual Behavior, 15*, 293–305.

Wincze, J. P., & Carey, M. P. (1991) *Sexual dysfunction*. New York: Guilford.

Wincze J. P., & Qualls, C. B. (1984). A comparison of structural patterns of sexual arousal in male and female homosexuals. *Archives of Sexual Behavior, 13*, 361–370.

Winton, R. (1998). Psychophysiological signs of faking in the phallometria test. *Sexual Abuse: A Journal of Research and Treatment* (in press).

Zuckerman, M. (1971). Physiological measures of sexual arousal in the human. *Psychological Bulletin, 75*, 297–329.

CHAPTER 16

ASSESSMENT OF CHILD BEHAVIOR PROBLEMS
INTERNALIZING DISORDERS

Wendy K. Silverman
Lourdes T. Serafini
Florida International University

The classification of child behavior problems has received its share of criticism, particularly with respect to its utility. Historically, classification in clinical settings has been done mostly for administrative reasons rather than for therapeutic purposes (Ross, 1980). In addition, it was argued that *children* were being classified rather than behaviors. Categorizing and labeling children were viewed as harmful and stigmatizing (Hobbs, 1975). The categories in classification schemes were also criticized as lacking utility because they were viewed as theoretical abstractions that showed little similarity to the behavior problems that children actually displayed (Hobbs, 1975; Ross, 1980).

Although many of these criticisms about the utility of classification of child behavior problems have merit, classification has a type of utility of communication that makes it useful to practitioners and clinical researchers. More specifically, in

practice and research it is essential to have a common language to be able to communicate effectively about child problems.

Because of the recognition of the need for a common language, efforts increased through the years to develop classification schemes that would better reflect the clinical reality of childhood emotional and behavioral problems and that would also better meet consensual scientific standards with respect to reliability and validity (e.g., Achenbach & Edelbrock, 1983; APA, 1980, 1987, 1994). Perhaps the two approaches to classification that have had the most impact on the mental health field are categorical approaches and dimensional approaches. *Categorical approaches* are typified by the *Diagnostic and Statistical Manual of Mental Disorders (DSM-IV*; APA, 1994) and the *International Classification of Diagnoses (ICD-10*; World Health Organization, 1992). *Dimensional approaches* are typified by the Child Behavior Checklist (CBCL; Achenbach & Edelbrock, 1983) and the Revised Behavior Problem Checklist (RBPC; Quay & Peterson, 1983), among others.

Preparation of this chapter was supported by Grants 44781 and 49680 from the National Institute of Mental Health.

A categorical approach to classification assumes that the diagnostic entities are qualitative and discrete, with distinct boundaries between them (Moras & Barlow, 1992; Silverman, 1992). This is a "yes/no" or "either/or" approach (Achenbach, 1980). A dimensional approach assumes that the entities are quantitative, continuous, and linear (Moras & Barlow, 1992). Each dimension is assumed to be relatively independent and to consist of a cluster of behaviors that tend to covary with one another, but not with behaviors from other dimensions. In this sense, a *syndrome* refers to a group of behaviors found to be statistically associated with one another. Therefore, a child is characterized in terms of his or her position along each possible behavioral dimension as compared to children in the normal population (Wells, 1981).

Seminal reviews on dimensional classification by Achenbach and Edelbrock (1978) and Quay (1979) showed that despite the diversity across factor- and cluster-analytic studies (with respect to assessment instruments, type of population, and type of respondent) two broad-band behavioral dimensions were reliably obtained across studies: externalizing and internalizing. *Externalizing* refers to a behavioral tendency toward acting out, aggression, and coercive behavior. *Internalizing* refers to behaviors such as anxiety, inhibition, shyness, immaturity, sadness, and social withdrawal. In categorical classification approaches, internalizing behavior problems are equated with anxiety and mood disorders.

In this chapter, the concepts and methods involved in the behavioral assessment of internalizing behavior problems of children are discussed. The focus is particularly on anxiety and mood (depression) problems, as these are the problems that have received the most attention by researchers and clinicians. The general approach to assessing anxiety and mood problems involves the use of multiple informants (child, parent, teacher) and multiple methods. The methods include interviews, behavior problem checklists, self-rating scales, observational procedures, self-monitoring procedures, and psychophysiological measurement. In the subsequent sections, evaluative descriptions of these methods are presented, with emphasis on the specific functions or goals of these methods (e.g.,

screening, diagnosis). The utility of these methods in research and clinic settings, respectively, is also noted. The chapter concludes with a case study that illustrates the major concepts and methods discussed.

ASSESSMENT METHODS

Interviews

The clinical interview provides for the most comprehensive assessment of a child's emotional and behavioral functioning relative to any other clinical method. Interviews are typically characterized as either unstructured (or nonstandardized) and structured (or standardized) (Richardson, Dohrenwend, & Klein, 1965). The nonstandardized interview makes no attempt to obtain the same information from respondents, and the unit of analysis is not necessarily individual (Richardson et al., 1965). Because of the problem of *criterion variance*, defined as the formal inclusion and exclusion criteria used to summarize patient data into psychiatric diagnoses (Spitzer, Endicott, & Robins, 1978), structured interviews were developed to help reduce interrater variability in diagnosis. As Richardson and colleagues (1965) explain:

> Because the standardized interview is designed to collect the same information from each respondent, the answers of all respondents must be comparable and classifiable—that is, they must deal with precisely the same subject matter—and differences or similarities between the responses must reflect actual differences or similarities between respondents and not differences due to questions they were asked or to the meanings that they attributed to the questions. (pp. 34–35).

In light of this, the structured interview schedule is the best method of assessment to use for accomplishing the goal of diagnosis.

In addition to diagnosis, structured interviews are useful for accomplishing the goal of identifying and quantifying symptoms and behaviors that coincide with *DSM* criteria. This goal can be accomplished by using particular sections of an interview schedule as a series of mini-modules. For example, for a researcher or clinician with an interest in a specific type of internalizing problem (i.e., a specific diagnosis), the interview questions that cover those problems may be asked of a child or parent and a "symptom summary score" derived (see Silverman & Eisen, 1992).

The first structured interview schedules to appear were for use with adults (e.g., the Schedule for Affective Disorders and Schizophrenia; Endicott & Spitzer, 1978, and the Diagnostic Interview Schedule; Robins, Helzer, Croughan, & Ratcliff, 1981), with similar schedules later developed for use with children. There are several child interview schedules currently available. These include the Schedule for Affective Disorders and Schizophrenia in School-Age Children (K-SADS; Puig-Antich & Chambers, 1978), the Diagnostic Interview for Children and Adolescents (DICA; Herjanic & Reich, 1982), the Interview Schedule for Children (ISC; Kovacs, 1982), the Child Assessment Schedule (CAS; Hodges, McKnew, Cytryn, Stern, & Kline, 1982), the Diagnostic Interview Schedule for Children (DISC; Costello, Edelbrock, Dulcan, Kalas, & Klaric, 1984), the Anxiety Disorders Interview Schedule for Children (ADIS-C; Silverman & Nelles, 1988), and the Child and Adolescent Psychiatric Assessment (CAPA-C; Angold & Costello, 1995). Of these interview schedules, the DISC and DICA are the most highly structured. The ISC and CAS are lowest in structure; the K-SADS, ADIS-C, and CAPA are intermediate in structure.

All of the interview schedules have accompanying parent versions, and most have undergone revision or modification to improve their diagnostic reliability. Work is currently ongoing on most of them to render compatibility with *DSM-IV*. The interviews are all appropriate for use with children across a wide age range (as young as 6 to 8 years of age and as old as 16 to 18 years of age). The interviews generally do not require the children to have extensive verbal expressive skills, and the interview questions tend to be geared toward the language capabilities of young children (La Greca & Stone, 1992).

Two of the structured interview schedules were specifically designed for the assessment of childhood internalizing problems: the K-SADS, for the mood disorders, and the ADIS-C, for the anxiety disorders. The questions contained on these schedules emphasize internalizing problems

more than the other schedules. Reliability of both schedules has been tested extensively. For example, for the ADIS-C/P, interrater reliability (Silverman & Nelles, 1988) and test-retest reliability of diagnoses, symptom summary scores (Silverman & Eisen, 1992), as well as the specific symptoms that comprise each diagnostic subcategory (Silverman & Rabian, 1995), have been studied and have been found to be satisfactory. Silverman and Eisen (1992) also studied how test-retest reliability varies by age for both child and parent informants, respectively. Reliability of the ADIS-C and ADIS-P has also been studied and found to be satisfactory in clinical research sites in other countries (e.g., Australia—Rapee, Barrett, Dadds, & Evans, 1994).

Although using a child-structured interview schedule, such as the ADIS-C/P, yields more reliable diagnoses than using an unstructured interview, clinician error or disagreement has not been totally eliminated. Specifically, reliability varies in terms of the specific diagnostic categories, as well as across such factors as the type of subjects (e.g., inpatient versus outpatient) and the type of interviewers (e.g., lay interviewers versus experienced clinicians) (see Silverman, 1991, 1994 for reviews). There is also some indication that the diagnosis of internalizing disorders in younger children may be more reliable than in older children and that child reports may be more reliable than parent reports (e.g., Lavigne et al., 1994; Silverman & Eisen, 1992; Silverman & Rabian, 1995). Not all studies support this conclusion, however (Silverman & Eisen, 1992). The recent study by Lavigne and associates (1994) further indicates the importance of base rate fluctuations in considering diagnostic reliability, thereby suggesting that future studies would benefit from designs that control base rates across developmental groupings or from using statistics that allow for an assessment of the impact of base rate variations (e.g., Yule's Y versus Cohen's kappa) (see Daleiden, Vasey, & Brown, in press, for further discussion.)

The issue of child/parent agreement is also important to consider in a discussion of interviewing procedures. In general, research findings suggest that the agreement between child and parent reports of internalizing problems increase as children get older. For example, in a cross-sectional analysis of clinic-referred 6- to 18-year-old youths (Edelbrock, Costello, Dulcan, Conover, & Kalas, 1986), it was found that child/parent agreement increased with age, especially between the 6- to 9-year-old and 10- to 13-year-old ages groups, with smaller increases for 14- to 18-year-olds. However, not all studies have found this type of age effect (e.g., Angold et al., 1987).

Finally, there is the issue of validity. Work in this area is sparse, perhaps because of uncertainty about the "gold standard" or the final criterion of validity that will stand as the basis for all comparison (Young et al., 1987). In some studies, for example, the criterion is the ability to discriminate between vastly different groups, such as psychiatrically referred and nonreferred samples. In other studies, a particular measure is taken as the best yardstick for testing the validity of the interview's diagnoses. Because there is no agreement on the single-best estimate diagnosis procedure for children, the yardstick is likely to involve one or several of the following clinician interview; parent, child, peer, or teacher ratings; and physical/neurological evaluations (Young et al., 1987).

Due to the elusive gold standard, studies that have selected a particular final criterion of validity have produced mixed results. Clinicians' diagnoses from unstructured interviews do not appear to relate well to structured interview diagnoses; scores on behavior rating scales and child self-rating scales relate better (see Silverman, 1994). However, the studies that have been conducted are limited in number, sample size, and scope. Studies using large, heterogenous samples of children with internalizing behavior problems that have compared assessments based on structured interviews with data obtained via multiple assessment procedures have not been conducted. There also has been little validation of interview-based diagnoses with respect to the etiology, course, prognosis, or treatment responsiveness of these disorders (Edelbrock & Costello, 1984).

Despite these concerns about validation, diagnostic interview schedules remain the best method to use for attaining the goal of diagnosis. Although in our view they are well suited for use in clinic settings (e.g., as templates that guide one's question-

ing), their use predominates in research rather than in clinic settings. Most of the interview schedules allow respondents to qualify or to elaborate on their responses; others provide alternative questions that can be asked on the basis of respondents' prior responses; and still others provide skip rules that can be followed so that not all questions need to be asked if it is clear that those questions are irrelevant. Research findings further show that children and their parents do not perceive the experience of a structured interviewing procedure as a negative or harmful one (Herjanic, Hudson, & Kotloff, 1976; Lewis, Gorsky, Cohen, & Hartmark, 1985).

Behavior Problem Checklists

Whereas child interview schedules were developed to primarily assist in diagnosis using categorical classification schemes (e.g., DSM, ICD), behavior problem checklists were developed primarily to assist in identifying and quantifying child problem behaviors using dimensional classification schemes. Thus, if identifying and quantifying child problem behaviors via a dimensional approach is one's primary goal, a behavior problem checklist is the best assessment method to use.

Several behavior problem checklists in which parents are asked to rate their child's behaviors have been developed and extensively studied. These include the Child Behavior Checklist (CBCL; Achenbach & Edelbrock, 1983), the Revised Behavior Problem Checklist (RBPC; Quay & Peterson, 1983), the Connors Parent Rating Scale (CPRS-R; Goyette, Conners, & Ulrich, 1978), and the Eyberg Child Behavior Inventory (ECBI; Eyberg, 1980). Some of these checklists have parallel forms in which teachers or the youths themselves serve as the raters, such as Achenbach's Teacher Report Form and the Youth Self-Report Form (Achenbach, 1991a, 1991b).

As noted earlier, in using behavior problem checklists, a child is characterized in terms of his or her position along each possible behavioral dimension as compared to children in the normal population. With respect to child internalizing behavior problems, using the measures developed by Achenbach, for example, a child aged 2 to 3 years may be characterized in terms of his or her position along social withdrawal and depressed (i.e., these are the "narrow-band factors" for this age group); a child aged 4 to 18 years may be characterized in terms of his or her position along withdrawn, somatic complaints, and anxious/depressed (i.e., these are the "narrow-band factors" for this age group). Examples of the types of specific behaviors that comprise these narrow-band factors include feeling worried, nervous, self-conscious or easily embarrassed, and too fearful or anxious.

Overall, behavior problem checklists have sound psychometric properties. With respect to reliability, mean retest reliabilities for the CBCL have been found to be .85 (ages 2–3) and .89 (ages 4–18), .92 for the Teacher Report Form, and .72 for the Youth Self-Report Form. Interrater reliability for the CBCL and the Teacher Report Form have been found to be adequate (e.g., ranging from .50 to .75). Internal consistency and long-term stability of these measures have also been found to be generally adequate (e.g., Koot & Verhulst, 1992; Rubio-Stipec et al., 1990; Spiker et al., 1992).

With respect to validity, both construct and concurrent validity have been found to be satisfactory (see Kearney & Socha, 1997, for review). For example, in terms of concurrent validity, correlations between scores on the CBCL and the Connors Parent Rating Scale, and between the CBCL and the Revised Behavior Problem Checklist, have ranged between .52 and .88. The utility of the internalizing subscales of these measures in differentiating among clinical groups, as well as between clinical and nonclinical groups, is not as clear (Jensen, Salzberg, Richters, & Watanabe 1993; McArdle & Mattison, 1989; Massey & Murphy, 1991). Part of the difficulty might be due to the high degree of comorbidity that exists in childhood psychopathology, and thus, the finding of significant correlations between the internalizing and externalizing subscale scores (e.g., Hinshaw, 1992).

Similar to interview schedules, the use of behavior problem checklists predominate in research rather than clinic settings. One reason for this may be because practitioners view it as a burden for parents to complete the checklists (although it takes only about 18 minutes to complete the CBCL). A second reason may be because practitio-

ners do not communicate among themselves using scores on checklists—they communicate using diagnoses. Similarly, insurance companies do not require children's scores on checklists; they require diagnoses. Third, the link between scores on behavior problem checklists and specific, prescribed treatments has not been made. In our view, investigators involved in developing and testing the various child behavior problem checklists need to improve their efforts in highlighting and promoting the clinical relevance of checklist scores to practitioners.

Self-Rating Scales

There are several child self-rating scales that have been developed to assess internalizing problems. The most widely used scales and their psychometrics are presented in Table 16.1. The self-rating scales listed in the table are best suited for accomplishing the following goals: (1) screening, (2) identifying and quantifying symptoms and behaviors, (3) evaluating treatment outcome, and (4) evaluating the role of mediators and moderators (Jensen & Haynes, 1986). A summary of how well the child self-rating scales accomplish each of these goals follows.

Screening means that the scale can differentiate a group of symptomatic children from the rest of the community (i.e., capable of identifying cases). In terms of screening for childhood internalizing behavior problems, the currently available self-rating scales are likely to select more false positives than true positives (Costello & Angold, 1988). Thus, youngsters identified as anxious or depressed at an initial screen are likely not to be anxious or depressed at the second stage of an investigation. For example, Asarnow and Carlson (1985) found sensitivity to be 54% with inpatient children (aged 8 to 13) using a child-completed measure of depression, indicating that 46% of the children were misclassified as depressed or nondepressed. Similar findings have been found by other investigators (e.g., Hodges, 1990; Kazdin, Colbus, & Rodgers, 1986; Mattison, Bagnato, & Brubaker, 1988).

In light of these findings, it appears that a useful and cost-efficient screening approach would be one

Table 16.1 Self-Rating Scales for Screening

SCALE	DESCRIPTION	PSYCHOMETRICS
Revised Children's Manifest Anxiety Scale (RCMAS; Reynolds & Richmond, 1978, 1985)	37 items; yields a total anxiety score and three factor scale scores (Physiological Anxiety, Worry/Oversensitivity, and Social Concerns/Contration) and a Lie Scale score	*Internal consistency:* Alpha coefficients were greater than .80 for the total scale score; alpha coefficients for each for each factor scale range from .64 to .76 *Reliability:* Test retest coefficients of .98 and .94 for the total scale score and Lie scale score using a 3-week interval; .68 and .58 using a 9-month interval *Validity:* Positive and significant correlations between RCMAS total scores and other anxiety/fear measures. Findings more mixed when multitrait multimethod methodology is used.
State-Trait Anxiety Inventory for Children (STAIC; Spielberger, 1973)	Two 20-item scales—the A-Trait Scale and A-State Scale. The A-Trait scale designed to measure chronic cross-situational anxiousness. The A-State scale designed to measur acute, transitory anxiousness	*Internal consistency:* Alpha coefficients range .80 to .90 for A-State and approximately .80 for A-Trait scale. *Reliability:* Test retest coefficients range from .65 to .72 for A-State, .44 to .94 for A-trait *Validity:* Positive and significant correlations between STAIC scores and other anxiety/fear measures. Findings more mixed when multitrait multimethod methodology is used.
Social Anxiety Scale for Children Revised, (SASC-R; La Greca & Stone, 1993)	22 items; yields a total score and three factor scale scores [Fear of Negative Evaluation (FNE), Social Avoidance and Distress in New Situiations (SAD-New), and General Social Avoidance and Distress (SAD-G)]	*Internal consistency:* Alpha coefficients for each of the SASC-R subscales reflected acceptable internal consistency with all coefficients greater than .65 *Reliability:* Standardized reliability coefficients were .86, .78, and .69 for the FNE, SAD-New, and SAD-G scales, respectively *Validity:* Confirmatory factor analysis rvealed a good fit for the three-factor model. Also, discriminant validity supported in that neglected and rejected children reported more social anxiety than accepted children
Social Phobia Anxiety Inventory for Children (SPAIC; Beidel, Turner, & Morris, 1995)	26 items; yields a total anxiety/distress score and three factor scale scores (Assertiveness/General Conversation, Traditional Social Encounters, and Public Performance)	*Internal consistency:* Alpha coefficients for the total scale score was .95 *Reliability:* Test–retest coefficient was .86 using a 2-week interval, .63 using a 9-month interval *Validity:* Positive and significant correlations between the SPAIC scores and other self-report anxiety/fear measures, with a range of .41 to .53
Test Anxiety Scale for children (TASC; Sarason et al., 1958)	30 items designed to measure children's anxsty in test-taking situations	*Internal consistency:* Alpha coefficients ranged from .82 to .90 *Reliability:* Test–retest coefficients ranged from .44 to .85 *Validity:* Positive and significant correlation with teaches' ratings from .09 to .31 for different grades
Child Anxiety Senstivity Index (CASI; Silverman et al., 1991)	18-item scale designed to measure aversive child views anxious symptoms	*Internal consistency:* Alpha coefficient of .87 *Reliability:* Test–retest coefficients range from .62 to .78 using a 1–2-week interval *Validity:* Explained variance in the prediction of trait anxiety unaccounted for by other anxiety/fear measures
Fear Survey Schedule for Children–Revised (FSSC-R; Ollendick, 1983)	80 items; yields a total fear score and five factor scale scores (Fear of Failure and Criticism, Fear of the Unknown, Fear of Danger and Death, Medical Fears)	*Internal consistency:* Alpha coefficients range from .92 to .95 *Reliability:* Test–retest coefficients were .82 using a 1-week interval and .55 using a 3-month interval *Validity:* Positive and significant correlations between FSSC-R total scores and other anxiety measures approximately .50

Source: From *Anxiety in Phobic Disorders: A Pragmatic Approach* by W. K. Silverman and W. M. Kurtines, 1996, New York: Plenum. Reprinted by permission.

that employs a multistage sampling design (e.g., Ialongo, Edelsohn, Werthamer-Larsson, Crockett, & Kellam, 1993; Kendall, Cantwell, & Kazdin, 1989; Roberts, Lewinsohn, & Seeley, 1991). At the first stage, a self-rating scale would be administered to all participants. This would thereby identify those cases that should undergo more precise and comprehensive assessments at the second or third stage of the research using one of the structured interview schedules discussed in the previous section.

Identifying and quantifying symptoms and behaviors is the goal that childhood self-ratings scales can best accomplish, as they were specifically designed for this purpose. To identify and quantify symptoms and behaviors, the scales are usually administered after diagnoses are derived from a structured interview, and a summary score is then obtained. This summary score is assumed to be a quantitative index of the degree to which internalizing problems, such as anxiety or depression is relevant to a child, or the probability that the child will emit one of a class of behaviors (e.g., worry/oversensitivity) (Jensen & Haynes, 1986). Departures from the norm can usually be determined based on standard deviation units that define a particular percentile of the sample.

Research findings have suggested, however, that a general negative affectivity component is common to both anxiety and depression disorders and measures in child (e.g., Lonigan, Carey, & Finch, 1994; Wolfe, Finch, Saylor, Blount, Pallmeyer, & Carek, 1987; see reviews by Finch, Lipovsky, & Casat, 1989, and King, Ollendick, & Gullone, 1991) and adult populations (e.g., Feldman, 1993; see review by Watson & Clark, 1984). Much of the evidence rests on the large number of studies (both monomethod and multimethod that have found large correlations between self-rating scales of anxiety and depression such that no meaningful discrimination between self-reported anxiety and depression could be identified (e.g., Norvell, Brophy, & Finch, 1985; Saylor, Finch, Spirito, & Bennett, 1984; Treiber & Mabe, 1987).

Although negative affectivity appears to be a common underlying feature of depression and anxiety, investigators have also found that one factor that may distinguish between anxiety and depression in both children and adults is positive affectivity (e.g., Lonigan et al., 1994; Watson, Clark, & Carey, 1988). That is, whereas negative affectivity is strongly related to both anxiety and depression, the absence of positive affectivity is associated only with depression. Accordingly, Watson and Kendall (1989) have suggested that a way to improve the distinctiveness of child anxiety and depression self-rating scales is to assess the degree to which respondents report high positive affective states and then to infer depression from the relative absence of such experiences. To accomplish this, it is important to ensure that an adequate number of items contained on a child self-rating scale is reflective of positive affectivity—not just negative affectivity. This issue is worthy of research attention.

Child self-rating scales also frequently serve as one of the main measures in the *evaluation of treatment outcome*. Significant change observed from pre- to posttreatment are interpreted to mean that the treatment was effective. Despite their widespread use in this way, self-rating scores need to be interpreted with caution in evaluating outcome. Research has shown that fluctuations occur in these scores, irrespective of treatment (e.g., Finch, Saylor, Edwards, & McIntosh, 1987; Nelson & Politano, 1990). Consequently, Finch and associates (1987) suggested that in using child self-rating scales in the evaluation of treatment outcome, the scales should be administered at least two times prior to the actual intervention—once at the initial screening or assessment and again immediately prior to treatment.

Finally, investigators are frequently interested in evaluating the role of *mediators and moderators* in treatment outcome. Self-rating scales also are the best methods of assessment to use for this function. A large number of variables can mediate or moderate outcome, including childhood internalizing problem behaviors. For example, La Greca, Dandes, Wick, Shaw, and Stone (1988) suggested that social anxiety may serve as an important moderator in children's peer relationships. Thus, an intstrument such as the Social Anxiety Scale for Children-Revised (La Greca & Stone, 1993) may serve as a useful measure to include in an outcome study.

Because of the many functions and goals of child self-rating scales, they are the most widely used methods of assessment in both research *and* clinical settings. They have other advantages as well, including (1) ease and low cost of administration; (2) face validity for targeted problem behaviors; (3) objective scoring procedures, thereby minimizing the role of clinical inference and interpretation in the assessment process; (4) utility for a wide range of populations and problems, and; (5) utility for obtaining information on multiple responses (e.g., behavior, cognitive, and physiological) (Jensen & Haynes, 1986; Mash & Terdal, 1988).

Despite these advantages, some may question whether children are capable of or willing to report on their internal states (e.g., Patterson & Stoolmiller, 1991). Recent data indicate, however, that children can provide internally consistent and relatively stable self-reports of internalizing problems, as early as first grade, and such reports are both concurrently and predictively related to adaptation on various developmentally salient tasks (Ialongo, Edelsohn, Werthamer-Larsson, Crockett, & Kellam, 1994; Kellam, Rebok, Ialongo, & Mayer, 1994). Of course, in an attempt to present themselves in a positive light to adult testers, some children may react to the demand characteristics of the assessment situation by responding in socially desirable ways (La Greca, 1990). Efforts have been taken to limit the potential of social desirability bias on the part of children by using carefully worded instructions (e.g., "There are no right or wrong answers") or some type of validity scale, such as a "lie scale" (La Greca, 1990).

Observational Procedures

Observational procedures are the best methods of assessment to use for determining the frequency and severity of symptoms/behaviors and their antecedents and consequences. Observational procedures also can be used in the initial stage of assessment to assist in the identification of target behaviors and symptoms. In working with children with internalizing problems, the types of symptoms and behaviors that might be identified can be classified as (1) verbal behavior, such as rate of speech, positive/negative self-references, and verbal social skills, and (2) overt behavior, such as head/gaze

aversions, head nods, posture, and eye contact. Although there are a number of ways to assess these behaviors, the most frequent strategies focus on discrete response occurrences (i.e., response rate or frequency) or the amount of time that the response occurs, (i.e., response duration) (Gelfand & Hartmann, 1984).

Several observational coding procedures have been developed for assessing anxiety in children. These procedures were developed to record discrete child behaviors in specific anxiety-provoking settings, such as in dental, medical or child/parent separation settings (e.g., Glennon & Weisz, 1978; Melamed & Siegel, 1975). For example, the Preschool Observation Scale of Anxiety (POSA) is a 30-item scale developed by Glennon and Weisz (1978). Glennon and Weisz (1978) used the POSA in a sample of 36 children (aged 32 to 59 months) enrolled in a university-based preschool program, who were observed during a forced separation from their mothers at the preschool. The children's verbal and physical behaviors—such as physical complaints, expression of fear or worry, scream, trembling lip, and trunk contortions—were observed. Interrater reliability for the 30 items on the POSA were found to be adequate ($r = .78$). In terms of validity, POSA scores significantly correlated with teachers' and parents' ratings of the children's anxiety ($r = .47$ and .37, respectively), but not with the children's self-ratings or an independent observer's ratings. These results suggest that the POSA may be a means of assessing situationally induced anxiety in children, particularly in very young children who may have difficulty in accurately reporting on their internal states via self-reports.

Kazdin, Esveldt-Dawson, Sherick, and Colbus (1985) developed an observational coding procedure for use with children with depression. Specifically, 62 child inpatients (aged 8 to 13 years) were observed for 35 minutes (using a 5-minute interval coding system) during a free-time period preceding lunchtime for 5 consecutive workdays. The children were re-observed 4 weeks later to assess stability of performance. During the free-time period, the children had the opportunity to engage in several different activities of their choice, such as watching television, playing games, or even doing nothing. The children were also free to come and go from their rooms to the activity room as frequently as they wished during the observation interval. The target behaviors that were observed for each child were Social Activity (talking, playing a game with at least one other person, participating in a group activity, and interacting with staff), Solitary Behavior (playing a game alone, working on an academic task, listening and watching television, straightening up one's room, grooming oneself), and Affect-Related Expression (smiling, frowning, arguing, and complaining). Behaviors were coded as either occurrences or non-occurrences during each 5-minute interval.

Interobserver agreement for ratings of Social Activity, Solitary Behavior, and Affect-Related Expression was high ($r = .98$, $.94$, and $.94$, respectively). Interobserver agreement for ratings of specific behaviors within each category was also high (e.g., r ranged from $.80$ to $.99$). The ratings of each category were also found to be internally consistent, with alphas of $.75$, $.59$, and $.70$ for Social Activity, Solitary Behavior and Affect-Related Expression, respectively. With respect to test-retest reliability, the correlations were in the moderate to high range: $r = .47$ for Social Activity, $r = .86$ for Solitary Behavior, and $r = .85$ for Affect-Related Expression. Similar to Glennon and Weisz (1978), parents' ratings of their child's depression were significantly related to the observations (higher ratings of depression related to lower rates of social activity and affect-related expression); child self-ratings were not related to the observations.

The studies of Glennon and Weisz (1978) and Kazdin and colleagues (1985) were among the first to show that internalizing symptoms associated with anxiety and depression can be observed in children's natural settings, and that the observations appear to be reliable and relatively valid. Investigators and clinicians can thus adopt (or adapt) these coding procedures for use in their own settings (see Kendall, 1994, for example).

Like structured interviews and child behavior checklists, however, observational procedures are used more frequently in research than in clinic settings. Most clinicians do not have the luxury to expend the time, cost, and effort involved in conducting observations in naturalistic settings. Indeed, doing so is cumbersome for many researchers, as

well. What is more feasible for practitioners and researchers is to conduct an analogue observation in which a situation that elicits the child's internalizing behaviors/symptoms is simulated in the clinic or research setting. To be most useful, the analogue situation should correspond as closely as possible to the situation that elicits the problem behavior in the child's natural environment. To accomplish this, it is necessary to obtain detailed information from the child and parent about the specifics of the child's internalizing problems, and then use this information to develop the analogue.

In working with children with fear and anxiety problems, for example, the most common type of analogue observation is the Behavioral Avoidance Test (BAT). The BAT represents a test of the child's behavioral limits as it measures the distance the child can approach the fear-provoking object. In our work in using BATs, we ask the children to confront the fearful object or situation for a total of 5 minutes. The children are informed that although they may stop the exposure task at any time, they should attempt the task for as long as they can. Because parents may serve as "safety signals" to their children (i.e., children are not afraid as long as they have their parents nearby), parents are not present in the room during the BAT. We assess either the amount of time that the child can participate in the task or the amount of distance that he or she can walk toward the object.

We also obtain a subjective rating of fear using the Fear Thermometer (depicted in Figure 16.1). Note that the BAT just described does not include an assessment of the consequences that follow the child's emission of the fear response. However, if it was important to obtain this information, the BAT could be administered with the parent present, thereby allowing the opportunity to observe parental behavior as a consequence of child fear or avoidance.

Other analogue behavioral exposure tasks can be developed for assessing children who present with other types of problems. For example, children with Social Phobia or Generalized Anxiety Disorder are usually most fearful in situations that involve social evaluation. For children with these disorders, an analogue situation would be developed in which the children are required to talk

Figure 16.1 The "Fear Thermometer" is a graphical measure used to obtain a subjective rating of fear.

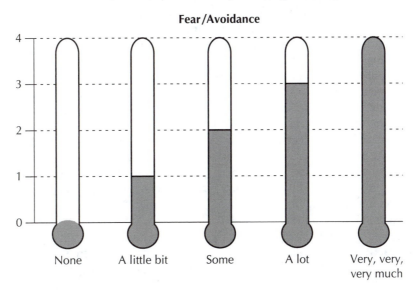

Fear/Avoidance

None   A little bit   Some   A lot   Very, very, very much

about themselves in front of a small group of people for 5 minutes. Analogues such as these can provide a rich picture of how children behave in anxiety-provoking situations (e.g., Can the child speak at all? Does the child display eye contact?). These behaviors can also be selected as targets for treatment.

Although analogue observation procedures provide clinically useful information, their psychometric properties, such as reliability and validity, have not been sufficiently studied. One exception is a study conducted by Hamilton and King (1991), who examined the temporal stability of an analogue observation procedure using 14 children (aged 2 to 11 years) with a specific phobia of dogs. The analogue procedure was comprised of a series of 14 performance tests. Each test required the child to engage in increasingly more difficult interactions with a dog. Two test administrations were conducted seven days apart prior to treatment. High test-retest reliability was obtained ($r = .97$), thereby providing support for the temporal stability of approach scores obtained on analogue observation procedures. Because of the small sample employed in this study and the wide age range, replication of this study would be worthwhile. Additional questions worth examining in the future include the role of differential levels of initial fear, the specific instructions employed (e.g., high demand versus low demand), and children's developmental level.

Self-Monitoring Procedures

Self-monitoring procedures require a child to self-observe and systematically record the occurrence of behavior. Research in behavioral assessment has demonstrated that individuals' continuous monitoring of behavioral and emotional events is far preferable to periodic retrospective recall of these events in terms of accuracy and reliability (e.g., Shapiro, 1984). That children can self-monitor across varied behaviors has been demonstrated in numerous research studies (e.g., Israel, Silverman, & Solotar, 1987; Ollendick, 1981).

In working with children with internalizing behavior problems, self-monitoring procedures are used to accomplish a goal similar to that of observational procedures—namely, to determine the frequency and severity of symptoms as well as their antecedents and consequences. As indicated earlier, however, in self-monitoring procedures the child is the observer and recorder of his or her own behaviors. Although this bypasses many of the difficulties involved in conducting direct behavioral observations, self-monitoring procedures have methodological difficulties of their own, particularly those relating to reactivity (i.e., the mere act of observing and recording one's behavior may lead to changes in that behavior) and accuracy. During assessment, it is important to minimize reactivity and maximize accuracy.

Clinically, we have found the "Daily Diary" a useful way to obtain self-monitoring data from children with anxiety disorders. The Daily Diary requires children to keep a record of the situations in which they experienced fear/anxiety, whether they confronted or avoided the situations, their accompanying cognitions, and a rating of fear. We ask children to begin monitoring and recording two weeks prior to the start of the treatment. To reduce the potential of reactivity during this phase, we emphasize to the children that they are "not to do anything different from what they usually do." The self-monitoring data obtained prior to treatment thereby serve as baseline information, which can be compared to the data obtained during the treatment phase (the children continue daily recording throughout treatment).

To maximize the accuracy of children's self-monitoring records, we provide the children with a detailed and thorough explanation of self-monitoring, with respect to both rationale and procedure. In terms of rationale, we emphasize the reasons why self-monitoring as accurately as possible is important. In terms of procedure, we emphasize the specific mechanics of self-monitoring. For example, in monitoring the situations that provoked anxiety, the children are instructed to specify the activity they were engaged in and the people who were in each situation with them. For example, children with a Specific Phobia of dogs are told to record each encounter with dogs, what they were doing at the time of the encounter, and who was with them. Samples of completed self-monitoring forms that we have received from children with whom we have worked are depicted in Figure 16.2.

For children whose self-monitoring data are unsatisfactory, researchers and practitioners might want to consider using a structured self-monitoring form. An example is the self-monitoring form described by Beidel, Neal, and Lederer (1991) in which children basically mark on a checklist whether certain events occurred and whether they experienced certain feelings. In a community sample of elementary school children involved in an investigation of test anxiety, Beidel and associates (1991) examined the reliability of the children's self-monitoring. They also compared the frequency and severity of anxiety-producing events during a two-week period for a text-anxious ($n = 17$) and nontest-anxious ($n = 17$) subsample. Compliance was also evaluated.

As Beidel and associates (1991) point out, assessing reliability for an event-orient assessment procedure is difficult, as events are variable and fluctuating. Not surprisingly, therefore, the resulting reliability coefficient (based on an N of 13) was relatively modest and not significant ($r = .50$). As preliminary support for validity, however, the test-anxious children reported significantly more emotional distress and more negative behaviors (e.g., crying, somatic complaints) than the nontest-anxious children. Compliance was found to be mixed, with 56% of the test-anxious children completing the forms 10 of the 14 days, and with the percentage of children completing the forms for all 14 days dropping to 31%. Beidel and colleagues (1991) suggest that perhaps compliance could be improved if self-monitoring was presented as an endeavor that requires involvement of the entire family. This has been found to enhance self-monitoring compliance among overweight children enrolled in weight reduction programs (Israel et al., 1987).

Self-monitoring procedures have also been used with children who suffer from depression (e.g., Stark, Reynolds, & Kaslow, 1987). For example, in Stark and colleagues (1987), children ($n = 29$) aged 9 to 12 years were asked to complete daily log sheets based on the Pleasant Events Schedule that was developed for use with adult depressed patients (MacPhillamy & Lewinsohn, 1974). The log sheets consisted of lists of pleasant events and various self-statements that the children were to endorse when relevant. The children were also required to rate their mood each day on a 0 to 10 rating scale. Because the focus of this study was on treatment outcome evaluation, the reliability and validity of the children's daily logs were not evaluated.

Figure 16.2 Sample selections of "Daily Diaries" in which children keep a record of the situations in which they experience fear/anxiety, whether they confront or avoid the situation, their accompanying cognitions, and their ratings of fear

Daily Diary

Name: *John S.* _____   Date: _____

TIME	SITUATION	WHAT DID YOU DO?	WHAT WERE YOU THINKING?	HOW AFRAID (0 to 4)
10:45 a.m.	It was a cold day. My teacher had all the doors & windows closed & had the heater on. It was hot and humid in the classroom.	nothing	What if I faint or something? What will the kids think of me?	2
9:00 p.m.	I was trying to fall asleep when I started to feel nervous about going to my friend's house who I'd never been to before.	I couldn't fall asleep. I kept on tossing and turning.	How about if I don't have fun? How about if my mom gets lost when she has to pick me up at his house? What if I start getting anxious there?	3

In sum, researchers and clinicians are likely to find self-monitoring the most useful way to obtain information about children's behavioral and emotional events before and during the course of treatment. However, these procedures are not without difficulties. Children's compliance with self-monitoring cannot be taken for granted, and efforts must be taken to minimize reactivity and increase accuracy. The basic psychometrics of self-monitoring data require further study, particularly with depressed children, including validity processing change from pre- to posttreatment.

Psychophysiological Measurement

Practical and conceptual knowledge about the use of psychophysiological measurement procedures with children has lagged behind knowledge about their use with adults. This is likely due to difficulties involved in using these procedures, including children's difficulty in sitting still and their fears of the test instrumentation (e.g., apprehension that the electrodes may shock them). There are also difficulties involved in the interpretive process with children, particularly as they relate to developmental level. For example, in relation to tonic heart rate in children, both heart rate and heart rate variability decrease with age (Shinebourne, 1974). Normative data with respect to psychophysiological measurement are also lacking (Venables, 1980).

The most widely used psychophysiological measures include heart rate, galvanic skin response and cortisol levels. A brief summary of these measures' utility in assessing childhood internalizing problems follows below.

Heart rate is the preferred cardiovascular index of fear and anxiety (Nietzel, Bernstein, & Russell, 1988). Heart rate can be measured as either beats per minute or as the interbeat interval (i.e., the measured time between consecutive heartbeats). In working with children with anxiety problems, the assessment of heart rate is perhaps most useful when done before, during, and after exposure to the anxiety-provoking stimulus during the behavioral exposure task (described earlier). Heart rate is less sensitive than the other visceral responses to measurement artifacts and can be monitored relatively easily. For example, in our work, we assess children's heart rate using a Computer Instruments Heart Watch, a device placed on the child's wrist during the behavioral exposure task. Following the task, the heart rate signals measured by the watch are counted by a computer. Data from our clinic indicate that this procedure yields reliable test-retest heart rate scores in phobic children (Chapinoff, 1992).

Beidel (1991) recently provided data showing that heart rate (assessed via pulse rate) could differentiate among children who met *DSM-III-R* diagnostic criteria for Social Phobia (SOP; $n = 18$), Overanxious Disorder (OAD; $n = 11$) and no diagnoses ($n = 18$). The children's pulse rate was monitored while they took an age-appropriate vocabulary test and while they read aloud before three research assistants. No information was presented concerning the reliability of the pulse rate assessment. Nevertheless, results revealed significant differences in the pulse rates of children diagnosed with OAD versus SOP during the baseline phase. The OAD children's pulse rates were significantly higher than those of the SOP ($p < .05$). No differences were found, however, in the baseline pulse rates of the normal controls and the two diagnostic groups. Although not significant, during the exposure phase there were trends for the groups to have different pulse rate changes. Specifically, during the vocabulary test the OAD children's pulse rate decreased an average of 6 BPM; the SOP children and normal controls had increases of 4 BPM and 1 BPM, respectively ($p < .09$). During the reading-aloud task, the OAD children had an increase of only 1 BPM, the SOP group had an increase of 6 BPM, and the normal controls had increases of 4 BPM ($p < .10$). Overall, Beidel (1991) concluded that children with SOP could be differentiated from other groups using heart rate indices.

Another measure of children's psychophysiological response is *galvanic skin response (GSR)*. The easiest and most convenient way to assess GSR in children is via the palmar sweat index (Johnson & Dabbs, 1967). Because the hands' sweat glands are mainly influenced by emotional factors and not other factors such as temperature, the number of active sweat glands provides an index of transitory physiological arousal (Johnson & Dabbs, 1967). The measurement of GSR using

the palmar sweat index involves dabbing a small amount of inklike solution on the child's fingertip, and then making a fingerprint by removing the solution with a small piece of transparent tape. The tape is then mounted on a microscope slide and projected onto a screen, which provides a permanent record of the number of active sweat glands (Melamed et al., 1978).

Melamed and colleagues used the palmar sweat index (PSI) as one of the outcome measures in their series of filmed modeling/medical-dental preparatory studies (Melamed et al., 1975, 1978). Of relevance here is the finding that initial PSI scores correlated with children's self-ratings of fear ($r = .30$) as well as their specific medical-dental fear scores ($r = .31$). The average interrater agreement for the PSI has been found to be high (e.g., 95%; Pinto & Hollandsworth, 1989). In addition, the test-retest reliability has also been found to be high (e.g., .99; Gilbert et al., 1982).

Finally, researchers have begun to focus on the stress reactivity of the hypothalamic-pituitary-adrenocortical (HPA) axis by measuring children's basal cortisol levels via saliva or urine (e.g., Granger, Stansbury, & Henker, 1994; Kagan, Reznick, & Snidman, 1987). McBurnett and associates (1991), for example, found that the combination of anxiety and conduct problems was linked to higher salivary cortisol levels in 67 boys (age 8 to 13 years) who were participants in an ongoing longitudinal study of conduct disorder. However, boys with anxiety and without comorbid conduct disorder were not found to have higher cortisol levels than boys with conduct disorder alone. The authors suggest that "cortisol may be a useful biological marker of arousal associated with the behavioral inhibition system activity in children with conduct disorder."

In a more recent study using 102 clinic referred children (aged 7 to 17 years old) with a range of behavioral and emotional problems, Granger, Weisz, and Kauneckis (1994) found cortisol reactivity in response to a parent/child conflict discussion task to be linked primarily to social anxiety and social inhibition rather than conduct problems. The relation between cortisol reactivity and levels of depression was also not significant. Procedural differences between the McBurnett and associates' and Granger and associates' studies make direct comparison of results difficult, but certainly these studies highlight the potential utility of using cortisol level as a psychophyiological measure in research concerned with the pathogenesis of children's internalizing problems.

In sum, despite the potential utility of psychophysiological measurements for research purposes, their clinical utility remains to be determined. For now, we are skeptical whether such measurements will become a part of the armamentarium of the clinician, especially vis-à-vis the other methods of assessment that are available.

Case Study

Joan, a 10-year-old girl, was referred to our center for treatment by a school counselor because of periodic episodes of crying during the school day, excessive social withdrawal, and an extreme need for reassurance. When Joan's mother called to schedule the initial assessment appointment for her daughter, she described Joan as being "scared of everything." Even ordinary things such as going to a restaurant were major events. (Joan refused to eat in public and she worried that she might get food poisoning from eating restaurant food. She had heard about this happening in a local restaurant in the local news.)

According to her mother, Joan, spent a lot of time worrying about little things and making these little things into big things. She worried about her grades even though she was an A student in a gifted program. Joan's mother told us how she was growing increasingly concerned about her daughter's behaviors, and she wished to be seen by us as soon as possible.

When Joan and her mother arrived at the center for their assessment appointment, they were each administered respective child and parent versions of the ADIS. Joan also completed several self-rating scales, including the RCMAS, the SASC-R, the FSSC-R, and the CDI. Joan's mother completed the CBCL on her daughter, and we obtained permission from her to send a teacher version of the CBCL to the school counselor who had referred Joan to our center. Joan's behavioral exposure task required her to talk about herself for five minutes in front of a small audience. During this time we also assessed Joan's heart rate using the

heart watch, and her level of subjective distress using the Fear Thermometer. Three minutes into the exposure task, Joan asked to stop, indicating that she was too upset to continue.

Based on Joan's and her mother's responses to the interviews, Joan was assigned a diagnosis of Generalized Anxiety Disorder, Major Depression, and Social Phobia (Social Anxiety Disorder). In addition, Joan's scores on all of the questionnaires were elevated, and her profile on both the parent and teacher versions of the CBCL indicated that she was in the clinical range on the internalizing subscales. Examples of items endorsed on the CBCLs were feeling worried, nervous, and self-conscious or easily embarrassed. Examples of items that Joan endorsed on her self-rating scales were often feeling sick to her stomach, worrying about what is going to happen, feeling that nothing will ever work out for her, and that nothing is fun at all.

We suggested to Joan and her mother that they become involved in treatment at our center. We asked Joan to complete Daily Diaries for the next two weeks prior to treatment. We told Joan we were particularly interested in her keeping track of all the times that she experienced feelings of anxiety and sadness, the situations that evoked these feelings, and the specific thoughts that she was having; we also asked her to rate her level of distress. We explained to Joan and her mother that this information would be useful before and during treatment as a way to monitor Joan's progress.

Two weeks later, we began treatment with Joan and her mother. We readministered the RCMAS and the SASC-R at the first treatment session. The intervention was a 12-week exposure-based cognitive-behavioral program in which Joan and her mother were seen individually and then briefly together by the therapist. The program, based on a transfer of control model of change (Silverman & Kurtines, 1996), involved first teaching Joan's mother the principles of contingency management (e.g., contingency contracting) and then teaching Joan and her mother child self-control strategies (e.g., cognitive coping skills). These strategies were then applied in gradual exposure tasks that involved Joan confronting various situations that provoked anxiety, such as going to and eating at restaurants.

The cognitive self-control strategies were also used to help Joan manage her excessive worrying and sad feelings. For example, Joan learned to recognize the specific cognitions associated with these feelings and to recognize the faulty and maladaptive nature of such cognitions. She also received practice in generating and in using more adaptive coping thoughts and behaviors, and in praising herself for doing so.

At the conclusion of treatment, all of the assessment measures were readministered to compare Joan's pre- to posttreatment functioning. Readministration of the ADIS-C and ADIS-P revealed that Joan no longer met diagnostic criteria for any *DSM* disorder, and there was no longer any interference in her daily functioning. In addition, her scores on the questionnaires decreased markedly and she was able to talk about herself in front of a small audience for the full five minutes of the in vivo behavioral exposure test. These gains were maintained at the 3-, 6- and 12-month follow-up assessment points.

ENDNOTE

1. Although according to the *DSM-IV*'s exclusionary rules, GAD is a common associated feature of mood disorders and should not be diagnosed separately if it occurs exclusively during the course of these conditions.. According to these rules, Joan would be assigned diagnoses of Major Depression and Social Phobia only. Because our center is a research clinic, however, for research purposes we assign all diagnoses that children are found to meet via the ADIS-C and ADIS-P.

REFERENCES

Achenbach, T. M. (1980). DSM-III in light of empirical research on the classification of child psychopathology. *Journal of the American Academy of Child and Adolescent Psychiatry, 19*, 395–412.

Achenbach, T. M. (1991a). *Manual for the Teacher's Report Form and 1991 profile.* Burlington: Department of Psychiatry, University of Vermont.

Achenbach, T. M. (1991b). *Youth Self-Report for ages 11–18.* Burlington: Department of Psychiatry, University of Vermont.

Achenbach, T. M., & Edelbrock, C. S. (1978). The classification of child psychology: A review and analysis of emirical efforts. *Psychological Bulletin, 85*, 1275–1301.

Achenbach, T. M., & Edelbrock, C. (1983). *Manual for the Child Behavior Checklist and Revised Child Behavior Profile.* Burlington: University of Vermont, Department of Psychology.

American Psychiatric Association. (1980). *Diagnostic and statistical manual of mental disorders* (3rd ed.). Washington, DC: Author.

American Psychiatric Association. (1987). *Diagnostic and statistical manual of mental disorders* (3rd ed., rev.). Washington, DC: Author.

American Psychiatric Association. (1994). *Diagnostic and statistical manual of mental disorders* (4th ed.). Washington, DC: Author.

Angold, A., & Costello, E. J. (1995). A test-retest reliability study of child-reported psychiatric symptoms and diagnoses using the Child and Adolescent Psychiatric Assessment (CAPA-C), *Psychological Medicine.*

Angold, A., Weissman, M. M., John, K., Marikangas, K. R., Prusoff, B. A., Wickramaratne, P., Gammon, G. D., & Warner, V. (1987). Parent and child reports of depressive symptoms in children at low and high risk of depression. *Journal of Child Psychology and Psychiatry and Allied Disciplines, 28*, 901–915.

Asarnow, J. R., & Carlson, G. A. (1985). Depression Self-rating Scale: Utility with child psychiatric inpatients. *Journal of Consulting and Clinical Psychology, 53*, 491–499.

Beidel, D. C. (1991). Social phobia and overanxious disorder in school-age children. *Journal of the American Academy of Child and Adolescent Psychiatry, 3*, 545–552.

Beidel, D. C., Neal, A. M., & Lederer, A. S. (1991). The feasibility and validity of a daily diary for the assessment of anxiety in children. *Behavior Therapy, 22*, 505–517.

Beidel, D. C., Turner, S. M., & Morris, T. L. (1995). A new inventory to assess childhood social anxiety and phobia: The Social Phobia Anxiety Inventory for Children. *Psychological Assessment, 7*, 73–79.

Chapinoff, A. (1992). *Test-retest reliability of heart response in children with phobic disorder.* Unpublished Master's thesis, Florida International University.

Costello, E. J., & Angold, A. (1988). Scales to assess child and adolescent depression: Checklists, screens, and nets. *Journal of the American Academy of Child and Adolescent Psychiatry, 27*, 726–737.

Costello, A. J., Edelbrock, C. S., Dulcan, M. K., Kalas, R., & Klaric, S. H. (1984). *Report to NIMH on the NIMH diagnostic interview schedule for children (DISC).* Washington, DC: National Institute of Mental Health.

Daleiden, E. L., Vasey, M. W., & Brown, L. M. (in press). Internalizing disorders. In W. K. Silverman & T. H. Ollendick (Eds.), *Developmental issues in the clinical treatment of children.* Boston: Allyn and Bacon.

Edelbrock, C., & Costello, A. (1984). Structured psychiatric interviews for children and adolescents. In G. Goldstein & M. Hersen (Eds.), *Handbook of psychological assessment* (pp. 276–290). New York: Pergamon.

Edelbrock, C., Costello, A. J., Dulcan, M. K., Conover, N. C., & Kalas, R. (1986). Parent-child agreement on child psychiatric symptoms assessed via structured interview. *Journal of Child Psychology and Psychiatry, 27,* 181–190.

Endicott, J., & Spitzer, R. L. (1978). A diagnostic interview: The schedule for affective disorders and schizophrenia. *Archives of General Psychiatry, 35,* 837–844.

Eyberg, S. M. (1980). Eyberg Child Behavior Inventory. *Journal of Clinical Child Psychology, 9,* 29.

Feldman, L. A. (1993). Distinguishing depression and anxiety in self-report: Evidence from confirmatory factor analysis on nonclinical and clinical samples. *Journal of Consulting and Clinical Psychology, 4,* 631–638.

Finch, A. J., Lipovsky, J. A., & Casat, C. D. (1989). Anxiety and depression in children and adolescents: Negative affectivity or separate constructs? In P. C. Kendall & D. Watson (Eds.), *Anxiety and depression: Distinctive and overlapping features* (pp. 171–196). San Diego, CA: Academic Press.

Finch, A. J., Saylor, C. F., Edwards, G. L., & McIntosh, J. A. (1987). Children's Depression Inventory: Reliability over repeated administrations. *Journal of Clinical Child Psychology, 16,* 339–341.

Gelfand, D. M., & Hartmann, D. P. (1984). *Child behavior analysis and therapy.* Boston: Allyn and Bacon.

Gilbert, B. O., Johnson, S. B., Spillar, R., McCallum, M., Silverstein, J. H., & Rosenbloom, A. (1982). The effects of a peer-modeling film on children learning to self-inject insulin. *Behavior Therapy, 13,* 186–193.

Glennon, B., & Weisz, J. R. (1978). An observational approach to the assessment of anxiety in young children. *Journal of Consulting and Clinical Psychology, 46,* 1246–1257.

Goyette, C. H., Conners, C. K., & Ulrich, R. F. (1978). Normative data on revised Conners Parent and Teacher Rating Scales. *Journal of Abnormal Child Psychology, 6,* 221–236.

Granger, D. A., Stansbury, K., & Henker, B. (1994). Preschoolers' behavioral and neuroendocrine responses to social challenge. *Merrill Palmer Quarterly, 10,* 190–211.

Granger, D. A., Weisz, J. R., & Kauneckis, D. (1994). Neuroendocrine reactivity, internalizing behavior problems, and control-related cognitions in clinic-referred children and adolescents. *Journal of Abnormal Psychology, 103,* 259–266.

Hamilton, D. I., & King, N. J. (1991). Reliability of a behavioral avoidance test for the assessment of dog phobic children. *Psychological Reports, 69,* 18.

Herjanic, B., Hudson, R., & Kotloff, K. (1976). Does interviewing harm children? *Research Communications in Psychology, Psychiatry, and Behavior, 1,* 523–531.

Herjanic, B., & Reich, W. (1982). Development of a structured psychiatric interview for children: Agreement between child and parent on individual symptoms. *Journal of Abnormal Child Psychiatry, 10,* 307–324.

Hinshaw, S. P. (1992). Externalizing behavior problems and academic underachievement in childhood and adolescence: Causal relationships and underlying mechanisms. *Psychological Bulletin, 111,* 127–155.

Hobbs, N. (1975). *The futures of children: Categories, labels, and their consequences.* San Francisco: Jossey-Bass.

Hodges, K. (1990). Depression and anxiety in children: A comparison of self-report questionnaires to clinical interview. *Psychological Assessment: A Journal of Consulting and Clinical Psychology, 2,* 376–381.

Hodges, K., McKnew, D., Cytryn, L., Stern, L., & Kline, J. (1982). The Child Assessment Schedule (CAS) Diagnostic Interview: A report on reliability and validity: *Journal of the American Academy of Child and Adolescent Psychiatry, 21,* 468–473.

Ialongo, N., Edelsohn, G., Werthamer-Larsson, L., Crockett, L., & Kellam, S. G. (1993). Are self-reported depressive symptoms in first-grade children developmentally transient phenomena? A further look. *Development and Psychopathology, 5,* 433–457.

Ialongo, N., Edelsohn, G., Werthamer-Larsson, L., Crockett, L., & Kellam, S. G. (1994). The significance of self-reported anxious symptoms in first grade children. *Journal of Abnormal Child Psychology, 22,* 441–455.

Israel, A. C., Silverman, W. K., & Solotar, L. C. (1987). Baseline adherence as a predictor of dropout in a children's weight reduction program. *Journal of Consulting and Clinical Psychology, 55,* 791–793.

Jensen, B. J., & Haynes, S. N. (1986). Self-report questionnaires and inventories. In A. R. Ciminero, K. S.

Calhoun, & H. E. Adams (Eds.), *Handbook of behavioral assessment* (pp. 150–175). New York: Wiley & Sons.

Jensen, P. S., Salzberg, A. D., Richters, J. E., & Watanbe, H. K. (1993). Scales, diagnoses, and child psychopathology: I. CBCL and DISC relationships. *Journal of the American Academy of Child and Adolescent Psychiatry, 32,* 397–406.

Johnson, R., & Dabbs, J. M. (1967). Enumeration of active sweat glands: A simple physiological indicator of psychological change's. *Nursing Research, 16,* 273–276.

Kagan, J., Reznick, J. S., & Snidman, N. (1987). The physiology and psychology of behavioral inhibition. *Child Development, 58,* 1459–1473.

Kazdin, A. E., Colbus, D., & Rodgers, A. (1986). Assessment of depression and diagnosis of depressive disorder among psychiatrically disturbed children. *Journal of Abnormal Child Psychology, 14,* 499–515.

Kazdin, A. E., Esveldt-Dawson, K., Sherick, R. B., & Colbus, D. (1985). Assessment of overt behavior and childhood depression among psychiatrically disturbed children. *Journal of Consulting and Clinical Psychology, 53,* 201–210.

Kearney, C. A., & Socha, K. E. (1997). Anxiety problems in childhood: Diagnostic and dimensional aspects. In J. A. den Boer (Ed.), *Clinical management of anxiety: Theory and practical applications.* New York: Marcel Dekker.

Kellam, S. G., Rebok, G. W., Ialongo, N., & Mayer, L. S. (1994). The course and malleability of aggressive behavior from early first grade into middle school: Results of developmental epidemiologically based prevention trial. *Journal of Child Psychology and Psychiatry and Allied Disciplines, 35,* 259–281.

Kendall, P. C. (1994). Treating anxiety disorders in children: Results of a randomized clinical trial. *Journal of Consulting and Clinical Psychology, 62,* 200–210.

Kendall, P. C., Cantwell, D. P., & Kazdin, A. E. (1989). Depression in children and adolescents: Assessment issues and recommendations. *Cognitive Therapy and Research, 13,* 109–146.

King, N. J., Ollendick, T. H., & Gullone, E. (1991). Negative affectivity in children and adolescents: Relations between anxiety and depression. *Clinical Psychology Review, 11,* 441–459.

Koot, H. M., & Verhulst, F. C. (1992). Prediction of children's referred to mental health and special education services from earlier adjustment. *Journal of Child Psychology and Psychiatry, 33,* 717–729.

Kovacs, M. (1982). *The longitudinal study of child and adolescent psychopathology: I. The semistructured psychiatric interview schedule for children (ISC).* Unpublished manuscript.

La Greca, A. M. (1990). Issues and perspectives on the child assessment process. In A. M. La Greca (Ed.), *Through the eyes of the child* (pp. 3–17). Boston: Allyn and Bacon.

La Greca, A. M., Dandes, S. K., Wick, P., Shaw, K., & Stone, W. L. (1988). Development of the Social Anxiety Scale for Children: Reliability and concurrent validity. *Journal of Clinical Child Psychology, 17,* 84–91.

La Greca, A. M., & Stone, W. L. (1992). Assessing children through interviews and behavioral observations. In C. E. Walker, & M. C. Roberts (Eds.), *Handbook of clinical child pychology* (pp. 63–83). New York: Wiley & Sons.

La Greca, A. M., & Stone, W. L. (1993). The Social Anxiety Scale for Children-Revised. Factor structure and concurrent validity. *Journal of Clinical Child Psychology, 22,* 17–27.

Lavigne, J. V., Arend, R., Rosenbaum, D., Sinacor, J., Ciccetti, C., Binns, H. J., Christoffel, K. K., Hayford, J. R., & McGuire, P. (1994). Interrater reliability of the DSM-III-R with preschool children. *Journal of Abnormal Child Psychology, 22,* 679–690.

Lewis, S. A., Gorsky, A., Cohen, P., & Hartmark, C. (1985). The reaction of youth to diagnostic interview. *Journal of the American Academy of Child and Adolescent Psychiatry, 24,* 750–755.

Lonigan, C. J., Carey, M. P., & Finch, A. J. (1994). Anxiety and depression in children and adolescents: Negative affectivity and the utility of self-reports. *Journal of Consulting and Clinical Psychology, 62,* 1000–1008.

MacPhillamy, D. J., & Lewinsohn, P. M. (1974). Depression as a function of levels of desired and obtained pleasure. *Journal of Abnormal Psychology, 83,* 651–657.

Mash, E. J., & Terdal, L. G. (Eds.). (1988). *Behavioral assessment of child disorders* (2nd ed.). New York: Guilford.

Massey, O. T., & Murphy, S. E. (1991). A study of the utility of the Child Behavior Checklist with residentially placed children. *Evaluation and Program Planning, 14,* 319–324.

Mattison, R. E., Bagnato, S. J., & Brubaker, B. M. (1988). Diagnostic utility of the Revised Children's Manifest Anxiety Scale in children with DSM-III anxiety disorders. *Journal of Anxiety Disorders, 2,* 147–155.

McArdle, J., & Mattison, R. E. (1989). Child behavior

profile types in a general population sample of boys 6 to 11 years old. *Journal of Abnormal Child Psychology, 17*, 597–607.

McBurnett, K., Lahey, B. B., Frick, P. J., Risch, C., Loeber, R., Hart, E. L., Christ, M. A. G., & Hanson, K. S. (1991). Anxiety, inhibition, and conduct disorder in children: II. Relation to salivary cortisol. *Journal of the American Academy of Child and Adolescent Psychiatry, 30*, 192–196.

Melamed, B. G., & Siegel, L. J. (1975). Reduction of anxiety in children facing hospitalization and surgery by use of filmed modeling. *Journal of Consulting and Clinical Psychology, 43*, 511–521.

Melamed, B. G., Yurcheson, R., Fleece, E. L., Hutcherson, S., & Hawes, R. (1978). Effects of filmed modeling on the reduction of anxiety-related behaviors in individuals varying in level of previous experience in the stress situation. *Journal of Consulting and Clinical Psychology, 40*, 1357–1367.

Moras, K., & Barlow, D. H. (1992). Dimensional approaches to diagnosis and the problem of anxiety and depression. In W. Feigenbaum, A. Ehlers, J. Margraf, & I. Florin (Eds.), *Perspectives and promises of clinical psychology* (pp. 23–37). New York: Plenum.

Nelson, W. M., III, & Politano, P. M. (1990). Children's Depression Inventory: Stability over repeated administrations in psychiatric inpatient children. *Journal of Clinical Child Psychology, 19*, 254–256.

Nietzel, M. T., Bernstein, D. A., & Russell, R. L. (1988). Assessment of anxiety and fear. In A. S. Bellack & M. Hersen (Eds.), *Behavioral assessment: A practical handbook* (3rd ed.) (pp. 280–312). New York: Pergamon.

Norvell, N., Brophy, C., & Finch, A. J. (1985). The relationship of anxiety to childhood depression. *Journal of Personality Assessment, 49*, 150–153.

Ollendick, T. H. (1981). Self-monitoring and self-administered overcorrection: The modification of nervous tics in children. *Behavior Modification, 5*, 75–84.

Ollendick, T. H. (1983). Reliability and validity of the revised Fear Survey Schedule for Children (FSSC-R). *Behaviour Research and Therapy, 21*, 395–399.

Patterson, G. R., & Stoolmiller, M. (1991). Replications of a dual failure model for boy's depressed mood. *Journal of Consulting and Clinical Psychology, 59*, 491–498.

Pinto, R. P., & Hollandsworth, J. G. (1989). Using videotape modeling to prepare children psychologically for surgery: Influence of parents and costs versus benefits of providing preparation services. *Health Psychology, 8*, 79–95.

Puig-Antich, J., & Chambers, W. (1978). *The Schedule for Affective Disorders and Schizophrenia for School-Aged Children.* New York State Psychiatric Institute.

Quay, H. C. (1979). Classification. In H. C. Quay & J. S. Werry (Eds.), *Psychopathological disorders of childhood* (2nd ed., pp. 1–42). New York: Wiley.

Quay, H. C., & Peterson, D. R. (1983). *Interim manual for the Revised Behavior Problem Checklist.* (Available from Herbert C. Quay, Box 248074, University of Miami, Coral Gables, FL 33124).

Rapee, R. M., Barret, P. M., Dadds, M. R., & Evans, L. (1994). Reliability of the DSM-III-R childhood anxiety disorders using structured interview: Interrater and parent-child agreement. *Journal of the American Academy of Child and Adolescent Psychiatry, 33*, 984–992.

Reynolds, C. R., & Richmond, B. O. (1978). What I think and feel: A revised measure of children's manifest anxiety. *Journal of Abnormal Child Psychology, 6*, 271–280.

Reynolds, C. R., & Richmond, B. O. (1985). *Revised Children's Manifest Anxiety Scale.* Los Angeles: Western Psychological Services.

Richardson, S. A., Dohrenwend, B. S., & Klein, D. (1965). *Interviewing: Its forms and functions.* New York: Basic Books.

Roberts, R. E., Lewinsohn, P. M., & Seeley, J. R. (1991). Screening for adolescent depression: A comparison of depression scales. *Journal of the American Academy of Child and Adolescent Psychiatry, 30*, 58–66.

Robins, L. N., Helzer, J. E., Croughan, J., & Ratcliff, K. S. (1981). National Institute of Mental Health diagnostic interview schedule. *Archives of General Psychiatry, 38*, 381–389.

Ross, A. O. (1980). *Psychological disorders of children.* New York: McGraw-Hill.

Rubio-Stipec, M., Bird, H., Canino, G., & Gould, M. (1990). The internal consistency and concurrent validity of a spanish translation of the Child Behavior Checklist. *Journal of Abnormal Child Psychology, 18*, 393–406.

Sarason, S., Davidson, K., Lighthall, F., & Waite, R. (1958). A test anxiety scale for children. *Child Development, 29*, 105–113.

Saylor, C. F., Finch, A. J., Jr., Spirito, A., & Bennett, B. (1984). The Children's Depression Inventory: A systematic evaluation of psychometric properties. *Journal of Consulting and Clinical Psychology, 52*, 955–967.

Shapiro, E . S. (1984). Self-monitoring procedures. In T. M. Ollendick & M. Hersen (Eds.), *Child behavioral assessment: Principles and procedures.* New York: Pergamon.

Shinebourne, E. A. (1974). Growth and development of the cardiovascular system. In J. A. Davis & J. Dobbing (Eds.), *Scientific foundations of pediatrics* (pp. 198–213). London: Heinemann.

Silverman, W. K. (1991). Diagnostic reliability of anxiety disorders in children using structured interviews. *Journal of Anxiety Disorders, 5,* 105–124.

Silverman, W. K. (1992). Taxonomy of anxiety disorders in children. In G. D. Burrows, R. Noyes, & S. M. Roth (Eds.), *Handbook of anxiety* (Vol. 5) (pp. 281–308). Amsterdam: Elsevier.

Silverman, W. K. (1994). Structured diagnostic interviews. In T. H. Ollendick, N. J. King, & W. Yule (Eds.), *International handbook of phobic and anxiety disorders in children and adolescents* (pp. 293–315). New York: Plenum.

Silverman, W. K., & Eisen, A. R. (1992). Age differences in the reliability of parent and child reports of child anxious symptomatology using a structured interview. *Journal of American Academy of Child and Adolescent Psychiatry, 31,* 117–124.

Silverman, W. K., Fleisig, W., Rabian, B., & Peterson, R. A. (1991). Childhood anxiety sensitivity index. *Journal of Clinical Child Psychology, 20,* 162–168.

Silverman, W. K., & Kurtines, W. K. (1996). *Childhood anxiety and phobic disorders: A pragmatic approach.* New York: Plenum.

Silverman, W. K., & Nelles, W. B. (1988). The Anxiety Disorders Interview Schedule for Children. *Journal of the American Academy of Child and Adolescent Psychiatry, 27,* 772–778.

Silverman, W. K., & Rabian, B. (1995). Test-retest reliability of the DSM-III-R anxiety childhood disorders symptoms using the Anxiety Disorders Interview Schedule for Children. *Journal of Anxiety Disorders, 9,* 1–12.

Spielberger, C. D. (1973). *Manual for the State-Trait Anxiety Inventory for Children.* Palo Alto, CA: Consulting Psychologists Press.

Spiker, D., Kraemer, H. C., Constantine, N. A., & Bryant, D. (1992). Reliability and validity of behavior problem checklist as measures of traits in low birth weight, premature preschoolers. *Child Development, 63,* 1481–1496.

Spitzer, R. L., Endicott, J., & Robins, E. (1978). Research diagnostic criteria: Rationale and reliability. *Archives of General Psychiatry, 35,* 773–782.

Stark K. D., Reynolds, W. M., & Kaslow, N. J. (1987). A comparison of the relative efficacy of self-control therapy and a behavioral problem-solving therapy for depression. *Journal of Abnormal Psychology, 15,* 91–113.

Treiber, F. A., & Mabe, P. A. (1987). Child and parent perceptions of children's psychopathology in psychiatric outpatient children. *Journal of Abnormal Child Psychology, 13,* 115–124.

Venables, P. H. (1980). Autonomic reactivity. In M. Rutter (Ed.), *Scientific foundations of developmental psychiatry* (pp. 165–175). London: Heinemann.

Watson, D., & Clark, L. A. (1984). Negative affectivity: The disposition to experience aversive emotional states. *Psychological Bulletin, 96,* 465–490.

Watson, D., Clark, L. A., & Carey, G. (1988). Positive and negative affectivity and their relation to anxiety and depressive disorders. *Journal of Abnormal Psychology, 97,* 346–353.

Watson, D., & Kendall, P. C. (1989). Common and differentiating features of anxiety and depression: Current findings and future directions. In P. C. Kendall & D. Watson (Eds.), *Anxiety and depression: Distinctive and overlapping features* (pp. 493–508). New York: Academic Press.

Wells, K. C. (1981). Assessment of children in outpatient Settings. In M. Hersen & A. S. Bellack (Eds.), *Behavioral assessment: A practical handbook* (pp. 484–533). New York: Pergamon.

Wolfe, V. V., Finch, A. J., Jr., Saylor, C. F., Blount, R. L., Pallmeyer, T. P., & Carek, D. J. (1987). Negative affectivity in children: A multitrait-multimethod investigation. *Journal of Consulting and Clinical Psychology, 55,* 245–250.

World Health Organization. (1992). *International classification of mental and behavioral disorders, clinical descriptions and diagnostic guidelines* (10th ed.). Geneva: Author.

Young, G., O'Brien, J. D., Gutterman, E. M., & Cohen, P. (1987). Research on the clinical interview. *Journal of the American Academy of Child and Adolescent Psychiatry, 26,* 613–620.

CHAPTER 17

ASSESSMENT OF CHILD BEHAVIOR PROBLEMS
EXTERNALIZING DISORDERS

Diane Franz
Alan M. Gross
University of Mississippi

The assessment of child behavior disorders is of relatively recent origins. Before the beginning of the twentieth century, disorders of children were viewed like those of adults. However, since the beginning of this century, there has been widespread examination of the development of behavior disorders during childhood. More recently, the advent of "developmental psychopathology" (Stroufe & Rutter, 1984) has greatly influenced the manner in which psychologists assess and treat children. Within this new found interest in the disorders of childhood, the field of behavioral assessment of children has evolved.

Behavioral assessment of children (Ollendick & Hersen, 1989) has been traditionally characterized by an adherence to an operant perspective that places the majority of its emphasis on observable events, current behavior, the situational determinants of behavior, and intra-individual differences. In this sense, behavioral assessment of children has been very similar to assessment of adults. Behavioral assessment relies on a description of current behavior and a specification of organismic and environmental conditions that elicit and maintain the behavior. The focus of behavioral assessment is what the child does in a given situation rather than what a child has (Mischel, 1973). Behavioral assessment of children has always been characterized by an empirical approach.

Behavioral assessment methods with children, like those with adults, have gradually evolved to include as their focus cognitive and affective components of behavior (Mash & Terdal, 1989). Children have also been acknowledged as active manipulators of their environment, rather than passive participants (Mischel, 1973). Similarly, children are now more likely to be assessed and treated in the context of the social environment of which they are a part. Finally, the impact of developmental level has become an important consideration when assessing children (Yule, 1993).

These changes in the manner in which child behavioral assessment has been conceptualized has led to the prevailing belief that multiple assessment strategies are useful in formulating effective treatments for children. A thorough assessment might include any or all of the following techniques: clinical interview; self-monitoring; behavioral observation; standardized testing; rating forms from parents, teachers, and peers; and self-report measures.

The purpose of the present chapter is to provide an overview of child behavioral assessment. Although this chapter reviews general methods of behavioral assessment, special attention will be paid to the assessment of behavior disorders that fall into the externalizing group. Following a discussion of developmental issues in child assessment, a review of the most commonly employed child behavioral assessment procedures will be presented. The first section will cover indirect methods, including behavioral interviews, behavioral rating scales, and self-report measures. The next section includes direct methods of behavioral assessment, including observation in natural settings and analog settings. Finally, the chapter will be concluded with a case example illustrating the use of multiple assessment procedures.

DEVELOPMENTAL CONSIDERATIONS

Developmental change is perhaps the most salient characteristic of childhood. Physical, emotional, and behavioral maturation rates must be taken into account during the assessment process (Yule, 1993). Behaviors that are viewed as appropriate at one point in a youngster's development may be considered problematic at another developmental level. For example, a eneuretic child at age 8 is more likely to cause concern as opposed to one at age 3 (Kimball, Nelson, & Politano, 1993). Furthermore, the loss of bladder control has different implications depending on the sex of the child, given that girls typically develop this control earlier than boys (Shaffer, 1985).

The recognition of developmental level as an important factor in assessment of children may be a result of the emergence of the field of developmental psychopathology (Yule, 1993). Developmental psychopathology is concerned with the origins and course of a disorder, including its precursors and sequelae, with respect to the child's developmental level (Stroufe & Rutter, 1984). Developmental psychopathologists examine so-called normal development to explain pathological development. Additionally, they are interested in continuities and changes in behavior over time. In terms of its impact on child behavioral assessment, developmental psychopathology illustrates the necessity of having an understanding of how a behavior compares to a set of developmental norms and fits into a child's sociocultural environment.

For example, direct observation, the hallmark of behavioral assessment, is very useful in the assessment of social behaviors in preschoolers (Bierman & Montminy, 1993). However, the increasing complexity of social behavior during the school-age years makes the use of behavioral observations as an assessment tool more difficult. Direct observation of children at this stage of development is likely to be obtrusive and ineffective at sampling the subtle social responses of importance. Peer ratings may be a more effective predictor of children's social behavior during the school-age years (Landau, Milich, & Whitten, 1984).

Developmental considerations are also important to the diagnostic process. Historically, child behavior therapists have attempted to minimize the use of formal diagnostic labels. However, the demands of many clinical environments necessitate expertise in using the DSM-IV (American Psychiatric Association, 1994). Developmental considerations are important when utilizing the diagnostic criteria listed in the DSM-IV for several disorders. Furthermore, developmental factors should be considered across several areas of functioning, such as motor skills, and cognitive and social development, when making a diagnosis.

For example, inattention and high levels of motor activity are listed as criteria for Attention Deficit Hyperactivity Disorder. However, these behavioral excesses must be inappropriate for the child's developmental level to meet the criteria for diagnosis. Many 3-year-olds might be described as very active yet do not meet the criteria for diagnosis since excessive motor activity is not atypical at the age of 3.

Concerns for the impact of developmental factors on diagnosis has led to the development of an alternative to the traditional classification scheme. An empirically based, multivariate classification strategy has been developed based on this concern (Achenbach & Edelbrock, 1987). This scheme is characterized by sampling a variety of behaviors, typically by administering behavior rating scales, and using factor-analytic procedures to determine which behaviors tend to occur together. These groupings of behaviors, being based on empirically derived data, are more consistent with the theoretical bent of the behavior therapist.

Achenbach and Edelbrock (1984) have reported two major grouping of behaviors that consistently have emerged in numerous studies utilizing this methodology: externalizing and internalizing. *Externalizing* disorders are those characterized by behavioral excess, and typically include those children referred for attentional problems, hyperactivity, aggression, and delinquency. Conversely, *internalizing* disorders are characterized by behavioral withdrawal and are also known as "overcontrolled." Children who typically fit into this category exhibit symptoms of depression and anxiety (Achenbach & Edelbrock, 1984).

Advantages of an empirically based assessment classification system include (1) facilitation of research aimed at identification of etiological factors in the development of a disorder, (2) development of effective interventions for specific syndromes of behavior disorders, and (3) development of interest in providing information regarding long-term prognosis for children with various behavior disorders (Wells, 1981). Furthermore, the use of an empirically based classification system takes into account developmental factors through its reliance on normative data.

INDIRECT METHODS

Behavioral Interview

Multimethod behavioral assessment of children encompasses a wide range of procedures, including those typically characterized as indirect methods– behavioral interviews, self-report, and other reports (Cone, 1977). These methods are usually referred to as indirect because, although they measure behaviors of clinical relevance, they are obtained at a time and place other than when the actual behaviors occurred. These procedures include those completed by the identified patient, as well as significant others (e.g., parents, teachers) in the child's life who can report on the behavior of interest. The most common and most widely used (Swann & MacDonald, 1978) is the behavioral interview. The behavioral interview is generally considered an indispensable part of the assessment process (Gross, 1984).

Behavioral interviews are constructed to obtain information about target behaviors and their controlling variables, to begin the formulation of treatment strategies, and to build rapport with the child and his or her family (Ollendick & Cerny, 1981). One of the primary reasons why the behavioral interview has gained such popularity is its practical utility (Gross, 1984). Direct observation of clinical behaviors of interest is often not feasible. Due to the demands of the typical outpatient clinical practice, the clinician must rely on the reports of the parent, child, and significant others during the assessment process.

The interview process also allows the clinician to obtain a broad band of information regarding overall functioning in addition to specific information about more isolated presenting problems. During an interview, an adept clinician may quickly obtain information about a child's academic, social, family, and medical functioning, as well as specific details regarding the specific presenting problem. The interview typically begins with an open-ended question ("What problems have you been having with your child?"). Since parents often begin listing a variety of concerns about their child using rather nonspecific terminology ("He just does not listen"), it is the job of the clinician to elicit information to determine frequency, duration, and intensity of the problem behaviors (Witt & Elliot, 1983).

Another important objective of the behavioral interview is to gather information regarding the conditions under which the child's problem behaviors are likely to occur. For example, asking parents if the behavior occurs only at home or at school, while the child is with one or both parents or other caregiver, or if the behavior occurs at particular times of the day or week. More specific questions may also be asked regarding the specific situational determinants of the problem behavior, such as how the parent reacts to the behavior.

As part of the broad band interview process, it is often recommended that the clinician ask about putative biological controlling variables (Nelson & Hayes, 1979). For example, some children take prescribed medication for asthma that sometimes produces hyperactivity as a side effect.

In addition to requesting information regarding problem behaviors and possible situational determinants, the clinician may encourage the parent to list acceptable alternative behaviors. It is important to note that parents sometimes seek assistance with behaviors that are typical for the child's age. For example, parents may seek help for a 4-year-old child with attentional difficulties or a 3-year-old who wets the bed. These referrals may be based on parental uneasiness or unrealistic expectations rather than genuine concerns (Campbell, 1989). Providing parents with information regarding normative developmental comparisons are often useful in these cases.

At this time, it is often helpful to elicit information regarding times when the child exhibits appropriate behavior, as this often is unnoticed by parents (e.g., "When does your child comply with your requests?"). These questions may help alleviate parental concerns as well as inform the therapist as to the child's capability for change.

The interview is also an appropriate time to determine potential reinforcers for the child (e.g., "Does your child enjoy video games?"). Moreover, this provides the opportunity to discuss the potentially powerful reinforcer of parental attention.

A portion of this interview session is reserved for the therapist's conceptualization of the problem. A discussion of additional assessment techniques that may be used (such as checklists and teacher interview) should also take place. Finally, since an important component of the interview process is developing a working relationship with the parent, some description of probable treatment alternatives might be mentioned and evaluated in terms of their acceptability.

The behavioral interview is often concluded with a brief meeting with the child (Gross, 1984). Though parents or other adults are typically the persons making the referral, the notion that children are active participants in their environment, rather than passive responders, has been gaining acceptance (Ollendick & Hersen, 1993). Consequently, some time should be spent with the child in order to foster rapport as well as gather information regarding his or her perception of the problem. This brief interview can be started by asking the child why he or she believes he or she has been brought to the clinic. Since children often believe they are being blamed for the family's difficulties, it is useful to discuss how both parents, and possibly teachers or other caregivers, will be involved in treatment. For example, the child might be told the treatment will result in "everyone at home getting along better" or some similar statement.

The interview with the child is also a time for a quick evaluation of the child's capabilities, including cognitive and social abilities. Some discussion of the limits of confidentiality are also suggested, particularly with older children who may fear everything they say will be reported back to parents. Both parents and child should be told that confidentiality will be maintained except in cases where the child is engaging in harmful behavior (Gross, 1984).

Structured Interviews

The successful use of structured interviews with adults led to the development of similar methods for use with children. Structured interviews differ from unstructured interviews in that they consist of a prearranged set of questions to asked in a certain order. Because of this characteristic, they have been subjected to more psychometric evaluation than unstructured interviews. Children have been found to self-report reliably on their own behaviors, cognitions, and affective experiences (Hodges, 1993). A number of structured interviews have recently been developed (Richman & Graham, 1971; Puig-Antich & Chambers, 1978; Kovacs, 1982; Costello, Edelbrock, Kalas, Kessler, & Klaric, 1982). However, only two devices will be discussed because of their applicability for the assessment of externalizing disorders.

Most structured interviews consist of an organized list of questions to which the child and/or parent is asked to respond. Most structured interviews can be used with children in the 6 to 12-year-old age range; preschool age children have been found to answer unreliably to a structured interview. The interview questions tend to be geared toward the child's language capabilities to facilitate understanding of the questions. Most structured interview take 60 to 90 minutes to administer (LaGreca & Stone, 1992).

The Child Assessment Schedule (CAS) (Hodges, Kline, Stern, Cytryn, & McKnew, 1982) is a semistructured interview for children aged 7 to 12. Typically administered to the child's parent, it is composed of 75 items regarding school, friends, family, self-image, behaviors, mood, and thought disorder. A considerable degree of clinical judgment is required and inference is required in administering and scoring the CAS items (Achenbach & Costello, 1988). The CAS yields scores in 11 content areas (e.g., school, friends, family) and 9 symptom areas corresponding to diagnostic categories (attention deficit disorder, conduct disorder, oppositional disorder). Inte-rater reliability has been found to be .90 for total symptom score. In terms of validity, total score has been found to discriminate significantly between inpatient, outpatient, and normal groups, and to correlate significantly ($r = .53, p < .001$) with total behavior problem score on the parent version of the Child Behavior Checklist (CBCL).

The Diagnostic Interview Schedule for Children (DISC), developed by NIMH, can be used with children ages 6 to 18 (Costello et al., 1982). The DISC is a highly structured interview, with both the wording and order of all items prespecified. Versions of the DISC have been developed for individual interviews with parents (DISC-P). The child version consists of 264 items, the parent version consists 302 items. It covers a wide range of child behaviors and symptoms, including their onset, duration, and severity. Questions were designed to assess diagnostic criteria in the *DSM-III*, and nearly all major childhood diagnoses are covered. The DISC-P yields symptom severity scores in 27 areas, such as overanxious, conduct disorder, and obsessive-compulsive.

Inter-rater reliability has been reported for symptom scores, with the average being $r = .98$.

Concurrent validity of the DISC has been supported by significant correlations with the parent and teacher versions of the Child Behavior Checklist (Costello Edelbrock, Kalas, Kessler, & Klaric, 1982).

Given the wide range of behavior disorders both of these structured interviews cover, both are viable options for assessing externalizing behavior disorders in children. However, more research is needed before structured interviews can be considered adequately reliable and valid (Hodges, 1993). While structured interviews provide some helpful information to the clinician, further research is needed before they may gain the acceptance of the traditional, unstructured interview.

Behavior Rating Scales

Often after the initial interview is completed and the presenting complaint has been discussed, significant others in the child's environment may be requested to complete rating forms or checklists. Most rating scales list various child behaviors, and the rater indicates which behaviors apply to the child in question. Most of the rating scales are relatively brief and can be completed in 15 to 20 minutes.

Rating scales offer several advantages over other methods of behavioral assessment besides their efficiency for both the rater and clinician. By utilizing rating scales, the clinician has the opportunity to gather information about the child from a variety of informants who have observed the child across a variety of settings (parents, teachers, babysitters, etc.). Behaviors that occur infrequently (e.g. fire setting) and may be missed by in vivo assessment methods can be indicated on a rating form. Additionally, many provide normative data for comparisons (Barkley, 1988). Often, if the child's behavior does not deviate significantly from the norm for his or her developmental level, apprehensive parents may only need be told that information to alleviate their concerns. Conversely, if the child's behavior deviates significantly from the norm, further assessment and intervention may be warranted. Finally, rating scales are often administered at the end of treatment to demonstrate treatment gains.

The following rating scales have been chosen because of their satisfactory psychometric properties and their applicability for the assessment of externalizing disorders.

Child Behavior Checklist

The parent and teacher versions of the Child Behavior Checklist (CBCL) (Achenbach, 1978; Achenbach & Edelbrock, 1979; Edelbrock & Achenbach, 1984) were developed to cover a broad range of child behaviors. A recent revision of the CBCL (Achenbach, 1991) was normed on a national sample of children ranging in age from 4 to 18 years of age. Norms are also available for children 2 to 3 years of age (Achenbach, 1992). Relatively unique to this scale is the inclusion of items covering positive child behaviors. This rating form consists of two scales: social competence and behavior problems scale (Barkley, 1988). The social competence portion of the checklist is comprised of 20 items that assess social competence in the following areas: activities (hobbies, sports, etc.), social (organizations, friendships), and school (performance problems). The behavior problems portion contains 113 items that are rated on a scale of 0 (not true), 1 (sometimes true), and 2 (very true). Raters should read at a fifth-grade level and it requires approximately 15 minutes to complete (Achenbach, 1991).

Responses from the behavior problem portion of the checklist are plotted on the Child Behavior Profile, which is used to generate percentile and *t* scores for the several subscales making up the scale. Each behavior profile is composed of eight or nine narrow-band factors grouped under one of the broad-band syndromes, either externalizing or internalizing. Normative data were collected on a randomly selected stratified sample of children who had not received mental health services in the previous year (Achenbach, 1991).

Excellent reliability has been reported for the parent version of the CBCL. Achenbach (1991) reported one-week test-retest reliability of .89 for the behavior problem component and .87 for the social competence portion of the scale. Interparent agreement has varied considerably, ranging from .52 (Garrsion & Earls, 1985) to .99 (Achenbach & Edelbrock, 1983) for the behavior problem portion.

Investigations regarding the validity of the CBCL have revealed positive results as well. The CBCL has demonstrated adequate discriminant validity in distinguishing between clinic-referred and nonreferred children (Achenbach & Edelbrock, 1983), and children diagnosed with attention deficit disorder and normal controls (Barkley, 1981; Edelbrock & Rancurello, 1985; Mash & Johnston, 1983). It has also been found to be useful in measuring behavior change following a parent training program focusing on child management skills (Webster-Stratton, 1984).

The CBCL is undoubtedly one of the most well-developed, empirically derived rating scales currently available for the behavioral assessment of children. Its broad item content allows it to cover a wide range of both externalizing and internalizing disorders. Furthermore, its provision of normative data for different age and sex groups allow the clinician to compare a child on a number a behavioral dimensions while acknowledging the influence of developmental factors.

Behavior Problem Checklist

The original Behavior Problem Checklist (Quay & Peterson, 1975) is one of the most commonly used and widely researched rating scales. It consists of 55 items and can be completed by parents, teachers, and other care-givers in approximately 15 minutes. The scale identifies broad dimensions of psychopathology based on four orthogonal factors: conduct disorder, personality disorder, inadequacy/immaturity, and socialized/delinquent personality.

The Revised Behavior Problem Checklist (RBPC) (Quay & Peterson, 1983, 1984) is a more recently developed version of the scale and it consists of 89 items. Each item is rated on a 3-point scale measuring severity of the behavior. The RBPC permits a broader assessment of psychopathology, including psychotic behavior. Normative data are available for both parent and teacher ratings on large samples of school-age children.

Test-retest coefficients have ranged between .49 and .85 (Quay & Peterson, 1984). Adequate discriminant validity has been reported in differentiating between clinic-referred and normal populations (Aman & Werry, 1984), and children with attention deficit disorders with and without hyperactivity (Lahey, Shaughency, Strauss, & Frame, 1984).

Conners' Rating Scales

The Conners' Rating Scales are perhaps the most widely used measures for assessment of childhood hyperactivity. It is important to note that several different versions of the scale exist and different factor structures have been reported for each. A manual is currently available (Connors, 1990) that describes the most current versions of the scale. The most frequently used version of the scale, the CPRS-48, consists of 48 items that require parents to rate items on a 4-point scale ranging from "not at all" to "very much." The CPRS-48 has five factors: Conduct Problem, Learning Problem, Psychosomatic, Impulsive-Hyperactive, and Anxiety. In addition to the empirically derived scales, the parent form can be scored on a 10-item Hyperkinesis Index, which consists of items most sensitive to the effects of pharmacological treatment for hyperactivity. Adequate test-retest reliability has been demonstrated for a slightly modified version on the CPRS (Glow, Glow, & Rump, 1982). The scale has also shown good concurrent and discriminant validity (Mash & Johnston, 1983; Kuehne, Kehle, & McMahon, 1987).

Eyberg Child Behavior Inventory

The Eyberg Child Behavior Inventory (ECBI) (Eyberg & Ross, 1978) has been developed as a behaviorally specific measure for the assessment of conduct disorders. The 36 items that comprise the ECBI are rated on a scale of 0 (never) to 7 (always) by the child's parent, which yields the Total Problem Score. The parent is then asked, for each item, whether this behavior is a problem. The sum of the positively endorsed items yield the Total Intensity Score. The items were developed based on the most frequent parental complaints listed in case records of conduct-disordered children.

Norms for the ECBI were collected on a clinic-referred population ranging from 2 to 12 years of age (Robinson, Eyberg, & Ross, 1980). Test-retest reliabilities have been reported in the satisfactory range (.86 for the Problem Score and .88 for the Intensity Score). Adequate inter-parental agree-ment has also been reported (Eyberg & Robinson, 1983; Eisenstadt, McElreath, Eyberg, & McNeil, 1994). A strong correlation has been found between the Problem and Intensity Score ($r = .75$, Robinson et al., 1980). The ECBI has been shown to demonstrate discriminant validity in differentiating between normal and behavior-disordered school-age (Eyberg & Ross, 1978) and adolescent children (Eyberg & Robinson, 1983).

Matson Evaluation of Social Skills (MESSY)

The Matson Evaluation of Social Skills with Youngsters (MESSY) (Matson, Rotatori, & Helsel 1983) is designed to measure deficiencies in social functioning as well as treatment gains after social skills training. It consists of 63 items focusing on both the verbal and nonverbal aspects of social behavior, which are rated on a Likert-type scale. The scale can be completed by either teachers or parents; however; norms are available only for teachers. Two factors have been identified: Inappropriate Assertiveness/Impulsiveness and Appropriate Social Skills. Validity studies have been reported to be satisfactory (Helsel & Matson, 1984; Raymond & Matson, 1989), but further psychometric validation is needed for the MESSY. Nevertheless, this measure provides an empirically based social skills assessment tool.

General Issues

This review has described some of most commonly employed rating scales used in the assessment of externalizing behavior disorders in children. All of the measures presented have been shown to demonstrate adequate reliability and validity; however, some might benefit from the collection of additional normative data. Each of these measures may be used as both a screening device and to measure the effectiveness of a treatment program. In particular, both the CPRS and the ECBI have been demonstrated to be sensitive to treatment intervention. Furthermore, these measures may be used to assess long-term follow-up assessment.

A few problems regarding the use of behavior rating scales should be discussed here. Despite the fact the structured rating scales are typically described as "objective" measures of children's behavior, they are susceptible to the errors and bias of the rater. An individual rater may respond in such a way as to make the child appear very deviant. Conversely, a parent who is not in favor of treatment may tend to minimize problem behaviors. A possible solution to this problem is the use of multiple raters who independently complete the checklist. If ratings differ substantially, alternative assessment methods might prove more useful in determining the course of treatment.

An additional problem with rating scales is that they offer no information as to the controlling contingencies of a child's behavior. Because knowledge of antecedents and consequences of behavior are essential to a behavior analyst's treatment plan, rating scales should always be used in conjunction with other assessment techniques better designed to identify these variables.

SELF-REPORT INSTRUMENTS

Relative to other behavioral assessment methods, the self-report measure has received the least attention and empirical support. Behavior analysts have traditionally eschewed self-report measures due to their dubious validity and reliability. However, self-report rating scales provide an efficient and convenient manner to assess children in need of treatment. They typically require only a few minutes to complete and may be used to supplement other assessment methods to derive information regarding a child's strengths and weaknesses.

Developmental factors are particularly important when utilizing self-report methods. Very few measures are designed for use with children below the age of 7 years, due to the limited reading ability of children at these ages. Also important in the use of self-report instruments with children is the expectation that the youngster is capable of reporting his or her behavior, affect, cognitions, and so on. This ability to self-monitor is developmentally sensitive; data suggest that although young children can monitor overt behaviors, they are less likely to be able to report on more internalized phenomena, such as feelings of sadness (Stone & Lemanek, 1990).

Many of the current self-report instruments are designed to assess specific areas of functioning,

such as social skills and aggressive behaviors (Nelson & Finch, 1978; Deluty, 1979; Michelson & Wood, 1982). Others have been developed that cover a wide range of behavioral and emotional problems (Beitchman, Raman, Carlson, Clegg, & Kruidenier, 1985). Only those that focus on externalizing disorders will be discussed here.

Several measures have been developed to assess aggression, anger, and assertiveness in children. The Children's Inventory of Anger (Nelson & Finch, 1978) is a measure designed to assess anger control problems in third- through eighth-grade children. The CIA consists of 71 items that use a 4-point response format. Each possible response is depicted by a facial expression, ranging from slightly angry to very angry. Finch and Rogers (1984) report the CIA possesses high internal consistency and test-retest reliability, as well as construct and criterion-related validity with normal and clinic-referred children.

The Children's Action Tendency Scale (CATS) measures several externalizing behaviors, such as aggressiveness, assertiveness, and submission in school-aged children. Its 30 items measure how a child might respond in situations involving provocation, loss, frustration, and conflict (Deluty, 1979). The child is presented with these situations and given a choice as to how he or she might respond (assertively, aggressively, or submissively). Scores on the CATS have been shown to correlate with peer and teacher reports of social behavior and to possess moderate split-half and test-retest reliabilities (Deluty, 1979). Moderate agreement has also been reported between CATS scores and measures of aggressiveness, assertiveness, and submissiveness obtained through direct observation of children in their school environments (Deluty, 1984).

The Children's Assertive Behavior Scale (CABS) (Michelson & Wood, 1982) is a 27-item self-report measure of assertive behavior for children in fourth through sixth grades. The child is presented with a social situation and chooses one of five possible responses ranging from very passive to very aggressive. The authors, in an unpublished paper, reported adequate validity and relatively high test-retest reliability for the CABS ($r = .87$). Furthermore, behavioral observations of assertive behavior correlated significantly with scores on the CABS and the CABS was shown to differentiate between fourth-grade children who had received social skills training and those who had not (Michelson & Wood, 1982).

The previously discussed scales focus primarily on social behaviors in children, but two scales have recently been developed that measure a wider range of behavioral and emotional features in children. The Children's Self-Report Rating Scale (Beitchman et al., 1985) is a 55-item measure that yields scores on the following dimensions: conduct problems, lie-immaturity, positive self-peer, worry, negative peer, antisocial-permissive, sensitive-emotional, and positive family factors. The measure is designed for use with children from 6 to 13 years. The CSRS has been reported to differentiate effectively between clinic-referred and normal children (Beitchman, Kruidenier, & Clegg, 1987).

The Youth Self-Report (YSR) (Achenbach & Edelbrock, 1987), similar to the Child Behavior Checklist, is a 102-item measure designed for use with children from 11 to 18 years. The YSR presents the respondent with items (e.g. "I cry a lot") to which the subject responds "not true," "somewhat or sometimes true," or "very true or often true." The YSR requires a fifth-grade reading level to complete.

Responses to the YSR are scored on the YSR Profile, which has separate forms for each sex for ages 11 to 18. The 1991 version of the profile provides scores for activities and social scales, total competence, total problems, internalizing and externalizing problems, and nine narrow-band syndrome scales. The scales of the 1991 YSR profile were normed on 1,315 randomly selected nonreferred youths. Adequate reliability and validity have been reported for the YSR (Achenbach, 1991). All of the YSR scales adequately differentiated between referred and nonreferred samples of children for both sexes.

Overall, the strengths and weaknesses for self-report measures and behavioral rating scales are similar. Although they provide a convenient method for gathering information, they are subject to rater bias and still require additional research regarding their psychometric properties (Ollendick

& Greene, 1990). Furthermore, they provide little information as to the controlling contingencies of targeted behaviors. To this end, direct methods of behavioral observation are better suited in identifying the variables contributing to the child's behavioral difficulties.

DIRECT METHODS

Direct observation of behavior in natural settings has been the hallmark of behavioral assessment with children. Although behavioral assessment has recently broadened its scope, direct observation has long been considered to be of greatest utility in behavioral assessment (LaGreca & Stone, 1992). Two major approaches will be discussed in this section: observation in the child's natural setting (e.g., at home or at school) and observation of parent/child interaction in analog (clinic) settings.

Observation in Natural Settings

Naturalistic observations of children have been conducted in a variety of settings, such as homes (Patterson; 1977; Wahler, House, & Stambaugh, 1976), classrooms (Reed & Edelbrock, 1983; Abikoff, Gittelman, & Klein, 1980), and playgrounds (LaGreca & Stark, 1986). Though they are expensive, inconvenient, and often intrusive, observations conducted in the natural setting often provide the most meaningful information. Both data on the child's behavior as well as on the child's social environment can be reliably gathered.

The utility of behavioral observations depends on the reliability and validity of the coding systems employed for conducting the observations. Well-validated observational codes have been reported to minimize observer bias (Abikoff, Gittleman-Klein, & Klein, 1977) and observer drift (Foster & Cone, 1986). A well-validated and clearly defined observational code is also advantageous for providing reliable diagnostic information (LaGreca & Stone, 1992).

Some of the most extensively validated codes have been designed to focus on parent/child interaction and externalizing behavior problems, such as aggression and attention deficits (Abikoff, Gittleman-Klein, & Klein, 1977; Reed & Edelbrock, 1983; Eyberg & Robinson, 1983; Foster & Robin, 1988). One of the most frequently used observation codes is the Family Interaction Coding System (FICS) (Patterson, Ray, Shaw, & Cobb, 1969), developed for observing family interactions in the home. This code has most often been used with children referred for conduct disorders and aggressive behavior disorders (Patterson, Reid, Jones, & Conger, 1975). Child and parent behaviors are coded into one of 29 behavior categories, such as command, compliance, destructive, and physical negative. Behaviors are coded sequentially so that antecedents and consequences of the child's behavior can be determined. The FICS is a relatively complex coding system, requiring approximately 50 hours of observer training time.

The FICS has been well validated, with the overall reliability estimate reported as .87 (Weinrott & Jones, 1984). The code reliably distinguishes between oppositional/conduct-disordered children and normal controls. The FICS has also been found to correlate moderately well with other assessment instruments (see Patterson, 1982, for review).

While the FICS is an example of an observational code developed for use in the home, Abikoff and associates (1977) developed a school-based code designed to assess children with Attention Deficit Hyperactivity Disorder. This code, designed to facilitate the identification of behavior problems in the classroom, can be used with children between 6 and 12 years of age. Children are observed in their classrooms for 4-minute periods, comprised of 15-second intervals. Fourteen total behavioral categories are coded, such as off-task, noncompliance, out of chair, and extended verbalization. Interobserver agreement has been reported as satisfactory. Twelve of the 14 behavior categories were shown to discriminate reliably between ADHD and normal children (Abikoff, Gittelman, & Klein, 1980).

Although these structured behavioral coding schemes are relevant for the assessment of many externalizing behavior disorders, at times behavior therapists must identify target behaviors for observation that are unique to a particular case (Foster &

Cone, 1986). In such cases, the first step in observational assessment is selecting appropriate target behavior for observation. Target behaviors can be determined via interview with the parents and/or teachers or by informal observations of the child during the initial visit (Barton & Ascione, 1984).

Once a target behavior has been selected and defined, observations should include evaluating specific antecedents and consequences of the target behavior. This information will allow the clinician to create a functional analysis of the behavior in question. For example, if a target behavior of hitting is selected, the observer should note what behaviors occur before and after the hitting is observed.

An important consideration when utilizing a behavioral observation scheme is selecting and training observers. Although many clinicians prefer to use trained assistants to conduct observations, many are training parents, teachers, and others already present in the child's environment to serve as observers (Loeber, Dishion, & Patterson, 1984). Regardless of who serves as an observer, two important issues should be discussed: observer drift and observer reactivity. *Observer drift* occurs when observers gradually depart from the original definitions of the target behaviors (Kent, O'Leary, Diament, & Dietz, 1974). Observer drift can be prevented by conducting periodic reliability checks and frequent observer training sessions (Kazdin, 1981). Furthermore, observer drift has been found to occur less frequently when behavioral categories are narrowly defined and observers are trained simultaneously in a group to minimize various code interpretations (Weinrott & Jones, 1984).

Observer reactivity may serve as a potential problem during observational assessment. Reactivity occurs when the behavior of the child or significant others is altered by the presence of the observer (Haynes & Horn, 1982). Solutions to combat observer reactivity include using covert observational procedures, using video or tape recorders, minimizing subject/observer interaction, using participant observers, and allowing a short amount of time for reactivity to dissipate before utilizing collected observation data.

Observations in Analog Settings

In many instances, it is not practical or feasible to observe the child and family in a naturalistic setting, yet observational assessment is warranted to facilitate treatment. These cases are especially conducive to structured observational formats, or analog assessments. Analog settings provide an opportunity to observe the parent or child in a standard situation that has been designed to elicit the behaviors of interest (LaGreca & Stone, 1992). Analog assessments have been used extensively in behaviorally oriented child clinical settings (Roberts & Forehand, 1978) and offer several advantages over naturalistic observations. They are often more convenient, cost effective, and less intrusive than naturalistic measures. Unlike naturalistic observations, they usually ensure the occurrence of the target behavior of interest since they are designed with this goal in mind.

An assessment procedure developed by Forehand and colleagues (Forehand, Cheney, Yoder, 1974; Forehand, Sturgis, McMahan, Aguar, Green, Wells, & Breiner, 1979) typifies the analog assessment method. This procedure involves observing mother and child in a clinic playroom and instructing the mother to spend the first five minutes engaged in whatever activity the child chooses (Child's game) and the following five minutes engaged in an activity of the mother's choosing (Mother's game). The child's behavior is scored for compliance, noncompliance, and inappropriate behavior (e.g., whining, crying) and the mother's behavior is scored for commands (direct and vague), warnings, questions, attention, and rewards (Forehand & MacMahon, 1981).

This code has been found to distinguish between referred and nonreferred children (Forehand et al., 1979) and has been demonstrated to be sensitive to treatment effects. For example, after participation in a parent training program, parents were observed to display lower rates of commands and higher rates of rewards utilizing this analog assessment (MacMahon & Forehand, 1988).

The ADHD Behavior Coding System (Barkely, 1990) was developed to assess ADHD symptoms in an analog setting. The child is placed alone in a playroom and requested to complete a packet of math problems. The child is asked to complete as many problems as possible within 15 minutes, not to leave the chair and table, and not to touch any of the toys in the playroom. Behavior is scored using five codes: "off task," "fidgets," "out of seat," "vocalizes," "plays with objects." Inter-rater agreement has been reported to range form .77 to .85. Normative data have not been reported as of yet for this coding system. Besides this assessment procedure, the Dyadic Parent-Child Interaction Coding System (Eyberg & Robinson, 1983) and the Parent-Adolescent Interaction Coding System (Foster & Robin, 1988) are other excellent examples of analog assessment formats.

Despite the utility of structured assessment formats such as these, some limitations have been cited. There has been a paucity of studies that focus on father/child and father/mother/child interactions (Hugh & Haynes, 1978). Future structured observational codes might include both parents, as well as all family members whenever possible. Developmental considerations are also just beginning to receive attention from clinicians interested in the developing analog formats. LaGreca and Stone (1992) suggest the establishment of developmental guidelines for so-called normal behavior when utilizing this assessment format.

Case Example

Amanda is a 7-year-old, second-grade girl who was referred to a behavior management clinic by her mother (Mrs. S.) due to reports of not following parental instructions and a "bad attitude." Furthermore, Mrs. S. reported that Amanda was frequently in trouble at school, often getting into physical fights with other children. Amanda lived at home with both parents and an older sister, age 10.

Mrs. S. brought Amanda to the clinic for the initial visit and was asked to complete the CBCL while Amanda played with other children in the playroom. The therapist conducted an unstructured interview with Mrs. S and began by inquiring when Amanda began having these behavior problems. Mrs. S. stated that Amanda has "always been difficult," but the problems had worsened since Amanda began school two years ago. Amanda's developmental history was reportedly unremarkable. Mrs. S.'s descriptions of Amanda's behavior problems were initially vague, so she was asked to clarify what she meant by Amanda's "bad attitude" in the following dialogue:

Therapist: What exactly is it that Amanda does that causes you to describe her as having a bad attitude?

Mrs. S.: I suppose it is the way she will not do the things I ask her to, even after I ask several times. Even if she does do what I ask, she usually does not do a good job, and sulks afterward.

Therapist: Is that what you mean by bad attitude?

Mrs. S.: Yes, I guess so. It's gotten so bad that I would rather do her chores for her rather than ask her to do them.

Therapist: So often Amanda does not have to do her chores because it is easier to do them yourself?

Mrs. S.: Yes, sometimes I would rather avoid yelling at her so I clean up her room myself.

Further discussion with Mrs. S indicated that the most problematic issues were Amanda's refusal to clean her room every day and putting the dishes in the dishwasher, her daily chore. She also stated that Amanda and her older sister often argued because Amanda did not do her chores, and the older sister was often left to do Amanda's chores. Thus, increasing the rate of compliance for daily chores were selected as initial goals.

When asked about Amanda's positive characteristics, Mrs. S. stated that Amanda was a very affectionate child, especially when she was not being asked to do her chores. She stated that she and Amanda often enjoyed doing activities together such as riding bikes or baking cookies. She stated that Amanda was a bright child and did well in school when she was not misbehaving. The therapist suggested to Mrs. S. that Amanda's sulking behavior probably resulted in positive gains for her (e.g., getting out of household chores). Furthermore, Mrs. S.'s completion of Amanda's chores for her probably resulted in the avoidance of

Amanda's sulking behavior, which was negatively reinforcing for Mrs. S.

The therapist informed Ms. S. that a parent training program might be suitable but that additional assessment should take place before beginning the program. Mrs. S. was scheduled for two clinic observation sessions and was also asked to record Amanda's behavior at home. Specifically, she was asked to record behavioral sequences when she asked Amanda to clean her room every day. She was instructed to code the following behaviors: command, compliance, noncompliance, additional command, and sulk/tantrum. Immediately following each episode, the coded sequence of behavior and the time of day were to be recorded.

After meeting with Mrs. S., the therapist spoke briefly with Amanda. Amanda stated that she was at the clinic because she was "bad" and fought with her mother and sister. The therapist explained that by working together, the entire family would learn how to get along better, and that no particular family member was at fault for their difficulties in getting along with each other. Amanda agreed to participate in treatment. When asked why she thought she and her mother fought, she stated that her mother was always asking her to clean her room when she wanted to go outside and ride her bike. In general, Amanda's descriptions of the problems seemed to coincide with Mrs. S's.

With Mrs. S's permission, the therapist contacted Amanda's teacher. The teacher reported that Amanda was a bright and hard-working child, but sometimes was noncompliant to teacher instructions. Furthermore, when frustrated with the teacher's reprimands, Amanda would often become angry and hit or pinch other children. The teacher agreed to complete a TRF and remained open to future contacts with the therapist if necessary.

Amanda's scores on the CBCL completed by Mrs. S. indicated that many of the scores were elevated in the externalizing domain, particularly on the aggressive scale. The teacher-completed TRF also indicated elevated scores in the aggressive domain. These data appeared consistent with information gathered from Amanda's mother during the initial interview.

During the next two meetings, Mrs. S. was instructed to interact with Amanda in the clinic playroom while their behavior was observed and recorded via a one-way mirror. During both observation periods, Mrs. S. was instructed to allow Amanda to do the interactive activity of her choosing for the first 10 minutes, and then to instruct Amanda to do the activity of her own (Mrs. S.'s) choosing (Forehand & MacMahon, 1981). Mother and child behavior was coded sequentially according to the structured code. Observational data revealed that Mrs. S. issued a large number of vague commands and Amanda typically ignored these commands, particularly when she was engaged in a task of her choosing.

Based on the information gathered from these observations, interviews, and behavior rating scales, Mrs. S. was encouraged to participate in a parent training program. The program focused on teaching parents the use of contingent attention and other forms of rewards for appropriate behavior, particularly phrasing commands in a clear manner and employing brief time-out for inappropriate behavior. Consistency of behavior management practices was also stressed, as this was a particular problem for Mrs. S. The same structured clinic observations were conducted on a weekly basis to assess Amanda's progress.

After several weeks of training, observations indicated that Mrs. S. had improved the clarity of her commands, was more consistent with her requests, and had become adept at utilizing time-out. Verbal reports from Amanda's teacher indicated that Amanda had become more compliant and less aggressive in the classroom. Further treatment focused on increasing Mrs. S.'s use of praise for Amanda's appropriate behavior, as well as incorporating favorite activities into her routine contingent on good behavior. Home observations conducted by Mrs. S. were designed to further monitor Amanda's progress.

At the conclusion of the parent training program, Mrs. S. reported that Amanda's behavior was much improved. This was corroborated with observational data collected in the clinic and at home. Mrs. S. was asked to complete the CBCL once again, which indicated that although Amanda continued to exhibit some aggressive behaviors, they fell within the normal range for girls her age.

SUMMARY

The field of behavioral assessment in children has evidenced rapid growth. Although behavioral assessment traditionally has focused on observable behaviors, cognitive and affective components of behavior are beginning to be incorporated into the assessment process. The field of developmental psychopathology has also had a great impact on child behavior assessment. The present chapter has described the range of techniques available to child behavior therapists and illustrated their application with a case example.

Classification of child behavior disorders has incorporated developmental factors through an empirically based system that addresses some of the criticisms of disease model classification systems. This system identifies two major syndromes of behavior: externalizing (characterized by behavioral excess) and internalizing (characterized by behavioral withdrawal). This chapter focused primarily on those disorders that fall within the externalizing domain.

The methods available for child behavioral assessment fall into two categories: indirect and direct. The indirect methods include the behavioral interview, behavioral rating scales, and self-report instruments for children. Whereas the unstructured behavioral interview is likely the most commonly used assessment method, structured interviews provide an alternative that has received more rigorous psychometric evaluation. Rating scales and self-report instruments can serve a useful screening function because of their reliance on normative data and the wide range of topics they cover. Their primary weakness is their inability to provide information as to the controlling variables of a child's behavior.

The direct methods include naturalistic and analog observations and are better suited to provide information as to the controlling variables of a child's behavior. Several coding systems were reviewed, as well as information regarding how to use them effectively. Guidelines for developing codes designed to monitor specific behaviors were also discussed.

REFERENCES

Abikoff, H., Gittelman, R., & Klein, D. F. (1980). Classroom observation code for hyperactive children: A replication of validity. *Journal of Consulting and Clinical Psychology, 45*, 772–783.

Abikoff, H., Gittelman-Klein, R., & Klein, D. F. (1977). Validation of a classroom observation code for hyperactive children. *Journal of Consulting and Clinical Psychology, 45*, 772–783.

Achenbach, T. M. (1978). The Child Behavior Profile: I. Boys aged 6–11. *Journal of Consulting and Clinical Psychology, 4*, 478–488.

Achenbach, T. M. (1991). *Manual for the Child Behavior Checklist/4–18 and 1991 Profile*. Burlington: University of Vermont, Department of Psychiatry.

Achenbach, T. M. (1991). *Manual for the Youth Self-Report and 1991 Profile*. Burlington: University of Vermont, Department of Psychiatry.

Achenbach, T. M. (1992). *Manual for the Child Behavior Checklist/2-3 and 1992 Profile*. Burlington, VT: University of Vermont Department of Psychiatry.

Achenbach, T. M., & Costello, A. J. (1988). Structured psychiatric interviews for children. In M. Rutter, A. Tuma, & I. Lann (Eds.), *Assessment and diagnosis in child psychopathology* (pp. 87–112). New York: Guilford.

Achenbach, T. M., & Edelbrock, C. S. (1979). The Child Behavior Profile II. Boys aged 12–16 and girls aged 6–11 and 12–16. *Journal of Consulting and Clinical Psychology, 47*, 223–233.

Achenbach, T. M., & Edelbrock, C. (1983). *Manual for the Child Behavior Checklist and Revised Child Behavior Profile*. Burlington: University of Vermont Department of Psychiatry.

Achenbach, T. M., & Edelbrock, C. S. (1984). Psychopathology of childhood. *Annual review of Psychology, 35*, 227–256.

Achenbach, T. M., & Edelbrock, C. S. (1987). *Manual for the youth self-report and profile*. Burlington: University of Vermont.

Achenbach, T. M., & McConaughy, S. H. (1987). *Empirically based assessment of child and adolescent psychopathology: Practical applications*. Newbury Park, CA: Sage.

Aman, M. G., & Werry, J. S. (1984). The Revised Behavior Problem Checklist in clinic attenders and nonattenders: Age and sex effects. *Journal of Clinical Child Psychology, 13*, 237–242.

American Psychiatric Association. (1994). *Diagnostic and statistical manual of mental disorders* (4th ed.). Washington, DC: Author.

Barkley, R. A. (1981). *Hyperactive children: A handbook for diagnosis and treatment*. New York: Guilford.

Barkley, R. A. (1988). Child behavior rating scales and checklists. In M. Rutter, A. Tuma, & I. Lann (Eds.), *Assessment and diagnosis in child psychopathology* (pp. 113–155). New York: Guilford.

Barkley, R. A. (1990). *Attention-Deficit Hyperactivity Disorder: A handbook for diagnosis and treatment*. New York: Guilford.

Barton, E. J., & Ascione, F. R. (1984). Direct observation. In T. H. Ollendick & M. Hersen (Eds.), *Child behavioral assessment* (pp. 166–194). New York: Pergamon.

Bierman, K., & Montminy, H. P. (1993). Developmental issues in social skills assessment and intervention with children and adolescents. *Behavior Modification, 17*, 229–254.

Beitchman, J. H., Kruidenier, B., & Clegg, M. (1987). The Children's Self-Report Rating Scale: Screening accuracy and predictive power reconsidered. *Journal of the American Association of Child and Adolescent Psychiatry, 26*, 49–52.

Beitchman, J. H., Raman, S., Carlson, S., Clegg, M., & Kruidenier, B. (1985). The development and validation of the Children's Self-Report Rating Scale: Screening accuracy and predictive power reconsidered. *Journal of the American Association of Child and Adolescent Psychiatry, 26*, 49–52.

Campbell, S. B. (1989). Developmental perspectives in child psychopathology. In T. H. Ollendick & M. Hersen (Eds.), *Handbook of child psychopathology* (2nd ed.) (pp. 5–28). New York: Plenum.

Cone, J. D. (1977). The relevance of reliability and validity for behavioral assessment. *Behavior Therapy, 8*, 411–426.

Connors, C. K. (1990). *Manual for Connors' Rating Scales*. Toronto: Multi-Health Systems, Inc.

Costello, A. J., Edelbrock, C., Dulcan, M. K., Kalas, R., & Klaric, S. H. (1984). *Development and testing of the NIMH Diagnostic Interview Schedule for Children in a clinic population*. Final report (Contract No. RFP-DB-81-0027). Rockville, MD: Center for Epidemiologic Studies, National Institute of Mental Health.

Costello, A. J., Edelbrock, C., Kalas, R., Kessler, M. D., & Klaric, S. H. (1982). *The NIMH Diagnostic Interview Schedule for Children (DISC)*. Unpublished interview schedule, Department of Psychiatry, University of Pittsburgh.

Deluty, R. H. (1979). Children's Action Tendency Scale: A self-report measure of aggressiveness, assertiveness, and submissiveness in children. *Journal of Consulting and Clinical Psychology, 47*, 1061–1071.

Deluty, R. H. (1984). Behavioral validation of the Children's Action Tendency Scale. *Journal of Behavioral Assessment, 6*, 115–130.

Edelbrock, C., & Achenbach, T. M. (1980). The teacher version of the Child Behavior Profile: I. Boys aged 6–11. *Journal of Consulting and Clinical Psychology, 52*, 207–217.

Edelbrock, C. S., & Achenbach, T. M. (1984). The teacher version of the Child Behavior Profile: I. Boys aged 6–11. *Journal of Consulting and Clinical Psychology, 52*, 207–217.

Edelbrock, C. S., & Rancurello, M. D. (1985). Childhood hyperactivity: An overview of rating scales and their applications. *Clinical Psychology Review, 5*, 429–445.

Eisenstadt, T. H., McElreath, L. H., Eyberg, S. M., & McNeil, C. B. (1994). Interparent agreement on the Eyberg Child Behavior Inventory. *Child and Family Behavior Therapy, 16*, 21–27.

Eyberg, S. M., & Robinson, E. A. (1983). Conduct problem behavior: Standardization of a behavioral rating scale with adolescents. *Journal of Clinical Child Psychology, 12*, 347–354.

Eyberg, S. M., & Ross, A. W. (1978). Assessment of child behavior problems: The validation of a new inventory. *Journal of Clinical Child Psychology, 12*, 347–354.

Finch, A. J., & Rogers, T. R. (1984). Self-report instruments. In T. H. Ollendick & M. Hersen (Eds.), *Child behavioral assessment: Principles and procedures* (pp. 106–123). New York: Particularly.

Forehand, R., Cheney, T., & Yoder, P. (1974). Parent behavior training: Effects of noncompliance of a deaf child. *Journal of Behavior Therapy and Experimental Psychiatry, 5*, 281–283.

Forehand, R., & MacMahon, R. J. (1981). *Helping the noncompliant child*. New York: Guilford.

Forehand, R., Sturgis, E. T., McMahon, R. J., Aguar, D., Green, K., Wells, K. C., & Breiner, J. (1979). Parent behavioral training to modify child noncompliance: Treatment generalization across time and from home to school. *Behavior Modification, 3*, 3–25.

Foster, S. L., & Cone, J. D. (1986). Design and use of direct observation procedures. In A. R. Ciminero, K. S. Calhoun, & H. E. Adams (Eds.). *Handbook of behavioral assessment* (2nd ed.) (pp. 253–324). New York: Wiley.

Foster, S. L., & Robin, A. L. (1988). Family conflict and communication in adolescence. In E. J. Mash & L. G. Terdal (Eds.), *Behavioral assessment of childhood disorders* (2nd ed.) (pp. 717–775). New York: Guilford.

Garrison, W. T., & Earls, F. (1985). The Child Behavior Checklist as a screening instrument for young children. *Journal of the American Academy of Child Psychiatry, 24*, 76–80.

Glow, R. A., Glow, P. A., & Rump, E. E. (1982). The stability of child behavior disorders: A one year test-retest study of adelaide versions of the Conners Teacher and Parent Rating Scales. *Journal of Abnormal Child Psychology, 10*, 33–60.

Gross, A. M. (1984). Behavioral Interviewing. In T. H. Ollendick & M. Hersen (Eds.), *Child behavioral assessment: Principles and procedures* (pp. 61–79). New York: Pergamon.

Haynes, S. N., & Horn, W. (1982). Reactivity in behavioral observation: A review. *Behavioral Assessment, 4*, 369–385.

Helsel, W. J., & Matson, J. L. (1984). The assessment of depression in children: The internal structure of the Child Depression Inventory (CDI). *Behaviour Research and Therapy, 22*, 289–298.

Hodges, K. (1993). Structured interviews for assessing children. *Journal of Child Psychology and Psychiatry, 34*, 49–68.

Hodges, K., Kline, J., Stern, L., Cytryn, L., & McKnew, D. (1982). The development of a child assessment interview for research and clinical use. *Journal of Abnormal Child Psychology, 10*, 173–189.

Hugh, H. M., & Haynes, S. N. (1978). Structured laboratory observation in the behavioral assessment of parent-child interaction: A methodological critique. *Behavior Therapy, 9*, 428–447.

Kazdin, A. E. (1981). Behavioral observations. In M. Hersen & A. S. Bellack (Eds.), *Behavioral assessment* (pp. 101–124). New York: Pergamon.

Kent, R. N., O'Leary, D. K., Diament, C., & Dietz, A. (1974). Expectation biases in observational evaluation of therapeutic change. *Journal of Consulting and Clinical Psychology, 42*, 774–780.

Kimball, W., Nelson, M. N., & Politano, M. P. (1993). The role of development variables in cognitive-behavioral interventions with children. In A. J. Fince, W. M. Nelson, & E. Ott (Eds.), *Cognitive-*

behavioral procedures with children and adolescents: A practical handbook (pp. 25–66). Boston: Allyn and Bacon.

Kovacs, M. (1982). The Interview Schedule for Children (ISC): Interrater and parent-child agreement. Unpublished manuscript.

Kuehne, C., Kehle, T. J., & McMahon, W. (1987). Differences between children with Attention Deficit Disorder, children with Specific Learning Disabilities, and normal children. Journal of School Psychology, 25, 161–166.

LaGreca, A. M., & Stark, P. (1986). Naturalistic observations of children's social behavior. In P. Strain, M. Guralnick, & H. Walker (Eds.), Children's social behavior: Developmental assessment and modification (pp. 181–213). New York: Academic Press.

LaGreca, A. M., & Stone, W. L. (1992). Assessing children through interviews and behavioral observations. In C. Walker & M. Roberts (Eds.), Handbook of clinical child psychology (2nd ed.) (pp. 63–84). New York: Wiley.

Lahey, B. B., Shaughency, E. A., Strauss, C. C., & Frame, C. L. (1984). Are attention deficit disorders with and without hyperactivity similar or dissimilar disorders? Journal of the American Academy of Child Psychiatry, 23, 302–309.

Landau, S., Milich, R., & Whitten, P. (1984). A comparison of teacher and peer assessment of social status. Journal of Clinical Child Psychology, 13, 44–49.

Loeber, R., Dishion, T. J., & Patterson, G. R. (1984). Multiple gating: A multistage assessment procedure for identifying youths at risk for delinquency. Journal of Research in Crime and Delinquency, 21, 7–32.

Mash, E. J., & Johnston, C. (1983). Parental perceptions of child behavior problems, parenting self-esteem, and mother's reported stress in younger and older hyperactive and normal children. Journal of Consulting and Clinical Psychology, 51, 68–99.

Mash, E. J., & Terdal, L. G. (1989). Behavioral assessment of childhood disturbance. In E. J. Mash & L. J. Terdal (Eds.), Behavioral assessment of childhood disorders (2nd ed.). New York: Guilford.

Matson, J. L., Rotatori, A. F., & Helsel, W. J. (1983). Development of a rating scale to measure social skills in children: The Matson Evaluation of Social Skills with Youngsters (MESSY). Behaviour Research and Therapy, 21, 335–340.

McMahon, R. J., & Forehand, R. (1988). Conduct disorders. In E. J. Mash & L. Terdal (Eds.), Behavioral assessment of childhood disorders (2nd ed.) (pp. 105–153). New York: Guilford.

Michelson, L., & Wood, R. (1982). Development and psychometric properties of the Children's Assertive Behavior Scale. Journal of Behavioral Assessment, 4, 3–13.

Mischel, W. (1973). Toward a cognitive social learning reconceptualization of personality. Psychological Review, 80, 252–283.

Nelson, W. M., & Finch, A. J. (1978). The children's inventory of anger. Unpublished manuscript. Cincinatti: Xavier University.

Nelson, R. O., & Hayes, S. C. (1979). Some current dimensions of behavioral assessment. Behavioral Assessment, 1, 1–16.

Ollendick, T. H., & Cerny, J. A. (1981). Clinical behavior therapy with children. New York: Plenum.

Ollendick, T. H., & Greene, R. (1990). Behavioral assessment of children. In G. Goldstein & M. Hersen (Eds.), Handbook of psychological assessment (2nd ed.) (pp. 403–422). New York: Pergamon.

Ollendick, T. H., & Hersen, M. (Eds.). (1989). Handbook of child psychopathology (2nd ed.). New York: Plenum.

Ollendick, T. H. & Hersen, M. (Eds.). (1993). Handbook of child and adolescent assessment. Boston: Allyn and Bacon.

Patterson, G. R. (1977). Naturalistic observation in clinical assessment. Journal of Abnormal Child Psychology, 5, 309–322.

Patterson, G. R. (1982). Coercive family process. Eugene, OR: Castalia.

Patterson, G. R., Ray, R. S., Shaw, D. A., & Cobb, J. A. (1969). Manual for coding family interactions (6th rev. ed.). Available from ASIS National Auxiliary Publication Service, c/o CCM Information Services, Inc., Third Ave., New York, N.Y. 10022 Document No. 01234.

Patterson, G. R., Reid, J. B., Jones, R. R., & Conger, R. (1975). A social learning approach to family intervention: Families with aggressive children (Vol. 1). Eugene, OR: Castalia.

Puig-Antich, J., & Chambers, W. (1978). The Schedule for Affective Disorders and Schizophrenia for school-aged children. New York State Psychiatric Institute.

Quay, H. C., & Peterson, D. R. (1975). Manual for the Behavior Problem Checklist. Unpublished manuscript, University of Miami.

Quay, H. C., & Peterson, D. R. (1983). Interim manual for the Revised Behavior Problem Checklist. Unpublished manuscript, University of Miami.

Quay, H. C., & Peterson, D. R. (1984). Appendix I to the interim manual for the Revised Behavior Problem

Checklist. Unpublished manuscript, University of Miami.

Raymond, K. I., & Matson, J. L. (1989). Social skills in the hearing impaired. *Journal of Clinical Child Psychology, 18*, 247–258.

Reed, M. L., & Edelbrock, C. (1983). Reliability and validity of the Direct Observation Form of the Child Behavior Checklist. *Journal of Abnormal Child Psychology, 11*, 521–530.

Richman, N., & Graham, P. (1971). A behavioral screening questionnaire for use with three-year old children: Preliminary findings. *Journal of Child Psychology and Psychiatry, 12*, 5–33.

Roberts, M. W., & Forehand, R. (1978). The assessment of maladaptive parent-child interaction by direct observation: An analysis of methods. *Journal of Abnormal Child Psychology, 6*, 257–270.

Robinson, E. A., Eyberg, S. M., & Ross, A. W. (1980). The standardization of an inventory of child conduct problem behaviors. *Journal of Clinical Child Psychology, 9*, 22–28.

Shaffer, D. (1985). Enuresis. In M. Rutter & L. Hersov (Eds.), *Child and adolescent psychiatry: Modern approaches* (2nd ed.) (pp. 465–481). Oxford: Blackwell Scientific Publications.

Stone, W. L., & Lemanek, K. L. (1990). Developmental issues in children's self-reports. In A. M. LaGreca (Ed.), *Through the eyes of the child: Obtaining self-reports from children and adolescents* (pp. 18–56). Boston: Allyn and Bacon.

Stroufe, L. A., & Rutter, M. (1984). The domain of developmental psychopathology. *Child Development, 55*, 17–29.

Swann, G. E., & MacDonald, M. L. (1978). Behavior therapy in practice: A rational survey of behavior therapists. *Behavior Therapy, 9*, 799–807.

Wahler, R. G., House, A. E., & Stambaugh, E. E. (1976). *Ecological assessment of child problem behaviors*. New York: Pergamon.

Webster-Stratton, C. (1984). Randomized trial of two parent training programs for families with conduct-disordered children. *Journal of Consulting and Clinical Psychology, 11*, 123–129.

Weinrott, M. R., & Jones, R. R. (1984). Overt versus covert assessment of observer reliability. *Child Development, 55*, 1125–1137.

Wells, K. C. (1981). Assessment of children in outpatient settings. In M. Hersen & A. S. Bellack (Eds.), *Behavioral assessment: A practical handbook* (2nd ed.) (pp. 484–533). New York: Pergamon.

Witt, J. C., & Elliot, S. N. (1983). Assessment in behavioral consultation: The initial interview. *School Psychology Review, 12*, 42–49.

Yule, W. (1993). Developmental considerations in child assessment. In T. H. Ollendick & M. Hersen (Eds.), *Handbook of child and adolescent assessment* (pp. 15–25). Boston: Allyn and Bacon.

CHAPTER 18

ASSESSMENT OF OLDER ADULTS

Barry A. Edelstein
Lisa Whipple Drozdick
Jane Null Kogan
West Virginia University

Our chapter is a new addition to the this book, which is in its fourth edition. Previous editions addressed behavioral assessment of children and younger adults, but neglected older adults. This neglect was more a function of the paucity of information on behavioral assessment of older adults than an egregious oversight by the book's editors. Indeed, it is a credit to the editors that this chapter is included in the current volume. Recent growth in the field of clinical geropsychology (Niederehe, Cooley, & Teri, 1995) and behavioral geropsychology (Carstensen, 1988) is ample evidence of increased interest in older adults and the need to more adequately address their mental health problems and needs.

One could argue that a separate chapter addressing the behavioral assessment of older adults is unnecessary. After all, the functional analysis of behavior is largely guided by an iterative process that is blind to the age of the individual being assessed. However, older adults bring somewhat unique repertoires, problems, and issues to the clinician that deserve attention if one is to competently assess older adults. In the interest of page economy

and reduction of redundancy with other chapters, we will address assessment issues and topics that are of particular relevance to older adults.

We will begin with a brief presentation of sensory changes occurring with age that can affect the assessment process and outcome. This will be followed by a discussion of ageism, one of many biases that can affect assessment of older adults. A discussion of multidimensional assessment provides an assessment perspective that lends itself to the multifaceted problems of many older adults. This is followed by psychometric considerations that are particularly important for older adult assessment instruments, succeeded by a discussion of some common assessment methods and instruments used with older adults. Finally, several assessment content areas frequently addressed in older adults will be discussed. This discussion will include assessment instruments commonly used for each of these content areas.

When we initially discussed the writing of this chapter, we tried to define what was meant by behavioral assessment, and therefore what would constitute a behavioral assessment instrument. We encountered the lack of an authoritative and complete definition of behavioral assessment. It is a concept that has come to be defined by its assumptions, purposes, and goals. This method of definition is inadequate for determining which instruments are or are not behavioral. We will continue to use the current approach to defining behavioral assessment and will define what constitutes a behavioral assessment instrument by how it is used rather than by its physical characteristics. Behavioral instruments directly and objectively measure overt behavior, physiological responses, or cognitive responses in a manner that results in identification of specific behavior problems and their functionally related variables. In behavioral assessment, assessment instruments are directly connected with treatment.

These criteria do not exclude an assessment instrument that is not developed and used exclusively by behavior therapists. Bellack and Hersen (1988) point out problems with calling a nonbehavioral instrument *behavioral* just because of the manner in which it is used, but there are many conditions in which this is unavoidable. Haynes (1978) notes that behavior therapy may need to use nonbehavioral instruments when there are no appropriate measures available or when the politics of publication and grant acquisition come into play. However, application of nonbehavioral assessment instruments should result in the same prescriptive information that leads one to appropriate intervention strategies.

In the sections in which we discuss particular assessment instruments, we will include an instrument if it (1) directly measures behavior, (2) quantifies variables or leads to the identification of more specific behavioral problems or their causal or maintaining variables, and/or (3) results in formulations that lead to specific treatment strategies.

SENSORY CHANGES ASSOCIATED WITH AGING

Older adults pose many unique challenges to the clinician who chooses to work with them, not the least of which is an understanding of the complex interplay of physiological changes, multiple medications, and situational factors unique to older adults. Accordingly, a working knowledge of the aging

process and awareness of potential problem areas common in older adults are essential. An appreciation of the physiological changes that often occur with aging and how these changes might contribute to presenting problems and even compromise the integrity of the assessment process is very important. Due to space limitations, we will address changes in only visual and auditory sensory systems. For a complete discussion of physiological changes associated with aging, see Whitbourne and Powers (in press).

Sensory deficits can have both direct and indirect effects on the physical and psychological integrity of the older adult, requiring the clinician's attention to factors that are less often encountered and perhaps of less importance or relevance for the assessment of healthy younger adults. Such sensory deficits (e.g., hearing loss) can influence information processing, mobility, independence, social behavior, and even self-concept. For example, prevalence of paranoia is higher among older adults whose hearing is impaired.

Hearing loss is a frequent problem among older adults, with estimates that more than 50% of Americans over age 65 are hearing impaired (Heckheimer, 1989; Vernon, 1989). Clinicians should be aware of clues to possible hearing impairment: a history of ear infections, loud speech, requests for the interviewer to repeat statements, inability to distinguish the speech of one individual in a group of speakers, and the tendency to watch intently the speaker's mouth (Vernon, 1989).

Background noise is a common problem for hearing impaired older adults that increases the likelihood that others will not be heard clearly. This phenomenon, known as *masking* highlights the need to minimize ambient background noise while interviewing older adults (Storandt, 1994). Hearing difficulties also increase at higher tone frequencies, which are employed in the articulation of consonants. Female interviewers with high-pitched voices should be sensitive to the fact that difficulty in hearing high frequencies may pose special communication problems with older adults, and in turn may need to consider lowering the pitch of their voices (Storandt, 1994).

Additional causes of hearing deficits include presbycusis (loss of auditory acuity associated with aging), drugs and allergies, circulatory disorders, central organic impairments, and occupational and recreational noise (Heckheimer, 1989; Storandt, 1994).

Further communication problems may result as individuals with hearing loss pretend to understand what is being said during the interview. More critical consequences of hearing loss include denial (Vernon, Griffin, & Yoken, 1981), isolation (Vernon, 1989), depression (Vernon, 1989), misleading diagnoses (Mindel & Vernon, 1987), and paranoid reactions (Zimbardo, Andersen, & Kabat, 1981).

Visual impairments, which sometimes accompany aging, can contribute to psychological problems and compromise some forms of psychological assessment. Approximately 80% of older adults have fair to adequate vision. For the remaining 20%, common visual impairments include decreases in visual acuity, depth perception, peripheral vision, adaptation to light change, tolerance for glare, accommodation, convergence, and ability to look up (Heckheimer, 1989). Cataracts, another common problem, can cause visual difficulties resulting from glare in brightly lit areas.

Changes in the visual system can lead to numerous changes in behavior/test performance that are of importance to a clinician. Decreased pupil size (miosis), pigmentation (opacification) and thickening of the lens, and loss of elasticity in the lens capsule can result in decreased visual acuity (usually presbyopia), with loss of lens elasticity accounting for approximately 90% of the loss in accommodation (Winograd, 1984). Increased lens thickness leads to reduced contrasts at the retina, causing increased light absorption and light scattering within the lens. This results in increased susceptibility to glare and problems resulting from abruptly changing light intensity (Marmor, 1992). As the aqueous humor becomes pigmented over time, the amount of light reaching the retina is reduced and shorter wavelengths of light are absorbed. This results in changes in color perception. The increased lens opacity and the decrease in pupil size that accompanies aging reduces the amount of light reaching the retina by as much as 66% between the ages of 20 and 65. The reduced pupil size combined with decreased retinal metabolism is associated with decreased adaptation to darkness and light (Winograd, 1984).

Decreased depth perception occurs with age, such differences being greatest at short distances where accommodation and convergences are most important. Various diseases (e.g., diabetes mellitus, cataracts, glaucoma, senile macular degeneration, myotonic dystrophy, hypoparathyroidism, Wilson's disease) and medications (phenothiazines, corticosteroids, antibiotics, antimalarials) can also compromise the integrity of the visual system (Hunt & Lindley, 1989; Winograd, 1984).

The foregoing visual deficits could result in diminished performance on tests requiring adequate vision, changes in social behavior resulting from a failure to recognize friends and acquaintances, reluctance to participate in any activity requiring reasonable visual acuity, falls resulting from poor visual acuity, and automobile accidents resulting from glare and rapid changes in light intensity.

The foregoing physiological changes can readily alter the behavior of the client and unwittingly contribute to erroneous conclusions by the clinician if he or she is ignorant of these changes and their concomitants. Similarly, erroneous assumptions made by clinicians with regard to characteristics of older adults can lead to faulty conclusions. If the clinician is to remain as objective as possible, potential sources of judgmental bias should be considered before pursuing the clinical assessment of an older adult.

AGEISM

Ageism is one of several biases that can affect the assessment process. We are focusing on ageism because it is something that is rarely discussed in the general assessment literature and yet it can have substantial effects on the assessment process and outcome. Ageism is discrimination based on age. This applies to discrimination toward any age group, but it is particularly prevalent with older adults. Butler (1980) describes three components of ageism with respect to older adults: (1) prejudicial attitudes toward older adults, old age, and the aging process, including those held by older adults; (2) discriminatory practices against older adults;

and (3) institutional practices and policies that perpetuate stereotypical beliefs about older adults, reduce their opportunities for a successful life, and undermine their personal dignity.

Ageism can significantly affect the professional relationship. The therapist must be aware of his or her perceptions and attitudes toward older adults and their impact on the therapeutic relationship. There are many misconceptions regarding older adults and each one influences how the aged are perceived and treated. Some examples drawn from Rodeheaver (1990) and Greene, Adelman, Charon, and Hoffman (1986) illustrate some of these myths. A common myth is that aging brings an end to productivity. Mandatory retirement age laws are an excellent example of the influence of this myth. Many adults work well into their seventies and eighties, living a productive life as determined by an industrial society. Even upon retirement, many older adults maintain active lifestyles and play significant roles in their communities.

A second myth is that the aged are infantile. A recent article referred to care-givers of older adults as "houseparents." This is not an uncommon perception in the health care industry. The recent development of age-appropriate programming in nursing homes demonstrates the desire to stop treating older adults as if they are children. A third myth is that senility is a normal part of aging. Although there is a normal, age-related loss in memory, only 5% of people over age 65 suffer from a dementing disorder (Crook, 1987). Another myth is that older adults are asexual. Though some change in the sexual response cycle can occur (i.e., decreased vaginal lubrication, increased time to achieve erection) (Masters & Johnson, 1966), older adults adjust to the changes and report high levels of sexual desire (O'Donohue, 1987) and continued participation in sexual activities (Fulton, 1992). A fifth and final myth is that older adults are unhealthy, they cannot hear, and they cannot care for themselves. Older adults do experience changes in physical and cognitive functioning as they age. These changes will be discussed in more detail later in the chapter.

It should be kept in mind, however, that the most common form of aging is healthy, vigorous old age. The majority of older adults live both in the community and independently. Disease is the main barrier to health and longevity, not age. However, chronic illnesses are more common in older adults (Kart, Metress, & Metress, 1992).

Belief in any of these myths, or others, can affect the therapeutic relationship. For example, believing that elderly people are set in their ways may lead to a belief that they cannot change and that therapy will not help them, when, in fact, therapy may benefit clients immensely.

In the treatment of older adults, there is a tendency for health and mental problems to be attributed to age rather than environmental sources (Rodin & Langer, 1980). For example, a fall by an older adult may be credited to old age instead of poor lighting. In fact, many older adults attribute their aches and pains to age. While some problems may be due to aging, the misattribution of problems to aging may be dangerous. Misattributing early signs of a serious illness to old age may lead to life-threatening illnesses that could be avoided. When a diagnosis is made, older adults are more likely to receive an organically based diagnosis and to receive medications as treatment than are younger adults (Rodin & Langer, 1980; Gatz & Pearson, 1988). This may contribute to the overmedication of many elderly persons. Reliance on medication as the primary treatment of mental disorders in the elderly leads to less referrals to other mental health professionals. Physicians are less likely to refer older patients for mental health consultations, especially for depression (Gatz & Pearson, 1988). Such failure to refer to mental health facilities is a contributing factor in the underutilization of these facilities by the elderly.

Perceptions of older adults can affect behavior toward the elderly, as well as behavior exhibited by the elderly (Rodeheaver, 1990). Ageism not only limits older adults' environmental opportunities, it also has an impact on their cognition and self-perceptions (Rodin & Langer, 1980). Older adults begin to act as they perceive they should act, thus fulfilling and perpetuating stereotypes of aged individuals. For example, one myth or stereotype discussed earlier stated that senility is a normal part of aging. The environment bombards older adults with images of senile adults, and age becomes associated with cognitive decline despite the more common pattern of aging without senility. Therefore, older adults are often concerned that they are becoming demented and, as Rodin and Langer (1980) discovered, they overestimate the possibility that they will become demented. The myth becomes a reality to the older adult.

PSYCHOMETRIC CONSIDERATIONS

It is important for clinicians and researchers to consider the psychometric properties of measures when considering an assessment endeavor. Such consideration is particularly important when using assessment instruments with older adults, because few instruments have undergone psychometric scrutiny with this population. Few instruments have been developed with consideration for older adults.

Though the relevance of traditional psychometric concepts for behavioral assessment has been debated (e.g., Haynes, 1991; Cone, 1977), consideration of those issues is beyond the scope of this chapter. We will assume, for our purposes, that traditional test theory is relevant to some of the instruments used for behavioral assessment. Reliability and validity are the most critical psychometric properties considered when estimating the value of a particular assessment measure (Hertzog & Schear, 1989). A measure is considered reliable if it is consistent either within or across situations. The most commonly examined forms of reliability are inter-rater reliability, test-retest reliability, and internal consistency. *Inter-rater reliability* refers to consistency of measurement between assessors within a given occasion (Kaszniak, 1990). When establishing inter-rater reliability of a measure with older adult samples, one should be aware that rater preconceptions (positive or negative) about the elderly may bias results (Edelstein, Northrup, Staats, & Packard, in press). For example, if the rater typically views the older adult population as frail, he or she may overlook issues associated with frailty and consider potential problems associated with this to be commonplace in his or her overall assessment.

Test-retest reliability (temporal stability) refers to the degree that a measure produces the same results on different testing occasions (Graziano & Raulin, 1989). Test-retest reliability is often difficult to establish for cognitively impaired or easily fatigued older adults because behavior is likely to change over time for these groups due to an expected decline in functioning. One must also be careful to apply the concept of test-retest reliability judiciously, as the behavior in question may inherently be unstable over time (Cone, 1977).

Internal consistency refers to the correlation among items within an instrument (Kaszniak, 1990). A strong relationship among items on an instrument depends on the reader's interpretation of each item. Different age groups may interpret the meaning of an item differently based on the phrasing or mode of presentation (e.g., computer assessment vs. written form) (Kaszniak, 1990). Moreover, cohort differences frequently exist as to social desirability of a response. Last, although measures with a greater number of items tend to have higher levels of internal consistency (Kaszniak, 1990), longer protocols are more time consuming, and, due to fatigue, may be more difficult for the older adult to complete. Given the potential age-associated differences, it is important to include older adult participants when obtaining internal consistency data (Kaszniak, 1990). Accordingly, those working with older adults should be cognizant of the standardization samples when considering the use of any assessment instrument.

Consistent measurement has no value if we fail to measure the construct or behavior we set out to measure. Validity is an index of the extent to which an instrument measures what it is intended to measure. Two types of validity of particular relevance to this discussion of older adults are construct and content validity. *Construct validity* refers to the degree that a measure accurately depicts the domain of the observable areas of interest (Nunnally & Bernstein, 1994). Constructs are defined by a consensually accepted domain of observables that are continually being modified based on the research findings (Kaszniak, 1990). Kaszniak (1990) has argued that construct validity must be established with particular age groups and with particular diagnostic groups, suggesting that validity estimates will vary across ages and diagnostic groups. For example, one cannot assume that factor structures obtained through factor analyses of measures using younger adult subjects would remain invariant for older adult groups. Age-specific validity estimates are often lacking with many clinical assessment instruments.

Content validity reflects the extent to which the items on a given measure are a thorough sample of the information needed (Cunningham, 1986). It is important that individual items in the measure that pertain to the behavior or situation of interest are appropriate to the age of the person with whom the measure is to be used. Psychological symptom-atology among older adults can be quite different as compared to other age groups (Himmelfarb & Murrell, 1983). Ignoring the fact that differences in both the presentation and etiology of a problem may exist between age groups could result in a threat to the content validity of a measure.

METHODS OF ASSESSMENT

Once one has attended to issues of reliability and validity, there remains the task of selecting assess-ment methods and instruments that will enable one to best represent the strengths and weaknesses of the client. This task is at times more complex with older adults, as they can present with problems arising from or maintained by a complicated array of contributing factors (e.g., losses, multiple medi-cations, chronic diseases).

The same advantages achieved through the utilization of multiple assessment methods with younger individuals accrue in the assessment of older adults. Assessment method variance must be considered when assessing individuals of all ages. We will briefly discuss the most popular assess-ment methods and address method content specific to older adults.

Clinical Interview

Interviews vary in their structure and function, from completely unstructured, free-flowing con-versations to carefully sequenced and branching questions leading to psychiatric diagnoses. An advantage of the more structured interviews is that they force one to consider issues and factors that might be overlooked if one were proceeding in an unstructured fashion, and they can lead to more reliable conclusions than one might reach with less structure. With regard to the former, structured interviews can serve as excellent guides for stu-dents and less experienced clinicians. The two principal disadvantages of structured and semi-structured interviews are the significant amount of time and training required to administer them.

The clinical interview relies on the self-report of individuals. To a large extent, accuracy and reli-ability of the clinical interview is a function of reli-ability and accuracy of self-reports by older adults. Self-reports are subject to the same environmental influences as other verbal behavior. They are shaped by the reinforcement contingencies opera-tive in the setting in which they are made. More-over, they are vulnerable to influences arising from cognitive deficits that are often present among older adults who suffer from dementia, physical ill-nesses, and/or medication side effects. Clinicians must be aware of many factors that can influence self-reports of older adults (Edelstein, Northrup, Staats, & Packard, in press). Sager, Dunham, Schwantes, Mecum, Halverson, and Harlowe (1992) suggest that responses to interviewer inquir-ies can be altered by affective response to acute ill-ness, changes from previous levels of physical functioning occurring during hospitalization, and presence of acute or chronic cognitive impairment. For example, Kuriansky, Gurland and Fleiss (1976) reported that affectively impaired older adults may underestimate their abilities.

Accuracy of self-reports may also be influ-enced by increases in cognitive impairment, as one might expect. Clients with severe dementia may not be able to comprehend questions or the nature of requested information. Older adults with dementia who deny memory loss also tend to deny the pres-ence of other symptoms (Feher, Larrabee, & Crook, 1992). Feher and associates (1992) assert that accu-rate self-report of recent mood requires only mini-mal memory ability, suggesting that individuals with mild to moderate dementia can be accurate in responding to questions requiring minimal memory ability.

Response sets can influence responses to ques-tions with older adults, much as they can with younger adults. However, there are some reported response biases that may be even more characteristic of older adults. Older adults may tend to be more cautious (Okun, 1976) and experience greater anxiety than younger adults regarding receipt of negative feedback, and engage in risk-avoiding behavior when anticipating evaluative information (Poon, Crook, Gurland, Davis, Kaszniak, Eisdorfer, & Thompson, 1986). Older adults are more likely than younger adults to respond to questions in a socially desirable fashion (Campbell, Converse, & Rodgers, 1976).

Accuracy of self-reported estimates of functional ability has been questioned by researchers, although the findings are mixed. Myers and Huddy (1985) found institutionalized older adults inaccurately reported current activities of daily living (ADL), physical ability, and estimates of functional capabilities in activities they no longer performed. Sager, Dunham, Schwantes, Mecum, Halverson, and Harlowe (1992) found that older adults both under- and overestimated their ability to complete activities of daily living compared to performance-based measures in a fourth study. Rubenstein, Schairer, Weiland, and Kane (1984) supported at least some of the Sagerand and associates' (1992) findings in their study where geriatric patients overestimated their functional ability. Finally, Sager and colleagues (1992) found that self-reported ADLs performed in home settings were accurate when self-reports were compared with more objective measures.

Accuracy of older adults' self-reports of memory impairment has also been questioned (e.g., Perlmutter, 1978; Rabbitt, 1982; Sunderland, Watts, Baddeley, & Harris, 1986; Zelinski, Gilewski, & Thompson, 1980), although some (e.g., Rodgers & Herzog , 1987) found that older adults are no less accurate than younger adults when queried about survey-type information.

Linguistic and semantic differences across generations (Kaszniak, 1990), genders, and ethnicities must be considered when evaluating responses to interview questions . Differences in what is considered socially desirable across generations may yield differences in responses to questions. For example, older adults often respond with less frankness to questions regarding sexuality than do younger adults (Yesavage, 1986).

Interviews are often conducted with significant others and/or care-givers of older adults, raising the question of the reliability and accuracy of reports by others. Staff, family members, and other individuals can be rich sources of primary and supplementary information. Reports by others are particularly helpful when the client is denying information suspected to be true, apparently overreporting symptoms, refusing to talk with a stranger (the interviewer), or unable to participate fully in the interview due to cognitive or physical impairment. Limitations and threats to accuracy and reliability are similar to those of self-report and direct observation. In addition, when multiple reports are involved, there is always the issue of which report constitutes the incontrovertible standard. Reliability and accuracy of such reports have been investigated with a variety of informants across a variety of content areas, yielding a mixture of findings.

Rubenstein, Schairer, Wieland, and Kane (1984) found that accuracy of functional status was greater with reports from a child, a relative, or a friend than with reports from a spouse. They also found that nurses and community proxies tended to rate patients as more dysfunctional than suggested by more objective indices. Silverman, Breitner, Mohs, and Davis (1986) found high levels of agreement among multiple informants from the same family when reporting the time of dementia onset for a relative. Similarly, Kukull, and Larson (1989) found that retrospective accounts of the symptoms of dementia could be recalled by close relatives of a deceased patient over an average of 2.9 years with reasonable accuracy, although the specificity for symptoms of primary degenerative dementia was only modest.

Finally, La Rue, Watson, and Plotkin (1992) examined the reliability of relatives' accounts of dementia symptoms by comparing current reports with those obtained retrospectively. Moderately reliable correlations were obtained between retrospective and initial ratings by relatives over a period of a few months. However, relatives recalled patients having fewer psychiatric symptoms in their retrospective accounts when compared with the initial reports. When retrospective reports were examined by type of relative (spouse vs. younger relatives), younger relatives reported higher levels of impairment of demanding functional skills, cognition, mood, and thought disturbance than did spouses.

Though there is evidence from the foregoing studies that reports by others can be accurate, sufficient evidence exists to warrant caution when using only single-source reports regarding the behavior of the client. Perhaps the best model of information gathering is one that includes as many sources as possible so that a convergence of information is accumulated.

We lack sufficient space to cover all available interviews of relevance to older adults, or even those developed specifically for older adults. Consequently, a few representative interviews will be briefly discussed for illustrative purposes.

The Geriatric Mental State Schedule (GMS; Copeland, Kelleher, Kellett, Gourlay, Gurland, Fleiss, & Sharpe, 1976) is a semistructured interview for examining the mental state of older adults. The GMS comprises items from the eighth edition of the Present State Examination (Wing, Birley, Cooper, Graham, & Isaacs, 1967) and the Present Status Schedule (Spitzer, Fleiss, Burdock, & Hardesty, 1964). The authors established good reliability among trained raters, recommending that one undertake 20 joint interviews with an instructor to establish adequate reliability.

The GMS formed the backbone for the psychiatric section of the Comprehensive Assessment and Referral Evaluation (CARE; Gurland, Kuriansky, Sharpe, Simon, Stiller, & Birkett, 1977–78). Its characteristics and psychometric properties are discussed later under the heading of Multidimensional Assessment.

The Cambridge Mental Disorders of the Elderly Examination (CAMDEX; Roth, Tym, Mountjoy, Huppert, Hendrie, Verma, & Goddard, 1986) is another example of a multielement assessment instrument that includes an interview component. It comprises three sections: (1) a structured clinical interview for obtaining family history as well as present and past history of the present problem(s), (2) a small battery of neuropsychological tests, and (3) a structured interview for a relative or other informant that addresses family history and the present and past history of the present problem(s). The CAMDEX focuses on the diagnosis of dementia, particularly in its early stages. Administration requires approximately 80 minutes, including 60 minutes for the client and 20 minutes for the informant.

Direct Observation

Though direct observation of behavior is costly, it remains the gold standard for behavioral assessment. The behaviors that clinicians most often examine through this method fall within the categories of adaptive and maladaptive behaviors.

Adaptive Behaviors

The focus of adaptive behavior assessment is typically the behaviors required for effective self-care and interaction with one's environment. These are termed *activities of daily living (ADLs)* and *instrumental activities of daily living (IADLs)*. For the sake of brevity, measures of IADLs will not be presented. They are constructed and utilized in a fashion quite similar to instruments intended for assessing ADLs. Though activities of daily living can often be easily observed and recorded, clinicians have generally turned to standardized observation instruments for noting and rating ADLs. ADL scales have been developed to measure basic self-care skills such as bathing, dressing, using the bathroom, getting in or out of a bed or chair, walking, feeding, and engaging in activities outside one's living quarters. The skills are often ordered in terms of decreasing dependency, forming a Guttman scale (Katz, Ford, Moskowitz, Jackson, & Jaffee, 1963).

The first ADL scale, or index, was developed by Katz and colleagues (Katz et al., 1963) for assessing chronically ill, institutionalized, older adults. Katz's index also became popular for the assessment of community-dwelling older adults in the 1980s (Kovar & Lawton, 1994). His theoretical formulation of ADLs characterized recovering patients as passing through three stages: (1) return of independence in feeding and continence, (2) recovery in transferring and going to the toilet, and (3) recovery of independence in dressing and bathing. Each of these activities was viewed as a function and defined in terms of the need or lack of need for assistance.

A variety of other instruments has been developed to assess adaptive behaviors. Domains sampled by these instruments varies, as there is no consensus on what should be included. The Older American Resources and Services methodology (OARS) (Pfeiffer, 1975) is the oldest and most popular multidimensional assessment instrument and the one most frequently cited in a survey by Edelstein, Northrup, and Staats (in press) for assessing adaptive behavior. The OARS comprises two instruments: the Multidimensional Functional Assessment Questionnaire (MFAQ) and the Services Assessment Questionnaire (SAG).

The MFAQ is designed to assess functional status and requires a 45- to 60-minute interview by a trained professional. Responses to an interview are rated on 6-point scales pertaining to the individual's well-being (1 = excellent functioning; 2 = severely impaired functioning) in the following categories: physical health, mental health (cognitive skill and psychological health), activities of daily living (physical and instrumental), social (time use and interaction with family and friends), and economic. Most of the questions are relevant to both community and institutional settings. Inter-rater reliability estimates have ranged from .67 to .87 across the five categories of functioning. Test-retest reliability over a five-week period resulted in identical scores for 91% of the items. Validity was demonstrated by comparing scores on four of the five categories (social resources excluded) with ratings by professionals, yielding coefficients ranging from .60 for physical health to .83 for ADL (George, 1994).

Maladaptive Behaviors

Two commonly targeted problem behaviors, particularly among institutionalized older adults, are wandering and aggressive behaviors. Wandering can impose risks to the older adult, leading one to becoming lost, frightened, and even panic stricken. Older adults may also be at greater risk for falling when wandering or pacing. Aggressive behavior can pose obvious risks for its targets.

Wandering is typically defined as aimless, non-goal-directed ambulation (Cohen-Mansfield, Werner, Culpepper, Wolfson, & Bickel, in press; Hussian, 1987). Rates of wandering vary across individuals and settings, ranging from 3% to 59% (Cohen-Mansfield et al., in press). Hussian (1987)

has identified four classes of wanderers: (1) akathisiacs: individuals whose pacing and restless behavior is induced by medications, (2) exit seekers: individuals who are often newly admitted to institutions and attempt to open locked exit doors, (3) self-stimulators: individuals who engage in wandering and other self-stimulatory behaviors, and (4) modelers: individuals who wander when in close contact with another wanderer.

Distance, frequency, and duration of wandering behavior may be obtained directly or through report of others. Such measurements may be obtained via reports by others using standard methods (e.g., time sampling) or via questionnaires (e.g., Wandering Observational Tool; Hoeffer, Rader, & Siemsen, 1987). Several general assessment instruments also contain one or more items pertaining to wandering or pacing (e.g., CMAI; Cohen-Mansfield, Marx, & Rosenthal, 1989; Disruptive Behavior Rating Scales; Mungas, Weiler, Franzi, & Henry, 1989), which can be used by trained observers.

No consensus exists for a definition of *aggressive behavior*, although some agreement seems to exist regarding three categories of aggression: physical, verbal and sexual. Though these categories can be useful at times, they can also create confusion and difficulties when attempting a functional analysis because they are not mutually exclusive. The following definition will suffice for our purposes: "Aggressive behavior is an overt act, involving the delivery of noxious stimuli (but not necessarily aimed at) another object, organism or self, which is clearly not accidental" (Patel & Hope, 1993, p. 458).

Reported rates of aggressive behavior among older adults varies from 8% to 91% among institutionalized older adults to 1% to 47% among community dwellers (Cohen-Mansfield et al., in press). As with wandering behavior, determination of the function of the behavior is important for designing a successful intervention program. It is easy to get caught up in the topographical features of a behavior and assume the intended function of the behavior. There is no substitute for a thorough functional analysis. Though some particular antecedents of aggressive behavior have been frequently implicated (e.g., touch by care-givers, requests for behavior), the discriminative stimulus for aggressive behavior is most often elusive and requires extensive observation and analysis.

Standard assessment instruments have been developed for the measurement of aggressive behavior, some requiring summary staff ratings and others requiring direct, systematic measurement of behavior by trained staff. The Ryden Aggression Scale (Ryden, 1988) is a 25-item rating instrument that includes three subscales: physically aggressive behavior, verbally aggressive behavior, and sexually aggressive behavior. It is intended for the measurement of aggressive behavior in the community. The Rating Scale for Aggressive Behavior in the Elderly (Patel & Hope, 1992) is an example of a rating instrument intended for use with psychogeriatric inpatients. Three factors are represented in this 23-item scale: antisocial behavior, verbally aggressive behavior, and physically aggressive behavior.

Several more broadly focused assessment rating instruments include items relevant to aggressive behavior (e.g., Cohen-Mansfield Agitation Inventory; Cohen-Mansfield, Marx, & Rosenthal, 1989; Nursing Home Behavior Problem Scale; Ray, Taylor, Lichtenstein, & Meador, 1992). Examples of instruments requiring systematic observation and description of aggressive behaviors include the Staff Observation Aggression Scale (Palmstierna & Wistedt, 1987) and the Pittsburgh Agitation Scale (Rosen, Burgio, Kollar, Cain, Allison, Fogelman, Michael, & Zubenko, 1994).

Multidimensional Assessment

As previously noted, the complexity of factors contributing to presenting problems of older adults often calls for a comprehensive, multifaceted approach to assessment. Unidimensional assessment, or assessment that evaluates only isolated aspects of client functioning, can lead to an oversimplification of such multifaceted problems, oversights in identification of problems, incomplete conceptualizations of the client's problems, and the neglect of related problems. Historically, psychologists have evaluated primarily cognitive and emotional functioning in their older clients, failing to acknowledge other factors such as environmental resources and physical health (Gallagher, Thompson, & Levy, 1980).

A multidimensional approach, one that considers all of these areas of functioning, is needed to determine which factors, based on the assessment of many possible factors, are contributing to the problem behavior(s). Over the past 20 years, multidimensional assessment of older adults has become a major cornerstone of geriatric medicine (Rubenstein, 1983). This approach to assessment includes a more thorough and cost-effective approach to understanding client deficiencies than does a haphazard administration of isolated instruments that, as a group, fail to cover all areas of client functioning. One method of multidimensional assessment combines many areas of client functioning (i.e., emotional, physical, financial) into a single instrument, thus allowing comprehensive analyses of multiple problem areas. Paralleling an ideographic approach, multidimensional assessment is also individualized and systematically considers each dimension for each individual.

The factors that are most frequently considered in multidimensional assessment are physical health, cognitive and mental functioning, activities of daily living, and social support (Rubenstein, 1983). The interrelationship of these domains tends to increase as one grows older (Gaitz & Baer, 1970). For example, debilitating health may lead to a decreased frequency of social interaction, decreased social support, and increased financial strain. By adopting a multidimensional approach, the geropsychologist is able to consider the importance of each individual dimension of client functioning and the relationship among these dimensions (George, 1994). This method of assessment has been especially useful in examining the individual needs of older adult clients, overall quality of life, and treatment outcome (George, 1994).

Three of the most popular multidimensional assessment instruments are discussed. These were also considered for inclusion in this chapter because each conceptualizes problem behavior in terms of functional rather than diagnostic categories (George, 1994).

The Older Americans Resources and Services (OARS) Methodology, developed at Duke University at the Center for the Study of Aging and Human Development (1978), has been the most popular assessment tool utilized by those interested in obtaining multidimensional information from older adults. The OARS Methodology comprises two major scales: the Multidimensional Functional Assessment Questionnaire (MFAQ) and the Service Assessment Questionnaire (SAQ).

The MFAQ evaluates the functional status (strengths and weaknesses) of various dimensions within the older adult's life. These dimensions are mental and physical health, economic and social resources, and activities of daily living. Both subjective and objective data are obtained through self-report of the older adult, reports provided by significant others, and interviewer's comments. A summary score ranging from excellent functioning to total impairment is tabulated for each of the aforementioned dimensions.

The OARS methodology can be used with lower-functioning older adults because information is obtained from significant others. Some investigators have extracted specific subscales from the MFAQ to look at dimensions such as mental status, activities of daily living, and mental health in isolation (see Pfeiffer, 1975, 1979; Lawton & Brody, 1969). However, Dalton, Pederson, Blom, and Holmes (1987) caution the interpretation of subscale data without considering the entire client presentation. Psychometric studies for the MFAQ have revealed moderate to high levels of reliability and validity (George & Fillenbaum, 1985; Gatz, Pederson, & Harris, 1987; Liang, Levin, & Krause, 1989). For example, George and Fillenbaum (1985) report internal consistency of all 11 scales to range from .52 to .87. In this same study, correlations between scores of each subscale and independent ratings of functioning made by relevant professionals revealed coefficients ranging from .60 to .83.

The Comprehensive Assessment and Referral Evaluation (CARE), developed by Gurland, Kuriansky, Sharpe, Simon, Stiller, and Birkett (1977), is a widely used multidimensional assessment tool. In its initial form with 1,500 items, the CARE was quite time consuming. However, the CARE has undergone significant refinement over the years, resulting in five new shorter versions designed for disparate uses (Gurland & Wilder, 1984). For example, the SHORT CARE (Gurland, Golden, Teresi, & Challop, 1984) is an abbreviated version of the original CARE. This version measures the severity of cognitive functioning and range of disability, and provides diagnostic information (Gurland et al., 1984).

Another instrument adapted from the CARE is the IN CARE (Gurland et al., 1979), which was originally designed for institutionalized older adults. This measure is hierarchical in that the interview leads to one of four protocols based on the respondent's initial performance. For example, after the initial interview, an interviewing method is continued for those older adults who are cognitively intact, whereas performance on daily living tasks are measured for those who are deemed as cognitively impaired. This approach is sensitive to the limitations of more frail and cognitively declining older adults, as it does not require each individual to sit through an assessment component that is not appropriate to his or her level of functioning.

Although this version appears to be quite useful in behavioral assessment for this particular population, gerontological literature citing the use of the IN CARE is sparse as compared to that of other CARE versions. Some research using the IN CARE with demented and long-term care residents is available indicating moderate levels of reliability (internal consistency) (Holmes, Teresi, Weiner, Monaco, Ronch, & Vickers, 1990; Teresi et al., 1993). In a study involving dementia patients, Holmes, Teresi, Weiner, Monaco, Ronch, and Vickers (1990) reported alpha levels that ranged from .60 to .95 for the IN CARE scales. Gurland, Teresi, Smith, Black, Hughes, and Edlavitch (1988) reported internal consistency reliability coefficients ranging from .51 to .84 for the SHORT CARE using a sample of older adults with heart disease. Golden and associates (1984) reported internal consistency alpha of .95 using all 22 scales of the original CARE with community-dwelling older adults.

The Multilevel Assessment Instrument (MAI) developed by Lawton, Moss, Fulcomer, and Kleban (1982) at the Philadelphia Geriatric Center is similar to the OARS-MFAQ. It also contains scales that assess various areas of functioning— including physical, cognitive, and emotional—but lacks an economic resources dimension. Subscale scores yield both subjective and objective ratings indicating level of functioning for each dimension (Lawton et al., 1982). This multidimensional measure has three forms varying in length, allowing for "flexibility" for varied levels of impairment (Gallagher et al., 1980). Psychometric studies reveal moderate to high levels of reliability and validity for all forms of the MAI (Lawton et al., 1982). Using a sample that consisted of community-dwelling older adults, older adults in short-term care, and older adults in long-term care, Lawton and colleagues (1982) reported test-retest reliability ranging from .73 to .95 and internal consistency ranging from .71 to .93.

In addition to considering the idiosyncrasies of these instruments and their applicability to various populations, one should also consider their efficiency. Multidimensional assessment can be quite time-consuming. Many researchers and clinicians opt for a less time-consuming strategy such as administering multiple screening measures in an effort to pinpoint problem areas (George, 1994). However, this method of assessment often fails to tap all integral areas of older adult functioning and problem areas may go unidentified. Although it seems prudent to consider the time pressures associated with multidimensional assessment, geropsychologists may also want to consider the inordinate amount of time that can be associated with a failure to identify specific problems because their initial assessment approaches were too narrow.

ASSESSMENT CONTENT AREAS

Neuropsychological Assessment

"Neuropsychological assessment is the attempt to relate behavioral deficits to underlying brain dysfunction, generally through the use of psychometric and other examinational procedures known as neuropsychological tests" (Goldstein, 1984, p. 1). Neuropsychologists tend to focus on diagnostic evaluation, assessment of impaired and preserved functions, and rehabilitation planning. The relationship between behavioral and neuropsychological assessment is informal but substantial. Neuropsychologists and behavioral psychologists are both interested in identifying functional relationships between organismic and environmental variables and behavior. The neuropsychologist relies on observations of individuals who have suffered insults to various parts of their nervous system and on ex-

perimental research in which various structures of the nervous system are disabled. In addition, neuropsychologists determine how individuals with particular lesions interact with their environment. This is not dissimilar to what the behavioral clinician does in observing the relationship between the client's history and current environment in determining particular behaviors.

The marriage of neuropsychological and behavioral assessment is most apparent in two contexts, both of which pertain to the assessment of functional competence. In the first context, assessment is performed to determine ecological competence (Heinrichs, 1990). Here, neuropsychologists formulate statements about the relation between neuropsychological test performance and activities of daily living (e.g., interpersonal behavior, occupational performance). Emphasis is on the individual's current behavioral repertoire. The goal of such assessment is to match individuals to environments in light of the individuals' strengths and weaknesses. In the second context, neuropsychological assessment is performed to determine an individual's potential for rehabilitation and determine what types of training experiences would benefit him or her. Here, the focus is on the capability of new learning in various domains.

In the foregoing cases, the neuropsychologist is less concerned with the localization of lesions and more with the individual's functional behavioral repertoire and the formulation of a prescription for rehabilitative efforts. In the case of ecological competence, the neuropsychologist must identify behavioral strengths and deficits, much as would a behavior analyst. A focus on rehabilitative efforts shifts the attention of the neuropsychologist to predictions of how effectively an individual will interact with his or her environment in light of nervous system insults. Unfortunately, neuropsychologists do not have the luxury of a history of client behavior under the new conditions of a nervous system insult.

Not every neuropsychologist approaches the assessment process in the same fashion. Two major traditions or approaches to neuropsychological assessment have emerged. These two approaches are the flexible, individualized process approach, as exemplified by the work of Kaplan and colleagues

(Kaplan, 1983), and the fixed battery approach, as exemplified by the Halstead-Reitan Battery (HRB; Reitan & Wolfson, 1985) and the Luria-Nebraska Neuropsychological Battery (LNNB; Moses, Golden, Ariel, & Gustavson, 1983).

Kaplan likens her process-oriented approach to that of Werner's (1956) organismic-developmental approach to the analysis of behavior. Werner (1937) "argued that it is erroneous to assume that any achievement, that is, the final solution to any problem, is an objective measure either of a developmental stage or of some unitary underlying mechanism" (Kaplan, 1983, p. 143). She favors this perspective because it encourages an individualized approach, much like that of the idiographic approach taken by most behavioral psychologists. This process-oriented, microgenetic (Werner, 1956) approach is particularly important when one is concerned with the development of prescriptions for rehabilitative efforts. Indeed, Kaplan (1983) argues that it is more effective for such purposes than a fixed-battery approach.

Kaplan (1983) illustrates her point in demonstrating that three individuals with lesions in three different areas of the brain go about the task of completing a block design task in three different fashions. All three individuals achieve the same score but through different performance strategies. From an operant perspective, one might liken the different methods of tackling the block design task as different operants, all of which accomplish the same function, but in different fashions. Kaplan would argue that the focus on topographical differences in behaviors increases our understanding of how the individual interacts with problems encountered in the environment. The approach also allows us to examine the strategies, adaptive and maladaptive, developed by an individual to compensate for his or her deficits. One can also use this approach to study how an individual responds to different task demands and determine what stimuli can set the occasion for more or less effective responding.

In contrast to the process-oriented approach, the fixed battery/achievement-oriented approach conceals the differences among performances and precludes the use of this information for determining current functioning and developing rehabilitation programs. In summary, the process-oriented

approach advocated by Kaplan and colleagues parallels the idiographic approach taken by behavior analysts, both in terms of its individualistic approach and its search for variables functionally related to behaviors of interest.

Neuropsychological Assessment Instruments

Few neuropsychological assessment instruments have demonstrated sound psychometric properties with older adult populations. Kaszniak (1990) and Lezak (1995) have noted that appropriate normative data are lacking for many of the popular neuropsychological tests, as well as the HRB and LNNB. Moreover, even though there is support for a test's validity, much validity will vary with the use to which a test is placed. For example, a test may have good validity when used to discriminate patients with Alzheimer's disease from elderly depressed persons, but may not identify young head trauma patients likely to benefit from rehabilitation (Heinrichs, 1990).

Two kinds of validity are of particular importance for neuropsychologists: face and predictive validity. *Face validity* is important when dealing with older adults who are willing to submit to tests that appear relevant (Cunningham, 1986; Mahurin & Pirozzolo, 1986), but who are more likely to reject tasks that seem nonsensical to them (Lezak, 1995). *Predictive validity* is particularly important because the neuropsychologist is interested in how assessment data translates into performance in the real world (Lezak, 1995).

Though most of the earlier assessment instruments used for neuropsychological assessment were developed for children or young adults, some progress has recently been made in the inclusion of norms for older adults recent years. These include, for example, the WAIS-R (Ivnik, Malec, Smith, Tangalos, Peterson, Kokmen, & Kurland, 1992a), the Wechsler Memory Scale-Revised (Ivnik, Malec, Smith, Tangalos, Peterson, Kokmen, & Kurland, 1992b), the Rey-Osterreith Complex Figure Test (Chiulli, Haaland, La Rue, & Garry, in press), and the Auditory Verbal Learning Test (Ivnik, Malec, Smith, Tangalos, Peterson, Kokmen, & Kurland, 1992c). A complete listing and discussion of all neuropsychological assessment instruments used with older adults is beyond the scope of this chapter. The clinician is likely to consider screening for cognitive impairment (see next section) and refer clients for formal neuropsychological assessment. Suffice it to say that the clinician should carefully examine the psychometric properties of any instrument being considered for use with older adults.

Cognitive Screening

One of the most common complaints made by older adults concerns a change in cognition, (i.e., memory). Although studies have shown that there is no correlation between subjective reports of problems with everyday memory and performance on memory tests (Sunderland, Watts, Baddeley, & Harris, 1986), it is a common concern among older adults. With prevalence of dementia increasing as age increases, it should also be a concern for clinicians. Cognitive screening provides a quick glimpse of the cognitive functioning of an older individual from which a decision on the necessity for further assessment can be made. Cognitive screening is not a thorough, comprehensive assessment of cognitive functioning, and none of the instruments discussed in this section should be viewed as affording such an assessment.

Cognitive screening instruments are difficult to classify as *behavioral* by the criteria we stated. This is in part due to the use of the term *cognitive*. Cognition, as a hypothetical construct, cannot be measured directly. Cognition is measured indirectly (inferred) by having the client perform a task that is believed to require a certain cognitive skill. Successful completion of this task indicates a lack of impairment. For example, a test item measuring the construct of comprehension might ask the client to read or listen to a sentence and then do what it instructs. Successful completion of the task would indicate the ability to comprehend. However, completion of the task involves observable behavior. Therefore, tests of cognitive abilities can be viewed as directly measuring behavioral skills. It is the ability to perform these skills that is important to the behaviorist, not the inferred underlying cognitive construct. Thus, in our earlier example, the skill of reading and following directions would be of interest, not necessarily the concept of comprehension.

Second, screening instruments, by their very nature, are not used to develop treatment strategies but to reveal whether further assessment is needed. They do, however, indicate which skill areas are in need of further evaluation, thus narrowing both the assessment and treatment focus (Harper, Chacko, Kotik-Harper, & Kirby, 1992). They also reveal what behavioral skill areas are in need of attention and which may be targeted later for intervention.

There are some changes in cognitive functioning that occur as individuals age. Botwinick (1984) describes the "classic aging pattern," in which over-learned skills and information such as reading and remote memory are maintained over time while abstract thinking and motor performance decline with age. Memory also declines, especially in acquiring and storing new information, as well as the ability to remember information exceeding six to seven items (Morin & Colecchi, in press). There also is a general slowing in reaction time as age increases, which affects speed but not necessarily accuracy. This should be taken into account on tests involving timed tasks. Since screening instruments assess only a small sample of a client's skills, certain precautions should be taken to avoid bias. Any physical or sensory impairments should be noted and appropriate measures taken to minimize their impact on test scoring (i.e., large-print materials for visually impaired clients). Individuals with cognitive impairment affecting language are a special problem since most of the screening tests are heavily language dependent (Albert, 1994). Other methods of assessment may be appropriate when language is significantly impaired.

Mood disorders also pose a problem because they may present as cognitive dysfunction. Depression is often difficult to distinguish from mild forms of cognitive impairment. Depressed mood can cause a decline in memory and cognitive functioning and therefore may give the initial appearance of a permanent cognitive impairment. A thorough history and assessment are necessary to differentiate the disorders. Differentiation is of vital importance because depression responds well to treatment, whereas many forms of severe cognitive dysfunction, such as that exhibited in dementia of the Alzheimer's type, tend to be resistant to treatment. A further complication is the co-occurrence of dementia and depression. Approximately 1% to 4% of people over the age of 65 suffer from both depression and dementia (Teri & Reifler, 1987). A tentative but helpful finding by Kaszniak (1990) suggests that depressed older adults complain about memory problems yet perform well on memory tests, whereas patients with dementia of the Alzheimer's type show clear impairment during testing, yet they overestimate their abilities. This is not a clear delineation for distinguishing clients but may aid in initial evaluations.

Cognitive Screening Instruments

The Mini-Mental State Examination (MMSE; Folstein, Folstein, & McHugh, 1975) is the most widely used instrument for assessing cognitive impairments (Albert, 1994; Ashford, Kolm, Colliver, Bekian, & Hsu, 1989); 89% of primary care physicians use it (Harper et al., 1992). It includes items covering orientation to time and place, registration, attention, recall, language, and praxis. The measure has been extensively researched and has good predictive validity (Uhlmann, Larson, & Buchner, 1987), convergent validity (Ashford et al., 1989; Starratt & Fields, 1988), test-retest reliability (Fillenbaum, Heyman, Wilkinson, & Haynes, 1987), and inter-rater reliability (Starratt & Fields, 1988).

Albert (1994) reports that the MMSE is a two-factor test, measuring Memory-Attention and Verbal Comprehension. The individual is rated on his or her ability to answer questions and perform tasks accurately. Each correct answer is worth a point, with a perfect score of 30. It is generally accepted that a score of 23 or less indicates the need for further testing. The MMSE contains items that bias it with regard to a client's educational level (e.g., counting backwards from 100 by 7s). Albert (1994) suggests that the cut-off scores be adjusted for different levels of education. For clients with less than 8 years of formal education, a cut-off of 17 is appropriate. For 8 or more years of education, the recommended cut-off score is 23, and for clients with high levels of schooling (i.e., more than 16 years) a cut-off score of 27 is recommended. These cut-off scores ensure the sensitivity of the test in detecting cognitive deficits in clients with various educational levels.

The MMSE was designed to briefly assess a person's general level of cognitive functioning. As a result, it loses the ability to detect focal impairment (Harper et al., 1992). Individuals with focal lesions can score in the normal range on the MMSE because they do not present with global impairment. For example, stroke victims often suffer from severe impairment in specific areas of functioning. The MMSE would not detect impairment in many stroke victims even when it is present.

The MMSE produces a high rate of false negatives. Many of these occur in younger, less globally impaired, and mildly impaired patients (Harper et al., 1992; Osato, Yang, & LaRue, 1993). Osato, Yang, and LaRue (1993) found a high rate of false positives in individuals over the age of 60 with less than eight years of education. A final problem that arises when assessing clients with severe dementia with the MMSE is the fact that clients can obtain a score of zero, the worst possible score, before complete functioning ability is lost (Ashford et al., 1989). When a patient obtains this score, he or she should then be assessed with a severe impairment battery, such as the Severe Impairment Battery developed by Saxton, McGonigle-Gibson, Swihart, Miller, and Boller (1990), or other forms of assessment.

As one of the oldest, widely used mental status examinations, the Blessed Dementia Scale (Blessed, Tomlinson, & Roth, 1968) has been through several modifications. The original version contained two sections: the first covering behavioral items similar to an activities of daily living scale, and the second covering cognitive functioning. The cognitive component is often referred to as the Blessed Information-Memory-Concentration test (BIMC). Unlike the Mini-Mental State Exam, the BIMC is unidimensional (Albert, 1994). It produces a single score that yields very little information on specific areas of functioning. The BIMC contains items measuring memory, orientation, and attention. Each incorrect answer is counted, with the possible score ranging from 0 to 33, with 0 being a perfect score. The test is highly reliable, with a test-retest coefficient of 0.89 (Villardita & Lomeo, 1992). Higher scores correlate highly with increasing numbers of senile plaques (Villardita & Lomeo, 1992), which is a sign of dementia of the Alzheimer's type. A shorter version of the BIMC, the Blessed Orientation-Memory-Concentration test (BOMC), also correlates with the physical signs of dementia. The BOMC correlates highly with the MMSE and demonstrates high test-retest reliability (Albert, 1994).

The Neurobehavioral Cognitive Status Examination (NCSE) (Kiernan, Mueller, Langston, & Van Dyke, 1987) is a relatively new measure of cognitive impairment in dementia patients. It evaluates orientation, attention, memory, language, constructional praxis, calculational ability, and higher-level reasoning. It is arranged so that when a particular item is failed, a follow-up item is given to determine the level of impairment. Unlike the MMSE, the NCSE produces a cognitive profile covering many cognitive abilities. It can be used to detect focal cognitive deficits, which the MMSE fails to detect. There is moderate support for its validity and its score correlates highly with age (Logue, Tupler, D'Amico, & Schmitt, 1993).

The NCSE has received considerable criticism. Logue and colleagues (1993) argue that the domains it measures are functionally unrelated and it contains inappropriate tasks that require specific materials. The NCSE also does not accurately assess highly educated people or people suffering from severe dementia (National Center for Cost Containment, 1993). The criterion for recommending further evaluation is reaching the impaired range in one or more of the subtests. Osato, Yang, and LaRue (1993) argue that this is too stringent and produces a high rate of false positives (72%). They recommend increasing the cut-off score to 2 or more subtests, which fall in the impaired range.

Although each of these tests has problems, all are highly useful for what they are designed to do: quickly assess functioning to determine the need for further evaluation. None of these instruments should be used alone for treatment purposes.

Social Support

Social support is not a topic commonly addressed in clinical assessment texts. Although it is quite common in research literature, it has not been developed as an assessment issue. Social support is included here because it is a pertinent construct for older adults. Inadequate social support is associated with depression and poorer physical health (Dean, Kolody, & Wood, 1991; Kogan, Van Hasselt, Hersen, & Kabacoff, 1995). Social support has also been found to reduce the effects of stressful events on mental health (Bolger & Eckenrode, 1990; Kasl & Cooper, 1987, as cited in Antonucci) and is also correlated with longevity (House, Robbins, & Metzer, 1982). Although early studies found positive effects of social support, many of the findings are coming into question as the research develops in this area. This should be kept in mind with regard to the research reported in this section.

There is not one universally accepted definition or measure of *social support*. For a thorough review of social support measures, the reader is directed to Rook (1994). Studies have incorporated physical contact, social network assessment, self-report questionnaires on perceived support, and other methods to measure social support. The different methods make results of studies difficult to interpret and compare. Krause (1986), in one of several conceptualizations of social support, suggests that the concept of social support is multidimensional, comprised of four dimensions: informational support, tangible help, emotional support, and integration. Informational support is simply providing information to older adults who may need help in remaining independent. Tangible, or instrumental, support is the most objectively measurable dimension and refers to physical (i.e., laundry, shopping) or financial assistance. Emotional support involves the behavior or personal characteristics of the supporter (i.e., warmth and empathy). The degree to which persons are involved in or feel that they belong to a certain group is known as integration. This type of support can have a negative impact on the individual if the group exerts pressure or high expectations on the stressed individual (Krause & Markides, 1990). Several other dimensions (i.e., frequency of social contact) have been proposed.

Assessment of social support should include an evaluation of both functional and structural support. Satisfaction with social support is based on perceived support and is associated with psychological well-being, perceptions of health, and outcome of depressive illness (Bowling, 1994). This type of social support is usually assessed with a self-report questionnaire or interview. This can then be contrasted with actual support, where direct measures can be created and used to assess support behaviors. A large discrepancy between perceived and actual support should be noted and can possibly be used as a target area during treatment. Content of interactions should also be assessed. Positive social interactions can positively influence health and well-being. However, negative interactions can have the opposite effect (see Rook, 1990).

Social support is not restricted to familial support, for friends and formal organizations also supply support. Matt and Dean (1993) demonstrated that friends exert a strong influence on measures of psychological distress and well-being. They found a strong gender difference, with women more likely to maintain old and develop new friendships than men. Men are more susceptible to loss of friends after retirement. Therefore, women have larger social networks and more close friendships.

Supportive relationships, such as friendships, are associated with lower illness rates, faster recovery rates, and higher levels of self-health care behavior (Nelson, 1993). In a comprehensive review, Bowling (1994) states that families are more likely to provide instrumental support whereas friends supply more emotional support. Frequent interactions with friends are positively associated with emotional well-being, yet frequency of familial contact has no association with well-being (Matt & Dean, 1993). This is not to suggest that family interactions are detrimental or unimportant, just that friends supply a significant amount of support to an older adult. Satisfaction with one's support network is related to degree of mental distress (Koenig, Westlund, George, Hughes, Blazer, & Hybels, 1993), regardless of the composition of the networks.

Depression

Epidemiological studies report prevalence rates for depressive disorders in later adulthood to be approximately 1% (Koenig & Blazer, 1992). However, prevalence rates of depression are frequently underreported for those over 65 years of age (Koenig & Blazer, 1992). Pachana, Gallagher-

Thompson, and Thompson (1994) suggest that this may be due to evaluating the depressive presentation as a full-blown syndrome rather than looking for specific symptoms that may not necessarily meet the traditional classifications of depression. The uniqueness of depressive disorders in the elderly is not fully captured by the *DSM-IV* nomenclature (Hassinger, Smith, & LaRue, 1989). This suggests a need for the geropsychologist to strongly consider an ideographic approach to the assessment of depression.

There are many special circumstances to consider in the assessment of depression with older adults. Two conditions that are often difficult to discriminate in older adulthood are depression and dementia. Cognitive decline among older adults is likely to interfere with accurate self-reporting, which may mask depression (La Rue, Dessonville, & Jarvik, 1985). Depressive symptoms (e.g., poor concentration) are frequently misunderstood as a decrease in mental functioning, referred to as *pseudodementia* (Hassinger, Smith, & La Rue, 1989). Additionally, physical problems and various medications contribute to depressive illness and obfuscate the assessment process. It is important to recognize that somatic complaints can be older individuals' means of expressing their depressed mood (Hassinger, Smith, & La Rue, 1989). Disentangling these concomitants of depression is the most difficult aspect of assessing depression in the elderly. Consequently, multidimensional, individualized assessment is needed to understand the role that these concurrent issues are playing in the clinical presentation of the older adult.

Complexities associated with determining clinical depression in older adults has contributed to poor measure development and refinement in this area (Pachana, Gallagher-Thompson, & Thompson, 1994). Though some researchers have developed measures that reflect the special needs of the older adults (e.g., Geriatric Depression Scale: Yesavage, Brink, & Rose, 1983), many widely used assessment devices were developed for the younger adult population. A relatively few investigations of the psychometric properties of these measures have been conducted over the past several years with older adult samples. The remainder of this section will focus on various self-report instruments and interviews that have been widely used and their utility with older adults.

The Geriatric Depression Scale (GDS), developed by Yesavage, Brink, and Rose (1983), is the only self-reported measure of depression designed specifically to accommodate older adults. For example, the GDS has a simple yes/no response format and minimal items endorsing somatic symptoms, ensuring easier and more accurate assessment (Yesavage et al., 1983). The GDS is more sensitive in detecting depressive symptoms in this population than any other measure of depression (e.g., Brink, Yesavage, Lunn, Hursema, Adey, & Rose, 1982; Hyer & Blount, 1984; Kiernan et al., 1986).

Examination of the psychometric properties of the GDS has yielded mixed results. Parmalee, Lawton, and Katz (1989) reported internal consistency of the GDS to be as high as .91 with a large sample of institutionalized older adults. The validity of the GDS with cognitively impaired older adults has been questioned (Kafonek, Ettinger, Roca, Kittner, Taylor, & German, 1989). It appears to be less valid for assessing depressive symptoms in older adults with moderate to severe cognitive impairment (Feher, Larrabee, & Crook, 1992; Burke, Houston, Boust, & Roccaforte, 1989). However, O'Neill, Rice, Blake, Walsh, and Coakley (1992) suggest that the mode of presentation can greatly affect the validity of the GDS in cognitively impaired older adults. Reading the items aloud rather than self-administration of the GDS may be a better alternative for assessing depression in cognitively impaired older adults.

The Beck Depression Inventory (BDI) (Beck, Ward, Mendelson, Mock, & Erbaugh, 1961) was originally created for younger adults but has been widely used with an older population (see Gallagher, 1986a, for review). Gallagher and colleagues (1983) concluded that depression is similar in old and young adults, suggesting that there is no need for disparate measures to assess for depression for each age group. In contrast, Weiss, Nagel, and Aronson (1986) believe that integral factors associated with depression in later adulthood (i.e., helplessness, loneliness, history of depressive symptoms) are ignored by the items on the BDI. Moreover, many items on the BDI ask the respondent to endorse somatic complaints. As discussed earlier, diagnosing depression in the older adult client based on a high endorsement of physical complaints may lead to misdiagnosis. Also, one should consider the difficulty of the Likert response format of the BDI requiring increased attention and memory of the older adult as compared to the simpler yes/no format of the GDS (Pachana, Gallagher-Thompson, & Thompson, 1994).

Deforge and Sobal (1988) created the Center for Epidemiological Studies-Depression Scale (CES-D) to assess levels of depression in the general population. This measure has been utilized by researchers to obtain prevalence rates of depression in older adult populations (see Murrell, Himmelfarb, & Wright, 1983; Phifer & Murrell, 1986). Hertzog and associates (1990) found the CES-D to be an effective screening device for depression in older adults. However, like the GDS, the CES-D has been criticized for use with cognitively impaired older adults. The response format of this measure requires the respondent to recall information from the past week, which may result in unreliable data collection (Gallagher, 1987). Therefore, use of the CED-S and BDI appear most appropriate with higher-functioning older adults (Pachana et al., 1994).

Blazer, Burchett, Service, and George (1991) also caution the use of the CES-D for clients who have many physical disabilities. Functional disability correlates highly with each item of the CES-D (Blazer et al., 1991). Consequently, a high number of somatic endorsements may be a threat to the validity of the CES-D. Stability coefficients with a general community population for two-, four-, six-, and eight-week periods have averaged .57 (Radloff, 1977). Coefficient alpha for the same population is .92 (Radloff, 1977). The CES-D has also been shown to discriminate well between clinical samples and general population samples (e.g., Himmelfarb & Murrell, 1983), and it correlates significantly with other measures of depression (e.g., Beck Depression Inventory, Zung Self-Rating Depression Scale; Weissman, Prusoff, & Newberry, 1975, as cited in Radloff & Teri, 1986). Radloff and Teri (1986) reported reliability and validity coefficients for the CES-D with older adults to be comparable to those obtained with younger populations.

Lewinsohn (1974) postulated that depression results from too few reinforcing or pleasant activities and/or too many negative or unpleasant activities in the individual's environment. Accordingly, MacPhillamy and Lewinsohn (1982) developed the Pleasant Events Scale (PES) and Lewinson, Mermelstein, Alexander, and MacPhillamy (1985) developed the Unpleasant Events Scale (UES). Both are checklists in which behavioral activities can be rated for frequency, pleasantness, and/or unpleasantness. Unlike the measures that assess depressive symptoms directly, the clinician may administer the PES or the UES to simply determine activity level. Results provide the clinician with information on specific depressive behaviors (e.g., low pleasant activity level, overinvolvement in unpleasant activities), resulting in a clear indication of treatment focus.

The PES and UES have been modified to evaluate behavioral activity in older age groups (Teri & Lewinsohn, 1982). Activities were included to reflect the interests of older adults, and items are briefer and easier to read (Teri, 1991). In addition, an "accessibility rating" was added so that the older adult could indicate if he or she was unable to engage in a particular activity due to physical or environmental limitations (Teri, 1991). Normative data for older adults are available for this measure (Teri & Lewinsohn, 1982).

The Structured Clinical Interview for *DSM-III-R* (SCID) (Spitzer, Williams, Gibbon, & First, 1992) is a semistructured clinical interview that is used to determine current and lifetime occurrences of major Axis I as well as Axis II disorders. One advantage of the SCID is its modular format, which decreases length in time of administration. Another advantage of using the SCID is having the immediate knowledge of whether the interviewee meets criteria for a given disorder. Although the psychometric properties of the SCID have been well studied with younger adult populations (e.g., Williams et al., 1992), it has received little empirical examination with older adults, and the paucity of research that has been conducted has resulted in conflicting findings.

Stukenberg, Dura, and Keicolt-Glaser (1990) found that the SCID adequately assessed the clinical syndrome of major depression in older adults, suggesting that it be used as the gold standard for assessing depression with the elderly. Additionally, Segal, Hersen, Van Hasselt, Kabacoff, and Roth (1993) demonstrated that the Major Depression module of the SCID had good interrater agreement (Kappa = .70) with residential and outpatient older adults. However, Stukenberg and associates (1990) concluded that the SCID did not sufficiently identify dysthymia or chronic depression. Further, Pachana and associates (1994) found that the SCID did not adequately identify either depression or anxiety disorders with elders. The paucity of data, as well as the mixed results, suggest that the psychometric properties of the SCID with older adults remain in question.

Developed by Spitzer and Endicott (1977), the Schedule for Affective Disorders and Schizophrenia (SADS) is a structured interview based on the *DSM* nomenclature. It yields a full-symptom picture of mood and/or psychotic disorders that may be present. Results from the SADS provide current information as well as historical information about symptomatology. Due to the schedule's lengthy administration (approximately two hours), one might consider using only those parts pertaining to Depressive Disorders. This strategy will not, however, yield a differential diagnosis. The SADS has been shown to be useful in distinguishing between depressed and nondepressed older adults (Gallagher, 1986b).

Because depression is so common in later adulthood, it is extremely important to screen for this disorder in both clinical and research settings. Pachana and colleagues (1994) recommend using the BDI and GDS for quick screening tools and the SADS for formulating diagnoses. Despite development of the GDS, there remains a great need for additional instruments that adequately measure the dimensions of depression that are unique to the elderly.

Regardless of their shortcomings, it is important to recognize the value that the aforementioned measures offer to the behavioral assessment of depression. Although these measures were developed out of a nomothetic model, each can be used within an ideographic framework by focusing on responses to individual items.

When possible, information should be obtained about the client's medical and medication history, cognitive functioning, and economic and social resources to clarify the etiology of symptoms. The CARE and OARS (see earlier part of this chapter for a discussion of these measures) can provide the clinician with information about depressive symptoms as well as these dimensions. If, upon completing a multidimensional assessment, depression is suspected, the clinician can rely on the individual assessment devices listed here for further, more precise measurement.

Anxiety

To date, the literature on behavioral assessment of anxiety in older adults is scant. Such void in the literature is difficult to understand, given the high prevalence rates of anxiety and related symptoms in late adulthood (Blazer, George, & Hughes, 1991; Himmelfarb & Murrell, 1984; Livingston & McNamara, 1992). Blazer and associates (1991) report that 2% to 4% of the older adult population suffer from Generalized Anxiety Disorder and approximately 10% of older adults report at least one specific phobia. Anxious older adults tend to present with an atypical symptom pattern, which in some cases is dramatically different from those of the general adult population with whom standards are set (Hersen & Van Hasselt, 1992). The symptom pattern of anxiety in older adulthood frequently comprises common anxiety symptoms, concomitant medical complaints, and additional psychological problems (Shamoian, 1991). The many concomitants of anxiety in older adults may preclude precise identification of this disorder and its related symptoms.

Comorbid medical conditions are common in older adults who are experiencing anxiety (Morrin & Colecchi, in press). In some cases, it is very difficult to determine whether anxiety is comorbid or primary in nature. Distinguishing the roles that physical ailments and the aging process play in the clinical presentation of anxiety in the older adult can also be very difficult (Morin & Colecchi, in press).

Behavioral clinicians have been very successful in identifying anxiety in younger populations. Although less is known about the manifestations of anxiety in older adults, gerontologists are beginning to recognize a need for change in the conceptualization and assessment of anxiety in older adults (Carstensen, 1988; Hersen & Van Hasselt, 1992;

Hersen, Van Hasselt, & Goreczny, 1993; Shamoian, 1991). Traditionally, behavioral assessment and treatment of children and adults have benefited from a tripartite conceptualization of anxiety (Cone, 1977). This approach is equally important when assessing older adults. Several instruments designed to measure anxiety in general adulthood have been developed with a consideration of the foregoing response modes, some of which are currently being used with anxious, older adults. Because no literature exists on the use of behavioral measures of anxiety with older adults, the following section will provide a discussion of the anxiety measures that have been reported are frequently utilized with older adults (see Edelstein et al., in press).

The Beck Anxiety Inventory (BAI) was developed by Beck, Epstein, Brown, and Steer (1988) to evaluate cognitive, somatic, and behavioral manifestations of anxiety in psychiatric populations. The BAI was also designed to discriminate generalized and panic anxiety from depression and has been proven effective in making this discrimination in younger adults (Beck et al., 1988). This measure is heavily loaded with somatic items, limiting its utility with older adults who have many physical complaints (Morin & Colecchi, in press). Unfortunately, psychometric data on older adult samples are not yet available.

The State Trait Anxiety Inventory (STAI) was developed by Spielberger, Gorsuch, and Lushene (1971) to measure anxiety both as a transient emotional state and as a stable personality trait. The STAI has been used to assess anxious symptoms in several studies with older adults who suffer from insomnia and memory impairments (see Morin, Kowatch, Barry, & Walton, 1993). However, use of this measure with older adults has been criticized because many older adults require a considerable amount of assistance completing it due to comprehension difficulties (McDonald & Spielberger, 1978). Patterson, O'Sullivan, and Spielberger (1980) responded to this criticism by utilizing a form of the STAI developed for children (STAIC; Spielberger, Edwards, Lushene, Montouri, & Platzek, 1973) with an older adult sample. Patterson and associates (1980) found the simplified three-choice format of the STAIC to be easier for the older adult to complete, and their investigation also revealed high convergent validity of the STAI-C with the STAI. Using a larger sample of older adults than Patterson and associates, Rankin, Gfeller, and Gilner (1993) reported the internal consistency of the STAI-C to be moderately high (alpha = .86) and test-retest reliability to be .81. Although more research is clearly needed, the STAI-C appears to be an adequate measure of anxiety in older adults.

The Minnesota Multiphasic Personality Inventory (MMPI) was originally published in 1943 and revised (MMPI-2) by Butcher, Dahlstrom, Graham, Tellegen, and Kaemmer (1989) as an objective assessment of personality and psychopathology. The MMPI-2 is comprised of 567 true/false items that provide the evaluator with results on 10 standard clinical scales as well as a number of validity, content, and supplemental scales (Graham, 1990). The clinical scale, Psychasthenia, most accurately reflects anxious symptomatology (Graham, 1990). Moreover, various content and supplemental scales also measure dimensions of anxiety (e.g., fears, obsessiveness). Several cohort comparison studies have been conducted using the MMPI to assess stability of personality during the aging process (e.g., Finn, 1986). More recently, Butcher and colleagues (1991), using a large sample of older males, concluded that special, age-related normative data for the MMPI-2 are not needed for this population.

The Structured Clinical Interview for the *DSM-III-R* (SCID) (Spitzer, Williams, Gibbon, & First, 1992) is a semistructured interview that provides the clinician or researcher with an Axis I or Axis II diagnosis for the client. The SCID contains sections that provide information on anxiety disorders and frequency of symptom occurrence. To avoid lengthy administration time, the anxiety sections of the SCID can be used in isolation to determine specific behaviors that are leading to distress. In one of two studies specifically evaluating the reliability of the SCID with older adults, Segal and associates (1993) report good inter-rater agreement (Kappa = .77) for the diagnosis of an anxiety disorder with a sample of residential and outpatient older adults.

As noted earlier, anxiety appears to differ in presentation across age groups (Shamoian, 1991). The current instruments used to evaluate anxiety in older adults have a strong emphasis on physical components of anxiety. Due to this emphasis, these instruments fail to differentiate anxious symptoms from concomitant medical problems in older clients, resulting in invalid assessment of anxiety in this population (Hersen & Van Hasselt, 1992). When measuring anxiety in the elderly, additional validity concerns are apparent. In accordance with the literature on younger adults, Rankin and colleagues (1993) found statistically significant, positive correlations between items on anxiety and depression measures frequently used with older adults. Therefore, one might question the discriminative validity of these measures (Morin & Colecchi, in press). However, consideration is increasingly being given to a mixed anxiety-depression syndrome. Until this issue of discrete anxiety and depressive disorders is resolved, we still need instruments that consider the unique variables (e.g., multiple physical problems, untoward effects from medications) associated with anxiety in later adulthood (Hersen & Van Hasselt, 1992).

SUMMARY

We have provided an overview of the assessment of older adults with a focus on methods and instruments that we considered behavioral.

We followed the approach of identifying behavioral assessment instruments by how they are used rather than by their physical characteristics. Behavioral instruments directly and objectively measure overt behavior, physiological responses, or cognitive responses in a manner that results in the identification of specific behavior problems and their functionally related variables. In behavioral assessment, such assessment instruments are directly connected with treatment.

We began with a brief presentation of sensory changes occurring with age that can affect the assessment process and outcome, noting how various physiological changes can. For example, hearing impairments can both compromise the validity of orally presented assessment material and even contribute to a presenting psychological problem (e.g., paranoia). This was followed by a brief discussion of how ageism, one of many biases that can affect assessment of older adults, can influence the assessment process and its outcome.

A discussion of multidimensional assessment then followed in which this comprehensive approach is advocated for the multifaceted problems of many older adults. Psychometric considerations that are particularly important for older adult assessment instruments were discussed, with particular attention to the paucity of psychometric data available for the most commonly used assessment instruments. Following several psychometric caveats, some of the more common assessment methods and instruments used with older adults were presented. Discussion of specific instruments focused on neuropsychological assessment, cognitive screening, and the assessment of social support, depression and anxiety. Characteristics and utility of these instruments/methods with older adults were discussed, with an eye to the adequacy of currently available psychometric information.

We hope that through a consideration of the information we have presented and the questions we have raised, the reader will be aware of the special considerations one must make for older adults, the paucity of psychometric data to support our current clinical assessment practices, and the need for the development of reliable and valid behavioral assessment measures for older adults.

REFERENCES

Albert, M. S. (1994). Brief assessments of cognitive function in the elderly. In M. P. Lawton & J. A. Teresi (Eds.), *Annual review of gerontology and geriatrics: focus on assessment techniques* (pp. 93–106). New York: Springer.

American Psychiatric Association. (1994). *Diagnostic and statistical manual of mental disorders* (4th ed.). Washington, DC: Author.

Antonucci, T. C. (1991). Attachment, social support and coping with stress in adulthood. In E. M. Cummings, E. Greene, & Karraker, K. H. (Eds.), *Lifespan development psychology: Perspectives on stress and coping* (pp. 261–276). Hillsdale: NJ: Erlbaum.

Ashford, J. W., Kolm, P., Colliver, J. A., Bekian, C., & Hsu, L. -N. (1989). Alzheimer patient evaluation and the mini-mental state: Item characteristic curve analysis. *Journals of Gerontology, 44*, P139–P146.

Beck, A. T. (1976). *Cognitive therapy and the emotional disorders*. New York: International University Press.

Beck, A. T., Epstein, N., Brown, G., & Steer, R. A. (1988). An inventory for measuring clinical anxiety: Psychometric properties. *Journal of Consulting and Clinical Psychology, 56*, 893–897.

Beck, A. T., Ward, C. H., Mendelson, M., Mock, J., & Erbaugh, J. (1961). An inventory for measuring depression. *Archives of General Psychiatry, 4*, 561–571.

Bellack, A. S., & Hersen, M. (1988). Future directions of behavioral assessment. In A. S. Bellack & M. Hersen (Eds.), *Behavioral assessment: A practical handbook* (3rd ed.) (pp. 610–615). Elmsford, NY: Pergamon.

Blazer, D., Burchett, B., Service, C., & George, L. K. (1991). The association of age and depression among the elderly: An epidemiologic exploration. *Journal of Gerontology, 46*, 210–215.

Blazer, D., George, L. K., & Hughes, D. (1991). The epidemiology of anxiety disorders: An age comparison. In C. Salzman & B. D. Lebowitz (Eds.), *Anxiety in the elderly: Treatment and research* (pp. 17–30). New York: Springer.

Blessed, G., Tomlinson, B. E., & Roth, M. (1968). Association between quanitative measures of dementia and of senile changes in the cerebral gray matter of elderly subjects. *British Journal of Psychiatry, 114*, 797–811.

Bolger, N., & Eckenrode, J. (1991). Social relationships, personality, and anxiety during a major stressful event. *Journal of Personality and Social Psychology, 61*, 440–449.

Botwinick, J. (1984). *Aging and behavior: A comprehensive integration of research findings*. New York: Springer.

Bowling, A. (1994). Social networks and social support among older people and implications for emotional well-being and psychiatric morbidity. *International Review of Psychiatry, 6*, 41–58.

Brink, T. L., Yesavage, J. A., Lunn, O., Huresma, P. H., Adey, M., & Rose, T. L. (1982). Screening tests for geriatric depression. *Clinical Gerontologist, 1*, 37–43.

Burke, W. J., Houston, M. J., Boust, S. J., & Roccaforte, W. H. (1989). Use of the Geriatric Depression Scale in dementia of the Alzheimer type. *Journal of the American Geriatrics Society, 37*, 856–860.

Butcher, J. N., Aldwin, C. M., Levenson, M. R., Ben-Porath, Y. S., Spiro, A., & Bosse, R. (1991). Personality and aging: A study of the MMPI-2 among older men. *Psychology and Aging, 6*, 361–370.

Butcher, J. N., Dahlstrom, W. G., Graham, J. R., Tellegen, A., & Kaemmer, B. (1989). *MMPI-2: Minne-*

sota Multiphasic Personality Inventory-2. Manual for administrative and scoring. Minneapolis: University of Minnesota Press.

Butler, R. N. (1980). Ageism: A foreword. Journal of Social Issues, 36, 8–11.

Campbell, A., Converse, P. E., & Rodgers, W. L. (1976). The quality of American life. New York: Sage.

Carstensen, L. L. (1988). The emerging field of behavioral gerontology. Behavior Therapy, 19, 259–281.

Chiulli, S. J, Haaland, K. Y., La Rue, A., & Garry, P. J. (in press). Impact of age on drawing the Rey-Osterrieth figure. The Clinical Neuropsychologist.

Cohen-Mansfield, J., Marx, M. S., Rosenthal, A. S. (1989). A description of agitation in a nursing home. Journal of Gerontology: Medical Sciences, 44, M77–M84.

Cohen-Mansfield, J., Werner, P., Culpepper II, W. J., Wolfson, M., & Bickel, E. (in press). In L. Carstensen, B. Edelstein, & L. Dornbrand (Eds.), Practice of clinical gerontology. Beverly Hills, CA: Sage.

Cone, J. (1977). The relevance of reliability and validity for behavioral assessment. Behavior Therapy, 8, 411–426.

Copeland, J. R., Kelleher, M. J., Kellett, J. M., Gourlay, A. J., Gurland, B. J., Fleiss, J. L., & Sharpe, L. (1976). A semistructured clinical interview for the assessment of diagnosis and mental state in the elderly: The Geriatric Mental State Schedule. I. Development and reliability. Psychological Medicine, 6, 439–449.

Crook, T. (1987). Dementia. In L. L. Carstensen & B. A. Edlestein (Eds.), Handbook of clinical gerontology. (pp. 96–111). Elmsford, NY: Pergamon.

Cunningham, W. R. (1986). Psychometric perspectives: Validity and reliability. In L. W. Poon (Ed.), Handbook of clinical memory assessment of older adults (pp. 27–31). Washington, DC: American Psychological Association.

Dalton, J. E., Pederson, S. L., Blom, B. E., & Holmes, N. R. (1987). Diagnostic errors using the Short Portable Mental Status Questionnaire with a mixed clinical population. Journal of Gerontology, 42, 512–514.

Dean, A., Kolody, B., & Wood, P. (1990). Effects of social support from various sources on depression in elderly persons. Journal of Health and Social Behavior, 31, 148–161.

DeForge, B. R., & Sobal, J. (1988). Self-report depression scales in the elderly: The relationship between the CES-D and Zung. International Journal of Psychiatry in Medicine, 18, 325–338.

Duke University Center for the Study of Aging and Human Development. (1978). Multidimensional functional assessment: The OARS Methodology (2nd ed.). Durham, NC: Author.

Edelstein, B., Northrup, L. E., Staats, N. & Packard, K. (in press). Assessment of older adults. In M. Hersen & V. B. Van Hasselt, (Eds.), Psychological treatment of older adults: An introductory textbook. New York: Plenum.

Feher, E. P., Larrabee, G. J., & Crook, T. H. (1992). Factors attenuating the validity of the geriatric depression scale in a dementia population. Journal of the American Geriatrics Society, 40, 906–909.

Fillenbaum, G. G., Heyman, A., Wilkinson, W. E., & Haynes, C. S. (1987). Comparison of two screening tests in Alzheimer's disease: The correlation and reliability of the Mini-Mental State Examination and the Modified Blessed Test. Archives of Neurology, 44, 924–927.

Finn, S.E. (1986). Stability of personality self-ratings over 30 years: Evidence for an age/cohort interaction. Journal of Personality and Social Psychology, 50, 813–818.

Folstein, M., Folstein, S. E., & McHugh, P. R. (1975). Mini-mental state : A practical method for grading the cognitive state of patients for the clinician. Journal of Psychiatric Research, 12, 189–198.

Fulton, G. B. (1992). Sexuality and aging. In C. S. Kart, E. K. Metress & S. P. Metress (Eds.), Human aging and chronic disease. (pp. 253–266). Boston: Jones & Bartlett.

Gallagher, D. (1986a). Assessment of depression by interview methods and psychiatric rating scales. In L. Poon (Ed.), Handook of clinical memory assessment of older adults (pp. 202–212). Washington, DC: American Psychological Association.

Gallagher, D. (1986b). The Beck Depression Inventory and older adults: Review of its development and utility. Clinical Gerontologist, 5, 149–163.

Gallagher, D. (1987). Assessing affect in the elderly. Clinics in Geriatric Medicine, 3, 65–85.

Gallagher, D., Breckenridge, J., Steinmetz, J., & Thompson, L. W. (1983). The Beck Depression Inventory and research diagnostic criteria: Congruence in an older population. Journal of Consulting and Clinical Psychology, 51, 945–946.

Gallagher, D., Thompson, W. W., & Levy, S. M. (1980). Clinical psychological assessment of older adults. In L. W. Poon (Ed.), Aging in the 1980's (pp. 19–40). Washington, DC: American Psychological Association.

Gaitz, C. M., & Baer, P. E. (1970). Diagnostic assessment of the elderly: A multifunctional model. The Gerontologist, 10, 47–52.

Gatz, M., & Pearson, C. G. (1988). Ageism revised and the provision of psychological services. *American Psychologist, 43*, 184–188.

Gatz, M., Pederson, N. L., & Harris, J. (1987). Measurement characteristics of the mental health scale from the OARS. *Journal of Gerontology, 42*, 332–335.

George, L. K. (1994). Multidimensional assessment instruments: Present status and future prospects. In M. P. Lawton & J. A. Teresi (Eds.), *Annual review of gerontology and geriatrics,* (Vol. 14) (pp. 353–376). New York: Springer.

George, L. K., & Fillenbaum, G .G. (1985). The OARS Methodology: A decade of experience in geriatric assessment. *Journal of the American geriatrics Society, 33*, 607–615.

Golden, R. R., Teresi, J. A., & Gurland, B. J. (1984). Development of indicator scales for the Comprehensive Assessment and Referral Evaluation (CARE) Interview Schedule. *Journal of Gerontology, 39*, 138–146.

Goldstein, G. (1984). Methodological and theoretical issues in neuropsychological assessment. In B. Edelstein & E. Couture (Eds.), *Behavioral assessment and rehabilitation of the traumatically brain-damaged* (pp. 1–21). New York: Plenum.

Graham, J. R. (1990). *MMPI-2: Assessing personality and psychopathology*. New York: Oxford Press.

Graziano, A. M., & Raulin, M. L. (1989). Hypothesis testing, validity, and threats to validity. In J. Rothman (Ed.), *Research methods: A process of inquiry* (pp. 153–177). New York: Harper and Row.

Greene, M. G., Adelman, R., Charon, R., & Hoffman, S. (1986). Ageism in the medical encounter: An exploratory study of the doctor-elderly patient relationship. *Language & Communication, 6*, 113–124.

Gurland, B., Cross, P., Defiguerido, J., Shannon, M., Mann, A. H., Jenkins, R., Bennett, R., Wilder, D., Wright, H., Keilleffer, E., Goodlove, C., Thompson, P., Ross, M., & Deming, W. E. (1979). A cross-national comparison of the institutionalized elderly in the cities of New York and London. *Psychological Medicine, 9*, 781–788.

Gurland, B., Golden, R. R., Teresi, J. A., & Challop, J. (1984). The SHORT-CARE: An efficient instrument for the assessment of depression, dementia, and disability. *Journal of Gerontology, 39*, 166–169.

Gurland, B., Kuriansky, J., Sharpe, L., Simon, R., Stiller, P., & Birkett, H. P. (1977–78). The Comprehensive Assessment and Referral Evaluation (CARE): Rationale, development and reliability. *International Journal of Aging and Human Development, 8*, 9–42.

Gurland, B. J., Teresi, J., Smith, W. M., Black, D., Hughes, G., & Edlavitch, S. (1988). Effects of treatment for isolated systolic hypertension on cognitive status and depression in the elderly. *Journal of American Geriatrics Society, 36*, 1015–1022.

Gurland, B. J., & Wilder, D. E. (1984). The CARE interview revisited: Development of an efficient, systematic, clinical assessment. *Journal of Gerontology, 39*, 129–137.

Harper, R. G., Chacko, R. C., Kotik-Harper, D., & Kirby, H. B. (1992). Comparison of two cognitive screening measures for efficacy in differentiating dementia from depression in a geriatric inpatient population. *Journal of Neuropsychiatry and Clinical Neurosciences, 4*, 179–184.

Hassinger, M., Smith, G., & LaRue, A. (1989). Assessing depression in older adults. In T. Hunt & C. J. Lindley (Eds.), *Testing older adults: A reference guide for geropsychological assessments*. Austin, TX: Pro-Ed.

Hayes, S. C., Nelson, R. O., & Jarrett, R. B. (1987). The treatment utility of assessment: A functional approach to evaluating assessment quality. *American Psychologist, 42,* 963–974.

Haynes, S. N. (1991). Behavioral assessment. In M. Hersen, A. Kazdin, & A. Bellack (Eds.), *The clinical psychology handbook* (pp. 430–264). Oxford: Pergamon Press.

Haynes, S. N. (1978). *Principles of behavioral assessment*. New York: Gardner Press.

Heckheimer, E. F. (1989). *Health promotion of the elderly in the community*. Philadelphia: W. B. Saunders.

Heinrichs, R. W. (1990). Current and emergent applications of neuropsychological assessment: Problems of validity and utility. *Professional Psychology: Research and Practice, 21*, 171–176.

Hersen, M., & Van Hasselt, V. B. (1992). Behavioral assessment and treatment of anxiety in the elderly. *Clinical Psychology Review, 12*, 619–640.

Hersen, M., Van Hasselt, V. B., & Goreczny, A. J. (1993). Behavioral assessment of anxiety in older adults. *Behavior Modification, 17*, 99–112.

Hertzog, C., & Schear, J. M. (1989). Psychometric considerations in testing the older person. In T. Hunt & C. J. Lindley (Eds.), *Testing older adults: A reference guide for geropsychology assessments* (pp. 24–50). Austin, TX: Pro-Ed.

Hertzog, C., Van Alstine, J., Usala, P. D., & Hultsch, D. F. (1990). Measurement properties of the Center for Epidemioloical Studies Depression Scale (CES-D) in older populations. *Psychological Assessment, 2*, 64–72.

Himmelfarb, S., & Murrell, S. A. (1983). Reliability and validity of five mental health scales in older persons. *Journal of Gerontology, 38*, 333–339.

Himmelfarb, S., & Murrell, S. A. (1984). The prevalence and correlation of anxiety symptoms in older adults. *Journal of Psychology, 116*, 159–167.

Hoeffer, B., Rader, J., & Siemsen, G. (November 1987). *An observational tool for studying the behavior of cognitively impaired nursing home residents who wander.* Paper presented at meeting of the Gerontological Society of America, Washington, DC.

Holmes, D., Teresi, J., Weiner, A., Monaco, C., Ronch, J., & Vickers, R. (1990). Impacts associated with special care units in long-term care facilities. *The Gerontologist, 30*, 178–183.

House, J. S., Robbins, C., & Metzer, H. L. (1982). The association of social relationships and activities with mortality. *American Journal of Epidemiology, 116*, 123–140.

Hunt, T. H., & Lindley, M. A. (1989). *Testing older adults*. Austin, TX: Pro-Ed.

Hussian, R. A. (1987). Wandering and disorientation. In L. Carstensen & B. Edelstein (Eds.), *Handbook of clinical gerontology* (pp. 177–189). New York: Pergamon.

Hyer, L., & Blount, J. (1984). Concurrent and discriminant validities of the Geriatric Depression Scale with older psychiatric inpatients. *Psychological Reports, 54*, 611–616.

Ivnik, R. J., Malec, J. F., Smith, G. E., Tangalos, E. G., Peterson, R. C., Kokmen, E., & Kurland, L. T. (1992a). Mayo's Older Americans Normative Studies: WAIS-R norms for ages 56 to 97. *Clinical Neuropsychologist, 6* (Suppl.), 1–30.

Ivnik, R. J., Malec, J. F., Smith, G. E., Tangalos, E. G., Peterson, R. C., Kokmen, E., & Kurland, L. T. (1992b). Mayo's Older Americans Normatiave Studies: WMS-R norms for ages 56-94. *Clinical Neuropsychologist, 6* (Suppl.), 49–82.

Ivnik, R. J., Malec, J. F., Smith, G. E., Tangalos, E. G., Peterson, R. C., Kokmen, E., & Kurland, L. T. (1992c). Mayo's Older Americans Normative Studies: Updated AVLT norms for ages 56 to 97. *Clinical Neuropsychologist, 6* (Suppl.), 83–104.

Kafonek, S., Ettinger, W. H., Roca, R., Kittner, S., Taylor, N., & German, P. S. (1989). Instruments for screening for depression and dementia in a long-term care facility. *Journal of the American Geriatrics Society, 37*, 29–34.

Kaplan, E. (1983). Process and achievement revisited. In S. Wapner & B. Kaplan (Eds.), *Toward a holistic developmental psychology* (pp. 143–155). Hillsdale, NJ: Lawrence Erlbaum.

Kart, C. S., Metress, E. K., & Metress, S. P. (1992). *Human Aging and Chronic Disease*. Boston: Jones & Bartlett.

Kaszniak, A. W. (1990). Psychological assessment of the aging individual. In J. E. Birren & K. W. Schaie (Eds.), *Handbook of the psychology of aging* (3rd ed.) (pp. 427–445). New York: Academic Press.

Katz, S. C., Ford, A. B., Moskowitz, R. W., Jackson, B. A., & Jaffee, M. W. (1963). Studies of illness in the aged. The Index of ADL: A standardized measure of biological and psychosocial function. *Journal of the American Medical Association, 185*, 914–919.

Kieman, B. U., Wilson, D., Suter, N., Naqvi, A., Moltzen, J., & Silver, G. (1986). Comparison of the Geriatric Depression Scale and Beck Depression Inventory in a nursing home setting. *Clinical Gerontologist, 6*, 54–56.

Kieman, R. J., Mueller, J., Langston, J. W., & Van Dyke, C. (1987). The neurobehavioral cognitive status examination: A brief but quantitative approach to cognitive assessment. *Annals of Internal Medicine, 107*, 481–485.

Koenig, H. G., & Blazer, D. G. (1992). Mood disorders and suicide. In J. E. Birren, R. B. Sloane, & G. D. Cohen (Eds.), *Handbook of mental health and aging* (2nd ed.) (pp. 379–407). San Diego, CA: Academic Press.

Koenig, H. G., Westlund, R. E., George, L. K., Hughes, D. C., Blazer, D. G., & Hybels, C. (1993). Abbreviating the Duke Social Support Index for use in chronically ill elderly individuals. *Psychosomatics, 34*, 61–69.

Kogan, E. S., Van Hasselt, V. B., Hersen, M., & Kabacoff, R. I. (1995). Relationship of depression, assertiveness, and social support in community-dwelling older adults. *Journal of Clinical Geropsychology 1*, 157–163.

Kovar, M. G., & Lawton, M. P. (1994). Functional disability: Activities and instrumental activities of daily living. In M. P. Lawton & J. A. Teresi (Eds.), *Annual review of gerontology and geriatrics* (Vol. 14) (pp. 57–75) New York: Springer.

Krause, N. (1986). Social support, stress, and well-being among older adults. *Journal of Gerontology, 41*, 512–519.

Krause, N., & Markides, K. S. (1990). Measuring social support among older adults. *International Journal of Aging and Human Development, 30*, 37–53.

Kukull, W. A., & Larson, E. B. (1989). Distinguishing Alzheimer's disease from other dementias: Questionnaire responses of close relatives and autopsy results. *Journal of the American Geriatrics Society, 37*, 521–527.

Kuriansky, J. B., Gurland, B. J., & Fleiss, J. L. (1976). The assessment of self-care capacity in geriatric psychiatric patients by objective and subjective methods. *Journal of Clinical Psychology, 32*, 95–102.

La Rue, A. (1995). *Neuropsychological assessment.* New York: Oxford University Press.

La Rue, A., Dessonville, C., & Jarvik, L. F. (1985). Aging and mental disorders. In J. E. Birren & K. W. Schaie (Eds.), *Handbook of the psychology of aging* (2nd ed.) (pp. 664–702). New York: Van Nostrand Reinhold.

La Rue, A., Watson, J., & Plotkin, D. A. (1992). Retrospective accounts of dementia symptoms: Are they reliable? *The Gerontologist, 32*, 240–245.

Lawton, M. P., & Brody, E. M. (1969). Assessment of older people: Self-maintaining and instrumental activities of daily living. *The Gerontologist, 9*, 179–186.

Lawton, M. P., Moss, M., Fulcomer, M., & Kleban, M. H. (1982). A research and service-oriented multi-level assessment instrument. *Journal of Gerontology, 37*, 91–99.

Lewinsohn, P. M. (1974). Clinical and theoretical aspects of depression. In K. S. Calhoun, H. E. Adams, & K. M. Mitchell (Eds.), *Innovative treatment methods in psychopathology.* New York: Wiley.

Lezak, M. D. (1995). *Nueropsychological assessment* (3rd ed.). New York: Oxford University Press.

Liang, J., Levin, J. S., & Krause, N. M. (1989). Dimensions of the OARS mental health measures. *Journals of Gerontology: Psychological Sciences, 44*, 127–138.

Livingston, M., & McNamara, R. (1992). Psychiatric status among the homebound elderly: An epidemiologic perspective. *Journal of American Geriatric Society, 40*, 561–566.

Logue, P. E., Tupler, L. A., D'Amico, C. J., & Schmitt, F. A. (1993). The Neurobehavioral Cognitive Status Examination: Psychometric properties in use with psychiatric inpatients. *Journal of Clinical Psychology, 49*, 80–89.

MacPhillamy, D. J., & Lewinsohn, P. M. (1982). The pleasant events schedule: Studies on reliability, validity, and scale intercorrelation. *Journal of Consulting and Clinical Psychology, 50*, 363–380.

Mahurin, R. K., & Pirozzolo, F. J. (1986). Chronometric analysis: Clinical applications in aging and dementia. *Developmental Neuropsychology, 2*, 345–362.

Marmor, M. (1992). Normal age-related vision changes and their effects on vision. In E. Faye & C. Stuen (Eds.), *The aging eye and low vision* (pp. 6–16). New York: The Lighthouse Inc.

Masters, W. H., & Johnson, V. E. (1966). *Human sexual response.* Boston: Little, Brown.

Matt, G. E., & Dean, A. (1993). Social support from friends and psychological distress among elderly persons: Moderator effects of age. *Journal of Health and Social Behavior, 34*, 187–200.

McDonald, R. J., & Spielberger, C. D. (1978). Measuring anxiety in hospitalized geriatric patients. In C. D. Spielberger & R. Diaz-Guerrero (Eds.), *Cross-cultural anxiety* (Vol. 2) (pp. 135–143). New York: Hemisphere.

McDonald, R. P. (1978). A simple comprehensive model for the analyses of covariance structures. *British Journal of Mathematical and Statistical Psychology, 31*, 59–72.

Mindel, E., & Vernon, M. (1987). *They grow in silence.* (2nd ed.). San Diego: College-Hill.

Morin, C. M., & Colecchi, C. A. (in press). Psychological assessment of older adults. In J. Butler (Ed.), *Clinical personality assessment: Practical approaches* (pp. 172–191). New York: Oxford University Press.

Morin, C. M., Kowatch, R. A., Barry, T., & Walton, E. (1993). Cognitive-behavior therapy for late-life insomnia. *Journal of Consulting and Clinical Psychology, 61*, 137–146.

Moses, J. A., Golden, C. J., Ariel, R., & Gustavson, J. L. (1983). *Interpretation of the Luria-Nebraska neuropsychological battery* (Vol. 1). New York: Grune & Stratton.

Mungas, D., Weiler, P., Franzi, C., & Henry, R. (1989). Assessment of disruptive behavior associated with dementia: The Distruptive Behavior Rating Scales. *Journal of Geriatric Psychiatry and Neurology, 2*, 196–202.

Murrell, S. A., Himmelfarb, S., & Wright, K. (1983). Prevalence of depression and its correlates in older adults. *American Journal of Epidemiology, 117*, 173–183.

Myers, A. M., & Huddy, L. (1985). Evaluating physical capabilities in the elderly: The relationship between ADL self-assessments and basic abilities. *Canadian Journal of Aging, 4*, 189–200.

National Center for Cost Containment, Department of Veterans Affairs. (1993). *Geropsychology assessment resource guide* (No. PB93-213684). Milwaukee, WI: Author.

Nelson, M. A. (1993). Race, gender, and the effect of social supports on the use of health services by the elderly individuals. *International Journal of Aging and Human Development, 37*, 227–246.

Niederehe, G., Cooley, S. G., & Teri, L. (1995). Research and training in clinical geropsychology: Advances and current opportunities. *The Clinical Psychologist, 48*, 37–44.

Nunnally, J. C., & Bernstein, I. H. (1994). *Psychometric theory* (3rd ed.). New York: McGraw-Hill.

O'Donohue, W. T. (1987). The sexual behavior and problems of the elderly. In L. L. Carstensen & B. A. Edelstein (Eds.), *Handbook of clinical gerontology* (pp 66–75). New York: Pergamon.

Okun, M. (1976). Adult age and cautiousness in decision: A review of the literature. *Human Development, 19*, 220–233.

O'Neill, D., Rice, I., Blake, P., Walsh, J. B., & Coakley, D. (1992). The Geriatric Depression Scale: Rater-administered or self-administered? *International Journal of Geriatric Psychiatry, 7*, 511–515.

Osato, S. S., Yang, J., & LaRue, A. (1993). The Neurobehavioral Cognitive Status Examination in an older psychiatric population: An exploratory study of validity. *Neuropsychiatry, Neuropsychology, and Behavioral Neurology, 6*, 98–102.

Pachana, N. A., Gallagher-Thompson, D., & Thompson, L. W. (1994). Assessment of depression. In M. P. Lawton & J. A. Teresi (Eds), *Annual review of gerontology and geriatrics* (pp. 234–256). New York: Springer.

Palmstierna, T., & Wistedt, B. (1987). Staff Observation Aggression Scale, SOAS: Presentation and evaluation. *Acta Psychiatrica Scandinvia, 76*, 657–663.

Parmalee, P. A., Katz, I. R., & Lawton, P. (1992). Incidence of depression in long-term care settings. *Journal of Gerontology, 47*, 189–196.

Parmelee, P. A., Lawton, M. P., & Katz, I. R. (1989). Psychometric properties of the Geriatric Depression Scale among the institutional aged. *Phychological Assessment: LA Journal of Consulting and Clinical Psychology, 1*, 331–338.

Patel, V., & Hope, R. A. (1992). A rating scale for aggressive behavior in the elderly—The RAGE. *Psychological Medicine, 22*, 211-221.

Patel, V., & Hope, R. A. (1993). Aggressive behavior in elderly people with dementia: A review. *International Journal of Geriatric Psychiatry, 8*, 457–472.

Patterson, R. L., O'Sullivan, M. J., & Spielberger, C. D. (1980). Measurement of state and trait anxiety in elderly mental health clients. *Journal of Behavioral Assessment, 2*, 89–97.

Pearlin, L. I., & Turner, H. A. (1987). The family as a context of the stress process. In S. V. Kasl & C. L. Cooper (Eds.), *Stress and health: Issues in research methodology* (pp. 143–165). New York: Wiley & Sons.

Perlmutter, M. (1978). What is memory aging the aging of? *Developmental Psychology, 14*, 330–345.

Pfeiffer, E. (1975). A short Portable Mental Status Questionnaire for the assessment of organic brain deficit in elderly patients. *Journal of the American Geriatrics Society, 23*, 433–441.

Pfeiffer, E. (1979). A short Psychiatric Evaluation Schedule: A new 15-item monotonic scale indicative of functional psychiatric disorder. In Bayer Symposium VII, *Brain function in old age* (pp. 228–236). New York: Springer.

Phifer, J. F., & Murrell, S. A. (1986). Etiologic factors in the onset of depressive symptoms in older adults. *Journal of Abnormal Psycholoogy, 95*, 282–291.

Poon, L., Crook, T., Gurland, B. J., Davis, K. L., Kaszniak, A., Eisdorfer, C., & Thompson, L. (Eds.) (1986). *Handbook for clinical memory assessment of older adults* (pp. 3–10). Washington, DC: American Psychological Association.

Rabbitt, P. (1982). Development of methods to measure changes in activities of daily living in the elderly. In S. Corkin, K. L. Davis, J. H. Growdon, E. Usdin, & R. J. Wurtman (Eds.), *Alzheimer's disease: A report of progress*. New York: Raven.

Radloff, L. (1977). The CES-D Scale: A self-report depression scale for research in the general population. *Applied Psychological Measurement, 1*, 385–401.

Radloff, L. S., & Teri, L. (1986). Use of the Center for Epidemiological Studies-Depression Scale with older adults. *Clinical Gerontologist, 5*, 119–136.

Rankin, E. J., Gfeller, J. D., & Gilner, F. H. (1993). Measuring anxiety states in the elderly using the State-Trait Anxiety Inventory for Children. *Journal of Psychiatric Research, 27*, 111–117.

Ray, W. A., Taylor, J. A., Lichtenstein, M. J., & Meador, K. G. (1992). The Nursing Home Behavior Problem Scale. *Journal of Gerontology, 47*, M9–M16.

Reitan, R. M., & Wolfson, D. (1985). *The Halsrtead-Reitan Neuropsychological Test Battery: Theory and clinical interpretation*. Tucson, AZ: Neuropsychology Press.

Rodeheaver, D. (1990). Ageism. In I. A. Parham, L. W. Poon, & I. C. Siegler (Eds.), *Access: Aging Curriculum Content for Education in the Social-Behaviorial Sciences* (pp. 7.1–7.43). New York: Springer.

Rodgers, W. L., & Herzog, A. R. (1987). Interviewing older adults: The accuracy of factual information. *Journal of Gerontology, 42*, 387–394.

Rodin, J., & Langer, E. J. (1980). Aging labels: The decline of control and the fall of self-esteem. *Journal of Social Issues, 36*, 12–29.

Rook, K. S. (1990). Stressful aspects of older adults'

social relationships: An overview of current theory and research. In M. A. P. Stephens, J. H. Crowther, S. E., Hobfoll, & D. L. Tennenbaum (Eds.), *Stress and coping in later-life families* (pp. 173–192). New York: Hemisphere.

Rook, K. S. (1994). Assessing the health-related dimensions of older adults social relationships. In M. P. Lawton & J. A. Teresi (Eds.), *Annual review of gerontology and geriatrics: Focus on assessment techniques* (Vol. 14) (pp. 142–181). New York: Springer.

Rosen, J., Burgio, L., Kollar, M., Cain, M., Allison, M., Fogelman, M., Michael, M., & Zubenko, G. S. (1994). The Pittsburgh Agitation Scale: A user-friendly instrument for rating agitation in dementia patients. *The American Journal of Geriatric Psychiatry, 2,* 52–59.

Roth, M., Tym, E., Mountjoy, C. Q., Huppert, F. A., Hendrie, F. A., Verma, S., & Goddard, R. (1986). A standardised instrument for the diagnosis of mental disorder in the elderly with special reference to the early detection of dementia. *British Journal of Psychiatry, 149,* 698–709.

Rubenstein, L. (1983). The clinical effectiveness of multidimensional geriatric assessment. *Journal of the American Geriatrics Society, 31,* 758–762.

Rubenstein, L. Z., Schairer, C., Wieland, G. D., & Kane, R. (1984). Systematic biases in functional status assessment of elderly adults: Effects of different data sources. *Journal of Gerontology, 39,* 686–691.

Ryden, M. B. (1988). Aggressive behavior in persons with dementia living in the community. *Alzheimer's Disease and Associated Disorders: International Journal, 2,* 342–355.

Sager, M. A., Dunham, N. C., Schwantes, A., Mecum, L., Halverson, K., & Harlowe, D. (1992). Measurement of activities of daily living in hospitalized elderly: A comparison of self-report and performance-based methods. *Journal of the American Geriatrics Society, 40,* 457–462.

Saxton, J., McGonigle-Gibson, K., Swihart, A., Miller, V., & Boller, F. (1990). Assessment of the severely impaired patient: Description and validation of a new neuropsychological test battery. *Psychological Assessment, 12,* 298–303.

Segal, D. L., Hersen, M., Van Hasselt, V. B., Kabacoff, R. I., & Roth, L. (1993). Reliability of diagnosis in older psychiatric patients using the Structured Clinical Interview for DSM-III-R. *Journal of Psychopathology and Behavioral Assessment, 15,* 347–356.

Shamoian, C. A. (1991). What is anxiety in the elderly? In C. Salzman & B. D. Lebowitz (Eds.), *Anxiety in the elderly: Treatment and research* (pp. 3–15). New York: Springer.

Silverman, J. M., Breitner, J. C. S., Mohs, R. C., & Davis, K. L. (1986). Reliability of the family history method in genetic studies of Alzheimer's disease and related dementias. *American Journal of Psychiatry, 143,* 1279–1282.

Spielberger, C. D., Edwards, C. D., Lushene, R. E., Montouri, J., & Platzek, D. (1973). *STAIC: Preliminary manual for the state-trait anxiety inventory for children.* Palo Alto, CA: Consulting Psychologists Press.

Spielberger, C. D., Gorsuch, R. L., & Lushene, R. E. (1971). *Manual for the State-Trait Anxiety Inventory.* Palo Alto, CA: Consulting Psychologists Press.

Spitzer, R. L., & Endicott, J. (1977). *SADS-change interview.* New York: New York State Psychiatric Institute.

Spitzer, R. L., Fleiss, J. L., Burdock, E. I., & Hardesty, A. (1964). The Mental Status Schedule: Rationale, reliability, and validity. *Comprehensive Psychiatry, 5,* 384–395.

Spitzer, R. L., Williams, J. B., Gibbon, M., & First, M. B. (1992). The structured clinical interview for DSM-III-R (SCID). I: History, rationale, and description. *Archives of General Psychiatry, 49,* 624–629.

Starratt, C., & Fields, R. B. (1988). Clinical Dementia Rating. In M. Hersen & A. S. Bellack (Eds.), *Dictionary of behavioral techniques* (pp. 115–117). Elmsford, NY: Pergamon.

Storandt, M. (1994). General principles of assessment of older adults. In M. Storandt, & G. Vandenbos (Eds.), *Neuropsychological assessment of dementia and depression in older adults: A clinician's guide* (pp. 7–31). Washington, DC: American Psychological Association.

Stukenberg, K. W., Dura, J. R., & Kiecolt-Glaser, J. K. (1990). Depression screening scale validation in an elderly, community-dwelling population. *Psychological Assessment, 2,* 134–138.

Sunderland, A., Watts, K., Baddeley, A. D., & Harris, J. E. (1986). Subjective memory assessment and test performance in elderly adults. *Journal of Gerontology, 41,* 376–384.

Teresi, J., Holmes, D., Benenson, E., Monaco, C., Barrett, V., Ramirez, M., & Koren, M. J. (1993). A primary care nursing model in long-term care facilities: evaluation and impact on affect, behavior, and socialization. *The Gerontologist, 33,* 667–674.

Teri, L. (1991). Assessment and treatment of depression.

In P. Wisocki (Ed.), *Handbook of clinical behavioral therapy with the elderly client* (pp. 225–243). New York: Plenum.

Teri, L., & Lewinsohn, P. M. (1982). Modification of the pleasant and unpleasant events schedules for use with the elderly. *Journal of Counseling and Clinical Psychology, 50*, 444–445.

Teri, L. & Reifler, B. V. (1987). Depression and dementia. In L. L. Carstensen & B. Edelstein (Eds.), *Handbook of clinical gerontology* (pp. 112–119). Elmsford, NY: Pergamon.

Uhlmann, R. F., Larson, E. B., & Buchner, D. M. (1987). Correlations of mini-mental state and modified Dementia Rating Scale to measures of transitional health status in dementia. *Journal of Genontology, 42*, 33–36.

Vernon, M. (1989). Assessment of persons with hearing disabilities. In T. Hunt & C. J. Lindley (Eds.), *Testing older adults: A reference guide for geropsychological assessments* (pp. 150–162). Austin, TX: Pro-Ed.

Vernon, M., Griffin, D. H., & Yoken, C. (1981). Hearing loss. *Journal of Family Practice, 12*, 1053–1058.

Villardita, C., & Lomeo, C. (1992). Alzheimer's disease: Correlational analysis of three screening tests and three behavioral scales. *Acta Neurologica Scandinavica, 86*, 603–608.

Weiss, I. K., Nagel, C. L., & Aronson, M. K. (1986). Applicability of depression scales to the old old person. *Journal of the American Geriatrics Society, 34*, 215–218.

Weissman, M. M., Prusoff, B. A., & Newberry, P. (1975). *Comparison of CES-D, Zung Self-Rating Depression Scale and Beck Depression Inventory.* Progress Report, Contract 42-74-83, NIMH.

Werner, H. (1937). Process and achievement: A basic problem of education and developmental psychology. *Harvard Educational Review, 7*, 353–368.

Werner, H. (1956). Microgenesis and aphasia. *Journal of Abnormal and Social Psychology, 52*, 347–353.

Whitbourne, S. (in press). Psychological manifestations of physical disease in the elderly. In L. Carstensen, B. Edelstein, & L. Dornbrand (Eds.), *Practical handbook of clinical gerontology*, Newbury Park, CA: Sage.

Williams, J. B., Gibbon, M., First, M. B., Spitzer, R. L., Davies, M., Borus, J., Howes, M. J., Kane, J., Pope, H. G., Rousaville, B., & Wittchen, W. (1992). The structured clinical interview for DSM-III-R (SCID). II: Multisite test-retest reliability. *Archives of General Psychiatry, 49*, 630–636.

Wing, J. L., Birley, J. L. T., Cooper, J. W., Graham, P., & Isaacs, A. (1967). Reliability of a procedure for measuring and classifying "Present Psychiatric State." *British Journal of Psychiatry, 113*, 499–515.

Winograd, I. R. (1984). Sensory changes with age: Impact on psychological well-being. *Psychiatric Medicine, 2*, 1–26.

Yesavage, J. A. (1986). The use of self-rating depression scales in the elderly. In L. Poon, T. Crook, B. J. Gurland, K. L. Davis, A. W. Kaszniak, C. Eisdorfer, & L. W. Thompson (Eds.), *Handbook for clinical memory assessment for older adults* (pp. 213–217). Washington, DC: American Psychological Association.

Yesavage, J. A., Brink, T. L., & Rose, T. L. (1983). Development and validation of a geriatric depression scale: A preliminary report. *Journal of Psychiatric Residents, 17*, 37–49.

Zelinski, E. M., Gilewski, M. J., & Thompson, L. W. (1980). Do laboratory tests relate to self-assessment of memory ability in the young and old? In L. W. Poon, J. L. Fozard, L. S. Cermak, D. Arenberg, & L. W. Thompson (Eds.), *New directions in memory and aging: Proceedings of the George A. Talland memorial conference.* Hillsdale, NJ: Erlbaum.

Zimbardo, P. G., Andersen, S. M., & Kabat, L. G. (1981). Induced hearing deficit generates experimental paranoia. *Science, 212*, 1529–1531.

CHAPTER 19

BEHAVIORAL NEUROPSYCHOLOGY

Michael D. Franzen
Laura Smith-Seemiller
Allegheny Neuropsychiatric Institute
Medical College of Pennsylvania and Hahnemann University

At first glance, behavioral assessment and neuro-psychological assessment may seem to have little in common. Their rationales seem to be divergent, their methods appear to be radically different, and their purposes seem to be inconsistent. If that were the actual case, this would be a very short chapter. Luckily for the reader, neuropsychological assessment and behavioral assessment do, in fact, share some common features, particularly in the area of treating people who have brain impairments. This chapter will attempt to describe some of the commonalities as well as some of the differences between the two areas of clinical neuropsychological assessment and behavioral assessment. These overlaps and disjunctions will be discussed in the context of conceptualizations, procedures, and methodologies. We will discuss factors that have led to a growing interface between these two disciplines, as well as the benefits of integrating behavioral assessment and treatment procedures with neuropsychological assessment. We will also address methods that have been employed to combine these two assessment and treatment modalities. Finally, we will review some specific target symptoms or problem areas in which the application of both assessment paradigms has resulted in positive effects.

PROCEDURAL DIFFERENCES BETWEEN BEHAVIOR THERAPY AND NEUROPSYCHOLOGY

Behavioral assessment and clinical neuropsychological assessment share the observation of discrete behaviors as their paramount assessment procedure. The clinician in both areas tends to use similar procedural methods. In both, the client is asked to perform some behavior. The clinician scores the client's response on the basis of latency, total response time, or accuracy with regard to some exemplar. The scoring of assessment results frequently requires a stopwatch, ruler, or protractor, as well as a scoring manual with examples of acceptable responses. In interpreting data, emphasis is on description of skill level or on some description of capacity to perform certain behaviors under certain situations.

There are also differences. The overt behaviors observed by behavior analysts are more likely to be similar to, or even identical with, behaviors that would be emitted in the natural environment. The behavior analyst may observe the client performing grooming behaviors or preparing a meal. Alternately, the clinical neuropsychologist may observe a client drawing a complex design from a model or naming objects from line drawing representations—behaviors that may be related to real-life situations but that are rarely elicited outside a laboratory assessment situation.

CONCEPTUAL DIFFERENCES BETWEEN BEHAVIOR THERAPY AND NEUROPSYCHOLOGY

Earlier writings (Franzen, 1991) on this topic have delineated differences between behavioral theory and the basic theoretical notions underlying much of clinical neuropsychology. Although clinical neuropsychology does not enjoy a central canon of principles, as does behaviorism, there are commonalities in the underlying epistemologies of the various approaches to clinical neuropsychological assessment.

The epistemology of neuropsychological assessment is essentially representational; that is, the numbers resulting from the use of neuropsychological assessment instruments are assumed to reflect some skill or process that is separate from the assessment method. The unit of interest may be a hypothetical construct or a physiological function. For example, the score on the Wisconsin Card Sorting Test might be interpreted as a reflection of either an abstract problem-solving skill or as an index of frontal lobe functioning.

In contrast, the epistemology of behavioral assessment is operational; that is, the numbers produced by the behavioral assessment method are assumed to be directly related only to the operation that produced the numbers and not reflective of any other construct. The meaning of the numbers is derived from their relation to numbers produced by other operations. The unit of interest is the observable phenomenon. Furthermore, although both neuropsychological and behavioral assessment assume that behavior is under the control of a wide range of variables, neuropsychological assessment places greater emphasis on the organismic, physiological controlling variables, and behavioral assessment places greater emphasis on the environmental variables.

Despite these seeming differences, clinical neuropsychology and behavioral assessment have a fair amount in common and a great deal to offer each other. Both neuropsychological and behavioral assessment have a basic grounding in the scientific method. Both have a strong relation to the basic science related to their respective areas, and increasingly, both are being used in rehabilitation settings.

THE DEVELOPMENT OF BEHAVIORAL NEUROPSYCHOLOGY

The frequent use of both behavior therapy and neuropsychological assessment in neurological rehabilitation settings is a significant factor behind the growing interface between these two disciplines. Particularly within the field of head injury rehabilitation, the role of neuropsychology has evolved as clinical and practical demands have changed. With the advent of neuroimaging procedures, the neuropsychology referral question is less likely to involve lesion localization and more likely to involve treatment recommendations. There is a high incidence of behavioral problems in individuals with acquired brain injury, and the consequent burden and strain imposed on the injured individual, family members, and rehabilitation staff are great (Jacobs, 1987). Incidence of behavior problems also leads to increasing demands for input as to evaluation and treatment of the behavioral consequences of brain injury.

The growing geriatric population is also likely to become an impetus for greater interface between neuropsychology and behavior therapy. Recent legislation restricting the use of mechanical or pharmacological restraints in nursing homes has resulted in an increased interest in behavioral techniques for use with geriatric nursing home residents (Lundervold & Jackson, 1992). This population has also been the focus of much neuropsychological investigation for reasons of clinical diagnosis, as well as for the interesting theoretical questions raised by some of the dementing illnesses. Given the increased involvement of both behaviorally and neuropsychologically oriented clinicians with older patients, it is somewhat surprising that there has been little work examining the interaction of these two fields. It is an area fecund with potential.

As this discussion illustrates, the merging of neuropsychology and behavior therapy is a natural evolution, given clinical demands. The subdiscipline of Behavioral Neuropsychology was first described in 1979, following the formation of a Special Interest Group, titled "Behavioral Neuropsychology" within the Association for Advancement of Behavior Therapy (Horton, 1979). Horton defined Behavioral Neuropsychology as "the application of Behavior Therapy techniques to problems of organically impaired individuals while using a neuropsychological assessment and intervention perspective" (p. 20).

Franzen (1991) more recently presented an exposition of the underlying principles of behavioral neuropsychology. He noted that there are differences between behavior therapy and traditional neuropsychology in conceptualization, but observed that the direct application may not be radically inconsistent. For example, although traditional clinical neuropsychology largely conceptualizes performance as related to *ability* (which is a theoretical construct), behavioral neuropsychology conceptualizes performance as being related to *skill*, which is the capacity to perform a behavior under defined conditions at some level relative to an external standard.

Benefits to Integrating Behavior Therapy and Neuropsychological Assessment

As elaborated on later, both neuropsychology and behavior therapy derive benefits from an integrated assessment. We will first describe the contributions that neuropsychological assessment can make to behavioral assessment and therapy, and then describe the contributions behavior therapy can offer to neuropsychology. Neuropsychological assessment can guide behavioral treatment programs in a variety of ways. Evaluation results can

be helpful in determining the etiology for a behavioral disorder (Horton, 1979). For example, noncompliance with medications may be a result of poor memory, lack of executive cognitive functions (with resultant decrease in self-monitoring and self-control), poor insight into deficits (leading to refusal), or other factors. Neuropsychological assessment can help to clarify factors behind such a behavioral problem, which will have implications for treatment.

Lawson-Kerr, Smith, and Beck (1990) note that neuropsychological assessment results can lead to hypotheses that will guide behavioral assessment and treatment. They note, for example, that an individual who suffers from acalculia on neuropsychological testing can be targeted for behavioral assessment and treatment of money management skills (e,g., the ability to keep a checkbook, etc.). Also, although standardized neuropsychological tests may not accurately predict performance in social behavior, results on these tests may help identify areas for further evaluation using behavioral means. For example, there may be relationships between performance on measures of cognitive executive function (Controlled Oral Word Association Test, the Stroop Color Word Test, and the Wisconsin Card Sorting Test) and social skill, whether the social interaction is measured using performance in a naturalistic setting (Marsh & Knight, 1991) or reports from significant others (Grattan & Eslinger, 1989).

A comprehensive neuropsychological evaluation, by providing a description of the individual's strengths and weaknesses, may help guide the selection of behavioral procedures that would be most effective. For example, identification of severe deficits in attention may lead to recommendations as to the importance of a nondistracting environment and frequent rest breaks. As noted by Hogan (1988), neuropsychological assessment can help identify residual strengths that can be utilized in treatment.

There has been some research suggesting that patients with varying neurological diagnoses differ in terms of their response to behavioral interventions. For example, Bleiberg and associates (1985) reported that individuals with CHI, in contrast to individuals with cerebral vascular accidents (CVA), show a deficit in their ability to learn from avoidance paradigms but not in their ability to learn from escape paradigms. Jackson and Bentall (1991) reported that their two amnesic patients (one with an etiology of a ruptured anterior communicating artery aneurysm and the other with an etiology of Korsakoff's disease) both demonstrated behavioral rigidity, in that they developed a high rate of responding to a fixed interval schedule and did not modify this response strategy when the schedules were changed to fixed ratio or differential reinforcement of low-rate responding. Impaired avoidance learning observed in closed head injury patients may be modified by increasing the negative valence of the stimulus to be avoided. Kosmidis and Fantie (1995) interpret this situation as reflecting the relatively intact capacity of the closed head injury individual to learn on the basis of classical conditioning.

These results seem to indicate that behavioral training of patients with certain types of brain impairment may need to be tailored to the effects that brain impairment has on the learning style of the patient. These studies highlight the potential relevance of neuropsychological deficits to behavioral treatment planning—an important area for future research.

The examples provided here emphasize the benefits neuropsychology offers to behavior therapy. However, neuropsychological treatment also benefits from the addition of behavioral procedures. Behavioral procedures have been described as showing promise for the treatment of deficits in attention (Peters, Gluck, & McCormick, 1992) and language deficits (Horton, 1979), for example. Horton and Wedding (1984) provided an early description of behavioral neuropsychology, which was heavily weighted to the practical considerations of using behavioral technology for treating the cognitive sequelae of brain impairment.

Lawson-Kerr and colleagues (1990) note that neuropsychological tests often lack ecological validity, and that integration of behavioral approaches to assessment and treatment can help to improve neuropsychologists, abilities to make specific predictions regarding the impact of neuropsychological deficits on adaptive functioning outside the testing room. Neuropsychologists are increasingly called on to make recommendations about driving, returning to work, or the need for supervision. Thus, the question of ecological validity is an extremely important one and is elaborated on in more detail.

Methodological Considerations in the Integration of Behavior Therapy and Neuropsychological Assessment

Although the preceding information reviewed provides strong support for a growing interface between neuropsychology and behavior therapy, specific strategies or models to guide the clinician in integrating these disciplines is relatively lacking. There have been some general models described, as well as more concrete procedures, however this is an area in need of greater attention.

Franzen and Iverson (1990) presented a framework for integrating behavioral and neuropsychological assessment in a multiple baseline design to evaluate the effects of behavioral interventions for remediating cognitive dysfunction. In this model, neuropsychological assessment is used to delineate the deficits and skills of the subject. After determining the relevant domains of skill to be treated, the interventions are applied to one skill area at a time and the untreated skills areas are conceptualized as the behaviors in the multiple baseline across behaviors design. Short standardized tests of neuropsychological skills are used as probe assessments and are administered between phase changes. The original model was conceptualized as being applicable to the treatment of the multiple deficits associated with closed head injury, but may be applied to other situations where multiple cognitive deficits exist in a single individual.

Diller and Gordon (1981) described an integrative model of behavioral rehabilitation that included a multidisciplinary team approach. Emphasis was placed on blending the independent domains of neuropsychology and behavior therapy (as well as other disciplines) when designing interventions. Lewinsohn, Danaher, and Kikel (1977) also described a model in which neuropsychological test results are used as a template for developing behavioral treatments. These models are useful as starting points, but the particulars of application need to be more fully explicated.

Another methodological concern has to do with implementation of behavioral principles and procedures within neuropsychological assessment. As already noted, clinical neuropsychologists are increasingly interested in the ecological validity of neuropsychological assessment instruments (Franzen & Wilhelm, in press). Part of that interest has translated into the development of new assessment instruments that have greater similarity to the behaviors that are to be predicted on the basis of the assessment results.

There are two basic concepts for determining the ecological validity of clinical neuropsychological assessment instruments. The first is *verisimilitude*, or whether the assessment task possesses a topographical resemblance to the behavior to be predicted. The second is *veridicality*, or whether the assessment task can actually empirically predict the behavior of interest. For example, a reaction time task being used to predict whether an individual has the necessary component skills to drive an automobile may be judged as possessing verisimilitude. Alternately, an assessment instrument may have an empirical relationship to the behavior in question, despite the lack of any obvious resemblance. One example is the use of the Trail Making Test Part B to predict ability to operate an automobile. Because many neuropsychologists are dissatisfied with the limited ability of standardized tests to predict free behavior, new instruments that more closely resemble behavioral assessment procedures are being developed.

The Loewenstein Direct Assessment of Functional Status (DAFS; Loewenstein, Amigo, Duara, Guterman, Hurwitz et al., 1989) is an example of a behavioral assessment instrument that was developed specifically for use in a neuropsychological setting. The DAFS is used to evaluate the capacity of an older individual to perform behaviors related to domains of functional behaviors, such as those involved in shopping, dressing, personal finances, and grooming. The individual is presented with standard test stimuli and asked to complete certain tasks. Specified criteria are used for scoring, in order to improve reliability and accuracy. Although this is a novel approach for clinical neuropsychol-

ogists to use, naturalistic assessment methods have been used extensively in the behavioral assessment literature. The naturalistic observation methods have been used by occupational therapists in the rehabilitation setting but without the perspective of a behavior-analytic approach.

PRACTICAL APPLICATIONS

So far, we have confined our review to studies that are strictly relevant to the interface between neuropsychological assessment and behavior therapy. However, in recent years there has been a significant growth in research devoted to the behavioral treatment of brain-injured people that does not include a formal neuropsychological assessment. Some of these studies discuss characteristics of neurologically compromised individuals that affect symptom expression and behavioral treatment. These studies are of interest to the neuropsychologist who is providing services to this population, and will be included in this review as well.

We will not provide a comprehensive review of all studies addressing these target areas. Instead, recent trends and important concepts will be highlighted. The topic of behavioral assessment and intervention with brain-injured people has been addressed in a number of other publications (Corrigan & Jakus, 1994; Franzen, 1991; Horton & Miller, 1985; Webster & Scott, 1988; Wood & Eames, 1981). There have also been a number of articles published that discuss some of the relevant issues and general procedures involved in performing behavioral assessment and intervention with people who have acquired brain injury (Burke, & Wesolowski, 1988; Eames, 1988; Page, Luce, & Willis, 1992; Wood, 1988; McGlynn, 1990).

Treatment of Cognitive Deficits

Earlier we described the development of a system in which neuropsychological assessment data are used to provide a baseline of cognitive functioning in a brain-impaired individual. Specific behavioral targets are then chosen for intervention in a modified multiple baseline across behaviors design. Short tests of specific neuropsychological function are used as probe assessments at phase changes, and the entire neuropsychological comprehensive evaluation is repeated at termination of treatment. The overall design, discussed in Franzen and Iverson (1990) will not be described in detail here. The utility of this modification of the multiple baseline design was demonstrated in the treatment of a closed head injured individual with deficits in memory and in organization planning (Franzen & Harris, 1993).

Treatment of Adaptive Behaviors

Silver, Boake, and Cavazos (1994) used a multiple baseline design to increase morning self-care behaviors in a 12-year-old child with neuropsychological impairment secondary to anoxic brain injury. During the neuropsychological evaluation, it was noticed that her performance on verbal arithmetic questions improved from 48% correct to 84% correct when she was given a penny for each correct answer. Therefore, pennies were incorporated into the behavioral contingencies. Six-month follow-up indicated maintenance of gains. Safir, Stravynski, and Jaffe (1981) presented a study in which behavior therapy was compared with traditional developmental therapy in the treatment of brain-damaged and severely mentally retarded children. Behavioral assessment techniques were used to monitor treatment, and more traditional child neuropsychological instruments were used as dependent measures. Using this combination of assessment strategies, the investigators were able to demonstrate the superiority of the behavioral interventions.

In 1988, Giles and Clarke-Wilson discussed the utility of behavioral-techniques to increase the functional capacity of severely brain injured individuals, but lamented the lack of specific information predicting the most effective behavioral schedules or paradigms for differing types of lesion location or cognitive impairment. Later, Giles and Shore (1989) reported that neuropsychological evidence for severe semantic/declarative memory deficits may be evidence that overlearning procedures for episodic memory processes are necessary.

In some instances, neuropsychological data have been used to match groups in a multiple baseline across groups designs. For example, Lalli, Pinter-Lalli, Mace, and Murphy (1991) used the Wechsler Intelligence Scale-Revised and score on the socialization-scale of the Vineland Adaptive Behavior Scale to ensure that changes in group performance on behavioral observation measures were not due to differences in level of social skill or intelligence. The Socialization scale of the Vineland was then readministered four months after termination of the treatment to evaluate maintenance of skills. Fox, Martella, and Marchand-Martella (1989) also used cognitive tests to demonstrate the equivalence of their two experimental groups of brain-injured individuals.

Treatment of Disruptive Behaviors

Presentation of disruptive behavior is common in moderate to severe closed head injury patients, as can be seen in the large number of articles that address the issue from a variety of perspectives (e.g., Andrewes, 1989; Franzen & Lovell, 1987; Lira, Carne, & Masri, 1983). Treatment of this problem involves a decrease in undesired behaviors, the description of which is much simpler than the execution. Disruptive behavior in brain-injured patients can take the form of everything from self-injurious behavior to physical aggression to loud vocalizations. Eliciting stimuli can vary from unpleasant internal states to discriminative stimuli. Range of behavioral responses in the repertoire of the change agent is limited, as frequently, negative consequences or intended punishers result in increases in aggressive responses and other adjunctive behaviors.

Disruptive behavior may not always be an aggressive action, but may instead involve inappropriate behaviors that would disrupt the environment. For example, Rolider, Williams, Cummings, and Van Houten (1991) report on the case of a brain-impaired individual who engaged in fecal smearing. Because time-out procedures and running water for cleaning the smears were apparently reinforcing to the individual, a period of brief movement restriction (20 seconds) and differential reinforcement of other behavior was implemented to reduce undesired behavior. For a second individual in the study, brief movement restriction was used to decrease the rate of aggressive outbursts. This study illustrates innovative approaches to treatment, where the most effective reinforcers and punishers may not conform to typical expectations. Although it is certainly true that all individuals are unique, the idiosyncratic nature of environmental controllers is frequently highlighted in people with brain impairment. There is often a tendency to think that brain-damaged individuals are more similar to each other than are those without brain damage; however, the opposite may be true.

On the other hand, one should not rule out more traditional behavioral treatment interventions just because an individual has brain impairment. For example, Wesolowski and Zencius (1992) reported using a point system with response cost and contingent home visits in an intervention to decrease the frequency of aggressive episodes in a brain-injured individual. The subject had significant frontal lobe damage, which, in many cases, would seem to argue against the use of a symbolic, abstract system-such as point accrual. To the contrary, the intervention worked quite well.

Similarly, Eames and Wood (1985) reported that token economy was effective in reducing disruptive behaviors in a group of 28 brain-injured individuals being treated in a residential behavioral unit. The program had a positive effect on behavior, and gains were maintained upon follow-up assessments conducted between six months and three years postdischarge from the residential unit. Unfortunately, the unit included social reinforcement as well as the token economy, so it is difficult to determine the relative contribution of each in the observed gains. However, maintenance of gains, as indicated by behavioral ratings as well as ratings of activities of daily living, is a promising finding. Pruneti, Cantini, and Baracchini-Muratorio (1989) also reported positive effects in the use of the token economy in the treatment of brain-damaged children. These authors reported a maintenance of gains at one-year follow-up.

As well as demonstrating the need to design behavioral programs individually, these studies remind us that one of the hallmarks of behavioral intervention is the use of the least restrictive method. Behavioral theory is at least partly based on William James's concepts of pragmatism, and we cannot rule out simple interventions until they have failed. More research needs to be completed on the relationship between types and degrees of cognitive impairment and the effectiveness of different types of behavioral schedules and methods before we can comfortably offer hypotheses regarding the appropriateness of different approaches in individual cases.

As an example of an empirical attempt to determine an effective method in an individual case, Lewis, Nelson, Nelson, and Reusink (1988) compared three feedback contingency methods in terms of their effect on the target behavior of inappropriate verbalization in an alternating treatments design. The subject had experienced a cardiac arrest with subsequent anoxia and brain damage. The neuropsychological test results indicated that the subject had significant impairment, especially in visual-spatial skills (which is fairly common in cardiac-induced anoxia). They found that correction was most effective in decreasing inappropriate verbalizations. The extent that these findings can be generalized to other people with similar etiologies and levels of skill is an empirical question. However, the method used to determine the most effective treatment in this case can easily be modified for use with other subjects and with other problems.

It is important to treat each person as a unique individual, but this does not mean previously established methods have no utility. Even strategies that have been developed for use in children might be successfully adapted for use with brain-injured adults. Papworth (1989) describes the application of Azrin and Thienes's (1978) method for treating enuresis in children to an enuretic adult with severe brain damage. Obviously, the point here is not to infantilize the brain-impaired adult, but instead to search behavioral literature in other populations for ideas on how to best treat problem behaviors.

Use of behavioral methods to reduce agitation appears to be a common phenomenon in rehabilitation settings and may be as common as the use of physical restraints or medication (Herbel, Schermerhorn, & Howard, 1990). However, there may be great variability in the type of behavioral interventions used as well as in the training and sophistication of the professionals responsible for designing such interventions. For example, use of time-out or redirection and differential reinforcement of other behavior (DRO) may be more helpful with individuals with greater levels of cognitive impairment, whereas strategies requiring greater self-direction and implementation may be more helpful with individuals with a greater level of cognitive skill. Crane and Joyce (1991) describe a "cool-down" procedure in which the patient practices lowering physiological arousal while role-playing disturbing events and situations. Clearly, this procedure would have significant limitations in attempting to reduce aggression in the individuals in the Rolider and colleagues' (1991) report.

Aggression is not the only form of disruptive behavior. Screaming can also be quite disruptive. Unfortunately, screaming elicits attention from staff and family that can be reinforcing. Andrewes (1989) describes the use of time-out on the spot (TOOTS) in response to screaming as well as the use of reinforcement via staff attention when the patient was quiet. This type of treatment can be difficult to implement since staff are accustomed to paying attention to the noisy patients and tend to adopt a more laissez-faire attitude toward quiet and essentially compliant patients. Differential reinforcement of other behavior (DRO) can help to reduce the frequency of disruptive behaviors by increasing the frequency of nondisruptive behaviors. An alternative method is to use differential reinforcement of low-rate behaviors (DRL) in which reinforcement is applied when the rate of undesired behavior falls below a certain criterion for a set period of time. Disruptive behaviors, such as inappropriate verbal statements, can be treated in this manner, by reinforcing a low frequency of behavior and reducing the standard in a changing criterion design (Turner, Green, & Braunling-McMorrow, 1990).

Treatment of Seizure Disorders

At first glance, seizure disorders appear to be the quintessential medical disorder for which pharmacology and, in extreme cases, surgery is the treatment modality of choice However, there is a growing body of literature documenting application of behavioral and other neurobehavioral treatment methods in reducing the effects of these

disorders. Franzen and Petrick (in press) have described behavioral interventions that have been used to remediate the cognitive deficits in individuals with seizure disorders. These attempts have been limited in number and have mainly involved the use of neuropsychological assessment to identify skill targets for which behavioral methods are then applied.

Yet another interaction between neuropsychology and behavioral assessment can occur in the context of these disorders. The concept of pseudoseizures, more appropriately called psychogenic seizures, involves manifestation of seizure behavior in the absence of abnormal electrical discharges from the brain. In other words, exhibition of seizure-related behaviors, including altered subjective states and abnormal motor patterns, is under the control of the environment. The individual is not purposefully producing these behaviors, nor is this an attempt to manipulate the social environment or gain access to medication. Instead, the individual has learned to emit seizure-like behavior under certain situations, following certain environmental events, or in eliciting certain environmental responses (Williams, Walczak, Berten, Nordli, & Bergtraum, 1993). Frequently, the psychogenic seizure is seen in an individual who also has a neurogenic seizure disorder or who has a relative or friend with a neurogenic seizure disorder (suggesting the influence of modeling). Behavioral assessment in the form of a functional analysis can be very helpful in the treatment of this disorder. In expanding the concept of seizure disorder to include a learned component, contingency management can be seen as potentially helpful in treating individuals with seizure disorders (Mostofsky, 1993).

Assessment and Treatment of Attention Deficit/Hyperactivity Disorder

We tend to compartmentalize approaches to psychological disorders, viewing them as either the result of physiological deficits or environmental stressors. However, life and science are rarely that neat. An example of the interactions possible among paradigms and etiologic agents is the phenomenon known as attention deficit/ hyperactivity disorder (ADHD). Even though many theories of ADHD posit a physiological, neurological basis for the emergence of ADHD (Barkley, 1990), and quite often specify neuropsychological deficits as defining characteristics, diagnosis of ADHD relies on behavioral observation and data (American Psychiatric Association, 1994). In this type of situation, an integrative model could be helpful in more fully delineating the disorder. For example, diagnostic criteria for ADHD include attention deficit and behavioral dyscontrol. Additionally, hyperactivity needs to be documented. The diagnostic criteria as stated are helpful, but may be insufficiently specific or precise.

Attention deficits could be more explicitly described with the use of clinical neuropsychological assessment data using traditional measures such as digit repetition procedures or computerized continuous performance tests. Behavioral disruptions and hyperactivity could be more explicitly described with use of behavioral assessment data that could document the level of hyperactivity with constructs such as "time out of classroom seat" or "time spent on an unsupervised task." Although presence of either an attention deficit or a behavioral problem could be indicative of the ADHD condition, neither by itself is sufficient. Similar to the situation regarding diagnosis, treatment of ADHD is more successful when there is a combination of pharmacological, behavioral, and psychosocial interventions (Teeter & Semrud-Clikeman, 1995).

SUMMARY

The information reviewed so far indicates that the merger of clinical neuropsychological and behavioral assessment can be advantageous for the individual client as well as for the clinical science of psychology. In fact, it would seem that not only does the individual client benefit from interaction of these two subfields, but the two subfields themselves would derive a beneficial outcome. Why, then, has progress been slow in this field? Part of the answer may lie in the fact that few graduate training programs are broad enough to allow the cross-fertilization of the these branches of clinical psychology in a way that will produce profession-

als who are trained in both paradigms. Interaction between these two subfields continues to be within the practical arena, where individual clinicians faced with the assessment and treatment of individuals with central nervous system dysfunction will continue to use whichever paradigm seems to be appropriate for the problem at hand. The situation is similar to that of the treatment of psychological disorders, in general, where practitioners are generally eclectic, and even an adherent of psychoanalytic theory may use systematic desensitization when appropriate.

The question is not whether application of the method is appropriate, but rather whether application of the method is competent and will achieve the desired goal. Jacobs (1988) accurately points out that although many behavioral programs can be implemented by individuals with limited formal training in behavior analysis, the design and conceptualization of such systems require the input of a professional with specific training in the area. Furthermore, it is likely that the success of future developments depends on the articulation of a coherent model that integrates neuropsychology and behavior therapy. The success of behavioral neuropsychology is still largely a promise.

REFERENCES

American Psychiatric Association. (1994). *Diagnostic and statistical manual of mental disorders*. Washington, DC: Author.

Andrewes, D. (1989). Management of disruptive behaviour in rain-damaged patient using selective reinforcement. *Journal of Behavior Therapy and Experimental Psychiatry, 20*, 261–264.

Azrin, N. H., & Thienes, P. M., (1978). Rapid elimination of enuresis by intensive learning without a conditioning apparatus. *Behavior Therapy, 9*, 342–354.

Barkley, R. A. (1990). *Attention deficit hyperactivity disorder: A handbook for diagnosis and treatment*. New York: Guiford.

Bleiberg, J., Freedman, P. E., Scheuneman, A. L., Merbitz, C., & Swartz, J. (1985). Anticipatory behavior deficits following brain injury. *International Journal of Clinical Neuropsychology, 7*, 153–156.

Burke, W. H., & Wesolowski, M. D. (1988). Applied behavior analysis in head injury rehabilitation. *Rehabilitation Nursing, 13*, 186–188.

Corrigan, P. W., & Jakus, M. R. (1994). Behavioral treatment. In J. M. Silver, S. C. Yudofsky, & R. E. Hales (Eds.), *Neuropsychiatry of traumatic brain injury* (pp. 733– 769). Washington, DC: American Psychiatric Press.

Crane, A. A. & Joyce, B. G. (1991). Brief report: Cool down: A procedure for decreasing aggression in adults with traumatic head injury. *Behavioral Residential Treatment, 6*, 65–75.

Diller, L., & Gordon, W. A. (1981). Rehabilitation and clinical neuropsychology. In S. B. Filskov & T. J. Boll (Eds.), *Handbook of clinical neuropsychology* (pp. 702–733). New York: Wiley.

Eames, P. (1988). Behavior disorders after severe head injury: Their nature and causes and strategies for management. *Journal of Head Trauma Rehabilitation, 3*, 1–6.

Eames, P., & Wood, R. (1985). Rehabilitation after severe brain injury: A follow-up study of a behaviour modification approach. *Journal of Neurology, Neurosurgery, and Psychiatry, 48*, 613–619.

Fox, R. M., Martella, R. C., & Marchand-Martella, N. E. (1989). The acquisition, maintenance, and generalization of problem-solving skills by closed head-injured adults. *Behavior Therapy, 20*, 61–76.

Franzen, M. D. (1991). Behavioral assessment and treatment of brain-impaired individuals. In M. Hersen, R. M. Eisler, & P. M. Miller (Eds.), *Process in behavior modification*: (Vol. 27) (pp. 56–85). Beverly Hills, CA: Sage.

Franzen, M. D., & Harris, C. V. (1993). Neuropsychological rehabilitation: Application of a modified multiple baseline design. *Brain Injury, 7*, 525–534.

Franzen, M. D., & Iverson, G. L. (1990). Applications of single subject design to cognitive rehabilitation. In A. M. Horton (Ed.), *Behavioral clinical neuropsychology across the life-span* (pp. 155–174) New York: Springer.

Franzen, M. D., & Lovell, M. R. (1987). Behavioral treatments of aggressive sequelae of brain injury. *Psychiatric Annals, 17*, 389–396.

Franzen, M. D., & Petrick, J. (in press). Cognitive rehabilitation in seizure disorders. In P. Corrigan & S. Yudofsky (Eds.), *Cognitive rehabilitation*. Washington, DC: American Psychiatric Press.

Franzen, M. D., & Wilhelm, K. L. (in press). Conceptual foundations of ecological validity in neuropsychological assessment. In R. Sbordonne and C. J. Long (Eds.), *The ecological validity of neuropsychological testing*. Winter Park, FL: GR Press.

Giles, G. M., & Clark-Wilson, J. (1988). The use of behavioral techniques in functional skills training after severe brain injury. *The American Journal of Occupational Therapy, 42*, 658–665.

Giles, G. M., & Shore, M. (1989). A rapid method for teaching severely brain injured adults how to wash and dress. *Archives of Physical Medicine and Rehabilitation, 70*, 156–158.

Grattan, L. M., & Eslinger, P. J. (1989). Higher cognition and social behavior: Changes in cognitive flexibility and empathy after cerebral lesions. *Neuropsychology, 3*, 175–185.

Herbel, K., Schermerhorn, L., & Howard, J. (1990). Management of agitated head-injured patients: A survey of current techniques. *Rehabilitation Nursing, 15*, 66–69.

Hogan, R. T. (1988). Behavior management for community reintegration. *Journal of Head Trauma Rehabilitation, 3*, 62–71.

Horton, A. M. (1979). Behavioral neuropsychology: Rationale and research. *Clinical Neuropsychology, 1*, 20–23.

Horton, A. M., & Miller, W. G. (1985). Neuropsychology and behavior therapy. In M. Hersen, R. M. Eisler, & P. M. Miller (Eds.) , *Progress in behavior modification*: (Vol. 19) (pp. 1–85). Orlando, FL: Academic Press.

Horton, A. M., & Wedding, D. (1984). *Clinical and behavioral neuropsychology*. New York: Praeger.

Jackson, H. F., & Bentall, R. P. (1991). Operant condition in amnesic subjects: Response patterning and sensitivity to schedule changes. *Neuropsychology, 5*, 89–105.

Jacobs, H. E. (1987). The Los Angeles head injury survey. *Journal of Head Trauma Rehabilitation, 2*, 37–50.

Jacobs, H. E. (1988). Yes, behaviour analysis can help, but do you know how to harness it? *Brain Injury, 2*, 339–346.

Kosmidis, M. H., & Fantie, B. D. (1995). Impaired avoidance learning after closed-head injury: Dissociation between two tasks due to classical conditioning. *Journal of Clinical and Experimental Neuropsychology. 17*, 622–633.

Lalli, J. S., Pinter-Lalli, E., Mace, F. C., & Murphy, D. M. (1991). Training interactional behaviors of adults with developmental disabilities: A systematic replication and extension. *Journal of Applied Behavior Analysis, 24*, 167–174.

Lawson-Kerr, K., Smith, S. S., & Beck, D. (1990). The interface between neuropsychology and behavior therapy. In A. M. Horton (Ed.), *Neuropsychology across the lifespan: Assessment and treatment* (pp. 103–131). New York: Springer.

Lewinsohn, P. M., Danaher, B, G., & Kikel, S. (1977). Visual imagery as a mnemonic aid for brain injured persons. *Journal of Consulting and Clinical Psychology, 45*, 717–723.

Lewis, F. D., Nelson, J., Nelson, C, & Reusink,, P. (1988). Effects of three feedback contingencies on the socially inappropriate talk of a brain-injured adult. *Behavior Therapy, 19*, 203–211.

Lira, F. T., Carne, W., & Masri, A. M. (1983). Treatment of anger and impulsivity in a brain damaged patient: A case study applying stress inoculation. *Clinical Neuropsychology, 5*, 159–160.

Loewenstein, D. A., Amigo, E., Duara, R., Guterman, A., Hurwitz, E., Berkowitz, N., Wilkie, F., Weinberg, G., Blakc, B., Gittelman, B., & Eisdorfer, C. (1989). A new scale for the assessment of functional status in Alzheimer's disease and related disorders. *Journal of Gerontology; Psychological Sciences, 44*, 114–121.

Lundervold, D. A., & Jackson, T. (1992). Use of applied behavior analysis in treating nursing home residents. *Hospital and Community Psychiatry, 43*, 171–173.

Marsh, N. V., Knight, R. G. (1991). Relationship between cognitive deficits and social skill after head injury. *Neuropsychology, 5*, 107–117.

McGlynn, S. M. (1990). Behavioral approaches to neuropsychological rehabilitation. *Psychological Bulletin, 108*, 420–441.

Mostofsky, D. I. (1993). Behavior modification and therapy in the management of epileptic disorders. In D.I. Mostofsky & Y. Loyning (Eds.), *The neurobehavioral treatment of epilepsy* (pp. 67–81). Hillsdale, NJ: Lawrence Erlbaum.

Page, T. J., Luce, S. C., & Willis, K. (1992). Rehabilitation of adults with brain injury. *Behavioral Residential Treatment, 7*, 169–179.

Papworth, M. A. (1989). The behavioural treatment of nocturnal enuresis in a severely brain-damaged client. *Journal of Behaviour Therapy and Experimental Psychiatry, 20*, 265–268.

Peters, M. D., Gluck, M., & McCormick, M. (1992). Behaviour rehabilitation of the challenging client in less restrictive settings. *Brain Injury, 6*, 299–314.

Pruneti, C. A., Cantini, R., Baracchini-Muratorio, G. (1989). Behavioral treatment of children after severe head injury: A pilot study. *Italian Journal of Neurological Science, 10*, 491–498.

Rolider, A., Williams, L., Cummings, A., & Van Houten, R. (1991). The use of a brief movement restriction procedure to eliminate severe inappropriate behavior. *Journal of Behavior Therapy and Experimental Psychiatry, 22*, 23–30.

Safir, M. P., Stravynski, A., & Jaffe, M. (1981). Comparison of operant and traditional treatment of severely retarded preschoolers in an out-patient setting. *Child Behavior Therapy, 3*, 121–139.

Silver, B. V., Boake, C., & Cavazos, D. I., (1994). Improving functional skills using behavioral procedures in a child with anoxic brain injury. *Archives of Physical Medicine and Rehabilitation, 75*, 742–745.

Teeter, P. A., & Semrud-Clikeman, M. (1995). Intergrating neurobiological, psychosocial, and behavioral paradigms: A transactional model for the study of ADHD. *Archives of Clinical Neuropsychology, 10*, 433–461.

Turner, J. M., Green, G., & Braunling-McMorrow, D. (1990). Differential reinforcement of low rates of responding (DRL) to reduce dysfunctional social behaviors of a head injured man. *Behavioral Residential Treatment, 5*, 15–27.

Webster, J. S., & Scott, R. R. (1988). Behavioral assessment and treatment of the brain-injured patient. In M. Hersen, R. M. Eisler, & P. M. Miller (Eds.), *Progress in behavior modification* (Vol. 22) (pp. 48–87). Orlando, FL: Academic Press.

Wesolowski, M. D., & Zencius, A. H. (1992). Treatment of aggression in a brain injured adolescent. *Behavioral Residential Treatment, 7*, 205–210.

Williams, D. T., Walczak, T., Berten, W., Nordli, D., Bergtraum, M. (1993). Psychogenic seizures. In D. I. Mostofsky & Y. Loyning (Eds.), *The neurobehavioral treatment of epilepsy* (pp. 83–106). Hillsdale, NJ: Lawrence Erlbaum.

Wood, R. (1988). Management of behavior disorders in a day treatment setting. *Journal of Head Trauma Rehabilitation, 3*, 53–61.

Wood, R., & Eames, P. (1981). Applications of behavior modification in the rehabilitation of traumatically brain-injured patients. In G. Davey (Ed.), *Applications of conditioning theory* (pp. 81–101). New York: Methuen.

CHAPTER 20

BIOLOGICAL ASSESSMENT

John A. Sweeney
Elizabeth L. Dick
Nalini M. Srinivasagam
University of Pittsburgh School of Medicine

Over the past several decades, significant advances have been achieved in the understanding of neurobiological aspects of severe mental disorders (Bloom & Kupfer, 1995). To date, this work has had minimal direct influence on the clinical assessment of patients presenting with mental disorders. This can be attributed to the novelty of the methods, the lack of validation data needed to justify use of new biomedical laboratory tests in general clinical practice, and the fact that the relationships between patterns of biological abnormalities and currently defined clinical syndromes remain uncertain. As a result, use of new laboratory procedures remains largely at the research/investigational level. However, with the major breakthroughs being achieved in basic and clinical neuroscience laboratories, a significant increase in the availability of biological laboratory tests for clinical purposes can be anticipated. These tests have the potential to be used for diagnostic purposes, for guiding treatment planning, for early prediction of course of illness, and ultimately for the early detection of genetic risk for mental illnesses.

The aim of this chapter is to review ongoing progress in biomedical research laboratories that may lead to the development of clinical laboratory tests relevant for the assessment of severe mental disorders. We provide brief introductions to relevant neurochemical, neurophysiologic, and neuroanatomic systems in which abnormalities are believed to play a role in different mental disorders, and to laboratory technologies used in the assessment of these brain systems.

This chapter is included in this text with both research and clinical considerations in mind. From a research perspective, studies examining relationships between psychological and biological aspects of severe mental illnesses almost certainly will be a major thrust of clinical investigations in the near future. In order for the meaning and implications of newly identified biological abnormalities to be clarified, they will need to be linked to selected domains of psychopathology. Studies designed to clarify such clinico-pathological relationships will require an informed integration of psychological and biological research strategies. For such an integration to occur, biologically informed behavioral investigators will need to play active roles in interdisciplinary research efforts.

An integrated understanding of biological and psychological domains of investigation will be important in treatment as well as in psychopathology research. Combined psychosocial and psychopharmacologic treatments have been shown to have advantages over unimodal therapies for many patients. The identification of patient characteristics that can be used to guide selection of optimal treatments will require studies assessing the potential significance of psychological, biological, and psychosocial patient characteristics.

The direct implications of neurobiological research for clinical work are more distant and therefore more difficult to predict. However, even in the near future, a working understanding of clinical psychobiologic research is essential in order to understand the rationale for and appropriate clinical conditions for use of psychopharmacologic treatments. This knowledge is important in order that clinicians can make informed decisions as to when pharmacologic treatments are needed as an adjunct or alternative to behavioral interventions. Similarly, findings from imaging studies of patients with dementing and other neurological illnesses can be useful for planning behavioral interventions, as they may point to particular areas of function likely to be compromised and suggest whether disabilities are likely to be static or progressive.

It is appropriate to present certain caveats at this point. First, space prohibits any in-depth presentation of the many neurochemical systems and neuroanatomic regions believed to be dysfunctional in different mental disorders, and any complete presentation of biomedical tests that may come to be useful in clinical diagnosis. Selectivity of coverage was required. Second, it is also not feasible to discuss the vast number of medical disorders that can lead to clinical symptoms that closely mimic mental disorders. Nearly all neurologic and endocrine disorders can cause psychiatric symptomatology, and reviews of the neuropsychiatric aspects of such illnesses are available elsewhere (Mesulam, 1985; Luria, 1962). Finally, we have oriented our presentation within a "medical model" framework. This was not done to endorse a view

that a biological viewpoint, in isolation, is sufficient to guide the evaluation of patients with mental disorders or to understand the etiology of such disorders. Rather, our intent was to provide a focused introduction to a range of promising findings from psychobiological research that are potentially relevant to patient care. Such developments are likely to come first in relation to dementing illnesses of late life and chronic illnesses such as schizophrenia and recurrent depression, where understanding of associated biological disturbances is most advanced. Therefore, these disorders receive the greatest attention in our review.

NEUROTRANSMITTERS AND NEUROPHARMACOLOGY

Effective functioning of the brain requires anatomic connectivity and functional interactions among neurons. Neurons "communicate" by releasing chemical neurotransmitters that initiate physiologic changes in other proximate neurons. Disturbances in processes by which neurons communicate across synaptic junctions are probably the most rigorously studied biological aspect of serious mental disorders. Nearly all currently available psychophamacological treatments exert their therapeutic influence by stimulating or inhibiting activity at the synaptic cleft in specific neurotransmitter system. For instance, antipsychotic medications block activity in synapses where dopamine is a transmitter, and most antidepressant medications alter serotonergic neurotransmission. By identifying disturbances in the specific neural systems altered by the medications, biochemical tests could feasibly identify patients who would be most likely to benefit from particular psychopharmacologic treatments. This could represent a considerable advance from the current practice of prescribing medications based on the presence of broadly defined clinical syndromes as in *DSM-IV* (American Psychiatric Association, 1994).

Figure 20.1 presents properties of neuronal function believed to be relevant in the biochemical pathophysiology of several severe mental disorders. Comprehensive discussions of neuronal physiology are available elsewhere (Kandel, Schwartz, & Jessell, 1991). In the simple model presented in

Figure 20.1   Schematic presentation of common aspects of neueronal
activity pertinent to many neurotransmitter systems

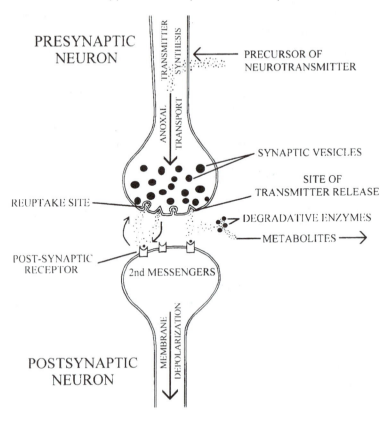

Figure 20.1, a neuron obtains the precursor of the neurotransmitter it will synthesize by absorbing or transporting it across its membrane from extracellular space. The precursor is enzymatically converted to an active neurotransmitter inside the neuron, and then taken into vesicles within which it is transported along the nerve axon to the synapses where it eventually will be released. Transmitters are released by "presynaptic" neurons and cross the small space between neurons (the synaptic cleft) to bind to receptors on nearby neurons. The binding of neurotransmitter to these receptors induces physiologic changes in "postsynaptic" neurons, which serve as the mechanism allowing information to be transmitted in multineuronal chains of communication.

Receptors for neurotransmitters are molecularly configured to be sensitive to specific neurotransmitters. There are multiple biochemically distinct forms of receptors for particular neurotransmitters and they have different distributions across brain regions. For example, 14 different receptors for the neurotransmitter serotonin have been identified (Roth, 1994). After binding of the neurotransmitter to a postsynaptic receptor has occurred for some brief period of time, the transmitter dissociates from the receptor. It can then be taken back into the presynaptic neuron at re-uptake sites. Alternatively, the transmitter can be enzymatically degraded in the synaptic cleft, after which metabolites of this enzymatic degradative process pass into the cerebrospinal fluid and bloodstream.

Two factors of synaptic connectivity have particular clinical importance. First, neurotransmitters need to be released from presynaptic neurons at rates that do not excessively or inadequately stimulate their postsynaptic neurons. Second, there must be an appropriate density of receptors in the synaptic cleft on postsynaptic neurons. If either of these aspects of synaptic connectivity is disturbed, the net communication between neurons becomes disrupted. In addition, synaptic connections are mediated by many different neurotransmitter systems, and brain regions differ in the density of neurons relying on a particular neurotransmitter system. Disturbances in different transmitter systems can therefore cause neurophysiological dysfunction in discrete regions of the brain, and thereby cause different disturbances in thinking, mood and behavior.

Clinical Assessment of Synaptic Activity

Clinical evaluation of biochemical processes at the neuronal level is limited by technical factors (i.e., the ability of available equipment to perform measurements of interest) as well as the necessity to conduct such studies in a noninvasive fashion to pose minimal health risks for patients. As a result of these considerations, measures of brain neurotransmitter activity obtained in clinical studies are typically indirect. The rationale for these studies depends on the fact that after being released into synapses, active metabolic processes quickly remove neurotransmitters from the cleft. Without such mechanisms, postsynaptic neurons would continue to be stimulated for long periods of time after a transmitter was released into the synaptic cleft. One of these clearance processes, mentioned earlier, is the active enzymatic degradative metabolism of neurotransmitter within the synaptic cleft and surrounding interneuronal space. Metabolites produced by this enzymatic degradation diffuse from the synaptic cleft into the cerebrospinal fluid (CSF) and bloodstream. Measuring these metabolites in CSF or blood therefore provides an accessible approach for clinically evaluating aggregate activity in brain neurotransmitter systems.

Cerebral Spinal Fluid Studies

Schizophrenia

Most efforts to study schizophrenia from a neurochemical perspective have focused on the dopam-ine neurotransmitter system, which is believed to play a key role in the pathophysiology of schizophrenia (Wiesel, 1994). The fact that all known clinically effective antipsychotic medications block dopamine receptors to reduce activity in the dopamine system provides the strongest support for this model. In addition, studies have demonstrated that dopamine agonists (drugs that increase dopaminergic activity) can cause an abrupt onset of psychotic symptoms in schizophrenic patients (Lieberman et al., 1984). This disturbance does not account for all manifestations of schizophrenia, as antipsychotic drugs that effectively block postsynaptic dopamine receptors fail to alleviate schizophrenic symptoms in a sizable minority of patients. Further, decreased rather than increased levels of homovanillic acid (HVA), a dopamine metabolite, have been reported in the cerebral spinal fluid of some chronically ill schizophrenic patients. Of interest, such patients often exhibit prominent negative symptoms, such as low levels of social interest and emotional reactivity (Bowers, 1974; Lindstrom, 1985). Davis, Kahn, Ko, and Davidson (1991) have proposed a more complex model of dopaminergic dysfunction in schizophrenia, suggesting that low levels of dopamine in prefrontal cortex are responsible for the negative symptoms of schizophrenia, while positive symptoms of acute psychosis (e.g., hallucinations and delusions) may be due to excessive dopamine activity in the limbic; system.

Depression

Studies of cerebrospinal fluid in depressed patients have focused primarily on reductions in levels of serotonin and norepinephrine metabolites. A metabolite of serotonin, 5-hydroxyindoleacetic acid (5-HIAA), has been the most widely studied neurotransmitter system in relation to depression (Risch & Nemeroff, 1992; Mann et al., 1992). Significantly lower levels of this metabolite have been found in the cerebral spinal fluid of patients with major depression. Interestingly, depressed patients who previously attempted suicide often have particularly low levels of 5-HIAA (Banki, Arato, & Kilts, 1986). In a prospective follow-up study, Traskman, Asberg, Bertilsso, and Sjostrand (1981) reported that 20% of depressed patients with markedly low levels of 5-HIAA committed suicide within one-year from assessment. These studies suggest that indices of reduced serotonergic function may prove useful as biological markers for depressed patients who are at particularly high risk to make suicide attempts.

Obsessive-Compulsive Disorder

Numerous studies have linked an abnormality in serotonergic activity with obsessive-compulsive disorder (OCD) (Murphy et al., 1989). As with other psychiatric disorders, much of the biochemical understanding of this illness is based on pharmacological data. Investigations have demonstrated that the administration of antidepressant medications known to block re-uptake of serotonin into presynaptic neurons can alleviate symptoms of this disorder (Altemus et al., 1994). While the immediate effect of these selective serotonergic re-uptake inhibitors is to increase net serotonergic transmission by blocking the re-uptake of serotonin into presynaptic neurons, in the longer term they can have the effect of reducing postsynaptic receptor density. Thus, in OCD, serotonin re-uptake inhibitors, by virtue of manipulating feedback regulation of pre- and postsynaptic receptors, may induce changes in postsynaptic receptors that have the longer-term effect of reducing net serotonergic transmission (Altemus et al., 1994; Barr, Goodman, Price, McDougle, & Charney, 1992). Consistent with a hyper-serotonergic model of OCD, administering a serotonin receptor agonist (which increases net serotonergic neurotransmission) can increase the severity of obsessive-compulsive behavior (Zohar, Mueller, Insel, Zohar-Kadouch, & Murphy, 1987). Results of pharmacologic challenge studies, wherein a drug is given and some physiologic index of drug effect is obtained (typically an endocrine response), have also suggested a role for serotonergic dysfunction in this disorder (Barr et al., 1992). Results of research in this area are not fully consistent, but generally indicate that increased serotonergic function is a component of the pathophysiology of OCD.

Eating Disorders

Investigations into the biological mechanisms of eating disorders have also focused on the role of the serotonergic system. This neurotransmitter system appears to exert control over appetite; specifically, increased serotonin activity results in feelings of satiety whereas lower levels reduce satiety (Kaye & Weltzin, 1991; Jimerson, Lesem, Hegg, & Brewerton, 1990). Further, studies have demonstrated the effectiveness of serotonin-enhancing antidepressants in the treatment of eating disorders (Pope & Hudson, 1986). Kaye, Ebert, Raleigh, and Lake (1984) reported a 20% reduction in the concentration of CSF 5-HIAA in anorectic patients, with metabolite levels returning to normal levels after behavioral treatment led to normal weight restoration. In contrast, low CSF 5-HIAA levels have been associated with frequent bingeing in patients with bulimia (Jimerson, Lesem, Kaye, & Brewerton, 1988). Accounting for the variation of behavior between some eating disorders, McBride, Anderson, Khait, Sunday, and Halmi (1991) suggested that postsynaptic serotonin receptor function may be reduced in both bulimic and anorectic patients, whereas levels of presynaptic transmitter release may be increased in anorexia but decreased in bulimia.

Plasma Studies

Conducting biochemical assays of blood plasma is another method for assessing activity of neurotransmitter systems. This method has the advantage of being obtained in a less invasive manner than the lumbar puncture required to withdraw cerebrospinal fluid. However, because peripheral neurons (those outside the brain and spinal cord) contribute metabolites to blood plasma, assays of plasma have the disadvantage of reflecting activity of peripheral neurons as well as neuronal activity in the brain.

The most successful line of research examining plasma levels of neurotransmitter metabolites has been studies of schizophrenia demonstrating a positive correlation between plasma homovanillic acid levels and severity of psychosis (Pickar et al., 1986; Davis et al., 1985). Research has also demonstrated that dopamine metabolite levels may be useful in predicting response to neuroleptic treatment. Bowers, Swigar, Jatlow, and Goicoechea (1984) found that patients with higher pretreatment levels of hornovanillic acid in plasma responded better to neuroleptic treatment than those with lower levels. In treatment-responsive patients, studies have reported an increase in plasma metabolite levels soon after neuroleptic treatment is discontinued (Pickar et al., 1986).

POSTMORTEM STUDIES OF BRAIN TISSUE

Postmortem investigation of brain tissue offers a precise way to examine biological changes in the central nervous system associated with mental disorders. There are two primary advantages of such studies in terms of the special information they can yield. First, this strategy provides a method for studying the anatomy of the brain in fine detail far beyond that possible with available brain imaging methodologies. Changes that occur at the neuronal level, such as cell death and disturbances of dendridic neuronal connections, cannot currently be measured by any other method. Second, providing the tissue is obtained and prepared very close to the time of death (typically frozen at low temperature), whole brain studies can be performed to clarify the regional distribution of neurotransmitter receptor abnormalities throughout the brain.

Suicide

In recent years, several studies have identified disturbances in specific neurotransmitter systems in individuals who have completed suicide. If the biological disturbances that contribute to suicidal behavior can be determined, it may be possible both to identify those at risk using in vivo clinical methods such as plasma, CSF, and neuroimaging studies, and to implement effective preventative treatments for such at-risk individuals.

As discussed earlier, studies of patients with affective disorders have linked abnormalities in serotonin to suicidal behavior (Molcho, Stanley, & Stanley, 1991). The knowledge that serotonergic innervation of the cerebral cortex comes from neurons whose cell bodies are in the brain stem led to an initial focus of postmortem studies on serotonergic cell bodies and biochemical indices of serotonergic function in the brain stems of suicide victims. Several studies reported decreased amounts of serotonin and its metabolite (5-HIAA) in the postmortem brain tissue of suicide victims (Ohmori, Arora, & Meltzer, 1992; Korpi et al., 1986). However, there are problems interpreting assays of serotonin and 5-HIAA in brain tissue, because levels of these chemicals are influenced by diet, activity levels, recent drug intake, and the length of time between death and tissue preparation.

Most recent postmortem studies of suicide victims studies have examined serotonin receptor sites in the cerebral cortex, which are significantly more stable than neurotransmitter and metabolite levels over the immediate postmortem period. Rather than providing information about serotonergic cell bodies in the brainstem, studies of receptor sites provide information about the distribution of receptors in cortical terminal fields to which the brain stem neurons project.

A process called *quantitative receptor autoradiography* can be used to determine the density of neurotransmitter receptor sites in different brain regions. Compounds known as *ligands*, radioactive chemicals that bind to receptor sites of a particular neurotransmitter system, are used to label specific receptor sites. After brain tissue is exposed to the ligand, the radioactively labeled ligand binds to receptors. The amount of radioactivity in a brain region reflects the density of receptors to which the ligand has bound. When the amount of neurotransmitter released by presynaptic neurons into synapses is reduced, feedback processes are initiated to increase (up-regulate) the density of postsynaptic receptors in an effort to maintain net effective synaptic transmission. For this reason, an increased density of postsynaptic transmitter sites can suggest a lower than normal level of presynaptic neurotransmitter release.

As with postmortem studies examining the brain stem, research investigating receptor sites in the cerebral cortex of suicide victims has linked suicidal behavior to disturbances in the serotonin system (Matsubara, Arora, & Meltzer, 1991; Mann, Stanley, McBride, & McEwen, 1986). Stanley and Mann (1983) found a significant increase in the number of postsynaptic serotonin receptor sites in the frontal cortex of suicide victims. The available literature suggests a parallel reduction in density of presynaptic serotonin receptor sites in the frontal cortex of suicide victims (Matsubara et al., 1991). Receptor binding studies of suicide victims have focused not only on serotonin receptors but also on receptors for noradrenaline. Arango, Underwood, and Mann (1992) reported an increase in β-adrenergic receptor binding in the temporal cortex of suicide victims with an increase in 5-HT$_2$ receptors in both prefrontal cortex and temporal cortex. More research is needed to provide a fuller picture of disturbances of different neurotransmitter systems in different brain regions that are associated with suicide.

Cortical Dementia

Alzheimer's disease is the most common form of dementia. About 11% of people over age 65 are diagnosed with this neurodegenerative disorder, and approximately 50% of the population who are age 85 and over have probable Alzheimer's disease (Moss & Albert, 1988). Because clinical dementia can be indicative of many disorders, it is not possible to make a positive diagnosis of Alzheimer's disease based solely on the presence of neuropsychological deficits. Clinical diagnoses of this illness are considered "probable" Alzheimer's disease. At present, the only definitive way to diagnose Alzheimer's disease is to perform an examination of brain tissue, which is typically done in postmortem studies. A biopsy of brain tissue from living patients can be obtained to confirm this diagnosis when it is suspected that another treatable neurological disorder might be causing the dementia. However, due to the invasiveness of this procedure, such brain biopsies are rarely performed.

Three markers in the brain have been identified that can be used to determine a positive diagnosis of Alzheimer's disease: neurofibrillary tangles, senile plaques, and neuronal degeneration (Mann, Neary, & Testa, 1994). Tangles are the result of the proliferation of small threads called fibrils that exist in the cytoplasm of nerve cells. Their growth causes a "tangle" of fibrils inside nerve cells. Senile plaques consist of degenerated components of nerve cells. A main component of these plaques is β-Amyloid protein.

Both tangles and plaques are a result of the degeneration of nerve cells that is associated with Alzheimers' disease. Plaques and tangles are observed to be most prominent in regions of cerebral cortex associated with integrative cognitive functions rather than basic sensory or motor processes. The severity of mental deterioration in patients with suspected Alzheimer's disease has been associated with the density of these plaques and tangles (Lamsback & Navrozov, 1993). Plaques and tangles, however, have been observed in other forms of dementia, and also appear (though much less extensively) in the brains of healthy aging subjects (Mann et al., 1994). There may also be a type of Alzheimer's disease occurring in older patients in which very few or no tangles exist (Lamsback & Navrozov, 1993). Nevertheless, plaques and tangles occur most often and with distinctively increased density in the brains of patients with Alzheimer's disease, and therefore provide the best available basis for making a diagnosis of this disorder.

Abnormalities in specific neurotransmitter systems have been associated with Alzheimer's disease. Many studies suggest that the cholinergic system is disturbed in Alzheimer's disease, which is consistent with the recognized importance of this neurotransmitter system in memory function (Geula & Mesulam, 1994). A decreased number of cholinergic neurons in multiple subcortical brain regions has been reported in postmortem studies of patients with Alzheimer's disease (Forstl, Levy, Burns, Luthert, & Cairns, 1994), and some investigators have suggested that plaques are a result of degenerated cholinergic fibers (Beach & McGeer, 1992). Gabriel and colleagues (1994) found a 65% increase in galanin, a peptide that inhibits cholinergic transmission, in the brains of Alzheimer's disease victims. Despite ample support for the importance of cholinergic abnormalities in Alzheimer's disease, it is clear that this is not the only disturbed neurotransmitter system in Alzheimer's disease. Lower than normal levels of serotonin and its metabolites have also been found in postmortem studies of Alzheimer's disease (Nazarali & Reynolds, 1992).

Basal Ganglia Diseases

A number of brain diseases disrupt the anatomy and physiology of the basal ganglia (the caudate nucleus, substantia nigra, globus pallidus, and putamen) and thereby cause movement disorders. The most common of these movement disorders is Parkinson's disease. The main clinical feature of this neurodegenerative disorder is decreased mobility, including rigidity of limb movement and tremor. The loss of dopamine-containing cells in the substantia nigra is the primary neuropathology in Parkinson's disease (Jenner, 1992). Out of every 100,000 persons, 41 suffer from Parkinson's disease with dementia, and after age 80, the incidence increases to approximately 800 out every 100,000 persons (Mayeux et al., 1992).

Huntington's disease is a movement disorder associated with gross atrophy of the caudate nucleus and the putamen (Lamsback & Navrozov, 1993). In contrast to Parkinson's disease, Huntington's disease is characterized by heightened rather than reduced activity in the dopaminergic pathway from the substantia nigra to the neostriatum (Spokes, 1980). Loss of neurons utilizing gamma-amino-butyric acid (GABA), the primary inhibitory neurotransmitter in the human brain, appears to be involved in the neurodegenerative processes of Huntington's disease. Consistent with this hypothesis, Bird and Iversen (1974) have found decreased levels of GABA and glutarnic acid decarboxylase (GAD), an enzyme that is responsible for the biosynthesis of GABA, in the brains of Huntington's patients.

GENETICS

The study of genetics has progressed at a rapid pace in the last decade (Gershon & Cloninger, 1992). Early studies into the hereditary basis of neuropsychiatric disorders focused on the incidence of particular disorders in monozygotic and dizygotic twins, adoptees, and other family members. Using these incidence rates, researchers estimated the degree of heritability associated with various psychiatric disorders. Research was limited, however, by the inability to directly examine genetic material. It was only recently that methods have been developed for studying abnormalities of specific genes and their relation to risk for various diseases. If genetic studies identify specific genetic configurations associated with risk for different mental disorders, genetic testing would be useful for identifying individuals at risk for particular disorders. This would provide the basis for identifying individuals who might benefit from preventive interventions that could be provided before individuals enter the period of risk for expression of the illness.

Huntington's Disease

The first neuropsychiatric disorder to be linked to a specific chromosomal abnormality was Huntington's disease, which has an autosomal dominant expression associated with a mutation on the short arm of chromosome 4 (Gusella et al., 1983). On this chromosome, there is a repeat of the trinucleotide sequence cytosine-adenine-guanine, a mutation referred to as a trinucleotide repeat amplification. Huntington's disease has a high likelihood of being manifest when the nucleotide sequence is repeated 36 times or more (The Huntington's Disease Collaborative Research Group, 1993). Detection of this abnormality has made it possible for at-risk individuals (those with a positive family history of the disorder) to learn with a fairly high degree of accuracy if they will develop the disease.

Alzheimer's Disease

Abnormalities on chromosome 21 have been detected in some families with a relative expressing Alzheimer's disease (St. George-Hyslop et al., 1987). This link was suggested by the frequent expression of an early-onset form of Alzheimer's disease in patients with Down's syndrome, a disease that is the result of an extra copy of chromosome 21. The amyloid precursor protein (APP) gene, which is responsible for the production of the amyloid protein found in neuronal plaques associated with Alzheimer's disease, is located on chromosome 21. This suggests a possible mechanism by which an abnormality on chromosome 21 might be involved in the pathogenesis of some forms of early-onset Alzheimer's disease.

Chromosome 14, which contains a site for proteins that promote amyloid precursor protein, has also been considered to be a marker for early-onset Alzheimer's disease. Several investigations have supported the link between chromosome 14 and

Alzheimer's disease. Kamboh, Sanghera, Ferrell, and DeKosky. (1995) have reported that the alpha-antichymotrypsin (ACT) gene on chromosome 14 influences the manifestation of Alzheimer's disease. A third genetic abnormality linked to early-onset Alzheimer's disease has recently been identified, Levy-Lahad and colleagues (1995) reported the existence of a marker on chromosome 1 that is linked to the presence of early-onset Alzheimer's disease in several families.

Cases of late-onset Alzheimer's have been linked to a mutation on chromosome 19 (Pericak-Vance et al., 1991). The allele for apolipoprotein E (Apo E), a substance which encourages the growth of plaques through amyloid deposition, is encoded by this gene. Specifically, it appears as if a duplication of the apolipoprotein E E4 allele causes an increased susceptibility to Alzheimer's disease (St. Clair, 1994).

Bipolar (Manic-Depressive) Disorder

One of the best-known investigations into the genetics of affective disorders was a study of a geographically isolated Amish community. Egeland and colleagues (1987) conducted family-genetic studies of manic-depressive members of an Amish community in Pennsylvania. Their initial findings suggested a link between manic-depression and a marker on chromosome 11, though this has not been replicated. The presence of a gene on chromosome 11 that encodes tyrosine hydroxylase—an enzyme that limits the synthesis rate of catecholamine neurotransmitters such as dopamine, norepinephrine and epinephrine—makes this preliminary finding one of particular interest.

In their review of genetic studies of bipolar disorder, Everman and Stoudemire (1994) noted a high incidence of bipolar disorder in individuals affected with Klinefielter's syndrome, a genetic disorder in males causing mental retardation and undeveloped testes. The presence of an extra X chromosome (XXY males) in Klinefelter's patients suggests that bipolar disorder might be linked to an abnormality on the X chromosome. However, there has been conflicting evidence regarding this association, and the effect may be present in only some families where there appears to be increased familial risk for the disorder (Baron et al., 1993).

Schizophrenia

Kendler and Diehl (1993) carefully analyzed seven large family studies of schizophrenia. Combining the results of these studies, they concluded that there was a 4.8% risk for developing schizophrenia for subjects who had a first degree relative with the disorder, compared to a 0.5% risk for relatives of healthy comparison subjects. They also noted that the concordance rate for monozygotic twins is close to 50%, further supporting the idea that schizophrenia is at least partially genetically determined.

The general acceptance of the idea that a familial/genetic component exists for at least some forms of schizophrenia has spurred efforts to identify the exact gene or genes that are responsible for, or create a susceptibility to, this disorder. Chromosomes 5, 11, 18, and 19 have all been identified as containing regions that may contain schizophrenia-related genes (Bassett, 1992). Inconsistent findings from schizophrenia genetic research have been the rule rather than the exception. This pattern of findings may result from etiological heterogeneity of the disorder. It is possible that the clinical syndrome of schizophrenia could be comprised of several disorders with similar clinical characteristics but distinct pathophysiology and genetic influences.

Determining whether or not schizophrenia is an etiologically heterogeneous disorder (as opposed to being only clinically heterogeneous) may help focus genetic studies by directing research to specific subgroups of families. An additional potential problem in schizophrenia genetic research is that this disorder may not have a simple mode of inheritance. If there are not a small number of genes exerting major effects, the identification of influential genes for research or clinical purposes becomes a very difficult task. Despite these potential problems, research into the genetics of schizophrenia remains a very active line of work. Success in this work would provide a basis for intervening early in a preventive way to reduce the likelihood of developing this severely disabling and chronic disorder.

Alcoholism

Alcoholism is another disorder in which genetic factors are believed to play a significant role. Several studies have identified genetic abnormalities related to alcoholism and other forms of substance abuse. The etiology of alcoholism is almost certainly heterogenous, consisting of genetic as well as environmental influences (Devor, 1993). A dopamine receptor gene, DRD2, located on chromosome 11 has been identified that may have an influence on the severity of alcoholism (Blum et al., 1990). Both Uhl, Persico, and Smith (1992) and Gelernter, Goldman, and Risch (1993) analyzed several studies concerning the relationship between alcoholism and the gene encoding DRD2. Uhl and colleagues found support for the association, but Gelernter and colleagues did not. This disparity might be explained by the results of a study by Noble (1993), which indicated an association between the presence of the Al allele for DRD2 and alcoholism only in families where there is an individual with severe alcoholism.

A genetic mutation protecting individuals from alcoholism, rather than predisposing one to the disease, has been proposed. It has been suggested that a mutation on a gene that encodes acetaldehyde dehydrogenase (ALDH) lowers an individual's risk of developing alcoholism (Harada, Agarwal, Goedde, Tagakai, & Ishikawa, 1982). A mutation on the ALDH2 gene, the products of which are involved in metabolism of alcohol, may make the development of alcoholism less likely because it leads to nausea, light-headedness, and flushing after the consumption of even small amounts of alcohol.

COMPUTERIZED AXIAL TOMOGRAPHY, MAGNETIC RESONANCE IMAGING, AND MAGNETIC RESONANCE SPECTROSCOPY

Magnetic resonance imaging (MRI) is a relatively new form of medical imaging technology. In the tradition of the computed tomographic (CT) scanning, magnetic resonance imaging has been used to examine the gross anatomic structure of the brain.

In most clinical magnetic resonance imaging, the patient is exposed to a large magnetic field that aligns water protons. A brief radiowave frequency (RF) pulse then pushes the protons out of alignment, and the rate of recovery back to the original alignment is measured. Image reconstruction takes advantage of the fact that the rate of recovery to the original magnetic alignment varies for different types of biological tissue. Magnetic resonance imaging provides high resolution in vivo images of the brain and, in contrast to CT, it does not expose patients to ionizing radiation.

Magnetic resonance spectroscopy (MRS) uses the measurement of isotopes such as hydrogen, carbon, sodium, and phosphorus in order to assess the density of molecules related to different physiologic processes and of cell membrane integrity. Information that can be obtained includes electrolyte balance and the metabolism of proteins, carbohydrates, phospholipids, and amino acids (Nasrallah & Pettegrew, 1995).

Schizophrenia

Enlargement of the lateral ventricles in schizophrenia has been repeatedly identified using CT scans (Weinberger, Torrey, Neopytides, & Wyatt, 1979; Klausner, Sweeney, Deck, Haas, & Kelly, 1992). The ventricles in the brain are filled with cerebrospinal fluid. They are under some pressure, and as a result, they expand to fill space created by the loss neural tissue. For this reason, ventricular enlargement implies some neuronal atrophy or an exaggeration of the normal pruning of dendritic connections that occurs during development. Although the observation of ventricular enlargement did not generate information regarding specific regional anatomic disturbances, it did provide the first clear and widely replicated demonstration of anatomic brain abnormalities in schizophrenia. Later, the high resolution of magnetic resonance imaging made possible the quantitative investigation of subtle regional changes in brain anatomy in schizophrenia. For instance, grey matter (the brain areas comprised of neuron cell bodies) has been reported to be decreased by approximately 20% in the frontal lobes of schizophrenic patients (Suddath et al., 1989).

Magnetic resonance imaging has also detected anatomic abnormalities in the superior temporal gyrus (McCarley et al., 1993). Studies have linked abnormalities in this area with auditory hallucinations (Barta, Pearlson, Powers, Richards, & Tune, 1990), thought disorder (Shenton et al., 1992) and thought and language disturbance (Vita et al., 1995). Seidman and colleagues (1994) reported a decrease in dorsolateral prefrontal cortex volume, particularly in the left hemisphere, in association with poor performance on tests of abstract reasoning, long-term memory, attention, and executive functions.

Magnetic resonance spectroscopy studies have been conducted to determine whether there are indications of degenerative processes in schizophrenia. In a study of prefrontal cortex in first episode, drug-naive schizophrenic patients, an increased level of phosphodiesters (end-products of nerve membrane degradation), along with a decreased level of phosphomonoesters (major building blocks in nerve membrane synthesis), has been demonstrated (Pettegrew et al., 1991). This observation is most consistent with a model that there is an exaggeration of the normal age-related selective pruning of the dendrites that connect different neurons in the brain.

Mood Disorders

Ventricular enlargement has also been observed in magnetic resonance imaging studies of depressed subjects, though somewhat less consistently (Kellner, Rubinow, & Post, 1986; Coffey et al., 1993). Several studies of depressed patients have reported an increased rate of white matter hyperintensities, which are small white regions observed in magnetic resonance imaging scans. These phenomena are believed to indicate small lesions in periventricular white matter, the tracts of long axons that connect different areas of the brain. Studies by Coffey and colleagues (1993) reported that such lesions were more common and more severe in elderly depressed patients than in normal elderly patients. Krishnan and colleagues (1988) found these lesions in both older and younger depressed patients, but the prevalence of lesions was greater in elderly patients.

An early CT study of bipolar disorder conducted by Pearlson and associates (1984) reported enlarged brain ventricles. Later, Aylward and associates (1994) replicated this result using magnetic resonance imaging, and also demonstrated deep white matter hyperintensities in bipolar disorder consistent with prior findings (Swayze, Andreasen, Alliger, Ehrhardt, & Yuh, 1990; McDonald & Krishnan, 1992),

Dementia

Magnetic resonance imaging has been used to assess brain atrophy, the shrinkage of brain volume resulting from the death of brain neurons. Decreases in grey matter (the superficial cortical layer comprised largely of neurons) has been demonstrated in Alzheimer's disease (Rusinek et al., 1991). Brain imaging studies have the potential to discriminate patients with dementia from those with late-life mood disorders because the former typically are associated with greater neuroanatomic abnormalities. This is clinically important because depression and early stage Alzheimer's disease can present with similar clinical features. Using magnetic resonance imaging, Zubenko and colleagues (1990) were able to distinguish depressed and demented subjects by comparing the amount of cortical atrophy present. Temporal lobe atrophy also has been used to discriminate between depressed and demented patients (OBrien, Ames, Schweitzer, Tuckwell, & Tress, 1994).

In contrast to Alzheimer's-type dementias, vascular dementias result from changes in vascular flow that adversely affect the brain. Pathologic events such as hemorrhages, thrombosis, and anoxia can lead to nerve cell death and thereby to neuropsychological deficits. Multi-infarct dementia can cause a relatively generalized disturbance of higher cognitive functions that can be similar to that of other diffuse dementias. Aside from postmortem examination, the only way to positively diagnose vascular dementia is to identify the presence of the resulting brain lesions through the use of neuroimaging techniques (Wahlund, 1994).

Magnetic resonance spectroscopy studies of demented patients have yielded two main findings. Levels of N-acetyl aspartate (NAA), a neuronal marker, have been shown to be reduced in the brains of patients with Alzheimer's disease (Shonk et al., 1995), indicating neuronal loss. Second, studies of Alzheimer's disease by Pettegrew and associates (1988) have demonstrated an increased level of phosphodiesters, which are a by-product of cell membrane degradation. They have associated this abnormality with the presence of senile plaques, with both levels increasing as the disease progresses.

BRAIN METABOLISM AND CEREBRAL BLOOD FLOW

Imaging techniques such as positron emission tomography (PET), single photon emission computed tomography (SPECT), and functional magnetic resonance imaging (fMRI) have made it possible to measure cerebral blood flow and/or metabolism in clinical studies. These techniques have the advantage of providing information about disturbances in active physiologic processes in the brain, such as the identification of brain regions where neuronal activity is reduced to an extent that could cause clinically apparent behavioral and cognitive problems.

In both PET and SPECT studies of brain activity, a radioactive material is injected into the blood stream at a dose low enough to impose minimal health risks for patients. The procedures differ in the way regional differences in radioactivity are measured, with the PET technique providing more precise measurements for most purposes. One way these procedures monitor regional neuronal activity is as follows. Blood flow increases in brain regions that are more active in relation to the increased metabolic demand. Increased blood flow brings greater amounts of the radioactive material that was injected into the bloodstream into the activated brain region. Regional brain activity can then be measured by monitoring the amount of radioactive material in various brain regions. Functional magnetic resonance imaging provides measurements of blood flow without exposure to radioactive material by taking advantage of the paramagnetic properties of deoxygenated hemoglobin. Use of all three of these functional brain imaging techniques has the potential to provide great advancements in understanding the pathophysiologic substrates of psychopathology.

Schizophrenia

It has been suggested that low levels of activity in the frontal lobes (referred to as *hypofrontality*) and increased activity in the left temporal lobe during periods of psychosis may be responsible for some clinical features of schizophrenia (Gur & Pearlson, 1993). A study demonstrating reduced metabolic activity in prefrontal cortex in schizophrenia was the first major finding from functional imaging investigations of psychiatric disorders (Ingvar & Franzen, 1974). More recent studies have replicated this effect (Buchsbaum et al., 1984), but findings have not been fully consistent (Gur & Gur, 1995). The hypofrontality effect has most consistently been demonstrated in studies of chronic patients who manifest significant negative symptoms. Some studies have linked episodes of acute psychosis to increased resting metabolic activity in the left temporal lobe (Gur et al., 1985).

Studies demonstrating reduced activation in prefrontal cortex of schizophrenic patients during performance of "frontal lobe" tests of executive cognitive functions have been more consistent. Using the Wisconsin Card Sorting Test (Heaton, 1981), a cognitive test that places neuronal demands on the prefrontal cortex and is known to increase neuronal activity in that brain region in healthy individuals, researchers have reported lower levels of task-related activation of prefrontal cortex in schizophrenic patients (Weinberger, Berman, & Zec, 1986; Rubin et al., 1991).

Obsessive-Compulsive Disorder

Functional imaging studies of patients with obsessive-compulsive disorder have revealed hyperactivity in orbital (ventral or inferior) prefrontal cortex and in the neostriatum (Machfin et al., 1991; Baxter et al., 1987). Swedo and colleagues (1989) found a posit positive correlation between the level of this hypermetabolism and severity of obsessive-compulsive symptoms. They have also reported a significant decrease in orbitofrontal metabolism associated with the reduction of symptoms after treatment with serotonergicly potent antidepressant medications (Swedo et al., 1992).

Dementia

The advent of functional neuroimaging techniques has aided in the difficult task of distinguishing different types of dementia. Previous techniques relied on examining structural anatomic abnormalities, but abnormalities of regional brain physiology often can be detected before gross anatomic changes are evident (Foster, 1994). Functional imaging studies of patients with suspected Alzheimer's disease reveal a bilateral decline in glucose metabolism in medial temporal and parietal cortex (Jagust, Budinger, & Reed, 1987). Such studies provide a strategy for diagnosing dementias earlier in their course than is possible with structural anatomic imaging, and thus can be used to initiate treatment interventions earlier in the course of illness. Functional neuroimaging studies of vascular dementia are characterized by a more patchy presentation of focal declines in regional brain activity (Kumar, 1993), because the effects of strokes are largely limited to the specific region where the cerebral vascular accident occurred.

Examinations of the intercorrelation of activation across brain regions provides a strategy for assessing functional connectivity of different brain regions. PET studies have highlighted the cooperative interaction of different brain regions in the performance of even simple behavioral tasks (Sweeney et al., in press). Studies have suggested that there is an alteration of cortical connectivity associated with aging (Grady et al., 1994) and after ischemic episodes (Mentis et al., 1994). Other data suggest that these disturbances in functional connectivity may occur early in the course of Alzheimer's disease, and that such deficits in effective integration of brain activity can be detected prior to the emergence of detectable atrophic changes in brain anatomy (Azari et al., 1993).

PET RECEPTOR STUDIES

In addition to gaining information on metabolism and blood flow, positron emission tomography can measure the density of neurotransmitter receptors throughout the brain. As in postmortem autoradiography studies, measurement of receptor binding is made possible by determining the amount and distribution of radioactive ligands that bind to particular receptors. In PET studies of neurotransmitter receptors, a very small dose of a radioactively labeled drug is injected that binds for relatively long periods of time to receptors of interest. This binding increases regional radioactivity and can be detected as such with a PET camera.

The earliest major positron emission tomography receptor studies of psychiatric disorders focused on schizophrenia and D_2 dopamine receptors (Sedvall, 1992). Wong and associates (1986) found an increased dopamine receptor density in neuroleptic-naive schizophrenic patients. Likewise, Pearlson and associates (1993) studied neuroleptic-naive patients with late-onset schizophrenia, and reported an increase in dopamine receptor density. However, a study by Farde and colleagues (1990) found no increased dopamine receptor density in never-treated schizophrenic patients.

Positron emission tomography receptor studies are not yet a widely applied clinical technique, in part because of the significant costs for equipment and multidisciplinary staffs needed to establish and maintain PET centers. However, unlike cerebral spinal fluid and plasma studies that provide net indices of transmitter activity in brain, PET and SPECT scanning can directly examine the regional distribution of receptors throughout the brain and the effects of treatments on regional receptor abnormalities. For these reasons, neuroimaging studies of neurotransmitter receptors may become an important diagnostic/assessment tool.

SUMMARY

Significant advances have been achieved in understanding biological aspects of severe mental disorders. At present, few such advances have led to the establishment of valid laboratory tests with direct clinical application. Any wide clinical application of such laboratory tests depends on ongoing developments in the basic understanding of brain anatomy, neurochemistry, and physiology, on technological developments, and on clinical studies using such knowledge and procedures to identify brain disturbances associated with severe mental disorders.

Although substantial progress has been realized in the understanding of basic brain physiology, the transfer of that knowledge into clinical studies is often a complex and arduous process because of the extensive validation studies that are required. Despite these limitations, the clinical application of various biochemical tests, brain imaging procedures, and genetic testing offer considerable promise not only for clarifying the understanding of psychopathologic conditions but also for improving the evaluation and treatment of patients suffering from severe mental illness.

REFERENCES

Altemus, M., Swedo, S. E., Leonard, H. L., Richter, D., Rubinow, D. R., Potter, W. Z., & Rapoport, J. L. (1994). Changes in cerebrospinal fluid neurochemistry during treatment of obsessive-compulsive disorder with clomipramine. *Archives of General Psychiatry, 51*, 794–803.

American Psychiatric Association. (1994). *Diagnostic and statistical manual of mental disorders* (4th ed.). Washington, DC: American Psychiatric Association.

Arango, V., Underwood, M. D., & Mann, J. J. (1992). Alterations in monoamine receptors in the brain of suicide victims. *Journal of Clinical Psychopharmacology, 12*, 85–125.

Aylward, E. H., Roberts-Twillie, J. V., Barta, P. E., Kumar, A, J., Harris, G. J., Geer, M., Peyser, C. E., & Pearlson, G. D. (1994). Basal ganglia volumes and white matter hyperintensities in patients with bipolar disorder. *American Journal of Psychiatry, 151*, 687–693.

Azari, N. P., Pettigrew, K. D., Schapiro, M. B., Haxby, J. V., Grady, C. L., Pietrini, P., Salerno, J. A., Heston, L. L., Rapoport, S. I., & Horwitz, B. (1993). Early detection of Alzheimer's disease: A statistical approach using positron emission tomographic data. *Journal of Cerebral Blood Flow and Metabolism, 13*, 438–447.

Banki, C. M., Arato, M., & Kilts, C. D. (1986). Aminergic studies and cerebrospinal fluid cations in suicide. *Annals of the New York Academy of Sciences, 487*, 221–230.

Baron, M., Freimer, N. F., Risch, N., Lerer, B., Alexander, J. R., Straub, R. E., Asokan, S., Das, K., Peterson, A., Amos, J., Endicott, J., Ott, J., & Gilliam, T. C. (1993). Diminished support for linkage between manic depressive illness and X-chromosome markers in three Israeli pedigrees. *Nature Genetics, 3*, 49–55.

Barr, L. C., Goodman, W. K., Price, L. H., McDougle, C. J., & Charney, D. S. (1992). The serotonin hypothesis of obsessive compulsive disorder: Implications of pharmacologic challenge studies. *Journal of Clinical Psychiatry, 53*, 17–28.

Barta, P. E., Pearlson, G. D., Powers, R. E., Richards, S. S., & Tune, L, E. (1990). Auditory hallucinations and smaller superior temporal gyral volume in schizophrenia. *American Journal of Psychiatry. 147*, 1457–1462.

Bassett, A. S. (1992). Chromosomal aberrations and schizophrenia. *British Journal of Psychiatry, 161*, 323–334.

Baxter, L. R., Phelps, M. E., Mazziotta, J. C., Guze, B. H., Schwartz, J. M., & Selin, C. E. (1987). Local cerebral glucose metabolic rates in obsessive-compulsive disorder. *Archives of General Psychiatry, 44*, 211–218.

Beach, T. G., & McGeer, E. G. (1992). Senile plaques, amyloid β-protein, and acetylcholinesterase fibres: Laminar distributions in Alzheimer's disease striate cortex. *Acta Neuropathology, 83*, 292–299.

Bird, E. D., & Iversen, L. L. (1974). Huntington's chorea. *Brain, 97*, 457–472.

Bloom, F. E., & Kupfer, D. J. (1995). *Psychopharmacology: The fourth generation of progress*. New York: Raven.

Blum, K., Noble, E. P., Sheridan, P., Montgomery, A., Ritchie, T., Jagadeeswaran, P., Nogami, H., Briggs, A. H., & Cohn, J. B. (1990). Allelic association of human dopamine D_2 receptor gene in alcoholism. *Journal of the American Medical Association, 263*, 2055–2060.

Bowers, M. B. (1974). Central dopamine turnover in schizophrenic syndromes. *Archives of General Psychiatry. 31*, 50–54,

Bowers, M. B., Swigar, M. E., Jatlow, P. I., & Goicoechea, N. (1984). Plasma catecholamine metabolites and early response to haloperidol. *Journal of Clinical Psychiatry, 45*, 248–251.

Buchsbaum, M. S., Delisi, L. E., Holcomb, H. H., Cappelletti, J., King, A. C., Johnson, J., Hazlett, E., Dowling-Zimmerman, S., Post, R. M., Morihisa, J., Carpenter, W., Cohen, R., Pickar, D., Weinberger, D. R., Margolin, R., & Kessler, R. M. (1984). Anteroposterior gradients in cerebral glucose use in schizophrenia and affective disorders. *Archives of General Psychiatry, 41*, 1159–1166.

Coffey, C. E., Wilkinson, W. E., Weiner, R. D., Parashos, I. A., Djang, W. T., Webb, M. C., Fiegiel, G. S., & Spritzer, C. E. (1993). Quantitative cerebral anatomy in depression. *Archives of General Psychiatry, 50*, 7–16.

Davis, K. L., Davidson, M., Mohs, R. C., Kendler, K. S., Davis, B. M., Johns, C. A., DeNignis, Y., & Horvath, T. B. (1985). Plasma homovanillic acid concentration and the severity of schizophrenic illness. *Science, 227*, 1601–1602.

Davis, K. L., Kahn, R. S., Ko, G., & Davidson, M. (1991). Dopamine in schizophrenia: A review and reconceptualization. *American Journal of Psychiatry, 148*, 1474–1486.

Devor, E. J. (1993). Why there is no gene for alcoholism. *Behavior Genetics, 23*, 145–149.

Egeland, J, A., Gerhard, D. S., Pauls, D. L., Sussex, J. N., Kidd, K. K., Allen, C. R., Hostetter, A. M., & Housman, D. E. (1987). Bipolar affective disorder linked to DNA markers on chromosome 11. *Nature, 325*, 783–787.

Everman, D. B., & Stoudemire, A. (1994). Bipolar disorder associated with Klinefelter's syndrome and other chromosomal abnormalities. *Psychosomatics, 35*, 35–40.

Farde, L., Wiesel, F., Stone-Elander, S., Halldin, C., Nordstrom, A., Hall, H., & Sedvall, G. (1990). D$_2$ Dopamine receptors in neuroleptic-naive schizophrenic patients. *Archives of General Psychiatry, 47*, 213–219.

Forstl, H., Levy, R., Burns, A., Luthert, P., & Cairns, N, (1994). Disproportionate loss of noradrenergic and cholinergic neurons as cause of depression in Alzheimer's disease—A hypothesis. *Pharmacopsychiatry, 27*, 11–15.

Foster, N. L. (1994). PET imaging. In R. D. Terry, R. Katzman, & K. L. Bick (Eds.), *Alzheimer disease* (pp. 87–103). New York: Raven.

Gabriel, S. M., Bierer, L. M., Davidson, M., Purohit, D. P., Perl, D. P., & Harotunian, V. (1994). Galanin-like immunoreactivity is increased in the postmortem cerebral cortex from patients with Alzheimer's disease. *Journal of Neurochemistry, 62*, 1516–1523.

Gelernter, J., Goldman, D., & Risch, N. (1993). The A1 allele at the D$_2$ dopamine receptor gene and alcoholism. *Journal of the American Medical Association, 269*, 1673–1677.

Gershon, E. S., & Cloninger, C. R. (1992). *Genetic approaches to mental disorders*. Washington, DC: American Psychiatric Press.

Geula, C., & Mesulam, M. M. (1994). Cholinergic systems and related neuropathological predilection patterns in Alzheimer disease, In R. D. Terry, R. Katzman, & K. L. Bick (Eds.), *Alzheimer disease* (pp. 263–291). New York: Raven.

Grady, C. L., Maisog, J. M., Horwitz, B., Ungerleider, L. G., Mentis, M. J., Salerno, J. A., Pietrini, P., Wagner, E., & Haxby, J. V. (1994). Age-related changes in cortical blood flow activation during visual processing of faces and location. *Journal of Neuroscience, 14*, 1450–1462.

Gur, R. C., & Gur, R. E. (1995). Hypofrontality in schizophrenia: RIP. *Lancet, 345*, 1383–1384.

Gur, R. E., Gur, R. C., Skolnick, B. E., Caroff, S., Obrist, W. D., Resnick, S. M., & Reivich, M. (1985). Brain function in psychiatric disorders: III. Regional cerebral blood flow in unmedicated schizophrenia. *Archives of General Psychiatry, 42*, 329–334.

Gur, R. E., & Pearlson, G. D. (1993). Neuroimaging in schizophrenia research. *Schizophrenia Bulletin, 19*, 337–353.

Gusella, J. F., Wexler, N. S., Conneally, P. M., Naylor, S. L., Anderson, M. A., Tanzi, R. E., Watkins, P. C., Ottina, K., Wallace, M. R., Sakaguchi, A. Y., Young, A. B., Shoulson, I., Bonilla, E., & Martin, J. B. (1983). A polymorphic DNA marker genetically linked to Huntington's disease. *Nature, 306*, 234–238.

Harada, S., Agarwal, D. P., Goedde, H. W., Tagakai, S., & Ishikawa, B. (1982). Possible protective role against alcoholism for aldehyde dehydrogenase isozyme deficiency in Japan. *Lancet, II*, 827.

Heaton, R. K. (1981). *Wisconsin Card Sorting Test Manual*. (unpub)

The Huntington's Disease Collaborative Research Group. (1993). A novel gene containing a trinucleotide repeat that is expanded and unstable on Huntington's disease chromosomes. *Cell, 72*, 971–983.

Ingvar, D. H., & Franzen, G. (1974). Abnormalities of cerebral blood flow distribution in patients with chronic schizophrenia. *Acta Psychiatrica Scandinavica 50*, 425–462.

Jagust, W. J., Budinger, T. F., & Reed, B. R. (1987). The diagnosis of dementia with single photon emission computed tomography. *Archives of Neurology, 44*, 258–262.

Jenner, P. (1992). What process causes nigral cell death in Parkinson's disease? *Neurologic Clinics of North America, 10*, 387–403.

Jimerson, D. C., Lesem, M. D., Hegg, A. P., & Brewerton, T. D. (1990). Serotonin in human eating disorders. *Annals of the New York Academy of Sciences, 600*, 532–544.

Jimerson, D. C., Lesem, M. D., Kaye, W. H., & Brewerton, T. D. (1988). Symptom severity and neurotransmitter studies in bulimia [Abstract]. *Psychopharmacology, 96,* S124.

Kamboh, M. I., Sanghera, D. K., Ferrell, R. E., & DeKosky, S. T. (1995). APOE*4-associated Alzheimer's disease risk is modified by α1-antichymotrypsin polymorphism. *Nature Genetics, 10,* 486–488.

Kandel, E. R., Schwartz, J. H., & Jessell, T. M. (1991). *Principles of neural sciences* (3rd ed.). Norwalk, CT: Appleton & Lange.

Kaye, W. H., Ebert, M. H., Raleigh, M., & Lake, R. (1984). Abnormalities in CNS monoamine metabolism in anorexia nervosa. *Archives of General Psychiatry, 41,* 350–355.

Kaye, W. H., & Weltzin, T. E. (1991). Serotonin activity in anorexia and bulimia nervosa: Relationship to the modulation of feeding and mood. *Journal of Clinical Psychiatry, 52,* 41–48.

Kellner, C. H., Rubinow, D, R., & Post, R. M. (I 986). Cerebral ventricular size and cognitive impairment in depression. *Journal of Affective Disorders, 10,* 215–219.

Kendler, K. S., & Diehl, S. R. (1993). The genetics of schizophrenia: A current genetic-epidemiologic perspective. *Schizophrenia Bulletin, 19,* 261–285.

Klausner, J. D., Sweeney, J. A., Deck, M. D. F., Haas, G. L., & Kelly, A. B. (1992). Clinical correlates of cerebral ventricular enlargement in schizophrenia. *Journal of Nervous and Mental Disease, 180,* 407–412.

Korpi, E. R., Kleinman, J. E., Goodman, S. I., Phillips, I., Delisi, L. E., Linnoila, M., & Wyatt, R, J, (1986). Serotonin and 5-hydroxyindoleacetic acid in brains of suicide victims. *Archives of General Psychiatry, 43,* 594–600.

Krishnan, K. R. R., Goli, V., Ellinwood, E. H., France, R. D., Blazer, D. G., & Nemeroff, C. B. (1988). Leukoencephalopathy in patients diagnosed as major depressive. *Biological Psychiatry, 23,* 519–522.

Kumar, A. (1993). Functional brain imaging in late-life depression and dementia. *Journal of Clinical Psychiatry, 54,* 21–25.

Lamsback, W. J., & Navrozov, M. (1993). Degenerative diseases of the nervous system. In R. D. Adams & M. Victor (Eds.), *Principles of neurology* (pp. 957–1009). New York: McGraw-Hill.

Levy-Lahad, E., Wijsman, E. M., Nemens, E., Anderson, L., Goddard, K. A. B., Weber, J. L., Bird, T. D., & Schellenberg, G. D. (1995). A familial Alzheimer's disease locus on chromosome I. *Science, 269,* 970–973.

Lieberman, J. A., Kane, J. M., Gadaleta, D., Brenner, R., Lesser, M. S., & Kinon, B. (1984). Methylpheni-

date challenge as a predictor of relapse in schizophrenia. *American Journal of Psychiatry, 141,* 633–638.

Lindstrom, L. H. (1985). Low HVA and normal 5HIAA CSF levels in drug-free schizophrenic patients compared to healthy volunteers: Correlations to symptomatology and family history. *Psychiatry Research, 14,* 265–273.

Luria, A. R. (1962). *Higher cortical functions in man* (2nd ed.). New York: Basic Books.

Machlin, S. R., Harris, G. J., Pearlson, G. D., Hoehn-Saric, R., Jeffery, P., & Camargo, E. E. (1991). Elevated medial-frontal cerebral blood flow in obsessive-compulsive patients: A SPECT study. *American Journal of Psychiatry, 148,* 1240–1242.

Mann, D. M. A., Neary, D., & Testa, H. (I 994). *Color atlas and test of adult dementia.* London: Mosby-Wolfe.

Mann, J. J., McBride, P. A., Brown, R. P., Linnoila, M., Leon, A. C., DeMeo, M., Mieczkowski, T., Myers, J. E., & Stanley, M. (1992). Relationship between central and peripheral serotonin indexes in depressed and suicidal psychiatric inpatients. *Archives of General Psychiatry, 49,* 442–446.

Mann, J. J., Stanley, M., McBride, P. A., & McEwen, B. S. (1986). Increased serotonin$_2$ and β-adrenergic receptor binding in the frontal cortices of suicide victims. *Archives of General Psychiatry, 43,* 954–959.

Matsubara, S., Arora, R. C., & Meltzer, H. Y. (1991). Serotonergic measures in suicide brain: 5-HT1A binding sites in frontal cortex of suicide victims. *Journal of Neural Transmission, 85,* 181–194.

Mayeux, R., Denaro, J., Hemenegildo, N., Marder, K., Tang, M. X., Cote, L. J., & Stern, Y. (1992). A population-based investigation of Parkinson's disease with and without dementia. *Archives of Neurology, 49,* 492–497.

McBride, P. A., Anderson, G. M., Khait, V. D., Sunday, S. R., & Halmi, K. A. (1991). Serotonergic responsivity in eating disorders. *Psychopharmacology Bulletin, 27,* 365–372.

McCarley, R. W., Shenton, M. E., O'Donnell, B. F., Faux, S. F., Kikinis, R., Nestor, P. G., & Jolesz, F. A. (1993). Auditory P300 abnormalities and left posterior superior temporal gyrus volume reduction in schizophrenia. *Archives of General Psychiatry, 50,* 190–197.

McDonald, W. M., & Krishnan, K. R. R. (1992). Magnetic resonance in patients with affective illness. *European Archives of Psychiatry and Clinical Neuroscience, 241,* 283–290.

Mentis, M. J., Salerno, J., Horwitz, B., Grady, C., Schapiro, M. B., Murphy, D. G. M., & Rapoport, S. I. (1994). Reduction of functional neuronal connectivity in long-term treated hypertension. *Stroke, 25,* 601–607.

Mesulam, M. M. (1985). *Principles of behavioral neurology.* Philadelphia: F.A. Davis.

Molcho, A., Stanley, B., & Stanley, M. (1991). Biological studies and markers in suicide and attempted suicide. *International Journal of Clinical Psychopharmacology, 6,* 77–92.

Moss, M. B., & Albert, M. S. (1988). Alzheimer's disease and other dementing disorders. In M. S. Albert & M. B. Moss (Eds.), *Geriatric neuropsychology* (pp. 145–178). New York: Guilford.

Murphy, D. L., Zohar, C., Benkelfat, C., Pato, M. T., Pigott, T. A., & Insel, T. R. (1989). Obsessive-compulsive disorder as a 5-HT subsystem-related behavioural disorder. *British Journal of Psychiatry, 155,* 15–24.

Nasrallah, H. A., & Pettegrew, J. W. (1995). *NMR spectroscopy in psychiatric brain disorders.* Washington DC: American Psychiatric Press.

Nazarali, A. J., & Reynolds, G. P. (1992). Monoamine neurotransmitters and their metabolites in brain regions in Alzheimer's disease: A postmortem study. *Cellular and Molecular Neurobiology, 12,* 581–587.

Noble, E. P. (1993). The D_2 dopamine receptor gene: A review of association studies in alcoholism. *Behavior Genetics, 23,* 119–129.

O'Brien, J. T., Ames, D, D., Schweitzer, I., Tuckwell, V., & Tress, B. (1994). The differentiation of depression from dementia by temporal lobe magnetic resonance imaging. *Psychological Medicine, 24,* 633–640.

Ohmori, T., Arora, R. C., & Meltzer, H. Y. (1992). Serotonergic measures in suicide brain: The concentration of 5-HIAA, HVA, and tryptophan in frontal cortex of suicide victims. *Biological Psychiatry, 32,* 57–71.

Pearlson, G. D., Garbacz, D. J., Tompkins, R. H., Ahn, H. S., Gutterman, D. F., Veroff, A. E., & DePaulo, J. R. (1984). Clinical correlates of lateral ventricular enlargement in bipolar affective disorder. *American Journal of Psychiatry, 141,* 253–256.

Pearlson, G. D., Tune, L. E., Wong, D. F., Aylward, E. H., Barta, P. E., Powers, R. E., Tien, A. Y., Chase, G. A., Harris, G. J., & Rabins, P. V. (1993). Quantitative D_2 dopamine receptor PET and structural MRI changes in late-onset schizophrenia. *Schizophrenia Bulletin, 19,* 783–795.

Pericak-Vance, M. A., Bebout, J. L., Gaskell, P. C., Yamaoka, L. H., Hung, W. Y., Alberts, M. J., Walker, A. P., Bartlett, R. J., Haynes, C. A., Welsh, K. A., Earl, N. L., Heyman, A., Clark, C. M., & Roses, A. D. (1991). Linkage studies in familial Alzheimer disease: Evidence for chromosome 19 linkage. *American Journal of Human Genetics, 48,* 1034–1050.

Pettegrew, J. W., Keshavan, M. S., Panchalingam, K., Strychor, S., Kaplan, D. B., Tretta, M. G., & Allen, M. (1991). Alterations in brain high-energy phosphate and membrane phospholipid metabolism in first-episode, drug-naive schizophrenia. *Archives of General Psychiatry, 48,* 563–568.

Pettegrew, J. W., Panchalingam, K., Moossy, J., Martinez, J., Rao, G., & Boller, F. (1988). Correlation of phosphorus-31 magnetic resonance spectroscopy and morphologic findings in Alzheimer's disease. *Archives of Neurology, 45,* 1093–1096.

Pickar, D., Labarca, R., Doran, A. R., Wolkowitz, O. M., Roy, A., Breier, A., Linnoila, M., & Paul, S. M. (1986). Longitudinal measurement of plasma homovanillic acid levels in schizophrenic patients. *Archives of General Psychiatry, 43,* 669–676.

Pope, H. G., & Hudson, J. I. (1986). Antidepressant drug therapy for bulimia: Current status. *Journal of Clinical Psychiatry, 47,* 339–345.

Risch, S. C., & Nemeroff, C. B. (1992). Neurochemical alterations of serotonergic neuronal systems in depression. *Journal of Clinical Psychiatry, 53,* 3–7.

Roth, B. L. (1994). Multiple serotonin receptors: Clinical and experimental aspects. *Annals of Clinical Psychiatry, 6,* 67–78.

Rubin, P., Holm, S., Friberg, L., Videbech, P., Andersen, H. S., Bendsen, B. B., Stromso, N., Larsen, J. K., Lassen, N. A., & Hemmingsen, R. (1991). Altered modulation of prefrontal and subcortical brain activity in newly diagnosed schizophrenia and schizophreniform disorder. *Archives of General Psychiatry, 48,* 98–995.

Rusinek, H., de Leon, M. J., George, A. E., Stylopoulos, L. A., Chandra, R., Smith, G., Rand, T., Mourino, M., & Kowalski, H. K. (1991). Alzheimer disease: Measuring loss of cerebral gray matter with MR imaging. *Radiology, 178,* 109–114.

St. Clair, D. (1994), Genetics of Alzheimer's disease. *British Journal of Psychiatry, 164,* 153–156.

Saint George-Hyslop, P. H., Tanzi, R. E., Polinsky, R. J., Haines, J. L., Nee, L., Watkins, P. C., Myers, R. H., Feldman, R. G., Pollen, D., Drachman, D., Growdon, J., Bruni, A., Foncin, J. F., Salmon, D., Frommelt, P., Amaducci, L., Sorbi, S., Piacentini, S.,

Stewart, G. D., Hobbs, W. J., Conneally, P. M., & Gusella, J. F. (1987). The genetic defect causing familial Alzheimer's disease maps on chromosome 21. *Science, 235*, 885–890.

Sedvall, M. D. (1992). The current status of PET scanning with respect to schizophrenia. *Neuropsychopharmacology, 7*, 41–54.

Seidman, L. J., Yurgelun-Todd, D., Kremen, W. S., Woods, B. T., Goldstein, J. M., Faraone, S. V., & Tsuang, M. T. (1994). Relationship of prefrontal and temporal lobe NM measures to neuropsychological performance in chronic schizophrenia, *Biological Psychiatry, 35*, 235–246.

Shenton, M. E., Kikinis, R., Jolesz, F. A., Pollak, S. D., LeMay, M., Wible, C. G., Hokama, H., Martin, J., Metcalf, D., Coleman, M., & McCarley, R. W. (1992). Abnormalities of the left temporal lobe and thought disorder in schizophrenia. *New England Journal of Medicine, 327*, 604–612.

Shonk, T. K., Moats, R. A., Gifford, P., Michaelis, T., Mandigo, J. C., Izumi, J., & Ross, B. D. (1995). Probable Alzheimer disease: Diagnosis with proton MR spectroscopy. *Radiology, 195*, 65–72.

Spokes, E. G. S. (1980). Neurochemical alterations in Huntington's chorea. *Brain, 103*, 179–210.

Stanley, M., & Mann, J. J. (1983). Increased serotonin-2 binding sites in frontal cortex of suicide victims. *Lancet, II*, 214–216.

Suddath, R. L., Casanova, M. F., Goldberg, T. E., Daniel, D. G., Kelsoe, J. R., & Weinberger, D. R. (1989). Temporal lobe pathology in schizophrenia: A quantitative magnetic resonance imaging study. *American Journal of Psychiatry, 146*, 464–472.

Swayze, V. W., Andreasen, N. C., Alliger, R. J., Ehrhardt, J. C., & Yuh, W. T. C. (1990). Structural brain abnormalities in bipolar affective disorder. *Archives of General Psychiatry, 47*, 1054–1059.

Swedo, S. E., Peitrini, P., Leonard, H. L., Schapiro, M. B., Rettew, D. C., Goldberger, E. L., Rapoport, S. I., Rapoport, J. L., & Grady, C. L. (1992). Cerebral glucose metabolism in childhood-onset obsessive-compulsive disorder: Revisualization during pharmacotherapy. *Archives of General Psychiatry, 49*, 690–694.

Swedo, S. E., Schapiro, M. B., Grady, C. L., Cheslow, D. L., Lenard, H. L., Kumar, A., Friedland, R., Rapoport, S. I., & Rapoport, J. L. (1989). Cerebral glucose metabolism in childhood onset obsessive-compulsive disorder. *Archives of General Psychiatry, 46*, 518–526.

Sweeney, J. A., Mintun, M. A., Kwee, S., Wiseman, M. B., Brown, D. L., Rosenberg, D. R., & Carl, J. R. (in press). A positron emission tomography study of voluntary saccadic eye movements and spatial working memory. *Journal of Neurophysiology.*

Traskman, L., Asberg, M., Bertilsson, L., & Sjostrand, L. (1981). Monoamine metabolites in CSF and suicidal behavior. *Archives of General Psychiatry, 38*, 631–636.

Uhl, G. R., Persico, A. M., & Smith, S. S. (1992). Current excitement with D$_2$ dopamine receptor gene alleles in substance abuse. *Archives of General Psychiatry, 49*, 157–160.

Vita, A., Dieci, M., Giobbio, G. M., Caputo, A., Ghiringhelli, L., Comazzi, M., Garbarini, M., Mendini, A. P., Morganti, C., Tenconi, F., Cesana, B., & Invernizzi, G. (1995). Language and thought disorder in schizophrenia: Brain morphological correlates. *Schizophrenia Research, 15*, 243–251.

Wahlund, L. O. (1994). Brain imaging and vascular dementia. *Dementia, 5*, 193–196.

Weinberger, D. R., Berman, K. F., & Zec, R. F. (I 986). Physiologic dysfunction of dorsolateral prefrontal cortex in schizophrenia: I. Regional cerebral blood flow evidence. *Archives of General Psychiatry, 43*, 114–124.

Weinberger, D. R., Torrey, E. F., Neopytides, N., & Wyatt, R. (1979). Lateral cerebral ventricular enlargement in chronic schizophrenia. *Archives of General Psychiatry, 36*, 735–739.

Wiesel, F. A. (1994). Neuroleptic treatment of patients with schizophrenia: Mechanisms of action and clinical significance. *British Journal of Psychiatry 164*, 65–70.

Wong, D. F., Wagner, H. N., Tune, L. E., Dannals, R. F., Pearlson, G. D., Links, J. M., Tamminga, C. A., Broussolle, E. P., Ravert, H. T., Wilson, A. A., Toung, J. K. T., Malat, J., Williams, J. A., O'Tuama, L. A., Snyder, S. H., Kuhar, M. J., & Gjedde, A. (1986). Positron emission tomography reveals elevated D$_2$ dopamine receptors in drug-naive schizophrenics. *Science, 234*, 1558–1563.

Zohar, J., Mueller, E. A., Insel, T. R., Zohar-Kadouch, R. C., & Murphy, D. L. (1987). Serotonergic responsivity in obsessive-compulsive disorder. *Archives of General Psychiatry, 44*, 946–951.

Zubenko, G. S., Sullivan, P., Nelson, J. P., Belle, S. H., Huff, F. T, & Wolf, G. L. (1990). Brain imaging abnormalities in mental disorders of late life. *Archives of Neurology, 47*, 1107–1111.

AUTHOR INDEX

SUBJECT INDEX